KING AND QUEEN COUNTY, VIRGINIA

LAND TAX LISTS

1782–1807

Wesley E. Pippenger

HERITAGE BOOKS
2021

HERITAGE BOOKS
AN IMPRINT OF HERITAGE BOOKS, INC.

Books, CDs, and more—Worldwide

For our listing of thousands of titles see our website
at
www.HeritageBooks.com

Published 2021 by
HERITAGE BOOKS, INC.
Publishing Division
5810 Ruatan Street
Berwyn Heights, Md. 20740

International Standard Book Number
Paperbound: 978-0-7884-0645-4

INTRODUCTION

This book contains a reproduction of the land tax lists for King and Queen County, Virginia for the years 1782 through 1807. It has been created from online copies at *FamilySearch.org*. For the years 1783 through 1786 only alterations were made to the 1782 and subsequent lists. The earliest list in King and Queen contains the name of the owners of the land (as the person taxed), the number of acres owned, the rate of value from which taxation was calculated, and the total value of the land. Initially the local sheriff(s) created the list.

In October 1786, an Act of Assembly established districts in each Virginia county, positions for Commissioners of Revenue, and for recordkeeping of land taxes to include persons names owning land, the number and yearly rent of lots where a town was involved, quantity of land, rate of land per acre, total value of land exclusive of lots, and amount of tax at 1½ percent of the value. The Commissioner made four copies: (1) one kept by him and forwarded to a successor, (2) one for the county clerk, (3) a copy certified by the clerk for use of the sheriff in determining taxes, and (4) one for the solicitor's office, later the Auditor of Public Accounts (in Richmond). Taxes were assessed between March and April each year and were payable by the end of December. Value and tax amounts were reflected in British pounds Sterling through 1797 after which the amount of tax was changed to 38 cents per 100 acres. In 1799 the amount increased to 48 cents per 100 acres. No tax records exist for 1808. Land was not valued in dollars until the 1809 list. The value per acre was determined by assistant assessors who prepared the land tax list by copying the previous year then making updates.

Recordkeepers often made notations to distinguish multiple persons with the same name. Entries for the same owner through the years may shift to including "Estate" or "Est." to indicate a recent death of the owner, and may remain on the list until the estate is settled. For this period tax was always shown in pounds, shillings and pence. One oddity noted is that the parts of a name were sometimes written out of sequence. For example, Robert B. Semple, is found Semple, B. Robert, and Semple, Robert B. Pages have been numbered multiple times on the originals, at bottom left or top.

For genealogical researchers, land tax records may help distinguish between individuals by the same name living in a locality at the same time. Land ownership may be tracked between family members. Some references, notations and estate divisions may be found here when not readily located in any of the few court records that have survived multiple fires at the King and Queen County courthouse.

Wesley E. Pippenger
Little Egypt
Tappahannock, Virginia
December 2020

A List of the valuation of Land return'd June 1st 1782
by Peter Dudley and William Courtney, Commissioners

[page 1, 1782]

Owner	Acres	Rate	[Value]	[Tax]
A				
[Allex]ander, Benjamin	[202]	4/6	£ 45.9.1	0.9.1
[Allex]ander, Elisha	[102]	3/6	17.13.1	0.3.6
[Alle]xander, Thomas	[50]	3/6	8.15.0	0.1.9
[A]llexander, John	[50]	4/6	11.5.0	0.2.3
Anderson, Churchill	[63]6	3/6	111.6.0	1.2.3
Anderson, Paulin	[49]8	7/	174.6.0	1.14.10
Atkins, John	[42]	3/6	7.7.0	0.1.5
Atkins, John Jr.	[12]0	2/	12.0.0	0.2.4
Abbott, Jacob	[112]	3/9	21.0.0	0.4.2
Anderson, Richard	[460]	2/6	57.10.0	0.11.6
B				
[Baylor], Gregory	[720]	7/	449.8.0	4.9.10
[B]land, Henry	[16]6	4/	33.4.0	0.6.7
[B]everley, Robert	[2]474	5/	668.10.0	6.13.8
[B]ates, James	[35]8	4/	17.12.0	0.14.6
[Ba]rton, John	[12]5	2/	12.10.0	0.2.6
[Bre]tt, John	[torn]9	5/	27.5.0	0.5.5
[B]arefoot, William	[torn]	3/	5.14.0	0.1.1
[torn]ll, James	[torn]9	2/6	24.17.6	0.4.11
Brooking, Frances	930	5/	232.10.0	2.6.[6]
Baylor, John	760	7/	266.0.0	2.19.[ ]
Boughton, Thomas (Essex)	130	4/6	29.5.0	0.5.10
Boughton, John	200	4/	40.0.0	0.8.0
Boughton, Henry (Essex)	88	3/	13.4.0	0.2.[ ]
Boughton, Thomas	100	4/	20.0.0	0.4.[ ]
Brown, Henry	296	3/6	51.16.0	0.10.[ ]
Burton, Thomas Est.	170	2/6	21.5.0	0.4.[ ]
Broache, Joh[n]	45	3/	6.15.0	0.10.[ ]
Bohannan, Benjamin	25	2/6	3.2.6	0.0.9
Bohannan, Ann	50	2/	5.0.0	0.1.[ ]
Bennett, Artaxerses	75	3/	11.5.0	0.2.[ ]
Brown, William	75	3/9	14.1.3	6.2.[ ]
Banks, Tunstall	230	3/9	43.2.6	0.8.7
Bagbey, John	630	3/6	110.5.0	1.2.0
Brown, George	26½	3/9	[0].17.6	0.0.11½
Brooke, George Est.	1539¾	14/	1077.16.6	10.15.[ ]
Bowers, Phill	329½	1/6	24.14.3	0.4.1
Bird, William	744	3/6	130.4.6	1.6.[ ]
Bird, Mary	619	3/	98.17.1	[ ]

[page 2, 1782]

Owner	Acres	Rate	[Value]	[Tax]
[Bi]rd, Philemon (Orphan)	1238	3/	185.14.0	1.17.1
Brett, John	446	12/	267.12.0	2.13.6
Brooks, William	[3]50	3/9	65.12.6	0.13.1
Bowers, William	[torn]1	3/6	12.5.0	0.2.5
Birch, Richard	[torn]0	1/6	3.15.0	0.0.9
Bowers, John	198	1/6	14.17.0	0.2.11½
Burch, James	190	1/6	14.5.0	0.2.10
Burch, Philip	[torn]00	1/6	7.10.0	0.1.6
Burch, Elizabeth	[7]0	2/	10.0.0	0.2.0
Burch, Henry	[ ]40	2/6	17.10.0	0.3.6
Bird, John	[2]75	1/6	20.12.6	0.4.1
Byne, John	[ ]36	2/	33.12.0	0.6.8½
Bird, Barbary	[ ]00	12/	480.0.0	4.16.0
Bourn, Richard	[ ]50	1/6	11.5.0	0.2.8
Byne, Edmond	[ ]01	2/6	62.12.6	0.12.6¼
Burch, William	[ ]7	2/9	35.6.9	0.7.0¾
[B]ourn, William	[ ]10	1/6	8.5.0	0.1.7¾
Boyd, James	115	9/	51.15.0	0.10.4
Bray, Richard	350	3/9	65.12.6	0.13.1
Brushwood, William	100	1/6	7.10.0	0.1.6
Bird, Hannah	[10]0	1/6	7.10.0	0.1.6
Bowers, Ann	[60]	1/6	4.10.0	0.0.10¾
Boyd, Lucy	52	5/	238.0.0	2.7.7
Bennett, James	[100]	1/6	7.10.0	0.1.6
Bowden, Sarah	180	5/	45.0.0	0.[ ]
Bowden, William	120	5/	30.0.0	0.[ ]
Bew, William	117	1/5	8.5.6	0.[ ]
Burke, Thomas	100	2/	10.0.0	[torn]
Bland, Richard	125	2/	12.10.0	[torn]
Berkley, Edmond	900	2/6	12.10.0	[torn]
Brushwood, Eliza.	180	2/	18.0.0	0.[ ]
Ballman, Thomas	100	2/6	12.10.0	0.[ ]
Bray, William	800	4/	160.0.0	1.1[ ]
Billups, John decd.	133	6/	39.18.0	0.7.[ ]
Bland, John	30	6/	9.0.0	0.[ ]
Briggs, John	170	2/	17.0.0	0.8.[ ]
Belote, Severn Esta.	172	2/	17.4.0	[smear]
Bland, William Senr.	120	2/	12.0.0	0.[ ]
Bowden, William Jr.	100	2/	10.0.0	0.[ ]
Bowden, George (Orphan)	100	2/	10.0.[ ]	[smear]
Bland, William Jr.	250	2/	25.0.0	0.[ ]
Bland, Thomas	200	2/	20.0.0	0.[ ]
Brooking, John	90	1/6	6.15.0	0.1.[ ]
Brown, James	140	3/9	26.5.0	0.5.[ ]
Bowden, Jno. (Orphan)	100	2/	10.0.0	0.2.[ ]

C

Owner	Acres	Rate	[Value]	[Tax]
Cook, Mary	200	4/	40.0.0	0.[ ]
Coleman, Thomas	572	3/	85.16.0	0.17.[ ]
Chick, Richard	491	3/6	85.18.6	[smear]
Chapman, George	200	3/9	37.10.0	0.7.[ ]

[page 3, 1782]

Owner	Acres	Rate	[Value]	[Tax]
Campbell, William	919	3/6	160.16.0	1.12.1¾
Carter, Wormley Robert	1036	12/	621.12.0	6.4.3¾
Chapman, Eliza.	800	3/9	37.10.0	0.7.6
Crane, Caty	[ ]50	2/6	6.5.0	0.1.3
Crane, John	[ ]6	2/6	0.18.0	0.0.2
Cleverus, Benjamin	[4]19	10/	209.10.0	2.1.10¾
Carlton, Henry Senr.	200	3/9	37.10.0	0.7.6
Crane, Ann	30	3/6	5.5.0	0.1.5
Clayton, Thomas	275	3/6	48.3.6	0.9.7½
Campbell, Whitaker	398	3/9	74.12.6	0.14.11
Crafton, Richard	[5]36	4/6	53.2.0	0.10.7¾
Coleman, Milley	196	5/	49.0.0	0.9.9½
Combs, Richard	[5]0	3/9	7.10.0	0.1.6
Carlton, John (King)	[ ]0	2/6	6.5.0	0.1.3
Carlton, Joel	3½	3/	8.0.6	0.1.7½
Courtney, Thomas	[1]75	2/6	21.17.6	0.4.4½
Carlton, Thomas (Swamp)	300	3/9	56.6.0	0.11.3
Carlton, John (School M.)	[ ]00	3/	15.0.0	0.3.0
Carlton, Robert (Bapt.)	26¾	2/	22.13.6	0.4.6¼
Campbell, Sarah	[3]96	6/	88.16.0	0.17.9
Carlton, Christopher	[ ]7½	3/	5.12.6	0.1.1½
[C]arlton, William	[ ]0¾	3/	13.12.3	0.2.8¼
Carlton, Robert (Buck)	93	2/	4.6.0	[blur]
Carlton, Richard	250	3/6	43.15.0	0.8.[ ]
Carlton, Christopher Jr.	100	3/6	17.10.0	0.3.6
Carlton, James	225	3/	33.15.0	0.6.9¾
Carlton, Henry	200	3/	30.0.0	0.6.0
Carlton, Phill	100	1/6	7.10.0	0.1.[ ]
Cooper, Henry	50	2/	5.0.0	0.1.[ ]
Carlton, Thomas (Taylor)	100	3/	15.0.0	0.3.0
Cardwell, John Esta.	600	2/	60.0.0	0.12.0
Cooke, John	300	2/	30.0.0	0.6.0
Collins, Thomas	150	2/	15.0.0	0.3.0
Campbell, William	238	1/6	17.17.0	0.3.6¾
Cook, Thomas	140	1/6	10.10.0	0.2.1
Collier, Charles	250	4/	50.0.0	0.10.0
Collins, John	355	2/	35.10.0	0.7.1
Colley, Charles	100	2/	10.0.0	0.2.0
Corbin, Richard	1868	5/	467.0.0	11.13.[ ]
Chowning, Saml.	150	2/6	18.15.0	0.3.[ ]
Cardwell, Richard	150	1/6	11.5.0	0.2.3
Collins, J[oyeux]	140	5/	35.0.0	0.7.[ ]
Crittenden, Richard [Senr.]	140	7/	49.0.0	0.9.9
Cary, [M.] Wilson	1820	8/	738.0.0	7.5.[ ]
Collier, John (Cobler)	150	2/6	18.15.0	0.3.0
Campbell, James	100	3/	15.0.0	0.3.0

[page 34 1782]

Owner	Acres	Rate	[Value]	[Tax]
Collawn, John	[ ]00	2/6	12.10.0	0.2.6
Crittenden, Rich^d. Jr.	178	2/6	22.5.0	0.4.5¼
Collier, Frances	400	2/	40.0.0	0.8.0
Collier, Benjamin	100	2/	10.0.0	0.2.0
Collier, Catharine	750	2/6	93.15.0	0.18.9
Corr, Averilla	[ ]40	2/6	17.10.0	0.3.6
Clegg, Isaiah	[2]48	2/	24.16.0	0.4.11½
Cook, Dawson	239	1/6	17.18.6	0.3.7
Curry, Ann	100	2/	10.0.0	0.2.0
Corr, Frances	175	1/6	13.2.6	0.2.7
C[ombs], Richard	[4]0	1/6	4.10.0	0.0.10¾
Courtney, William	190	3/9	35.12.6	0.7.1½

D

Owner	Acres	Rate	[Value]	[Tax]
Dew, William	935	7/	327.5.0	3.5.5¼
Duling, William	164	4/	32.16.0	0.6.6½
Deshazo, Richard	152	1/6	11.8.0	0.2.3½
Deshazo, John	160	2/	16.0.0	0.3.2½
Deshazo, William	162	2/	16.4.0	0.3.2¾
Durham, Joseph	76	2/	7.12.0	0.1.6
Draper, John	287	3/	43.1.0	0.8.7¼
Deshazo, Peter	180	3/	27.1.0	0.5.4¾
Dickie, James	512	4/	102.1.0	1.0.5½
Dunbar[r], David	366	4/	73.4.0	0.14.7½
Deshazo, James	30	3/	4.10.0	3.0.0
Dalley, John	200	1/6	15.0.0	0.3.[ ]
Dalley, Ann	224	1/6	16.16.0	0.3.[ ]
Dobbins, Charles	147	2/6	18.17.6	0.3.9
Dean, Benjamin	50	2/6	6.5.0	0.1.3
Dillard, William Jr.	100	1/6	7.10.0	0.1.6
Dudley, Christopher	120	2/	12.0.0	0.2.4
Davis, Jane	100	2/	10.0.0	0.2.[ ]
Didlake, Margret	65	2/	6.10.0	0.1.3¾
Durham, Robert Esta.	50	2/	5.0.0	0.1.[6]
Dunn, Thomas	30	3/	4.10.0	0.0.10½
Dillard, William	276	6/	82.16.0	0.16.6
Durham, George	50	2/	5.0.0	0.1.[3]
Dillard, Ann	70	2/	7.0.0	0.1.4
Durham, Thomas	85	1/6	6.12.6	0.1.[3]
Diggs, Isaac	175	2/6	21.17.6	0.4.4½
Didlake, George	114	5/	28.10.0	0.5.8¼
Dillard Ann (Tassetine)	260	2/6	32.10.0	0.6.6
Dungie, John	110	1/6	8.5.0	3.1.7½
Davis, Zachy.	130	1/6	9.15.0	0.1.11
Dudley, William (Ferry)	290	7/	101.10.0	1.0.[3]
Damm, John	55	3/	8.5.0	0.1.7½
Dudley, William Senr.	180	3/8	33.15.0	0.6.9

[page 5, 1782]

Owner	Acres	Rate	[Value]	[Tax]
Duglass, John	106	3/	1[5].0.0	0.3.0
Didlake, John	200	3/6	210.0.0	2.1.0
Dudley, Thomas	352	3/	52.16.0	0.10.6½
Dudley, B. Robert	421	3/6	73.13.6	0.14.8¼
Dillard, Nicholas	75	2/	7.10.0	0.1.6
Dillard, Delphia	133	2/6	16.13.6	0.3.3¾
Drummond, Thos. Sen[r.]	150	3/	22.10.0	0.4.6
Didlake, James	131	1/6	24.16.6	0.4.11½
Dillard, Thomas	377	2/6	47.2.6	0.9.5
Dillard, Eliza.	449	4/	157.3.0	1.11.5
Dudley, Banks	246	1/6	18.9.0	0.3.8½
Dillard, Wm. (son of Thomas)	150	2/	15.0.0	0.3.0
Dudley, Peter	370	3/9	69.7.6	0.13.10½
E				
Eubank, John	[2]00	7/	175.0.0	1.15.0
Eubank, Susanna	200	4/	40.0.0	0.8.0
Eubank, Major	45	4/	9.0.0	0.1.9½
Eubank, Henry	171	2/6	21.7.6	0.4.3½
Edwards, Thomas Esta.	66	2/	6.12.0	0.1.3
Eubank, George	235	2/	23.10.0	0.4.8¼
Eubank, Phill Sen[r.]	[smear]	1/6	8.5.0	0.1.7¾
Eubank, Jane	28¾	2/6	3.11.10	0.0.8½
Eubank, Richard Sen[r.]	227	2/	22.14.0	0.4.6¼
Eubank, Rachel	75	6/6	2[4].7.6	0.4.10¾
Emmons, James	180	3/6	31.10.0	0.6.3½
Edwards, Charles	192	1/6	14.8.0	0.2.10½
Eubank, Rich[d.]	90¾	2/6	11.1.10½	0.2.2½
F				
Falconer, Thomas	155	3/	23.5.0	0.4.7½
Fogg, James	320	3/	48.0.0	0.9.7
Farthing, Dudley	422	3/9	79.2.6	0.15.9¾
Fisher, Benjamin	190	3/	28.10.0	0.5.8¼
Feronholtz, William	146	3/	21.18.0	0.4.4½
Frazer, William (Kg. Wm.)	45	10/	22.10.0	0.4.[4]
Fleet, William	296¼	10/	148.2.6	1.9.7
Fleet, Henry	665	10/	332.[10].0	3.6.6
Fisher, James Esta.	110	1/6	8.5.0	0.1.7¾
Foster, Thomas	214	2/	21.8.0	0.4.3¼
Faulkner, Mary	333	3/	49.19.0	0.9.11¾
Field, Stephen	855	3/6	149.12.6	1.9.11
G				
Grafton, Thomas	132	4/6	29.14.0	0.5.11¼
Grafton, James	111	3/	16.13.0	0.3.3¾
Gayle, John	180	5/	45.0.0	0.9.0
Gayle, William	20	5/	5.0.0	0.1.0
Garnet, John	72	5/	18.0.0	0.3.7
Goldman, Thomas (Essex)	714	4/6	160.13.0	1.12.17

[page 6, 1782]

Owner	Acres	Rate	[Value]	[Tax]
Garnet, [Rice]	[2]97	3/6	51.19.6	0.10.4½
Gatewood, Chaney	[8]66	5/	216.10.0	2.3.3½
Garnet, Joshua	322	4/	64.8.0	0.12.10½
Gardner, James Jr.	100	3/6	[1]7.10.0	0.3.6
Graves, Edward	200	3/	30.0.0	0.6.0
Gatewood, Joseph	445	5/	111.5.0	1.2.3
Gayle, Matthew	32[8]	5/6	88.16.6	0.17.9
Gatewood, John	160	4/	32.0.0	0.6.4¾
Glen, Thomas	183	3/	29.9.0	0.5.5¾
Gwathmey, Temple	600	17/	510.0.0	5.2.0
Garlick, Samuel	454	12/	272.8.0	2.14.4¾
Griffith, Joseph	[5]0	3/	7.10.0	0.1.6
Gresham, Samuel	400	3/6	70.0.0	3.14.0
Gresham, Thomas	339¼	3/	50.17.9	0.10.2
Gaines, Harry	1580	10/	790.0.0	7.18.0
Gordon, James	19	1/6	14.5.0	0.2.10
Gresham, Phill	200	3/	30.0.0	0.6.0
Gresham, John (Docr.)	200	3/9	37.10.0	0.7.6
Gaines, Robert	225	2/6	28.2.6	0.5.7½
Gresham, William	100	2/	10.0.0	0.2.0
Gardner, Eliza.	100	3/	15.0.0	0.3.0
Gains, Frances	360	3/	180.0.0	1.16.0
Gibson, Richard	113	1/6	8.9.6	0.1.8¼
Gibson, John	219¾	1/6	16.9.7½	0.3.3½
Gordon, John	[ ]60	1/6	4.10.0	0.0.10¾
Griffith, Milley	[torn]	3/	7.10.0	0.1.6
Gresham, Ruth	250	2/6	31.5.0	0.6.3
Gresham, Job	235	3/	35.5.0	0.7.[0]
Gardner, John	672	3/3	109.4.0	1.1.10
Gardner, James	649	5/	162.5.0	1.12.5
Gaines, Betty	410	7/	143.10.0	7.8.8
Griffin, William	840	7/	294.0.0	2.18.0
Garlick, Camm	1100	3/	165.0.0	1.13.0
Garrett, Richard	100	1/6	7.10.0	0.1.6
Garrett, William Esta.	330	2/	33.0.0	0.6.7
Gardner, Anthony Docr.	220	5/	55.0.0	0.11.0
Green, Robert Esta.	150	2/	15.0.0	0.3.0
Garrett, Humphrey	450	6/	135.0.0	1.7.0
Guthrie, James	120	6/	36.0.0	0.7.2
Molly Guthrie Jr.	30	6/	9.0.0	0.1.9
Mary Guthrie	30	2/6	3.15.0	0.0.9
Goldman, Martin	140	2/	14.0.0	0.8.9½
Groom, Mary	273	1/6	20.9.0	0.4.1
Groom, Barbery	100	1/6	7.10.0	0.1.6
Groom, Zachy.	187	1/6	14.0.6	0.2.9½

H

Owner	Acres	Rate	[Value]	[Tax]
Harwood, Agness	225	2/	22.10.0	0.4.6
Holt, Richard	400	3/	60.0.0	0.12.0
Hind, William	126	2/	12.12.0	0.2.6
Hill, William	1591	7/	556.17.0	5.11.5

[page 7, 1782]

Owner	Acres	Rate	[Value]	[Tax]
Harrison, William	75	5/	18.5.0	0.3.9
Hutcherson, Charles	[101]	3/6	87.13.6	0.17.6¼
Hall, Corbin	188	11/	37.12.0	0.7.6
Hitchcock, Thomas	146	2/	14.0.0	0.2.9½
Hoskins, Samuel	75	2/6	21.17.6	0.4.4½
Hoskins, William	160	5/	40.0.0	0.8.0
Holloway, George	750	6/6	243.15.0	2.8.9
Herndon, Margt.	100	3/6	17.10.0	0.3.6
Holderbey, William	210	3/9	39.7.6	0.7.10¼
Heskew, John	61	2/6	7.12.6	0.1.6¼
Howell, John	100	5/	25.0.0	0.5.0
Hurt, West	100	2/	10.0.0	0.2.0
Hill, Robert	1600	4/	320.0.0	3.4.0
Holderbey, Joseph	3 Lotts in Walkerton, £5		10.0.0	0.2.0
Hoomes, Benjamin	640	9/	288.0.0	2.17.7
Hill, Edward	1200	9/	540.0.0	5.8.0
Hodges, Salley	462	2/1	[1]6.4.0	0.9.2¾
Hutson, William	224	1/6	16.16.0	0.3.4¼
[Hem]ingway, Daniel	[torn]	2/	80.0.0	0.16.0
[Ha]rwood, Christopher	300	12/	180.0.0	1.16.0
Harwood, John	[4]00	12/	240.0.0	2.8.0
Harwood, Joseph	354½	5/	88.12.6	0.17.8½
Hill, Thomas Majr.	300	13/	195.0.0	1.19.0
Hart, James	150	1/6	11.5.0	0.8.[ ]
Hart, Robert	190	2/6	24.5.0	0.4.9
Hart, Anthony	200	1/6	15.0.0	0.3.0
Hart, William	218	1/6	16.7.0	0.3.3
Hare, William Docr.	109	2/6	13.12.6	0.2.8¼
Hunt, William	730	3/	109.10.0	1.1.10
Holderbey, Eliza.	100	2/	10.0.0	0.2.0
Henry, James	1900	7/	665.0.0	6.13.[ ]
Halyard, William	320	2/6	40.0.0	0.8.0
Hoskins, John	540	5/	135.5.0	1.7.0½

J

Owner	Acres	Rate	[Value]	[Tax]
Jones, John	505	4/	101.0.0	1.0.2¾
Jeffries, Edward	70	1/6	5.5.0	0.1.0½
Jones, Erasmus	462	3/	69.6.0	0.13.10¼
Jones, James	160	7/	56.0.0	0.11.2½
James Jones' Esta.	196	5/	49.0.0	0.9.9 [ ]
Jones, William	335	6/6	108.17.6	1.1.9
Jeffries, Ambrose	210	3/9	39.7.6	0.7.10½
Jeffries, Bernard	30	2/	3.0.0	0.0.7
Jordon, William	100	1/6	7.10.0	0.1.6
Jordon, Eliza.	120	2/	12.0.0	0.2.4½
John, Thomas Est.	100	2/	10.0.0	0.2.0
Johnson, Achebald	100	2/	10.0.0	0.2.0

[page 8, 1782]

Owner	Acres	Rate	[Value]	[Tax]
K				
Keeling, William	150	2/	15.2.0	0.3.0
Keeling, James	300	3/6	55.0.0	0.11.0
Kemp, John	87	3/9	16.6.3}	
", (Thos. Wiltshire Est.)	60	3/9	11.5.0}	0.5.6
Kauffman, George	583	7/	204.1.0	2.0.9½
Kauffman, John	471	9/	211.19.0	2.2.4¼
Kauffman, John Jr.	200	4/	40.0.0	0.8.0
Kennedy, Alexander	580	6/	174.0.0	1.14.9½
Kercheval, Charles	60	4/	12.0.0	0.2.4¾
Kemp, John (Lower Parish)	100	2/6	12.10.0	0.2.6
Kidd, Barthow.	100	1/6	7.10.0	0.1.6
Kidd, John	370	3/6	64.15.0	0.12.11¼
L				
Lumpkin, Henry	620	4/6	139.14.0	1.7.10¾
Lumpkin, John	130	3/	19.12.0	0.3.10¾
Lyon, Dixon	150	3/6	26.5.0	0.5.3
Lumpkin, William	305	7/	106.15.0	1.1.4
Lefon, Wm. & Francis	[4]17	4/	83.8.0	0.16.8
Lankford, Thomas	100	2/	10.0.0	[0].2.[0]
Lyne, William	1[5]78	4/	295.1[3].0	2.19.1¾
Lyne, George	110	3/6	19.5.0	0.3.10
Lumpkin, Anthony	338	4/6	76.1.0	0.15.2½
Lumpkin, Robert	90	4/	18.0.0	0.3.7
Lumpkin, Sarah	375	4/	70.0.0	0.14.0
Langham, William	707	3/9	132.11.3	1.6.6
Longest, Lewis	23	2/6	4.2.6	0.0.9
Lumpkin, Robt. (St. Stephens)	430	3/6	75.5.0	0.15.0
Longest, Caleb	103	3/9	19.6.3	0.3.10
Longest, Dorathy	100	3/9	18.15.0	0.3.9
Lumpkin, Joyce	287	3/9	53.16.3	0.10.9
Lumpkin, Mary	108	3/	16.4.0	0.3.2¾
Lumpkin, Anthony	108	3/	16.4.0	0.3.2¾
Lumpkin, Jacob	916	3/	137.8.0	1.7.5¾
Lewis, Ivesin	606	7/	212.2.0	2.2.5
Lewis, Eliza.	100	2/	10.0.0	0.2.0
Leigh, Richard	300	12/	180.0.0	1.16.0
Lyne, John	507	3/	76.1.0	0.15.2
Lambeth, Thomas	200	1/6	15.0.0	0.3.0
Leigh, Richard Jr.	266	6/	79.16.0	0.15.11
Lumpkin, Robt. (Orphan)	183	2/	18.6.0	0.3.7¾
M				
Mehon, James	60	3/6	10.10.0	0.2.1
Motley, Edwin	747	5/	186.15.0	1.7.[ ]
Martin, John	80	4/6	18.0.0	0.3.[ ]
McKintosh, William	66	2/	6.12.0	0.1.3
May, Benjamin	22[0]	1/6	16.10.0	0.3.3½
Minor, Joseph	170	3/6	29.15.0	0.5.1¾

[page 9, 1782]

Owner	Acres	Rate	[Value]	[Tax]
Martin, Thomas	680	7/	238.0.0	2.7.7
Minor, William	149	4/	29.16.0	0.5.11½
Minor, John	137	4/	27.8.0	0.5.5½
Mann, Augustine	400	4/	80.0.0	0.16.0
Miller, Thomas	[5]27	3/9	98.16.3	0.19.9
Mitchel, John Senr.	197	4/	30.8.0	0.7.10¼
Mitchel, Robert	50	10/	25.0.0	0.5.0
Mitchel, John	50	3/	7.10.0	0.1.6
Mitchel, James	750	6/	225.0.0	2.5.0
McKendree, Eliza.	323	2/6	40.7.6	0.8.0¾
Moore, Phill	100	2/	10.0.0	0.2.0
McKendree, John	100	1/6	7.10.0	0.1.6
Mitchel, Susanna	170	1/6	17.5.0	0.3.6½
Moore, John	100	1/6	7.10.0	0.1.6
Meredith, William	530	7/	185.10.5	1.17.1
Mitchel, John	270	2/6	33.15.0	0.6.9
Morris, William	50	1/6	3.15.0	0.0.9
Metcalf, Thomas	700	7/	245.0.0	2.9.0
Meredith, Saml. Esta.	340	7/	119.0.0	1.3.9½
Meredith, Ralph	227	3/	34.1.0	0.6.9½
Muire, Richard	93	[7]/	27.18.0	0.5.6¾
Muire, John	182	3/6	31.17.0	0.6.4¼
Major, Joseph	100	2/	10.0.0	0.2.[ ]
Major, Mary	175	3/6	30.12.6	0.6.1[7]
Moore, Richard	145	3/	21.15.0	0.4.1[8]

N

Owner	Acres	Rate	[Value]	[Tax]
Nunn, Jane	180	3/6	31.10.0	[torn]
Newill, John	100	4/	20.[ ]	[torn]
Nunn, Thomas	174	3/6	30.[ ]	[torn]
Nunn, James	110	4/	22.0.0	[torn]
Newbill, George	500	4/	100.0.0	1.[ ]
Nash, John	100	3/	15.0.0	0.3.0
Nowell, Reuben & Oliver and John Ball	296	3/	44.8.0	0.8.10
Newcomb, Benjamin	73	1/6	5.9.6	0.1.1
Newcomb, Eliza.	109	1/6	8.3.6	0.1.7½

O

Owner	Acres	Rate	[Value]	[Tax]
Oneal, John	450	4/6	101.5.0	1.0.3
Olliver, John	320	2/6	40.0.0	0.8.0
Orvill, John & Lawrence	100	3/	15.0.0	0.3.0
Overstreet, Mitchel	170	2/	17.0.0	0.3.4¾
Overstreet, Gabriel	414	2/	48.8.0	0.8.3¾
O'Dear, Stephen	70	6/	21.0.0	0.4.2
O'Dear, Major	700	6/	21.0.0	0.4.2
O'Dear, Edith	50	2/6	6.5.0	0.1.3

[page 10, 1782]

Owner	Acres	Rate	[Value]	[Tax]
Oakes, Henry	100	2/	10.0.0	0.2.0

P

Owner	Acres	Rate	[Value]	[Tax]
Pitts, David	420	4/6	94.10.0	0.18.10¼
Pitts, Ann	100	3/	15.0.0	0.3.0
Philip, Richard	[ ]0	3/6	40.5.0	0.8.0¼
[torn]d, John	[torn]	4/6	52.17.6	0.10.6¾
[torn], [Fr]ances	[torn]	4/6	22.5.6	0.4.5¼
[torn], [W]illiam	[torn]	3/	37.10.0	0.7.6
[torn], [A]nn	[torn]	3/6	6.2.6	0.1.2½
[Pendle]ton, Phill	[torn]	5/	102.0.0	1.0.4¾
Perryman, Anthony	30	3/6	22.15.0	0.4.6½
Pollard, Richard	432	4/	86.8.0	0.17.3¼
Pollard, Edmund	100	3/	15.0.0	0.3.0
Prince, Francis	113	3/9	21.3.9	0.4.2¾
Pendleton, Benjamin	450	3/9	84.7.6	0.16.10½
Pynes, Benjamin	[4]00	3/	60.0.0	0.12.0
Pemberton, John	386	3/	57.18.0	0.11.6¾
P[a]ce, Benjamin	263	3/6	46.0.6	0.9.2½
Pickels, John	225	3/6	39.7.6	0.7.10½
Price, Robert	630	3/	94.10.0	0.18.10¾
Peachey, Samuel	[1]00	3/	15.0.0	0.3.0
Palmer, Eliza.	[3]50	3/6	61.5.0	0.12.3
Pigg, Rachel	[1]08	7/	37.16.0	0.7.6½
Pigg, John	276	7/	75.12.0	0.15.1¼
Paget, Samuel	36	3/9	6.15.0	0.1.4
Pryor, John	200	3/	30.0.0	0.6.0
Peirce, Thomas	160	2/	16.0.0	0.3.2¼
Pollard, William	95	3/6	16.12.6	0.3.3¾

R

Owner	Acres	Rate	[Value]	[Tax]
Richards, William	510	6/	153.0.0	1.10.7
Roane, Thomas	3567	9/	1605.3.0	16.1.0
Richards, John	1020	4/6	229.10.0	2.5.10
Robinson, Donald	155	6/	46.10.0	0.9.3½
Row, Joseph	450	3/	67.10.0	0.13.6
Row, Thomas Majr.	1652	3/6	289.2.0	2.17.9¾
Read, Robert	14	2/6	1.15.0	0.0.4
Row, Richard	550	4/	110.0.0	1.2.0
Roane, William	1600	12/	960.0.0	9.12.0
Row[e], Eliza.	120	1/6	9.0.0	0.1.9½
Richerson, Elias	86	2/	8.12.0	0.1.8½
Row, John Est.	100	3/	15.0.0	0.3.0
Richards, John	221½	2/	22.3.[0]	0.4.5
Richards, Mary Esta.	200	2/	20.0.0	0.4.0
Richards, George	100	2/	10.0.0	0.2.0
Richards, William	296	2/6	37.0.0	0.7.4¾
Richerson, James	180	2/	18.0.0	0.3.7
Richerson, William	181	2/	18.2.0	0.3.7½
Richerson, Rachel	101½	2/	10.3.0	0.2.0½

[page 11, 1782]

Owner	Acres	Rate	[Value]	[Tax]
Roane, Thomas	150	1/6	11.5.0	0.2.3
Roane, Major	260	2/	16.0.0	0.3.2½
Rootes, Philip Esta.	700	6/	210.0.0	2.2.0
Robinson, Benjamin	1300	4/	260.0.0	2.12.0
Roane, Charles	200	7/	70.0.0	0.14.0

S

Owner	Acres	Rate	[Value]	[Tax]
Smith, John	406	3/6	71.1.0	0.14.2½
Satterwhite, George	164	3/	24.12.0	0.4.11
Samuel, Henry Jr.	78	3/6	13.13.0	0.2.8¾
Samuel, Henry	85	3/	12.15.0	0.2.6½
Samuel, Andrew	72	3/6	12.12.0	0.2.6
Satterwhite, William	100	2/	10.0.0	0.2.0
Smithey, Leonard	384	3/6	67.0.0	0.13.5
Spencer, Edward	392½	4/	78.10.0	0.15.8
School[s], Gabriel	169	3/	25.7.0	0.5.0¾
Shelton, William	132	4/6	29.14.0	0.5.11
Smith, Ann	85	3/6	14.17.6	0.2.11½
Starling, Jane	360	3/9	67.10.0	0.13.6
Shelton, Thomas	294	4/	58.16.0	0.11.9¼
Scott, Benjamin	200	4/6	45.0.0	0.9.0
Saunders, Joseph Est.	200	3/6	35.0.0	0.7.0
Shepherd, William	140	4/6	23.8.0	0.4.8
Semple, Eliza.	786	7/	275.2.0	2.15.0
Smith, John	30	2/	3.0.0	0.0.[ ]
Smith, John	100	2/6	12.10.0	0.2.6
Smith, Lewis	113½	3/6	19.17.3	0.3.11
Stone, Sarah	300	3/6	52.10.0	0.10.6
Story, Mary	5 Lotts in Walkerton @ £5		25.0.0	0.5.0
Smith, Larkin	1290	15/	967.10.0	9.13.6
Smith, Henry	400	3/	60.0.0	0.12.0
Smith, William	140	3/9	26.5.0	0.5.3
Smith, William	364	3/	54.12.0	0.18.11
Smith, James Senr.	80	1/6	6.0.0	0.1.2½
Shepherd, Mary	100	2/6	12.10.0	0.2.6
Stevens, Thomas	609½	3/9	114.[5].1½	1.2.[ ]
Stevens, George	627½	3/9	117.13.1½	1.3.6¾
Shackelford, John	236	3/6	40.16.0	0.8.17
Starke, Richard	250	3/	37.10.0	0.7.6
Soans, James	191	12/	114.12.0	1.2.[1]
Soans, John Est.	191	12/	114.12.0	1.2.11
Stone, Robert	300	2/	30.10.0	0.6.0
Stone, John	357	2/6	44.12.6	0.8.1[6]
Shackelford, Leonard	250	3/6	43.15.0	0.8.[ ]
Smith, Robert	879	5/	219.15.0	2.3.11
Smith, Guy	189½	1/6	14.4.3	0.2.[4]

[page 12, 1782]

Owner	Acres	Rate	[Value]	[Tax]
Simkins, Nimrod	60	1/6	4.10.0	0.0.10¼
Southerland, William	283¼	2/6	35.8.9	0.7.1
Sears, Philip	83	2/	8.6.0	0.1.7¾
Seward, Mary Esta.	260	2/	26.0.0	0.5.2¼
Shackelford, William	700	7/	245.0.0	2.9.0
Seward, Benjamin	115	1/6	8.12.6	0.1.8½
Steadman, Christopher	191	2/6	23.17.6	0.4.9
Sadler, John	150	3/	22.10.0	0.4.6
Shackelford, Robinson	200	1/6	15.0.0	0.3.0
Shackelford, Drusilla	500	5/	125.0.0	1.5.0
Steadman, Christo[r.] J[r.]	265	3/	30.15.0	0.7.11¼
Smith, Gregory	585	7/	204.15.0	2.0.11¼
Shackelford, Thomas	508	4/	101.2.0	1.0.0¼
Shackelford, Lyne	607	3/	91.1.0	0.18.[2]
Shackelford, John (W.C.?)	100	2/	10.0.0	0.2.0
Standard, George	243	2/6	30.7.6	0.6.0¾
Scott, Anderson	330	8/	132.0.0	1.6.4¾
Saunders, George	200	1/6	15.0.0	0.3.0

T

Owner	Acres	Rate	[Value]	[Tax]
[Trice?], William	70	3/6	12.5.0	0.2.5¼
Trice, Betty	70	3/6	12.5.0	0.2.5¼
Taylor, John Esta.	50	3/	7.10.0	0.1.6
Taylor, Saml.	50	2/	5.[ ].0	0.1.1
Tignor, William	370	5/	92.10.0	0.18.6
Taylor, Edmond	294	4/	58.16.0	0.11.7
Todd, William Esta.	1776	8/	710.8.0	7.2.0¾
Temple, Joseph	918	5/	229.10.0	2.5.10¾
Tunstall, Ann	223	3/9	41.16.3	0.8.4¼
Tunstall, Molley	490	5/	122.10.0	1.4.6
Tunstall, Rich[d.] Col. (Esta.)	12[6]3	10/	6[07].10.0	6.0.3½
Tunstall, Salley	200	9/	90.0.0	0.18.0
Tunstall, Richard (Best.)	357	4/	71.8.0	0.14.[3]
Todd, Henry (Doctr.)	919	7/	321.13.0}	
", (Barrom?)	250	1/6	18.15.0}	3.8.0¾
Trice, James	210	2/6	26.5.0	0.5.3
Tureman, Benjamin	120	1/6	9.0.0	0.1.9½
Taliaferro, William	1000	7/	350.0.0	3.10.0
Townley, Robert	350	7/	122.10.0	1.4.6
Taliaferro, Phill	990	4/	198.0.0	1.19.7
Taliaferro, Richard	300	2/6	37.10.0	0.7.6

V

Owner	Acres	Rate	[Value]	[Tax]
Vass, Thomas	250	2/6	31.5.0	0.6.3

W

Owner	Acres	Rate	[Value]	[Tax]
Wyatt, John	200	3/6	35.0.0	0.7.0
White, Henry	100	4/	20.0.0	0.4.0
Willmore, Thomas	150	5/	37.10.0	0.7.6

[page 13, 1782]

Owner	Acres	Rate	[Value]	[Tax]
Wright, James	124½	2/6	15.11.3	0.3.0½
Wyatt, Joseph	60	4/	12.0.0	0.2.4¾
Walding, John	105	6/	31.10.0	0.6.3
Wood, Thomas	260	3/9	48.15.0	0.9.9
Wilson, Isaac	200	3/	30.0.0	0.6.0
Wilson, Benjamin Esta.	200	3/6	35.0.0	0.7.0
Wyatt, Thomas Esta.	480	5/	120.0.0	1.4.0
Wyatt, John	100	3/9	18.15.0	0.3.9
White, John	957	14/	669.18.0	6.13.11¾
Wheeley, John	50	3/	7.10.0	0.1.6
Watkins, William	37	2/	3.14.0	0.0.8¾
Watkins, Phill	65	2/	6.10.0	0.1.3½
Wiltshire, Joseph	[ ]3	3/6	23.5.6	0.4.7¾
Walding, James	100	3/9	18.15.0	0.3.9
Wheeley, Phill	150	2/6	18.15.0	0.3.9
Ware, John	562	3/6	98.7.0	0.19.8
Weston, Edward	1 Lott in Walkerton		5.0.0	0.1.0
Whiteing, George	1 Lott in Walkerton		5.0.0	0.1.0
Walker, Frances	880	16/	704.0.0	7.0.9½
Whayne, William	13½	3/9	2.10.7½	0.0.6½
Watts, John	293	3/9	54.18.9	0.[ ]
Watts, William	480	3/9	90.0.0	0.18.[ ]
Watts, Kauffman	300	2/6	37.10.0	0.7.6
Williams, Howard Jr.	283	2/	28.6.0	0.5.7¾
Williams, Wyatt Senr.	125	3/6	21.17.6	0.4.4
Wyatt, Thomas	106	3/9	19.17.6	0.3.11¼
Wyatt, John	103	3/	15.9.0	0.3.10
Wyatt, William Jr.	52	3/6	9.2.0	0.1.9¾
Williams, Howard	300	3/	45.0.0	0.9.0
Williams, Charles	550	2/	55.0.0	0.11.0
Walton, James	80	2/	8.0.0	0.1.7
Walton, Mary	60	2/	6.0.0	0.1.2¾
Walton, Eliza.	60	1/6	4.10.0	0.0.10
Walton, John	176	2/6	22.0.0	0.4.[4]
Walton, William	66	2/	6.12.0	0.1.3¾
Walton, Thomas	66	2/	6.12.0	0.1.3¾
Ware, John	75	2/6	9.7.6	0.1.[ ]
Watts, Auther	350	2/0	35.0.0	2.7.0
Ware, Auther	83	2/	8.6.0	0.1.[7]

[page 14, 1782]

Owner	Acres	Rate	[Value]	[Tax]
Walding, Richard	75	6/6	24.7.6	0.4.10
Ware, Robert Est.	100	2/	14.0.0	0.2.0
Ware, Sarah	175	2/	17.10.0	0.3.6
Williams, Eliza.	50	1/6	3.15.0	0.0.9
White, James	200	3/	30.0.0	0.6.0
Watkins, Humphrey	476	5/	119.0.0	1.3.9½
Warren, Cathe.	175	1/6	13.2.6	0.2.7½
Ware, Robert (Bishop)	112	1/6	8.11.0	0.6.7¾
Wyatt, Richard	150	6/	45.0.0	0.9.0
Whiteing, Mary	1100	5/	[2]75.0.0	2.15.0
Ware, Christopher	500	6/	15[3].0.0	1.10.0
Wedderburn, Alexander	350	3/	52.10.0	0.10.6
Whiteing, Beverley	1400	3/9	262.10.0	2.12.6
Webley, John	173	2/6	21.12.6	0.4.3¾
Walding, Edward	373	2/6	46.12.6	0.9.3¾
Wright, William	100	2/	10.0.0	0.2.0
Walding, Lewis	150	1/6	11.5.0	0.2.3
Waller, Edward	133½	1/6	10.0.3	0.2.0
Waller, John	66½	1/6	4.19.9	0.0.11¾

Y

Owner	Acres	Rate	[Value]	[Tax]
Younger, Marcus	94	1/6	7.1.0	0.1.4¾

We the Subscribers have asses'd. the Lands of Capt. Peter Dudley to three Shillings & 9d. p. Acre and Capt. William Courtney's the same price given from under our Hands this 29 Day of May 1782. [signed] Tunstall Banks, Harry Gaines. A copy Test Rich[d.] Tunstall [Jr.], Clk.

A Return made by the Commissioners of King & Queen
County Agreeable to an Act of Assembly passed October 1782
of all Alterations or Additions of Land in the sd. County for the year
1783

Present Proprietors Names	[Acres]		Former Proprietors Names
Brown, Henry	197	acres land	Jn°. Mitchell Senr.
Brooke, Rich^d.	1539¾	do.	Geo. Brooke Est.
Brumley, Jn°.	329½	do.	Phil Bowers
Corr, William Est.	200	do.	Robinson Shackelford
Cook, Thomas	100	do.	James Bennett
Crane, William	75	do.}	Rachel Eubank
do.	25	do.} from	Richard Walding
Campbell, William Junr.	[9]19	do. do.	Wm. Campbell Senr.
Campbell, William	60	do. added and taken from Jos. Row	
Cleaveley, Thomas, a Town Lott		do.	Mary Story
Carlton, Danl. Est.	350	do. do.	Auther Watts
Dillard, Wm.	60	do. added	Jn°. Gordon
Davis, Thomas	150	do.	taken from Thomas Roane
Dalley, Thomas	30	do.	Ann Crane
Eubank, James	75	do.	Wm. Harrison
Fleet, Edwin	360	do.	Frans. Gaines
Fleet, Baylor	350	do.	Wm. Brookes
Fauntleroy, G. Saml.	[885]	do.	part of Wm. Todd's decd.
Garrett, Jn°.	100	do.	Phil. Moore
Gaines, Fleming	640	do.	Benjamin Hoomes
Gardner, Jn°.	26	do. added	taken from James Gardner
Gaines, Fras.	410	do.	Betty Gains
Gulley, Phil	250	do.	taken from Henry Todd
Hoskins, Robert	370	do.	Wm. Tignor
Hoomes, Benjamin	230	do.	Tunstall Banks
Hendley, Thomas	40	do.	part of Wm. Todd [Est.]
Ison, Lucy	60	do.	Charles Kerchaval
Kemp, Thomas	40	do.	part of Wm. Todd Est.
Lumpkin, Richard	450	do.	Jn°. O'Neal
Longest, Richard	140	do.	James Brown
Meredith, W^m.	243	do.	Geo. Standard
Major, Joseph	100	do. added	Jn°. Shackelford [tear]
Moore, Phil	50	do.	Wm. Morris
Macon, Jn°.	1092	do.	part of Wm. Todd [tear]
Mansfield, Wm.	75	do.	do. do.
Manley, Peter	40	do.	Richard Combs
O'Neal, Jn°.	75 do.}		Artax. Bennett
do.	100 do.}		Edmond Pollard
O'Dear, Major	70		charged last year instead of 70, £5.18.[1] to be deducted from [this year land] tax

Carried forward

[1783 Alterations, page 2]

Brought Over

Present Proprietors Names	[Acres]		Former Proprietors Names
Pitts, David	20	acres land	added Wm. Gayle
Phillips, Jno.	143	do.	part of Wm. Todd Est.
Robins, William	40	do.	do. of Lyne Shackelford
Richards, Geo.	200	do.	Mary Richards
Shackelford, Jno. (M)	40	do.	part of Beverley Whiteing's
Starke, Richard	100	do. added	Geo. Richards
Stevens, Geo.	25½	do.	deducted, a mistake 3/ deductd.
Smith, Gregory	100	do.	do. do.
Tunstall, Richard Jr.	665		part of Col. Richd. Tunstall's Est.
Tunstall, Richard Col. Est.	538		
Taylor, Saml.	80	do.	added Jno. Martin
Tunstall, Molley	100	do.	added
Ware, Robert (Bishop)	130		added part of Wm. Halyard's
Watts, Edward	250	do.	Leonard Shackelford
Watts, W^m.	100	do.	deducted, a mistake, deduct 11/9

There has been a Survey of Wm. Todd's Land since the valuation last year and there appears to be [2270] instead of 1776 which now is in the hands of several people.

[arithmetic omitted]

Peter Dudley}
& Commissioners
Wm. Courtney}

A List of Alterations of Land in King & Queen County for the year 1784,
Agreeable to an Act of Assembly passed October 1792.
Return'd. to the Auditor's Office
(Alterations 1784)

Present Proprietors Names	Qty. Land	Price	Amt. Land	Amt. Tax	Of Whom Had
William Banks, 165 acres more than} Richards had last year which on a} survey appears to be	365	4/2	76.0.[ ]	1.2.9¾	Geo. Richards
Jane Carter	60	3/2	9.10.[ ]	2.11	Wm. Dillard
Richard Row, 71 acres added	71	10/5	36.19.7	11.1	deduct from Phil Pendleton
Henry Todd, 75 acres added	75	6/9	25.6.3	7.7	deduct from Jno. Gardner
Joseph Watkins	65	4/2	13.10.10	4.1	Phil Watkins
James Deshazo, 160 added	160	4/2	33.6.8	0.10	Jno. Deshazo
Wilson Cary	1820	16/7	1509.1.8	22.12.9	Wilson Miles Cary
James Halbert	462	6/3	144.7.6	2.3.4	Erasmus Jones
Jno. Carter	126	4/2	26.5.0	7.11	Wm. Hind
Henry Wyatt	200	7/3	72.10.--	1.1.9	Jno. Wyatt
William Tignor	150	7/3	54.7.6	16.4	Dixon Lyon
Wm. Lyne, 110 acres added	110	7/3	39.17.6	12.--	Geo. Lyne
Dixon Lyon	45	8/4	18.15.0	5.8	Major Eubank
Robert Hill, 223 acres added	223	7/10	87.6.10	1.6.8	Ann Tunstall
Wm. Campbell Senr., added	419	7/3	154.17.9	2.5.6	Wm. Campbell Junr.
Gabriel Overstreet, 130 added	130	5/3	34.2.6	10.2	Robert Ware (Bishop)
Thomas Moore	700	12/6	437.10.--	6.14.3	Phil Rootes Est.
Thos. Row, 665 added	665	20/9	689.18.9	10.7.0	Henry Fleet
Baylor Fleet, 360 added	360	20/9	373.10.0	5.12.0	Edwin Fleet here apear'd to be a mistake in the lt. year [ ]
Mary Soanes	382	24/10	474.6.4	7.2.4	James & Jno. Soane's Est.
Richd. Walding, 25 acres added	25	13/6	16.17.6	5¾	deduct from Wm. Crane
Matthew Kemp	100	5/4	26.13.4	8.--	Jno. Kemp (Lower Parish)
Jno. Kemp (L. Parish)	200	6/3	62.[ ]	18.9	Jno. Pryor
Joseph Wiltshire Jr.	60	7/10	23.12.--	7.1	deduct from Jno. Kemp
Agrippa Dunn	140	5/3	36.[ ]	11.1	Henry Burch
Peter Dudley, 160 acres added	160	5/3	42.1.0	12.7	deduct from Molley Tunstall
William Wright	110	8/4	45.16.8	13.9	deduct from Richd. Deshazo

Peter Dudley & Wm. Courtney, Comrs.

[arithmetic omitted]

King & Queen Return from Commrs. of Land, for 1784

£1362.12.8

A List of Alterations of Land in King & Queen County for the year 1785.

Present Proprietors Names	Qty. Land	Price	Amt. Land	Amt. Tax	Of Whom Had
James Eubank	150	14/6	108.15.0	1.12.7½	Jno. Eubank
Thomas Eubank	150	14/6	108.15.0	1.12.7½	Jno. Eubank
Joseph Cross	38	6/3	11.17.6	3.7	William Barefoot
James Bates	42	4/2	8.15.0	2.7½	Saml. Taylor
Chaney Gatewood	100	7/3	36.5.0	10.11	James Gardner
Jno. Lumpkin	70	6/3	18.7.6	5.6	William Phillips
Rachel Robinson	150	7/3	54.7.6	16.4	William Tignor
Humphrey Temple	one Lot in Walkerton		5.0.0	1.6	Edwd. Weston
do.	do.		5.0.0	1.6	Geo. Whiteing
do.	four do.		20.0.0	6.--	Mary Story
do.	one do.		5.0.0	1.6	Thomas Cl[e]veley
do.	70	33/2	116.1.8	1.14.9½	Frans. Walker
Humpr. Walker	325	do.	538.19.2	8.1.8	do
William Jones	35¾	31/1	55.11.2½	16.8	Larkin Smith
Jno. Roane	450	10/	225.--.--	3.7.6	William Hill
Christopher Kay (there is part of his land lay Essex and this is the part only in K&Q)	116	6/3	30.9.0	9.1½	Benja. Fisher (rest in Essex)
Jno. Kemp	53	7/3	19.4.3	5.9	Joseph Wiltshire
Jno. Garlick	957	29/	1387.13.0	20.16.4	John White
William Newbill	450	9/4	210.--.--	3.3.--	Richard Lumpkin
William Gatewood	220	3/2	34.16.8	10.6	Benjamin May
William Haws	72	10/5	37.10.--	11.3	Jno. Garnett
Reubin Garnett	183	6/3	57.3.9	17.2	Thomas Glenn
Robert Lumpkin, added	375	8/4	156.5.0	2.6.11	Sarah Lumpkin
Samuel Crittenden	199	5/3	52.4.9	15.9	James Ball
Isbell Taylor	100	4/2	20.16.8	6.3	West Hurt
Henry Oaks	350	do.	72.18.4	1.1.11	Daniel Carlton's Est.
William McKintosh	126	do.	26.5.0	7.11	Jno. Carter
James Walden, added	54	7/10	21.3.--	6.4	Eliza. Semple
Robert Mitchell (to be deducted on a survey)	33	20/9	34.4.9	10.3	x
Eliza. Semple, to be deducted, in do.	212	14/6	153.14.2	2.6.1	x
Geo. Stevens, added	43	7/6	16.16.10	5.0½	William Langham
William Whayne	194	do.	75.19.8	1.2.9½	do.
James Smith Jr.	101	do.	39.11.2	11.10	do.
Ambrose Jeffries, added	169	do.	66.3.10	19.10	do.
Batcheldor Thurston	100	3/2	15.16.8	4.9	Phil Gulley
Jno. Tucker	180	7/3	65.5.0	19.7	James Emmons
Joseph McCarty	73	3/2	11.11.2	3.6	Benja. Newcombe
Lucy Boyd	476	10/5	247.18.4	3.14.5	Humpy. Watkins
Eliza. Watkins	100	3/2	15.16.8	4.9	[Phil Birch]
Michal Mills	50	do.	7.18.4	2.5	Richard Birch
William Harwood	501	5/3	131.10.3	1.19.6	Edwd. Byne
Margt. Gilmore	354½	10/5	184.12.9	2.15.5	Joseph Harwood
Humpy. Carlton	125	7/3	45.6.3	13.8	William Wyatt Senr.
James Laughlin	126¾	4/2	26.8.2	8.0	Robert Carlton (Bapt.)
Anthony Hart	190	5/3	49.17.6	15.--	Robert Hart
do.	94	3/2	14.17.8	4.6	Marcus Younger
Thomas Roane, added	200	6/3	62.10.--	18.9	Henry Carlton
Thomas Row, do.	296	do.	92.10.0	1.7.9	Reubin & Oliver Nowel, Jno. Ball
James Martin	332½	20/9	344.19.4½	5.3.5¾	Richard Tunstall Jnr.
Richard Tunstall Jr.	1097	7/3	397.13.3	5.19.3	Thomas Row
do.	200	18/8	186.13.4	2.16.0	Salley Tunstall
Robert Gaines	235	6/3	73.8.9	1.2.1	Job Gresham
	Carried Forward				

Alterations of Land for the year [1785] *continued*

Present Proprietors Names	Qty. Land	Price	Amt. Land	Amt. Tax	Of Whom Had
Molley Smith	30	4/2	6.5.0	1.11	Jn°. Smith
Gabriel Dix	338	6/3	105.12.6	1.11.8	James Halbert
William Duling, mistake added	100	8/4	41.13.4	12.6	
Jn°. Merideth	500	10/5	260.8.4	3.18.2	Drusilla Shackelford
Jn°. Bland	30	12/6	18.15.--	5.8	Molley Guthrie
Richard Guthrie	60	do.	37.10.--	11.3	James Guthrie
Dawson Cook (overcharged)	39	3/2	6.3.6	1.10	
Edward Brooke	100	do.	15.16.8	4.9	Barthw. Kidd
Thomas Bland	100	do.	15.16.8	4.9	William Brushwood
Thos. Metcalf	132½	6/3	41.8.1½	12.5½	Christopher Steadman
Alexander Wedderburn	311½	do.	97.3.9	1.9.1¾	Thomas Metcalf

A list of Grants issued & Recd. from the Land Office

Jn°. Payne	20¾				no such man to be found in the County
the Same	14¾		do. do. do.		
Benja. Freeman	902		do. do. do.		
x Jn°. Thomson	18½	5/3	4.17.1½	1.5¼	
x William Bird	10½	17/	8.18.6	2.8	
x do.	51	do.	43.7.0	13.--	
x do.	27	do.	17.19.--	5.4	purchased of James Dunlop
x Anthony Gardner	42½	do.	36.2.6	10.10	
x Henry Todd	130	do.	110.10.--	1.13.1¾	
x Jn°. Byne	2¼	do.	1.18.3	6¾	
William Dillard	76	appears to be land that has always been incl. in his other lands			
Robert Hill	75	8/4	31.5.0	9.4½	Wm. Keeling

[arithmetic omitted]

Peter Dudley & William Courtney, Commrs.
King & Queen Return for 1785
Warrant issd. 30 Augt. '85
£1.5.8 to add

A List of Alterations of Land in King & Queen County for the year 1786.

Present Proprietors Names	Qty. Land	Price	Amt. Land	Amt. Tax	Of Whom Had
Thomas Fogg	200	6/3	62.10.0	0.18.9	James Fogg
Theoderick Nowel	248	8/4	124.3.4	1.17.3	Fras. & Wm. Lefon
Jn[o.] Parker	116½	7/10	45.12.7	13.9	Dudley Farthing
Jn[o.] Schools	83½	--	32.14.2	9.9½	Do.
Thomas Wilmore	19	--	7.8.10	2.2½	Do.
John Hoskins (addition)	170	7/3	61.12.6	18.6	Joseph Minor
Henry Brown, do.	50	6/3	15.12.6	4.9	Jn[o.] Wheeley
Do., this land has been Surveyed and [ ] 21 acres	54	--	16.17.6	5.0	Jn[o.] O'Neale, ¼ deduct
Do., addition	60	7/10	23.10.0	7.1	Joseph Wiltshire
Eliza. Semple, do.	100	10/5	52.1.8	15.8	Jn[o.] Howel
William Gatewood	109	--	56.15.5	17.1	Jas. Ball
Jn[o.] Fleet	370	--	192.14.2	2.17.10	Robt. Hoskins
Do.	180	6/3	56.5.0	16.10½	Wm. Phillips
Reuben Garnett, addition	33	5/3	8.13.3	2.8	Lewis Longest
Henry Carlton, Do.	80	7/10	31.6.8	7.4¾	Wm. Holderby
Wm. Tignor	130	--	50.18.4	15.4¼	Do.
Jn[o.] Pollard, add.	384	7/3	139.4.0	[2].1.10	Leo[d.] Smithey
Humphry Temple, all Lands of Walkerton} both improv'd and unimprov'd [ ]} the Lotts charg'd last year Included}	108	30/	162.0.0	2.8.7	Given to public, taken away and made private property
Thomas Roane Junr.	1600	24/10	1926.13.4	28.18.0	Wm. Roane
Augt[e.] Owin	100	6/3	31.5.0	9.5	Jn[o.] O'Neal
Mrs. Lucy Leigh, £125.8.2	101	24/10	12.[8.2]	1.17.7	Rich[d.] Leigh
Jn[o.] Leigh	199	--	247.1.10	3.14.2	Do.
Joel Willis	63	20/9	65.7.3	19.7	Harry Gaines
Major Roane, added	190	4/2	38.8.2	10.8	Mitchell Overstreet
Rob[t.] Armstead	200	7/10	78.6.8	1.3.6	Beverly Whiteing
Mitchell Overstreet	90	4/2	18.15.0	5.7½	Major Roane
Rich[d.] Deshazo	52	3/2	8.4.8	2.5½	not before enter'd.
Wm. Hart	40	5/3	10.10.0	3.1¾	Benj[a.] Bohannon 15a more than was enter'd [ ] survey

Carried Over

Alterations [1786] *continued*

Present Proprietors Names	Qty. Land	Price	Amt. Land	Amt. Tax	Of Whom Had
Wm. Damm	25	4/2	5.4.2	1.6½	Geo. Bowden [acpt.?]
Robt. Carlton B added	100	6/3	31.5.0	9.4½	Jno. Pemberton
Jno. Watts, Do.	45	--	14.1.3	4.2½	Robt. Carlton
Jno. Jones, Do.	200	10/5	104.3.4	1.11.3	Robt. Beverley
Thomas Dew	600	14/6	435.0.0	6.10.6	Wm. Dew
Do.	577	13/6	389.9.6	5.16.10	Geo. Holloway
Peter Deshazo, added	45	8/4	18.15.0	5.7½	Robt. Hill
Frankey Seayers	338	9/4	157.14.8	2.7.2	Anthony Lumpkin
Ralph G. Merideth	155	14/6	108.10.0	1.12.6	Saml. Merideth Est.
Benja. Bohannon	160	4/2	33.6.8	10.--	James Deshazo
Richd. Row, as it apeared} it so much more than he} ought to be charg'd. with}	71	10/5	36.19.7	11.1	
Jno. Mitchell, added	300	12/6	187.10.0	2.16.3	Thomas [Moore]
Thomas Cleveley	80	7/10	31.6.8	9.4¾	[Whitacar] Campbell
Henry Oaks Senr.	110	3/2	17.8.4	5.3	William Bourn
Moore Fauntleroy	1036	24/10	1286.7.4	19.5.11	Robt. W. Carter
Thomas Fauntleroy	800	8/4	333.6.2	5.0.0	Wm. Bray

Wm. Courtney & Peter Dudley, Commrs.

[arithmetic omitted]

King & Queen, July 20th 1786.
D. Sir
I am Exceeding sorry to Trouble you with the inclos'd return of the Changes of the Land in the County, but seeing M. Wood's advertisement was glad to make use of the first opportunity to make the return, and must beg the favour of you to do it for me, and likewise should be much oblige to you to get the warrent [blot] for doing that service, in sepperates ones your favour will greatly Oblige Sir.

Your Hble. servant, Wm. Courtney.

1786. Commissioners of the Land tax in King & Queen.

Warrt. issd. & [ ] to Mr. Jno. Lyne, 2nd July '86.
1.15.7 add.
£1365.13.11
end'd. 6th June 1787.

[envelope face addressed to] f.post.
Capt. John Lyne, Richmond

List of the land Tax within the County of King and Queen for the year 1787, with Alterations Included.

This List apears to be a just state of Land in this County as possibly can be come to.

[pages 1-2, 1787]

Present Proprietors Names	Qty. Land	Price	Amt. Land	Amt. Tax
Alexander, Benjamin	202	9/4	94.5.4	1.8.4
Alexander, Elisha	102	7/3	36.12.3	11.6
Alexander, Thomas	50	"	18.2.6	5.6
Alexander, John	50	9/4	23.6.8	7.0
Anderson, Churchill	636	7/3	230.11.0	3.9.2
Anderson, Pauling	498	14/6	361.1.0	5.9.4
Atkins, John Este.	42	7/3	15.4.6	4.7
Atkins, John Jun$^{r.}$	120	4/2	25.0.0	7.6
Abbott, Jacob	112	7/10	43.17.4	13.2
Anderson, Richard	460	5/3	120.15.0	1.16.3
Armstead, Rob$^{t.}$	200	7/10	78.6.8	1.3.6
Beverley, Robert	2474	10/5	1288.8.10	19.6.7
Brown, Henry	657	7/5½	245.8.1	3.13.7½
Baylor, Gregory Este.	720	14/6	522.0.0	7.16.7
Bland, Henry	166	8/4	69.3.4	1.0.9
Bates, James	358	"	149.3.4	2.4.9
do.	42	4/2	8.15.0	2.7½
Barton, John	125	"	26.0.10	7.10
Banks, William	365	"	76.0.10	1.2.9¾
Brooking, Fra$^{s.}$	930	10/5	484.7.6	7.5.4
Baylor, John Este.	760	14/6	551.0.0	8.5.4
Boughton, Thomas, Essex	130	9/4	60.13.4	18.3
[Bou]ghton, John	200	8/4	83.6.8	1.[5]
Boughton, Henry, Essex	88	6/3	27.10.0	[8.3]
Boughton, Tho$^{s.}$	100	8/4	41.13.4	12.[6]
Broach, John	45	6/3	14.1.3	4.3
Burton, Tho$^{s.}$ Este.	170	5/3	44.12.6	13.5
Bohannon, Benjamin	160	4/2	33.6.8	10.0
Bohannon, Ann	50	"	10.8.4	3.2
Brown, W$^{m.}$	75	7/10	29.7.6	8.10
Bagby, John	110	7/3	39.17.6	11.11
Bagby, Richard	260	"	94.5.0	1.8.3½
Bagby, Tho$^{s.}$	260	"	94.5.0	1.8.3½
Brooke, Richard	1539¾	29/-	2232.12.9	33.9.10
Brumley, John	329½	3/2	52.3.5	15.[8]
Bird, William	744	7/3	269.14.0	4.0.[11]
do., Dragon	88½	17/1-	70.4.6	1.1.0
Bird, Mary	619	6/3	19[3].8.9	2.18.1
Bird, Philemon	1238	"	386.17.6	5.16.1
Brett, John	446	18/	401.8.0	6.0.5
Bowers, William	70	7/3	25.7.6	7.8
Bowers, John	198	3/2	31.7.0	9.5
Birch, James	190	"	30.1.8	9.1
Birch, Eliz$^{h.}$	100	4/2	20.16.8	6.3
Bird, Anthony	275	3/2	43.10.10	13.1
	Carried forw$^{d.}$			132.1.2¾
There must be an addition to}				
John Bagbey, 1 above Quant$^{y.}$ of}	220	7/3	79.15.0	1.3.[ ]

[page 3, 1787]

Present Proprietors Names	Qty. Land	Price	Amt. Land	Amt. Tax
Brought Forw[d.]				132.1.2¾
Byne, John Este.	336	4/2	70.0.0	1.1.0
do., Dragon	2¼	17/	1.18.3	6¾
Bird, Barbara	$266_{2/3}$	24/10	331.2.2½	4.16.0
Bird, Robert	$533_{1/3}$	--	662.4.5½	9.12.0
Bourn, Richard	150	3/2	23.15.0	7.2
Burch, Wm. Este.	257	5/9	73.17.9	1.2.2
Boyd, James Este.	115	18/8	107.6.8	1.12.3
Bray, Richard	350	7/10	137.1.8	2.1.2
Bird, Hanah	100	3/2	15.16.8	4.9
Bowers, Ann	60	"	9.10.0	2.11
Bowden, Wm.	403	6/9	136.0.3	2.0.9½
Bew, William	117	3/2	18.10.6	5.7½
Burk, Tho[s.]	100	4/2	20.16.8	6.3
Bland, Richard	125	"	26.0.0	7.10
Boyd, Spencer Este.	1428	10/5	770.15.0	11.11.2
Berkley, Edm[d.]	762	5/3	200.0.6	3.0.0
Bland, John	60	12/6	37.10.0	11.3
Bullman, Tho[s.] Este.	100	5/3	26.5.0	7.11
Billups, John	133	12/6	83.02.6	1.5.0
Briggs, John	170	4/2	35.8.4	10.8
Belote, Severn Este.	172	--	35.16.8	10.9
Bland, William Jun[r.]	120	"	25.0.0	7.6
do., Edw[d.] Brookes	30	3/2	4.15.0	1.5
Bowden, William Jun[r.]	100	4/2	20.16.8	6.3
Bowden, John	100	--	20.16.8	6.3
[Bland], Wm. Jr.	250	--	52.1.8	15.8
Bland, Thomas	300	3/2	57.10.0	17.3
Brooking, John	90	--	14.5.0	4.4
Bowden, George	75	--	15.12.6	4.9½
Butler, Reuben	380	7/3	137.15.0	2.1.4
Burch, William	45	3/2	7.2.6	2.1½
Cook, Mary	200	8/4	83.6.8	1.5.0
Coleman, Thomas	572	6/3	178.15.0	2.13.8
Chick, Richard	491	7/3	177.19.9	2.13.5
Chapman, George	200	7/10	78.6.8	1.3.6
Campbell, William	1029	7/3	373.0.3	5.11.9
Chapman, Eliz[a.]	200	7/10	78.6.8	1.3.6
Craine, Catharine	50	5/3	13.2.6	4.0
Craine, John	6	--	1.10.6	.6
Cleverius, Benjamin	419	20/9	434.14.3	6.10.5
Carlton, Henry	280	7/10	109.13.4	1.12.10
Clayton, Thomas	275	7/3	99.13.9	1.9.11
Campbell, Whitaker	318	7/10	124.11.0	1.17.6
	Carried forw[d.]			205.11.4

[page 4, 1787]

Present Proprietors Names	Qty. Land	Price	Amt. Land	Amt. Tax
Brought Forw[d.]				205.11.4
Clevely, Thomas	80	7/10	36.6.8	9.4¾
Crafton, Richard	236	9/4	110.2.8	1.13.1
Craine, George	30	7/3	10.7.6	3.4
Coleman, Milley	196	10/5	102.1.8	1.10.8
Carlton, John	50	5/3	13.2.6	4.0
Carlton, Joel	53½	6/3	16.14.5	5.1
Carter, Jane	60	3/2	9.10.0	2.11
Courtney, Thomas	175	5/3	45.18.9	13.10
Carlton, Thomas (S)	300	7/10	117.10.0	1.15.3
Carlton, John (SM)	100	6/3	31.5.0	9.5
Campbell, Sarah	296	12/6	185.0.0	2.15.6
Carlton, Christ[r.] Sen[r.]	37½	6/3	11.14.5	3.7
Carlton, Wm. (Shoe)	90¾	"	28.7.3	8.7
do., Wm. Harwood	160	15/	120.0.0	1.16.0
Carlton, Robert Este.	93	4/2	19.7.6	5.10
do., Jn[o.] Pemberton	55	6/3	17.3.9	5.2
Carlton, Richard	250	7/3	90.12.6	1.7.3
Carlton, Christ[r.] Jun[r.]	100	"	36.5.0	10.11
Carlton, James	225	6/3	70.6.3	1.1.2
Carlton, Philemon	100	3/2	15.16.8	4.9
Cooper, Henry	50	4/2	10.8.4	3.2
Carlton, Thomas (T)	100	6/3	31.5.0	9.5
Cardwell, John Este.	600	4/2	125.0.0	1.17.6
Cook, John Este.	300	"	62.10.0	18.9
Collins, Thomas	150	"	31.5.0	9.5
do., Palmers	350	7/3	126.17.6	1.18.1
Carlton, John Jun[r.] (Carp[r.])	235	4/2	48.19.2	14.9
Campbell, William (St.)	238	3/2	[37].13.8	11.4
Collier, Charles	250	8/4	104.3.4	1.11.3
Collins, John	100	4/2	20.16.8	6.3
Colley, Charles	100	"	20.16.8	6.3
Corbin, Richard	1868	10/5	972.18.4	14.11.11
Chowning, Samuel	150	5/3	39.7.6	11.1[6]
Collins, Joyeux	140	10/5	72.18.4	1.1.10
Crittenden, Zachariah	140	14/6	101.10.0	1.10.6
Cary, W. Miles	1820	16/7	1509.1.8	22.12.9
Collier, John (Cobler)	150	5/3	39.7.6	11.10
Campbell, James	100	6/3	31.5.0	9.5
Collawn, John	100	5/3	26.5.0	7.11
Crittenden, Rich[d.] Jun[r.]	178	"	46.14.6	14.1
Collier, Fra[s.] Este.	400	4/2	83.6.8	1.5.0
Corr, Averilla	140	"	36.15.0	11.1
Collier, Catharine	750	5/3	196.17.6	2.19.1
Clegg, Isaiah	248	4/2	56.13.4	15.6
Cook, Dawson	40	3/2	6.6.6	1.1[0]
do., Step[n.] Field	296	7/3	107.3.0	1.12.[ ]
Curry, Ann	100	4/2	20.16.8	6.3
	Carried Forw[d.]			281.6.1¼

[page 5, 1787]

Present Proprietors Names	Qty. Land	Price	Amt. Land	Amt. Tax
Brought Forward				281.6.1¼
Corr, Fran[s.]	175	3/2	27.14.2	8.4
Courtney, W[m.]	190	7/10	74.8.4	1.2.4
Corr, Wm. Este.	200	3/2	31.13.4	9.6
Craine, William	75	13/6	50.12.6	15.2¼
Cooke, Thomas	240	3/2	38.0.0	11.5
Cross, Joseph	38	6/3	11.17.6	3.7
Crittenden, Lemuel	199	5/3	52.4.9	15.9
Carlton, Humph[y.]	125	7/3	45.6.3	13.8
Carlton, Thos. (Join[r.])	235	6/3	73.8.9	1.2.1
Dew, William	935	14/6	677.17.6	10.3.5
Dowling, William	264	8/4	110.0.0	1.13.0
Dix, Gabrial	338	6/3	105.12.6	1.11.8
Deshazo, James	30	--	9.7.6	2.10
Deshazo, Richard	204	3/2	32.6.0	9.8½
Deshazo, William	162	4/2	33.15.0	10.2
Durham, Joseph	76	"	15.16.8	4.9
Draper, John Este.	287	6/3	89.13.9	1.6.11
Deshazo, Peter	180	--	56.5.0	16.11
do., Rt. Hill	45	8/4	18.15.0	5.7½
Dickie, James	512	--	213.6.8	3.4.0
Dunbar, David	366	"	152.10.0	2.5.9
Dally, John	200	3/2	31.13.4	9.6
Dally, Ann	224	--	35.9.4	10.8
Dobbins, Charles	147	5/3	38.11.9	11.7
Dean, Benjamin	50	"	13.2.6	4.0
Dillard, William Jr.	100	3/2	15.16.8	4.9
Dunn, Agrippa	140	5/3	36.15.0	11.1
Dudley, Peter Este.	370	7/10	144.18.4	2.3.6
do., of Jn[o.] Baylor	160	5/3	42.0.0	12.7
Davis, Jane	100	4/2	20.16.8	6.3
Didlake, Margt.	65	"	13.10.10	4.1
Durham, Robert Este.	50	"	10.8.4	3.2
Dunn, Thomas	30	6/3	9.7.6	2.10
Dillard, William Senr.	276	12/6	172.10.0	2.11.9
Durham, George	50	4/2	10.8.4	3.2
Dillard, Ann	70	"	14.11.8	4.5
Durham, Tho[s.]	85	3/2	13.9.2	4.1
Diggs, Isaac Este.	175	5/3	45.18.9	13.10
Didlake, George Este.	114	10/5	59.7.6	17.10
Dungie, John	110	3/2	17.8.4	5.3
Davis, Zachariah	130	"	20.11.8	6.3
Dudley, William (Ferry)	290	14/6	210.5.0	3.3.1
do. Lidia Wedderburn's	315½	6/3	98.11.10½	1.9.6¾
Damm, John	55	6/3	17.3.9	5.2
Damm, William	25	4/2	5.4.2	1.6½
Dudley, William Senr.	180	7/10	70.10.0	1.1.2
		Amo[t.] Carried Forw[d.]		320.3.10¼

[page 6, 1787]

Present Proprietors Names	Qty. Land	Price	Amt. Land	Amt. Tax
Amo[t.] Brought Forw[d.]				320.3.10¼
Douglass, John	100	6/3	31.5.0	9.5
do., Stn. Field	139	7/3	50.7.9	15.1¼
Didlake, John	1200	"	435.0.0	6.10.6
Dudley, B. Robert Est.	421	"	152.12.3	2.5.10
Dudley, Thomas	267½	6/3	81.17.8½	1.4.7
Dillard, Nichs.	75	4/2	15.12.6	4.9
Dillard, Benjn. Este.	133	5/3	34.18.4	10.6
Drummond, Thomas	150	6/3	46.17.6	14.6
Didlake, James Este.	131	3/2	20.14.10	6.3
Dillard, Tho[s.]	377	5/3	98.19.3	1.9.9
Dillard, Eliz[h.]	449	14/6	325.10.6	
Dudley, Banks	246	3/2	38.19.--	
Dillard, William (Son T.)	150	4/2	31.5.0	
Davis, Thomas	150	7/3	50.12.6	
Eubank, James	75	10/5	39.1.3	11.9
do.	150	14/6	108.15.0	1.12.7½
Eubank, Thomas	150	14/6	108.15.0	1.12.7½
Eubank, John	200	"	145.0.0	2.3.6
do., H. Samuel	78	7/3	28.5.6	8.6
Eubank, Henry	171	5/3	44.17.9	13.6
Edwards, Thomas	66	4/2	13.15.0	4.2
Eubank, Jane	28¾	5/3	7.11.0	2.4
Eubank, Richard	65	3/2	10.5.10	3.1½
do.	90¾	5/3	23.16.6	7.2
Eubank, Richard Este.	227	4/2	47.5.10	14.3
Edwards, Charles	192	3/2	30.8.0	9.2
Fleet, Baylor	360	20/9	373.10.0	5.12.0
do., Whiteings	350	7/10	137.1.8	2.1.2
Fauntleroy, G. Samuel	880	16/7	729.13.4	10.18.1
Fauntleroy, Moore	1006	24/10	1231.2.4	18.14.8¾
Fleet, John	326	10/5	165.12.6	2.9.7
do.	180	6/3	56.6.--	16.10
Faulkner, Thomas	155	"	48.8.9	14.7
Fogg, Thomas	200	"	62.10.--	18.9
Fogg, James	120	"	37.10.--	11.3
Faurinholtz, Wm. Este.	146	"	45.12.6	13.9
Frazer, Wm. Este.	45	20/9	46.13.9	14.1
Fleet, William	296¼	20/9	307.7.3	4.12.3
Fisher, James Este.	110	3/2	17.18.4	5.3
Foster, Tho[s.]	214	4/2	44.11.8	13.5
Faulkner, Mary	333	6/3	104.1.4	1.11.3
		Amo[t.] Carried Forw[d.]		401.18.7¾

[page 7, 1787]

Present Proprietors Names	Qty. Land	Price	Amt. Land	Amt. Tax
Amo$_{t.}$ bro$^{t.}$ forw$^{d.}$				401.18.7¾
Fauntleroy, Thomas	800	8/4	333.6.8	5.0.0
do., Doct$^{r.}$ Todd	496	18/	456.8.0	6.16.11
Farthing, Dudley	203	7/10	79.10.2	1.3.10
Grafton, Thomas	132	9/4	61.12.0	18.6
Grafton, James	111	6/3	34.13.9	10.5
Gale, John	180	10/5	93.15.0	1.8.5
Goldman, Thomas, Essex	714	9/4	333.4.0	5.0.0
Garnett, Rice	297	7/3	107.13.7	1.12.4
Gatewood, Chaney	860	10/5	451.0.10	6.15.4
do., of Gardners	100	7/3	36.5.0	10.11
Garnett, Joshua	322	8/4	134.3.4	2.0.3
Graves, Edward	200	6/3	62.10.0	18.9
Gatewood, Joseph	445	10/5	231.15.5	3.9.7
Gale, Mathew	323	11/5	184.7.7	2.15.4
Gatewood, John	160	8/4	66.13.4	1.0.0
Garnett, Reuben	183	6/3	57.3.9	17.2
do., Lewis Longest	33	5/3	8.13.3	2.8
Gwathmey, Temple	600	35/3	1057.10.--	15.17.3
Garlick, Samuel	454	24/10	563.14.4	8.9.2
Garlick, John	957	29/	1387.13.0	20.16.4
Griffith, Joseph	50	6/3	15.12.6	4.9
Gresham, Sam$^{l.}$	400	7/3	145.0.0	2.3.6
Garrett, John	100	4/2	20.16.8	6.3
Gardner, John Est.	623	6/9	20.5.3	3.2.9
[G]aines, Fran$^{s.}$	410	14/6	297.5.0	4.9.3
Gaines, Harry	1517	20/4	1542.5.8	23.2.8
Gresham, Tho$^{s.}$	339¼	6/3	106.0.4	1.11.10
Gresham, Phil	200	"	62.10.0	18.9
Gresham, John (D)	200	7/10	78.6.8	1.3.6
Gaines, Robert	225	5/3	59.1.3	17.9
Gresham, William	100	4/2	20.16.8	6.3
Gardner, Eliza	100	6/3	31.5.0	9.5
Gibson, Richard	113	3/2	17.17.10	5.5
Gibson, John	219¾	--	34.15.11	10.6
Griffith, Milly	50	6/3	15.12.6	4.9
Gresham, Ruth	250	5/3	65.12.6	19.9
Griffin, William	840	14/6	609.0.0	9.2.9
Garlick, Camm Este.	1100	6/3	343.15.0	5.3.2
Garrett, Richard	100	3/2	15.16.8	4.9
Garrett, William Est.	330	4/2	68.15.0	1.0.8
Gardner, Anthy. (Doct$^{r.}$)	623	10/5	324.9.7	4.17.4
do., of Doc$^{t.}$ Todd	215	12/6	134.7.6	2.0.3
do., Dragon	42½	17/	36.2.6	10.10
Gresham, William Jun$^{r.}$	200	8/4	83.6.8	1.5.0
Gatewood, Wm.	105	10/5	54.13.9	16.8
Gatewood, Wm. (*Tuckahoe*)	220	3/2	34.16.8	10.6
[G]reen, Robert	150	4/2	31.5.0	9.5
		Amot. Carried Forw$^{d.}$		555.10.2¾

[page 8, 1787]

Present Proprietors Names	Qty. Land	Price	Amt. Land	Amt. Tax
Amount Brought Forward				555.10.2¾
Garrett, Humphry	450	12/6	281.5.0	4.4.9
Guthrie, James	60	"	37.10	11.3
Guthrie, Richard	60	"	37.10	11.3
Guthrie, Richard Jun[r.]	160	3/2	25.6.8	7.7
Glaspe, James	210	5/3	55.2.6	16.7
Guthrie, Mary Sen[r.]	30	--	7.17.6	2.5
Groom, Mary	273	3/2	43.4.6	13.0
Goldman, Martin	140	4/2	29.3.4	8.9
Groom, Barbara	100	3/2	15.16.8	4.9
Groom, Zach[h.]	187	"	29.12.2	8.7
Gulley, Philip	150	"	23.15.0	7.2
Gilmore, Ruth	354	10/5	184.12.9	2.15.5
Garrett, William (Shoe)	200	3/2	31.13.4	9.6
Halbert, James	124	6/2	38.15.0	11.7½
Harwood, Agness	225	4/2	46.17.6	14.1
Holt, Richard	400	6/3	125.0.0	1.17.6
Hill, William	1191	14/6	928.9.6	13.18.7
Hutcherson, Charles	501	7/3	181.12.6	2.14.6
Hall, Corbin	188	8/4	78.6.8	1.3.6
Hitchcock, Tho[s.]	140	4/2	29.3.4	8.9
Hoskins, Samuel	175	5/3	45.18.9	13.10
Hoskins, W[m.]	160	10/5	83.6.8	1.5.0
Herndon, Mary	100	7/3	36.5.0	10.11
Heskew, John	61	5/3	16.0.3	4.10
Hoomes, Benj[n.]	230	7/10	90.1.8	1.7.1
Hendley, Thomas	40	10/5	[2]0.16.8	6.[ ]
Hill, Robert	1555	8/4	647.8.4	9.14.4½
do., Ann Tunstall	223	7/10	87.6.10	1.6.3
Hill, Edward	1200	18/8	1120.0.0	16.16.0
Hart, Wm. Sen[r.]	40	5/3	10.10.0	3.1¼
Hodges, Sally	462	4/2	96.5.0	1.8.11
Hudson, Wm.	112	3/2	17.14.8	5.4
Hemmingway, Daniel Est.	800	4/2	166.13.4	2.0.0
Harwood, Christ[r.]	300	24/10	372.10.--	5.11.9
Harwood, John	501	5/3	131.10.3	1.19.6
Harwood, William	240	30/	360.0.0	5.8.0
Hill, Tho[s.]	300	26/11	403.15.0	6.1.2
Hart, James	150	3/2	23.15.0	7.2
Hart, Anthony	294	"	46.11.0	14.0
do., R. Hart	190	5/3	49.17.6	15.0
do., M. Younger	94	3/2	14.17.8	4.6
Hare, William	109	5/3	28.12.3	8.8
Hunt, William	730	6/3	228.2.6	3.8.6
Holderby, Elizabeth	100	4/2	20.16.8	6.8
Hart, William	218	3/2	34.10.4	10.5
do., H. Jordan	32	4/2	6.13.4	2.0
		Amo[t.] Carried Forw[d.]		650.18.5

[page 9, 1787]

Present Proprietors Names	Qty. Land	Price	Amt. Land	Amt. Tax
Amo^t. bro^t. Forw^d.				650.18.5
Henry, James	1900	14/6	1377.10.0	20.13.3
Halyard, W^m.	190	5/3	49.17.6	15.0
Hoskins, John	540	10/5	281.5.0	4.4.4½
do., J. Minors	170	7/3	61.12.6	18.6
Hawes, William	72	10/5	37.10.0	11.3
Hoskins, Robert	100	6/3	31.5.0	9.5
do., C. Dudley's	120	4/2	25.0.0	7.6
do., J. Oliver	157	5/3	41.4.3	12.4¼
Hardy, Joseph	100	3/2	15.16.8	4.9
Jones, John	505	8/4	210.8.4	3.3.2
do., R. Beverly	200	10/5	104.3.4	1.11.3
Jeffries, Edward	70	3/2	11.1.8	3.4
Jones, James	160	14/6	116.0.0	1.14.10
Jones, James Est.	196	10/5	102.1.8	1.10.8
Jones, William	335	13/6	226.2.6	3.7.11
do., L. Smith	35¾	31/1	55.11.2	16.8
Jeffries, Ambrose	397	7/10	148.8.10	2.4.7
Jeffries, Bernard	30	4/2	6.5.0	
Jordan, Eliz^a.	88	"	18.6.8	
Jordan, Wm.	100	3/2	15.16.8	
Jordan, Thomas Est.	100	4/2	20.16.8	
Johnson, Archibald	100	--	20.16.8	
[Johnson], Lucy	60	8/[4]	25.0.0	
Johnson, Thomas	112	3/2	17.14.8	[blur]
Keeling, William	150	4/2	31.5.0	9.5
Keeling, James	300	7/3	108.15.0	1.12.8
Kemp, John	87	7/10	34.7.6	10.3
do., Jos^h. Wiltshire	53	7/3	19.4.3	5.9
Kauffman, George	583	14/6	422.13.6	6.6.10
Kemp, Thomas	40	10/5	20.16.8	6.3
Kauffman, John	471	18/8	439.12.0	6.11.11
Kennedy, Alex^r.	580	12/6	362.10.0	5.8.9
Kemp, Mathew	100	5/4	26.13.4	8.0
Kemp, Jos. (SM)	200	6/3	62.10.0	18.9
Kidd, John	370	7/3	134.2.6	2.0.3
do., Thos. Peirce	25	4/2	5.4.2	1.7
Kay, Christ^r.	116	6/3	30.9.0	9.1½
Kidd, Barthow.	136	5/3	35.14.0	10.8
Kidd, Benjn.	111	13/6	74.18.2	1.2.5½
Lumpkin, Henry (C)	620	9/4	289.6.8	4.6.10
Lumpkin, John	200	6/3	59.0.0	17.9
Lyne, William Col.	1480	8/4	610.14.2	9.3.3
Lyne, William Junr.	108	8/4	45.0.0	13.6
		Amo^t. Car^d. Forw^d.		738.8.8¾

[page 10, 1787]

Present Proprietors Names	Qty. Land	Price	Amt. Land	Amt. Tax
Amo[t.] Brou. forward				738.8.8¾
Lyon, Dixon	55	8/4	18.15.0	5.8
Lumpkin, William	305	14.6	221.2.6	3.6.5
Lefon, Frans.	119	8/4	49.11.8	14.10½
Lankford, Thomas	100	4/2	20.16.8	6.3
Lumpkin, Robert Jun[r.]	465	8/4	193.15.0	2.18.2
Langham, Wm.	200	7/10	78.6.8	1.3.6
Lumpkin, Robert Sen[r.]	430	7/3	155.17.6	2.6.10
Longest, Caleb	97	7/10	37.19.10	11.6
Longest, Richard	140	"	54.16.8	16.6
Longest, Dorathy	100	"	39.3.4	11.9
Lumpkin, Joyce	287	"	112.8.2	1.13.9
Lumpkin, Mary	108	6/3	33.15.0	10.2
Lumpkin, Anthony	108	"	33.15.0	10.2
Lumpkin, Jacob	916	"	286.5.0	4.5.11
Lewis, Iverson	606	14/6	439.11.--	6.11.11
Lewis, Elizabeth	100	4/2	20.16.8	6.3
Leigh, Lucy	101	24/10	125.8.2	1.17.7
[Leigh], John	199	"	247.1.10	3.14.2
[Lyne], John	507	6/3	158.8.9	2.7.7
[Lambeth], Thomas	200	3/2	31.11.4	9.6
[Lumpkin], Robert (Orphan)	183	4/8	38.2.6	11.6
[Laughlin], [J]ames	126¾	4/2	26.8.2	8.--
[Motley] [E]dwin	740	10/5	389.1.3	5.16.[ ]
McKintosh, William	192	4/2	40.0.0	
Martin, Thomas	680	14/6	493.0.0	7.7.[ ]
Minor, William	149	8/4	62.1.8	18.8
Minor, John	137	"	57.1.8	17.2
Miller, Thomas	527	7/10	206.8.2	3.2.0
Mann, August[e.]	400	8/4	166.13.4	2.10.0
Mitchell, Robert	17	20/9	17.17.9	5.4
Mitchell, John	50	6/3	15.12.6	4.9
Mitchell, James	750	12/6	468.15.0	7.0.8
McKendree, Eliz[a.]	323	5/3	84.15.9	1.5.6
McKendree, John	100	3/2	15.16.8	4.9
Meredith, William (Leach)	243	5/3	63.15.9	19.2
Mitchell, Susanah	170	3/2	26.18.4	8.1
Moore, John	100	"	15.16.8	4.9
Major, Joseph	200	4/2	41.13.4	12.6
Moore, Thomas	400	12/6	250.0.0	3.15.0
Meredith, William Est.	530	14/6	384.5.0	5.15.4
Mitchell, John (S. Major)	270	5/3	70.17.6	1.1.4
do., Rootes's	300	12/6	187.10.0	2.16.3
Moore, Phil	50	3/2	7.18.4	2.5
Macon, John	1092	16/7	905.9.0	13.11.7
Mansfield, William	75	"	62.3.9	18.7
		Amo[t.] carried forward		835.2.3¼

[page 11, 1787]

Present Proprietors Names	Qty. Land	Price	Amt. Land	Amt. Tax
Amo[t.] Bro[t.] for.				835.2.3¼
Manley, Peter	40	7/10	15.13.4	4.9
Meredith, G. Ralph	382	14/6	273.1.6	4.2.--½
[Me]redith, Samuel Est.	185	"	138.0.0	2.1.5½
Muire, Richard	93	12/6	58.2.6	17.6
Major, Mary	175	7/3	63.8.9	19.1
Moore, Richard	145	6/3	45.6.3	13.8
Martin, James	332½	20/9	344.19.4	5.3.5¾
Meredith, John	500	10/5	260.8.4	3.18.2
McCarty, Joseph	73	3/2	11.11.2	3.6
Mills, Michal	50	"	7.18.4	2.5
Metcalf, Thomas	521	14/6	377.14.6	5.13.3¾
Martin, John	80	9/4	37.6.8	11.3
Nowel, Theodrick	298	8/4	124.3.4	1.17.3
Nunn, Jane	180	7/3	65.5.0	19.7
Newbill, George Est.	500	8/4	208.6.8	3.2.6
Newbill, William	450	9/4	210.0.0	3.3.0
Nunn, Thomas	174	7/3	63.1.6	1."."
Nash, John	100	6/3	31.5.0	9.5
Newcombe, Eliz[a].	109	3/2	17.5.2	5.2
Newcombe, William	60	"	9.10.0	2.11
Oliver, John	163	5/3	42.15.9	12.10¾
Orvill, John	100	6/3	31.5.[ ]	9.5
Overstreet, Mitchell	90	4/2	18.5.0	5.7½
Overstreet, Gabriel	414	4/2	86.5.0	1.5.11
do., Eliz[a.] Brushwood	120	"	25.0.0	7.6
do., Haynes	130	5/3	34.2.6	10.2
Odear, Edith	50	5/3	13.2.6	4.0
Oakes, Henry Sen[r.]	110	3/2	17.8.4	5.3
Oakes, Henry Jun[r.]	100	4/2	20.16.8	6.3
Owen, Augustine	100	6/3	31.5.0	9.5
Pitts, David	420	9/4	196.0.[ ]	2.18.10
Pitts, Obadiah	20	10/5	10.8.4	3.2
Philips, John	143	"	74.9.7	1.2.4
Pitts, Ann Est.	100	6/3	31.5.0	9.5
Philips, Richard	230	7/3	83.7.6	1.5.1
Pollard, John	235	9/4	109.13.4	1.12.11
do., Leo[d.] Smithey	384	7/3	139.4.0	2.1.10
Pruett, Frans.	99	9/4	46.4.[ ]	13.11
Parker, John	116½	7/10	45.12.7	13.9
Peirce, Ann	35	7/5	12.3.9	3.8
Pendleton, Philip	337	10/5	175.10.5	2.12.8
Perryman, Anthony	130	7/3	47.2.6	14.2
		Carried Forward		890.1.11

[page 12, 1787]

Present Proprietors Names	Qty. Land	Price	Amt. Land	Amt. Tax
Amot. ~~Carried~~ brot. forwd.				890.0.11
Pollard, Richard	432	8/4	180.0.0	2.14.0
Prince, Frans.	113	7/10	40.5.2	13.4
Pendleton, Benjamin	450	"	176.5.0	2.12.11
Pynes, Benja.	400	6/3	125.0.0	1.17.6
Pemberton, John	286	"	89.7.6	1.6.11½
Pace, Benjn.	263	7/3	95.6.9	1.[ ].8
Pickels, John	225	"	81.11.3	1.4.6
Price, Robert	630	6/3	196.17.6	2.19.1
Pigg, Rachel	108	14/6	78.6.0	1.3.6
Pigg, John	216	"	156.12.0	2.7.0
Paggett, Samuel	36	7/10	14.2.[ ]	4.2
Pollard, William	95	7/3	34.8.9	10.5
Pierce, Thomas	135	4/2	28.1.11	8.5
Prior, John	150	3/2	23.15.0	7.8
Richards, William	510	12/6	318.15.0	4.15.8
Robertson, Donald Est.	155	"	96.17.6	1.9.1
do.	210	7/3	76.2.6	1.2.11
Richards, George	564	14/6	408.18.[ ]	6.2.9
Roane, Thomas Col.	3417	18/8	3189.4.[ ]	47.16.9
do., Henry Carlton's	200	6/3	63.10.[ ]	18.[ ]
do. Richards John Est.	1020	9/4	476.[8].8	
Row, Joseph	390	6/3	12[1].17.6	1.16.[ ]
Row, Thomas Major	555	7/3	201.3.9	3.0.4
do., Fleet's	665	20/9	689.18.9	10.7.0
do., Nowel's	296	6/3	92.10.0	1.7.2
Read, Robert	14	5/3	3.13.6	1.1
Row, Richard	550	8/4	229.3.4	3.8.9
Roane, Thomas Junr.	1600	24/10	1926.13.4	28.18.0
Rowzee, Eliza.	120	3/2	19.0.0	5.9
Richerson, Elias	86	4/2	17.18.4	5.5
Row, John Est.	100	6/3	31.5.0	9.5
Richards, John	221½	4/2	46.3.0	13.11
Richards, Williams	296	5/3	77.14.0	1.3.4
Richerson, James	180	4/2	37.10.0	11.3
Richerson, William	181	"	37.14.2	11.4
Richerson, Rachel	101½	"	21.2.11	6.5
Roane, Thos. (LP)	150	3/2	23.15.0	7.2
Roane, Major	340	4/2	71.1.8	1.1.8
Robinson, Benjn. Est.	1300	8/4	541.13.4	8.2.6
do., Richd. Leigh's	266	12/6	166.5.0	2.9.11
Roane, Charles	200	14/6	145.0.0	2.3.6
Robins, William	40	6/3	12.10.0	3.9
Roane, John	450	10/-	225.1.0	3.7.6
	Amot. carried forwd.			1049.9.4½

[page 13, 1787]

Present Proprietors Names	Qty. Land	Price	Amt. Land	Amt. Tax
Amo$^{t.}$ bro$^{t.}$ forw$^{d.}$				1049.9.4½
Smith, John (drisdale)	406	7/3	147.3.6	2.4.2
Satterwhite, George	164	6/3	51.5.[ ]	15.1
Satterwhite, Wm.	100	4/2	20.16.8	6.3
Samuel, Henry	85	6/3	26.11.6	8.0
Samuel, Andrew	72	7/3	26.2.0	7.10
Spencer, Edward	392½	8/4	163.10.10	2.9.1
Schools, John	83½	7/10	32.14.1	9.9½
Sears, Franky	338	9/4	157.14.8	2.7.2
Schools, Gabriel	169	6/3	52.16.3	15.11
Skelton, Wm.	132	9/4	61.12.0	18.6
Smith, Ann	85	7/3	30.16.3	9.3
Starling, Jane	360	7/10	141.0.0	2.2.4
Skelton, Tho$^{s.}$	294	8/4	122.10.0	1.16.9
Scott, Benj$^{n.}$	200	9/4	93.6.8	1.8.0
Saunders, Joseph Est.	200	7/3	72.10.[ ]	1.1.0
Shepherd, Wm.	140	9/4	65.6.8	19.8
Semple, Eliz$^{h.}$	674	14/6	488.4.8	7.6.7
Smith, Molly	30	4/2	6.5.0	1.11
Smith, John (Lhead)	100	5/3	26.5.0	7.11
Smith, Lewis	113½	7/3	41.12.11	12.6
Swinton, Geo:	750	13/6	506.5.0	7.11.11
Stone, Sarah	300	7/3	108.15.0	1.12.8
Smith, Larkin	1254¼	31/1	1949.6.3½	29.4.10
Smith, Henry	400	6/3	125.0.0	1.17.6
Smith, Wm.	140	7/10	54.16.8	16.8
Smith, Wm. (Son Jas.)	300	6/3	113.15.[ ]	1.14.2
Smith, James Sen$^{r.}$	80	3/2	12.13.4	3.10
Smith, James Jun$^{r.}$	101	7/10	39.11.2	11.10½
Shepherd, Mary	100	5/3	26.5.[ ]	7.11
Stephens, Tho$^{s.}$ Est.	609½	7/10	238.14.5	3.11.8
Stephens, George	645	"	252.12.6	3.15.9½
Shackelford, John	236	7/3	85.11.0	1.5.8
Starke, Richard Est.	250	6/3	78.2.6	1.3.6
do., Geo: Richards	100	4/2	20.16.8	6.3
Soans, Mary	382	24/10	474.6.4	7.2.4
Stone, Robert	300	4/2	62.10.0	18.9
Stone, John	357	6/3	93.14.3	1.8.2
Smith, Robert	879	10/5	457.19.3	6.17.5
Smith, Guy	189½	3/2	30.0.1	9.1
Simpkins, Nimrod	60	"	9.10.[ ]	2.11
Southerland, Wm. Est.	283½	5/3	73.18.5	1.2.3
Sears, Philip	83	4/2	17.5.10	5.3
Seward, Mary Est.	260	"	54.3.4	16.3
Spencer, Tho$^{s.}$	300	10/5	156.5.0	2.6.11
do., Jn$^{o.}$ Collins	255	4/2	53.2.6	15.11
Shackelford, Wm. Est.	700	14/6	527.10.[ ]	7.18.6
Seward, Benjamin	115	3/2	18.4.2	5.6
Stedman, Christ$^{r.}$	191	5/3	50.2.9	15.1
Saddler, John	150	6/3	46.17.6	14.6
Shackelford, Alex$^{r.}$	60	4/2	12.10.0	3.9
		Amo$^{t.}$ Carried forw$^{d.}$		1163.4.8

[page 14, 1787]

Present Proprietors Names	Qty. Land	Price	Amt. Land	Amt. Tax
Amo[t.] bro[t.] forward				1163.4.8
Stedman, Christ[r.] Jun[r.]	133½	6/3	41.18.1½	12.6½
do., of Ann Dillard (T)	260	5/3	65.6.0	1.0.6
Smith, Gregory	485	14/6	351.12.6	5.5.5
Shackelford, John (R)	508	8/4	211.13.4	3.3.6
Shackelford, Lyne	567	6/3	177.3.9	2.13.1
Shackelford, Jn[o.] (M)	40	7/10	15.13.4	4.8
do., of Jn[o.] Muire	182	7/3	65.19.6	19.10
Scott, Anderson	330	16/7	273.12.6	4.2.2
Shepherd, Isaac	190	3/2	30.1.8	9.3
Trice, William	70	7/3	25.7.6	7.8
Trice, Betty	70	"	25.7.6	7.8
Taylor, John Est.	50	6/3	15.12.6	4.9
Taylor, Edmond	294	8/14	122.10.[ ]	1.16.9
Temple, Joseph	918	10/5	478.2.6	7.3.6
Tunstall, Molly	430	"	233.19.2	3.7.2½
Tunstall, Richard Jun[r.]	1097	7/3	397.13.3	5.19.3
do., Sally Tunstall	200	18/8	186.13.4	2.16.0
Trice, Jane	170	5/3	44.12.6	13.5
Tignor, William	130	7/10	50.18.4	15.4½
Tureman, Benj[n.]	120	3/2	19.0.0	5.9
Taliaferro, Wm.	1000	14/6	725.0.0	10.17.6
Townley, Robert	350	"	235.15.0	3.16.2
Taliaferro, Philip	990	8/4	412.10.0	6.3.9
Taliaferro, Richard	300	5/3	78.15.0	1.3.8
Taylor, Isbell	100	4/2	20.16.8	6.3
Thruston, Batchelder	100	3/2	15.16.8	4.[ ]
Tucker, John	180	7/3	65.5.0	19.7
Temple, Humphy.	70	33/2	116.1.8	1.14.9¾
do., Walkertown	108	30/	162.0.0	2.8.7
Tunstall, Rich[d.] Est.	538	20/9	558.3.6	8.7.5
Tunstall, Richard (Best[d.])	357	8/4	148.15.0	2.4.8
Vass, Thomas	250	5/3	65.12.6	19.9
Wyatt, Henry	200	7/3	72.10.[ ]	1.1.9
White, Henry	100	8/4	41.13.4	12.6
Wilmore, Tho[s.]	150	10/5	78.2.6	1.3.6
do., Dudley Farthing	19	7/10	7.8.10	2.2½
Wright, James	124½	5/3	32.13.8	9.10
Wyatt, Joseph	60	8/4	25.0.0	7.6
Walden, John	105	12/6	65.12.6	19.9
Wood, Thomas	260	7/10	111.16.8	1.10.8
Wilson, Isaac	200	6/3	62.10.0	18.9
Wilson, Benj[a.] Est.	200	7/3	72.18.0	1.1.9
Wiltshire, Joseph	133	"	48.4.3	14.6
Wyatt, Tho[s.] Est.	480	10/5	250.0.0	3.15.0
Wyatt, John	100	7/10	39.3.4	11.9
Wheeley, John	50	6/3	15.12.6	4.9
Watkins, William	37	4/2	7.14.2	2.4
Watkins, Joseph	65	"	13.10.10	4.2
		Amo[t.] Carried up		1259.0.6¾

[page 15, 1787]

Present Proprietors Names	Qty. Land	Price	Amt. Land	Amt. Tax
Amo^t. bro^t. forward				1259.0.6¾
Willis, Joel	63	31/1	97.12.3	1.9.4½
Walden, James	154	7/10	60.6.4	18.1
Walker, Henry Est.	150	5/3	39.7.6	11.10
Ware, John	562	7/3	203.14.6	3.3.2
Walker, Frans.	495	33/2	216.15.0	12.6.3
Walker, Humphy.	325	"	538.19.2	8.1.8
Whayne, Wm.	13½	7/3	4.17.11	1.6
do., Langham's	194	7/10	75.19.8	1.2.9
Watts, Edward	250	7/3	90.12.6	1.7.3
Watts, Jno.	293	7/10	114.15.2	1.14.6
do., of Jno. Pemberton	45	6/3	14.1.3	4.2½
Watts, Wm.	380	7/10	184.16.8	2.4.7
Watts, Kauffman	300	5/3	78.15.0	1.3.8
Williams, Howard	283	4/2	58.19.2	17.9
Wyatt, Thos.	106	7/10	41.10.4	12.6
Wyatt, John (Blind)	103	6/3	32.3.9	9.8
Wyatt, Wm.	29¾	7/3	10.15.8	3.3
Williams, Howard Est.	300	6/3	93.15.0	1.8.2
Williams, Charles	550	4/2	114.11.8	1.14.5
Walton, James	80	"	16.3.4	5.0
Walton, Mary	60	"	12.10.0	3.9
Walton, Eliz^a.	60	3/2	9.10.[ ]	2.11
Walton, John	176	5/3	46.4.0	13.11
Walton, Wm.	66	4/2	13.15.0	4.2
Walton, Thos.	66	"	13.15.0	4.2
Ware, John	75	5/3	19.13.9	5.11
Ware, Auther	83	4/2	17.5.10	5.3
Watts, James	350	"	72.18.4	1.1.11
[Walden], Richard	180	10/[ ]	93.15.0	1.8.1½
[Wa]lden, Lewis	150	3/2	23.15.0	7.3
do., of Thos. Dudley	84½	6/3	28.2.3½	8.5
Wyatt, Richard	175	12/6	109.7.6	1.12.9¾
Wyatt, William	125	"	78.2.6	1.3.5
Ware, Robert Est.	100	4/2	20.16.8	6.3
Ware, Sarah	175	"	36.9.2	11.0
Williams, Eliz^a.	50	3/2	7.18.4	2.5
White, James	200	6/3	62.10.[ ]	18.9
Watkins, Eliz^a.	100	3/2	15.16.8	4.9
Warrin, Cathe.	175	"	27.14.2	8.4
Ware, Robert (Bishop)	112	"	17.14.8	5.4
Whitting, Peter	1100	10/5	572.18.4	8.11.11
Ware, Christ^r. Est.	500	12/6	312.10.[ ]	4.13.9
Weddisburn, Lydia [should be Ledderburn]	350	6/3	109.7.6	1.12.10
Whitting, Beverley	1360	7/10	532.13.4	7.19.9
Webley, John	173	5/3	45.8.3	13.8
do., of B. Collier	100	4/2	20.16.8	6.3
Walden, Edward	373	5/3	97.18.3	1.9.5
Wright, William	100	4/2	20.16.8	6.3
Waller, Edward	133½	3/2	21.2.9	6.5
Waller, John	66½	"	10.10.7	3.2
Young, Henry	640	18/8	597.6.8	8.19.3
Total Amount of Land Tax in K. & Queen				1345.1.3
mistake in Harry Gaines Calculation				9.7
				1344.11.8

[page 16, 1787]

Amo$^{t.}$ of Tax brought Over	1344.11.8
Mistake in Jn$^{o.}$ Bagbey brought here	1.3.11
	£1345.15.7

William Fleet & William Courtney, Commissions

A List of Alterations of Land in King & Queen County for the year 1787.

[page 17, 1787]

Present Proprietors Names	Qty. Land	Price	Amt. Land	Amt. Tax	from whom and to have
Bowden, William	403	6/9	136.0.3	[ ].0.9½	Henry Todd
Bland, William	30	3/2	4.15.0	[ ].1.5	Edw$^{d.}$ Brooks
Bird, Rob$^{t.}$	533 1/3	24/10	662.4.5	9.12.0	Barbara Bird
Brett, Jn$^{o.}$, Cr. for 6/10 p. acre as we suppose} there must have been some mistake in} the former valuation}					
Butler, Reubin	380	7/3	137.15.0	[2].1.4	Stephen Field
Bird, Anthony	275	3/2	43.10.10	13.1	Jn$^{o.}$ Bird
Bagbey, Richard	260	7/3	94.5.0	1.8.3½	Jn$^{o.}$ Bagbey
Bagbey, Thomas	260	"	94.5.[ ]	1.8.3½	Do.
Berkley, Edmond, deduct 138 acres from 900	762	5/3	200.0.6	3.0.0	
Birch, Wm.	45	3/2	7.2.[8]	2.1½	Phil Eubank
Boyd, Spencer Est.	1428	10/5	770.15.0	1.11.2	Lucy Boyd
Crittenden, Zachy.	140	14/6	101.10.0	1.10.6	Richard Crittenden
Carlton, Jn$^{o.}$ J$^{r.}$	235	4/2	48.19.2	14.9	Geo. Eubank
Cook, Dawson	296	7/3	107.3.0	[1].12.1	Stephen Field
Collins, Jn$^{o.}$, Cr. for 255 acres to Thos. Spencer	100	4/2	20.16.8	6.3	what he has remaining
Crane, Geo.	30	7/3	10.7.6	[ ].3.4	Tho$^{s.}$ Dalley
Carlton, Wm.	160	15/	120.0.0	1.16.0	Wm. Harwood
Douglass, Jn$^{o.}$	139	7/3	50.7.0	15.1¼	Stephen Field
Dudley, Wm. (ferry)	315½	6/3	98.11.10½	1.9.6¾	Alexander Wedderburn's Est.
[Dew], Wm.	600	[ ]	[4]25.[ ]	6.10.6	[Thomas] Dew
Eubank, John	78	7/3	28.5.6	8.6	Henry Samuel J$^{r.}$
Eubank, Richard	65	3/2	10.5.10	3.1½	Phil Eubank Sen$^{r.}$
Fauntleroy, Thomas	496	18/	456.8.0	[ ].16.11	Henry Todd
Fleet, John, charged with 44 acres too much	44	10/5	22.18.4	[ ].6.10½	
Fauntleroy, Moore, w$^{th.}$ 30 do. too much	30	24/10	37.5.0	11.2	
Farthing, Dudley, formerly Omitted	203	7/10	79.10.2	1.3.10	
Guthrie, Richard Jr.	160	3/2	25.6.8	7.7	Dawson Cook
Glaske, James	210	5/3	55.2.6	16.7	James Trice Est.
Gatewood, William, deduct 4 acres	4	10/5	2.1.8	7½	
Gatewood, William (*Tuckahoe*)	220	3/2	34.16.8	[1]0.6	Wm. Gatewood
Gresham, William Jun$^{r.}$	200	8/4	83.6.8	5.0	Susan$^{h.}$ Eubank
Harwood, Jn$^{o.}$	501	5/3	131.10.3	1.19.6	William Harwood
Harwood, William	400	24/10	496.13.4	7.9.0	Jn$^{o.}$ Harwood
Hoskins, Rob$^{t.}$	100	6/3	31.5.0	9.5	Sam$^{l.}$ Peachey
do.	120	4/2	25.0.0	7.6	Chris$^{r.}$ Dudley
do.	157	5/3	41.4.3	12.4½	Jn$^{o.}$ Olliver
Hart, William	32	4/2	6.13.4	2.0	Eliz$^{a.}$ Jordon
Hardy, Joseph	100	3/2	15.16.8	4.9	Edw$^{d.}$ Brooks
~~Jordon, Henry~~	~~88~~	~~4/2~~			~~Eliza. Jordon~~
Kidd, Barthw.	136	5/3	35.14.0	10.8	Edw$^{d.}$ Walden
Kidd, Jn$^{o.}$	25	4/2	5.4.2	1.7	Tho$^{s.}$ Peirce
Kidd, Benj$^{a.}$	75	13/6	50.12.6	15.1¾	Richard Walding
Longest, Caleb, deduct 6 acres	6	7/10	2.7.0	8¼	
[Lyne], William Jun$^{r.}$	108	8/4	45.0.0	13.6	Lyne William Col.

Carried Forward

[page 18, 1787]
[Amo$^{t.}$] brought over & continued

Present Proprietors Names	Qty. Land	Price	Amt. Land	Am$^{t.}$ Tax	from whom and to have
Newcombe, William	60	3/2	9.10.0	2.11	Richard Clerk
Overstreet, Gabriel	120	4/2	25.0.0	7.6	Eliz$^{a.}$ Brushwood
Pitts, Obadiah	20	10/5	10.8.4	3.2	David Pitts
Prior, John	150	3/2	2[0].15.0	7.8	Rich$^{d.}$ Cardwell
Richards, George	564	14/6	408.18.0	6.2.9	Gregory Baylor
Spencer, Thomas	180	10/5	93.15.0	1.8.2	Sarah Bowden
do.	120	"	62.10.0	18.9	Wm. Bowden Sen$^{r.}$
do.	255	4/2	53.2.6	[5].11	[Jn$^{o.}$] Collins
Shackelford, Alexander	60	4/2	12.10.0	3.9	Eliz$^{a.}$ Brushwood
Shackelford, John (Roman)	508	8/4	211.13.4	[ ].3.6	Frans. Shackelford
Steadman, Christ$^{r.}$ J$^{r.}$	260	5/3	68.5.0	1.0.6	Ann Dillard (Ta.)
Shackelford, Jn$^{o.}$ (M)	182	7/3	54.19.6	19.10	Jn$^{o.}$ Muire
Smith, Wm. (son of James) deduct}					
more than he ought to be charg'd. wth.}	64	6/3	20.0.0	0.6.0	
Swinton, George	750	13/6	506.5.0	7.11.11	Tho$^{s.}$ Dew & Geo. Holloway
Wyatt, William	140	12/6	87.10.0	1.6.4	Stephen Odear & Major Odear
Walding, Richard	180	10/5	93.8.[ ]	8.1½	Anthoy. Gardner
Walding, Lewis	84½	6/3	28.2.3½	8.5	Tho$^{s.}$ Dudley
Wyatt, Richard	25	12/6	15.12.6	4.8	Wm. Wyatt
Watts, James	350	4/2	78.18.4	.11	Henry Oaks Sen$^{r.}$
Wyatt, William, deduct}	22¼	7/3	8.1.0	2.5	
[illegible line]}					
[Web]ley, John	100	4/2	20.16.8	6.3	Benjamin Collier
Young, Henry	640	18/8	597.6.8	8.19.3	Benj$^{a.}$ Hoomes

Wm. Fleet & Wm. Courtney, Commissioners

A List of the Land Tax within the County of King & Queen for the year 1788

[page 2, 1788]

Present Proprietors Names	Qty. Land	Price	Amt. Land	Amt. Tax
Alexander, Benj[a.]	202	9/4	94.5.4	1.8.4
Alexander, Elisha	102	7/3	36.12.3	11.--
Alexander, Tho[s.]	50		18.2.6	5.6
Alexander, John	50	9/4	23.6.8	7.--
Anderson, Churchill Est.	636	7/3	230.11.0	3.9.2
Anderson, Pauling	498	14/6	361.1.0	5.9.4
Atkins, Jn[o.] Est.	42	7/3	15.4.6	4.7
Atkins, Jn[o.] J[r.]	120	4/2	25.0.0	7.6
Abbott, Jacob	112	7/10	43.17.4	13.2
Anderson, Richard Est.	460	5/3	120.15.0	1.16.3
Beverley, Robert	2474	10/5	1288.8.10	19.6.7
Brown, Henry	657	7/5½	245.8.1	3.13.7½
do. of James Keeling	103½	7/3	37.10.4½	11.3
Baylor, Gregory Est.	720	14/6	522.0.0	7.16.7
Bland, Henry	166	8/4	69.3.4	1.0.9
Bates, James	358	"	149.3.4	2.4.9
do.	42	4/2	8.15.0	2.7½
Barton, John	125	"	26.0.10	7.10
Banks, William	365	"	76.0.10	1.2.9¾
Brooking, Francis	930	10/5	484.7.6	7.5.[4]
Baylor, John Est.	760	14/6	551.0.0	[8.5.4]
Boughton, Tho[s.] (Essex)	130	9/4	60.13.4	18.3
Boughton, John	200	[8]/4	83.6.8	1.5.0
Boughton, Henry (Essex)	88	6/3	27.10.0	8.3
Boughton, Thomas	100	8/4	41.13.4	12.6
Broach, John	45	6/3	14.1.3	4.3
Burton, Tho[s.] Est.	170	5/3	44.12.6	13.5
Bohannon, Benj[a.]	160	4/2	33.6.8	10.-
Bohannon, Ann	50	"	10.8.4	3.2
Brown, William	75	7/10	29.7.6	8.10
Bagbey, John	330	7/3	119.12.6	1.15.10½
Bagbey, Richard	260	"	94.5.0	1.8.3½
Bagbey, Thomas	260	"	94.5.0	1.8.3½
Brooke, Richard	1539¾	29/-	2232.12.9	33.9.10
Brumley, John	329½	3/2	52.3.5	15.8
Bird, William	532	7/3	192.17.-	2.18.0¼
do., Dragon	88½	17/	70.4.6	1.1.0
Bird, Mary	619	6/3	193.8.9	2.18.1
Bird, Philemon	1238	"	386.17.6	5.16.1
Brett, Jn[o.]	446	18/	401.8.0	6.0.5
Bowers, William	70	7/3	25.7.6	7.8
Bowers, John	198	3/2	31.7.0	9.5
Burch, James	190	"	30.1.8	9.1
Burch, Eliz[a.]	100	4/2	20.16.8	6.3
Bird, Anthony	275	3/2	43.10.10	13.1
	Carried Forw[d.]			131.10.0½

[page 3, 1788]

Present Proprietors Names	Qty. Land	Price	Amt. Land	Amt. Tax
Brought Forw[d.]				131.10.0½
Byne, Jn[o.] Est.	336	4/2	70.0.0	1.1.0
do., Dragon	2¼	17/	1.18.3	6¾
Bird, Barbara	266 3/4	24/10	331.2.2½	4.16.0
Bird, Robert	533 1/3	--	662.4.5½	9.12.0
Bourn, Richard	150	3/2	23.15.0	7.2
Burch, William Est.	257	5/9	73.17.9	1.2.2
Boyd, James Est.	115	18/8	107.6.8	1.12.3
Bray, Richard	350	7/10	137.1.8	2.1.2
Bird, Hannah	100	3/2	15.16.8	4.9
Bowden, William	403	6/9	136.0.3	2.0.9½
Bew, William	117	3/2	18.10.6	5.7
Burk, Thomas	100	4/2	20.16.8	6.3
Boyd, Spencer's Est.	1428	10/5	770.15.0	11.11.2
Berkley, Edmond	762	5/3	200.0.6	3.0.0
Bland, Jn[o.]	60	12/6	37.10.0	11.3
Bullman, Thomas Est.	100	5/3	26.5.0	7.11
Briggs, John (W. Finny)	170	4/2	35.8.4	10.8
Belote, Severn Est.	172	--	35.16.8	10.9
Bland, William Sen[r.]	120	--	25.0.0	7.6
do. of Edw[d.] Brooks	30	3/2	4.15.0	1.5
Bowden, William Jr.	100	4/2	20.16.8	6.3
Bowden, John	--	--	--	6.3
Bland, William Jr.	250	"	52.1.8	15.8
[Bland], Thomas	300	3/2	57.10.0	17.3
Bowden, George	75	4/2	15.12.6	4.9½
Burch, William	45	3/2	7.2.6	2.1½
Cook, Mary	200	8/4	83.6.8	1.5.0
Coleman, Thomas	572	6/3	178.15.0	2.13.8
Chick, Richard	491	7/3	177.19.9	2.13.5
Chapman, George	200	7/10	78.6.8	1.3.6
Campbell, William	1029	7/3	373.0.3	5.11.9
Chapman, Eliz[a.]	200	7/10	78.6.8	1.3.6
Crane, Cath[e.]	50	5/3	13.2.6	4.0
Crane, John	6	--	1.10.6	.6
Cleverius, Benj[a.]	419	20/9	434.14.3	6.10.5
Carlton, Henry	280	7/10	109.13.4	1.12.10
Clayton, Thomas Est.	275	7/3	99.13.9	1.9.11
Campbell, Whitacar	318	7/10	124.11.-	1.17.6
	Carri[d.] Forw[d.]			201.8.8¾

[page 4, 1788]

Present Proprietors Names	Qty. Land	Price	Amt. Land	Amt. Tax
Brought Forward				201.8.8¾
Cleaveley, Thos.	80	7/10	36.6.8	9.4¾
do. Langham's	200		78.6.8	1.3.6
Crafton, Richard	236	9/4	110.2.8	1.13.1
Crane, George	30	7/3	10.7.6	3.4
Coleman, Milley	196	10/5	102.1.8	1.10.8
Carlton, John (King)	50	5/3	13.2.6	4.-
Carlton, Joel	53½	6/3	16.14.5	5.1
Carter, Jane	60	3/2	9.10.0	2.11
Carlton, Thomas (Swamp)	300	7/10	117.10.0	1.15.3
Carlton, John (SM)	100	6/3	31.5.0	9.5
Campbell, Sarah	296	12/6	185.0.0	2.15.6
Carlton, Christr. Senr.	37½	6/3	11.14.5	3.7
Carlton, William (shoe)	90¾		28.7.3	8.7
do. of Wm. Harwood	160	15/	120.0.0	1.16.0
Carlton, Robt. Est.	93	4/2	19.7.6	5.10
do. of Jno. Pemberton	55	6/3	17.3.9	5.2
Carlton, Richard	250	7/3	90.12.6	1.7.3
Carlton, Christr. Jr.	100		36.5.0	10.11
Carlton, James	225	6/3	70.6.3	1.1.2
Carlton, Philemon	100	3/2	15.16.8	4.9
Cooper, Henry	50	4/2	10.8.4	3.2
Carlton, Thomas (T)	100	6/3	31.5.0	[smear]
Cardwell, Jno. Est.	150	4/2	31.5.0	9.5
Cardwell, Jno.	150		31.5.0	9.5
Cardwell, Thos.				9.5
Cardwell, William				9.5
Cook, John Est.	300	4/2	62.10.0	18.9
Collins, Thomas	150		31.5.0	9.5
do., Palmers	350	7/3	126.17.6	1.18.1
Carlton, Jno. Junr. (Carpr.)	235	4/2	48.19.2	14.9
Campbell, Wm. (Stratn.)	238	3/2	37.13.8	11.4
Collier, Charles	250	8/4	104.3.4	1.11.3
Collins, John	100	4/2	20.16.8	6.3
~~Colley, Charles~~	~~100~~	"	~~20.16.8~~	~~6.3~~
Corbin, Richard	1868	10/5	972.18.4	14.11.11
do. Thos. Moore	400	12/6	250.--.--	3.15.0
Collins, Joy[eux] Est.	140	10/5	72.18.4	1.1.10
Crittenden, Zachy.	140	14/6	101.10.0	1.10.6
Cary, W. Miles	1820	16/7	1509.1.8	22.12.9
Collier, Jno. (Cobler)	150	5/3	39.7.6	11.10
Campbell, James	100	6/3	31.5.0	9.5
Collawn, Jno.	100	5/3	26.5.0	7.11
Crittenden, Richard Jr. Est.	178		46.14.6	14.1
Collier, Frans. Est.	400	4/2	83.6.8	1.5.0
Corr, Averalla	140		36.15.0	11.1
Collier, Cathe.	750	5/3	196.17.6	2.19.1
Clegg, Isaah	248	4/2	56.13.4	15.6
Cook, Dawson, (S. Field)	296	7/3	107.3.0	1.12.[ ]
Curry, Ann	100	4/2	20.16.8	6.3
Corr, Frans.	175	3/2	27.14.2	8.4
	Carried Forwd.			280.16.9½

[page 5, 1788]

Present Proprietors Names	Qty. Land	Price	Amt. Land	Amt. Tax
Brought Forward				280.16.9½
Courtney, William	190	7/10	74.8.4	1.2.4
Crane, William	75	13/6	50.12.6	15.2¼
Cook, Thos.	240	3/2	38.0.0	11.5
Cross, Joseph	38	6/3	11.17.6	3.7
Crittenden, Lemuel	199	5/3	52.4.9	15.9
Carlton, Humphy.	125	7/3	45.6.3	13.8
Carlton, Thomas (Joynr.)	235	6/3	73.8.9	1.2.1
Crouch, Edward Est.	130	3/2	20.11.8	6.3
Campbell, Alexander	125	12/6	78.2.6	1.3.5
Dew, William	935	14/6	677.17.6	10.3.5
Dowling, William	264	8/4	110.--.--	1.13.0
Dix, Gabriel	338	6/3	105.12.6	1.11.8
Deshazo, Richard	204	3/2	32.6.0	9.8½
Deshazo, William	162	4/2	33.15.0	10.2
Durham, Joseph	76		15.16.8	4.9
Draper, Jno. Est.	287	6/3	89.13.9	1.6.11
Deshazo, Peter	172		53.15.0	16.2
do., Robt. Hill	45	8/4	18.15.0	5.7½
Dickie, James	512		213.6.8	3.4.0
Dunbar, David	366		152.10.0	2.5.9
Dalley, John	200	3/2	31.13.4	9.6
Dalley, Ann	224		35.9.4	10.8
Dobbins, Charles	147	5/3	38.11.9	11.7
Dean, Benjamin	50		13.2.6	4.--
[Dilla]rd, William Jr.	100	3/2	15.16.8	4.9
Dunn, Agrippa	140	5/3	36.15.0	11.1
Dudley, Peter Est.	370	7/10	144.18.4	2.3.6
do. of Jno. Baylor	160	5/3	42.0.0	12.7
Davis, Jane	100	4/2	20.16.8	6.3
Didlake, Margret	65		13.10.10	4.1
Durham, Robt. Est.	50		10.8.4	3.2
Dunn, Thos.	30	6/3	9.7.6	2.10
Dillard, William Senr.	276	12/6	172.10.--	2.11.9
Durham, George	50	4/2	10.8.4	3.2
Dillard, Ann	70		14.11.8	4.5
Durham, Thomas	85	3/2	13.9.2	4.1
Diggs, Isaac Est.	175	5/3	45.18.9	13.10
Didlake, George Est.	114	10/5	59.7.6	17.10
Dungie, John	110	3/2	17.8.4	5.3
~~Davis, Zachy.~~	~~130~~	~~"~~	~~20.11.8~~	~~6.3~~
Dudley, William (Ferry)	290	14/6	210.5.0	3.3.1
do., Lidia Wedderburn's	315½	6/3	98.11.10½	1.9.6¾
Damm, John	55		17.3.9	5.2
Damm, William	25	4/2	5.4.2	1.6½
Dudley, William Senr.	180	7/10	70.10.--	1.1.2
Dunbar, Mary	450	9/4	210.--.--	3.3.0
		Carried forward		330.10.6

[page 6, 1788]

Present Proprietors Names	Qty. Land	Price	Amt. Land	Amt. Tax
Brought Forward				330.10.6
Douglass, John	100	6/3	31.5.0	9.5
do. of S. Field	139	7/3	50.7.9	15.1¼
Didlake, John	1200		435.--.--	6.10.6
Dudley, B. Robert Est.	421		152.12.3	2.5.10
Dudley, Thomas	267½	6/3	81.17.8½	1.4.7
Dillard, Nicholas	75	4/2	15.12.6	4.9
Dillard, Benj[a.] Est.	133	5/3	34.18.4	10.6
Drummond, Tho[s.]	150	6/3	46.17.6	14.6
Didlake, James Est.	131	3/2	20.14.10	6.3
Dillard, Thomas	377	5/3	98.19.3	1.9.9
Dillard, Eliz[a.]	449	14/6	325.10.6	4.17.8
Dudley, Banks	246	3/2	38.19.0	11.8
Dillard, William (son Tho[s.])	150	4/2	31.5.0	9.5
Davis, Tho[s.]	150	7/3	50.12.6	15.2
Eubank, James	75	10/5	39.1.3	11.9
do.	150	14/6	108.15.0	1.12.7½
Eubank, Thomas	150		108.15.0	1.12.7½
Eubank, John	200		145.--.--	2.3.6
do. Harry Samuel	78	7/3	28.5.6	8.6
Eubank, Henry	171	5/3	44.17.9	13.6
Edwards, Tho[s.] Est.	66	4/2	13.15.0	4.[2]
Eubank, William Est.	28¾	5/3	7.11.0	2.4
Eubank, Richard	65	3/2	10.5.10	3.1½
do.	90¾	5/3	23.16.6	7.2
Eubank, Richard Est.	227	4/2	47.5.10	14.3
Edwards, Charles	192	3/2	30.8.0	9.2
Fleet, Baylor	360	20/9	373.10.0	5.12.0
do., not taken up	152	5/	38.0.0	11.5
do. Whitings	350	7/10	137.1.8	2.1.2
Fauntleroy, G. Samuel	880	16/7	729.13.4	10.18.1
do. Jn[o.] Phillips & Henley's	183	10/5	95.6.3	1.8.7
Fauntleroy, Moore	1006	24/10	1231.2.4	18.14.8¾
Fleet, John	326	10/5	165.12.6	2.9.7
do.	180	6/3	56.6.0	16.10
Faulkner, Thomas	155		48.8.9	14.7
Fogg, Thomas	200		62.10.0	18.9
Fogg, James	120		37.10.0	11.3
Farrenholtz, Wm. Est.	146		45.12.6	13.9
Frazer, William Est.	45	20/9	46.13.9	14.1
Fleet, William	296¼		307.7.3	4.12.3
Fisher, James Est.	110	3/2	17.18.4	5.3
Foster, Thomas	214	4/2	44.11.8	13.5
Faulkner, Mary	333	6/3	104.1.4	1.11.3
		Carried Forward		414.5.3½

[page 7, 1788]

Present Proprietors Names	Qty. Land	Price	Amt. Land	Amt. Tax
Brought Forward				414.5.3½
Fauntleroy, Thomas	800	8/4	333.6.8	5.0.0
do. Henry Todd	500	18/	460.0.0	6.18.0
Farthing, Dudley	203	7/10	79.10.2	1.3.10
Grafton, Thomas	132	9/4	61.12.0	18.6
Grafton, James	111	6/3	34.13.9	10.5
Gale, John Est.	180	10/5	93.15.0	1.8.5
Goleman, Tho[s.] (Essex)	714	9/4	333.4.0	5.--.--
Garnett, Rice	297	7/3	107.13.7	1.12.4
Gatewood, Chaney	860	10/5	451.0.10	6.15.4
do. J. Gardners	100	7/3	36.5.0	10.11
Garnett, Joshua	322	8/4	134.3.4	2.0.3
Graves, Edward	200	6/3	62.10.--	18.9
Gatewood, Joseph	445	10/5	231.15.5	3.9.7
Gale, Matthew	323	11/5	184.7.7	2.15.4
Gatewood, John	160	8/4	66.13.4	1.--.--
Garnett, Reubin	33	5/3	8.13.3	2.8
Gwathmey, Temple	600	35/3	1057.10.0	15.17.3
Garlick, Samuel	454	24/10	563.14.4	8.9.2
Garlick, John	957	29/	1387.13.0	20.16.4
Griffith, Joseph	50	6/3	15.12.6	4.9
Gresham, Samuel	400	7/3	145.0.0	2.3.6
do of Rich[d.] Tunstall	87½	8/4	3.9.2	10.11
Garrett, Richard Jr. Est.	100	4/2	20.16.8	6.3
Gardner, John Est.	623	6/9	20.5.3	3.2.9
Gaines, Fran[s.]	410	14/6	297.5.0	4.9.3
Gaines, Harry	1517	20/4	1542.5.8	23.2.8
Gresham, Thomas	339¼	6/3	106.0.4	1.11.10
Gresham, Phil	200		62.10.--	18.9
Gresham, John (D)	200	7/10	78.6.8	1.3.6
Gaines, Robert	225	5/3	59.1.3	17.9
Gresham, William	100	4/2	20.16.8	6.3
Gardner, Eliz[a.]	100	6/3	31.5.0	9.5
Gibson, Richard Est.	113	3/2	17.17.10	5.5
Gibson, John	219¾		34.15.11	10.6
Griffith, Milley	50	6/3	15.12.6	4.9
Gresham, Ruth	250	5/3	65.12.6	19.9
Griffin, William	840	14/6	609.--.--	9.2.9
Garlick, Camm Est.	1100	6/3	343.15.0	5.3.2
Garrett, Henry	50	3/2	7.8.4	2.4½
Garrett, Richard	50		7.8.4	2.4½
Garrett, William Est.	330	4/2	68.15.0	1.0.8
Gardner, Antho[y.] Doct[r.]	623	10/5	324.9.7	4.17.4
do. of Henry Todd	215	12/6	134.7.6	2.0.3
do. Dragon	42½	17/	36.2.6	10.10
Gresham, William Jr.	200	8/4	83.6.8	1.5.0
do. Dixon Lyon's	42	8/4	17.10.0	5.3
Gatewood, William	105	10/5	54.13.9	16.8
Gatewood, William (*Tuck.*)	220	3/2	34.16.8	10.6
Green, Rob[t.] Est.	150	4/2	31.5.0	9.5
		Carried forward		567.7.11½

[page 8, 1788]

Present Proprietors Names	Qty. Land	Price	Amt. Land	Amt. Tax
Bl. Forward				567.6.11½
Garrett, Humph[y.]	450	12/6	281.5.0	4.4.9
Guthrie, James	60		37.10.--	11.3
Guthrie, Richard			37.10.0	11.3
Guthrie, Richard Jr.	200	3/2	31.13.4	9.6
Glaspe, James	210	5/3	55.2.6	16.7
Guthrie, Mary	30		7.17.6	2.5
Groom, Mary	273	3/2	43.4.6	13.--
Goldman, Martin	140	4/2	29.3.4	8.9
Groom, Barbara	100	3/2	15.16.8	4.9
Groom, Zach[y.]	187		29.12.2	8.7
Gulley, Phil	150		23.15.0	7.2
Gilmore, Ruth	354	10/5	184.12.9	2.15.5
Garrett, William (sho)	200	3/2	31.13.4	9.6
Halbert, James	124	6/2	38.15.0	11.7½
Harwood, Agness	225	4/2	46.17.6	14.1
Holt, Richard Jr.	400	6/3	125.--.--	1.17.6
Hill, William	1191	14/6	928.9.6	13.18.7
Hutcherson, Charles	501	7/3	181.12.6	2.14.6
Hall, Corbin	188	8/4	78.6.8	1.3.6
Hitchcock, Thomas	140	4/2	29.3.4	8.9
Hoskins, Samuel	175	5/3	45.18.9	13.10
Hoskins, William	160	10/5	83.6.8	1.5.1
Herndon, Margret Est.	100	7/3	36.5.0	10.11
Heskew, Jn[o.]	61	5/3	16.0.3	4.10
Heskew, Jn[o.] Jr.	50	6/3	15.12.6	4.8
Hoomes, Benjamin	230	7/10	90.1.8	1.7.1
Hill, Robert	1555	8/4	647.8.4	9.14.4½
do. Ann Tunstall	223	7/10	87.6.10	1.6.3
do. James Keeling	42½	7/3	15.8.1½	0.4.7
Hill, Edward	1200	18/8	1120.--.--	16.16.0
Hart, W[m.] Sen[r.]	40	5/3	10.10.0	3.1¼
Hodges, Salley	462	4/2	96.5.0	1.8.11
Hudson, William	112	3/2	17.14.8	5.4
Hemmingway, Daniel Est.	800	4/2	166.13.4	2.0.0
Harwood, Christopher	300	24/10	372.10.0	5.11.9
Harwood, John	501	5/3	131.10.3	1.19.6
Harwood, William	240	30/	360.--.--	5.8.0
Hill, Thomas	300	26/11	403.[15].0	6.1.2
Hart, James	150	3/2	23.15.0	7.2
Hart, Anthony	94		14.17.8	4.0
do. Rob[t.] Hart's	190	5/3	49.17.6	15.--
do. M. Younger's	94	3/2	14.17.8	4.6
Hart, Gregory	200	3/2	31.13.4	9.6
Hart, William	218		34.10.4	10.5
do. H. Jordon	32	4/2	6.13.4	2.--
Hare, William Doct[r.]	109	5/3	28.12.3	8.8
Hunt, William	730	6/3	228.2.6	3.8.6
Holderby, Eliz[a.]	100	4/2	20.16.8	6.8
Hudson, Mary (of C. Colly)	100	"		6.8
		Carried forward		663.8.6

[page 9, 1788]

Present Proprietors Names	Qty. Land	Price	Amt. Land	Amt. Tax
Amo[t.] bro[t.] Forw[d.]				663.8.6
Henry, James Esq[r.]	1900	14/6	1377.10.0	20.13.3
Halyard, William	190	5/3	49.17.6	15.--
Hoskins, John	540	10/5	281.5.0	4.4.4½
do. J. Minors	170	7/3	61.12.6	18.6
Haws, William	72	10/5	37.10.0	11.3
Hoskins, Robert	100	6/3	31.5.0	9.5
do. C. Dudley's	120	4/2	25.--.--	7.6
Hardy, Joseph	75	3/2	11.17.6	3.6¼
Jones, John	505	8/4	210.8.4	3.3.2
do. Mr. Beverley	200	10/5	104.3.4	1.11.3
Jeffries, Edward	70	3/2	11.1.8	3.4
Jones, James	160	14/6	116.--.--	1.14.10
Jones, James Est.	196	10/5	102.1.8	1.10.8
Jones, William	335	13/6	226.2.6	3.7.11
do. of L. Smith	35¾	31/1	55.11.2	16.8
Jeffries, Ambrose	397	7/10	148.8.10	2.4.7
Jeffries, Bernard	30	4/2	6.5.0	1.11
Jordan, Henry	88		18.6.8	5.6
Jordan, William	100	3/2	15.16.8	4.9
Jordan, Thomas Est.	100	4/2	20.16.8	6.3
Johnson, Archl[d.]	100		20.16.8	6.3
[Johns]on, Lucy	60	8/[4]	25.0.0	7.6
Johnson, Thomas	112	3/2	17.14.8	5.4
Jameson, David (York)	50		7.18.4	2.5
Keeling, James	113¼	7/3	41.1.0¾	12.4
Keeling, William	150	4/2	31.5.0	9.5
Kemp, John	87	7/10	34.7.6	10.3
do. of Joseph Wiltshire	53	7/3	19.4.3	5.9
Kauffman, George	583	14/6	422.13.6	6.6.10
Kemp, Thomas	40	10/5	20.16.8	6.3
Kauffman, Jn[o.]	471	18/8	439.12.0	6.11.11
Kennedy, Alex[r.]	580	12/6	362.10.0	5.8.9
Kemp, Matthew	100	5/4	26.13.4	8.--
Kemp, Jos. (SM)	200	6/3	62.10.0	18.9
Kidd, John	370	7/3	134.2.6	2.0.3
do. Tho[s.] Peirce	25	4/2	5.4.2	1.7
Kay, Christ[r.]	116	6/3	30.9.0	9.1½
Kidd, Barthow.	136	5/3	35.14.--	10.8
Kidd, Benj[a.] (Middlesex)	111	13/6	74.18.2	1.2.5½
Lumpkin, Henry	620	9/4	289.6.8	4.6.10
Lumpkin, John	200	6/3	59.--.--	17.9
Lyne, William Col.	1480	8/4	610.14.2	9.3.3
Lyne, William Jun[r.]	108	8/4	45.--.--	13.6
Lumpkin, William	305	14/6	221.2.6	3.6.5
		Amo[t.] Car[d.] Forw[d.]		752.13.9¼

[page 10, 1788]

Present Proprietors Names	Qty. Land	Price	Amt. Land	Amt. Tax
Brought Forward				742.13.9¼
Lefon, Fran[s.]	119	8/4	49.11.8	14.10½
Lankford, Thomas	100	4/2	20.16.8	6.3
Lumpkin, Robert Jr.	465	8/4	193.15.0	2.18.2
Lumpkin, Robert Sen[r.]	430	7/3	155.17.6	2.6.10
Longest, Caleb	97	7/10	37.19.10	11.6
Longest, Richard	140		54.16.8	16.6
Longest, Dorathy	100		39.3.4	11.9
Lumpkin, Joyce	287		112.8.2	1.13.9
Lumpkin, Mary	108	6/3	33.15.0	10.2
Lumpkin, Anthony	"	"	33.15.0	10.2
Lumpkin, Jacob	916	"	286.5.0	4.5.11
do. Southerlands	271	5/3	71.2.9	1.1.4
Lewis, Iverson	356	14/6	258.2.-0	3.17.4¼
Lewis, Eliz[a.]	100	4/2	20.16.8	6.3
Leigh, Lucy	101	24/10	125.8.2	1.17.7
Leigh, John	199	"	247.1.10	3.14.2
Lyne, John	507	6/3	158.8.9	2.7.7
Lambouth, Thomas	200	3/2	31.11.4	9.6
Lumpkin, Rob[t.] (orp[a.])	183	4/8	38.2.6	11.6
Laughlin, James	126¾	4/2	26.8.2	8.—
Leigh, Richard (of Campbell's)	400	12/6	250.0.0	3.15.0
Motley, Edwin	740	10/5	389.1.3	5.16.9
McKentosh, William	192	4/2	40.--.--	7.1
Martin, Thomas Capt.	680	14/6	493.--.--	7.7.11
Minor, William	149	8/4	62.1.8	18.8
Minor, John	137	"	57.1.8	17.2
Miller, Thomas	527	7/10	206.8.2	3.2.0
Mann, August[e.] Est.	400	8/4	166.13.4	2.10.0
Mitchell, Robert	17	20/9	17.17.9	5.4
Mitchell, John	50	6/3	15.12.6	4.9
Mitchell, James	750	12/6	468.15.0	7.0.8
McKendree, Eliz[a.]	323	5/3	84.15.9	1.5.6
McKendree, John	100	3/2	15.16.8	4.9
Meredith, William (Leach)	243	5/3	63.15.9	19.2
Mitchell, Susanah	170	3/2	26.18.4	8.1
Moore, Jn[o.]	100		15.16.8	4.9
Major, Joseph	200	4/2	41.13.4	12.6
Merideth, William Est.	530	14/6	384.5.0	5.15.4
Mitchell, Jn[o.] (S. Major)	270	5/3	70.17.6	1.1.4
do. of Rootes	300	12/6	187.10.0	2.16.3
Moore, Phill	50	3/2	7.18.4	2.5
Macon, John	1092	16/7	905.9.0	13.11.7
Mansfield, William	75	"	62.3.9	18.7
Manley, Peter	40	7/10	15.13.4	4.6
Merideth, G. Ralph	382	14/6	273.1.6	4.2.--
		Carried forw[d.]		847.7.8

[page 11, 1788]

Present Proprietors Names	Qty. Land	Price	Amt. Land	Amt. Tax
Brought Forward				847.7.8
Meredith, Samuel Est.	185	14/6	138.--.--	2.1.5½
Muire, Richard	93	12/6	58.2.6	17.6
Major, Mary	175	7/3	63.8.9	19.1
Moore, Richard	145	6/3	45.6.3	13.8
Martin, James	332½	20/9	344.19.4	5.3.5¾
McCarty, Joseph	73	3/2	11.11.2	3.6
Metcalf, Thomas	521	14/6	377.14.6	5.13.3¾
Martin, John	80	9/4	37.6.8	11.3
Nowell, Theodrick	298	8/4	124.3.4	1.17.3
Nunn, Jane	180	7/3	65.5.0	19.7
Newbill, George Est.	500	8/4	208.6.8	3.2.6
Nunn, Thomas	174	7/3	63.1.6	1.--.--
Nash, John	100	6/3	31.5.0	9.5
Newcombe, Eliz[a.]	109	3/2	17.5.2	5.2
Newcombe, William	60	"	9.10.0	2.11
Olliver, John	320	5/3	84.0.0	1.5.3
Orvill, John	100	6/3	31.5.0	9.5
Overstreet, Mitchell	90	4/2	18.5.0	5.7½
Overstreet, Gabriel	386	"	80.10.9	5.2
do. Eliz[a.] Brushwood	120	"	25.0.0	7.6
do. Haynes	130	5/3	34.2.6	10.2
Osburn, John	90	3/2	14.5.0	4.4
O'Dear, Edith	50	5/3	13.2.6	4.--
Oaks, Henry Sen[r.]	110	3/2	17.8.4	5.3
Oaks, Henry Jr.	100	4/2	20.16.8	6.3
Owin, Aug[te.]	100	6/3	31.5.0	9.5
Pitts, David Est.	420	9/4	196.--.--	2.18.10
Pitts, Obadiah	20	10/5	10.8.4	3.2
Pitts, Ann Est.	100	6/3	31.5.0	9.5
Phillips, Richard	230	7/3	83.7.6	1.5.1
Pollard, John	235	9/4	109.13.4	1.12.11
do. Leo[d.] Smithey	384	7/3	139.4.0	2.1.10
Pruett, Fran[s.]	99	9/4	46.4.0	13.11
Parker, John	116½	7/10	45.12.7	13.9
Peirce, Ann	35	7/5	12.3.9	3.8
Pendleton, Phil	337	10/5	175.10.5	2.12.8
Perryman, Anthony	130	7/3	47.2.6	14.2
Pollard, Richard	432	8/4	180.--.--	2.14.—
do. of W[m.] Wood	32½	7/3	11.15.7½	3.6
P[r]ince, Francis	113	7/10	44.5.2	13.4
Pendleton, Benjamin	450	"	176.5.0	2.12.11
[Py]nes, Benjamin	400	6/3	125.--.--	1.17.6
Pemberton, John	286	"	89.7.6	1.6.11
		Carried forw[d.]		899.16.9

[page 12, 1788]

Present Proprietors Names	Qty. Land	Price	Amt. Land	Amt. Tax
Amo[t.] ~~Carried~~ bro[t.] forw[d.]				899.16.9
Pace, Benjamin	263	7/3	95.6.9	1.8.8
Pickels, John (G. Carlton's Est.)	225	"	81.11.3	1.4.6
Price, Robert	630	6/3	196.17.6	2.19.1
Pigg, Rachel	108	14/6	78.6.0	1.3.6
Pigg, John	216	"	156.12.0	2.7.0
Padgett, Sam[l.] Est.	36	7/10	14.2.0	4.2
Pollard, William	95	7/3	34.8.9	10.5
Pierce, Thomas	135	4/2	28.1.11	8.5
Prior, John	150	3/2	23.15.0	7.8
Richards, William	510	12/6	318.15.0	4.15.8
Robertson, Donald Est.	155	"	96.17.6	1.9.1
do.	210	7/3	76.2.6	1.2.11
Richards, George	362½	14/6	262.16.3	3.18.10
Roane, Thomas Col.	3417	18/8	3189.4.0	47.16.9
do. Henry Carlton's	200	6/3	63.10.0	18.9
do. of Geo. Richards	201½	14/6	146.1.9	2.3.11
Richards, John Est.	1020	9/4	476.0.0	7.2.10
Row, Joseph Est.	390	6/3	121.17.6	1.16.5
Row, Thomas Maj[r.]	555	7/3	201.3.9	3.0.4
do. Fleet's	665	20/9	689.18.9	10.7.0
do. Nowel's	296	6/3	92.10.0	1.7.2
Read, Robert	14	5/3	3.13.6	1.1
Row, Richard	550	8/4	229.3.4	3.8.9
Roane, Thomas Jun[r.]	1600	24/10	1926.13.4	[28.18.0]
Rowzee, Eliz[a.]	120	3/2	19.0.0	5.9
Richerson, Elias	86	4/2	17.18.4	5.5
Row, Jn[o.] Est.	100	6/3	31.5.0	9.5
Richards, John	221½	4/2	46.3.0	13.11
Richards, William Jr.	296	5/3	77.14.0	1.3.4
Richerson, James	180	4/2	37.10.0	11.3
Richerson, William	181	"	37.14.2	11.4
Richerson, John Est.	101½	"	21.2.11	6.5
Roane, Thomas (LP)	150	3/2	23.15.0	7.2
Reigns, Giles	60		9.10.0	2.11
Roane, Major	367½	4/2	76.16.7	1.10.5
Robinson, Benj[a.] Est.	1300	8/4	541.13.4	8.2.6
do. a new Entry, dragon	70	17/	59.10.0	17.11
Robins, William	40	6/3	12.10.0	3.9
Roane, John [J. Pendleton]	450	10/	225.0.0	3.7.6
Smith, John (Drisd[e.])	406	7/3	147.3.6	2.4.2
Satterwhite, Geo.	164	6/3	51.5.--	15.1
Satterwhite, William	100	4/2	20.16.8	6.3
Samuel, Henry	85	6/3	26.11.6	8.--
Samuel, Andrew	60	7/3	21.15.0	6.--
Spencer, Edward	392½	8/4	163.10.10	2.9.1
do. Butlers	380	7/3	137.15.0	2.1.4
		Carried forw[d.]		1058.10.7

[page 13, 1788]

Present Proprietors Names	Qty. Land	Price	Amt. Land	Amt. Tax
Brought Forward				1058.10.7
Schools, John	83½	7/10	32.14.1	9.9½
Sears, Frankey	338	9/4	157.14.8	2.7.2
Schools, Gabriel	169	6/3	52.16.3	15.11
Skelton, William	132	9/4	61.12.0	18.6
Smith, Ann	85	7/3	30.16.3	9.3
Starling, Jane	360	7/10	141.--.--	2.2.4
Skelton, Thomas	294	8/4	122.10.0	1.16.9
Scott, Benjamin	200	9/4	93.6.8	1.8.--
Saunders, Joseph Est.	200	7/3	72.10.--	1.1.9
Shepherd, William	140	9/4	65.6.8	19.8
Semple, Eliz[a.]	674	14/6	488.4.8	7.6.7
Smith, Molley	30	4/2	6.5.0	1.11
Smith, John (LHead)	100	5/3	26.5.0	7.11
Smith, Lewis	113½	7/3	41.12.11	12.6
Swinton, George	750	13/6	506.5.0	7.11.11
Stone, Sarah	300	7/3	108.15.0	1.12.8
Smith, Larkin Col.	1254¼	31/1	1949.6.3½	29.4.10
Smith, Henry	400	6/3	125.--.--	1.17.6
Smith, William	140	7/10	54.16.8	16.8
Smith, William (son James)	300	6/3	113.15.0	1.14.2
Smith, James Sen[r.]	80	3/2	12.13.4	3.10
Smith, James Jun[r.]	101	7/10	39.11.2	11.10½
Shepherd, Mary	100	5/3	26.5.0	7.11
Stephens, Thomas Est.	609½	7/10	238.14.5	3.11.8
Stevens, George	645	"	252.12.6	3.15.9½
Shackelford, John	214	7/3	77.11.6	1.3.3½
Starke, Richard Est.	250	6/3	78.2.6	1.3.6
do. Geo: Richards	100	4/2	20.16.8	6.3
Soans, Mary	382	24/10	474.6.4	7.2.4
Stone, Robert	300	4/2	62.10.--	18.9
Stone, John Est.	357	6/3	93.14.3	1.8.2
Smith, Robert	879	10/5	457.19.3	6.17.5
Smith, Guy	189½	3/2	30.0.1	9.1
Simkins, Nimrod	60	"	9.10.0	2.11
Sears, Phil	83	4/2	17.5.10	5.3
Seward, Mary Est.	260	"	54.3.4	16.3
Spencer, Thomas	300	10/5	156.5.0	2.6.11
do. of Jn[o.] Collins	255	4/2	53.2.6	15.11
Shackelford, William Est.	700	14/6	527.10.0	7.18.6
Seward, Benjamin	115	3/2	18.4.2	5.6
Steadman, Christ[r.]	191	5/3	50.2.9	15.1
Saddler, John	150	6/3	46.17.6	14.6
Shackelford, Alexander	60	4/2	12.10.0	3.9
Steadman, Christ[r.] Jr.	133½	6/3	41.18.1½	12.6½
do. of Ann Dillard (T)	260	5/3	65.5.--	1.0.6
Smith, Gregory	485	14/6	351.12.6	5.5.5
Shackelford, John (R)	308	8/4	128.6.8	1.18.6
Shackelford, Benja.	200		83.6.8	1.5.0
		Carried forward		1174.12.9½

[page 14, 1788]

Present Proprietors Names	Qty. Land	Price	Amt. Land	Amt. Tax
Brought Forward				1174.12.9½
Shackelford, Robinson	500	10/5	260.8.4	3.18.2
do. William Corr Est.	200	3/2	31.13.4	9.6
Shackelford, Lyne	567	6/3	177.3.9	2.13.1
Shackelford, John (M), B. Whitting's Est.	~~40~~	~~7/10~~	~~15.13.4~~	~~4.8~~
do. of Jn$^{o.}$ Muire	182	7/3	65.19.6	19.10
Scott, Anderson	330	16/7	273.12.6	4.2.2
Shepherd, Isaac	190	3/2	30.1.8	9.3
Trice, William	70	7/3	25.7.6	7.8
Trice, Bettey	70		25.7.6	7.8
Taylor, John Est.	50	6/3	15.12.6	4.9
Taylor, Edmond	294	8/14	122.10.0	1.16.9
Temple, Joseph	918	10/5	478.2.6	7.3.6
Tunstall, Molley	430	"	233.19.2	3.7.2½
Tunstall, Richard Jr.	1097	7/3	397.13.3	5.19.3
do. Salley Tunstall	200	18/8	186.13.4	2.16.0
Trice, Jane	170	5/3	44.12.6	13.5
Tignor, William	130	7/10	50.18.4	15.4½
Tureman, Benj$^{a.}$	120	3/2	19.--.--	5.9
Taliaferro, William	1000	14/6	725.--.--	10.17.6
Townley, Robert	350	"	235.15.0	3.16.2
Taliaferro, Phil Col.	990	8/4	412.10.0	6.3.9
do. of P. Whiteing	75	1/46	54.18.6	16.4
Taliaferro, Richard	300	5/3	78.15.0	1.3.8
Taylor, Isbell	100	4/2	20.16.8	6.3
Thurston, Batcheldor	100	3/2	15.16.8	4.9
Tucker, John	180	7/3	65.5.0	19.7
Temple, Humph$^{y.}$	70	33/2	116.1.8	1.14.9¾
do. Walkerton	108	30/	162.--.--	2.8.7
Tunstall, Richard Est.	538	20/9	558.3.6	8.7.5
Tunstall, Richard (Best$^{d.}$)	269½	8/4	112.15.10	1.13.9
Vass, Thomas	250	5/3	65.12.6	19.9
Wyatt, Henry	200	7/3	72.10.0	1.1.9
White, Henry	100	8/4	41.13.4	12.6
Willmore, Thomas	150	10/5	78.2.6	1.3.6
do. of Dudley Farthing	19	7/10	7.8.10	2.2½
Wright, James	124½	5/3	32.13.8	9.10
Wyatt, Joseph	60	8/4	25.0.0	7.[ ]
Walding, John	105	12/6	65.12.6	19.9
Wood, Thomas	260	7/10	111.16.8	1.10.8
Wilson, Isaac	200	6/3	62.10.0	18.9
Wilson, Benj$^{a.}$ Est.	200	7/3	72.18.0	1.1.9
Wiltshire, Joseph	133	"	48.4.3	14.6
Wyatt, Tho$^{s.}$ Est.	480	10/5	250.--.--	3.15.0
Wyatt, John	100	7/10	39.3.4	11.9
Wheeley, John	50	6/3	15.12.6	4.9
Watkins, William	37	4/2	7.14.2	2.4
Watkins, Joseph	65	"	13.10.10	4.2
Walding, James	154	7/10	60.6.4	18.1
		Carried forw$^{d.}$		1260.10.4¾

[page 15, 1788]

Present Proprietors Names	Qty. Land	Price	Amt. Land	Amt. Tax
Amo[t.] bro[t.] forward				1260.10.4¾
Walker, Henry Est.	150	5/3	39.7.6	11.10
Ware, John	562	7/3	203.14.6	3.3.2
Walker, Fran[s.]	475	33/2	783.9.6	11.17.3
Walker, Humph[y.]	345	"	572.4.8	8.10.7
Wright, William	175	5/3	45.18.9	13.10
Whayne, William	13½	7/3	4.17.11	1.6
do. Langham's	194	7/10	75.19.8	1.2.9
Watts, Edward	250	7/3	90.12.6	1.7.3
Watts, Jn[o.]	293	7/10	114.15.2	1.14.6
do. Pemberton's	45	6/3	14.1.3	4.2½
Watts, William	380	7/10	184.16.8	2.4.7
Watts, Kauffman	300	5/3	78.15.0	1.3.8
Williams, Howard	283	4/2	58.19.2	17.9
Wyatt, Thomas	106	7/10	41.10.4	12.6
Wyatt, Jn[o.] (Blind)	103	6/3	32.3.9	9.8
Wyatt, William	29¾	7/3	10.15.8	3.3
Williams, Howard Est.	300	6/3	93.15.0	1.8.2
Williams, Charles	550	4/2	114.11.8	1.14.5
Walton, James	80	"	16.3.4	5.--
Walton, Mary	60	"	12.10.0	3.9
Walton, Eliz[a.]	60	3/2	9.10.0	2.11
Walton, John	176	5/3	46.4.0	13.11
Walton, William Est.	66	4/2	13.15.0	4.2
Walton, Thomas	"	"	"	4.2
Ware, John	75	5/3	19.13.9	5.11
Ware, Auther	83	4/2	17.5.10	5.3
Watts, James	350	"	72.18.4	1.1.11
Walding, Richard	180	10/5	93.15.0	1.8.1½
[Wa]lden, Lewis	150	3/2	23.15.0	7.3
do. of Thomas Dudley	84½	6/3	28.2.3½	8.5
Wyatt, Richard	175	12/6	109.7.6	1.12.9¾
Ware, Robert Est.	100	4/2	20.16.8	6.3
Ware, Sarah	175	"	36.9.2	11.--
Williams, Eliz[a.]	50	3/2	7.18.4	2.5
White, James Est.	200	6/3	62.10.--	18.9
Watkins, Eliz[a.]	100	3/2	15.16.8	4.9
Warrin, Cath[e.]	175	"	27.14.2	8.4
Ware, Rob[t.] (Bishop)	112	"	17.14.8	5.4
Whiteing, Peter	325	14/6	235.11.6	3.10.8¼
Ware, Christ[r.] Est.	500	12/6	312.10.0	4.13.9
Wedderburn, Lidia	350	6/3	109.7.6	1.12.10
Whiteing, Beverley's Est.	2447¾	7/10	866.18.9½	13.0.0
Webley, John	173	5/3	45.8.3	13.8
do. of B. Collier	100	4/2	20.16.8	6.3
Ware, Leo[d.] Est.	200	8/4	83.6.8	1.5.0
Walding, Edw[d.]	373	5/3	97.18.3	1.9.5
Wright, William (S. Major)	100	4/2	20.16.8	6.3
Waller, Edward	133½	3/2	21.2.9	6.5
Waller, Jn[o.]	66½	"	10.10.7	3.2
Willis, Joel	63	31/1	93.18.3	1.9.4½
Young, Henry	640	18/8	597.6.8	8.19.3
	Total Amount of tax			1350.14.11½

[page 16, 1788]

Examined
For Leyton Wood Esqr., Solicitor

A true copy, Test.
Wm. Fleet & Wm. Courtney, Commissrs. Tax

A List of the Land Tax within the County of King & Queen for the year 1789

[page 1, 1789]

Present Proprietors Names	Qty. Land	Price	Amt. Land	Amt. Tax
Alexander, Benjamin	202	9/4	94.5.4	1.8.4
Alexander, Elisha	102	7/3	36.12.3	0.11.--
Alexander, John	50	9/4	23.6.8	0.7.--
Anderson, Churchill's Est.	636	7/3	230.11.0	3.9.2
Anderson, Pauling	498	14/6	361.1.0	5.9.4
Atkins, John's Estate	42	7/3	15.4.6	0.4.7
Atkins, John Jun[r.]	120	4/2	25.0.0	0.7.6
Abbott, Jacob	112	7/10	43.17.4	0.13.2
Anderson, Richard's Est.	460	5/3	120.15.0	1.16.3
Atkins, Lewis	60	8/4	25.0.0	0.7.6
Anderson, Francis (home)	233	14/6	168.18.6	2.10.7
do. Mary Guthrie's & Odears	225	6/10	76.17.6	1.3.1
Beverley, Robert	2474	10/5	1288.8.10	19.6.7
Brown, Henry	657	7/5½	245.8.1	3.13.7½
do. of James Keeling	103½	7/3	37.10.4½	0.11.3
do. of John Wheeley	50	6/3	15.12.6	0.4.9
Baylor, Gregory Estate	720	14/6	522.0.0	7.16.7
Bland, Henry Estate	166	8/4	69.3.4	1.0.9
Bates, James	358	"	149.3.4	2.4.9
do.	42	4/2	8.15.0	2.7½
Barton, John	125	"	26.0.10	0.7.10
Banks, William	365	"	76.0.10	1.2.9¾
Brooking, Francis	930	10/5	484.7.6	7.5.4
Baylor, John Estate	760	14/6	551.0.0	8.5.4
Boughton, Thomas (Essex)	130	9/4	60.13.4	0.18.3
Boughton, John	200	[8]/4	83.6.8	1.5.4
Boughton, Henry (Essex)	88	6/3	27.10.0	0.18.3
Boughton, Thomas	100	8/4	41.13.4	0.12.6
Broach, John	45	6/3	14.1.3	0.4.3
Burton, Thomas Estate	170	5/3	44.12.6	0.13.5
Bohannon, Benjamin	160	4/2	33.6.8	0.10.0
Bohannon, Ann	150	"	31.17.6	0.9.6¾
Brown, William	75	7/10	29.7.6	0.8.10
Bagbey, John	330	7/3	119.12.6	1.15.10½
Bagbey, Richard	260	"	94.5.0	1.8.3½
Bagbey, Thomas	260	"	94.5.0	1.8.3½
Brooke, Richard	1539¾	29/-	2232.12.9	33.9.10
Brumley, John	329½	3/2	52.3.5	0.15.8
Bird, William	532	7/3	192.17.0	2.18.0¼
do., Dragon	88½	17/	70.4.6	1.1.0
Bird, Mary	619	6/3	193.8.9	2.18.1
Bird, Philemon	1238	"	386.17.6	5.16.1
Brett, John	446	18/	401.8.0	6.0.5
Bowers, John	70	7/3	25.7.6	0.7.8
Burch, Elizabeth	100	4/2	20.16.8	0.6.3
Bird, Anthony	275	3/2	43.10.10	0.13.1
Byne, John's Estate	336	4/2	70.0.0	1.1.0
do., Dragon	2¼	17/	1.18.3	0.06¾
Bird, Barbara	266 3/4	24/10	331.2.2½	4.16.0
Bird, Robert	533 2/3	--	662.4.5½	9.12.0

[page 2, 1789]

Present Proprietors Names	Qty. Land	Price	Amt. Land	Amt. Tax
Amount Brought forward				150.7.11¼
Bourn, Richard	150	3/2	23.15.0	0.7.2
Burch, William Est.	257	5/9	73.17.9	1.2.2
Boyd, John	115	18/8	107.6.8	1.12.3
Bray, Richard estate	93	7/10	36.8.6	0.10.11
Bird, Hannah	100	3/2	15.16.8	0.4.9
Bowden, William	403	6/9	136.0.3	2.0.9½
Bew, William	117	3/2	18.10.6	0.5.7
Boyd, Spencer estate	1428	10/5	770.15.0	11.11.2
Berkley, Edmond	762	5/3	200.0.6	3.0.0
Bland, John	60	12/6	37.10.0	0.11.3
Bullman, Thomas este.	100	5/3	26.5.0	0.7.11
Briggs, John (W. Finney)	170	4/2	35.8.4	0.10.8
Belote, Severn estate	172	--	35.16.8	0.10.9
Bland, William Sen[r.]	120	--	25.0.0	0.7.6
do. of Edward Brooks & Hardy's	105	3/2	16.12.6	0.5.0
Bowden, William jun[r.]	100	4/2	20.16.8	0.6.3
Bowden, John	--	--	--	0.6.3
Bland, William jun[r.] este.	250	"	52.1.8	0.15.8
Bland, Thomas	300	3/2	57.10.0	0.17.3
Bowden, George	75	4/2	15.12.6	0.4.9½
Bird, William jun[r.]	300	6/3	113.15.0	1.14.2
Cook, Mary	200	8/4	83.6.8	1.5.0
Coleman, Thomas	572	6/3	178.15.0	2.13.8
Chick, Richard	491	7/3	177.19.9	[2.13.5]
Chapman, George estate	200	7/10	78.6.8	1.3.6
Campbell, William	1029	7/3	373.0.3	5.11.9
Chapman, Elizabeth	200	7/10	78.6.8	1.3.6
Crane, Cath[e.]	50	5/3	13.2.6	0.4.0
Crane, John	6	--	1.10.6	0.0.6
Cleverius, Benjamin	419	20/9	434.14.3	6.10.5
Carlton, Henry	280	7/10	109.13.4	1.12.10
Clayton, Thomas estate	275	7/3	99.13.9	1.9.11
Campbell, Witacar	318	7/10	124.11.-	1.17.6
Clevely, Thomas	80	7/10	36.6.8	0.9.4¾
do. Langham's	200		78.6.8	1.3.6
Crafton, Richard	236	9/4	110.2.8	1.13.1
Crane, George	30	7/3	10.7.6	0.3.4
Coleman, Milly	196	10/5	102.1.8	1.10.8
Carlton, Joel	53½	6/3	16.14.5	0.5.1
[Ca]rter, Jane	60	3/2	9.10.0	0.2.11
[C]arlton, Thomas (Swamp)	300	7/10	117.10.0	1.15.3
[Ca]rlton, John (School[r.])	100	6/3	31.5.0	0.9.5
[C]ampbell, Sarah	296	12/6	185.0.0	2.15.6
[Ca]rlton, Christ[r.] Sen[r.]	37½	6/3	11.14.5	0.3.7
[Ca]rlton, William (Shoe)	90¾		28.7.3	0.8.[7]
do. of W[m.] Harwood	160	15/	120.0.0	1.1[6.0]
Carlton, Robert est.	93	4/2	19.7.6	0.5.10
do. of John Pemberton	55	6/3	17.3.9	0.5.2
Carlton, Richard	250	7/3	90.12.6	1.7.3
Carlton, Christopher	100		36.5.0	0.10.[11]

[page 3, 1789]

Present Proprietors Names	Qty. Land	Price	Amt. Land	Amt. Tax
Brought Forward				220.6.5¾
Carlton, James	225	6/3	70.6.3	1.1.2
Carlton, Philemon	100	3/2	15.16.8	0.4.9
Cooper, Henry	50	4/2	10.8.4	0.3.2
Carlton, Thomas (Taylor)	100	6/3	31.5.0	0.9.5
Cardwell, John estate	150	4/2	31.5.0	0.9.5
Cardwell, John	150		31.5.0	0.9.5
Cardwell, Thomas				0.9.5
Cardwell, William				0.9.5
Cook, John estate	300	4/2	62.10.0	0.18.9
Collins, Thomas	150		31.5.0	0.9.5
ditto Palmers	350	7/3	126.17.6	1.18.1
Carlton, John Junr. (Carp^r.^)	235	4/2	48.19.2	0.14.9
Campbell, William (Strat^n.^ Major)	238	3/2	37.13.8	0.11.4
Collier, Charles	250	8/4	104.3.4	1.11.3
Collins, John	100	4/2	20.16.8	0.6.3
Corbin, Richard Esqr.	1868	10/5	972.18.4	14.11.11
Corbin, John, Taylor [ ]	400	12/6	290.0.0	4.7.0
do of Wm. [Meredith]	124	11/3	69.13.0	1.0.10½
Collins, Joyeux este.	140	10/5	72.18.4	1.1.10
Crittenden, Zachariah	140	14/6	101.10.0	1.10.6
Cary, W. Miles	1820	16/7	1509.1.8	22.12.9
Collier, John (Cobler)	150	5/3	39.7.6	0.11.10
Campbell, James	100	6/3	31.5.0	0.9.5
do. of Thos. Burk	100	4/2	20.16.8	0.6.3
Crittenden, Richard jr. este.	178		46.14.6	0.14.1
Collier, Fran^s.^ este.	400	4/2	83.6.8	1.5.0
Corr, Avarilla	140		36.15.0	0.11.1
Collier, Catharine	750	5/3	196.17.6	2.19.[1]
Clegg, Isaiah	248	4/2	56.13.4	0.15.6
Cook, Dawson	296	7/3	107.3.0	1.12.1
do. Christ^r.^ Ware's este.	500	12/6	312.10.0	4.13.9
Curry, Ann	100	4/2	20.16.8	0.6.3
Corr, Frances	175	3/2	27.14.2	0.8.4
Courtney, William	190	7/10	74.8.4	1.2.4
Crane, William	75	13/6	50.12.6	0.15.2¼
do dragon swamp	36	17/	30.18.0	0.9.2
Cook, Thomas	240	3/2	38.0.0	0.11.5
Carlton, Humph^y.^	125	7/3	45.6.3	0.13.8
Carlton, Thos. (Joyn^r.^) este.	235	6/3	73.8.9	1.2.1
Campbell, Alex^r.^ (R^d.^ Corbins)	125	12/6	78.2.6	1.3.5
Carlton, Beverly	210	4/2	43.15.0	0.13.1½
Corr, John Senr.	38	3/2	6.0.4	0.1.9½
Campbell, John	400	12/6	250.0.0	3.15.0
Dew, William	935	14/6	677.17.6	10.3.5
Dowling, William	264	8/4	110.0.0	1.13.0
Dix, Gabriel	338	6/3	105.12.6	1.11.8
Deshazo, Richard	204	3/2	32.6.0	0.9.8½
				3[16.14.11¾]

[page 4, 1789]

Present Proprietors Names	Qty. Land	Price	Amt. Land	Amt. Tax
Amount bro. forward				316.14.11¾
Deshazo, William	162	4/2	33.15.0	0.10.2
Durham, Joseph	76	"	15.16.8	0.4.9
Deshazo, Peter	217	7/2	72.15.2	1.1.9½
Dickie, James	512	8/4	213.6.8	3.4.0
Dunbar, David	366	"	152.10.0	2.5.9
Dalley, John	200	3/2	31.13.4	0.9.6
Dalley, William	224	"	35.9.4	0.10.8
Dobbins, Charles	147	5/3	38.11.9	0.11.7
Dean, Benjamin	50	"	13.2.6	0.4.0
Dillard, William Jr.	100	3/2	15.16.8	0.4.9
Dunn, Agripia	140	5/3	36.15.0	0.11.1
Dudley, Peter estate	370	7/10	144.18.4	2.3.6
do. of Jno. Baylor	160	5/3	42.0.0	0.12.7
Davis, Jane	100	4/2	20.16.8	0.6.3
Didlake, Margrett	65	"	13.10.10	0.4.1
Durham, Robert est.	50	"	10.8.4	3.2
Dunn, Thomas	30	6/3	9.7.6	2.10
Dillard, William Senr.	276	12/6	172.10.--	2.11.9
Durham, George	50	4/2	10.8.4	0.3.2
Durham, Thomas	85	3/2	13.9.2	0.4.1
Dumagin, Richard est.	237	5/5	64.3.9	0.19.3
Diggs, Frances	175	5/3	45.18.9	0.13.10
Didlake, George estate	114	10/5	59.7.6	0.17.10
Dungie, John	110	3/2	17.8.4	0.5.3
Dudley, William (ferry)	290	14/6	210.5.0	3.3.1
do. of Lydia Wedderburn	315½	6/3	98.11.10½	1.9.6¾
[Da]mm, John est.	55	"	17.3.9	0.5.2
Dudley, William Senr.	180	7/10	70.10.--	1.1.2
Damm, William	25	4/2	5.4.2	0.1.6½
Dunbar, Mary	450	9/4	210.--.--	3.3.0
Douglass, John	100	6/3	31.5.0	0.9.5
do. of S. Field	139	7/3	50.7.9	0.15.1¼
Didlake, John	1200	"	435.--.--	6.10.6
Dudley, Robert B. Est.	421	"	152.12.3	2.5.10
Dudley, Thomas	267½	6/3	81.17.8½	1.4.7
Dillard, Nicholas	75	4/2	15.12.6	0.4.9
Dillard, Benjamin este.	133	5/3	34.18.4	0.10.6
Drummond, Thomas	150	6/3	46.17.6	0.14.6
Didlake, James este.	131	3/2	20.14.10	0.6.3
Dillard, Thomas	377	5/3	98.19.3	1.9.9
Dillard, Elizabeth	449	14/6	325.10.6	4.17.8
Dillard, William (Son Thos.)	150	4/2	31.5.0	0.9.5
Davis, Thomas	150	7/3	50.12.6	0.15.2
Dixon, Michael	406	15/6	314.13.0	4.14.4
Dabney, Benjamin	325	14/6	25.12.6	3.10.8¾

[page 5, 1789]

Present Proprietors Names	Qty. Land	Price	Amt. Land	Amt. Tax
Amount bro. forward				£372.2.7[ ]
Eubank, James	75	10/5	39.1.3	0.11.9
do.	150	14/6	108.15.0	1.12.7½
Eubank, Thomas	150		108.15.0	1.12.7½
Eubank, John	200		145.--.--	2.3.6
do. Harry Samuel	78	7/3	28.5.6	0.8.6
Eubank, Henry	171	5/3	44.17.9	0.13.6
Edwards, Thomas Est.	66	4/2	13.15.0	0.4.2
Eubank, Wm. estate	28¾	5/3	7.11.0	0.2.4
Eubank, Richard	65	3/2	10.5.10	0.3.1½
do.	90¾	5/3	23.16.6	0.7.2
Eubank, Richard este.	227	4/2	47.5.10	0.14.3
Edwards, Charles	192	3/2	30.8.0	0.9.2
Fleet, Baylor	360	20/9	373.10.0	5.12.0
do. Marsh	152	5/	38.0.0	0.11.5
do. Whittings	350	7/10	137.1.8	2.1.2
Fauntleroy, Samuel G.	880	16/7	729.13.4	10.18.1
do. Philips & Henley's	183	10/5	95.6.3	1.8.7
Fauntleroy, Moore	1006	24/10	1231.2.4	18.14.8¾
Fleet, John	326	10/5	165.12.6	2.9.7
do.	180	6/3	56.6.0	0.16.10
Faulkner, Thomas	155		48.8.9	0.14.7
Fogg, Thomas	200		62.10.0	0.18.9
Fogg, James	120		37.10.0	0.11.3
[Farr]enholtz, Wm. Est.	146		45.12.6	0.13.[9]
Frazer, William este.	45	20/9	46.13.9	0.14.[1]
Fleet, William	296¾		307.7.3	4.12.3
Fisher, James este.	110	3/2	17.18.4	0.5.3
Foster, Thomas	214	4/2	44.11.8	0.13.5
Faulkner, Mary	333	6/3	104.1.4	1.11.3
Fauntleroy, Thomas	800	8/4	333.6.8	5.0.0
do. of Henry Todd	500	18/	460.0.0	6.18.0
Farthing, Dudley	203	7/10	79.10.2	1.3.10
Grafton, Thomas	132	9/4	61.12.0	0.18.6
Grafton, James	111	6/3	34.13.9	0.10.5
Gale, John estate	180	10/5	93.15.0	1.8.5
Goleman, Thomas (Essex)	714	9/4	333.4.0	5.0.0
Garnett, Rice	297	7/3	107.13.7	1.12.4
Gatewood, Chaney	860	10/5	451.0.10	6.15.4
ditto Gardners	100	7/3	36.5.0	0.10.11
Garnett, Joshua	322	8/4	134.3.4	2.0.3
Graves, Edward	200	6/3	62.10.0	0.18.9
Gatewood, Joseph	445	10/5	231.15.5	3.9.7
Gale, Matthew	323	11/5	184.7.7	2.15.4
Gatewood, John	160	8/4	66.13.4	1.0.0
Garnett, Reubin	33	5/3	8.13.3	0.2.8
	Carried forw[d.]			£473.[16.7¼]

[page 6, 1789]

Present Proprietors Names	Qty. Land	Price	Amt. Land	Amt. Tax
Amount bro[t.] forward				473.16.7¼
Gwathmey, Temple	600	35/3	1057.10.0	15.17.3
Garlick, Samuel	454	24/10	563.14.4	8.9.2
Garlick, John	893	29/	1294.17.0	19.8.5
Griffith, Joseph	50	6/3	15.12.6	0.4.9
Gresham, Samuel	400	7/3	145.0.0	2.3.6
do. of R[d.] Tunstall	87½	8/4	3.9.2	0.10.11
Garrett, Rich[d.] jr. este.	100	4/2	20.16.8	0.6.3
Gardner, John este.	623	6/9	20.5.3	3.2.9
Gaines, Francis	391	14/6	283.9.6	4.5.1½
Gaines, Harry este.	1517	20/4	1542.5.8	23.2.8
Gresham, Thomas	339¼	6/3	106.0.4	1.11.10
Gresham, Philemon	200		62.10.0	0.18.9
Gresham, John (D)	200	7/10	78.6.8	1.3.6
Gaines, Robert	225	5/3	59.1.3	0.17.9
Gresham, William	100	4/2	20.16.8	0.6.3
Gardner, Elizabeth	100	6/3	31.5.0	0.9.5
Gibson, Richard este.	113	3/2	17.17.10	0.5.5
Gibson, John	219¾		34.15.11	0.10.6
Griffith, Milley	50	6/3	15.12.6	0.4.9
Gresham, Ruth	250	5/3	65.12.6	0.19.9
Griffin, William	859	14/6	622.15.6	9.6.10½
Garlick, Camm este.	1100	6/3	343.15.0	5.3.2
Garrett, Henry	50	3/2	7.8.4	0.2.4½
Garrett, Richard	50		7.8.4	0.2.4½
Garrett, William este.	330	4/2	68.15.0	1.0.8
[Gar]dner, Anthony	623	10/5	324.9.7	4.17.4
do. of H. Todd	215	12/6	134.7.6	2.0.3
do. of dragon swamp	42½	17/	36.2.6	0.10.10
Gresham, William jun[r.]	242	8/4	100.16.8	1.10.3
Gatewood, William	105	10/5	54.13.9	0.16.8
Gatewood, William (*Tuck[o.]*)	220	3/2	34.16.8	0.10.6
Garrett, Hump[y.]	450	12/6	281.5.0	4.4.9
Guthrie, James	60		37.10.0	0.11.3
Guthrie, Richard Sen[r.] este.	60			0.11.3
Guthrie, Richard Jun[r.]	162	3/2	25.13.0	0.7.8½
Glaspe, James	210	5/3	55.2.6	0.16.7
Groom, Robert	100	3/2	15.16.8	0.4.9
Groom, Mary	173	3/2	27.17.10	0.8.5
Garrett, George & Edward	170	5/3	44.12.6	0.13.5
Goldman, Martain	140	4/2	29.3.4	0.8.9
Groom, Barbara	100	3/2	15.16.8	0.4.9
Groom, Zachariah	187		29.12.2	0.8.7
Gulley, Philip	150		23.15.0	0.7.2
Garrett, William (Shoe)	200		31.13.4	0.9.6
Gramshill, Henry	25		3.19.2	0.1.2

[page 7, 1789]

Present Proprietors Names	Qty. Land	Price	Amt. Land	Amt. Tax
Amount brought forward				594.16.7
Halbert, James	124	6/2	38.15.0	0.11.7½
Harwood, Agness	225	4/2	46.17.6	0.14.1
Holt, Richard Jun[r.]	400	6/3	125.--.--	1.17.6
Hill, William	1191	14/6	928.9.6	13.18.7
Hutcherson, Charles	501	7/3	181.12.6	2.14.6
Hall, Corbin	188	8/4	78.6.8	1.3.6
Hitchcock, Thomas	140	4/2	29.3.4	8.9
Hoskins, Samuel	175	5/3	45.18.9	13.10
Hoskins, William	160	10/5	83.6.8	1.5.0
do. of Richard Bray	366	7/10	143.7.0	2.3.0
Herndon, Margrett Est.	100	7/3	36.5.0	10.11
Heskew, John	61	5/3	16.0.3	4.10
Heskew, John Jun[r.]	50	6/3	15.12.6	4.8
Hoomes, Benjamin	230	7/10	90.1.8	1.7.1
Hill, Robert	1555	8/4	647.8.4	9.14.4½
do. Ann Tunstall	223	7/10	87.6.10	1.6.3
do. James Keeling	42½	7/3	15.8.1½	0.4.7
Hill, Edward	1200	18/8	1120.--.--	16.16.0
Hart, William Sen[r.]	40	5/3	10.10.0	3.1¼
Hodges, Sally (J.H. Norton)	462	4/2	96.5.0	1.8.11
Hudson, William	112	3/2	17.14.8	5.4
Hemmingway, Danl. est.	800	4/2	166.13.4	2.0.0
Harwood, Christ[r.]	300	24/10	372.10.0	5.11.9
Harwood, John	501	5/3	131.10.3	1.19.6
Harwood, William	240	30/	360.--.--	5.8.0
Hill, Thomas	300	26/11	403.[15].0	6.1.2
Hart, James	150	3/2	23.15.0	0.7.2
Hart, Anthony	190	5/3	[49.17.6]	[15.0]
do.	1[8]8	3/2	29.15.4	9.0
Hart, Gregory	200		31.13.4	9.6
Hart, William	218		34.10.4	0.10.5
do. of H. Jordon	32	4/2	6.13.4	0.2.0
Harwood, John	354	10/5	184.12.9	2.15.5
Hare, William Doctor	109	5/3	28.12.3	8.8
Hunt, William	730	6/3	228.2.6	3.8.6
Holderby, Eliz[a.]	100	4/2	20.16.8	0.6.8
Hudson, Mary	100	"		0.6.8
Henry, James Esq[r.]	1900	14/6	1377.10.0	20.13.3
Halyard, William	190	5/3	49.17.6	0.15.0
do. Edward Crouch	130	3/2	20.11.8	0.6.3
Hoskins, John	540	10/5	281.5.0	4.4.4½
do. Jos. Minors	170	7/3	61.12.6	0.18.6
Haws, William	72	10/5	37.10.0	0.11.3
Hoskins, Robert	100	6/3	31.5.0	0.9.5
do. C. Dudley's	120	4/2	25.0.0	0.7.6
				£711.14.10¾

[page 8, 1789]

Present Proprietors Names	Qty. Land	Price	Amt. Land	Amt. Tax
Amo[unt] brought forw[d.]				711.14.10¾
Jones, John Est.	360	8/11	168.10.0	2.8.2
Jeffries, Edward	70	3/2	11.1.8	0.3.4
Jones, James	160	14/6	116.--.--	1.14.10
Jones, James Est.	196	10/5	102.1.8	1.10.8
Jones, William	335	13/6	226.2.6	3.7.11
do. of L. Smith	35¾	31/1	55.11.2	0.16.8
Jeffries, Ambrose	397	7/10	148.8.10	2.4.7
Jeffries, Bernard	30	4/2	6.5.0	0.1.11
Jordan, Henry	88		18.6.8	0.5.6
Jordan, William	100	3/2	15.16.8	0.4.9
Jordan, Thomas Est.	100	4/2	20.16.8	0.6.3
Johnson, Archibald	100			0.6.3
Johnson, Thomas	120	3/2	17.14.8	0.5.4
Jamerson, David (York)	50		7.18.4	0.2.5
Keeling, James	113¼	7/3	41.1.0¾	0.12.4
Kemp, John	87	7/10	34.7.6	0.10.3
do. of Jos: Wiltshire	53	7/3	19.4.3	0.5.9
Kauffman, George	583	14/6	422.13.6	6.6.10
Kauffman, John	471	18/8	439.12.0	6.11.11
Kennedy, Alex[r.]	600	12/6	379.3.4	5.12.9
Kemp, Matthew	100	5/4	26.13.4	0.8.0
Kemp, John (S. Major)	200	6/3	62.10.0	0.18.9
Kidd, John	370	7/3	134.2.6	2.0.3
do. Tho[s.] Peirce	25	4/2	5.4.2	0.1.7
Kay, Christ[r.]	116	6/3	30.9.0	[9.1½]
Kidd, Bartholomew	136	5/3	35.14.--	0.10.8
Kidd, Benj[a.] (Midd[x.])	111	13/6	74.18.2	1.2.5½
Lumpkin, Henry	620	9/4	289.6.8	4.6.10
Lumpkin, John	200	6/3	59.--.--	0.17.9
Lyne, William Col.	1480	8/4	610.14.2	9.3.3
Lyne, William Jun[r.]	108	8/4	45.--.--	13.6
Lumpkin, William	305	14/6	221.2.6	3.6.5
Lefon, Fran[s.]	119	8/4	49.11.8	0.14.10½
Lankford, Thomas	100	4/2	20.16.8	0.6.3
Lumpkin, Robert jr.	465	8/4	193.15.0	2.18.2
Lumpkin, Robert Sen[r.]	430	7/3	155.17.6	2.6.10
Longest, Caleb	97	7/10	37.19.10	0.11.6
Longest, Richard	140		54.16.8	0.16.6
Longest, Dorathy	100		39.3.4	0.11.9
Lumpkin, Joyce	287		112.8.2	1.13.9
Lumpkin, Mary	108	6/3	33.15.0	0.10.2
Lumpkin, Anthony	"	"	33.15.0	0.10.2
Lumpkin, Jacob	916	"	286.5.0	4.5.11
do. Southerlands	271	5/3	71.2.9	1.1.4
Lewis, Iveson	356	14/6	258.2.0	3.17.4¼
				£78[9.16.5]

[page 9, 1789]

Present Proprietors Names	Qty. Land	Price	Amt. Land	Amt. Tax
Brought Forward				789.16.5[ ]
Lewis, Elizabeth	100	4/2	20.16.8	0.6.3
Lumpkin, Richard	22	7/3	7.19.6	0.2.4½
do. Jn[o.] Carlton (King)	50	5/3	13.2.6	0.4.0
Leigh, Lucy	101	24/10	125.8.2	1.17.7
Leigh, John	199	"	247.1.10	3.14.2
Lyne, John	507	6/3	158.8.9	2.7.7
Lambeth, Thomas	200	3/2	31.11.4	9.6
Lumpkin, Robert (orpn[n.])	183	4/8	38.2.6	11.6
Laughlin, James	126¾	4/2	26.8.2	8.—
Motley, Edwin	740	10/5	389.1.3	5.16.9
McKentosh, William	192	4/2	40.--.--	7.1
Martain, Tho[s.] Capt.	680	14/6	493.--.--	7.7.11
do. Ann Peirce	35	7/3	12.3.9	0.3.8
Minor, William	149	8/4	62.1.8	18.8
Minor, John	137	"	57.1.8	17.2
Miller, Thomas	527	7/10	206.8.2	3.2.0
Man[n], Augustine Est.	400	8/4	166.13.4	2.10.0
Mitchell, John (Const[e.])	50	6/3	15.12.6	4.9
Mitchell, Robert	17	20/9	17.17.9	5.4
Mitchell, James	750	12/6	468.15.0	7.0.8
Mann, Robert	399	6/	119.14.0	1.15.10¾
McKendree, Eliz[a.]	323	5/3	84.15.9	1.5.6
McKendree, [John]	100	3/2	15.16.8	4.9
[Meredith, William (Leach)	243	5/3	63.15.9	19.2]
Mitchell, Susannah	170	3/2	26.18.4	8.1
Moore, Thomas	260	4/2	54.3.4	0.16.3
Moore, John	100	3/2	15.16.8	0.4.9
Major, Joseph	200	4/2	41.13.4	12.6
Mitchell, John (S. Major)	270	5/3	70.17.6	1.1.4
do. Rootes	300	12/6	187.10.0	2.16.3
Moore, Philip	50	3/2	7.18.4	2.5
Macon, John	1092	16/7	905.9.0	13.11.7
Mansfield, William	75	"	62.3.9	18.7
Manley, Peter	40	7/10	15.13.4	4.9
Merideth, Ralph G.	382	14/6	273.1.6	4.2.0
Meredith, Samuel Est.	185	14/6	138.0.0	2.1.5½
Muire, Richard	93	12/6	58.2.6	17.6
Moore, Richard	145	6/3	45.6.3	13.8
Martain, James	332½	20/9	344.19.4	5.3.5¾
McCarty, Jos:	73	3/2	11.11.2	3.6
Metcalf, Thomas	521	14/6	377.14.6	5.13.3¾
Martain, John	80	9/4	37.6.8	11.3
do. of John Jones	345	8/11	153.16.3	2.6.1½
Noel, Theoderick	298	8/4	124.3.4	1.17.3
Nunn, Jane	180	7/3	65.5.0	19.7
Newbill, Geo: Est.	500	8/4	208.6.8	3.2.6
				£880.[15.1¼]

[page 10, 1789]

Present Proprietors Names	Qty. Land	Price	Amt. Land	Amt. Tax
Amount bro[t.] forw[d.]				£880.15.1¼
Nunn, Thomas	174	7/3	63.1.6	1.0.0
Nash, John	100	6/3	31.5.0	0.9.5
Newcombe, Elizabeth	109	3/2	17.5.2	0.5.2
Newcombe, William	60	"	9.10.0	0.2.11
Olliver, John	320	5/3	84.0.0	1.5.3
Orvill, John	100	6/3	31.5.0	0.9.5
Overstreet, Mitchell	90	4/2	18.5.0	0.5.7½
Overstreet, Gabriel	286	"	61.13.4	0.18.6
do. Haynes	130	5/3	34.2.6	0.10.2
Osburn, John	90	3/2	14.5.0	0.4.4
Oakes, Henry Sen[r.]	110	3/2	17.8.4	0.5.3
Oakes, Henry Jr.	100	4/2	20.16.8	0.6.3
Owin, Augustine	100	6/3	31.5.0	0.9.5
Pendleton, James	450	10/	225.0.0	3.7.6
Pitts, David Est.	420	9/4	196.--.--	2.18.10
Pitts, Obadiah	20	10/5	10.8.4	0.3.2
Pitts, William	100	6/3	31.5.0	0.9.5
Phillips, Richard	230	7/3	83.7.6	1.5.1
Pollard, John	235	9/4	109.13.4	1.12.11
do. of Leo[d.] Smithy	384	7/3	139.4.0	2.1.10
Pruett, Fran[s.]	99	9/4	46.4.0	0.13.11
Parker, John	116½	7/10	45.12.7	0.13.9
Pendleton, Phil	337	10/5	175.10.5	2.12.8
Perryman, Anthony	[130]	[7/3]	[47.2].6	0.14.2
Pollard, Richard	[389]	8/4	1[62]1.8	2.8.7½
do. of W[m.] Wood	32½	7/3	11.15.7½	0.3.6
P[r]ince, Francis	113	7/10	44.5.2	0.13.4
Pendleton, Benjamin	450	"	176.5.0	2.12.11
Pynes, Benjamin	400	6/3	125.--.--	1.17.6
Pemberton, John	286	"	89.7.6	1.6.11½
Pace, Benjamin	143	6/	42.18.0	0.12.10½
Pace, John	120	8/6	51.0.0	0.15.5½
Pickels, John (G.C. Est.)	225	7/3	81.11.3	1.4.6
Price, Robert	630	6/3	196.17.6	2.19.1
Pigg, Rachel	108	14/6	78.6.0	1.3.6
Pigg, John	216	"	156.12.0	2.7.0
Padgett, Samuel Est.	36	7/10	14.2.0	0.4.2
Pollard, William	95	7/3	34.8.9	0.10.5
Pierce, Thomas	135	4/2	28.1.11	0.8.5
Pryor, John	150	3/2	23.15.0	0.7.8
Poole, Micajah	282	6/3	89.13.9	1.6.11
Richards, William	510	12/6	318.15.0	4.15.8
Robertson, Donald Est.	155	"	96.17.6	1.9.1
do.	260	7/3	94.5.0	1.8.5
Richards, George	362½	14/6	262.16.3	3.18.10

[page 11, 1789]

Present Proprietors Names	Qty. Land	Price	Amt. Land	Amt. Tax
Amount bro[t.] forward				936.14.8[ ]
Roane, Thomas Col.	2033	18/8	1897.9.4	28.8.3
do. H. Carlton's	200	6/3	63.10.0	0.18.9
do. of Geo. Richards ([W]R)	201½	14/6	146.1.9	2.3.11
Roane, William	1384	18/8	1[0]91.14.8	19.7.6
Richards, John Est.	1020	9/4	476.0.0	7.2.10
Row, Hansford & Wilson	390	6/3	121.17.6	1.16.5
Row, Thomas Major.	555	7/3	201.3.9	3.0.4
do. of H. Fleet	665	20/9	689.18.9	10.7.0
do. of Noel	296	6/3	92.10.0	1.7.2
do. Bowers & Burches	388	3/8	61.8.8	[1].18.6
Read, Robert	14	5/3	3.13.6	0.1.1
Row, Richard	550	8/4	229.3.4	3.8.9
Roane, Thomas jun[r.]	1600	24/10	1926.13.4	[28.18.0]
Rowzee, Elizabeth	120	3/2	19.0.0	0.5.9
Richerson, Elias	86	4/2	17.18.4	0.5.5
Row, John Est.	100	6/3	31.5.0	0.9.5
Richards, John	221½	4/2	46.3.0	0.13.11
Richards, William jr.	296	5/3	77.14.0	1.3.4
Richerson, James	180	4/2	37.10.0	0.11.3
Richerson, William	181	"	37.14.2	0.11.4
Richerson, John est.	101½	"	21.2.11	0.6.5
Roane, Tho[s.] Est. (S. Major)	150	3/2	23.15.0	0.7.2
Reigns, Giles	60		9.10.0	0.2.11
Roane, Major	367½	4/2	76.16.7	1.10.5
Robinson, Benj[a.] Est.	1300	8/4	541.13.4	8.2.6
[Roane, Charles]	200	14/6	145.0.0	2.3.6
do. dragon	70	17/	59.10.0	0.17.11
Robbins, William	40	6/3	12.10.0	0.3.9
Segar, Richard	406	7/3	147.3.6	2.4.2
Satterwhite, George	164	6/3	51.5.0	0.15.1
Satterwhite, William	100	4/2	20.16.8	0.6.3
Samuel, Henry	85	6/3	26.11.6	0.8.0
Samuel, Andrew	60	7/3	21.15.0	0.6.6
Spencer, Edward	392½	8/4	163.10.10	2.9.1
do. of Butler's	380	7/3	137.15.0	2.1.4
Schools, John	83½	7/10	32.14.1	0.9.9½
Sears, Frankey	338	9/4	157.14.8	2.7.2
Schools, Gabriel	169	6/3	52.16.3	0.15.11
Skelton, William	132	9/4	61.12.0	0.18.6
Smith, Ann	85	7/3	30.16.3	0.9.3
Starling, Jane	360	7/10	141.--.--	2.2.4
Skelton, Thomas	294	8/4	122.10.0	1.16.9
Scott, Benjamin	200	9/4	93.6.8	1.8.0
Saunders, George	100	7/3	36.5.0	0.10.10½
Saunders, Alex[r.]	100			0.10.10½
Shepherd, William	140	9/4	65.6.8	0.19.8
				£1083.6.11

[page 12, 1789]

Present Proprietors Names	Qty. Land	Price	Amt. Land	Amt. Tax
Amount bro[t.] forward				1083.6.11
Semple, Elizabeth	674	14/6	488.4.8	7.6.7
Semple, W. John	52		37.14.0	0.11.4
Smith, Molly	30	4/2	6.5.0	0.1.11
Smith, John (LHead)	100	5/3	26.5.0	0.7.11
Smith, Lewis	113½	7/3	41.12.11	0.12.6
Swinton, George	750	13/6	506.5.0	7.11.11
Stone, Sarah	300	7/3	108.15.0	1.12.8
Smith, Larkin	1254¼	31/1	1949.6.3½	29.4.10
Smith, Henry	400	6/3	125.0.0	1.17.6
Smith, William	140	7/10	54.16.8	0.16.8
Smith, James	80	3/2	12.13.4	0.3.10
Smith, James j[r.]	101	7/10	39.11.2	0.11.10½
Stevens, Thomas Est.	609½	7/10	238.14.5	3.11.8
Stevens, George	645	"	252.12.6	3.15.9½
Shackelford, John (taylor)	214	7/3	77.11.6	1.3.3½
Starke, Richard est.	250	6/3	78.2.6	1.3.6
do. Geo: Richards	100	4/2	20.16.8	0.6.3
Soanes, Mary	382	24/10	474.6.4	7.2.4
Stone, Robert	300	4/2	62.10.0	0.18.9
Stone, John Est.	357	6/3	93.14.3	1.8.2
Smith, Robert	879	10/5	457.19.3	6.17.5
Smith, Guy	189½	3/2	30.0.1	0.9.1
Simpkins, Nimrod	60	"	9.10.0	0.2.11
Sears, Philip	83	4/2	17.5.10	0.5.3
Spencer, Thomas	300	10/5	156.5.0	2.6.11
do.	255	4/2	53.2.6	0.15.11
Shackelford, William Est.	700	14/6	527.10.0	7.18.6
Seward, Benj[a.]	115	3/2	18.4.2	0.5.6
Steadman, Christ[r.]	191	5/3	50.2.9	0.15.1
Saddler, John	150	6/3	46.17.6	0.14.6
Shackelford, Alex[r.]	60	4/2	12.10.0	0.3.9
Steadman, Christ[r.] jun[r.]	133½	6/3	41.18.1½	0.12.6½
do. Dillard's	260	5/3	65.5.--	1.0.6
Smith, Gregory	485	14/6	351.12.6	5.5.5
Shackelford, John (Roman)	308	8/4	128.6.8	1.18.6
Shackelford, Benjamin	200		83.6.8	1.5.0
Shackelford, Robinson	500	10/5	260.8.4	3.18.2
do. Wm. Corr's Est.	200	3/2	31.13.4	0.9.6
Shackelford, Lyne	567	6/3	177.3.9	2.13.1
Shackelford, John (MacG.)	182	7/3	65.19.6	0.19.10
Scott, Anderson	330	16/7	273.12.6	4.2.2
Shepherd, Isaac	190	3/2	30.1.8	0.9.3
Trice, William	140	7/3	50.15.0	0.15.3
Taylor, James	50	6/3	15.12.6	0.4.9
				£[1197.13.]

[page 13, 1789]

Present Proprietors Names	Qty. Land	Price	Amt. Land	Amt. Tax
Amount bro[t.] forw[d.]				1197.13.[ ]
Taylor, Edmond	294	8/14	122.10.0	1.16.9
Temple, Joseph	918	10/5	478.2.6	7.3.6
Tunstall, Molley	250	"	130.4.2	1.19.0¾
Tunstall, Richard jr.	1097	7/3	397.13.3	5.19.3
Tunstall, John	200	18/8	186.13.4	2.16.0
Tunstall, Gregory & Rich[d.]	332½	20/9	344.19.4	5.3.5¾
Tignor, William	130	7/10	50.18.4	0.15.4½
Tureman, Benjamin	120	3/2	19.--.--	0.5.9
Taliaferro, Wm.	1000	14/6	725.--.--	10.17.6
Townley, Robert	117	"	84.16.6	1.5.5
Taliaferro, Philip	990	8/4	412.10.0	6.3.9
do. of P. Whiting	75	1/46	54.18.6	16.4
Taliaferro, Richard	300	5/3	78.15.0	1.3.8
Thruston, Batcheldor	100	3/2	15.16.8	0.4.9
Tucker, John Est.	180	7/3	65.5.0	0.19.7
Temple, Humph[y.]	70	33/2	116.1.8	1.14.9¾
do. Walkerton	108	30/	162.--.--	2.8.7
Tunstall, Richard Est.	538	20/9	558.3.6	8.7.5
Tunstall, Richard (Best[d.])	269½	8/4	112.15.10	1.13.9
Vass, Thomas	250	5/3	65.12.6	0.19.9
Wyatt, Henry	200	7/3	72.10.0	1.1.9
White, Henry	100	8/4	41.13.4	0.12.6
[Wi]lmore, Thomas	150	10/5	78.2.6	1.3.6
do. of Dudley Farthing	19	7/10	7.8.10	0.2.2½
Wright, James	124½	5/3	32.13.8	0.9.10
Wyatt, Joseph	60	8/4	25.0.0	0.7.6
Waldin, John	105	12/6	65.12.6	0.19.9
Wood, Thomas	260	7/10	111.16.8	1.10.8
Wilson, Isaac	200	6/3	62.10.0	0.18.9
Wilson, Benjamin Est.	200	7/3	72.18.0	1.1.9
Wiltshire, Joseph	80	"	29.0.0	0.8.9
Wright, Isaac	183	6/3	57.3.9	0.17.2
Wyatt, Thomas Est.	480	10/5	250.--.--	3.15.0
Wyatt, John	100	7/10	39.3.4	0.11.3
Watkins, William	37	4/2	7.14.2	0.2.4
Watkins, Joseph	65	"	13.10.10	0.4.2
Waldin, James	154	7/10	60.6.4	0.18.1
Walker, Henry Est.	150	5/3	39.7.6	0.11.10
Ware, John	562	7/3	203.14.6	3.1.2
Walker, Frances	475	33/2	783.9.6	11.17.3
Walker, Humph[y.]	345	"	572.4.8	8.10.7
Wright, William	175	5/3	45.18.9	0.13.10
Whayne, William	13½	7/3	4.17.11	0.1.6
do. Langham's	194	7/10	75.19.8	1.2.9
				£1301.11.10¾

[page 14, 1789]

Present Proprietors Names	Qty. Land	Price	Amt. Land	Amt. Tax
Amount of tax bro[t.] forward				£1301.11.10¾
Watts, Edward	250	7/3	90.12.6	1.7.3
Watts, John	293	7/10	114.15.2	1.14.6
do. of Pemberton	45	6/3	14.1.3	0.4.2½
Watts, William	380	7/10	184.16.8	2.4.7
Watts, Kauffman	300	5/3	78.15.0	1.3.8
Williams, Howard	283	4/2	58.19.2	0.17.9
Wyatt, Thomas	206	7/10	81.2.0	1.4.4½
Wyatt, John (blind)	103	6/3	32.3.9	0.9.8
Wyatt, William	29¾	7/3	10.15.8	0.3.3
Williams, Howard Est.	300	6/3	93.15.0	1.8.2
Williams, Charles	550	4/2	114.11.8	1.14.5
Walton, James	80	"	16.3.4	0.5.0
Walton, Mary	60	"	12.10.0	0.3.9
Walton, Eliz[a.]	60	3/2	9.10.0	0.2.11
Walton, John	176	5/3	46.4.0	0.13.4
Walton, William Est.	66	4/2	13.15.0	0.4.2
Walton, Thomas est.	"	"	"	0.4.2
Ware, John	75	5/3	19.13.9	0.5.11
Ware, Auther	83	4/2	17.5.10	0.5.3
Watts, James	350	"	72.18.4	1.1.11
Walding, Richard	180	10/5	93.15.0	1.8.1½
Walden, Lewis	150	3/2	23.15.0	0.7.3
do. of T. Dudley	84½	6/3	28.2.3½	0.8.5
Wyatt, Richard	175	12/6	109.7.6	1.12.9¾
do. [illegible]	1[20]	7/2	[101.16.8]	[ ]
Ware, Sarah	175	"	36.9.2	0.11.0
Williams, Eliz[a.]	50	3/2	7.18.4	0.2.5
White, James Est.	200	6/3	62.10.--	0.18.9
Watkins, Eliz[a.]	100	3/2	15.16.8	0.4.9
Warren, Catharine	175	"	27.14.2	0.8.4
Ware, Robert (bishop)	112	"	17.14.8	0.5.4
Wedderburn, Lydia	350	6/3	109.7.6	1.12.10
Whiting, Beverly Est.	2447¾	7/10	866.18.9½	13.0.0
Webley, John	173	5/3	45.8.3	0.13.8
do. of B. Collier	100	4/2	20.16.8	0.6.3
Ware, Leo[d.] est.	200	8/4	83.6.8	1.5.0
Walden, Edward	373	5/3	97.18.3	1.9.5
Wright, William (S. Major)	100	4/2	20.16.8	0.6.3
Waller, Edward este.	133½	3/2	21.2.9	0.6.5
Waller, John	66½	"	10.10.7	0.3.2
Willis, Joel	63	31/1	93.18.3	1.9.4½
Wyatt, John	30	5/3	7.17.6	0.2.5
Young, Henry	640	18/8	597.6.8	8.19.3
Total Amot. of land tax @ 1½ per cent				£[ ]

We do hereby certify that the foregoing is a Just statement of the land and tax thereon @ one and a half percent on the value [ ]. Wm. Fleet & Wm. Courtney, Commrs. the tax. King & Queen July 1789.
Amount of Land Tax at ¾ p.ct. £679.2[ ].

[cover] For Leyton Wood, Esquire, Solicitor, Richmond.

A list of the land within the County of King and Queen
for the year 1790

[page 1, 1790]

Present Proprietors Names	Qty. Land	Price	Amt. Land	Amt. Tax
Alexander, Benjamin	202	9/4	94.5.4	1.8.[4]
Alexander, Elisha	102	7/3	36.12.3	11.[ ]
Alexander, John	50	9/4	23.6.8	7.[ ]
Anderson, Churchill's est.	636	7/3	230.11.0	3.9.[2]
Anderson, Paulin	498	14/6	361.1.0	5.9.[4]
Atkins, John's est.	42	7/3	15.4.6	4.[7]
Atkins, John jr.	120	4/2	25.0.0	7.[6]
Abbott, Jacob	112	7/10	43.17.4	13.2
Anderson, Richard est.	460	5/3	120.15.0	1.16.3
Atkins, Lewis	60	8/4	25.0.0	7.6
Anderson, Francis [home]	233	14/6	168.18.6	2.10.8
do. high land	225	6/10	76.17.6	1.3.1
Beverley, Robert	2474	10/5	1288.8.10	19.6.7
Brown, Henry	657	7/5½	245.8.1	3.13.7½
do. of James Keeling	103½	7/3	37.10.4½	11.3
do. of John Wheeley	50	6/3	15.12.6	4.9
Baylor, Gregory est.	720	14/6	522.0.0	7.16.7
Bland, Henry est.	166	8/4	69.3.4	1.0.9
Bates, James	358	"	149.3.4	2.4.9
do.	42	4/2	8.15.0	2.7½
Barton, John	125	"	26.0.10	7.10
Banks, William est.	365	"	76.0.10	1.2.9¾
Brooking, Frances	930	10/5	484.7.6	7.5.4
Baylor, John est.	760	14/6	551.0.0	8.5.4
Boughton, Thomas, Essex	130	9/4	60.13.4	18.3
Boughton, John [torn page]	200	8/4	83.6.8	[1].5.[0]
Boughton, Henry, Essex	88	6/3	27.10.0	[8.3]
Boughton, Thomas	100	8/4	41.13.4	12.6
Broach, John	45	6/3	14.1.3	4.3
Burton, Thomas est.	170	5/3	44.12.6	13.5
Bohannon, Benjamin	160	4/2	33.6.8	10.0
Bohannon, Ann	150	"	31.17.6	9.6¾
Brown, William	75	7/10	29.7.6	8.10
Bagby, John	330	7/3	119.12.6	1.15.10½
Bagby, Richard	260	"	94.5.0	1.8.3½
Bagby, Thomas	260	"	94.5.0	1.8.3½
Brooke, Richard	1539¾	29/-	2232.12.9	33.9.[10]
Brumley, John	329½	3/2	52.3.5	15.[8]
Bird, William	532	7/3	192.17.0	2.18.1
do. Dragon swamp	88½	17/	70.4.6	1.1.[ ]
Bird, Mary	619	6/3	193.8.9	2.18.1
Bird, Philemon	1238	"	386.17.6	5.16.1
Brett, John	446	18/	401.8.0	6.--.5
Bowers, John	70	7/3	25.7.6	7.8
Burch, Eliz[a.]	100	4/2	20.16.8	6.3
Bird, Anthony A.	275	3/2	43.10.10	13.1
Byne, John est.	336	4/2	70.0.0	1.1.[ ]
do. Dragon	2¼	17/	1.18.3	6¾
Bird, Barbara	266 3/4	24/10	331.2.2½	4.16.[ ]
				£140.16.[2]

[page 2, 1790]

Present Proprietors Names	Qty. Land	Price	Amt. Land	Amt. Tax
Bird, Robert	533 1/3	24/10	662.4.5½	9.12.[ ]
Bourn, Richard	150	3/2	23.15.0	7.2
Burch, William est.	257	5/9	73.17.9	1.2.2
Boyd, John	115	18/8	107.6.8	1.12.3
do. Mary Soanes	382	24/10	474.6.4	7.2.4
Bray, Richard est.	93	7/10	36.8.6	10.11
Bird, John	100	3/2	15.16.8	4.9
Bowden, William	253	7/	88.11.0	1.6.6¼
Bew, William	117	3/2	18.10.6	5.7
Boyd, Spencer est.	1428	10/5	770.15.0	11.11.2
Berkley, Edmond	762	5/3	200.0.6	3.0.0
Bohannon, William	130		34.2.6	10.[ ]
Bland, John	60	12/6	37.10.0	11.[3]
Bullman, Thomas est.	100	5/3	26.5.0	7.[11]
Briggs, John (Wm. Finney)	170	4/2	35.8.4	10.[8]
Belote, Laban	384½		80.2.1	1.4.0
Bland, William Senr.	120	--	25.0.0	7.6
do. of Brooks & Hardy	105	3/2	16.12.6	5.--
Bowden, William jr.	100	4/2	20.16.8	6.3
do. of G. Sykes & B. Dudley	34	3/2	5.7.8	1.8
Bowden, John	--	--	--	6.3
Bland, William jr. est.	250	"	52.1.8	15.8
Bland, Thomas	300	3/2	57.10.0	17.3
Bowden, George	75	4/2	15.12.6	4.9½
Burch, Will	45	3/2	7.2.6	2.1½
Brown, Thomas	212		34.11.4	10.4
Cary, Martha	462	4/2	96.5.--	1.8.11
Cook, Mary	200	8/4	83.6.8	1.5.0
Coleman, Thomas [tear across page]	[572]	[6/3]	[178.15.0]	[2.13.8]
Chick, Richard	491	7/3	177.19.9	2.13.5
Chapman, George est.	200	7/10	78.6.8	1.3.6
Campbell, William	1029	7/3	373.0.3	5.11.9
Chapman, Elizabeth	200	7/10	78.6.8	1.3.6
Crane, Catharine	50	5/3	13.2.6	4.0
Crane, John	6	--	1.10.6	6
Cleverius, Benja.	419	20/9	434.14.3	6.10.5
Carlton, Henry	280	7/10	109.13.4	1.12.10
Clayton, Thomas est.	275	7/3	99.13.9	1.9.11
Campbell, Whitacar	318	7/10	124.11.-	1.17.6
Clevely, Thomas	80	7/10	36.6.8	9.4
do. Langham's	200		78.6.8	1.3.6
Crow, Nathaniel	200	6/3	62.10.0	18.9
Crafton, Richard	236	9/4	110.2.8	1.13.1
Crane, George	30	7/3	10.7.6	3.4
Coleman, Milley	196	10/5	102.1.8	1.10.8
Carlton, Joel	53½	6/3	16.14.5	5.1
Carter, Jane	60	3/2	9.10.0	2.11
Carlton, Thomas (Swamp)	300	7/10	117.10.0	1.15.3
Carlton, John (Schoolr.)	100	6/3	31.5.0	9.5
Campbell, Sarah	296	12/6	185.0.0	2.15.6
Carlton, Christr. Sr.	37½	6/3	11.14.5	3.7
				83.1.5

[page 3, 1790]

Present Proprietors Names	Qty. Land	Price	Amt. Land	Amt. Tax
Carlton, Will$^{m.}$ (Shoe$^{r.}$)	90¾	6/3	28.7.3	8.7
do. of W$^{m.}$ Harwood	160	15/	120.0.0	1.1[6.0]
Carlton, Robert est.	93	4/2	19.7.6	5.10
do. of J. Pemberton	55	6/3	17.3.9	5.2
Carlton, Richard	250	7/3	90.12.6	1.7.3
Carlton, Christ$^{r.}$ jr.	100		36.5.0	10.11
Carlton, James est.	225	6/3	70.6.3	1.1.2
Carlton, Philemon	150	6/6	48.15.0	14.7½
Cooper, Henry	50	4/2	10.8.4	3.2
Carlton, Thomas (tay$^{r.}$)	100	6/3	31.5.0	9.5
Cardwell, John est.	150	4/2	31.5.0	9.5
Cardwell, John				9.5
Cardwell, Thomas				9.5
Cardwell, William				9.5
Cook, John est.	300	4/2	62.10.0	18.9
Collins, Thomas	150		31.5.0	9.5
do. Palmers	350	7/3	126.17.6	1.18.1
Carlton, John j$^{r.}$ (Carp$^{r.}$)	235	4/2	48.19.2	14.9
Campbell, W$^{m.}$ (Strat$^{n.}$ M.)	238	3/2	37.13.8	11.4
Collier, Charles	250	8/4	104.3.4	1.11.3
Collins, John	100	4/2	20.16.8	6.3
Corbin, Richard est.	1868	10/5	972.18.4	14.11.11
Corbin, John, T [Rosewall]	400	12/6	290.0.0	4.7.0
do of Wm. Meredith	124	11/3	69.13.0	1.0.10½
Corrie, John exors.	500	10/5	260.8.	3.18.2
do. [W. Corr's est.] [torn page]	200	[3/2]	3.31.4	[9.6]
Crittenden, Thomas	75	13/6	50.12.6	15.2¼
do Dragon Swamp	72	17/	61.4.0	18.4
Collins, Joyeux est.	140	10/5	72.18.4	1.1.10
Crittenden, Zachariah	34 1/3	14/6	24.17.10	7.6
Cary, W. Miles	1820	16/7	1509.1.8	22.12.9
Collier, John (Cob~~b~~ler)	150	5/3	39.7.6	11.1[0]
Campbell, James	100	6/3	31.5.0	9.5
do. Tho$^{s.}$ Burk	100	4/2	20.16.8	6.[3]
Crittenden, Rich$^{d.}$ jr. est.	178		46.14.6	14.1
Collier, Fran$^{s.}$ est.	400	4/2	83.6.8	1.5.[0]
Corr, Avarilla	140		36.15.0	11.1
Collier, Catharine	750	5/3	196.17.6	2.19.[1]
Clegg, Isaiah	241	4/2	50.4.2	15.0½
Cook, Dawson	296	7/3	107.3.0	1.12.1
do. C. Ware's est.	500	12/6	312.10.0	4.13.9
Curry, Ann	100	4/2	20.16.8	6.3
Corr, Frances	175	3/2	27.14.2	8.4
Courtney, William	190	7/10	74.8.4	1.2.4
Cooke, Thomas	240	3/2	38.0.0	11.5
Carlton, Humph$^{y.}$	125	7/3	45.6.3	13.8
Carlton, Tho$^{s.}$ est. (Carp$^{r.}$)	235	6/3	73.8.9	1.2.1
Carlton, Beverly	210	4/2	43.15.0	13.1½
Corr, John Sen$^{r.}$	38	3/2	6.0.4	1.9½
Campbell, John	400	12/6	250.0.0	3.15.0
Crittenden, Francis Jr.	105 2/3	14/6	76.12.2	1.3.0
				£89.7.4

[page 4, 1790]

Present Proprietors Names	Qty. Land	Price	Amt. Land	Amt. Tax
Dew, William	935	14/6	677.17.6	10.3.5
Dowling, William est.	264	8/4	110.0.0	1.13.0
Dix, Gabriel	338	6/3	105.12.6	1.11.8
Deshazo, William	162	4/2	33.15.0	10.2
Durham, Joseph	76	"	15.16.8	4.9
Deshazo, Peter	217	7/2	72.15.2	1.1.9½
Dickie, James	512	8/4	213.6.8	3.4.0
Dunbar, David	366	"	152.10.0	2.5.9
Dalley, John	200	3/2	31.13.4	9.6
Drumright, Thomas	224	"	35.9.4	10.8
Dobbins, Charles	147	5/3	38.11.9	11.7
Dean, Benjamin	50	"	13.2.6	4.0
Dillard, William jr.	100	3/2	15.16.8	4.9
Dunn, Agrippia	140	5/3	36.15.0	11.1
Draper, Thos. & Thos. Nunn	87	6/3	27.3.9	8.2
Dudley, Peter est.	370	7/10	144.18.4	2.3.6
do. of J. Baylor	160	5/3	42.0.0	12.7
Davis, Jane	100	4/2	20.16.8	6.3
Didlake, James	311	6/9	105.2.7½	1.11.4½
Didlake, Margrett	65	"	13.10.10	4.1
Durham, Robert est.	50	"	10.8.4	3.2
Dunn, Thomas	30	6/3	9.7.6	2.10
Dillard, William Senr.	276	12/6	172.10.--	2.11.9
Durham, George	50	4/2	10.8.4	3.2
Durham, Thomas	85	3/2	13.9.2	4.1
Dumagin, Richard est.	237	5/5	64.3.9	19.3
Diggs, Frances	175	5/3	45.18.9	13.10
Didlake, George estate [tear in page]	[114]	10/5	59.7.6	[17.10]
Dungie, John	110	3/2	17.8.4	5.3
Dudley, William jr.	290	14/6	210.5.0	3.3.1
do. of L. Wedderburn	315½	6/3	98.11.10½	1.9.6¾
Damm, John est.	55	"	17.3.9	5.2
Dudley, William Senr.	180	7/10	70.10.--	1.1.2
Damm, William	25	4/2	5.4.2	1.6½
Dunbar, Mary	450	9/4	210.--.--	3.3.0
Douglass, John	100	6/3	31.5.0	9.5
do. of S. Field	139	7/3	50.7.9	15.1¼
Didlake, John	1200	"	435.--.--	6.10.6
Dudley, Robert B. est.	421	"	152.12.3	2.5.10
Dudley, Thomas	267½	6/3	81.17.8½	1.4.7
Dillard, Nicholas	75	4/2	15.12.6	4.9
Dillard, Benja. est.	133	5/3	34.18.4	10.6
Drummond, Thomas est.	150	6/3	46.17.6	14.6
Didlake, James est.	131	3/2	20.14.10	6.3
Dillard, Thomas	377	5/3	98.19.3	1.9.9
Dillard, Elizabeth	449	14/6	325.10.6	4.17.8
Dillard, Wm. (son Thos.)	150	4/2	31.5.0	9.5
Davis, Thomas	150	7/3	50.12.6	15.2
Dixon, Michael	406	15/6	314.13.0	4.14.4
Dabney, Benjamin	325	14/6	25.12.6	3.10.8¾
				£72.15.3

[page 5, 1790]

Present Proprietors Names	Qty. Land	Price	Amt. Land	Amt. Tax
Eubank, John	200		145.--.--	2.3.6
do. H. Samuel & W.H. [Hill]	209	7/3	75.15.3	1.2.9
Eubank, Thomas	300	14/6	217.10.0	3.5.3
Eubank, Henry	171	5/3	44.17.9	13.6
Edwards, Thomas est.	66	4/2	13.15.0	4.2
Eubank, William est.	28¾	5/3	7.11.0	2.4
Eubank, Richard	65	3/2	10.5.10	3.1½
do.	90¾	5/3	23.16.6	7.2
do. of J. Harwood jr.	39½	10/5	20.11.5½	6.2
Eubank, Richard est.	227	4/2	47.5.10	14.3
Edwards, Charles	192	3/2	30.8.0	9.2
Fogg, Frederick	298	8/4	124.3.4	1.17.3
Fleet, Baylor	360	20/9	373.10.0	5.12.0
do. Marsh	152	5/	38.0.0	11.5
do. Whitings	350	7/10	137.1.8	2.1.2
Fauntleroy, Sam[l.] G.	880	16/7	729.13.4	10.18.1
do. Jn[o.] Philips & Hendley	183	10/5	95.6.3	1.8.7
Fauntleroy, Moore	1006	24/10	1231.2.4	18.14.8¾
Fleet, John	326	10/5	165.12.6	2.9.7
do.	180	6/3	56.6.0	16.10
Faulkner, Thomas	155		48.8.9	14.7
Fogg, Thomas est.	200		62.10.0	18.9
Fogg, James	120		37.10.0	11.3
Farrenholtz, W[m.] est.	146		45.12.6	13.9
Frazer, William est.	45	20/9	46.13.9	14.1
Fleet, William [page tear]	296¾	23/9	307.7.3	4.[12.3]
Fisher, James est.	110	3/2	17.18.4	5.3
Foster, Thomas	214	4/2	44.11.8	13.5
Faulkner, Mary	333	6/3	104.1.4	1.11.3
Fauntleroy, Thomas	800	8/4	333.6.8	5.0.0
do. of H. Todd	500	18/	460.0.0	6.18.0
Farthing, Dudley	203	7/10	79.10.2	1.3.10
Grafton, Thomas	132	9/4	61.12.0	18.6
Grafton, James	111	6/3	34.13.9	10.5
Gale, John est.	180	10/5	93.15.0	1.8.5
Goleman, Thomas (Essex)	714	9/4	333.4.0	5.0.0
Garnett, Rice	297	7/3	107.13.7	1.12.4
Gatewood, Chaney	860	10/5	451.0.10	6.15.4
do. Gardners	100	7/3	36.5.0	10.11
Garnett, Joshua	322	8/4	134.3.4	2.0.3
Graves, Edward	200	6/3	62.10.0	18.9
Gatewood, Joseph	445	10/5	231.15.5	3.9.7
Gale, Matthew	323	11/5	184.7.7	2.15.4
Gatewood, John	160	8/4	66.13.4	1.0.0
Garnett, Reubin	33	5/3	8.13.3	2.8
do. of J. Richards est.	407	9/4	189.18.8	2.17.0
				£107.16.11

[page 6, 1790]

Present Proprietors Names	Qty. Land	Price	Amt. Land	Amt. Tax
Gwathmey, Temple	600	35/3	1057.10.0	15.17.3
Garlick, Samuel	454	24/10	563.14.4	8.9.2
Garlick, John	893	29/	1294.17.0	19.8.5
Griffith, Joseph	50	6/3	15.12.6	4.9
Gresham, Samuel	400	7/3	145.0.0	2.3.6
do. of Richard Tunstall	87½	8/4	3.9.2	10.11
Garrett, Richard jr. est.	100	4/2	20.16.8	6.3
Gardner, Elizabeth M.	311	6/9	105.2.7½	1.11.4½
Gaines, Francis	391	14/6	283.9.6	4.5.1½
Gaines, Harry est.	1517	20/4	1542.5.8	23.2.8
Gresham, Thomas	339¼	6/3	106.0.4	1.11.10
Gresham, Philemon	200		62.10.0	18.9
Gresham, John (D)	200	7/10	78.6.8	1.3.6
Gaines, Robert	225	5/3	59.1.3	17.9
Gresham, William	100	4/2	20.16.8	6.3
Gardner, Elizabeth	100	6/3	31.5.0	9.5
Gibson, Richard	100	3/2	15.16.8	4.9
Gibson, Richard est.	113		17.17.10	5.5
Gibson, John	219¾		34.15.11	10.6
Griffith, Milley	50	6/3	15.12.6	4.9
Gresham, Ruth	250	5/3	65.12.6	19.9
Griffin, William	859	14/6	622.15.6	9.6.10½
Garlick, Camm est.	1100	6/3	343.15.0	5.3.2
Garrett, Henry	50	3/2	7.8.4	2.4½
do. of A. Campbell (J.T.C.)	125	12/6	78.2.6	1.3.5
Garrett, Richard	50	3/2	7.8.4	2.4½
Garrett, William est. [page tear]	330	4/2	68.15.0	1.0.8
Gardner, Anthony	623	10/5	324.9.7	4.17.4
do. H. Todd	215	12/6	134.7.6	2.0.3
do. Dragon	42½	17/	36.2.6	10.10
Gresham, William jr.	242	8/4	100.16.8	1.10.3
Gatewood, William	105	10/5	54.13.9	16.8
Gatewood, W^m.^ (*Tuck^o.^*)	220	3/2	34.16.8	10.6
Garrett, Humphry	450	12/6	281.5.0	4.4.9
Guthrie, James	60		37.10.0	11.3
Guthrie, Rich^d.^ est.	60			11.3
Guthrie, Richard	162	3/2	25.13.0	7.8½
Glaspe, James	210	5/3	55.2.6	16.7
Groom, Robert	100	3/2	15.16.8	4.9
Groom, Mary	173	3/2	27.17.10	8.5
Garrett, George & Edward	170	5/3	44.12.6	13.5
Goldman, Martain	140	4/2	29.3.4	8.9
Groom, Barbara	100	3/2	15.16.8	4.9
Groom, Zachariah	187		29.12.2	8.7
Gulley, Philip	50		7.18.4	2.4
				1[1]9.19.4

[page 7, 1790]

Present Proprietors Names	Qty. Land	Price	Amt. Land	Amt. Tax
Amount brought forward				594.16.7
Gulley, Benjamin	100	3/2	15.16.8	4.9
Garrett, W[m.] (Shoe[m.])	200		31.13.4	9.6
Gramshill, Henry	25		3.19.2	1.2¼
Halbert, James	124	6/2	38.15.0	11.7½
Harwood, Agness	225	4/2	46.17.6	14.1
Holt, Richard jr.	400	6/3	125.--.--	1.17.6
Hill, William	1191	14/6	928.9.6	13.18.7
Hutcherson, Charles	501	7/3	181.12.6	2.14.6
Hall, Corbin	188	8/4	78.6.8	1.3.6
Hitchcock, Thomas	140	4/2	29.3.4	8.9
Hoskins, Samuel	175	5/3	45.18.9	13.10
Hoskins, William	160	10/5	83.6.8	1.5.0
do. of R[d.] Bray	366	7/10	143.7.0	2.3.0
Heskew, John	61	5/3	16.0.3	4.10
Heskew, John jr.	50	6/3	15.12.6	4.8
Hill, Robert	1555	8/4	647.8.4	9.14.4½
do. A. Tunstalls	223	7/10	87.6.10	1.6.3
do. J. Keeling	42½	7/3	15.8.1½	4.7
Hoomes, Benjamin	230	7/10	90.1.8	1.7.1
Hill, Edward	1200	18/8	1120.--.--	16.16.0
Hudson, William	112	3/2	17.14.8	5.4
Hemmingway, Dan[l.] est.	800	4/2	166.13.4	2.0.0
Harwood, Christ[r.]	294	24/10	365.1.0	5.[ ]
Harwood, John	501	5/3	131.10.3	1.19.6
Harwood, William est.	240	30/	360.--.--	5.8.0
Hill, Thomas	300	26/11	403.[15].0	6.1.2
Hart, James	150	3/2	23.15.0	7.2
Hart, Anthony	190	5/3	49.17.6	15.0
do.	259½	3/2	41.1.9	12.4
Hart, Gregory	200		31.13.4	9.6
Hart, William	218		34.10.4	10.5
do. of H. Jordon	32	4/2	6.13.4	2.0
Harwood, John jr.	314½	10/5	164.1.4½	2.9.3
Hare, William	109	5/3	28.12.3	8.8
Hunt, William	730	6/3	228.2.6	3.8.6
Holderby, Eliz[a.]	100	4/2	20.16.8	6.8
Hudson, Mary	100	"		6.8
Henry, James	1900	14/6	1377.10.0	20.13.3
Halyard, William	190	5/3	49.17.6	15.0
do. of Edward Crouches	130	3/2	20.11.8	6.3
Hoskins, John	540	10/5	281.5.0	4.4.4½
do. Jos. Minor	170	7/3	61.12.6	18.6
				£114.0.8

[page 8, 1790]

Present Proprietors Names	Qty. Land	Price	Amt. Land	Amt. Tax
Haws, William	72	10/5	37.10.0	0.11.3
Hoskins, Robert	100	6/3	31.5.0	9.5
do. C. Dudley	120	4/2	25.0.0	7.6
Jones, John est.	360	8/11	168.10.0	2.8.2
Jeffries, Edward	70	3/2	11.1.8	3.4
Jones, James	160	14/6	116.--.--	1.14.10
Jones, James est.	196	10/5	102.1.8	1.10.8
Jones, William	241	15/10	190.15.10	2.17.3
do. of L. Smith	35¾	31/1	55.11.2	16.8
Jeffries, Ambrose	397	7/10	148.8.10	2.4.7
Jeffries, Bernard	30	4/2	6.5.0	1.11
Jordan, Henry	88		18.6.8	5.6
Jordan, William	100	3/2	15.16.8	4.9
Jordan, Thomas est.	100	4/2	20.16.8	6.3
Johnson, Arch[d.]	100	"		6.3
Johnson, Thomas	112	3/2	17.14.8	5.4
Jameson, David (York)	50	"	7.18.4	2.5
Jones, Rawleigh	63	31/1	93.18.3	1.9.4½
Keeling, James	113¼	7/3	41.1.0¾	12.4
Kemp, John	87	7/10	34.7.6	10.3
do. Jos: Wiltshire	53	7/3	19.4.3	5.9
[Kauffman], George	583	14/6	422.13.6	6.6.10
Kauffman, John	471	18/8	439.12.0	6.11.11
Kennedy, Alex[r.] est.	300	12/6	189.11.8	2.16.4½
do. M. Overstreet	90	4/2	18.15.0	5.7½
Kennedy, Arch[d.]	300	12/6	189.11.8	2.16.4½
Kemp, Matthew	100	5/4	26.13.4	8.--
Kemp, John (A. Price to pay)	200	6/3	62.10.0	18.9
Kay, Christ[r.]	116	6/3	30.9.0	[9.1½]
Kidd, Barth[o.]	136	5/3	35.14.--	10.8
Kidd, Benjamin	111	13/6	74.18.2	1.2.5½
Lumpkin, Henry	620	9/4	289.6.8	4.6.10
Lumpkin, John	200	6/3	59.--.--	17.9
Lyne, William Col.	1480	8/4	610.14.2	9.3.3
Lyne, William jr.	108	8/4	45.--.--	13.6
Lumpkin, William	305	14/6	221.2.6	3.6.5
Lefon, Fran[s.]	119	8/4	49.11.8	14.10½
Lankford, Tho[s.] est.	100	4/2	20.16.8	6.3
Lumpkin, Ro. jr.	465	8/4	193.15.0	2.18.2
Lumpkin, Ro. Sen[r.]	430	7/3	155.17.6	2.6.10
Longest, Caleb	97	7/10	37.19.10	11.6
Longest, Richard	140		54.16.8	16.6
				66.1.9

[page 9, 1790]

Present Proprietors Names	Qty. Land	Price	Amt. Land	Amt. Tax
Longest, Doratha	100	7/10	39.3.4	11.9
Lumpkin, Mary	108	6/3	33.15.0	10.2
Lumpkin, Joyce	213	7/10	83.8.2	1.5.0
Lumpkin, Anthony	108	6/3	33.15.0	10.2
Lumpkin, Jacob	916	"	286.5.0	4.5.11
do. Southerlands	271	5/3	71.2.9	1.1.4
Lewis, Iveson	356	14/6	258.2.0	3.17.4¼
Lewis, Eliz[a.]	100	4/2	20.16.8	6.3
Lumpkin, Richard	22	7/3	7.19.6	2.4½
do. J. Carlton	54¼	5/3	14.4.9½	4.4
Leigh, Lucy	101	24/10	125.8.2	1.17.7
Leigh, John	199	"	247.1.10	3.14.2
Lyne, John	507	6/3	158.8.9	2.7.7
Lambeth, Thomas	200	3/2	31.11.4	9.6
Lambeth, Charles	50		7.18.4	2.5
Lumpkin, Ro. (orphan)	183	4/8	38.2.6	11.6
Laughlin, James	126¾	4/2	26.8.2	8.0
Motley, Edwin	815	10/5	428.2.6	6.8.6
McKentosh, William	192	4/2	40.0.0	12.0
Martain, Thomas	680	14/6	493.0.0	7.7.11
do. Ann Peirce	35	7/3	12.3.9	3.8
Minor, William	149	8/4	62.1.8	18.8
Minor, John	137	"	57.1.8	17.2
Miller, Thomas	527	7/10	206.8.2	3.2.0
Mann, Augustine est.	400	8/4	166.13.4	2.10.0
Mitchell, Robert	17	20/9	17.17.9	5.4
Mitchell, John	50	6/3	15.12.6	4.9
Mitchell, James	650	13/	422.10.0	6.6.9
Mann, Robert	399	6/	119.14.0	1.15.10¾
do. of W. Bird jr.	300	6/3	113.15.0	1.14.2
McKendrie, Eliz[a.]	323	5/3	84.15.9	1.5.6
McKendrie, John	100	3/2	15.16.8	4.9
Meredith, William	343	5/3	90.0.9	1.7.1
Mitchell, Susannah	170	3/2	26.18.4	8.1
Moore, Thomas	150	4/2	31.5.0	9.4½
Moore, John	100	3/2	15.16.8	4.9
Major, Joseph	200	4/2	41.13.4	12.6
Mitchell, John est.	270	5/3	70.17.6	1.1.4
do. Rootes	300	9/11	148.15.0	2.4.7
Macon, John	1092	16/7	905.9.0	13.11.7
Mansfield, William	75	"	62.3.9	18.7
Manley, Peter	40	7/10	15.13.4	4.9
Merideth, Ralph G.	382	14/6	273.1.6	4.2.0
Meredith, Sam[l.] est.	185	14/6	138.--.--	2.1.5½
Muire, Richard	93	12/6	58.2.6	17.6
Moore, Richard	145	6/3	45.6.3	13.8
Martain, James	332½	20/9	344.19.4	5.3.5¾
				90.3.[2]

[page 10, 1790]

Present Proprietors Names	Qty. Land	Price	Amt. Land	Amt. Tax
McCarty, Joseph	73	3/2	11.11.2	3.6
Metcalf, Thomas	521	14/6	377.14.6	5.13.3¾
Morgan, William	26	8/4	10.16.8	3.3
Martain, John	80	9/4	37.6.8	11.3
do. of J. Jones	345	8/11	153.16.3	2.6.1½
Mann, Mary	100	5/3	26.5.0	7.11
Noel, Theoderick	362½	14/6	262.16.3	3.18.10
Nunn, Jane	180	7/3	65.5.0	19.7
Newbill, George est.	500	8/4	208.6.8	3.2.6
Nunn, Thomas	174	7/3	63.1.6	1.0.0
Nash, John	100	6/3	31.5.0	9.5
Newcombe, Eliz[a.]	109	3/2	17.5.2	5.2
Newcombe, William	60	"	9.10.0	2.11
Newell, John	100	7/10	39.3.4	11.9
Olliver, John (SL)	320	5/3	84.0.0	1.5.3
Orvill, John	100	6/3	31.5.0	9.5
Overstreet, Gabriel	296	4/2	61.13.4	18.6
do. Haynes	130	5/3	34.2.6	10.2
Osburn, John	90	3/2	14.5.0	4.4
Oakes, Henry Sen[r.]	110	3/2	17.8.4	5.3
Oakes, Henry Jr.	100	4/2	20.16.8	6.3
Owin, Augustine	100	6/3	31.5.0	9.5
Pendleton, James	450	10/	225.0.0	3.7.6
Pitts, David est.	420	9/4	196.--.--	2.18.10
Pitts, Obadiah	20	10/5	10.8.4	3.2
Pitts, William	100	6/3	31.5.0	9.5
Phillips, Richard	230	7/3	83.7.6	1.5.1
Pollard, John	235	9/4	109.13.4	1.12.11
do. of Leo[d.] Smithey	384	7/3	139.4.0	2.1.10
Prewett, Fran[s.]	99	9/4	46.4.0	13.11
Parker, John	116½	7/10	45.12.7	13.9
Pendleton, Philip	337	10/5	175.10.5	2.12.8
Perryman, Anthony	130	7/3	47.2.6	14.2
Pollard, Richard	389	8/4	162.1.8	2.8.7½
do. of W. Wood	32½	7/3	11.15.7½	3.6
P[r]ince, Francis	113	7/10	44.5.2	13.4
Pendleton, Benjamin	450	"	176.5.0	2.12.11
Pynes, Robert	199¼	3/2	31.10.11½	9.5½
Pynes, Benjamin	400	6/3	125.--.--	1.17.6
Pemberton, John	286	"	89.7.6	1.6.11½
Pace, Benjamin	143	6/	42.18.0	12.10½
Pace, John	120	8/6	51.0.0	15.5½
Pollard, Robert	6	24/10	7.9.0	2.2¾
Pickels, John (G. Carlton's est.)	225	7/3	81.11.3	1.4.6
				53.4.6

[page 11, 1790]

Present Proprietors Names	Qty. Land	Price	Amt. Land	Amt. Tax
[Pr]ice, Robert	630	6/3	196.17.6	2.19.1
[Pi]gg, Rachel	108	14/6	78.6.0	1.3.6
Pigg, John	216	"	156.12.0	2.7.--
Paggett, Samuel est.	36	7/10	14.2.0	4.2
Pollard, William	95	7/3	34.8.9	10.5
Pierce, Thomas	135	4/2	28.1.11	8.5
Pryor, John	150	3/2	23.15.0	7.8
Richards, William	510	12/6	318.15.0	4.15.8
Robertson, Donald est.	155	"	96.17.6	1.9.6
do.	260	7/3	94.5.0	1.8.5
Roane, Thomas Col.	2033	18/8	1897.9.4	28.8.3
do. H. Carlton's	200	6/3	63.10.0	18.9
Roane, William	1384	18/8	1291.14.8	19.7.6
do Geo. Richards	201½	14/6	146.1.9	2.3.11
Richards, John est.	423	9/4	197.8.0	2.19.2
Row, Hansford & Wilson	390	6/3	121.17.6	1.16.5
Row, Thomas G.	555	7/3	201.3.9	3.0.4
Row, Elizabeth	665	20/9	689.18.9	10.7.0
Row, Francis	296	6/3	92.10.0	1.7.2
do. Bowers & Burch	316½	3/2	50.2.3	15.0
Read, Robert	14	5/3	3.13.6	1.1
Row, Richard	550	8/4	229.3.4	3.8.9
Roane, Thomas jr.	1600	24/10	1926.13.4	[28.18.0]
Richerson, Elias	86	4/2	17.18.4	5.5
Row, John est.	100	6/3	31.5.0	9.5
Richards, John	221½	4/2	46.3.0	13.11
Richards, William jr.	296	5/3	77.14.0	1.3.4
Richerson, James	180	4/2	37.10.0	11.3
Richerson, William	181	"	37.14.2	11.4
Richerson, John est.	101½	"	21.2.11	6.5
Roane, Tho[s.] Est. (SM)	150	3/2	23.15.0	7.2
Reigns, Giles	60		9.10.0	2.11
Roane, Major	367½	4/2	76.16.7	1.10.5
Robinson, Benj[a.] est.	1300	8/4	541.13.4	8.2.6
Roane, Charles	200	14/6	145.0.0	2.3.6
do. dragon	70	17/	59.10.0	17.11
do. of R[d.] Trice	130½	7/3	57.6.1½	17.2
Robbins, William	40	6/3	12.10.0	3.9
Segar, Richard	406	7/3	147.3.6	2.4.2
Satterwhite, George	164	6/3	51.5.0	15.1
Satterwhite, William	100	4/2	20.16.8	6.3
Samuel, Henry	85	6/3	26.11.6	8.0
Samuel, Andrew	60	7/3	21.15.0	6.6
				£141.11.7

[page 12, 1790]

Present Proprietors Names	Qty. Land	Price	Amt. Land	Amt. Tax
Spencer, Edward	392½	8/4	163.10.10	2.9.1
do. Butler's	380	7/3	137.15.0	2.1.4
Schools, John	83½	7/10	32.14.1	9.9½
Sears, Frankey	338	9/4	157.14.8	2.7.2
Schools, Gabriel	169	6/3	52.16.3	15.11
Skelton, William	132	9/4	61.12.0	18.6
do M. Herndon's	100	7/3	36.5.0	10.11
Smith, Ann	85	7/3	30.16.3	9.3
Smith, John (Drisd[e.])	190	9/4	88.13.4	1.6.7
Starling, Jane	360	7/10	141.--.--	2.2.4
Skelton, Thomas	294	8/4	122.10.0	1.16.9
Scott, Benjamin	200	9/4	93.6.8	1.8.0
Saunders, George	100	7/3	36.5.0	10.10
Saunders, Alexr.	"	"	"	10.10
Shepherd, William	140	9/4	65.6.8	19.8
Semple, John W.	674	14/6	488.4.8	7.6.7
Smith, Molley	30	4/2	6.5.0	1.11
Smith, John (LHead)	100	5/3	26.5.0	7.11
Smith, Lewis	113½	7/3	41.12.11	12.6
Swinton, George	750	13/6	506.5.0	7.11.11
Stone, Sarah	300	7/3	108.15.0	1.12.8
Stone, Daniel	52	3/2	8.4.8	2.6
Smith, Larkin	1254¼	31/1	1949.6.3½	29.4.10
Smith, Henry	400	6/3	125.0.0	1.17.6
Smith, William	140	7/10	54.16.8	16.8
Smith, James	80	3/2	12.13.4	3.10
Smith, James j[r.]	101	7/10	39.11.2	11.10½
Stevens, Thomas est.	609½	7/10	238.14.5	3.11.8
Stevens, George est.	645	"	252.12.6	3.15.9½
Shackelford, John (taylor)	214	7/3	77.11.6	1.3.3½
Starke, Richard est.	250	6/3	78.2.6	1.3.6
do. G. Richards	100	4/2	20.16.8	6.3
Stone, Robert	300	4/2	62.10.0	18.9
Stone, John est.	357	6/3	93.14.3	1.8.2
Smith, Robert	879	10/5	457.19.3	6.17.5
Smith, Guy	189½	3/2	30.0.1	9.1
Simpkins, Nimrod	60	"	9.10.0	2.11
Sears, Philip	83	4/2	17.5.10	5.3
Spencer, Thomas	300	10/5	156.5.0	2.6.11
do.	255	4/2	53.2.6	15.11
Shackelford, W[m.] est.	700	14/6	527.10.0	7.18.6
Seward, Benjamin	115	3/2	18.4.2	5.6
				100.16.7

[page 13, 1790]

Present Proprietors Names	Qty. Land	Price	Amt. Land	Amt. Tax
[St]edman, Christ[r.]	191	5/3	50.2.9	15.1
[Sa]ddler, John	150	6/3	46.17.6	14.6
[Sh]ackelford, Alexander	60	4/2	12.10.0	3.9
[Ste]dman, Christ[r.] jr.	133½	6/3	41.18.1½	12.6½
do. Dillard's	260	5/3	65.5.--	1.0.6
[S]mith, Gregory	485	14/6	351.12.6	5.5.5
[S]hackelford, John (R)	282	8/4	117.10.0	1.15.3
[S]hackelford, Benj[a.]	200		83.6.8	1.5.0
[S]hackelford, Lyne	567	6/3	177.3.9	2.13.1
[S]hackelford, John (Mac)	182	7/3	65.19.6	19.10
Scott, Anderson	330	16/7	273.12.6	4.2.2
Shepherd, Isaac	190	3/2	30.1.8	9.3
Seward, Mary & Lucy	110	4/2	22.18.4	6.10
Trice, William	140	7/3	50.15.0	15.3
Taylor, James	50	6/3	15.12.6	4.9
Taylor, Edmond	294	8/14	122.10.0	1.16.9
Temple, Joseph	918	10/5	478.2.6	7.3.6
Tunstall, Molley	250	"	130.4.2	1.19.0¾
Tunstall, Richard jr.	1097	7/3	397.13.3	5.19.3
Tunstall, John	200	18/8	186.13.4	2.16.0
Tunstall, Rich[d.] G.	332½	20/9	344.19.4	5.3.5¾
Tignor, William	130	7/10	50.18.4	15.4½
Tureman, Benjamin	120	3/2	19.--.--	5.9
Taliaferro, William	1000	14/6	725.--.--	10.17.6
Townley, Robert	117	"	84.16.6	1.5.5
Taliaferro, Philip	990	8/4	412.10.0	6.3.9
do. P. Whiting	75	1/46	54.18.6	16.4
Taliaferro, Richard est.	300	5/3	78.15.0	1.3.8
Thruston, Batchelder	100	3/2	15.16.8	4.9
Trice, Richard	269½	7/3	97.13.10½	1.9.3½
Tucker, John est.	180	7/3	65.5.0	19.7
Temple, Humphry	70	33/2	116.1.8	1.14.9¾
do. Walkerton	108	30/	162.--.--	2.8.7
Tunstall, Richard est.	538	20/9	558.3.6	8.7.6
Tunstall, Rich[d.] (Best[d.])	269½	8/4	112.15.10	1.13.9
Vass, Thomas	250	5/3	65.12.6	19.9
Wyatt, Henry	200	7/3	72.10.0	1.1.9
White, Henry	100	8/4	41.13.4	12.6
Willmore, Thomas	150	10/5	78.2.6	1.3.6
do. of D. Farthing	19	7/10	7.8.10	2.2½
Wright, James	124½	5/3	32.13.8	9.10
				£88.16.10

[page 14, 1790]

Present Proprietors Names	Qty. Land	Price	Amt. Land	Amt. Tax
Wyatt, Joseph	60	8/4	25.0.0	7.6
Waldin, John	105	12/6	65.12.6	19.9
Wood, Thomas	260	7/10	111.16.8	1.10.8
Wilson, Isaac	200	6/3	62.10.0	18.9
Wilson, Benjamin est.	200	7/3	72.18.0	1.1.9
Wiltshire, Joseph	74	"	26.16.6	8.0
Wright, Isaac	183	6/3	57.3.9	17.2
Wyatt, Thomas est.	480	10/5	250.--.--	3.15.0
Wyatt, John	100	7/10	39.3.4	11.3
Watkins, William	37	4/2	7.14.2	2.4
Watkins, Joseph	65	"	13.10.10	4.2
Waldin, James	154	7/10	60.6.4	18.1
Walker, Henry est.	150	5/3	39.7.6	11.10
Ware, John	562	7/3	203.14.6	3.1.2
Walker, Frances	475	33/2	783.9.6	11.17.3
Walker, Humphry	345	"	572.4.8	8.10.7
Wright, William	175	5/3	45.18.9	13.10
Whayne, William	13½	7/3	4.17.11	1.6
do. Langham	194	7/10	75.19.8	1.2.9
Watts, Edward	250	7/3	90.12.6	1.7.3
Watts, John	293	7/10	114.15.2	1.14.6
do. Pemberton	45	6/3	14.1.3	4.2½
Watts, William	380	7/10	184.16.8	2.4.7
Watts, Kauffman	300	5/3	78.15.0	1.3.8
Williams, Howard	283	4/2	58.19.2	17.9
Wyatt, Thomas	206	7/10	81.2.0	1.4.4½
Wyatt, John, blind	103	6/3	32.3.9	9.8
Wyatt, William	29¾	7/3	10.15.8	3.3
Williams, Howard est.	300	6/3	93.15.0	1.8.1
Williams, Charles	550	4/2	114.11.8	1.14.5
Walton, James	80	"	16.3.4	5.--
Walton, Mary	60	"	12.10.0	3.9
Willis, Joel	94	7/10	35.5.0	10.7
Walton, Elizabeth	60	3/2	9.10.0	2.11
Walton, John	176	5/3	46.4.0	13.11
Walton, William est.	66	4/2	13.15.0	4.2
Walton, Thomas est.	"	"	"	4.2
Ware, John	75	5/3	19.13.9	5.11
Ware, Auther	83	4/2	17.5.10	5.3
Watts, James	350	"	72.18.4	1.1.11
Waring, Robert P. (birds)	212	7/3	76.17.0	1.2.10¾
do. of Lewis	330	13/	214.10.0	3.4.4
Walden, Richard	180	10/5	93.15.0	1.8.1½
				59.1[0].--

[page 15, 1790]

Present Proprietors Names	Qty. Land	Price	Amt. Land	Amt. Tax
[W]alden, Lewis	150	3/2	23.15.0	7.3
do. of T. Dudley	84½	6/3	28.2.3½	8.5
[W]yatt, Richard	175	12/6	109.7.6	1.12.9¾
[W]are, Robert est.	100	4/2	20.16.8	6.3
[Wa]re, Sarah	175	"	36.9.2	11.--
[Wi]lliams, Elizabeth	50	3/2	7.18.4	2.5
[W]hite, James est.	200	6/3	62.10.--	18.9
[W]atkins, Elizabeth	100	3/2	15.16.8	4.9
[W]arren, Catharine	175	"	27.14.2	8.4½
[W]are, Robert (B.P.)	112	"	17.14.8	5.4
[W]edderburn, Lydia	350	6/3	109.7.6	1.12.10
[W]hiting, Beverly est.	2447¾	7/10	866.18.9½	13.0.0
Webbley, John	173	5/3	45.8.3	13.8
do. of B. Colliers	100	4/2	20.16.8	6.3
Ware, Leonard est.	200	8/4	83.6.8	1.5.0
Walden, Edward	373	5/3	97.18.3	1.9.5
Wright, W[m.] (S.M.)	100	4/2	20.16.8	6.3
Waller, Edward est.	133½	3/2	21.2.9	6.5
Waller, John	66½	"	10.10.7	3.2
Wyatt, John (S.M.)	30	5/3	7.17.6	2.5
Young, Henry	640	18/8	597.6.8	8.19.3
				£33.9.[11]
deduct ¼ being Amt. qty. Tax				£3[torn]

William Courtney}
William Fleet} Commissrs.

[arithmetic omitted]

A list of the land and the tax thereon at one and a half percent within the County of King & Queen for 1791

[page 1, 1791]

Present Proprietors Names	Qty. Land	Price	Amt. Land	Amt. Tax
	[35]			
Alexander, Benjamin	202	9/4	94.5.4	1.8.4
Alexander, Elisha	102	7/3	36.12.3	11.0
do. of Wm. Gatewood	105	10/2	54.13.9	16.8
Alexander, John	50	9/4	23.6.8	7.0
Anderson, Churchill est.	636	7/3	230.11.0	3.9.2
Anderson, Paulin	498	14/6	361.1.0	5.9.4
Atkins, John jr.	120	4/2	25.0.0	7.6
Abbott, Jacob	112	7/10	43.17.4	13.2
Anderson, Richard est.	460	5/3	120.15.0	1.16.3
Atkins, Lewis	60	8/4	25.0.0	7.6
Anderson, Francis, home	233	14/6	168.18.6	2.10.8
do. Mary Guthrie & O'Dears	225	6/10	76.17.6	1.3.1
12				
Beverley, Robert esqr.	2474	10/5	1288.8.10	19.6.7
Brown, Henry	657	7/5½	245.8.1	3.13.7½
do. Keeling	103½	7/3	37.10.4½	11.3
do. of Wheeley	50	6/3	15.12.6	4.9
do. of John W. Semple	100	12/	60.0.0	18.0
Baylor, Gregory est.	720	14/6	522.0.0	7.16.7
Bland, Henry est. do.	166	8/4	69.3.4	1.0.9
Bates, Maredy	50	6/3	15.12.6	4.9
Bates, James	35[8]	11/	149.3.4	2.4.9
do.	42	4/2	8.15.0	2.7½
				55.3.4
Barton, John	125	"	26.0.10	7.10
Banks, William est.	365	"	76.0.10	1.2.9¾
Brooking, Frances	930	10/5	484.7.6	7.5.4
Baylor, John est.	503	14/6	364.13.6	5.9.4
Boughton, Thomas, Essex	130	9/4	60.13.4	18.3
Boughton, John	200	8/4	83.6.8	1.5.0
Boughton, Henry, Essex	88	6/3	27.10.0	8.3
Boughton, Thomas	100	8/4	41.13.4	12.6
Broach, John	45	6/3	14.1.3	4.3
Burton, Thomas est.	170	5/3	44.12.6	13.5
Bohannon, Ann	150	"	31.17.6	9.6¾
do. of Wm. Deshazo	80	4/3	16.13.4	5.0
Brown, William	75	7/10	29.7.6	8.10
Bagby, John	330	7/3	119.12.6	1.15.10½
Bagby, Richard	260	"	94.5.0	1.8.3½
Bagby, Thomas	260	"	94.5.0	1.8.3½
Brooke, Richard	1539¾	29/-	2232.12.9	33.9.10
Brumley, Robert	225	5/3	59.1.3	17.9
Brumley, John	329½	3/2	52.3.5	15.8
Bird, B. George	60	6/3	18.5.0	5.7½
Bird, William	532	7/3	192.17.0	2.18.0¼
do. dragon swamp	88½	17/	70.4.6	1.1.0
Bird, Mary	619	6/3	193.8.9	2.18.1
				£121.12.1¾

[page 2, 1791]

Present Proprietors Names	Qty. Land	Price	Amt. Land	Amt. Tax
Bird, Philemon	1173	6/3	368.2.6	5.14.9½
Brett, John	446	18/	401.8.0	6.0.5
Bowers, John	70	7/3	25.7.6	7.8
Burch, Vincent	100	4/2	20.16.8	6.3
Bird, Anthony A.	275	3/2	43.10.10	13.1
Byne, John est.	336	4/2	70.0.0	1.1.0
do. dragon swamp	2¼	17/	1.18.3	6¾
Bird, Barbara	266 2/3	24/10	331.2.2½	4.16.0
Bird, Robert	533 1/3	24/10	662.4.5½	9.12.0
Bourn, Richard	150	3/2	23.15.0	7.2
Burch, William est.	100	5/9	28.15.0	8.7½
Boyd, John	115	18/8	107.6.8	1.12.3
do. Mary Sones [sic]	382	24/10	474.6.4	7.2.4
Bray, Richard est.	93	7/10	36.8.6	10.11
Bird, John est.	100	3/2	15.16.8	4.9
Bowden, William	253	7/	88.11.0	1.6.6¾
Bew, William	117	3/2	18.10.6	5.7
Boyd, Spencer est.	1428	10/5	770.15.0	11.11.2
Berkley, Edmond	762	5/3	200.0.6	3.0.0
Bland, John	60	12/6	37.10.0	11.3
Bohannon, William	130		34.2.6	10.3
Bullman, Thomas est.	100	5/3	26.5.0	7.11
Briggs, John (W. Finney's)	170	4/2	35.8.4	10.8
Belote, Laban	384½		80.2.1	1.4.0
Bland, William Sen[r.]	120	--	25.0.0	7.6
do. Edw[d.] Brooks & Hardy	105	3/2	16.12.6	5.—
				58.17.8½
Bowden, William jr.	100	4/2	20.16.8	6.3
do. of Sykes & Dudley	34	3/2	5.7.8	1.8
Bowden, John	100	4/2	20.16.8	6.3
Bland, William jr. est.	250	"	52.1.8	15.8
Bland, Thomas	412	3/2	75.4.8	1.2.6¾
Bowden, George	75	4/2	15.12.6	4.9½
Burch, William	45	3/2	7.2.6	2.1½
Brown, Thomas	212		34.11.4	10.4
34				
Cary, Martha	462	4/2	96.5.--	1.8.11
Cook, Mary	200	8/4	83.6.8	1.5.0
Coleman, Thomas	572	6/3	178.15.0	2.13.8
Chick, Richard	491	7/3	177.19.9	2.13.5
Chapman, George est.	200	7/10	78.6.8	1.3.6
Campbell, William	1029	7/3	373.0.3	5.11.9
Chapman, Elizabeth	200	7/10	78.6.8	1.3.6
Crane, Cath[e.] est.	50	5/3	13.2.6	4.0
Crane, John	6	--	1.10.6	6
do. of Tho[s.] Draper	130	6/3	4[8].12.6	12.2
Cleverius, Benjamin	419	20/9	434.14.3	6.10.5
Carlton, Henry	280	7/10	109.13.4	1.12.10
do of John Baylor's est.	257	14/6	186.6.6	2.15.10¾
Clayton, Thomas est.	275	7/3	99.13.9	1.9.11
Campbell, Whitacar	318	7/10	124.11.-	1.17.6
[49]				£93.10.4

[page 3, 1791]

Present Proprietors Names	Qty. Land	Price	Amt. Land	Amt. Tax
	[36]			
Clevely, Thomas	80	7/10	36.6.8	9.4½
do. Langham's	200	"	78.6.8	1.3.6
Crow, Nathaniel est.	200	6/3	62.10.0	18.9
Crafton, Richard est.	236	9/4	110.2.8	1.13.1
Crane, George	30	7/3	10.7.6	3.4
Coleman, Milley	196	10/5	102.1.8	1.10.8
Carlton, Joel	53½	6/3	16.14.5	5.1
Carter, Jane	60	3/2	9.10.0	2.11
Carlton, Thomas (Swamp)	300	7/10	117.10.0	1.15.3
Carlton, John (School[r.])	100	6/3	31.5.0	9.5
Campbell, Sarah	296	12/6	185.0.0	2.15.6
Carlton, Christ[r.] Sen[r.]	37½	6/3	11.14.5	3.7
Carlton, Richard jr.	139	7/	48.13.0	14.7
Carlton, W[m.] (Shoe)	90¾	6/3	28.7.3	8.7
do. of W. Harwood	160	15/	120.0.0	1.16.0
Carlton, Robert est.	93	4/2	19.7.6	5.10
do. of John Pemberton	55	6/3	17.3.9	5.2
Carlton, Richard	250	7/3	90.12.6	1.7.3
Carlton, Christopher jr.	100		36.5.0	10.11
Carlton, Philemon	150	6/6	48.15.0	14.7½
Cooper, Henry	50	4/2	10.8.4	3.2
Carlton, Thomas (taylor)	100	6/3	31.5.0	9.5
Cardwell, John est.	150	4/2	31.5.0	9.5
				18.15.5
Cardwell, John	"			9.5
Cardwell, Thomas	"			9.5
Cardwell, William	"			9.5
Cooke, John est.	300	4/2	62.10.0	18.9
Collins, Thomas	150		31.5.0	9.5
do. Palmers	350	7/3	126.17.6	1.18.1
do. dragon Swamp	39½	14/	27.13.0	8.3½
Carlton, John j[r.] (Carp[r.])	235	4/2	48.19.2	14.9
Campbell, William (S.M.)	238	3/2	37.13.8	11.4
Collier, Charles	250	8/4	104.3.4	1.11.3
do John Pryor's	200	3/2	31.13.4	9.6
Curtis, Ann	464	5/3	121.16.0	1.16.6
Collier, John	100	4/2	20.16.8	6.3
Corbin, John, T	1868	10/5	972.18.4	14.11.11
do. Rosewall	400	12/6	290.0.0	4.7.0
do of Meredith's est.	124	11/3	69.13.0	1.0.10½
Corrie, John exors.	500	10/5	260.8.	3.18.2
do. W. Corr's est.	200	3/2	31.13.4	9.6
Crittenden, Thomas	126	13/6	85.1.0	1.5.6
do dragon Swamp	36	17/	30.12.0	9.2
Collins, Joyeux est.	140	10/5	72.18.4	1.1.10
Crittenden, Zach[h.]	34 1/3	14/6	24.17.10	7.6
Cary, Wilson M.	1820	16/7	1509.1.8	22.12.9
Collier, John (Cobler)	150	5/3	39.7.6	11.10
Campbell, James	100	6/3	31.5.0	9.5
do. Tho[s.] Burk's	100	4/2	20.16.8	6.3
				80.19.6

[page 4, 1791]

Present Proprietors Names	Qty. Land	Price	Amt. Land	Amt. Tax
Crittenden, Richard jr. est.	178	5/3	46.14.6	14.1
Collier, Francis est.	400	4/2	83.6.8	1.5.0
Corr, Avarilla	140	5/3	36.15.0	11.1
Collier, Catharine	750	"	196.17.6	2.19.1
Clegg, Isaiah	241	4/2	50.4.2	15.0½
Cooke, Dawson	296	7/3	107.3.0	1.12.1
do. of Charles Edwards est.	192	3/2	30.8.0	9.2
Curry, Ann	100	4/2	20.16.8	6.3
Corr, Frances	175	3/2	27.14.2	8.4
Courtney, William	200	7/10	78.6.8	1.3.6
Cooke, Thomas	240	3/2	38.0.0	11.5
Carlton, Humphry	125	7/3	45.6.3	13.8
do. of James Carlton's	50	6/	15.0.0	4.6
Carlton, Thos. (Carpr.) est.	235	6/3	73.8.9	1.2.1
Carlton, Beverly	210	4/2	43.15.0	13.1½
Corr, John Senr.	38	3/2	6.0.4	1.9½
Campbell, John	400	12/6	250.0.0	3.15.0
Crittenden, Francis Senr.	105 2/3	14/6	76.12.2	1.3.0
Clayton, James	100	9/11	49.11.8	14.10¼
19				
Dew, William	935	14/6	677.17.6	10.3.5
Dowling, William est.	264	8/4	110.0.0	1.13.0
Dix, Gabriel	338	6/3	105.12.6	1.11.8
Deshazo, William	82	4/2	17.1.8	5.1½
Durham, Joseph	76	"	15.16.8	4.9
do. of Ben. Bohannan	160	4/3	33.6.8	10.0
Deshazo, Peter	217	7/2	72.15.2	1.1.9½
Dickie, James	512	8/4	213.6.8	3.4.0
Dunbar, David	366	"	152.10.0	2.5.9
				40.2.6¾
Dalley, John est.	200	3/2	31.13.4	9.6
Drumright, Thomas	224	"	35.9.4	10.8
Dobbins, Charles est.	147	5/3	38.11.9	11.7
Dean, Benjamin	50	"	13.2.6	4.0
Dillard, William jr.	100	3/2	15.16.8	4.9
Dunn, Agrippia	140	5/3	36.15.0	11.1
Dudley, Peter est.	370	7/10	144.18.4	2.3.6
do. of John Baylor	160	5/3	42.0.0	12.7
Didlake, James	311	6/9	105.2.7½	1.11.4½
Didlake, Margrett	65	"	13.10.10	4.7
Durham, Robert est.	50	"	10.8.4	3.2
Dunn, Thomas	30	6/3	9.7.6	2.10
Dillard, William Senr.	276	12/6	172.10.--	2.11.9
Durham, George	50	4/2	10.8.4	3.2
Durham, Thomas	85	3/2	13.9.2	4.1
Dumagin, Richard est.	237	5/5	64.3.9	19.3
Digges, Frances	175	5/3	45.18.9	13.10
Didlake, George est.	114	10/5	59.7.6	17.10
Dungie, John	110	3/2	17.8.4	5.3
Dudley, William (Ferry)	290	14/6	210.5.0	3.3.1
do. of Lydia Wedderburn	315½	6/3	98.11.10½	1.9.6¾
[49]				57.19.6

[page 5, 1791]

Present Proprietors Names	Qty. Land	Price	Amt. Land	Amt. Tax
	[37]			
Damm, John est.	55	"	17.3.9	5.2
Dudley, William Senr.	180	7/10	70.10.--	1.1.2
Damm, William	25	4/2	5.4.2	1.6½
Dunbar, Mary	450	9/4	210.--.--	3.3.0
Douglass, John	100	6/3	31.5.0	9.5
do. of Stephen Field	139	7/3	50.7.9	15.1¼
Didlake, John	1200	"	435.--.--	6.10.6
Dudley, B. Robert	421	"	152.12.3	2.5.2
Dudley, Thomas	267½	6/3	81.17.8½	1.4.7
Dillard, Nicholas	75	4/2	15.12.6	4.9
Dillard, Benjamin est.	248	5/3	75.2.0	1.2.6
Drummond, Thomas est.	150	6/3	46.17.6	14.6
Didlake, James est.	131	3/2	20.14.10	6.3
Dillard, Thomas	377	5/3	98.19.3	1.9.9
Dillard, Elizabeth	449	14/6	325.10.6	4.17.8
Dillard, W^m. (son of Thos.)	150	4/2	31.5.0	9.5
Dixon, Michael	406	15/6	314.13.0	4.14.4
Dabney, Benjamin	400	14/6	290.0.0	4.7.0
18				
Eubank, John	200		145.--.--	2.3.6
do. of Samuel & Hill	209	7/3	75.15.3	1.2.9
Eubank, Thomas	300	14/6	217.10.0	3.5.3
				40.13.3¾
Eubank, Henry	171	5/3	44.17.9	13.6
Edwards, Thomas est.	66	4/2	13.15.0	4.2
Eubank, William est.	28¾	5/3	7.11.0	2.4
Eubank, Richard	65	3/2	10.5.10	3.1½
do.	90¾	5/3	23.16.6	7.2
do. of John Harwood jr.	39½	10/5	20.11.5½	6.2
Eubank, Richard est.	227	4/2	47.5.10	14.3
Eubank, Richard jr.	36	6/	10.16.0	3.2¾
Edwards, William	125	12/6	78.2.6	1.3.5
12				
Fogg, Frederick	298	8/4	124.3.4	1.17.3
Fleet, Baylor	350	20/9	373.10.0	5.12.0
do. Marsh	152	5/	38.0.0	11.5
do. Whitings	350	7/10	137.1.8	2.1.2
Fauntleroy, Saml. G.	880	16/7	729.13.4	10.18.1
do. Phillips & Hendley's	183	10/5	95.6.3	1.8.7
Fauntleroy, Moore	1006	24/10	1231.2.4	18.14.8¾
Fleet, John Capt.	408½	7/6	153.3.9	2.5.11
Faulkner, Thomas	155	6/3	48.8.9	14.7
Fogg, Thomas est.	200	"	62.10.0	18.9
Fogg, James	120	"	37.10.0	11.3
Faurenholtz, Wm. est.	146	"	45.12.6	13.9
Frazer, William	45	20/9	46.13.9	14.1
do. Marsh	11	3/6	1.18.6	0.7
Fleet, William	352	20/9	365.4.0	5.9.6½
				97.2.4¼

[page 6, 1791]

Present Proprietors Names	Qty. Land	Price	Amt. Land	Amt. Tax
Fisher, James est.	110	3/2	17.18.4	5.3
Foster, Thomas	214	4/2	44.11.8	13.5
Faulkner, Mary	333	6/3	104.1.4	1.11.3
Fauntleroy, Thomas	800	8/4	333.6.8	5.0.0
do. of Henry Todd	500	18/	460.0.0	6.18.0
Grafton, Thomas	132	9/4	61.12.0	18.6
Grafton, James	111	6/3	34.13.9	10.5
Gale, John est.	180	10/5	93.15.0	1.8.5
Goleman, Thomas, Essex	714	9/4	333.4.0	5.0.0
Garnett, Rice	297	7/3	107.13.7	1.12.4
Gatewood, Chaney	860	10/5	451.0.10	6.15.4
do. Gardners	100	7/3	36.5.0	10.11
do. Theodk. Noel	362½	14/6	262.16.3	3.18.10
Garnett, Joshua	322	8/4	134.3.4	2.0.3
Graves, Edward	200	6/3	62.10.0	18.9
Gatewood, Joseph	445	10/5	231.15.5	3.9.7
Gale, Matthew	323	11/5	184.7.7	2.15.4
Gatewood, John	160	8/4	66.13.4	1.0.0
Garnett, Reubin	33	5/3	8.13.3	2.8
do. of John Richards est.	407	9/4	189.18.8	2.17.0
do. of Dudley Farthing	262	7/10	102.12.4	1.10.9
Gwathmey, Temple	600	35/3	1057.10.0	15.17.3
Garlick, Samuel	454	24/10	563.14.4	8.9.2
Garlick, John	893	29/	1294.17.0	19.8.5
Griffith, Joseph	50	6/3	15.12.6	4.9
Gresham, Samuel	400	7/3	145.0.0	2.3.6
do. of R. Tunstall	87½	8/4	3.9.2	10.11
Garrett, Richard jr.	100	4/2	20.16.8	6.[3]
				9[6].17.3
Gardner, Elizabeth M.	311	6/9	105.2.7½	1.11.4
Gaines, Francis	356	14/6	258.2.0	3.17.5
Gaines, Harry est.	1517	20/4	1542.5.8	23.2.8
Gresham, Thomas	339¼	6/3	106.0.4	1.11.10
Gresham, Philemon	200		62.10.0	18.9
Gresham, John (D)	200	7/10	78.6.8	1.3.6
Gresham, William	100	4/2	20.16.8	6.3
Gardner, Elizabeth	100	6/3	31.5.0	9.5
Gibson, Richard	100	3/2	15.16.8	4.9
Gibson, Richard est.	113	"	17.17.10	5.5
Gibson, John	219¾	"	34.15.11	10.6
Griffith, Milley	50	6/3	15.12.6	4.9
Gresham, Ruth	250	5/3	65.12.6	19.9
Griffin, William	859	14/6	622.15.6	9.6.10
Garlick, Camm est.	1100	6/3	343.15.0	5.3.2
Garrett, Henry	50	3/2	7.8.4	2.4½
do. of A. Campbell (J.T.C.)	125	12/6	78.2.6	1.3.5
Garrett, Richard	50	3/2	7.8.4	2.4½
Garrett, Wm. est.	330	4/2	68.15.0	1.0.8
Gardner, Anthony	423	10/5	216.16.3	3.5.0½
do. H. Todd	215	12/6	134.7.6	2.0.3
do. dragon Swamp	42½	17/	36.2.6	10.10
[50]				154.18.6½

[page 7, 1791]

Present Proprietors Names	Qty. Land	Price	Amt. Land	Amt. Tax
	[38]			
Gresham, Lumpkin	315	7/3	114.3.9	1.13.3
Garrett, Robert	200	7/	70.0.0	1.1.0
Gresham, William jr.	242	8/4	100.16.8	1.10.3
Gatewood, William	105	10/5	54.13.9	16.8
Gatewood, Wm. (*Tucko.*)	220	3/2	34.16.8	10.6
Garrett, Humphry	450	12/6	281.5.0	4.4.9
Guthrie, James	60	"	37.10.0	11.3
Guthrie, Richard est.	60	"		11.3
Guthrie, Richard	162	3/2	25.13.0	7.8½
Glaspe, James	210	5/3	55.2.6	16.7
Groom, Mary	173	3/2	27.17.10	8.5
Garrett, George & Edward	170	5/3	44.12.6	13.5
Goldman, Martin	140	4/2	29.3.4	8.9
Groom, Barbara	100	3/2	15.16.8	4.9
Groom, Zachariah	187	"	29.12.2	8.7
Gulley, Philip	50	"	7.18.4	2.4
Garrett, Esther	100	4/2	20.16.8	6.8
Gulley, Benjamin	100	3/2	15.16.8	4.9
Garrett, William (Shoe)	200	5/3	31.13.4	9.6
do. Jno. Harwood	25	5/3	6.11.3	1.11½
Gramshill, Henry	25	3/2	3.19.2	1.2¼
Garrett, Watts Ann	112	5/	28.0.0	8.4¾
22				16.1.6
Halbert, James	124	6/2	38.15.0	11.7½
Harwood, Agness est.	225	4/2	46.17.6	14.1
Holt, Richard jr.	252	6/3	78.15.0	1.3.7
Hill, William	1191	14/6	928.9.6	13.18.7
Hutcherson, Charles	501	7/3	181.12.6	2.14.6
Hall, Corbin	188	8/4	78.6.8	1.3.6
Hitchcock, Thomas	140	4/2	29.3.4	8.9
Hoskins, Samuel	175	5/3	45.18.9	13.10
Hoskins, William	160	10/5	83.6.8	1.5.0
do. of Rd. Bray	360	7/10	143.7.0	2.3.0
Heskew, John	61	5/3	16.0.3	4.10
Heskew, John jr.	50	6/3	15.12.6	4.8
Hill, Robert	1820½	8/2	743.7.5	11.3.0
Hoomes, Benjamin	230	7/10	90.1.8	1.7.1
Hill, Edward	1200	18/8	1120.0.0	16.16.0
Hutson, William	112	3/2	17.14.8	5.4
Hemmingway, Danl. est.	534	4/2	111.5.0	1.13.4½
Hemmingway, John	266	"	55.8.4	16.7½
Hare, William	217	5/3	56.19.3	16.1
Harwood, Christr.	294	24/10	365.1.0	5.9.6
Harwood, John	75	5/3	19.13.9	5.10¾
Harwood, William est.	240	30/	360.0.0	5.8.0
Hill, Thomas	300	26/11	403.15.0	6.1.2
Hart, James	150	3/2	23.15.0	7.2
Holderby, John	100	4/2	20.16.8	6.3
[47]				92.2.11¼

[page 8, 1791]

Present Proprietors Names	Qty. Land	Price	Amt. Land	Amt. Tax
Hart, Anthony	190	5/3	49.17.6	15.0
do. Sundry people	259½	3/2	41.1.9	12.4
Hart, Gregory	200	"	31.13.4	9.6
Hart, William	218	"	34.10.4	10.5
do. of H. Jordon	32	4/2	6.13.4	2.0
Harwood, John jr.	314½	10/5	164.1.4½	2.9.3
Hunt, William	730	6/3	228.2.6	3.8.6
Holderby, Elizabeth	100	4/2	20.16.8	6.[3]
Hutson, Mary	100	"		6.[3]
Henry, James	1900	14/6	1377.10.0	20.13.3
Halyard, William	190	5/3	49.17.6	15.0
do. of Ed. Crouch	130	3/2	20.11.8	6.3
Hoskins, John	540	10/5	281.5.0	4.4.[4½]
do. of Jo$^{s.}$ Minor	170	7/3	61.12.6	18.6
Haws, William	72	10/5	37.10.0	11.3
Hoskins, Robert	100	6/3	31.5.0	9.5
do. of C. Dudley	120	4/2	25.0.0	7.6
17				
Jones, John est.	360	8/11	168.10.0	2.8.2
Jeffries, Edward	70	3/2	11.1.8	3.4
Jones, James	160	14/6	116.0.0	1.14.10
Jones, James est.	196	10/5	102.1.8	1.10.8
Jones, William est.	241	15/10	190.15.10	2.17.3
do. of L. Smith	35¾	31/1	55.11.2	16.8
Jeffries, Ambrose	397	7/10	148.8.10	2.4.7
				49.0.6½
Jeffries, Bernard	30	4/2	6.5.0	1.11
Jordan, Henry	88		18.6.8	5.[6]
Jordan, William	100	3/2	15.16.8	4.9
Jordan, Thomas est.	100	4/2	20.16.8	6.3
Johnson, Archibald	100	"		6.3
Johnson, Thomas	112	3/2	17.14.8	5.4
Jameson, David (York)	50	"	7.18.4	2.5
Jones, Rawleigh	63	31/1	93.18.3	1.9.4½
15				
Keeling, James	113¼	7/3	41.1.0¾	12.4
Kemp, John	178	"	64.2.2	19.2¾
Kauffman, John jr.	38	10/5	19.15.10	5.11½
Kauffman, George	583	14/6	422.13.6	6.6.10
Kauffman, John	471	18/8	439.12.0	6.11.[11]
Kennedy, Alex$^{r.}$ est.	300	12/6	189.11.8	2.16.4½
do. of M. Overstreet	90	4/2	18.15.0	5.7½
Kennedy, Archibald	300	12/6	189.11.8	2.16.4½
Kay, Christopher	116	6/3	30.9.0	9.1½
Kidd, Bartholomew	136	5/3	35.14.--	10.8
Kidd, Benj$^{a.}$ (Mid$^{x.}$)	111	13/6	74.18.2	1.2.5½
do. of T. Crittenden	60	13/6	40.10.0	12.1¾
do. Dragon Swamp	36	17/	30.12.0	9.2
Kidd, John	370	7/3	134.2.6	2.0.3
do. of Lumpkin & Pierce	60	4/2	12.10.0	3.9
				78.4.6½

[page 9, 1791]

Present Proprietors Names	Qty. Land	Price	Amt. Land	Amt. Tax
	[39]			
Lumpkin, Joyce	213	7/10	85.8.2	1.5.0
Lumpkin, Henry	620	9/4	289.6.8	4.6.10
Lumpkin, John	200	6/3	59.--.--	17.9
Lyne, William Col.	1480	8/4	610.14.2	9.3.3
Lyne, William jr.	108	8/4	45.0.0	13.6
Lumpkin, William	305	14/6	221.2.6	3.6.5
Lefon, Francis	119	8/4	49.11.8	14.10
Lankford, Thomas est.	100	4/2	20.16.8	6.3
Lumpkin, Robert (D)	465	8/4	193.15.0	2.18.3
Longest, Caleb	97	7/10	37.19.10	11.6
Longest, Richard	140	"	54.16.8	16.6
Longest, Doratha	100	7/10	39.3.4	11.9
Lumpkin, Mary	108	6/3	33.15.0	10.2
Lumpkin, Anthony	108	6/3	33.15.0	10.2
Lumpkin, Jacob	916	"	286.5.0	4.5.11
do. Southerlands	271	5/3	71.2.9	1.1.4
Lewis, Iveson	356	14/6	258.2.0	3.17.4¼
Lewis, Betty	100	4/2	20.16.8	6.3
Lumpkin, Richard est.	22	7/3	7.19.6	2.4½
do. of John Carlton	54¼	5/3	14.4.9½	4.4
				36.9.8¾
Leigh, Lucy	101	24/10	125.8.2	1.17.7
Leigh, John	199	"	247.1.10	3.14.2
Lyne, John	507	6/3	158.8.9	2.7.7
Lambeth, Thomas	200	3/2	31.11.4	9.6
Lumpkin, Robert jr.	183	4/8	38.2.6	11.6
Laughlin, James	126¾	4/2	26.8.2	8.0
Lambeth, Charles est.	50	3/2	7.18.4	2.5
27				
Motley, Edwin	815	10/5	428.2.6	6.8.6
McKentosh, William	192	4/2	40.0.0	12.0
Martin, Thomas C.	680	14/6	493.0.0	7.7.11
do.	134½	7/3	48.15.1½	14.7½
Morgan, William	26	8/4	10.16.8	3.3
Mitchel, Ralph	193	10/5	100.10.5	1.10.1½
Minor, William	149	8/4	62.1.8	18.8
Minor, John	137	"	57.1.8	17.2
Miller, Thomas	527	7/10	206.8.2	3.2.0
Mann, Augustine est.	400	8/4	166.13.4	2.10.0
Mitchell Robert	17	20/9	17.17.9	5.4
Mitchell, John	50	6/3	15.12.6	4.9
Mitchell, James	650	13/	422.10.0	6.6.9
Mann, Robert	399	6/	119.14.0	1.15.10¾
do. of Wm. Bird jr.	300	6/3	113.15.0	1.14.2
McKendrie, Eliza.	323	5/3	84.15.9	1.5.6
McKendrie, John	100	3/2	15.16.8	4.9
Meredith, Wm.	343	5/3	90.0.9	1.7.1
Moore, Philip	150	4/2	31.5.0	9.4½
Moore, John	100	3/2	15.16.8	4.9
				84.3.[1]

[page 10, 1791]

Present Proprietors Names	Qty. Land	Price	Amt. Land	Amt. Tax
Major, Josiah	200	4/2	41.13.4	12.6
Mitchell, John est.	270	5/3	70.17.6	1.1.4
do. part of Rootes	200	9/11	99.3.4	1.9.8½
Macon, John	1092	16/7	905.9.0	13.11.7
Mansfield, William	75	"	62.3.9	18.7
Manley, Peter	40	7/10	15.13.4	4.9
Merideth, Ralph G.	382	14/6	273.1.6	4.2.0
Meredith, Samuel est.	185	14/6	138.--.--	2.1.5½
Muire, Richard	93	12/6	58.2.6	17.6
Moore, Richard	145	6/3	45.6.3	13.8
Martin, James	332½	20/9	344.19.4	5.3.5¾
McCarty, Joseph	73	3/2	11.11.2	3.6
Metcalfe, Thomas	521	14/6	377.14.6	5.13.3¾
Martin, John	80	9/4	37.6.8	11.3
do. of John Jones	345	8/11	153.16.3	2.6.1½
Mann, Mary	100	5/3	26.5.0	7.11
16				
Nunn, Jane	180	7/3	65.5.0	19.7
Newbill, George est.	500	8/4	208.6.8	3.2.6
Nunn, Thomas	174	7/3	63.1.6	1.0.0
Nash, John est.	100	6/3	31.5.0	9.5
Newcombe, Elizabeth	109	3/2	17.5.2	5.2
Newcombe, William	60	"	9.10.0	2.11
Newill, John	100	7/10	39.3.4	11.9
7				46.10.0¼
Olliver, John	320	5/3	84.0.0	1.5.3
Orvill, John	100	6/3	31.5.0	9.5
Overstreet, Gabriel	296	4/2	61.13.4	18.6
do. Haynes's	130	5/3	34.2.6	10.2
Osburn, John	90	3/2	14.5.0	4.4
Oakes, Henry	110	3/2	17.8.4	5.3
Oakes, Henry jr.	100	4/2	20.16.8	6.3
Owin, Augustine	100	6/3	31.5.0	9.5
8				
Pendleton, James	450	10/	225.0.0	3.7.6
Pitts, David est.	420	9/4	196.0.0	2.18.10
Pitts, Obadiah	20	10/5	10.8.4	3.2
Pitts, William	100	6/3	31.5.0	9.5
Phillips, Richard	230	7/3	83.7.6	1.5.1
Pollard, John	235	9/4	109.13.4	1.12.11
do. of Ld. Smithey	384	7/3	139.4.0	2.1.10
Prewett, Francis	99	9/4	46.4.0	13.11
Parker, John	116½	7/10	45.12.7	13.9
do. of Rd. Holt jr.	147¾	6/3	46.3.5¼	13.10
Pendleton, Philip	337	10/5	175.10.5	2.12.8
Perryman, Anthony	130	7/3	47.2.6	14.2
P[erry]man, Philip	109	9/3	50.8.3	15.1¼
[Pitts], Benjamin G.	100	5/4	26.13.4	8.0
Pynes, Clement	199¼	3/2	31.10.11½	9.5½
				69.18.3

[page 11, 1791]

Present Proprietors Names	Qty. Land	Price	Amt. Land	Amt. Tax
	[40]			
Pace, Benjamin	143	6/	42.18.0	12.10½
do. of John Pace	120	8/6	51.0.0	15.3½
Pollard, Richard	389	8/4	162.1.8	2.8.7½
do. of W. Wood	32½	7/3	11.15.7½	3.6
Prince, Francis	113	7/10	44.5.2	13.4
Pendleton, Benj[a.]	450	"	176.5.0	2.12.11
Pynes, Benj[a.]	400	6/3	125.0.0	1.17.6
Pemberton, John	286	"	89.7.6	1.6.11½
Pollard, Robert	6	24/10	7.9.0	2.2¾
Pickels, John (G. Carltons est.)	225	7/3	81.11.3	1.4.6
Price, Robert	630	6/3	196.17.6	2.19.1
Pigg, Rachel	108	14/6	78.6.0	1.3.6
Pigg, John	216	"	156.12.0	2.7.0
do. of Tucker	180	7/3	65.5.0	19.7
Paggett, Samuel est.	36	7/10	14.2.0	4.2
Pollard, William	95	7/3	34.8.9	10.5
Pierce, Thomas	135	4/2	28.1.11	8.5
17				
Richards, William est.	510	12/6	318.15.0	4.15.8
Robertson, Donald est.	155	"	96.17.6	1.9.6
do.	260	7/3	94.5.0	1.8.5
Roane, Thomas	2033	18/8	1897.9.4	28.8.3
do. H. Carlton's	200	6/3	63.10.0	18.9
do new entry	260	3/6	45.10.0	13.7¾
Roane, William	1384	18/8	1291.14.8	19.7.6
do of Geo. Richards	201½	14/6	146.1.9	2.3.11
Richards, John est.	423	9/4	197.8.0	2.19.2
				82.14.8½
Row, Hansford & Wilson	390	6/3	121.17.6	1.16.5
Row, Thomas G. (orphan)	555	7/3	201.3.9	3.0.4
Row, Elizabeth	665	20/9	689.18.9	10.7.0
Row, Francis (orphan)	296	6/3	92.10.0	1.7.2
do. Bowers & Burch	316½	3/2	50.2.3	15.0
Read, Robert	14	5/3	3.13.6	1.1
Row, Richard est.	550	8/4	229.3.4	3.8.9
Roane, Spencer	1600	24/10	1926.13.4	28.18.0
Richerson, Elias	86	4/2	17.18.4	5.5
Row, William and Moses	100	6/3	31.5.0	9.5
Richards, John	221½	4/2	46.3.0	13.11
Richards, William	296	5/3	77.14.0	1.3.4
Richerson, James	180	4/2	37.10.0	11.3
Richerson, William	181	"	37.14.2	11.4
Richerson, John est.	101½	"	21.2.11	6.5
Roane, Major	367½	4/2	76.16.7	1.10.5
do. of T. Roane & J. Mitchell	320	3/2	50.3.4	15.3
Raines, Giles	60		9.10.0	2.11
Robinson, Benj[a.] est.	1300	8/4	541.13.4	8.2.6
Roane, Charles	200	14/6	145.0.0	2.3.6
do. dragon swamp	70	17/	59.10.0	17.11
Robbins, William	40	6/3	12.10.0	3.9
Richerson, William jr.	80	10/5	41.13.4	12.6
				150.18.3½

[page 12, 1791]

Present Proprietors Names	Qty. Land	Price	Amt. Land	Amt. Tax
Segar, Richard	406	7/3	147.3.6	2.4.2
Satterwhite, George	164	6/3	51.5.0	15.1
Satterwhite, William	100	4/2	20.16.8	6.3
Samuel, Henry	85	6/3	26.11.6	8.0
Samuel, Andrew	60	7/3	21.15.0	6.6
Spencer, Edward	392½	8/4	163.10.10	2.9.1
do. Butler's	380	7/3	137.15.0	2.1.4
Schools, John	83½	7/10	32.14.1	9.9½
Seayres, Franky	338	9/4	157.14.8	2.7.2
Schools, Gabriel	169	6/3	52.16.3	15.11
Skelton, William	132	9/4	61.12.0	18.6
do M. Herndon's	100	7/3	36.5.0	10.11
do. of Thos. Wood	130	7/10	50.18.4	15.4
Smith, Ann	85	7/3	30.16.3	9.3
Smith, John (Drisdale)	190	7/6	71.5.0	1.1.4
Sterling, Jane	360	7/10	141.0.0	2.2.4
Skelton, Thomas	294	8/4	122.10.0	1.16.9
Scott, Benjamin	200	9/4	93.6.8	1.8.0
Saunders, George	100	7/3	36.5.0	10.10½
Saunders, Alexander	100	"	"	10.10½
Shepherd, William	140	9/4	65.6.8	19.8
Semple, John W.	574	14/6	430.10.0	6.9.1
Smith, Molley	30	4/2	6.5.0	1.11
Smith, John (L.H.)	100	5/3	26.5.0	7.11
Smith, Lewis	113½	7/3	41.12.11	12.6
				30.18.6½
Swinton, George	750	13/6	506.5.0	7.11.11
Stone, Sarah	300	7/3	108.15.0	1.12.8
Stone, Daniel	52	3/2	8.4.8	2.6
Smith, Larkin	1254¼	31/1	1949.6.3½	29.4.10
Smith, Henry	400	6/3	125.0.0	1.17.6
Smith, William	140	7/10	54.16.8	16.8
Smith, James	80	3/2	12.13.4	3.10
Smith, James jr.	101	7/10	39.11.2	11.10½
Stevens, George est.	645	"	252.12.6	3.15.9½
Stevens, Thomas est.	609½	"	238.14.5	3.11.8
Shackelford, John (tayr.)	214	7/3	77.11.6	1.3.3½
Starke, Richard est.	250	6/3	78.2.6	1.3.6
do. of Geo. Richards	100	4/2	20.16.8	6.[3]
Stone, Robert	300	4/2	62.10.0	18.9
Stone, John est.	357	6/3	93.14.3	1.8.2
Smith, Robert	648	10/5	337.10.0	5.1.3
Smith, Guy	189½	3/2	30.0.1	9.1
Simpkins, Nimrod	60	"	9.10.0	2.11
Sears, Philip	83	4/2	17.5.10	5.3
Spencer, Thos.	300	10/5	156.5.0	2.6.11
do.	255	4/2	53.2.6	15.11
Shackelford, Wm. est.	700	14/6	527.10.0	7.18.6
Seward, Benjamin	115	3/2	18.4.2	5.6
[48]				102.13.1

[page 13, 1791]

Present Proprietors Names	Qty. Land	Price	Amt. Land	Amt. Tax
	[41]			
Stedman, Christ[r.] [Sr.]	191	5/3	50.2.9	15.1
Saddler, John	150	6/3	46.17.6	14.6
Shackelford, Alex[r.]	60	4/2	12.10.0	3.9
Stedman, Christ[r.] jr.	133½	6/3	41.18.1½	12.6½
do. Dillard's	260	5/3	65.5.0	1.0.6
Smith, Thomas (orphan)	485	14/6	351.12.6	5.5.5
Shackelford, John (Roman)	282	8/4	117.10.0	1.15.3
Shackelford, Benj[a.]	200		83.6.8	1.5.0
Shackelford, Lyne	517	6/3	161.11.3	2.8.5
Shackelford, Lyne jr.	50	"	15.12.6	4.8
Shackelford, John (Mac)	183	7/3	65.19.6	19.10
Scott, Anderson	330	16/7	273.12.6	4.2.2
Shepherd, Isaac	190	3/2	30.1.8	9.3
Seward, Lucy & Eliza. est.	110	4/2	22.18.4	6.10
14				20.3.2½
Trice, William	140	7/3	50.15.0	15.3
Taylor, James	50	6/3	15.12.6	4.9
Taylor, Edmond	294	8/14	122.10.0	1.16.9
Temple, Joseph	918	10/5	478.2.6	7.3.6
Tunstall, Molley	250	"	130.4.2	1.19.0¾
Tunstall, Richard jr.	1097	7/3	397.13.3	5.19.3
Tunstall, John	200	18/8	186.13.4	2.16.0
Tunstall, Richard G.	332½	20/9	344.19.4	5.3.5¾
Tignor, William	130	7/10	50.18.4	15.4½
Tureman, Benj[a.]	120	3/2	19.0.0	5.9
Taliaferro, William	1000	14/6	725.0.0	10.17.6
Townley, Ro. (A. Price to pay)	200	6/3	62.10.0	18.9
do. Anderson's	117	"	84.16.6	1.5.5
Taliaferro, Philip	990	8/4	412.10.0	6.3.9
do. of D. Cooke	374½	12/6	234.7.6	3.10.4
Trice, Edward	210	5/3	55.2.6	16.6¼
Thruston, William	140	4/3	29.15.0	8.11
Taliaferro, Richard est.	300	5/3	78.15.0	1.3.8
Thruston, Batchelder	100	3/2	15.16.8	4.9
Temple, Humphry	70	33/2	116.1.8	1.14.9¾
do. Walkerton	108	30/	162.0.0	2.8.7
do. of W[m.] Tunstall	100	15/	75.0.0	1.2.6
Tunstall, Richard est.	438	21/	459.18.0	6.18.0
Tunstall, Richard (Best[d.])	269½	8/4	112.15.10	1.13.9
Vass, Thomas	250	5/3	65.12.6	19.9
				87.9.4½

[page 14, 1791]

Present Proprietors Names	Qty. Land	Price	Amt. Land	Amt. Tax
Wyatt, Henry	200	7/3	72.10.0	1.1.9
White, Henry	100	8/4	41.13.4	12.6
Willmore, Thomas	150	10/5	78.2.6	1.3.6
do. of Dudley Farthing	19	7/10	7.8.10	2.2½
Wright, James	124½	5/3	32.13.8	9.10
Wyatt, Joseph	68	8/4	25.0.0	7.6
Waldin, John	105	12/6	65.12.6	19.9
Wood, Thomas	130	7/10	50.18.4	15.4
Wilson, Isaac	200	6/3	62.10.0	18.9
Wilson, Benjamin est.	200	7/3	72.18.0	1.1.9
Wiltshire, Joseph	74	"	26.16.6	8.0
Wright, Isaac	183	6/3	57.3.9	17.2
Wyatt, Thomas est.	480	10/5	250.0.0	3.15.0
Wyatt, John	100	7/10	39.3.4	11.3
Watkins, William	37	4/2	7.14.2	2.4
Watkins, Joseph	65	"	13.10.10	4.2
Walden, James	154	7/10	60.6.4	18.1
Walker, Henry est.	150	5/3	39.7.6	11.10
Ware, John	562	7/3	203.14.6	3.1.2
Walker, Frances	475	33/2	783.9.6	11.17.3
Walker, Humphry	345	"	572.4.8	8.10.7
Wright, William	175	5/3	45.18.9	13.10
Whayne, William	13½	7/3	4.17.11	1.6
do.	194	7/10	75.19.8	1.2.9
Watts, Edward	250	7/3	90.12.6	1.7.3
do. of W. Watts	113	5/	28.5.0	8.5½
				42.3.6
Watts, John	293	7/10	114.15.2	1.14.6
do. of Pemberton	45	6/3	14.1.3	4.2½
Watts, Kauffman	300	5/3	78.15.0	1.3.8
do. of W. Burch's est.	157	5/9	45.2.9	13.6¼
Watts, James	350	4/2	72.18.4	1.1.11
do. of W$^{m.}$ Watts	60	15/	45.0.0	13.6
Watts, Jane	144	5/	36.0.0	10.9½
Williams, Howard	283	4/2	58.19.2	17.9
Wyatt, Thomas	206	7/10	81.2.0	1.4.4½
Wyatt, John (Blind)	103	6/3	32.3.9	9.8
Wyatt, William	29¾	7/3	10.15.8	3.3
Williams, Howard est.	300	6/3	93.15.0	1.8.1
Williams, Charles	550	4/2	114.11.8	1.14.5
Walton, James	80	"	16.3.4	5.0
Walton, Mary	60	"	12.10.0	3.9
Willis, Joel	94	7/10	35.5.0	10.7
Walton, Elizabeth	60	3/2	9.10.0	2.11
Walton, John	176	5/3	46.4.0	13.11
Walton, William est.	66	4/2	13.15.0	4.2
Walton, Thomas est.	66	"	"	4.2
[46]				56.7.7¾

[page 15, 1791]

Present Proprietors Names	Qty. Land	Price	Amt. Land	Amt. Tax
	[42]			
Ware, John	75	5/3	19.13.9	5.11
Ware, Auther est.	83	4/2	17.5.10	5.3
Waring, Robert P. (Birds)	212	7/3	76.17.0	1.2.10¾
do. of Lewis	330	13/	214.10.0	3.4.4
Walden, Richard	180	10/5	93.15.0	1.8.1½
Walden, Lewis	150	3/2	23.15.0	7.3
do. of T. Dudley	84½	6/3	28.2.3½	8.5
Wright, Edward	141½	7/3	51.5.10½	15.2
Ware, Robert S.	50	10/	25.0.0	7.6
do. dragon swamp	39½	14/	27.13.0	8.3½
Ware, Anna (orphan)	80	10/5	41.13.4	12.6
Ware, Rebecca (do.)	80	"	"	12.6
Wyatt, Richard	175	12/6	109.7.6	1.12.9¾
Ware, Robert jr. est.	100	4/2	20.16.8	6.3
Williams, Eliz[a.]	50	3/2	7.18.4	2.5
White, James est.	200	6/3	62.10.0	18.9
Watkins, Eliz[a.]	100	3/2	15.16.8	4.9
				13.3.1½
Warren, Catharine	175	"	27.14.2	8.4
Ware, Robert (Bishop)	112	"	17.14.8	5.4
Wedderburn, Lydia	350	6/3	109.7.6	1.12.10
Whiting, Beverly est.	2447¾	7/10	866.18.9½	13.0.0
Webbley, John	173	5/3	45.8.3	13.8
do. of B. Collier	100	4/2	20.16.8	6.3
Ware, Leonard est.	200	8/4	83.6.8	1.5.0
Walden, Edward est.	373	5/3	97.18.3	1.9.5
Wright, William (S.M.)	100	4/2	20.16.8	6.3
Waller, Edward est.	133½	3/2	21.2.9	6.5
Waller, John est.	66½	"	10.10.7	3.2
Wyatt, John (S.M.)	30	5/3	7.17.6	2.5
Young, Henry	640	18/8	597.6.8	8.19.3
				£42.1.5½

Errors Excepted by
William Fleet & William Courtney}, Commissrs. of the tax

[arithmetic omitted]

1370.1.0½ @ 1½ p'cent.
¼ is £342.10.3 Nett amount

King & Queen 1791
For Mr. Solicitor

A list of the Land within the County of King and Queen for the year 1792

[page 1, 1792]

Present Proprietors Names	Qty. Land	Price	Amt. Land	Amt. Tax
	[43]			
Atkins, Joseph	66	4/2	13.15.0	4.1½
Alexander, Benjamin	202	9/4	94.5.4	1.8.4
Alexander, Elisha	102	7/3	36.12.3	11.0
do. of Wm. Gatewood	105	10/2	54.13.9	16.8
Alexander, John	50	9/4	23.6.8	7.--
Anderson, Churchill est.	636	7/3	230.11.0	3.9.2
Anderson, Paulin	498	14/6	361.1.0	5.9.4
Atkins, John	120	4/2	25.0.0	7.6
do. of Wm. Campbell	15	7/3	5.8.9	1.7½
Abbott, Jacob	112	7/10	43.17.4	13.2
Anderson, Richard est.	460	5/3	120.15.0	1.16.3
Atkins, Lewis	60	8/4	25.0.0	7.6
Anderson, Francis, Home	233	14/6	168.18.6	2.10.8
do.	225	6/10	76.17.6	1.3.1
Brown, Henry Junr.	100	12/	60.0.0	18.0
Beverley, Robert esqr.	2474	10/5	1288.8.10	19.6.7
Brown, Henry	657	7/5½	245.8.1	3.13.7½
do. Keeling's	103½	7/3	37.10.4½	11.3
do. of Wheeley	50	6/3	15.12.6	4.9
Baylor, Gregory est.	720	14/6	522.0.0	7.16.7
Bland, Henry est. [torn page]	166	8/4	69.3.4	1.0.9
Bates, Meridy	50	6/3	15.12.6	4.9
Bates, James	358	11/	149.3.4	2.4.9
do.	42	4/2	8.15.0	2.7½
Barton, John est.	125	"	26.0.10	7.10
Banks, William est.	365	"	76.0.10	1.2.9¾
Brooking, Frances	930	10/5	484.7.6	7.5.4
Baylor, John est.	503	14/6	364.13.6	5.9.4
Boughton, Thomas (Essex)	130	9/4	60.13.4	18.3
Boughton, John	200	8/4	83.6.8	1.5.0
Boughton, Henry (Essex)	88	6/3	27.10.0	8.3
Broach, John	45	6/3	14.1.3	4.3
Burton, Thomas est.	170	5/3	44.12.6	13.5
Bohannon, Ann	197	4/6	44.6.6	13.3½
Brown, William	75	7/10	29.7.6	8.10
Bagby, John	330	7/3	119.12.6	1.15.10½
Bagby, Richard	260	"	94.5.0	1.8.[3½]
Bagby, Thomas	"	"	"	1.8.3½
Brooke, Richard	1539¾	29/-	2232.12.9	33.9.10
Brumley, Robert	225	5/3	59.1.3	17.9
Brumley, John	329½	3/2	52.3.5	15.8
Bird, George B.	60	6/3	18.5.0	5.7½
Bird, William	532	7/3	192.17.0	2.18.0¼
do. dragon swamp	88½	17/	70.4.6	1.1.0
				118.6.0½

[page 2, 1792]

Present Proprietors Names	Qty. Land	Price	Amt. Land	Amt. Tax
Bird, Mary	619	6/3	193.8.9	2.18.[ ]
Bird, Philemon	1178	6/3	368.2.6	5.14.[9½]
Brett, John	446	18/	401.8.0	6.0.5
Bowers, John	70	7/3	25.7.6	7.8
Burch, Vincent	100	4/2	20.16.8	6.3
Bird, Anthony A.	275	3/2	43.10.10	13.1
Byne, John est.	336	4/2	70.0.0	1.1.[0]
do. dragon swamp	2¼	17/	1.18.3	6¾
Bird, Barbara	266 2/3	24/10	331.2.2½	4.16.[0]
Bird, Robert	533 1/3	24/10	662.4.5½	9.12.[0]
do. Guy Smith	189½	3/2	30.0.1	9.0
Bourn, Richard est.	150	3/2	23.15.0	7.[2]
Burch, William est.	100	5/9	28.15.0	8.7
Boyd, John	115	18/8	107.6.8	1.12.3
do. Soanes	382	24/10	474.6.4	7.2.4
Bray, Richard est.	93	7/10	36.8.6	10.11
Bird, John est.	100	3/2	15.16.8	4.9
Bowden, William	253	7/	88.11.0	1.6.6¾
Bew, William	117	3/2	18.10.6	5.7
Boyd, Spencer est.	1428	10/5	770.15.0	11.11.2
Edmond Berkely	762	5/3	200.0.6	3.0.0
Bland, John	60	12/6	37.10.0	11.3
Bohannon, William	130		34.2.6	10.3
				59.0.8
Bullman, Thomas est.	100	5/3	26.5.0	7.11
Briggs, John (W. Finney's)	170	4/2	35.8.4	10.[8]
Belote, Laban	384½		80.2.1	1.4.0
Bland, William Senr.	120	--	25.0.0	7.6
do. Brooks and Hardy	105	3/2	16.12.6	5.--
Bowden, William jr.	100	4/2	20.16.8	6.3
do. of Sykes & Dudley	34	3/2	5.7.8	1.8
Bowden, John	100	4/2	20.16.8	6.3
Bland, William jr. est.	250	"	52.1.8	15.8
Bland, Thomas	412	3/2	75.4.8	1.2.6¾
Bowden, George	236	5/3	61.19.--	18.7
Burch, William	45	3/2	7.2.6	2.1½
Brown, Thomas	450	12/6	281.5.0	4.4.9
do. Ed. Trice	4	5/	1.0.0	.3
Banks, James	282	7/3	102.4.6	1.10.8
Bristow, Barthow.	33½	3/2	5.6.1	1.7
Beard, David	450	9/4	210.0.0	3.3.0
Crafton, Thomas	119	"	55.10.8	17.7¾
Crafton, James	59	"	27.6.0	8.9½
Crafton, John	"	"	"	8.9½
Clayton, James	100	9/11	49.11.8	14.10¼
do. of Thos. Lambeth	100	3/2	15.16.8	4.9
Cary, Martha	462	4/2	96.5.--	1.8.11
Cooke, Mary	200	8/4	83.6.8	1.5.0
Coleman, Thomas	572	6/3	178.15.0	2.13.8
				82.11.6

[page 3, 1792]

Present Proprietors Names	Qty. Land	Price	Amt. Land	Amt. Tax
	[44]			
Chick, Richard	491	7/3	177.19.9	2.13.5
Chapman, George est.	200	7/10	78.6.8	1.3.6
do. of Wm. Hoskins	39	10/5	20.6.3	6.1
Campbell, William	1014	7/3	367.11.6	5.10.1½
Chapman, Elizabeth	200	7/10	78.6.8	1.3.6
Crane, Catharine est.	50	5/3	13.2.6	4.--
Crane, John	136	6/3	42.0.0	12.7
Cleverius, Benjamin	419	20/9	434.14.3	6.10.5
Carlton, Henry	280	7/10	109.13.4	1.12.10
do of John Baylor's est.	257	14/6	186.6.6	2.15.10¾
Clayton, Thomas est.	275	7/3	99.13.9	1.9.11
Campbell, Whitacar	318	7/10	124.11.-	1.17.6
Clevely, Thomas	80	7/10	36.6.8	9.4½
do. Langham's	200	"	78.6.8	1.3.6
Crow, Nathaniel est.	200	6/3	62.10.0	18.9
Crane, George	30	7/3	10.7.6	3.4
Coleman, Milley	196	10/5	102.1.8	1.10.8
Carlton, Joel	53½	6/3	16.14.5	5.1
Carter, Jane	60	3/2	9.10.0	2.11
Carlton, Thomas (Swamp)	300	7/10	117.10.0	1.15.3
Carlton, John (Schoolmr.)	100	6/3	31.5.0	9.5
Campbell, Sarah	296	12/6	185.0.0	2.15.6
Carlton, Christr. Senr.	37½	6/3	11.14.5	3.7
Carlton, Richard jr.	139	7/	48.13.0	14.7
				[ ]6.11.8¾
Cothern, James	36½	3/2	5.15.7	1.8
Carlton, William (Shoe)	309¼	11/6	178.1.2½	2.13.5
Carlton, Robert est.	93	4/2	19.7.6	5.10
do. of John Pemberton	55	6/3	17.3.9	5.2
Carlton, Richard	250	7/3	90.12.6	1.7.3
Carlton, Christr. jr.	100		36.5.0	10.11
Carlton, Philemon	150	6/6	48.15.0	14.7½
Cooper, Henry	50	4/2	10.8.4	3.2
Carlton, Thomas (taylor)	100	6/3	31.5.0	9.5
Cardwell, John est.	150	4/2	31.5.0	9.5
Cardwell, John	"			9.5
Cardwell, Thomas	"			9.5
Cardwell, William	"			9.5
Cooke, John est.	300	4/2	62.10.0	18.9
Collins, Thomas	329½	7/	115.6.6	1.14.7
do. Palmers	350	7/3	126.17.6	1.18.1
Carlton, John jr.	235	4/2	48.19.2	14.9
Campbell, William	238	3/2	37.13.8	11.4
Collier, Charles	200	3/2	31.13.4	9.6
Curtis, Ann	414	5/3	108.13.6	1.12.[ ]
Collier, John	100	4/2	20.16.8	6.3
Corbin, John, T	1868	10/5	972.18.4	14.11.11
do. Rosewall	400	12/6	290.0.0	4.7.[0]
do of Meredith's est.	124	11/3	69.13.0	1.0.10½
				73.6.0½

[page 4, 1792]

Present Proprietors Names	Qty. Land	Price	Amt. Land	Amt. Tax
Crittenden, Thomas	126	13/6	85.1.0	1.5.6
do dragon Swamp	36	17/	30.12.0	9.2
Collins, Joyeux est.	140	10/5	72.18.4	1.1.10
Crittenden, Zachariah	$34_{1/3}$	14/6	24.17.10	7.6
Cary, Wilson M.	1820	16/7	1509.1.8	22.12.9
Collier, John (Cobler)	150	5/3	39.7.6	11.10
Campbell, James	100	6/3	31.5.0	9.5
do. Burk's	100	4/2	20.16.8	6.3
Crittenden, Richard jr. est.	178	5/3	46.14.6	14.1
Collier, Fran[s.] est.	400	4/2	83.6.8	1.5.0
Corr, Avarilla	140	5/3	36.15.0	11.[1]
Collier, Catharine	750	"	196.17.6	2.19.1
Clegg, Isaiah	241	4/2	50.4.2	15.0½
Cooke, Dawson	296	7/3	107.3.0	1.12.1
do. Edwards est.	192	3/2	30.8.0	9.2
Curry, Ann	100	4/2	20.16.8	6.3
Corr, Frances	175	3/2	27.14.2	8.4
Courtney, William	200	7/10	78.6.8	1.3.6
Cooke, Thomas	240	3/2	38.0.0	11.5
Carlton, Humphry	125	7/3	45.6.3	13.8
do. James Carlton's est.	50	6/	15.0.0	4.[6]
Carlton, Thomas est.	235	6/3	73.8.9	1.2.[1]
Carlton, Beverly	210	4/2	43.15.0	13.[1½]
Corr, John Sen[r.]	38	3/2	6.0.4	1.9½
Campbell, John [torn page]	400	12/6	250.0.0	3.15.0
				44.9.[ ]
Crittenden, Francis (River)	$105_{2/3}$	14/6	76.12.2	1.3.[0]
Clarke, John	144	5/	36.0.0	10.[ ]
Dew, William estate	935	14/6	677.17.6	10.3.5
Dowling, William este.	264	8/4	110.0.0	1.13.0
Dix, Gabriel	338	6/3	105.12.6	1.11.8
Deshazo, William	82	4/2	17.1.8	5.1½
Durham, Joseph	76	4/2	15.16.8	4.9
do. of Ben. Bohannan	155	4/3	32.5.5	9.8¼
Deshazo, Peter	217	7/2	72.15.2	1.1.9½
Dickie, James est.	512	8/4	213.6.8	3.4.0
Dunbar, David	366	"	152.10.0	2.5.9
Dalley, John est.	200	3/2	31.13.4	9.6
Drumright, Thomas	224	"	35.9.4	10.8
Dobbins, Charles est.	147	5/3	38.11.9	11.7
Dean, Benjamin	50	"	13.2.6	4.0
Dillard, William jr.	100	3/2	15.16.8	4.9
Dunn, Agrippia	140	5/3	36.15.0	11.1
Dudley, Peter est.	370	7/10	144.18.4	2.3.6
do. of John Baylor	160	5/3	42.0.0	12.7
				72.10.1¼

[page 5, 1792]

Present Proprietors Names	Qty. Land	Price	Amt. Land	Amt. Tax
	[45]			
Didlake, James	311	6/9	105.2.7½	1.11.4½
Didlake, Margrett	65	"	13.10.10	4.[7]
Durham, Robert est.	50	"	10.8.4	3.2
Dunn, Thomas	30	6/3	9.7.6	2.10
Dillard, William Sen[r.]	276	12/6	172.10.--	2.11.9
Durham, George	50	4/2	10.8.4	3.2
Durham, Thomas	85	3/2	13.9.2	4.1
Dumagin, Richard est.	237	5/5	64.3.9	19.3
Digges, Frances	175	5/3	45.18.9	13.10
Didlake, George est.	114	10/5	59.7.6	17.10
Dungie, John	110	3/2	17.8.4	5.3
Dudley, William (Ferry)	290	14/6	210.5.0	3.3.1
do. of L. Wedderburn	315½	6/3	98.11.10½	1.9.6¾
Damm, John est.	55	"	17.3.9	5.2
Dudley, William Sen[r.]	180	7/10	70.10.--	1.1.2
Damm, William	25	4/2	5.4.2	1.6½
Douglass, John	100	6/3	31.5.0	9.5
do. of S. Field	139	7/3	50.7.9	15.1¼
Didlake, John	1200	"	435.--.--	6.10.6
Dudley, Ann	141	7/3	50.16.3	15.2¼
Dudley, Banks	230	3/2	36.8.4	10.11
Didlake, William	26¼	4/2	7.9.4½	2.2¾
Didlake, William jr.	278	8/4	115.16.0	1.14.9
				24.15.3½
Downey, Michael	50	10/5	26.0.10	7.9¾
Didlake, Royston	75	4/2	15.12.6	4.9½
Dillard, Thomas	449	14/6	325.10.6	4.17.8
Dudley, Thomas	267½	6/3	81.17.8½	1.4.7
Dillard, Nicholas	75	4/2	15.12.6	4.9
Dillard, Benjamin est.	248	5/3	75.2.0	1.2.6
Drummond, Thomas est.	150	6/3	46.17.6	14.6
Didlake, James est.	131	3/2	20.14.10	6.3
Dillard, William (son of Tho[s.])	150	4/2	31.5.0	9.5
Dixon, Michael	406	15/6	314.13.0	4.14.4
Dabney, Benjamin	400	14/6	290.0.0	4.7.0
Davis, Staige	311	6/9	105.2.7½	1.11.4½
Eubank, John	200	14/6	145.0.0	2.3.6
do. of Samuels & Hill	269	7/3	97.10.3	1.9.3
Eubank, Thomas	300	14/6	217.10.0	3.5.3
Eubank, Henry	171	5/3	44.17.9	13.6
Edwards, Thomas est.	66	4/2	13.15.0	4.2
Eubank, William est.	28¾	5/3	7.11.0	2.4
Eubank, Richard Sen[r.]	196	7/	68.12.0	1.0.7
Edmonson, William	280	10/5	145.16.8	2.3.9
Eubank, Richard est.	227	4/2	47.5.10	14.3
Eubank, Richard jr.	112¼	7/	39.5.7½	11.9
Edwards, William	125	12/6	78.2.6	1.3.5
				58.12.0

[page 6, 1792]

Present Proprietors Names	Qty. Land	Price	Amt. Land	Amt. Tax
Fogg, Frederick	298	8/4	124.3.4	1.17.3
Fleet, Baylor	862	12/6	538.15.--	8.1.7½
Fauntleroy, Samuel G.	880	16/7	729.13.4	10.18.1
do.	183	10/5	95.6.3	1.8.7
do. Moore Fauntleroy	1006	24/10	1231.2.4	18.14.8¾
Fleet, John	408½	7/6	153.3.9	2.5.11
Faulkner, Thomas	155	6/3	48.8.9	14.7
Fogg, Thomas est.	200	"	62.10.0	18.9
Fogg, James	120	"	37.10.0	11.3
Frazer, William	45	20/9	46.13.9	14.1
do. Marsh	11	3/6	1.18.6	.7
Fleet, William	352	20/9	365.4.0	5.9.6½
Fisher, James est.	110	3/2	17.18.4	5.3
Foster, Thomas	137¾	4/2	28.10.10	8.6¾
Falkner, Mary	333	6/3	104.1.4	1.11.3
Fauntleroy, Thomas	800	8/4	333.6.8	5.0.0
do. of Hy. Todd	500	18/	460.0.0	6.18.0
Grafton, Thomas est.	132	9/4	61.12.0	18.6
Grafton, James	111	6/3	34.13.9	10.5
Gale, John est.	180	10/5	93.15.0	1.8.5
Goleman, Thomas (Essex)	714	9/4	333.4.0	5.0.0
Garnett, Rice	297	7/3	107.13.7	1.12.4
Gatewood, Chaney	860	10/5	451.0.10	6.15.4
do. Gardners	100	7/3	36.5.0	10.[11]
do. Noel's	362½	14/6	262.16.3	3.18.[10]
Garnett, Joshua	322	8/4	134.3.4	2.0.3
				83.13.0½
Graves, Edward	200	6/3	62.10.0	18.9
Gatewood, Joseph	445	10/5	231.15.5	3.9.7
Gale, Mathew	323	11/5	184.7.7	2.15.4
Gatewood, John	160	8/4	66.13.4	1.0.0
Garnett, Reuben	990	8/9	433.15.3	6.10.1½
Gwathmey, Temple	600	35/3	1057.10.0	15.17.3
Garlick, Samuel	454	24/10	563.14.4	8.9.2
Garlick, John	893	29/	1294.17.0	19.18.5
Griffith, Joseph	50	6/3	15.12.6	4.9
Gresham, Samuel	400	7/3	145.0.0	2.3.6
Garrett, Richard jr.	100	4/2	20.16.8	6.3
Gaines, Francis	356	14/6	258.2.0	3.17.5
Gaines, Harry est.	1517	20/4	1542.5.8	23.2.8
Gresham, Thomas	339¼	6/3	106.0.4	1.11.10
Gresham, Philemon	200	"	62.0.0	18.9
Gresham, John (D)	200	7/10	78.6.8	1.3.6
Gresham, William	100	4/2	20.16.8	6.3
Gardner, Elizabeth	100	6/3	31.5.0	9.5
				176.16.0

[page 7, 1792]

Present Proprietors Names	Qty. Land	Price	Amt. Land	Amt. Tax
	[46]			
[Gibs]on, Richard	156½	3/2	24.16.7	7.4
[Gi]bson, Banks	56½	"	8.18.[11]	2.7
Gibson, John	219¾	"	34.15.11	10.6
Griffith, Milley	50	6/3	15.12.6	4.9
Gresham, Ruth	250	5/3	65.12.6	19.9
Griffin, William	859	14/6	622.15.6	9.6.10
Garlick, Camm est.	1100	6/3	343.15.0	5.3.2
Garrett, Henry	50	3/2	7.8.4	2.4½
do. of John T. Corbin's	125	12/6	78.2.6	1.3.5
Garrett, Richard	50	3/2	7.8.4	2.4
Garrett, William est.	330	4/2	68.15.0	1.0.8
Gardner, Anthony	423	10/5	216.16.3	3.5.0½
do. H. Todd	215	12/6	134.7.6	2.0.3
do. dragon Swamp	42½	17/	36.2.6	10.10
Gresham, Lumpkin	315	7/3	114.3.9	1.13.3
Garrett, Robert	200	7/	70.0.0	1.[1.0]
Gresham, William jr.	329½	8/4	137.5.10	2.[torn]
Gaines, Robert	537¾	20/9	558.8.7¾	8.[torn]
do. [Ro.] Curtis	50	5/3	13.2.6	[torn]
Gatewood, W[m.] (*Tuck[o.]*)	220	3/2	34.16.8	10.6
Gatewood, William	105	10/5	54.13.9	16.8
do. Ro. Hoskins (part Glebe)	132	"	68.15.0	1.0.7½
Guthrie, James	60	12/6	37.10.0	11.3
[Guthri]e, Richard est.	"	"	"	11.3
				41.1[6]11¾
[Guthri]e, Richard	162	3/2	25.13.0	7.8½
Glaspe, James	210	5/3	55.2.6	16.7
Groom, Mary	173	3/2	27.17.10	8.5
Garrett, Geo. & Edward	170	5/3	44.12.6	13.5
Goldman, Martin	140	4/2	29.3.4	8.9
Groom, Barbara est.	100	3/2	15.16.8	4.9
Groom, Zachariah	187	"	29.12.2	8.7
Gulley, Philip est.	50	"	7.18.4	2.4
Garrett, Esther est.	100	4/2	20.16.8	6.3
Garrett, William (Shoe)	200	5/3	31.13.4	9.6
do. John Harwood	25	5/3	6.11.3	1.11½
Gramshill, Henry est.	25	3/2	3.19.2	1.2¼
Garrett, Ann Watts	112	5/	28.0.0	8.4¾
Gatewood, Gabriel	78	10/5	40.17.6	12.2¼
Halbert, James	124	6/2	38.15.0	11.7½
Harwood, Agness est.	225	4/2	46.17.6	14.1
Holt, Richard jr.	252	6/3	78.15.0	1.3.7
Hill, William	1191	14/6	928.9.6	13.18.7
Hall, Corbin	188	8/4	78.6.8	1.3.6
				84.18.4½

[page 8, 1792]

Present Proprietors Names	Qty. Land	Price	Amt. Land	Amt. Tax
Hitchcock, Thomas [est.]	140	4/2	29.3.4	[torn]
Hoskins, Samuel	175	5/3	45.18.9	13.[10]
do. of John Hoskins	170	7/3	61.12.6	18.[ ]
Hutcherson, Charles	501	7/3	181.12.6	2.14.[ ]
do. of Thos. Roane	61	5/3	16.0.3	4.[3]½
Hoskins, William	360	7/10	143.7.0	2.3.0
Heskew, John	61	5/3	16.0.3	4.10
Heskew, John junr.	50	6/3	15.12.6	4.8
Hill, Robert	1820½	8/2	743.7.5	11.3.0
Hoomes, Benjamin	230	7/10	90.1.8	1.7.1
do. of Durham & Bohannan	42	4/2	8.15.0	2.7½
Hill, Edward	1200	18/8	1120.0.0	16.16.0
Hutson, William	112	3/2	17.14.8	5.4
Hemmingway, Daniel est.	534	4/2	111.5.0	1.13.4½
Hemmingway, John	266	"	55.8.4	16.7½
Hare, William	217	5/3	56.19.3	16.1
[Har]wood, Christr.	294	24/10	365.1.0	5.9.6
[Har]wood, John	75	5/3	19.13.9	5.10¾
[Harw]ood, William est.	240	30/	360.0.0	5.8.0
[Hill], Thomas	300	26/11	403.15.0	6.1.2
[Hart], James	150	3/2	23.15.0	7.2
[H]olderby, John	100	4/2	20.16.8	6.3
Hart, Anthony	190	5/3	49.17.6	15.--
				50.5.11¾
do. Sundry people	259½	3/2	41.1.9	[torn]
Hart, Gregory	200	"	31.13.4	[torn]
Hart, William	218	"	34.10.4	[torn]
do. of H. Jordon	32	4/2	6.13.4	2.--
Harwood, John junior	196½	10/5	102.6.10½	1.10.8½
Hunt, William	730	6/3	228.2.6	3.8.6
Hutson, Mary	100	"		6.3
Henry, Samuel Hugh	1900	14/6	1377.10.0	20.13.3
Halyard, William	190	5/3	49.17.6	15.--
do. of Edwd. Crouch's	130	3/2	20.11.8	6.3
Hoskins, John	740	10/5	385.8.4	5.15.7
do. of Boughton	100	8/4	41.13.4	12.6
Haws, William	72	10/5	37.10.0	11.3
Hoskins, Robert	100	6/3	31.5.0	9.5
do. of C. Dudley	120	4/2	25.0.0	7.6
Hart, Alden	50	"	10.8.4	3.1½
Howerton, Heritage	122¾	20/9	126.16.7¼	1.18.--½
Jeffries, Thomas	75¾	7/3	27.9.2¼	8.2¾
Jones, John est.	360	8/11	168.10.0	2.8.2
Jeffries, Edward	70	3/2	11.1.8	3.4
				100.17.3¾

[page 9, 1792]

Present Proprietors Names	Qty. Land	Price	Amt. Land	Amt. Tax
	[47]			
Jones, James	160	14/6	116.0.0	1.14.10
[Jones], James est.	196	10/5	102.1.8	1.10.8
Jones, William est.	241	15/10	190.15.10	2.17.3
do. of L. Smith	35¾	31/1	55.11.2	16.8
Jeffries, Ambrose	397	7/10	148.8.10	2.4.7
[J]effries, Bernard	30	4/2	6.5.0	1.11
[J]ordan, Henry	88		18.6.8	5.6
Jordan, William	100	3/2	15.16.8	4.9
Jordan, Thomas est.	100	4/2	20.16.8	6.3
Johnson, Archibald	100	"		6.3
Johnson, Thomas	112	3/2	17.14.8	5.4
Jameson, David (York)	50	"	7.18.4	2.5
Jones, Rawleigh	63	31/1	93.18.3	1.9.4
Keeling, James	113¼	7/3	41.1.0¾	12.4
Kemp, John	178	"	64.2.2	19.2
Kauffman, John jr.	38	10/5	19.15.10	5.11½
Kauffman, George	583	14/6	422.13.6	6.6.10
Kauffman, John	471	18/8	439.12.0	6.11.11
Kennedy, Archibald	330	12/6	206.5.0	3.1.10½
do. of Eliz[a.] Holderby	38¼	4/2	7.19.4	2.4½
[Ke]nnedy, Ann	120	12/6	75.0.0	1.2.6
				31.8.8
do. Overstreet	70¼	4/2	14.11.8	4.6¾
Kennedy, Ann jr.	150	12/6	97.10.0	1.9.3
do. of Eliz[a.] Holderby	33¾	4/2	7.0.6	2.1¼
Kennedy, Lucy	37½	"	7.16.2	2.4
Kay, Christopher	116	6/3	30.9.0	9.1½
Kidd, Barthol[w.]	136	5/3	35.14.--	10.8
Kidd, Benj[a.] (Midd[x.])	111	13/6	74.18.2	1.2.5½
do. of Crittenden	60	13/6	40.10.0	12.1¾
do. dragon Swamp	36	17/	30.12.0	9.2
Kidd, John	370	7/3	134.2.6	2.0.3
do. of Lumpkin & Pierce	60	4/2	12.10.0	3.9
Lumpkin, Joyce	213	7/10	85.8.2	1.5.0
Lumpkin, Henry	620	9/4	289.6.8	4.6.10
Lumpkin, John	200	6/3	59.--.--	17.9
Lyne, William Col.	1480	8/4	610.14.2	9.3.3
Lyne, William jr.	108	8/4	45.0.0	13.6
Lumpkin, William	305	14/6	221.2.6	3.6.5
Lefon, Fran[s.]	119	8/4	49.11.8	14.10
				59.2.1¼

[page 10, 1792]

Present Proprietors Names	Qty. Land	Price	Amt. Land	Amt. Tax
Lankford, Thomas est.	100	4/2	20.16.8	6.3
Lumpkin, Robert (D)	465	8/4	193.15.0	2.18.3
Longest, Caleb	97	7/10	37.19.10	[11.6]
Longest, Richard	140	"	54.16.8	16.6
Longest, Doratha	100	7/10	39.3.4	11.9
Lumpkin, Mary est.	108	6/3	33.15.0	10.[2]
Lumpkin, Anthony	108	6/3	33.15.0	10.[2]
Lumpkin, Jacob	916	"	286.5.0	4.5.11
do. Southerlands	271	5/3	71.2.9	1.1.4
Lewis, Iveson	356	14/6	258.2.0	3.17.4¼
Lewis, Betty	100	4/2	20.16.8	6.3
Lumpkin, Richard est.	22	7/3	7.19.6	2.4½
do. of J. Carlton	54¼	5/3	14.4.9½	4.4
Leigh, Lucy	101	24/10	125.8.2	1.17.7
Leigh, John	199	"	247.1.10	3.14.2
Lyne, John	507	6/3	158.8.9	2.7.7
Lambeth, Thomas	100	3/2	15.16.8	4.9
Lumpkin, Robert jr.	183	4/8	38.2.6	11.6
Laughlin, James	126¾	4/2	26.8.2	8.--
Lambeth, Charles est.	50	3/2	7.18.4	2.5
				[4]5.8.[ ]
Motley, Edwin	815	10/5	428.2.6	6.8.[6]
McKentosh, William	126	4/2	[2]6.5.0	7.10½
Martin, Thomas C.	680	14/6	493.0.0	7.7.11
do.	134½	7/3	48.15.1½	14.7½
Morgan, William	26	8/4	10.16.8	3.3
Mitchel, Ralph est.	193	10/5	100.10.5	1.10.1½
Minor, William	149	8/4	62.1.8	18.8
Minor, John	137	"	57.1.8	17.2
Miller, Thomas	527	7/10	206.8.2	3.2.0
Mann, Augustine est.	400	8/4	166.13.4	2.10.0
Mitchell, Robert	17	20/9	17.17.9	5.4
Mitchell, John	50	6/3	15.12.6	4.9
Mitchell, James	650	13/	422.10.0	6.6.9
Mann, Robert	399	6/	119.14.0	1.15.10¾
do. of Wm. Bird jr.	300	6/3	113.15.0	1.14.2
McKendrie, Eliza.	323	5/3	84.15.9	1.5.6
McKendrie, John	100	3/2	15.16.8	4.9
Meredith, William	343	5/3	90.0.9	1.7.1
Moore, Philip	150	4/2	31.5.0	9.4½
Moore, John	100	3/2	15.16.8	4.9
Major, Josiah	200	4/2	41.13.4	12.6
				63.19.0¾

[page 11, 1792]

Present Proprietors Names	Qty. Land	Price	Amt. Land	Amt. Tax
	[48]			
Mitchell, John est.	270	5/3	70.17.6	1.1.4
do. part of Rootes	200	9/11	99.3.4	1.9.8¾
Macon, John	1092	16/7	905.9.0	13.11.7
Mansfield, William	75	"	62.3.9	18.7
Manley, Peter	40	7/10	15.13.4	4.9
Merideth, Ralph G.	382	14/6	273.1.6	4.2.0
Meredith, Samuel est.	185	14/6	138.0.0	2.1.5½
Muire, Richard	93	12/6	58.2.6	17.6
Moore, Richard	145	6/3	45.6.3	13.8
McCarty, Joseph	73	3/2	11.11.2	3.6
Metcalfe, Thomas	521	14/6	377.14.6	5.13.3¾
Martin, John	80	9/4	37.6.8	11.3
do. of John Jones	345	8/11	153.16.3	2.6.1½
Mann, Mary	100	5/3	26.5.0	7.11
Nunn, Jane	180	7/3	65.5.0	19.7
Newbill, George est.	500	8/4	208.6.8	3.2.6
Nunn, Thomas	174	7/3	63.1.6	1.0.0
Nash, John est.	100	6/3	31.5.0	9.5
Newcombe, Eliz[a.]	109	3/2	17.5.2	5.2
Newcombe, William	60	"	9.10.0	2.11
Newill, John	100	7/10	39.3.4	11.9
				40.14.11½
[O]lliver, John	320	5/3	84.0.0	1.5.3
Orvill, John	100	6/3	31.5.0	9.5
Overstreet, Gabriel	296	4/2	61.13.4	18.6
do. of Haynes	130	5/3	34.2.6	10.2
Osburn, John	90	3/2	14.5.0	4.4
Oakes, Henry	73½	"	11.12.9	3.5¾
Oakes, Henry jr.	100	4/2	20.16.8	6.3
Owin, Augustine est.	100	6/3	31.5.0	9.5
Pendleton, James	450	10/	225.0.0	3.7.6
do. of [H.] Samuel	100	6/3	31.5.0	9.5
Pitts, David est.	420	9/4	196.0.0	2.18.10
Pitts, Obadiah	20	10/5	10.8.4	3.2
Pitts, William	100	6/3	31.5.0	9.5
Phillips, Richard	230	7/3	83.7.6	1.5.1
Pollard, John	235	9/4	109.13.4	1.12.11
do. of L[d.] Smithey	384	7/3	139.4.0	2.1.10
Prewett, Fran[s.]	99	9/4	46.4.0	13.11
Parker, John	116½	7/10	45.12.7	13.9
do. of R[d.] Holt jr.	147¾	6/3	46.3.5¼	[13.10]
				59.[smear]

[page 12, 1792]

Present Proprietors Names	Qty. Land	Price	Amt. Land	Amt. Tax
Pendleton, Philip	337	10/5	175.10.5	2.12.[8]
do. of Farrinholtz est.	146	6/6	45.12.6	13.[ ]
Perryman, Anthony	130	7/3	47.2.6	14.2
Perryman, Philip	109	9/3	50.8.3	15.1¼
Pitts, Benjamin G.	100	5/4	26.13.4	8.--
Pynes, Clement	199¼	3/2	31.10.11½	9.5½
Pace, Benjamin	143	6/	42.18.0	12.10½
do. of John Pace	120	8/6	51.0.0	15.3½
Pollard, Richard	389	8/4	162.1.8	2.8.7½
Prince, Fran[s.]	113	7/10	44.5.2	13.4
Pendleton, Benjamin	450	"	176.5.0	2.12.[11]
Pynes, Benjamin	400	6/3	125.0.0	1.17.6
Pemberton, John	286	"	89.7.6	1.6.11½
Pollard, Robert	6	24/10	7.9.0	2.2¾
Price, Robert	630	6/3	196.17.6	2.19.1
Pigg, Rachel	108	14/6	78.6.0	1.3.6
Pigg, John	216	"	156.12.0	2.7.0
do.	180	7/3	65.5.0	19.7
Paggett, Samuel est.	36	7/10	14.2.0	4.2
Pollard, William	95	7/3	34.8.9	10.5
Pierce, Thomas Estate	87	4/2	18.2.6	5.5¼
Richards, William est.	510	12/6	318.15.0	4.15.[8]
Robertson, Rachel	155	"	96.17.6	1.9.6
do.	260	7/3	94.5.0	1.8.5
Roane, Thomas	2033	18/8	1897.9.4	28.8.3
do. H. Carlton's	200	6/3	63.10.0	18.9
Roane, William	1384	18/8	1291.14.8	19.7.6
do Geo. Richards	201½	14/6	146.1.9	2.3.11
Richards, John est.	215	9/4	100.6.8	1.10.1
Row, Hansford & Wilson	390	6/3	121.17.6	1.16.5
Row, Thomas G. (orphan)	555	7/3	201.3.9	3.0.4
Row, Elizabeth	665	20/9	689.18.9	10.7.0
Row, Francis (orphan)	296	6/3	92.10.0	1.7.2
do. Bowers & Burch	316½	3/2	50.2.3	15.[0]
Read, Robert	14	5/3	3.13.6	1.1
Row, Richard est.	550	8/4	229.3.4	3.8.9
Roane, Spencer	1600	24/10	1926.13.4	28.18.0
Richerson, Elias	86	4/2	17.18.4	5.5
Row, William & Moses	100	6/3	31.5.0	9.5
Richards, John	221½	4/2	46.3.0	13.11
Richards, William	296	5/3	77.14.0	1.3.4
Richerson, James	180	4/2	37.10.0	11.3
Richerson, William	181	"	37.14.2	11.4
Richerson, John est.	101½	"	21.2.11	6.5
				138.8.11¾

[page 13, 1792]

Present Proprietors Names	Qty. Land	Price	Amt. Land	Amt. Tax
	[49]			
Roane, Major	367½	4/2	76.16.7	1.10.5
do.	320	3/2	50.3.4	15.3
[Ra]ines, Giles	60		9.10.0	2.11
Robinson, Benjamin est.	1300	8/4	541.13.4	8.2.6
Roane, Charles	200	14/6	145.0.0	2.3.6
do. dragon Swamp	70	17/	59.10.0	17.11
Robbins, William	40	6/3	12.10.0	3.9
Roy, Beverly	700	8/4	291.13.4	4.7.6
Ross, John (Ben Minor to pay)	100	5/3	26.5.0	7.11
Segar, Richard	406	7/3	147.3.6	2.4.2
[Satte]rwhite, George	164	6/3	51.5.0	15.1
Satterwhite, William	100	4/2	20.16.8	6.3
Spencer, Edward	392½	8/4	163.10.10	2.9.1
do. Butler's	380	7/3	137.15.0	2.1.4
Schools, John	83½	7/10	32.14.1	9.9½
Seayres, Franky	338	9/4	157.14.8	2.7.2
Schools, Gabriel	169	6/3	52.16.3	15.11
Skelton, William	132	9/4	61.12.0	18.6
do Herndon's	100	7/3	36.5.0	10.11
do. Wood's	130	7/10	50.18.4	15.4
Smith, Ann	85	7/3	30.16.3	9.3
Smith, John (Drisdale)	190	7/6	71.5.0	1.1.4
Starling, Jane	360	7/10	141.0.0	2.2.4
				35.18.1½
[Skelton], Thomas	294	8/4	122.10.0	1.16.9
Scott, Benjamin	200	9/4	93.6.8	1.8.0
Saunders, George	100	7/3	36.5.0	10.11
Saunders, Alexander	"	"	"	10.11
Shepherd, William	140	9/4	65.6.8	19.8
Semple, John W.	574	14/6	430.10.0	6.9.1
Smith, Molley	30	4/2	6.5.0	1.11
Smith, John (L.H.)	100	5/3	26.5.0	7.11
Smith, Lewis	113½	7/3	41.12.11	12.6
Swinton, George	750	13/6	506.5.0	7.11.11
Stone, Sarah	300	7/3	108.15.0	1.12.8
Stone, Daniel	52	3/2	8.4.8	2.6
Smith, Larkin	1254¼	31/1	1949.6.3½	29.4.10
Smith, Henry	400	6/3	125.0.0	1.17.6
Smith, William	193	7/10	73.9.4	1.2.3
Smith, James	80	3/2	12.13.4	3.10
Smith, James jr.	101	7/10	39.11.2	11.10½
Stevens, George est.	645	"	252.12.6	3.15.9½
Stevens, Thomas est.	609½	"	238.14.5	3.11.8
Shackelford, John (taylor)	214	7/3	77.11.6	1.3.3½
				99.13.11

[page 14, 1792]

Present Proprietors Names	Qty. Land	Price	Amt. Land	Amt. Tax
Starke, Richard est.	250	6/3	78.2.6	1.3.6
do. of G. Richards	100	4/2	20.16.8	6.3
Stone, Robert	300	4/2	62.10.0	18.9
Stone, John est.	357	6/3	93.14.3	1.18.2
Smith, Robert	509	10/5	311.9.2	4.13.5¼
Simpkins, Nimrod	60	"	9.10.0	2.11
Sears, Philip	83	4/2	17.5.10	5.3
Spencer, Thomas	300	10/5	156.5.0	2.6.11
do.	255	4/2	53.2.6	15.11
Shackelford, William est.	700	14/6	527.10.0	7.18.6
Seward, Benjamin	115	3/2	18.4.2	5.6
Stedman, Christopher Senr.	191	5/3	50.2.9	15.[1]
Smith, Thomas (orphan)	485	14/6	351.12.6	5.5.5
Saddler, John	150	6/3	46.17.6	14.6
Shackelford, Alexander	60	4/2	12.10.0	3.9
Stedman, Christ[r.] jr.	133½	6/3	41.18.1½	12.6½
do. Dillards	260	5/3	65.5.0	1.0.6
Shackelford, John (Roman)	282	8/4	117.10.0	1.15.3
Shackelford, Benjamin	200		83.6.8	1.5.0
Shackelford, Lyne	517	6/3	161.11.3	2.8.5
Shackelford, Lyne jr.	50	"	15.12.6	4.8
Shackelford, John (Mac)	183	7/3	65.19.6	19.10
Scott, Anderson	330	16/7	273.12.6	4.2.2
Shepherd, Isaac	190	3/2	30.1.8	[9.3]
Seward, Lucy & Eliza. est.	110	4/2	22.18.4	6.[10]
Semple, Robert B.	154	7/10	60.6.4	18.1
				41.[10].[ ]
Trice, William	140	7/3	50.15.0	15.3
Taylor, James	50	6/3	15.12.6	4.9
Taylor, Edm[d.]	294	8/14	122.10.0	1.16.9
Temple, Joseph	918	10/5	478.2.6	7.3.6
Tunstall, Molley	250	"	130.4.2	1.19.0¾
Tunstall, Richard jr. est.	1097	7/3	397.13.3	5.19.3
Tunstall, John	200	18/8	186.13.4	2.16.0
Tignor, William	130	7/10	50.18.4	15.4
Tureman, Benjamin	120	3/2	19.0.0	5.6
Taliaferro, William	1000	14/6	725.0.0	10.17.9
Townley, Ro. (E. Williams to pay)	200	6/3	62.10.0	18.5
do. Anderson's	117	"	84.16.6	1.5.9
Taliaferro, Philip	990	8/4	412.10.0	6.3.4
do. D. Cooke	374½	12/6	234.7.6	3.10.3
Trice, Edward	206	5/3	54.2.6	16.11
Thruston, William	140	4/3	29.15.0	8.8
Taliaferro, Richard est.	300	5/3	78.15.0	1.3.6
Thruston, Batchelder	200	3/2	31.13.4	9.3
Turner, Benjamin	36	4/2	7.10.0	2.--
				89.8.5

[page 15, 1792]

Present Proprietors Names	Qty. Land	Price	Amt. Land	Amt. Tax
	[50]			
[Te]mple, Humphry	70	33/2	116.1.8	1.14.9¾
do. Walkerton	108	30/	162.0.0	2.8.7
do. of W. Tunstall	100	15/	75.0.0	1.2.6
[Tu]nstall, Richard est.	438	21/	459.18.0	6.18.0
[Tu]nstall, Richard (Best[d.])	269½	8/4	112.15.10	1.13.9
[V]ass, Thomas	250	5/3	65.12.6	19.9
Wyatt, Henry	200	7/3	72.10.0	1.1.9
White, Henry	100	8/4	41.13.4	12.6
Willmore, Thomas	150	10/5	78.2.6	1.3.6
do. of D. Farthing	19	7/10	7.8.10	2.2½
Wright, James	124½	5/3	32.13.8	9.10
Wyatt, Joseph	68	8/4	25.0.0	7.6
Waldin, John	105	12/6	65.12.6	19.9
Wood, Thomas	130	7/10	50.18.4	15.4
Wilson, Isaac	200	6/3	62.10.0	18.9
Wilson, Benjamin est.	200	7/3	72.18.0	1.1.9
Wiltshire, Joseph	74	"	26.16.6	8.--
Wright, Isaac	183	6/3	57.3.9	17.2
Wyatt, John	100	7/10	39.3.4	11.3
Watkins, William	37	4/2	7.14.2	2.4
Watkins, Joseph	65	"	13.10.10	4.2
Walker, Henry est.	150	5/3	39.7.6	11.10
Ware, John	562	7/3	203.14.6	3.1.2
Walker,				
Walker				
Wright				
Whayne				
Watts				
do. of W.				
Watts, J				
do. of P				
Watts, K				
o. of W.				
Watts				
do. of				
Williams				
Wyatt				
Wyatt				
Wyatt				
Williams				
Williams				
Walton				
Walton				
Willis				
Walton				

Note: The bottom right portion of the page is cut away.

[page 16, 1792]

Present Proprietors Names	Qty. Land	Price	Amt. Land	Amt. Tax
Walton, John	176	5/3	46.4.0	13.11
Walton, William est.	66	4/2	13.15.0	4.2
Walton, Thomas est.	66	"	"	4.2
Ware, John	75	5/3	19.13.9	5.11
Ware, Auther est.	83	4/2	17.5.10	5.3
Waring, Robert P.	212	7/3	76.17.0	1.2.10¾
do.	330	13/	214.10.0	3.4.4
Walden, Richard	180	10/5	93.15.0	1.8.1½
Walden, Lewis	150	3/2	23.15.0	7.3
do. of T. Dudley	84½	6/3	28.2.3½	8.5
Wright, Edward	141½	7/3	51.5.10½	15.2
Ware, Robert S.	50	10/	25.0.0	7.6
do. dragon swamp	39½	14/	27.13.0	8.3½
Williams, George	80	10/5	41.13.4	12.6
Wyatt, Richard	175	12/6	109.7.6	1.12.9¾
Ware, Robert jr. est.	100	4/2	20.16.8	6.3
Williams, Elizabeth	50	3/2	7.18.4	2.5
White, James est.	200	6/3	62.10.0	18.9
Watkins, Elizabeth	100	3/2	15.16.8	4.9
Warren, Catharine	175	"	27.14.2	8.4
Ware, Robert (B.P.)	112	"	17.14.8	5.4
Wedderburn, Lydia	350	6/3	109.7.6	1.12.10
Whiting, Beverly est.	2447¾	7/10	866.18.9½	13.0.0
Webbley, John	173	5/3	45.8.3	13.8
do. of B. Collier	100	4/2	20.16.8	6.3
Ware, Leonard est.	200	8/4	83.6.8	1.5.0
Walden, Edward est.	373	5/3	97.18.3	1.9.5
Wright, William (S.M.)	100	4/2	20.16.8	6.3
Waller, Edward est.	133½	3/2	21.2.9	6.5
Waller, John est.	66½	"	10.10.7	3.2
Wyatt, John (S.M.)	30	5/3	7.17.6	2.5
Young, Henry	640	18/8	597.6.8	8.19.3
				£42.1.6¼

Note: The lower left portion of the page is cut away.

A list of the Land within the County of King & Queen with
the Tax thereon at one and a half pr. cent for the year 1793

[page 1, 1793]

Present Proprietors Names	Qty. Land	Price	Amt. Land	Amt. Tax
	[51]			
Atkins, Joseph	66	4/2	13.15.0	4.1½
Alexander, Benjamin	202	9/4	94.5.4	1.8.4
do. of James Halbert	124	6/2	38.15.0	11.7½
Acree, Seaton	52	9/4	24.5.4	7.3½
Alexander, Elisha	102	7/3	36.12.3	11.0
do. of W^m. Gatewood	105	10/2	54.13.9	16.8
Anderson, Churchill est.	636	7/3	230.11.0	3.9.2
Anderson, Pauling	498	14/6	361.1.0	5.9.4
Atkins, John	120	4/2	25.0.0	7.6
do. of William Campbell	15	7/3	5.8.9	1.7½
Abbott, Jacob	112	7/10	43.17.4	13.2
Anderson, Richard est.	460	5/3	120.15.0	1.16.3
Atkins, Lewis	60	8/4	25.0.0	7.6
Anderson, Francis (Home)	233	14/6	168.18.6	2.10.8
do.	225	6/10	76.17.6	1.3.1
Brown, Henry jr.	100	12/	60.0.0	18.0
Beverley, Robert	2474	10/5	1288.8.10	19.6.7
Brown, Henry	657	7/5½	245.8.1	3.13.7½
do. Keeling's	103½	7/3	37.10.4½	11.3
do. of Wheeley	50	6/3	15.12.6	4.9
Baylor, Gregory Est.	720	14/6	522.0.0	7.16.7
Bland, Henry est.	166	8/4	69.3.4	1.0.9
Bates, James	358	11/	149.3.4	2.4.9
do.	42	4/2	8.15.0	2.7½
Barton, John Est.	125	"	26.0.10	7.10
Banks, William Est.	365	"	76.0.10	1.2.9¾
Brooking, Frances	930	10/5	484.7.6	7.5.4
Baylor, John Est.	380	14/3	270.15.0	4.1.2½
Boughton, Thomas, Essex	130	9/4	60.13.4	18.3
Boughton, John	200	8/4	83.6.8	1.5.0
Boughton, Henry, Essex	88	6/3	27.10.0	0.8.3
Broach, John	45	6/3	14.1.3	4.3
Burton, Thomas Est.	170	5/3	44.12.6	13.5
Bohannon, Ann	197	4/6	44.6.6	13.3½
Brown, William	75	7/10	29.7.6	8.10
Bagby, John Est.	330	7/3	119.12.6	1.15.10½
Bagby, Richard	260	"	94.5.0	1.8.3½
Bagby, Thomas	"	"	"	1.8.3½
Brooke, Richard	1539¾	29/-	2232.12.9	33.9.10
Brumley, Robert	225	5/3	59.1.3	17.9
Brumley, John	20	7/10	7.16.8	2.4
Bird, B. George	60	6/3	18.5.0	5.7½

[page 2, 1793]

Present Proprietors Names	Qty. Land	Price	Amt. Land	Amt. Tax
Bird, William	532	7/3	192.17.0	2.18.0¼
do. Dragon Swamp	88½	17/	70.4.6	1.1.0
Bird, Philemon	1157½	6/3	361.14.4½	5.8.6
Bird, Mary	619	6/3	193.8.9	2.18.1
Brett, John	446	18/	401.8.0	6.0.5
Burch, James	70	7/3	25.7.6	7.8
Burch, Vincent	100	4/2	20.16.8	6.3
Bird, A. Anthony	275	3/2	43.10.10	13.1
Byne, John Est.	336	4/2	70.0.0	1.1.0
do. dragon swamp	2¼	17/	1.18.3	6¾
Bird, Barbara	266 2/3	24/10	331.2.2½	4.16.0
Bird, Robert	533 1/3	24/10	662.4.5½	9.12.0
do. Guy Smith	189½	3/2	30.0.1	9.0
Bourn, Richard Est.	150	3/2	23.15.0	7.2
Burch, William Est.	100	5/9	28.15.0	8.7
Boyd, John	115	18/8	107.6.8	1.12.3
do. Soanes	382	24/10	474.6.4	7.2.4
Bray, Richard Est.	93	7/10	36.8.6	10.11
Bird, John Est.	100	3/2	15.16.8	4.9
Bowden, William	253	7/	88.11.0	1.6.6¾
Bew, William	117	3/2	18.10.6	5.7
Boyd, Spencer Est.	1428	10/5	770.15.0	11.11.[2]
Berkeley, Edmund	762	5/3	200.0.6	3.0.0
Bland, John	60	12/6	37.10.0	11.3
Bohannon, William	130		34.2.6	10.3
Bullman, Thomas est.	100	5/3	26.5.0	7.11
Briggs, John (W. Finney)	170	4/2	35.8.4	10.8
Belote, Laban	384½	"	80.2.1	1.4.[0]
Bland, William Senr.	225	3/8¼	41.9.8¼	12.[ ]
do. Merideth	146	5/3	38.6.6	11.6
Bowden, William jr.	100	4/2	20.16.8	6.3
do. of Sykes & Dudley	34	3/2	5.7.8	1.8
Bowden, John	100	4/2	20.16.8	6.3
Bland, William Est.	250	"	52.1.8	15.8
Bland, Thomas	412	3/2	75.4.8	1.2.6¾
Bowden, George	236	5/3	61.19.--	18.7
Burch, William	45	3/2	7.2.6	2.1½
Brown, Thomas	450	12/6	281.5.0	4.4.9
do. Edwd. Trice	4	5/	1.--.--	.3
Banks, James	98	7/3	35.10.6	10.7[¾]
Bristow, Bartho^w.	33½	3/2	5.6.1	1.7
Beard, David	450	9/4	210.0.0	3.3.0
Bristow, George	100	3/2	15.16.8	4.9
Broach, James & W^m. Mansfield	200	16/7	165.16.8	2.9.9
Bates, William	50	6/3	15.12.6	4.9
Banks, Andrew	125	12/6	78.2.6	1.3.5
Crafton, Thomas	145	9/4	67.13.4	1.0.3½
Crafton, ~~Thomas~~ James	59	"	27.6.0	8.9½

[page 3, 1793]

Present Proprietors Names	Qty. Land	Price	Amt. Land	Amt. Tax
	[52]			
Crafton, John	59	9/4	27.6.0	8.9½
Clayton, James	100	9/11	49.11.8	14.10¼
Cary, Martha	462	4/2	96.5.--	1.8.11
Cook, Mary	200	8/4	83.6.8	1.5.0
Coleman, Thomas	507	6/3	158.8.9	2.7.6¼
Chick, Richard Est.	491	7/3	177.19.9	2.13.5
Chapman, George Est.	200	7/10	78.6.8	1.3.6
do. of William Hoskins	39	10/5	20.6.3	6.1
Campbell, William	1014	7/3	367.11.6	5.10.1½
Chapman, Eliz[a.]	200	7/10	78.6.8	1.3.6
Crane, John	136	6/3	42.0.0	12.7
Cleverius, Benjamin	419	20/9	434.14.3	6.10.5
Carlton, Henry	280	7/10	109.13.4	1.12.10
do of John Baylor's Est.	257	14/6	186.6.6	2.15.10¾
Clayton, Thomas Est.	275	7/3	99.13.9	1.9.11
Campbell, Whitacar	318	7/10	124.11.-	1.17.6
Cleveley, Thomas	200	"	76.6.8	1.3.6
Crow, Nathaniel Est.	200	6/3	62.10.0	18.9
Crane, George Est.	30	7/3	10.7.6	3.4
Coleman, Milley Est.	196	10/5	102.1.8	1.10.8
Carlton, Joel	53½	6/3	16.14.5	5.1
Cooper, Ann	60	3/2	9.10.0	2.11
Carlton, Thomas (Swamp)	200	7/10	78.6.8	1.3.6
Carlton, Noah	100	"	39.3.4	11.9
Carlton, John (School[r.])	100	6/3	31.5.0	9.5
Campbell, Sarah	296	12/6	185.0.0	2.15.6
Carlton, Christ[r.] Sen[r.]	37½	6/3	11.14.5	3.7
Carlton, Richard jr.	139	7/	48.13.0	14.7
Cothern, James	36½	3/2	5.15.7	1.8¾
Carlton, William (Shoe)	309¼	11/6	178.1.2½	2.13.5
Carlton, Robert Est.	93	4/2	19.7.6	5.10
do. of Pemberton	55	6/3	17.3.9	5.2
Carlton, Richard	250	7/3	90.12.6	1.7.3
Carlton, Christ[r.] jr.	100		36.5.0	10.11
Carlton, Philemon	150	6/6	48.15.0	14.7½
Cooper, Henry	50	4/2	10.8.4	3.2
Carlton, Thomas (Taylor)	100	6/3	31.5.0	9.5
Cardwell, John Est.	150	4/2	31.5.0	9.5
Cardwell, John	"			9.5
Cardwell, William	77	"	15.11.6	4.7¼
Cardwell, Thomas	150	"	31.5.0	9.5
Cooke, John Est.	300	4/2	62.10.0	18.9
Collins, Thomas	329½	7/	115.6.6	1.14.7
do. Palmers	350	7/3	126.17.6	1.18.1
Carlton, John j[r.]	235	4/2	48.19.2	14.9
Campbell, William	238	3/2	37.13.8	11.4
Collier, Charles	200	3/2	31.13.4	9.6
Curtis, Ann	414	5/3	108.13.6	1.12.7
Collier, John	100	4/2	20.16.8	6.3
Corbin, T. John	2390	11/1¾	1332.11.4	19.19.9½
do. new dragon bridge	125	12/8	78.2.6	1.3.5

[page 4, 1793]

Present Proprietors Names	Qty. Land	Price	Amt. Land	Amt. Tax
Crittenden, Thomas	126	13/6	85.1.0	1.5.6
do. Dragon Swamp	36	17/	30.12.0	9.2
Collins, Joyeux Est.	140	10/5	72.18.4	1.1.10
Crittenden, Zachariah	34¾	14/6	24.17.10	7.6
Cary, M. Wilson	1820	16/7	1509.1.8	22.12.9
Collier, John (Cobler)	150	5/3	39.7.6	11.10
Campbell, James	100	6/3	31.5.0	9.5
do. Burk's	100	4/2	20.16.8	6.3
Crittenden, Richard jr. est.	178	5/3	46.14.6	14.1
Corr, Avarilla	79	"	20.14.9	6.2½
Collier, Catharine	750	"	196.17.6	2.19.1
Clegg, Isaiah	241	4/2	50.4.2	15.0½
Cooke, Dawson	296	7/3	107.3.0	1.12.1
do. Edwards & Osburn	282	3/2	44.13.0	13.6
Curry, Ann	100	4/2	20.16.8	6.3
Corr, Frances Est.	175	3/2	27.14.2	8.4
Courtney, William	200	7/10	78.6.8	1.3.6
Cooke, Thomas	240	3/2	38.0.0	11.5
Cook, Thomas jr.	96	"	15.0.4	4.6½
Carlton, Humphry	125	7/3	45.6.3	11.5
do. James Carlton's Est.	50	6/	15.0.0	4.6
Carlton, Thomas Est.	235	6/3	73.8.9	1.2.1
Carlton, Beverley	160	4/2	33.6.8	10.1
Corr, John jr.	184	7/5	66.14.0	1.10.0
Campbell, John	400	12/6	250.0.0	3.15.0
Crittenden, Francis (River)	105 2/3	14/6	76.12.2	1.3.0
Clark, John	144	5/	36.0.0	10.9¼
Cannaday, William	100	6/3	31.5.0	9.5
Corr, Thomas	157½	5/3	41.6.10½	12.4¼
Corr, John Sen[r.]	38	3/2	6.1.4	1.9½
Dew, William Est.	935	14/6	677.17.6	10.3.5
Dowling, William Est.	264	8/4	110.0.0	1.13.0
Dix, Gabriel	338	6/3	105.12.6	1.11.8
Deshazo, William	82	4/2	17.1.8	5.1½
Durham, Joseph	76	4/2	15.16.8	4.9
do. of Ben. Bohannan	155	4/3	32.5.5	9.8¼
Deshazo, Peter Est.	217	7/2	72.15.2	1.1.9½
do. Robert Hill	46	8/2	18.15.8	5.7
Dickie, James Est.	512	8/4	213.6.8	3.4.[0]
Dunbar, David	366	"	152.10.0	2.5.9
Dalley, John Est.	200	3/2	31.13.4	9.6
Drumright, Thomas	224	"	35.9.4	10.8
Dobbins, Charles Est.	147	5/3	38.11.9	11.7
Dean, Benjamin	50	"	13.2.6	4.0
Dillard, William Est.	100	3/2	15.16.8	4.9
Dunn, Agrippia	140	5/3	36.15.0	11.1
Dudley, Peter Est.	370	7/10	144.18.4	2.3.6
do. of Jn[o.] Baylor	160	5/3	42.0.0	12.7

[page 5, 1793]

Present Proprietors Names	Qty. Land	Price	Amt. Land	Amt. Tax
	[53]			
Didlake, James	311	6/9	105.2.7½	1.11.4½
do. of William Didlake jr.	278	8/4	115.16.8	1.14.9
Didlake, Margrett	65	"	13.10.10	4.1
Durham, Robert Est.	50	"	10.8.4	3.2
Dunn, Thomas	50½	6/3	15.15.7½	4.9
Dillard, William Senr.	276	12/6	172.10.0	2.11.9
Durham, George	50	4/2	10.8.4	3.2
Durham, Thomas	85	3/2	13.9.2	4.1
Dumagin, Richard Est.	237	5/5	64.3.9	19.3
Digges, Frances	175	5/3	45.18.9	13.10
Didlake, George Est.	114	10/5	59.7.6	17.10
Dungee, John	110	3/2	17.8.4	5.3
Dudley, William (Ferry)	290	14/6	210.5.0	3.3.1
do. of L. Wedderburn	315½	6/3	98.11.10½	1.9.6¾
Damm, John Est.	55	6/3	17.3.9	5.2
Dudley, William Senr.	180	7/10	70.10.0	1.1.2
Damm, William	25	4/2	5.4.2	1.6½
Douglass, John	100	6/3	31.5.0	9.5
do. of S. Field	139	7/3	50.7.9	15.1¼
Didlake, John	1200	"	435.0.0	6.10.6
Dudley, Ann	141	7/3	51.2.3	15.4
Dudley, Banks	230	3/2	36.8.4	10.11
Didlake, William	26¼	4/2	7.9.4½	2.2¾
Downey, Michael	50	10/5	26.0.10	7.9¾
Didlake, Royston	75	4/2	15.12.6	4.9¾
do. James Didlake's Est.	131	3/2	20.14.10	6.3
Dillard, Thomas	404	14/6	292.18.0	4.7.10½
Dudley, Thomas	267½	6/3	81.17.8½	1.4.7
Dillard, Nicholas	75	4/2	15.12.6	4.9
Dillard, Benjamin Est.	248	5/3	75.2.0	1.2.6
Drummond, John	150	6/3	46.17.6	14.6
Dillard, William (son of Thos.)	150	4/2	31.5.0	9.5
Dixon, Michael	406	15/6	314.13.0	4.14.4
do. Arch^d. Kennedy	8¾	12/6	5.9.4½	1.10
Dabney, Benjamin	400	14/6	290.0.0	4.7.0
Davis, Staige	311	6/9	105.2.7½	1.11.4½
Dally, George	174¼	3/2	27.11.9½	8¾
Eubank, John	200	14/6	145.0.0	2.3.6
do. of Samuel & Hill	269	7/3	97.10.3	1.9.6
Eubank, Thomas	300	14/6	217.10.0	3.5.3
Eubank, Henry	171	5/3	44.17.9	13.6
Edwards, Thomas Est.	66	4/2	13.15.0	4.2
Eubank, William Est.	28¾	5/3	7.11.0	2.4
Eubank, Richard Senr.	196	7/	68.12.0	1.0.7

[page 6, 1793]

Present Proprietors Names	Qty. Land	Price	Amt. Land	Amt. Tax
Edmonson, William	253	10/5	131.15.5	1.19.6½
Eubank, Richard Est.	227	4/2	47.5.10	14.3
Eubank, Richard jr.	118¼	7/	39.5.7½	11.9¼
Fogg, Frederick	298	8/4	124.3.4	1.17.3
Fleet, Baylor	862	12/6	538.15.--	8.1.7½
Fauntleroy, G. Samuel	880	16/7	729.13.4	10.18.1
do. do.	183	10/5	95.6.3	1.8.7
do. Moore Fauntleroy	1006	24/10	1231.2.4	18.14.8¾
Fleet, John	338½	7/6	126.18.9	1.18.1
Faulkner, Thomas	220	6/3	68.15.0	1.0.6¼
Fogg, Thomas Est.	200	"	62.10.0	18.9
Fogg, James	120	"	37.10.0	11.3
Frazer, William Est.	45	20/9	46.13.9	14.1
do. Marsh	11	3/6	1.18.6	.7
Fleet, William	352	20/9	365.4.0	5.9.6½
Fisher, James	110	3/2	17.18.4	5.3
Foster, Thomas	137¾	4/2	28.10.10	8.6¾
Faulkner, Mary	333	6/3	104.1.4	1.11.3
Fauntleroy, Thomas	800	8/4	333.6.8	5.0.0
do. of Hy. Todd	500	18/	460.0.0	6.18.0
Grafton, Thomas Est.	132	9/4	61.12.0	18.6
Grafton, James	111	6/3	34.13.9	10.5
Gale, John Est.	180	10/5	93.15.0	1.8.5
Goleman, Thomas (Essex)	714	9/4	333.4.0	5.0.0
do. of Spencer & Holt jr.	234½	7/3½	88.5.3	1.7.5½
Garnett, Rice	297	7/3	107.13.7	1.12.4
Gatewood, Chaney	860	10/5	451.0.10	6.15.4
do. Gardners	100	7/3	36.5.0	10.11
do. Theodk. Noel	362½	14/6	262.16.3	3.18.10
Garnett, Joshua	322	8/4	134.3.4	2.0.3
Graves, Edward	200	6/3	62.10.0	18.9
Gatewood, Joseph	445	10/5	231.15.5	3.9.7
Mathew Gale	323	11/5	184.7.7	2.15.4
Gatewood, John	160	8/4	66.13.4	1.0.0
Garnett, Reuben	990	8/9	433.15.3	6.10.7
do. Wm. Haws	72	10/5	37.10.0	11.3
Gwathmey, Temple	600	35/3	1057.10.0	15.17.3
Garlick, Samuel	454	24/10	563.14.4	8.9.2
Garlick, John	893	29/	1294.17.0	19.18.5
Griffith, Joseph	50	6/3	15.12.6	4.9
Gresham, Samuel	400	7/3	145.0.0	2.3.6
Garrett, Richard jr.	100	4/2	20.16.8	6.3
Gaines, Francis	356	14/6	258.2.0	3.17.5
Gaines, Harry Est.	1517	20/4	1542.5.8	23.2.8
Gresham, Thomas	339¼	6/3	106.0.4	1.11.10

[page 7, 1793]

Present Proprietors Names	Qty. Land	Price	Amt. Land	Amt. Tax
	[54]			
Gresham, Philemon	200	6/3	62.10.0	18.9
Gresham, John (D)	200	7/10	78.6.8	1.3.6
Gresham, William	100	4/2	20.16.8	6.3
Gardner, Elizabeth	100	6/3	31.5.0	9.5
Gibson, Richard	156½	3/2	24.16.7	7.4
Gibson, Banks	56½	"	8.18.[11]	2.7
Gibson, John Est.	219¾	"	34.15.11	10.6
Griffith, Milley	50	6/3	15.12.6	4.9
Gresham, Mitchem	100	5/3	26.5.9	7.10½
Gresham, Ambrose	80	"	21.0.0	6.3½
do. new entry	30	17/	25.1.0	7.6
Gresham, John jr.	80	5/3	21.0.0	6.3½
Graves, Thomas	50½	7/3	18.6.1½	5.5½
Griffin, William Est.	859	14/6	622.15.6	9.6.10
Garlick, Camm Est.	1100	6/3	343.15.0	5.3.2
Garrett, Richard	50	3/2	7.8.4	2.4
Garrett, William Est.	330	4/2	68.15.0	1.0.8
Gardner, Anthony	638	11/	350.11.8	5.5.3
do. dragon Swamp	67½	17/	57.7.6	17.2½
Gresham, Lumpkin	315	7/3	114.3.9	1.13.3
Garrett, Robert	200	7/	70.0.0	1.1.0
Gresham, William jr.	329½	8/4	137.5.10	2.1.2¼
Gaines, Robert	537¾	20/9	558.8.7¾	8.7.6
do. of A. Curtis	50	5/3	13.2.6	3.11
Gatewood, William (*Tuck*[o.])	220	3/2	34.16.8	10.6
Gatewood, Gabriel	78	10/5	40.12.6	12.2¼
Gatewood, William	237	"	123.8.9	1.17.3½
Guthrie, James	60	12/6	37.10.0	11.3
Guthrie, Richard Est.	60	"	"	11.3
Guthrie, Richard	162	3/2	25.13.0	7.8½
Glaspe, James	210	5/3	55.2.6	16.7
Gro[o]m, Mary	173	3/2	27.17.10	8.5
Garrett, George	88½	5/3	23.4.7½	6.11½
Goldman, Martin	140	4/2	29.3.4	8.9
Groom, Zachariah	187	3/2	29.12.2	8.10½
Gulley, Phil Est.	50	"	7.18.4	2.4
Garrett, Easter Est.	100	4/2	20.16.8	6.3
Garrett, William (Shoe)	200	5/3	31.13.4	9.6
do. John Harwood	25	5/3	6.11.3	1.11½
Gramshill, Henry	25	3/2	3.19.2	1.2¼
Garrett, Watts Ann	112	5/	28.0.0	8.4¾

[page 8, 1793]

Present Proprietors Names	Qty. Land	Price	Amt. Land	Amt. Tax
Harwood, Agness	225	4/2	46.17.6	14.1
Hill, William	1191	14/6	928.9.6	13.18.7
Hall, Corbin	188	8/4	78.6.8	1.3.6
Hitchcock, Thomas	140	4/2	29.3.4	8.9
Hoskins, Samuel	345	6/3	107.16.3	1.12.3
Hutcherson, Charles	647	7/0¾	228.9.5¼	3.8.6½
Hoskins, William	360	7/10	143.7.0	2.3.0
Heskew, John	61	5/3	16.0.3	4.10
Heskew, John jr.	50	6/3	15.12.6	4.8
Hill, Robert	1751¼	8/2	715.1.10	10.14.6¼
Hoomes, Benj[a.]	272	7/3½	99.3.4	1.9.9
Hill, Edward	1200	18/8	1120.0.0	16.16.0
Hutson, William (S. Step[n.])	112	3/2	17.14.8	5.4
Hemmingway, Daniel	534	4/2	111.5.0	1.13.4½
Hemmingway, John	266	"	55.8.4	16.7½
Hare, William	217	5/3	56.19.3	16.1
Harwood, Christ[r.] Est.	294	24/10	365.1.0	5.9.6
Harwood, John	75	5/3	19.13.9	5.10¾
Harwood, William Est.	240	30/	360.0.0	5.8.0
Hill, Thomas	300	26/11	403.15.0	6.1.2
Hart, James	150	3/2	23.15.0	7.2
Holderby, John	100	4/2	20.16.8	6.3
Hart, Anthony	190	5/3	49.17.6	15.0
do. Sundry persons	259½	3/2	41.1.9	12.4
Hart, Gregory	200	11/	31.3.4	9.6
Hart, William	250	3/3½	41.2.11	12.4
Harwood, John jr.	196½	10/5	102.6.10½	1.10.8¼
Hunt, William	730	6/3	228.2.6	3.8.6
Hutson, Mary Est.	100	4/2	20.16.8	6.3
Henry, H. Samuel	1900	14/6	1377.10.0	20.13.3
Halyard, William	190	5/3	49.17.6	15.0
do. of E. Crouches	130	3/2	20.11.8	6.3
Hoskins, John	767	10/7	399.9.7	5.19.10
do. Boughtons	100	8/4	41.13.4	12.6
Hoskins, Robert	100	6/3	31.5.0	9.5
do. of C. Dudley	120	4/2	25.0.0	7.6
Hart, Alden	127	"	26.9.2	7.11¼
Howerton, Heritage	122¼	20/9	126.16.7¼	1.18.0½
Holt, Richard	123	14/3	87.12.9	1.6.3½
Hutson, William	50	4/2	10.8.4	3.1½
Jeffries, Thomas	75¾	7/3	27.9.2¼	8.2¾
Jones, John Est.	300	8/11	133.15.0	2.0.1½
Jeffries, Edward	70	3/2	11.1.8	3.4
Jones, James	160	14/6	116.0.0	1.14.10
Jones, James Est.	196	10/5	102.1.8	1.10.8
Jones, William Est.	241	15/10	190.15.10	2.17.3
do. L. Smith	35¾	31/1	55.11.2	16.8

[page 9, 1793]

Present Proprietors Names	Qty. Land	Price	Amt. Land	Amt. Tax
	[55]			
Jeffries, Ambrose	397	7/10	148.8.10	2.4.7
Jeffries, Bernard	30	4/2	6.5.0	1.11
Jordan, William	100	3/2	15.16.8	4.9
Jordan, Henry	88	4/2	18.6.8	5.6
Jordan, Thomas Est.	100	"	20.16.8	6.3
Johnson, Archibald	100	"	"	6.3
Johnson, Thomas	112	3/2	17.14.8	5.4
Jameson, David (York)	50	"	7.18.4	2.5
Jones, Rawleigh	63	31/1	93.18.3	1.9.4
Keeling, James	113¼	7/3	41.1.0¾	12.4
Kemp, John	178	"	64.2.2	19.2
Kauffman, John jr.	38	10/5	19.15.10	5.11½
Kauffman, George	583	14/6	422.13.6	6.6.10
Kauffman, John	471	18/8	439.12.0	6.11.11
Kennedy, Archibald	321¼	12/6	200.5.7½	3.0.2¾
do. of Eliz[a.] Holderby	38¼	4/2	7.19.4	2.4½
Kennedy, Ann	120	12/6	75.0.0	1.2.6
do. Overstreet	70¼	4/2	14.11.8	4.6¾
Kennedy, Ann jr.	150	12/6	97.10.0	1.9.3
do. of Eliz[a.] Holderby	33¾	4/2	7.0.6	2.1¼
Kennedy, Lucy	37½	"	7.16.2	2.4
Kay, Christopher	116	6/3	30.9.0	9.1½
Kidd, Bartho[w.]	136	5/3	35.14.--	10.8
Kidd, Benjamin (Middle[x.])	111	13/6	74.18.2	1.2.5½
do. of Crittenden	60	13/6	40.10.0	12.1¾
do. Dragon Swamp	36	17/	30.12.0	9.2
Kidd, John	370	7/3	134.2.6	2.0.3
do. of Lumpkin & Peirce	60	4/2	12.10.0	3.9
do. Tho[s.] Dillard	45	14/6	32.12.6	9.10
Lumpkin, Joyce	213	7/10	85.8.2	1.5.0
Lumpkin, Henry	620	9/4	289.6.8	4.6.10
Lumpkin, John Est.	200	6/3	59.--.--	17.9
Lyne, William Col.	1480	8/4	610.14.2	9.3.3
Lyne, William jr.	108	8/4	45.0.0	13.6
Lumpkin, William	305	14/6	221.2.6	3.6.5
Lefon, Frances	119	8/4	49.11.8	14.10
Lumpkin, Robert (D)	374	"	155.16.8	2.6.9
Lankford, Thomas Est.	100	4/2	20.16.8	6.3
Longest, Caleb	97	7/10	37.19.10	11.6
Longest, Richard	140	"	54.16.8	16.6
Longest, Dorathy Est.	100	"	39.3.4	11.9
Lumpkin, Anthony	216	6/3	67.10.0	1.0.4
Lumpkin, Jacob	916	"	286.5.0	4.5.11
do. Southerlands	271	5/3	71.2.9	1.1.4

[page 10, 1793]

Present Proprietors Names	Qty. Land	Price	Amt. Land	Amt. Tax
Lewis, Iveson	356	14/6	258.2.0	3.17.4¼
Lewis, Betty	100	4/2	20.16.8	6.3
Lumpkin, Richard Est.	22	7/3	7.19.6	2.4½
do. of J. Carlton	54¼	5/3	14.4.9½	4.4
Leigh, Lucy	101	24/10	125.8.2	1.17.7
Leigh, John Est.	199	"	247.1.10	3.14.2
Lyne, John	507	6/3	158.8.9	2.7.7
Lambeth, Thomas	100	3/2	15.16.8	4.9
Lumpkin, Robert jr.	183	4/8	38.2.6	11.6
Laughlin, James	126¾	"	26.8.2	8.0
Lambeth, Charles Est.	50	3/2	7.18.4	2.5
Motley, Edwin	815	10/5	428.2.6	6.8.6
McKentosh, William	126	4/2	[2]6.5.0	7.10½
Martin, C. Thomas	680	14/6	493.0.0	7.7.11
do.	134½	7/3	48.15.1½	14.7½
Morgan, William	26	8/4	10.16.8	3.3
Mitchel, Ralph Est.	193	10/5	100.10.5	1.10.1½
Minor, William	149	8/4	62.1.8	18.8
Minor, John	137	"	57.1.8	17.2
Miller, Thomas	527	7/10	206.8.2	3.2.0
Mann, Augustine Est.	400	8/4	166.13.4	2.10.0
Mitchell, Robert	17	20/9	17.17.9	5.4
Mitchell, John	50	6/3	15.12.6	4.9
Mitchell, James	650	13/	422.10.0	6.6.9
Mann, Robert	399	6/	119.14.0	1.15.10¾
do. of William Bird	300	6/3	113.15.0	1.14.2
McKendree, Eliz[a.]	323	5/3	84.15.9	1.5.6
Meredith, William	197	"	51.14.3	15.7
Moore, Phil	150	4/2	31.5.0	9.4½
Moore, John	100	3/2	15.16.8	4.9
Major, Josiah	200	4/2	41.13.4	12.6
Mitchel, John Est.	270	5/3	70.17.6	1.1.4
do. part of Rootes	200	9/11	99.3.4	1.9.8¾
Macon, John	892	16/7	739.12.4	11.1.10
Mansfield, William	75	"	62.3.9	18.7
Merideth, Ralph G.	382	14/6	273.1.6	4.2.0
Merideth, Samuel Est.	185	"	138.0.0	2.1.5½
Muire, Richard	93	12/6	58.2.6	17.6
Moore, Richard	145	6/3	45.6.3	13.8
McCarty, Joseph	73	3/2	11.11.2	3.6
Metcalfe, Thomas Est.	521	14/6	377.14.6	5.13.3¾
Mann, Mary	100	5/3	26.5.0	7.11
Martin, John	80	9/4	37.6.8	11.3
do. of John Jones	395	8/11	176.2.1	2.12.9¾
Mann, Joseph (son of Augt[e.])	72	4/2	15.0.0	4.6

[page 11, 1793]

Present Proprietors Names	Qty. Land	Price	Amt. Land	Amt. Tax
	[56]			
Nunn, Jane	180	7/3	65.5.0	19.7
Newbill, George Est.	500	8/4	208.6.8	3.2.6
Nunn, Thomas	130	7/3	47.2.6	14.1½
Nash, John Est.	100	6/3	31.5.0	9.5
Newcombe, Eliz[a.]	109	3/2	17.5.2	5.2
Newcombe, William	60	"	9.10.0	2.11
Newill, John	100	7/10	39.3.4	11.9
Orvill, John	100	6/3	31.5.0	9.5
Olliver, John	320	5/3	84.--.--	1.5.3
Overstreet, Gabriel	296	4/2	61.13.4	18.6
do. Haynes	130	5/3	34.2.6	10.2
Oakes, Henry	73½	3/2	11.12.9	3.5¾
Oakes, Henry jr.	100	4/2	20.16.8	6.3
Owin, Augustine Est.	100	6/3	31.5.0	9.5
Pendleton, James	450	10/	225.0.0	3.7.6
do. of H. Samuel	100	6/3	31.5.0	9.5
Pitts, David Est.	420	9/4	196.--.--	2.18.10
Pitts, Obadiah	20	10/5	10.8.4	3.2
Phillips, Richard	230	7/3	83.7.6	1.5.1
Pollard, John	235	9/4	109.13.4	1.12.11
do. of L. Smithey	384	7/3	139.4.0	2.1.10
Prewett, Frances	99	9/4	46.4.0	13.11
Parker, John	116½	7/10	45.12.7	13.9
do. of Rich[d.] Holt jr.	147¾	6/3	46.3.5¼	13.10
Pendleton, Phil	337	10/5	175.10.5	2.12.8
do. of Farenholtz Est.	146	6/6	45.12.6	13.9
Perryman, Anthony	130	7/3	47.2.6	14.2
Perryman, Phil	109	9/3	50.8.3	15.1¼
Pitts, Benjamin G.	100	5/4	26.13.4	8.--
Pynes, Clement	199¼	3/2	31.10.11½	9.5½
Pace, Benjamin	263	7/3	95.6.9	1.8.8
Pollard, Richard	389	8/4	162.1.8	2.8.7½
Prince, Frances	113	7/10	44.5.2	13.4
Pendleton, Benjamin	450	"	176.5.0	2.12.11
Pynes, Benjamin	400	6/3	125.0.0	1.17.6
Pemberton, John	286	"	89.7.6	1.6.11½
Pollard, Robert	6	24/10	7.9.0	2.2¾
Price, Robert	630	6/3	196.17.6	2.19.1
Pigg, Rachel	108	14/6	78.6.0	1.3.6

[page 12, 1793]

Present Proprietors Names	Qty. Land	Price	Amt. Land	Amt. Tax
Pigg, John Est.	216	14/6	156.12.0	2.7.0
do.	180	7/3	65.6.0	19.7
Pollard, William	95	7/3	34.8.9	10.5
Pierce, Thomas Est.	87	4/2	18.2.6	5.5¼
Peirce, Philip	100	3/2	15.16.8	4.9
Richards, William Est.	510	12/6	318.15.0	4.15.8
Robertson, Rachel Est.	155	"	96.17.6	1.9.6
do.	260	7/3	94.5.0	1.8.5
Roane, Thomas	2033	18/8	1897.9.4	28.8.3
do. H. Carlton's	200	6/3	63.10.0	18.9
Roane, William	1384	18/8	1291.14.8	19.7.6
do Geo. Richards	201½	14/6	146.1.9	2.3.11
Richards, John Est.	215	9/4	100.6.8	1.10.1
Row, Hansford & Wilson	390	6/3	121.17.6	1.16.5
Row, Thomas G. (orphan)	555	7/3	201.3.9	3.0.4
Row, Eliz[a].	665	20/9	689.18.9	10.7.0
Row, Francis (orphan)	296	6/3	92.10.0	1.7.2
do. Bowers & Burch	316½	3/2	50.2.3	15.0
Read, Robert	14	5/3	3.13.6	1.1
Row, Richard Est.	550	8/4	229.3.4	3.8.9
Roane, Spencer	1600	24/10	1926.13.4	28.18.0
Richerson, Elias	86	4/2	17.18.4	5.[5]
Row, William & Moses	100	6/3	31.5.0	9.5
Richards, John	221½	4/2	46.3.0	13.11
Richards, William	296	5/3	77.14.0	1.3.4
Richerson, James	180	4/2	37.10.0	11.3
Richerson, William	181	"	37.14.2	11.4
Richerson, John Est.	101½	"	21.2.11	6.5
Roane, Major	367½	4/2	76.16.7	1.10.5
do.	320	3/2	50.3.4	15.3
Raines, Giles	60		9.10.0	2.11
Robinson, Benjamin Est.	1300	8/4	541.13.4	8.2.6
Roane, Charles	200	14/6	145.0.0	2.3.6
do. Dragon Swamp	70	17/	59.10.0	17.11
Robbins, William	40	6/3	12.10.0	3.9
Roy, Beverly	700	8/4	291.13.4	4.7.6
Ross, John (Ben Minor to pay)	100	5/3	26.5.0	7.11
Richards, George	21	17/	17.17.0	5.4¼

[page 13, 1793]

Present Proprietors Names	Qty. Land	Price	Amt. Land	Amt. Tax
	[57]			
Segar, Richard	406	7/3	147.3.6	2.4.2
Satterwhite, George	164	6/3	51.5.0	15.1
Satterwhite, William	100	4/2	20.16.8	6.3
Spencer, Edward	245½	8/4	96.5.10	1.8.11
do. in Stratton Major	582	7/3	210.19.6	3.3.3½
Schools, John	83½	7/10	32.14.1	9.9½
Seayres, Frankey	338	9/4	157.14.8	2.7.2
Schools, Gabriel	169	6/3	52.16.3	15.11
Skelton, William	132	9/4	61.12.0	18.6
do Herndon's	100	7/3	36.5.0	10.11
do. Wood's	130	7/10	50.18.4	15.4
Smith, John (D)	190	7/6	71.5.0	1.1.4
Starling, Jane	360	7/10	141.0.0	2.2.4
Skelton, Thomas	294	8/4	122.10.0	1.16.9
Scott, Benjamin	200	9/4	93.6.8	1.8.0
Saunders, George	100	7/3	36.5.0	10.11
Saunders, Alexander	"	"	"	10.11
Shepherd, William	140	9/4	65.6.8	19.8
Semple, W. John	574	14/6	430.10.0	6.9.1
Smith, Molley	30	4/2	6.5.0	1.11
Smith, John (L.H.)	100	5/3	26.5.0	7.11
Smith, Lewis	113½	7/3	41.12.11	12.6
do. of Ro. Hill	234	8/2	9.9.10½	2.10
Swinton, George	750	13/6	506.5.0	7.11.11
Stone, Sarah	300	7/3	108.15.0	1.12.8
Stone, Daniel	52	3/2	8.4.8	2.6
Smith, Larkin	1254¼	31/1	1949.6.3½	29.4.10
Smith, Henry	400	6/3	125.0.0	1.17.6
Smith, William	53	7/10	20.15.2	6.3½
Smith, James	80	3/2	12.13.4	3.10
Smith, James jr.	101	7/10	39.11.2	11.10½
Stevens, George Est.	645	"	252.12.6	3.15.9½
Stevens, Thomas Est.	609½	"	238.14.5	3.11.8
Shackelford, Jno. (Taylor)	214	7/3	77.11.6	1.3.3½
Starke, Richard Est.	350	5/8	99.3.4	1.9.9
Stone, Robert	300	4/2	62.10.0	18.9
Stone, Jno. Est.	357	6/3	93.14.3	1.18.2
Smith, Robert	488	10/5	243.3.4	3.16.3
Smith, Samuel	110	"	57.5.10	17.2¼
Simpkins, Nimrod	60	"	9.10.0	2.11
Sears, Phil	83	4/2	17.5.10	5.3
Spencer, Thomas	300	10/5	156.5.0	2.6.11
do.	255	4/2	53.2.6	15.11
Shackelford, William Est.	700	14/6	527.10.0	7.18.6

[page 14, 1793]

Present Proprietors Names	Qty. Land	Price	Amt. Land	Amt. Tax
Seward, Benjamin	115	3/2	18.4.2	5.6
Stedman, Christ[r.] Sen[r.]	191	5/3	50.2.9	15.1
Smith, Thomas (orphan)	485	14/6	351.12.6	5.5.5
Saddler, John	150	6/3	46.17.6	14.6
Shackelford, Alexander	60	4/2	12.10.0	3.9
Stedman, Christ[r.] jr.	133½	6/3	41.18.1½	12.6½
do. Dillards	260	5/3	65.5.0	1.0.6
Shackelford, Jn[o.] (Roman)	282	8/4	117.10.0	1.15.3
Shackelford, Benj[a.]	200		83.6.8	1.5.0
Shackelford, Lyne	351	6/3	109.13.9	1.12.10¼
Shackelford, Lyne jr.	50	"	15.12.6	4.8
Shackelford, John (Mac)	183	7/3	65.19.6	19.10
Scott, Anderson	330	16/7	273.12.6	4.2.2
do. of Charles Williams	214	11/2	44.14.8	[ ]½
Shepherd, John	190	3/2	30.1.8	9.3
Seward, Lucy & Eliza. Est.	110	4/2	22.18.4	6.10
Semple, B. Robert	154	7/10	60.6.4	18.1
Stone, William	74¼	3/2	11.15.3½	3.6½
Seward, Edward	81½	5/3	21.6.6¾	6.4¾
Sthreshley, William	155½	6/3	48.11.10½	14.7
Sears, Thomas	23	17/	19.11.0	5.10¼
Trice, William	140	7/3	50.15.0	15.3
Taylor, James	50	6/3	15.12.6	4.9
Taylor, Edmond	294	8/14	122.10.0	1.16.9
Temple, Joseph	918	10/5	478.2.6	7.3.6
Tunstall, Molley	250	"	130.4.2	1.19.0¾
Tunstall, Richard jr. Est.	1097	7/3	397.13.3	5.19.3
Tunstall, John	200	18/8	186.13.4	2.16.0
Tignor, William	130	7/10	50.18.4	15.4½
Tureman, Benjamin	70	3/2	11.1.8	3.4
Tureman, George	50	"	7.18.4	2.4½
Taliaferro, William	1000	14/6	725.0.0	10.17.6
Townley, Ro. (E. Williams to pay)	200	6/3	62.10.0	18.9
do. Anderson's	117	"	84.16.6	1.5.5
Taliaferro, Phil	990	8/4	412.10.0	6.3.9
do. D. Cook	374½	12/6	234.7.6	3.10.4
Trice, Edward	206	5/3	54.2.6	16.3
Thruston, William	140	4/3	29.15.0	8.11
Taliaferro, Richard Est.	300	5/3	78.15.0	1.3.8
Thruston, Batchelder	200	3/2	31.13.4	9.6
Turner, Benjamin	36	4/2	7.10.0	2.3
Temple, Humphry	178	31/3	278.2.6	4.3.5¼
do. of William Tunstall	100	15/	75.0.0	1.2.6

[page 15, 1793]

Present Proprietors Names	Qty. Land	Price	Amt. Land	Amt. Tax
	[58]			
Tunstall, William	438	21/	459.18.0	6.18.0
Tunstall, Richard (Bestl[d.])	269½	8/4	112.15.10	1.13.9
Townley, Ann	79	4/2	16.9.2	5.--
Vass, Thomas	250	5/3	65.12.6	19.9
Wyatt, Henry	200	7/3	72.10.0	1.1.9
White, Henry	100	8/4	41.13.4	12.6
Willmore, Thomas	150	10/5	78.2.6	1.3.6
do. of D. Farthing	19	7/10	7.8.10	2.2½
Wright, James	124½	5/3	32.13.8	9.10
Wyatt, Joseph	68	8/4	25.0.0	7.6
Walding, John Est.	105	12/6	65.12.6	19.9
Wood, Thomas	130	7/10	50.18.4	15.4
Wilson, Isaac	200	6/3	62.10.0	18.9
Wilson, Benj[a.] Est.	200	7/3	72.18.0	1.1.9
Wiltshire, Joseph	74	"	26.16.6	8.--
Wright, Isaac	183	6/3	57.3.9	17.2
Wyatt, John	100	7/10	39.3.4	11.3
Watkins, William	37	4/2	7.14.2	2.4
Watkins, Joseph	156	6/7	51.7.0	15.5
Walker, Henry Est.	150	5/3	39.7.6	11.10
Ware, John Est.	562	7/3	203.14.6	3.1.2
Walker, Frances	475	33/2	783.9.6	11.17.3
Walker, Humphry	345	"	572.4.8	8.10.7
Wright, William	175	5/3	45.18.9	13.10
Whayne, William	154½	7/6	60.10.3	18.1¾
Watts, Edward	250	7/3	90.12.6	1.7.3
do. of W. Watts Est.	113	5/	28.5.0	8.5½
Watts, John	293	7/10	114.15.2	1.14.6
do. of Pemberton	45	6/3	14.1.3	4.2½
Watts, Kauffman	300	5/3	78.15.0	1.3.8
do. of W. Burch's Est.	157	5/9	45.2.9	13.6¼
Watts, James	350	4/2	72.18.4	1.1.11
do. of W[m.] Watts Est.	60	15/	45.0.0	13.6
Williams, Howard	283	4/2	58.19.2	17.9
do. new entry	43	17/	36.11.--	10.11½
Wyatt, Thomas	206	7/10	81.2.0	1.4.4½
Wyatt, John (Blind)	103	6/3	32.3.9	9.8
Wyatt, William	29¾	7/3	10.15.8	3.8
Williams, Howard Est.	300	6/3	93.15.0	1.8.1
Williams, Charles	336	4/2	70.0.0	1.1.--
Walton, James	80	"	16.3.4	5.--
Walton, Mary	60	"	12.10.0	3.9
Willis, Joel	94	7/10	35.5.0	10.7
Walton, Elizabeth	60	3/2	9.10.0	2.11
Walton, John	176	5/3	46.4.0	13.11
Walton, William Est.	66	4/2	13.15.0	4.2

[page 16, 1793]

Present Proprietors Names	Qty. Land	Price	Amt. Land	Amt. Tax
Walton, Thomas Est.	66	4/2	13.15.0	4.2
Ware, John	75	5/3	19.13.9	5.11
Ware, Arther Est.	83	4/2	17.5.10	5.3
Waring, P. Robert	212	7/3	76.17.0	1.2.10¾
do.	330	13/	214.10.0	3.4.4
Walden, Richard	180	10/5	93.15.0	1.8.1½
Walden, Lewis	150	3/2	23.15.0	7.3
do. of T. Dudley	84½	6/3	28.2.3½	8.5
Wright, Edward	60½	6/8	20.3.4	6.0¾
Wright, James	124	"	41.6.8	12.4¾
Ware, S. Robert	50	10/	25.0.0	7.6
do. Dragon Swamp	39½	14/	27.13.0	8.3½
Williams, George	80	10/5	41.13.4	12.6
Wyatt, Richard	175	12/6	109.7.6	1.12.9¾
Ware, Robert jr. Est.	100	4/2	20.16.8	6.3
Williams, Elizabeth	16½	3/2	2.12.9	9½
White, James Est.	200	6/3	62.10.0	18.9
Watkins, Elizabeth	100	3/2	15.16.8	4.9
Warren, Catharine	175	"	27.14.2	8.4
Ware, Robert (B.P.)	112	"	17.14.8	5.4
Wedderburn, Lydia	350	6/3	109.7.6	1.12.10
Whiting, Beverly Est.	2447¾	7/10	866.18.9½	13.0.0
Webbley, John	173	5/3	45.8.3	13.8
do. of B. & F. Collier	268½	4/2	55.18.9	16.9¼
Ware, Leonard Est.	200	8/4	83.6.8	1.5.0
Walden, Edward Est.	373	5/3	97.18.3	1.9.5
Wright, William Senr.	100	4/2	20.16.8	6.3
Waller, Edward Est.	133½	3/2	21.2.9	6.5
Waller, Robert	48	4/2	10.--.--	3.--
do. of John Waller's Est.	65	3/2	10.5.10	3.1
Wyatt, John (Taylor)	30	5/3	7.17.6	2.5
Ware, Nicholass	100	3/2	15.16.8	4.9
Wilmore, Henry	70	7/6	26.5.0	7.10½
Williamson, Abner	100	3/2	15.16.8	4.9
Walding, Samuel	80	7/10	36.6.8	9.4½
Young, Henry	640	18/8	597.6.8	8.19.3

Errors Excepted by
William Fleet and William Courtney, Commrs.
£227.11.6

List of the land tax within the County of King and Queen for the year 1794

[page 1, 1794] Persons names owning lands	quantity of land	rate per acre	Amount of Value	Tax at 1½ percent
	[59]			
Atkins, Joseph	66	4/2	13.15.0	4.1½
Alexander, Benjamin	202	9/4	94.5.4	1.8.4
do. of James Halbert	124	6/2	38.15.0	11.7½
Acree, Seaton	52	9/4	24.5.4	7.3½
Alexander, Elisha	102	7/3	36.12.3	11.0
do. Wm. Gatewood	105	10/2	54.13.9	16.8
Anderson, Churchill est.	636	7/3	230.11.0	3.9.2
Anderson, Paulin	498	14/6	361.1.0	5.9.4
Atkins, John	120	4/2	25.0.0	7.6
Abbott, Jacob	112	7/10	43.17.4	13.2
Anderson, Richard est.	460	5/3	120.15.0	1.16.3
Atkins, Lewis	60	8/4	25.0.0	7.6
Anderson, Francis	233	14/6	168.18.6	2.10.8
Brown, Henry Junr.	100	12/	60.0.0	18.0
Beverley, Robert	2474	10/5	1288.8.10	19.6.7
Brown, Henry	657	7/5½	245.8.1	3.13.7½
Baylor, Gregory est.	720	14/6	522.0.0	7.16.7
Bland, John [& Lucy]	166	8/4	69.3.4	1.0.9
Bates, James [page torn]	358	11/	149.3.4	2.4.9
do.	42	4/2	8.15.0	2.7½
Barton, John est.	125	"	26.0.10	7.10
Banks, William est.	365	"	76.0.10	1.2.9¾
Brooking, Frances	930	10/5	484.7.6	7.5.4
Baylor, John est.	380	14/3	270.15.0	4.1.2½
Boughton, Thomas (Essex)	130	9/4	60.13.4	18.3
Boughton, John	200	8/4	83.6.8	1.5.0
Boughton, Henry (Essex)	88	6/3	27.10.0	0.8.3
Broach, John	45	6/3	14.1.3	4.3
Burton, Thomas est.	170	5/3	44.12.6	13.5
Bohannon, Ann	197	4/6	44.6.6	13.3½
Brown, William	75	7/10	29.7.6	8.10
Bagby, John est.	330	7/3	119.12.6	1.15.10½
Bagby, Richard	260	"	94.5.0	1.8.3½
Bagby, Thomas	"	"	"	1.8.3½
Brooke, Richard	1539¾	29/-	2232.12.9	33.9.10
Brumley, Robert	225	5/3	59.1.3	17.9
Brumley, John	20	7/10	7.16.8	2.4
Bird, George B.	60	6/3	18.5.0	5.7½
Bird, William	532	7/3	192.17.0	2.18.0¼
do. Dragon Swamp	88½	17/	70.4.6	1.1.0
Brown, John	50	7/4½	18.8.9	0.5.6½

[page 2, 1794] Persons names owning lands	quantity of land	rate per acre	Amount of Value	Tax at 1½ percent
Bird, Philemon	1157½	6/3	361.14.4½	5.8.6
Bird, Mary	619	"	193.8.9	2.18.1
Brett, John	446	18/	401.8.0	6.--.5
Burch, James	70	7/3	25.7.6	7.8
Burch, Vincent	100	4/2	20.16.8	6.3
Bird, Anthony A.	275	3/2	43.10.10	13.1
Byne, John est.	336	4/2	70.0.0	1.1.--
do. dragon swamp	2¼	17/	1.18.3	6¾
Bird, Barbara	266 2/3	24/10	331.2.2½	4.16.--
Bird, Robert	533 1/3	24/10	662.4.5½	9.12.--
do. Guy Smith	189½	3/2	30.0.1	9.--
Bourn, Richard est.	150	"	23.15.0	7.2
Burch, Shepherd	50	5/9	14.7.6	0.4.3¾
Burch, Samuel	50	5/9	14.7.6	4.3¾
Boyd, John	115	18/8	107.6.8	1.12.3
do. Sones's	382	24/10	474.6.4	7.2.4
Bray, Richard est.	93	7/10	36.8.6	10.11
Bird, John est.	100	3/2	15.16.8	4.9
Bowden, William	220¼	6/6	71.11.7½	1.1.6
Bew, William	117	3/2	18.10.6	5.7
Boyd, Spencer est.	1428	10/5	770.15.0	11.11.2
Berkeley, Edmund	762	5/3	200.0.6	3.0.0
Bland, John	60	12/6	37.10.0	11.3
Bohannan, William	130	5/3	34.2.6	10.3
Bullman, Ann	100	"	26.5.0	7.11
Briggs, John (W. Finney's)	170	4/2	35.8.4	10.8
Belote, Laban	384½	"	80.2.1	1.4.0
Bland, William Sen[r.]	225	3/8¼	41.9.8¼	12.6
Bland, Ralph	146	5/3	38.6.	11.6
Bowden, William jr.	100	4/2	20.16.8	6.3
do. of Sykes & Dudley	34	3/2	5.7.8	1.8
Bowden, John	100	4/2	20.16.8	6.3
Bland, William est.	250	"	52.1.8	15.8
Bland, Thomas	412	3/2	75.4.8	1.2.6¾
Bowden, George	236	5/3	61.19.--	18.7
Burch, William	45	3/2	7.2.6	2.1½
Brown, Thomas	454	12/6	283.15.--	4.5.10
Banks, James	98	7/3	35.10.6	10.7¾
Bristow, Bartho[w.]	33½	3/2	5.6.1	1.7
Beard, David	450	9/4	210.0.0	3.3.0
Bristow, George	100	3/2	15.16.8	4.9
Broach, Ja[s.] & W[m.] Mansfield	200	16/7	165.16.8	2.9.9
Bates, William	81	7/9½	31.10.1	9.5¼
Banks, Andrew	125	12/6	78.2.6	1.3.5
Brightwell, John est.	70	4/2	14.11.8	4.4½
Crafton, Thomas	145	9/4	67.13.4	1.0.3½
Crafton, James	59	"	27.6.0	8.9½

[page 3, 1794] Persons names owning lands	quantity of land	rate per acre	Amount of Value	Tax at 1½ percent
	[60]			
Crafton, John	176	9/4	81.16.8	1.4.6½
Clayton, James	100	9/11	49.11.8	14.10¼
Cary, Martha	462	4/2	96.5.--	1.8.11
Cooke, Mary	200	8/4	83.6.8	1.5.0
Chick, Richard	491	7/3	177.19.9	2.13.5
Chapman, George est.	200	7/10	78.6.8	1.3.6
do. of W. Hoskins	39	10/5	20.6.3	6.1
Campbell, William	1014	7/3	367.11.6	5.10.1½
Crane, John	136	6/3	42.0.0	12.7
Cleverius, Benjamin	419	20/9	434.14.3	6.10.5
Carlton, Henry	280	7/10	109.13.4	1.12.10
do John Baylor's est.	257	14/6	186.6.6	2.15.10¾
Clayton, Thomas est.	275	7/3	99.13.9	1.9.11
Campbell, Whitacar	318	7/10	124.11.-	1.17.6
Cleveley, Thomas	200	"	76.6.8	1.3.6
Crow, Nathaniel est.	200	6/3	62.10.0	18.9
Crane, George est.	30	7/3	10.7.6	3.4
Coleman, Milley est.	196	10/5	102.1.8	1.10.8
Carlton, Joel	53½	6/3	16.14.5	5.1
Cooper, Ann	60	3/2	9.10.0	2.11
Carlton, Thomas (Swamp)	200	7/10	78.6.8	1.3.6
Carlton, Noah	100	"	39.3.4	11.9
Carlton, John (School[r.])	100	6/3	31.5.0	9.5
Campbell, Sarah	296	12/6	185.0.0	2.15.6
Carlton, Christ[r.] Sen[r.]	37½	6/3	11.14.5	3.7
Carlton, Richard est.	139	7/	48.13.0	14.7
Cothern, James	36½	3/2	5.15.7	1.8¾
Carlton, William (Shoe)	309¼	11/6	178.1.2½	2.13.5
Carlton, Robert est.	148	5/	37.--.--	11.1
Carlton, Richard	250	7/3	90.12.6	1.7.3
Carlton, Christopher jr.	100		36.5.0	10.11
Cooper, Henry	50	4/2	10.8.4	3.2
Carlton, Thomas (Taylor)	100	6/3	31.5.0	9.5
Cardwell, John est.	150	4/2	31.5.0	9.5
Cardwell, John	"			9.5
Cardwell, William	77	"	15.11.6	4.7¼
Cardwell, Thomas	15	"	31.5.0	9.5
Cooke, John Est.	300	4/2	62.10.0	18.9
Collins, Thomas	329½	7/	115.6.6	1.14.7
do. Palmers	350	7/3	126.17.6	1.18.1
Carlton, John j[r.]	235	4/2	48.19.2	14.9
Campbell, William	238	3/2	37.13.8	11.4
Collier, Charles	200	3/2	31.13.4	9.6
Curtis, Ann	414	5/3	108.13.6	1.12.7
Collier, John	100	4/2	20.16.8	6.3
Corbin, John T. est.	2390	11/1¾	1332.11.4	19.19.9½
do. new dragon bridge	125	12/8	78.2.6	1.3.5
Crouch, James	130	3/8	20.11.8	6.3
Chapman, Elizabeth	200	7/10	78.6.8	1.3.6

[page 4, 1794] Persons names owning lands	quantity of land	rate per acre	Amount of Value	Tax at 1½ percent
Crittenden, Thomas	126	13/6	85.1.0	1.5.6
do. dragon swamp	36	17/	30.12.0	9.2
Collins, Joyeux est.	140	10/5	72.18.4	1.1.10
Crittenden, Zachariah	34 1/3	14/6	24.17.10	7.6
Cary, Wilson est.	1820	16/7	1509.1.8	22.12.9
Collier, John (Cobler)	150	5/3	39.7.6	11.10
Campbell, James	130	5/9¼	37.10.0	11.3
Crittenden, Rich[d.] est.	178	5/3	46.14.6	14.1
Corr, Avarilla	79	"	20.14.9	6.2½
Collier, Catharine	750	"	196.17.6	2.19.1
Clegg, Isaiah	241	4/2	50.4.2	15.0½
Cooke, Dawson	282	3/2	44.13.0	13.6
Curry, Ann	100	4/2	20.16.8	6.3
Courtney, William	200	7/10	78.6.8	1.3.6
Cooke, Thomas	240	3/2	38.0.0	11.5
Cook, Thomas jr.	96	"	15.0.4	4.6½
Carlton, Humphry	175	7/	61.5.0	18.4
Carlton, Thomas est.	235	6/3	73.8.9	1.2.1
Carlton, Beverley est.	160	4/2	33.6.8	10.1
Corr, John jun[r.]	184	7/5	66.14.0	1.10.0
Campbell, John	400	12/6	250.0.0	3.15.0
Crittenden, Fran[s.] (River)	105 2/3	14/6	76.12.2	1.3.0
Clarke, John	144	5/	36.0.0	10.9¼
Cannaday, William	100	6/3	31.5.0	9.5
Corr, Thomas	157½	5/3	41.6.10½	12.4¼
Corr, John Sen[r.]	213	3/2	33.15.6	10.1½
Cooke, William	65	5/5	17.12.1	5.3¼
Cooke, James	65	8/9	28.8.9	8.6½
Dew, William est.	935	14/6	677.17.6	10.3.5
Dew, Thomas	535	12/6	334.7.6	5.--.3¾
Dowling, William est.	264	8/4	110.0.0	1.13.--
Dix, Gabriel	338	6/3	105.12.6	1.11.8
Deshazo, William	82	4/2	17.1.8	5.1½
Durham, Joseph	155	4/3	32.5.5	9.8.¾
Deshazo, Peter est.	192	7/4	70.8.0	1.1.1½
Deshazo, Larkin	71	7/2	25.8.10	7.7¾
Dickie, James est.	512	8/4	213.6.8	3.4.0
Dunbar, David	366	"	152.10.0	2.5.9
Dalley, John est.	200	3/2	31.13.4	9.6
Drumright, Thomas	224	"	35.9.4	10.8
Dobbins, Charles est.	147	5/3	38.11.9	11.7
Dean, Benjamin	50	"	13.2.6	4.--
Dillard, William jr. est.	100	3/2	15.16.8	4.9
Dunn, Agrippia	140	5/3	36.15.0	11.1
Dudley, Peter est.	530	7/0¾	186.18.4	2.16.1

[page 5, 1794] Persons names owning lands	quantity of land	rate per acre	Amount of Value	Tax at 1½ percent
	[61]			
Didlake, Mary	311	6/9	105.2.7½	1.11.4½
do. of Wm. Didlakes	278	8/4	115.16.8	1.14.9
Didlake, Margrett	65	4/2	13.10.10	4.1
Durham, Robert est.	50	"	10.8.4	3.2
Dunn, Thomas	50½	6/3	15.15.7½	4.9
Dillard, William Senr.	276	12/6	172.10.0	2.11.9
Durham, George	50	4/2	10.8.4	3.2
Durham, Thomas est	85	3/2	13.9.2	4.1
Dumagin, Richard est.	172	5/5	46.11.8	14.--
Digges, Frances	175	5/3	45.18.9	13.10
Didlake, George est.	114	10/5	59.7.6	17.10
Dungee, John	110	3/2	17.8.4	5.3
Dudley, William jr.	290	14/6	210.5.0	3.3.1
do. L. Wedderburn	315½	6/3	98.11.10½	1.9.6¾
Damm, John est.	55	6/3	17.3.9	5.2
Dudley, William	180	7/10	70.10.0	1.1.2
Damm, William	25	4/2	5.4.2	1.6½
Douglass, John	239	7/	83.13.0	1.5.1
Didlake, John	1200	7/3	435.0.0	6.10.6
Dudley, Ann	141	7/3	51.2.3	15.4
Dudley, Banks	230	3/2	36.8.4	10.11
Didlake, William	26¼	4/2	7.9.4½	2.2¾
Downey, Michael	50	10/5	26.0.10	7.9¾
Didlake, Royston	206	3/6½	36.7.4	11.1
Dillard, Thomas	349	15/	261.15.0	3.18.6¼
Dillard, William jr.	150	4/2	31.5.0	9.5
do. Thos. Dillard	56	10/1¾	31.3.--	9.4
Dudley, Thomas	267½	6/3	81.17.8½	1.4.7
Dillard, Nicholas	75	4/2	15.12.6	4.9
Dillard, Benja. est.	148	5/3	48.17.0	14.7¾
Drummond, John	150	6/3	46.17.6	14.6
Dixon, Michael	414¾	15/5	320.--.--	4.16.0
Dabney, Benjamin	400	14/6	290.--.--	4.7.0
Davis, Staige	311	6/9	105.2.7½	1.11.4½
Dally, George	174¼	3/2	27.11.9½	8¾
Eubank, John	469	10/4	242.6.4	3.12.9
Eubank, Thomas	300	14/6	217.10.0	3.5.3
Eubank, Henry	171	5/3	44.17.9	13.6
Edwards, Thomas est.	66	4/2	13.15.0	4.2
Eubank, William est.	28¾	5/3	7.11.0	2.4
Eubank, Richard Senr.	196	7/	68.12.0	1.0.7
Edmonson, William	253	10/5	131.15.5	1.19.6½
Eubank, Richard est.	227	4/2	47.5.10	14.3
Eubank, Richard jr.	112¼	7/	39.5.7½	11.9¼

[page 6, 1794] Persons names owning lands	quantity of land	rate per acre	Amount of Value	Tax at 1½ percent
Fogg, Frederick	298	8/4	124.3.4	1.17.3
Fleet, Baylor	862	12/6	538.15.--	8.1.7½
Fauntleroy, Samuel G.	2069	20/	2069.0.0	31.0.8½
Fleet, John	260	6/3	81.5.0	1.6.4½
Falkner, Thomas	220	"	68.15.0	1.0.6¼
Fogg, Thomas est.	200	"	62.10.0	18.9
Fogg, James	120	"	37.10.0	11.3
Frazer, William est.	45	20/9	46.13.9	14.1
Fleet, William	352	"	365.4.0	5.9.6½
Fisher, James est.	110	3/2	17.18.4	5.3
Foster, Thomas	137¾	4/2	28.10.10	8.6¾
Faulkner, Mary	333	6/3	104.1.4	1.11.3
Fauntleroy, Thomas	486	10/	243.--.--	3.12.10¾
do. of Hy. Todd	500	18/	460.0.0	6.18.0
do. Wm. Bowden	183	7/	64.1.--	0.19.2½
Grafton, Sally & Ann	132	9/4	61.12.0	18.6
Grafton, James	111	6/3	34.13.9	10.5
Gale, John	615	7/5½	229.13.9	3.8.8½
Goleman, Thomas (Essex)	948½	9/-	426.16.6	6.8.--
Garnett, Rice	297	7/3	107.13.7	1.12.4
Gatewood, Chaney	829	10/5	437.17.11	4.10.6
do. Gardners	100	7/3	36.5.0	10.11
do. Theodk. Noel	362½	14/6	262.16.3	3.18.10
Garnett, Joshua	322	8/4	134.3.4	2.0.3
Graves, Edward	200	6/3	62.10.0	18.9
Gatewood, Joseph	445	10/5	231.15.5	3.9.7
Gale, Mathew	323	11/5	184.7.7	2.15.4
Gatewood, John	160	8/4	66.13.4	1.0.0
Garnett, Reuben	1131¾	8/10	499.17.1½	7.9.11¼
Gwathmey, Temple	600	35/3	1057.10.0	15.17.3
Garlick, Samuel	454	24/10	563.14.4	8.9.2
Garlick, John	893	29/	1294.17.0	19.18.5
Griffith, Joseph	50	6/3	15.12.6	4.9
Gresham, Samuel	400	7/3	145.0.0	2.3.6
Guthrie, William	40¾	"	14.15.5¼	4.5
Garrett, Robert (Estate)	100	4/2	20.16.8	6.3
Gaines, Francis	356	14/6	258.2.0	3.17.5
Gaines, Harry est.	1517	20/4	1542.5.8	23.2.8
Gresham, Thomas	339¼	6/3	106.0.4	1.11.10
Gresham, Philemon	200	"	62.10.0	18.9
Gresham, John (D)	200	7/10	78.6.8	1.3.6
Gresham, William	100	4/2	20.16.8	6.3
Gardner, Elizabeth	100	6/3	31.5.0	9.5
Gibson, Richard	156½	3/2	24.16.7	7.4
Gibson, Banks	56½	"	8.18.[11]	2.7

[page 7, 1794] Persons names owning lands	quantity of land	rate per acre	Amount of Value	Tax at 1½ percent
	[62]			
Gibson, John est.	219¾	"	34.15.11	10.6
Griffith, Milley	50	6/3	15.12.6	4.9
Gresham, Michem	100	5/3	26.5.0	7.10½
Gresham, Ambrose	80	"	21.0.0	6.3½
do. new entry	30	17/	25.1.0	7.6
Gresham, John jun^r.	80	5/3	21.0.0	6.3½
Graves, Thomas	50½	7/3	18.6.1½	5.5½
Griffin, William est.	859	14/6	622.15.6	9.6.10
Garlick, Camm est.	1100	6/3	343.15.0	5.3.2
Garrett, Richard	50	3/2	7.8.4	2.4
Garrett, James	230	4/2	47.18.4	14.4½
Garrett, William jr.	500	"	20.16.8	6.3
Gardner, Anthony	638	11/	350.11.8	5.5.3
do. dragon swamp	67½	17/	57.7.6	17.2½
Gresham, Lumpkin	315	7/3	114.3.9	1.13.3
Garrett, Robert	200	7/	70.0.0	1.1.--
Gresham, William jr.	329½	8/4	137.5.10	2.1.2¼
Gaines, Robert	537¾	20/9	558.8.7¾	8.7.6
do. Ann Curtis	50	5/3	13.2.6	3.11
Gatewood, W^m. (*Tuck^o.*)	220	3/2	34.16.8	10.6
Gatewood, Gabriel	78	10/5	40.12.6	12.2¼
Gatewood, William	237	"	123.8.9	1.17.3½
Guthrie, James	60	12/6	37.10.0	11.3
Guthrie, Richard est.	"	"	"	11.3
Guthrie, Richard	162	3/2	25.13.0	7.8½
Glaspe, James	210	5/3	55.2.6	16.7
Groom, Mary	173	3/2	27.17.10	8.5
Garrett, George	88½	5/3	23.4.7½	6.11½
Goldman, Martin	140	4/2	29.3.4	8.9
Groom, Zachariah est.	187	3/2	29.12.2	8.10½
Gulley, Philip est.	50	"	7.18.4	2.4
Garrett, William (Shoe^r.)	225	3/4¾	37.19.4½	11.4½
Gramshill, Henry	25	3/2	3.19.2	1.2¼
Garrett, Ann Watts	112	5/	28.0.0	8.4¾
Garrett, Richard	100	4/2	20.16.8	6.3
Harwood, Agness est.	225	4/2	46.17.6	14.1
Hill, William	1191	14/6	928.9.6	13.18.7
Hall, Corbin	188	8/4	78.6.8	1.3.6
Hitchcock, Thomas	140	4/2	29.3.4	8.9
Hoskins, Samuel	345	6/3	107.16.3	1.12.3
Hutcherson, Charles	547	7/1	193.14.7	2.18.1½
Hoskins, William	360	7/10	143.7.0	2.3.0
Heskew, John	61	5/3	16.0.3	4.10
Heskew, John jun^r.	50	6/3	15.12.6	4.8
Hill, Robert	1515¼	8/2	618.14.6	9.5.7¼
Hill, Edward	1200	18/8	1120.0.0	16.16.--

[page 8, 1794] Persons names owning lands	quantity of land	rate per acre	Amount of Value	Tax at 1½ percent
Hoomes, Benjamin	272	7/3½	99.3.4	1.9.9
do. Durham & Bohannan	115	4/2	23.19.2	7.2½
Hutson, William (S.S.)	112	3/2	17.14.8	5.4
Hemmingway, John jr.	267	4/2	55.12.6	16.8¼
Hemmingway, Samuel	267	"	55.12.6	16.8¼
Hemmingway, John Sen[r.]	266	"	55.8.4	16.7½
Hare, William	217	5/3	56.19.3	16.1
Harwood, Christ[r.] est.	294	24/10	365.1.0	5.9.6
Harwood, John Sen[r.]	75	5/3	19.13.9	5.10¾
Harwood, William est.	240	30/	360.0.0	5.8.0
Hill, Thomas	300	26/11	403.15.0	6.1.2
Hart, James	150	3/2	23.15.0	7.2
Holderby, John	100	4/2	20.16.8	6.3
Hart, Anthony	190	5/3	49.17.6	15.0
do. of Sundry persons	259½	3/2	41.1.9	12.4
Hart, Gregory	200	11/	31.3.4	9.6
Hart, William	250	3/3½	41.2.11	12.4
Harwood, John jr.	196½	10/5	102.6.10½	1.10.8¼
Hunt, William est.	730	6/3	228.2.6	3.8.6
Hutson, Mary est.	100	4/2	20.16.8	6.3
Henry, Samuel H. est.	1900	14/6	1377.10.0	20.13.3
Halyard, William	190	5/3	49.17.6	15.--
Hoskins, John	767	10/7	399.9.7	5.19.10
do. Boughtons	100	8/4	41.13.4	12.6
Hoskins, Robert	287	6/	86.2.0	1.5.10
Hart, Alden	127	"	26.9.2	7.11¼
Howerton, Heritage	122¼	20/9	126.16.7¼	1.18.0½
Holt, Richard	123	14/3	87.12.9	1.6.3½
Hutson, William (S.M.)	50	4/2	10.8.4	3.1½
Hutcherson, John	73¼	8/9	32.0.11¼	9.7¼
Jeffries, Thomas	75¾	7/3	27.9.2¼	8.2¾
Jones, John est.	300	8/11	133.15.0	2.0.1½
Jeffries, Edward	70	3/2	11.1.8	3.4
Jones, James	160	14/6	116.0.0	1.14.10
Jones, James est.	196	10/5	102.1.8	1.10.8
Jones, William est.	241	15/10	190.15.10	2.17.3
do. L. Smith	35¾	31/1	55.11.2	16.8
Jeffries, Ambrose	337	7/10	124.18.10	1.17.6
Jeffries, Robert	60	"	23.10.0	7.1
Jeffries, Bernard	30	4/2	6.5.0	1.11
Jordan, Henry	88	4/2	18.6.8	5.6
Jordan, William	100	3/2	15.16.8	4.9
Jordan, Thomas est.	100	4/2	20.16.8	6.3

[page 9, 1794] Persons names owning lands	quantity of land	rate per acre	Amount of Value	Tax at 1½ percent
	[63]			
Johnson, Thomas	112	3/2	17.14.8	5.4
Jameson, David est.	50	"	7.18.4	2.5
Jones, Rawleigh	63	31/1	93.18.3	1.9.4
Keeling, James	113¼	7/3	41.1.0¾	12.4
do. Ro. Hill	23	8/2	9.7.10	2.10
Kemp, John	178	7/3	64.2.2	19.2
Kauffman, John jr.	38	10/5	19.15.10	5.11½
Kauffman, George	583	14/6	422.13.6	6.6.10
Kauffman, John	471	18/8	439.12.0	6.11.11
Kennedy, Archibald	321¼	12/6	200.5.7½	3.0.2¾
do. Holderby's	38¼	4/2	7.19.4	2.4½
Kennedy, Ann	120	12/6	75.0.0	1.2.6
do. Overstreet's	70¼	4/2	14.11.8	4.6¾
Kennedy, Ann jr.	150	12/6	97.10.0	1.9.3
do. Holderby	33¾	4/2	7.0.6	2.1¼
Kennedy, Lucy	37½	"	7.16.2	2.4
Kay, Christopher	116	6/3	30.0.9	9.1½
Kidd, Bartholomew	136	5/3	35.14.--	10.8
Kidd, Benjamin	111	13/6	74.18.2	1.2.5½
do. Crittenden	60	"	40.10.0	12.1¾
do. dragon swamp	36	17/	30.12.0	9.2
Kidd, John	370	7/3	134.2.6	2.0.3
do. Lumpkin & Peirce	60	4/2	12.10.0	3.9
do. Thos. Dillard	45	14/6	32.12.6	9.10
Lumpkin, Joyce	213	7/10	85.8.2	1.5.0
Lumpkin, Henry	620	9/4	289.6.8	4.6.10
Lumpkin, John	200	6/3	59.--.--	17.9
Lyne, William	1480	8/4	610.14.2	9.3.3
Lyne, William jr.	108	"	45.0.0	13.6
Lumpkin, William	305	14/6	221.2.6	3.6.5
Lefon, Francis	119	8/4	49.11.8	14.10
Lankford, Thomas est.	100	4/2	20.16.8	6.3
Lumpkin, Robert (D)	374	8/4	155.16.8	2.6.9
Longest, Caleb	97	7/10	37.19.10	11.6
Longest, Richard	140	"	54.16.8	16.6
Longest, Doratha	100	"	39.3.4	11.9
Lumpkin, Anthony	216	6/3	67.10.0	1.0.4
Lumpkin, Jacob	916	"	286.5.0	4.5.11
do. Southerlands	271	5/3	71.2.9	1.1.4
Lewis, Iveson	356	14/6	258.2.0	3.17.4¼
Lumpkin, Richard est.	76¼	6/	22.17.6	6.10¼
Leigh, Lucy	101	24/10	125.8.2	1.17.7

[page 10, 1794] Persons names owning lands	quantity of land	rate per acre	Amount of Value	Tax at 1½ percent
Leigh, John est.	199	"	247.1.10	3.14.2
Lyne, John	507	6/3	158.8.9	2.7.7
Lambeth, Thomas	100	3/2	15.16.8	4.9
Lumpkin, Robert jun[r.]	183	4/8	38.2.6	11.6
Laughlin, James	126¾	"	26.8.2	8.--
Lambeth, Charles est.	50	3/2	7.18.4	2.5
Motley, Edwin	815	10/5	428.2.6	6.8.6
McKentosh, William	126	4/2	[2]6.5.0	7.10½
Martin, Thomas C.	680	14/6	493.0.0	7.7.11
do.	134½	7/3	48.15.1½	14.7½
Morgan, William	26	8/4	10.16.8	3.3
Mitchel, Ralph est.	193	10/5	100.10.5	1.10.1½
Minor, William	149	8/4	62.1.8	18.8
Minor, John	137	"	57.1.8	17.2
Miller, Thomas	527	7/10	206.8.2	3.2.0
Mann, Augustine est.	400	8/4	166.13.4	2.10.0
Mitchell, Robert	17	20/9	17.17.9	5.4
Mitchell, John	50	6/3	15.12.6	4.9
Mitchell, James est.	650	13/	422.10.0	6.6.9
Mann, Robert	699	6/3	218.8.9	3.5.6½
McKendrie, Elizabeth	323	5/3	84.15.9	1.5.6
Meredith, William	197	"	51.14.3	15.7
Moore, Lambeth	70	4/2	14.11.8	4.3¼
Morris, William	10	"	2.1.8	.7½
Moore, Benjamin	100	"	[15].16.8	6.3
Merideth, Samuel	215	7/10	84.4.2	1.5.3
Moore, John	100	3/2	15.16.8	4.9
Major, Josiah	200	4/2	41.13.4	12.6
Mitchell, John est.	270	5/3	70.17.6	1.1.4
do. part Rootes	200	9/11	99.3.4	1.9.8¾
Macon, John est.	892	16/7	739.12.4	11.1.10
Mansfield, William	75	"	62.3.9	18.7
Merideth, Ralph G.	567	14/6	411.1.6	6.3.5½
Muire, Richard	93	12/6	58.2.6	17.6
Moore, Richard	145	6/3	45.6.3	13.8
McCarty, Joseph est.	73	3/2	11.11.2	3.6
Metcalfe, Thomas est.	521	14/6	377.14.6	5.13.3¾
Mann, Mary	100	5/3	26.5.0	7.11
Martin, John	475	9/	312.15.0	3.3.1½
Mann, Joseph (son of Augustine)	72	4/2	15.0.0	4.6
Nunn, Jane	180	7/3	65.5.0	19.7
Newbill, George est.	500	8/4	208.6.8	3.2.6
Nunn, Thomas	130	7/3	47.2.6	14.1½
Nash, John est.	100	6/3	31.5.0	9.5

[page 11, 1794] Persons names owning lands	quantity of land	rate per acre	Amount of Value	Tax at 1½ percent
	[64]			
Newcombe, Elizabeth	109	3/2	17.5.2	5.2
Newcombe, William	60	"	9.10.0	2.11
Newill, John	100	7/10	39.3.4	11.9
Orvill, John	100	6/3	31.5.0	9.5
Olliver, John	320	5/3	84.--.--	1.5.3
Overstreet, Gabriel	296	4/2	61.13.4	18.6
do. Haynes's	130	5/3	34.2.6	10.2
Oakes, Henry	73½	3/2	11.12.9	3.5¾
Oakes, Henry Jun[r.]	100	4/2	20.16.8	6.3
Owin, Augustine est.	100	6/3	31.5.0	9.5
Pendleton, James	888½	8/7½	383.3.3¾	5.14.11½
Pitts, David est.	420	9/4	196.--.--	2.18.10
Pitts, Obadiah	20	10/5	10.8.4	3.2
Phillips, Richard	230	7/3	83.7.6	1.5.1
Pollard, John est.	235	9/4	109.13.4	1.12.11
do. of L. Smithey	384	7/3	139.4.0	2.1.10
Prewett, Francis	99	9/4	46.4.0	13.11
Parker, John	264¼	7/	92.9.9	1.7.9
Pendleton, Philip	483	9/2	221.7.6	3.6.5
Perryman, Anthony	130	7/3	47.2.6	14.2
Perryman, Philip	230	7/2	82.8.4	1.4.9
Pitts, Benjamin G.	100	5/4	26.13.4	8.0
Pynes, Clement	199¼	3/2	31.10.11½	9.5½
Pace, Benjamin	263	7/3	95.6.9	1.8.8
Pollard, Richard	389	8/4	162.1.8	2.8.7½
Prince, Francis	113	7/10	44.5.2	13.4
Pendleton, Benjamin	450	"	176.5.0	2.12.11
Pynes, Benjamin	164	6/3	51.5.0	15.4½
Pynes, Benjamin jr.	100	"	31.5.0	9.5
Pynes, Robert	136	"	42.10.0	12.9
Pemberton, John	286	"	89.7.6	1.6.11½
Pollard, Robert	6	24/10	7.9.0	2.2¾
Price, Robert	630	6/3	196.17.6	2.19.1
Pigg, Rachel	100	14/6	78.6.0	1.3.6
Pigg, John est.	216	14/6	156.12.0	2.7.0
do.	180	7/3	65.5.0	19.7
Pollard, William	95	7/3	34.8.9	10.5
Peirce, Philip	100	3/2	15.16.8	4.9
Pierce, Thomas est.	87	4/2	18.2.6	5.5¼
Price, Andrew	314	6/	94.4.0	1.8.3

[page 12, 1794] Persons names owning lands	quantity of land	rate per acre	Amount of Value	Tax at 1½ percent
Robertson, Rachel est.	155	12/6	96.17.6	1.9.6
do.	260	7/3	94.5.0	1.8.5
Roane, Thomas	2033	18/8	1897.9.4	28.8.3
do. H. Carlton's	200	6/3	63.10.0	18.9
Roane, William	1585½	18/1½	1436.17.2	21.11.1
Row, Hansford & Wilson	390	6/3	121.17.6	1.16.5
Row, Thomas G. (orphan)	555	7/3	201.3.9	3.0.4
Row, Elizabeth	665	20/9	689.18.9	10.7.0
Row, Francis (orphan)	612½	4/8	142.16.0	2.2.10
Read, Robert	14	5/3	3.13.6	1.1
Row, Richard est.	550	8/4	229.3.4	3.8.9
Roane, Spencer	1600	24/10	1926.13.4	28.18.0
Richeson, Elias	86	4/2	17.18.4	5.5
Row, William & Moses	100	6/3	31.5.0	9.5
Richards, John	521½	4/8	124.18.--	1.17.6
Richeson, James	180	4/2	37.10.0	11.3
Richeson, William	181	"	37.14.2	11.4
Richeson, John est.	101½	"	21.2.11	6.5
Roane, Major	687½	3/8	128.18.1½	1.18.8
Raines, Giles	60	3/2	9.10.0	2.11
Robinson, Benjamin est.	1300	8/4	541.13.4	8.2.6
Roane, Charles	200	14/6	145.0.0	2.3.6
do. dragon Swamp	70	17/	59.10.0	17.11
Robbins, William	40	6/3	12.10.0	3.9
Roy, Beverly	700	8/4	291.13.4	4.7.6
Ross, John (Ben Minor to pay)	100	5/3	26.5.0	7.11
Richards, George	21	17/	17.17.0	5.4¼
Richeson, W[m.] & R. Shepherd	80	10/5	41.13.4	12.6
Segar, Richard	406	7/3	147.3.6	2.4.2
Satterwhite, George	164	6/3	51.5.0	15.1
Satterwhite, William	200	5/7½	56.5.0	16.10½
Spencer, Edward	245½	8/4	96.5.10	1.8.11
do. (S. Major)	582	7/3	210.19.6	3.3.3½
Schools, John	83½	7/10	32.14.1	9.9½
Seayres, Frankey	338	9/4	157.14.8	2.7.2
Schools, Gabriel	169	6/3	52.16.3	15.11
Skelton, William	362	8/2½	148.11.5	2.4.7
Smith, John (D)	190	7/6	71.5.0	1.1.4
Starling, Jane	360	7/10	141.0.0	2.2.4
Starling, Rodderick	213	8/2	86.19.6	1.6.2
Skelton, Thomas	294	8/4	122.10.0	1.16.9
Scott, Benjamin	200	9/4	93.6.8	1.8.0
Sanders, George	200	7/3	72.10.0	1.1.9
Shepherd, William	140	9/4	65.6.8	19.8

[page 13, 1794] Persons names owning lands	quantity of land	rate per acre	Amount of Value	Tax at 1½ percent
	[65]			
Semple, John W.	574	15/	430.10.0	6.9.1
Smith, Molley	30	4/2	6.5.0	1.11
Smith, John (L.H.)	100	5/3	26.5.0	7.11
Smith, Lewis	96	7/6	36.0.0	10.9¾
Swinton, George	750	13/6	506.5.0	7.11.11
Stone, Sarah	300	7/3	108.15.0	1.12.8
Stone, Daniel	52	3/2	8.4.8	2.6
Smith, Larkin	1254¼	31/1	1949.6.3½	29.4.10
Smith, Henry	400	6/3	130.--.--	1.18.0
Smith, William	193	7/10	20.15.2	6.3½
Smith, James	80	3/2	12.13.4	3.10
Smith, James Jun[r.]	101	7/10	39.11.2	11.10½
Stevens, George est.	430	7/10	168.8.4	2.10.6½
Stevens, Thomas est.	609½	"	238.14.5	3.11.8
Shackelford, John (taylor)	214	7/3	77.11.6	1.3.3½
Starke, Richard est.	350	5/8	99.3.4	1.9.9
Stone, Robert est.	200	4/2	41.13.4	12.6
Stone, Job	100	"	20.16.8	6.3
Stone, John est.	357	6/3	93.14.3	1.18.2
Smith, Robert	421	10/5	219.5.5	3.5.10
Smith, Samuel	110	"	57.5.10	17.2¼
Simpkins, Nimrod	60	3/2	9.10.0	2.11
Sears, Philip	83	4/2	17.5.10	5.3
Spencer, Thomas	300	10/5	156.5.0	2.6.11
do.	225	4/2	53.2.6	15.11
Shackelford, W[m.] est.	700	14/6	527.10.0	7.18.6
Seward, Benjamin	115	3/2	18.4.2	5.6
Stedman, Christ[r.] Sen[r.]	191	5/3	50.2.9	15.1
Smith, Thomas (orphan)	485	14/6	351.12.6	5.5.5
Saddler, John	150	6/3	46.17.6	14.6
Shackelford, Alex[r.]	60	4/2	12.10.0	3.9
Stedman, Christ[r.] jr.	260	5/3	65.5.0	1.0.6
Shackelford, John (R)	482	8/4	200.16.8	3.0.3
Shackelford, Lyne	351	6/3	109.13.9	1.12.10¾
Shackelford, Lyne jr.	50	"	15.12.6	4.8
Shackelford, John (Mac)	283	6/2	87.5.2	1.6.2½
Scott, Anderson	330	16/7	273.12.6	4.2.2
do. of Cha[s.] Williams	214	11/2	44.14.8	13.4½
Shepherd, John	190	3/2	30.1.8	9.3
Seward, Lucy & Eliza. est.	110	4/2	22.18.4	6.10
Semple, Robert B.	154	7/10	60.6.4	18.1
Stone, William	74¼	3/2	11.15.3½	3.6½
Seward, Edward	81½	5/3	21.6.6¾	6.4¾
Sthreshley, William	155½	6/3	48.11.10½	14.7
Sears, Thomas	123	6/7	40.9.9	12.2

[page 14, 1794] Persons names owning lands	quantity of land	rate per acre	Amount of Value	Tax at 1½ percent
Trice, William	140	7/3	50.15.0	15.3
Taylor, James	50	6/3	15.12.6	4.9
Taylor, Edmund	294	8/14	122.10.0	1.16.9
Temple, Joseph	918	10/5	478.2.6	7.3.6
Tunstall, Molley	250	"	130.4.2	1.19.--¾
Tunstall, Rich[d.] jr. est.	1097	7/3	397.13.3	5.19.3
Tunstall, John	200	18/8	186.13.4	2.16.0
Tignor, William	130	7/10	50.18.4	15.4½
Tureman, Benj[a.]	70	3/2	11.1.8	3.4
Tureman, George	50	"	7.18.4	2.4½
Taliaferro, William	1000	14/6	725.0.0	10.17.6
Townley, Robert (Ed. Wms. to pay)	200	6/3	62.10.0	18.9
do. Anderson's	117	"	84.16.6	1.5.5
Taliaferro, Philip	990	8/4	412.10.0	6.3.9
do. D. Cook	374½	12/6	234.7.6	3.10.4
Trice, Edward	206	5/3	54.2.6	16.3
Thruston, William	140	4/3	29.15.0	8.11
Taliaferro, Richard est.	300	5/3	78.15.0	1.3.8
Thruston, Batcheld[r.]	200	3/2	31.13.4	9.6
Turner, Benjamin	36	4/2	7.10.0	2.3
Temple, Humphry	178	31/3	278.2.6	4.3.5¼
do. of W. Tunstall	100	15/	75.0.0	1.2.6
Tunstall, William	438	21/	459.18.0	6.18.0
Tunstall, Richard (Bestl[d.])	269½	8/4	112.15.10	1.13.9
Townley, Ann	79	4/2	16.9.2	5.0
Turner, Henry	100	"	20.16.8	6.3
Vass, Thomas	250	5/3	65.12.6	19.9
Wyatt, Henry	200	7/3	72.10.0	1.1.9
White, Henry	100	8/4	41.13.4	12.6
Willmore, Thomas	150	10/5	78.2.6	1.3.6
do. D. Farthing	19	7/10	7.8.10	2.2½
Wright, James	124½	5/3	32.13.8	9.10
Wyatt, Joseph	68	8/4	25.0.0	7.6
Walden, John	105	12/6	65.12.6	19.9
Wilson, Isaac	200	6/3	62.10.0	18.9
Wilson, Benjamin est.	200	7/3	72.10.0	1.1.9
Wiltshire, Joseph	74	"	26.16.6	8.--
Wright, Isaac	183	6/3	57.3.9	17.2
Wyatt, John	100	7/10	39.3.4	11.3
Watkins, William	37	4/2	7.14.2	2.4
Watkins, Joseph	156	6/7	51.7.0	15.5
Walker, Henry est.	150	5/3	39.7.6	11.10
Ware, John est.	562	7/3	203.14.6	3.1.2
Walker, Humphry	820	33/2	1355.14.2	20.7.10
Wright, William	175	5/3	45.18.9	13.10
Watts, Edward	250	7/3	90.12.6	1.7.3
do. W. Watts	113	5/	28.5.0	8.5½

[page 15, 1794] Persons names owning lands	quantity of land	rate per acre	Amount of Value	Tax at 1½ percent
	[66]			
Watts, John	293	7/10	114.15.2	1.14.6
do. Pemberton's	45	6/3	14.1.3	4.2½
Watts, Kauffman	300	5/3	78.15.0	1.3.8
do. Burch's est.	157	5/9	45.2.9	13.6¼
Watts, James	350	4/2	72.18.4	1.1.11
do. W. Watts est.	60	15/	45.0.0	13.6
Williams, Howard	283	4/2	58.19.2	17.9
do. new entry	43	17/	36.11.--	10.11½
Wyatt, Thomas	206	7/10	81.2.0	1.4.4½
Wyatt, John (blind)	103	6/3	32.3.9	9.8
Wyatt, William	29¾	7/3	10.15.8	3.8
Williams, Howard est.	300	6/3	93.15.0	1.8.1
Williams, Charles	336	4/2	70.0.0	1.1.--
Walton, James	80	"	16.3.4	5.--
Walton, Mary	60	"	12.10.0	3.9
Willis, Joel	94	7/10	35.5.0	10.7
Walton, Elizabeth	60	3/2	9.10.0	2.11
Walton, John	176	5/3	46.4.0	13.11
Walton, William est.	66	4/2	13.15.0	4.2
Walton, Thomas est.	66	"	"	4.2
Ware, John	75	5/3	19.13.9	5.11
Ware, Arther estate	83	4/2	17.5.10	5.3
Waring, Robert P.	542	10/9	291.6.6	4.7.3¾
Walden, Richard	180	10/5	93.15.0	1.8.1½
Walden, Lewis	150	3/2	23.15.0	7.3
do. T. Dudley	84½	6/3	28.2.3½	8.5
Wright, Edward	60½	6/8	20.3.4	6.3¼
Wright, James	124	"	41.6.8	12.4¾
Ware, Robert S.	89½	11/9	52.13.--	15.10
Wyatt, Richard	175	12/6	109.7.6	1.12.9¾
Ware, Robert jr. est.	100	4/2	20.16.8	6.3
Williams, Eliz[a.]	16½	3/2	2.12.9	9½
White, James est.	200	6/3	62.10.0	18.9
Watkins, Eliz[a.]	100	3/2	15.16.8	4.9
Warren, Catharine	175	"	27.14.2	8.4
Ware, Robert (B.P.)	112	"	17.14.8	5.4
Wedderburn, Lydia	350	6/3	109.7.6	1.12.10
Whitting, Beverly est.	2447¾	7/10	866.18.9½	13.0.0
Webbley, John	173	5/3	45.8.3	13.8
do. F. Collier	268½	4/2	55.18.9	16.9¼
Ware, Robert ~~Robert~~ jr.	100	8/4	41.13.4	12.6
Ware, William	"	"	"	12.6
Walden, Edward est.	373	5/3	97.18.3	1.9.5
Waller, Edward est.	133½	3/2	21.2.9	6.5

[page 16, 1794] Persons names owning lands	quantity of land	rate per acre	Amount of Value	Tax at 1½ percent
Waller, Robert	113	3/7	20.5.11	6.1
Wyatt, John (taylor)	30	5/3	7.17.6	2.5
Ware, Nicholas	100	3/2	15.16.8	4.9
Wilmore, Henry	70	7/6	26.5.0	7.10½
Williamson, Abner	100	3/2	15.16.8	4.9
Walden, Samuel	80	7/10	36.6.8	9.4½
Walden, John Sen$^{r.}$	100	5/3	26.5.--	7.10½
Ware, John (son of Kit)	296	7/3	107.3.0	1.12.1
Young, Henry	640	18/8	597.6.8	8.19.3
				£136[5].12.0
				~~£227.10.10~~
[arithmetic omitted]				~~£37.10.6?~~

Errors Excepted by
William Fleet and Wm. Courtney, Commrs. tax
£227.12 @ 5/

List of the Land within the County of King & Queen with
the Tax thereon at one and a half percent for the year 179 five

[page 1, 1795] Persons owning lands	Quantity of land	Price per acre	Tot. Amt. Value Land	Tax on land 1½ percent
	[67]			
Atkins, Joseph	66	4/2	13.15.--	4.1½
Alexander, Benj[a.]	202	9/4	94.5.4	1.8.4
do. James Halbert	124	6/2	38.15.--	11.7½
Acre, Seaton	52	9/4	24.5.4	7.3½
Alexander, Elisha	102	7/3	36.12.3	11.--
do. William Gatewood	105	10/2	54.13.9	16.8
Anderson, Churchill Est.	636	7/3	230.11.--	3.9.2
Anderson, Pauling	498	14/6	361.1.--	5.9.4
Atkins, John	135	4/6	30.7.6	9.1½
Abbott, Jacob	112	7/10	43.17.4	13.2
Anderson, Richard Est.	460	5/3	120.15.--	1.16.3
Atkins, Lewis	60	8/4	25.--.--	7.6
Anderson, Francis	458	10/9	246.3.6	3.13.10½
Bray, James	234	7/10	91.13.--	1.7.6
Brown, Henry jr.	100	12/	60.--.--	18.--
Beverley, Robert	2474	10/5	1288.8.10	19.6.7
Brown, Henry	760½	7/4½	280.8.8¼	4.4.1½
Baylor, Gregory Est.	720	14/6	522.--.--	7.16.7
Bland, John & Lucy	166	8/4	69.3.4	1.0.9
Bates, James [page torn]	358	11/	149.3.4	2.4.9
do.	42	4/2	8.15.--	2.7½
[Bar]ton, John Est.	125	"	26.0.10	7.10
[Ba]nks, William Est.	365	"	76.0.10	1.2.9¾
[Br]ooking, Frances	930	10/5	484.7.6	7.5.4
Baylor, John Est.	380	14/3	270.15.--	4.1.2½
Boughton, Thomas (Essex)	130	9/4	60.13.4	18.3
Boughton, John	200	8/4	83.6.8	1.5.--
Boughton, Henry (Essex)	88	6/3	27.10.--	8.3
Broach, John	45	6/3	14.1.3	4.3
Burton, Thomas Est.	170	5/3	44.12.6	13.5
Bohannon, Ann	197	4/6	44.6.6	13.3½
Brown, William	75	7/10	29.7.6	8.10
Bagby, John Est.	330	7/3	119.12.6	1.15.10½
Bagby, Richard	260	"	94.5.--	1.8.3½
Bagby, Thomas	"	"	"	1.8.3½
Brooke, Richard	1539¾	29/-	2232.12.9	33.9.10
Brumley, Robert	225	5/3	59.1.3	17.9
Brumley, John	60	7/10	23.10.--	7.--½
Bird, George B.	60	6/3	18.5.--	5.7½
Broach, William	20	7/10	7.16.8	2.4
Bird, William	532	7/3	197.17.--	2.18.--¼
do. Dragon Swamp	88½	17/	70.4.6	1.1.--
Brown, John	50	7/4½	18.8.9	0.5.6½
Bird, Philemon	1157½	6/3	361.14.4½	5.8.6
[Bird], Mary	619	"	193.8.9	2.18.1
[Brett], John Est.	446	18/	401.8.--	6.0.5
[Burch, James]	70	7/3	25.7.6	7.8

[page 2, 1795] Persons owning lands	Quantity of land	Price per acre	Tot. Amt. Value Land	Tax on land 1½ percent
Burch, Vincent	100	4/2	20.16.8	6.3
Bird, Anthony A.	275	3/2	43.10.10	13.1
Byne, John Est.	336	4/2	70.0.0	1.1.--
do. Dragon Swamp	2¼	17/	1.18.3	6¾
Barbara Bird	266 2/3	24/10	331.2.2½	4.6
Bird, Robert	533 1/4	24/10	662.4.5½	9.12.[6]
do. Guy Smith	189½	3/2	30.0.1	9.--
Bourn, Richard Est.	150	"	23.15.0	7.2
Boyd, John	115	18/8	107.6.8	1.12.3
do. Sones's	382	24/10	474.6.4	7.2.4
Bray, Richard Est.	93	7/10	36.8.6	10.11
Bird, John Est.	100	3/2	15.16.8	4.9
Bowden, William	69	6/6	22.2.9	6.8
Bew, William	117	3/2	18.10.6	5.7
Boyd, Spencer Est.	1428	10/5	770.15.0	11.11.2
Berkeley, Edmond	762	5/3	200.0.6	3.0.0
Bland, John	60	12/6	37.10.0	11.3
Bohannan, William	130	5/3	34.2.6	10.3
Bullman, Ann	100	"	26.5.0	7.11
Briggs, John (Wm. Finney to pay)	170	4/2	35.8.4	10.8
Belote, Laban	384½	"	80.2.1	1.4.--
Bland, William Senr.	225	3/8¼	41.9.8¼	12.6
Bland, Ralph	146	5/3	38.6.6	11.6
Bowden, William jr.	100	4/2	20.16.8	6.3
do. of Sykes & Dudley's	34	3/2	5.7.8	1.[8]
Bowden, John [page torn]	100	4/2	20.16.8	6.[3]
Bland, William Est.	250	"	52.1.8	15.[8]
Bland, Thomas	412	3/2	75.4.8	1.2.[6¾]
Bowden, George	236	5/3	61.19.--	18.[7]
Burch, William	45	3/2	7.2.6	2.1½
Brown, Thomas Est.	454	12/6	283.15.0	4.5.1
Banks, James	98	7/3	35.10.6	10.7¾
Bristow, Barthow.	33½	3/2	5.6.1	1.7
Beard, David	450	9/4	210.--.--	3.3.--
Bristow, George	100	3/2	15.16.8	4.9
Broach, James & Wm. Mansfield	200	16/7	165.16.8	2.9.9
Bates, ~~James~~ William	81	7/9½	31.10.1	9.5¼
Banks, Andrew	125	12/6	78.2.6	1.3.5
Brightwell, John Est.	70	4/2	14.11.8	4.4½
Crafton, Thomas	145	9/4	67.13.4	1.0.3½
Crafton, James	59	"	27.6.0	8.9½
Crafton, John	171	9/4	81.16.8	1.4.[6½]
Clayton, James	100	9/11	49.11.8	14.10¼
Cook, Mary	200	8/4	83.6.8	1.5.0
~~Carter~~ Chick, Richard Est.	491	7/3	177.19.9	2.13.1
Chapman, George Est.	200	7/10	78.6.8	1.3.6
do. of Wm. Hoskins	39	10/5	20.6.3	[6.1]
Campbell, William	1014	7/3	367.11.6	5.[10.1½]

[page 3, 1795] Persons owning lands	Quantity of land	Price per acre	Tot. Amt. Value Land	Tax on land 1½ percent
	[68]			
Crane, John	136	6/3	42.--.--	12.7
Cleverius, Benjamin	419	20/9	434.14.3	6.10.5
Carlton, Henry	280	7/10	109.13.4	1.12.10
do Jn°. Baylor's Est.	257	14/6	186.6.6	2.15.10¾
Clayton, Thomas Est.	275	7/3	99.13.9	1.9.11
Campbell, Whitacar	318	7/10	124.11.-	1.17.6
Cleveley, Thomas	200	"	76.6.8	1.3.6
Crow, Nathaniel Est.	200	6/3	62.10.--	18.9
Crane, George Est.	30	7/3	10.7.6	3.4
Carlton, Joel	53½	6/3	16.14.5	5.1
Cooper, Ann	60	3/2	9.10.--	2.11
Carlton, Thomas (Swamp)	200	7/10	78.6.8	1.3.6
Carlton, Noah	100	"	39.3.4	11.9
Carlton, John (Schoolm^r.)	100	6/3	31.5.--	9.5
Campbell, Sarah	296	12/6	185.--.--	2.15.6
Carlton, Christopher Senr.	37½	6/3	11.14.5	3.7
Carlton, Richard Est.	139	7/	48.13.--	14.7
Cothern, James	36½	3/2	5.15.7	1.8¾
Carlton, William (Shoe^r.)	309¾	11/6	178.1.2½	2.13.5
Carlton, Robert Est.	148	5/	37.--.--	11.1
Carlton, Richard	250	7/3	90.12.6	1.7.3
Carlton, Christ^r. jr.	100		36.5.--	10.4
Cooper, Henry	50	4/2	10.8.4	3.2
Carlton, Thos. (Taylor)	100	6/3	31.5.--	9.[5]
Cardwell, John Est.	150	4/2	31.5.--	9.[5]
Cardwell, John	"	"	"	9.5
Cardwell, William	77	"	15.11.6	4.7½
Cardwell, Thomas	110	"	22.18.4	6.11
Cooke, John Est.	300	4/2	62.10.--	18.9
Collins, Thomas	329½	7/	115.6.6	1.14.7
do. Palmers	350	7/3	126.17.6	1.18.[1]
Carlton, John j^r.	235	4/2	48.19.2	14.9
Campbell, William	238	3/2	37.13.8	11.4
Collier, Charles	200	3/2	31.13.4	9.6
Curtis, Ann	414	5/3	108.13.6	1.12.7
Collier, John	100	4/2	20.16.8	6.3
Corbin, John T Est.	2390	11/1¾	1332.11.4	19.19.9½
do. new dragon bridge	125	12/8	78.2.6	1.3.5
Crouch, James	130	3/8	20.11.8	6.3
Chapman, Phil	200	7/10	78.6.8	1.3.6
Crittenden, Thomas	126	13/6	85.1.0	1.5.6
do Dragon Swamp	36	17/	30.12.--	9.2
Collins, Joyeux Est.	140	10/5	72.18.4	1.1.10
Crittenden, Zach^h.	34 1/3	14/6	24.17.10	7.6
Cary, Wilson Est.	1820	16/7	1509.1.8	22.12.9
Collier, John (Cobler)	150	5/3	39.7.6	11.10
Campbell, James	130	5/9¼	37.10.--	11.3
Crittenden, Richard Est.	178	5/3	46.14.6	14.1
Corr, Avarilla	79	"	20.14.9	6.2½

[page 4, 1795] Persons owning lands	Quantity of land	Price per acre	Tot. Amt. Value Land	Tax on land 1½ percent
Collier, Catharine	750	5/3	196.17.6	2.19.[1]
Clegg, Isaiah	241	4/2	50.4.2	15.[0½]
Cook, Dawson	282	3/2	44.13.--	13.6
Curry, Ann	100	4/2	20.16.8	6.3
Courtney, William	200	7/10	78.6.8	1.3.6
Cooke, Thomas	240	3/2	38.0.0	11.5
Cook, Thomas jr.	96	"	15.0.4	4.6[½]
Carlton, Humph^y.	175	7/	61.5.--	18.4
Carlton, Thos. Est.	235	6/3	73.8.9	1.2.1
Carlton, Beverley Est.	160	4/2	33.6.8	10.1
Corr, John jr.	94	7/3	34.1.6	10.[2]
Campbell, John	400	12/6	250.--.--	3.15.--
Curry, James	70	4/2	18.16.--	4.7
Corr, John Senr.	2[1]3	3/2	33.15.6	10.1½
do. of Jno. Corr jr.	90	7/3	32.12.6	9.9
Cook, Henry	49¼	10/5	25.10.5	7.8
Crittenden, Francis (river)	105 2/3	14/6	76.12.2	1.3.--
Clarke, John	144	5/	36.--.--	10.9½
Cannady, William	100	6/3	31.5.--	9.5
Corr, Thomas R.	157½	5/3	41.6.10¼	12.4¼
Cook, William	65	5/5	17.12.1	5.3¼
Cook, James	65	8/9	28.8.9	8.6½
Carter, Jesse	525	10/	2[4]2.10.--	3.18.9
Dew, William Est.	935	14/6	677.17.6	10.3.5
Dew, Thomas	535	12/6	334.7.6	5.--.3¾
Dowling, William Est.	264	8/4	110.--.--	1.13.--
Dix, Gabriel	338	6/3	105.12.6	1.11.8
Deshazo, William	82	4/2	17.1.8	5.1½
Durham, Joseph	155	4/3	32.5.5	9.8.¾
Deshazo, Peter Est.	192	7/4	70.8.--	1.1.1½
Deshazo, Larkin	71	7/2	25.8.10	7.7¾
Dickie, James Est.	512	8/4	213.6.8	3.4.--
Dunbar, David	366	"	152.10.--	2.5.9
Dunn, Richard	150	4/2	31.5.--	9.4
Dalley, John Est.	200	3/2	31.13.4	9.6
Dobbins, Charles Est.	147	5/3	38.11.9	11.7
Dean, Benjamin	50	"	13.2.6	4.--
Dillard, William jr. Est.	100	3/2	15.16.8	4.9
Dunn, Agrippia	140	5/3	36.15.--	11.1
Dudley, Peter Est.	530	7/3¼	186.18.4	2.16.1
Didlake, Mary	311	6/9	105.2.7½	1.11.4½
do. W^m. Didlake	278	8/4	115.16.8	1.14.9
Durham, Robert Est.	50	"	10.8.4	3.2
Didlake, Margret	65	4/2	13.10.10	4.1
Dunn, Thomas	50½	6/3	15.15.7½	4.9
Dillard, William Senr.	276	12/6	172.10.--	2.11.9
Durham, George	50	4/2	10.8.4	3.2

[page 5, 1795] Persons owning lands	Quantity of land	Price per acre	Tot. Amt. Value Land	Tax on land 1½ percent
	[69]			
Durham, Thomas Est.	85	3/2	13.9.2	[4].1
Dumagin, Richard Est.	172	5/5	46.11.8	14.--
Digges, Frances Est.	175	5/3	45.18.9	13.10
Didlake, George Est.	114	10/5	59.7.6	17.10
Dungee, John	110	3/2	17.8.4	5.3
Dudley, William jr.	290	14/6	210.5.--	3.3.1
do. L. Wedderburn	315½	6/3	98.11.10½	1.9.6¾
Damm, John Est.	55	6/3	17.3.9	5.2
Dudley, William	180	7/10	70.10.--	1.1.2
Damm, William	25	4/2	5.4.2	1.6½
Douglass, John	239	7/	83.13.--	1.5.1
Didlake, John	1200	7/3	435.--.--	6.10.6
Dudley, Ann	141	7/3	51.2.3	15.4
Dudley, Banks	230	3/2	36.8.4	10.11
Didlake, William	26¼	4/2	7.9.4½	2.2¾
Downey, Michael	50	10/5	26.0.10	7.9¾
Didlake, Royston	206	3/6½	36.7.4	11.1
Dillard, Thomas	49	15/	36.15.--	11.--
Dillard, William jr.	61½	4/2	18.12.11	5.7
do. Thos. Dillard	300	15/	225.--.--	3.7.6¼
do. of Do.	56	10/4¾	31.3.--	9.4
Dudley, Thomas	267½	6/3	81.17.8½	1.4.7
Dillard, Nicholas	75	4/2	15.12.6	4.[9]
Dillard, Benja. Est.	148	5/3	48.17.0	14.[7¾]
Drummond, John	150	6/3	46.17.6	14.[6]
Dixon, Michael	414¾	15/5	320.--.--	4.16.[0]
Dabney, Benjamin	400	14/6	290.--.--	4.7.[0]
of. Phil Taliaferro	72	8/4	30.--.--	10.[ ]
Davis, Stage	311	6/9	105.2.7½	1.11.[4½]
do. of Thos. Foster	50	4/2	10.8.4	3.[ ]
Dally, George	174¼	3/2	27.11.9½	8[¾]
Dudley, Henry F.	50	5/3	13.2.6	3.[ ]
Eubank, John	469	10/4	242.6.4	3.12.9
Eubank, Thomas	300	14/6	217.10.--	3.5.3
Eubank, Henry	171	5/3	44.17.9	13.6
Edwards, Thomas Est.	66	4/2	13.15.--	4.2
Eubank, William Est.	28¾	5/3	7.11.--	2.4
Eubank, Richard Senr.	196	7/	68.12.--	1.0.7
Edmondson, William	253	10/5	131.15.5	1.19.6½
Eubank, Thomas (St. S.)	100	5/9	28.15.--	8.7½
Eubank, Richard Est.	227	4/2	47.5.10	14.3
Eubank, Richard jr.	11[2]¼	7/	39.5.7½	11.9¼
Evans, Ambrose	234½	7/10	91.13.--	1.7.[ ]
Fogg, Frederick	298	8/4	124.3.4	1.17.3
Fleet, Baylor	862	12/6	538.15.8	8.1.7½
Fauntleroy, Samuel G.	2069	20/	2069.--.--	31.--.8½
Fleet, John	260	6/3	81.5.0	1.6.4½
Falkner, Thomas	220	"	68.15.--	1.--.6¼
Fogg, Thomas Est.	200	"	62.10.--	18.9

[page 6, 1795] Persons owning lands	Quantity of land	Price per acre	Tot. Amt. Value Land	Tax on land 1½ percent
Fogg, James	120	6/3	37.10.0	11.3
Frazer, William Est.	45	20/9	46.13.9	14.1
Fleet, William	352	"	365.4.0	5.9.6[½]
Fisher, James Est.	110	3/2	17.18.4	5.3
Foster, Thomas	87¾	4/2	18.2.6	5.5¼
Faulkner, Mary	333	6/3	104.1.4	1.11.3
Fauntleroy, Thomas	486	10/	243.--.--	3.12.10¾
do. of H. Todd	500	18/	460.--.--	6.18.--
do. William Bowden	183	7/	64.1.--	19.2½
Farrenholtz, David	151¼	6/6	49.1.6	14.8½
Faulkner, Benjamin	100	4/2	20.16.8	6.3
Grafton, Sally & Ann	132	9/4	61.12.0	18.6
Grafton, James	111	6/3	34.13.9	10.5
Gale, John	615	7/5½	229.13.9	3.8.8½
Goleman, Thomas (Essex)	948½	9/-	426.16.6	6.8.--
Garnett, Rice	297	7/3	107.13.7	1.12.4
Gatewood, Chaney	829	10/5	437.17.11	6.10.6
do. Gardners	100	7/3	36.5.--	10.11
do. Theodk. Noel	362½	14/6	262.16.3	3.18.10
do. from Wm. Harwood	225	4/2	46.17.6	14.1
[Ga]rnett, Joshua Est.	322	8/4	134.3.4	2.0.3
[Gr]aves, Edward Est.	200	6/3	62.10.0	18.9
[Ga]tewood, Joseph	445	10/5	231.15.5	3.9.7
[Ga]le, Mathew	323	11/5	184.7.7	2.15.4
[Ga]tewood, John	160	8/4	66.13.4	1.--.--
[Gar]nett, Reuben	1131¾	8/10	499.17.1½	7.9.11¼
[Gw]athmey, Temple	600	35/3	1057.10.--	15.17.3
[Ga]rlick, Samuel	454	24/10	563.14.4	8.9.2
[Ga]rlick, John	893	29/	1294.17.--	19.18.5
[Gr]iffith, Joseph	50	6/3	15.12.6	4.9
[Gr]esham, Samuel	400	7/3	145.--.--	2.3.6
[Gu]thrie, William	40¾	"	14.15.5¼	4.5
~~Gresham, Samuel~~	~~400~~	~~7/3~~	~~145.--.--~~	~~2.3.6~~
Garrett, Robert	100	4/2	20.16.8	6.3
Gaines, Francis	356	14/6	258.2.0	3.17.5
Gaines, Harry Est.	1517	20/4	1542.5.8	23.2.8
Gresham, Thomas	339¼	6/3	106.0.4	1.11.10
Gresham, Philemon	200	"	62.10.--	18.9
Gresham, John D	200	7/10	78.6.8	1.3.6
Gresham, William	100	4/2	20.16.8	6.3
Gardner, Eliza.	100	6/3	31.5.0	9.5
Gibson, Richard	156½	3/2	24.16.7	7.4
Gibson, Banks	56½	"	8.18.[11]	2.7
Gibson, John Est.	219¾	"	34.15.11	10.6
Griffith, Milley	50	6/3	15.12.6	4.9
Gresham, Machem	100	5/3	26.5.0	7.10½
Gresham, Ambrose	80	"	21.--.--	6.3½
do. new entry	30	17/	25.1.--	7.6

[page 7, 1795] Persons owning lands	Quantity of land	Price per acre	Tot. Amt. Value Land	Tax on land 1½ percent
	[70]			
Gresham, John jr.	80	5/3	21.--.--	6.3½
Graves, Thomas	50½	7/3	18.6.1½	5.5½
Griffin, William Est.	859	14/6	622.15.6	9.6.10
Garlick, Camm Est.	1100	6/3	343.15.--	5.3.2
Garrett, Richard	50	3/2	7.8.4	2.4
Garrett, James	230	4/2	47.18.4	14.4½
Garrett, William jr.	100	"	20.16.8	6.3
Gardner, Anthony	638	11/	350.11.8	5.5.3
do. dragon swamp	67½	17/	57.7.6	17.2½
Gresham, Lumpkin	315	7/3	114.3.9	1.13.3
Garrett, Robert	200	7/	70.--.--	1.1.--
Gresham, William	329½	8/4	137.5.10	2.1.2¼
Gaines, Robert Est.	537¾	20/9	558.8.7¾	8.7.6
do. Ann Curtis	50	[5/3]	13.2.6	3.11
Gatewood, William (*Tuck^o.*)	220	[3/2]	34.16.8	10.6
Gatewood, Gabriel	78	10/5	40.12.6	12.2¼
Gatewood, William	237	"	123.8.9	1.17.3½
Guthrie, James	60	12/6	37.10.--	11.3
Guthrie, Richard Est.	"	"	"	11.3
Guthrie, Richard	162	3/2	25.13.--	7.8½
Glaspe, James	210	5/3	55.2.6	16.7
Groom, Mary	173	3/2	27.17.10	8.5
Garrett, George	88½	5/3	23.4.7½	6.11½
Goldman, Martin	140	4/2	29.3.4	8.9
Groom, Zach^y. Est.	187	3/2	29.12.2	8.10½
Gulley, Philip Est.	50	"	7.18.4	2.4
Garrett, William (Shoe)	225	3/4¾	37.19.4	11.4½
Gramshill, Henry	25	3/2	3.19.2	1.2¼
Garrett, Ann Watts	112	5/	28.--.--	8.4¾
Garrett, Richard	100	4/2	20.16.8	6.3
Hill, William	1191	14/6	928.9.6	13.18.7
Hitchcock, Thomas	140	4/2	29.3.4	8.9
Hoskins, Samuel	345	6/3	107.16.3	1.12.3
Hutcherson, Charles	547	7/1	193.14.7	2.18.1½
Hoskins, William	360	7/10	143.7.--	2.3.--
Heskew, John	61	5/3	16.0.3	4.10
Heskew, John jr.	50	6/3	15.12.6	4.8
Hill, Robert	1515¼	8/2	618.14.6	9.5.7¼
Hill, Edward	1200	18/8	1120.--.--	16.16.--
Hoomes, Benjamin	447	12/6	2[7]9.8.4	4.3.9¾
do. of Martha Cary	462	4/4	96.5.--	1.8.11
Hutson, William Est.	112	3/2	17.14.8	5.4
Hemmingway, John jr.	267	4/2	55.12.6	16.8¼
Hemmingway, Samuel	"	"	"	16.8¼
Hemming, John Senr.	266	"	55.8.4	16.7½
Hare, William	217	5/3	56.19.3	16.1
Harwood, Christ^r. Est.	294	24/10	365.1.--	5.9.6
Harwood, John Senr.	25	5/3	4.7.6	1.3½
Harwood, William Est.	240	30/	360.--.--	5.8.--
Hill, Thomas	300	26/11	403.15.--	6.1.2

[page 8, 1795] Persons owning lands	Quantity of land	Price per acre	Tot. Amt. Value Land	Tax on land 1½ percent
Hart, James	150	3/2	23.15.--	7.2
Holderby, John	100	4/2	20.16.8	6.3
Hart, Anthony	190	5/3	49.17.6	15.--
do. of Sundry Persons	259½	3/2	41.1.9	12.4
Hart, Gregory	200	11/	31.3.4	9.6
Hart, William	250	3/3½	41.2.11	12.4
Harwood, John jr.	109	10/5	56.15.5	17.--
Hunt, William Est.	730	6/3	228.2.6	3.8.6
Henry, Samuel H.	1900	14/6	1377.10.0	20.13.3
Halyard, William	190	5/3	49.17.6	15.--
Hoskins, John	767	10/7	399.9.7	5.19.10
do. Boughtons	100	8/4	41.13.4	12.6
Hoskins, Robert	287	6/	86.2.--	1.5.10
Hart, Alden	127	"	26.9.2	7.11¼
Howerton, Heritage Est.	122¼	20/9	126.16.7¼	1.18.--½
Holt, Richard	123	14/3	87.12.9	1.6.3½
Hutson, William (S.M.)	50	4/2	10.8.4	3.1½
Hutcherson, John	73¼	8/9	32.0.11¼	9.7¼
Jeffries, Thomas	75¾	7/3	27.9.2¼	8.2¾
do. Jno. Harwood Jr.	38¼	10/5	19.15.10¾	5.11
Jones, John Est.	300	8/11	133.15.--	2.--.1½
Jeffries, Edward	70	3/2	11.1.8	3.4
Jones, James	160	14/6	116.--.--	1.14.10
Jones, James Est.	196	10/5	102.1.8	1.10.8
Jones, William Est.	241	15/10	190.15.10	2.17.3
do. L. Smith	35¾	31/1	55.11.2	16.8
Jeffries, Ambrose	337	7/10	124.18.10	1.17.6
Jeffries, Robert	60	"	23.10.0	7.1
Jeffries, Bernard Est.	30	4/2	6.5.--	1.11
Jordan, Henry	88	4/2	18.6.8	5.6
Jordan, Thomas Est.	100	4/2	20.16.8	6.3
Johnson, Thomas	112	3/2	17.14.8	5.4
Jameson, David Est.	50	"	7.18.4	2.5
Jones, Rawleigh	63	31/1	93.18.3	1.9.4
Keeling, James	113¼	7/3	41.0.0	12.4
do. Robt. Hill	23	8/2	9.7.10	2.10
Kemp, John	178	7/3	64.2.2	19.2
Kauffman, John jr.	38	10/5	19.15.10	5.11½
Kauffman, John	471	18/8	439.12.0	6.11.11
do. Geo. Kauffman	583	14/6	422.13.6	6.6.10
Kennedy, Archibald	38¼	4/2	7.19.4	2.4½
do. Hoomes	[230]	7/[3]	[90].1.8	1.7.1
do. " [page torn]	100	10/3	17.--.--	[smear]6
Kennedy, Ann	70¼	4/2	14.11.8	4.6¾
Kennedy, Ann jr.	33¾	"	7.0.6	2.1¼
do.	150	12/6	97.10.--	1.[9]3
Kennedy, Lucy	37½	"	7.16.2	2.4
Kay, Christr.	116	6/3	30.0.9	9.1½
Kidd, Barthw.	136	5/3	35.14.0	10.8
Kidd, Benja.	111	13/6	74.18.2	1.2.5½
do. Crittenden	60	"	40.10.0	12.1¾
do. Dragon Swamp	36	17/	30.[12.0]	9.2

[page 9, 1795] Persons owning lands	Quantity of land	Price per acre	Tot. Amt. Value Land	Tax on land 1½ percent
	[71]			
Kidd, John	370	7/3	134.2.6	2.0.3
do. Lumpkin & Peirce	60	4/2	12.10.--	3.9
do. Tho[s.] Dillard	45	14/6	32.12.6	9.10
Lumpkin, Joyce	213	7/10	85.8.2	1.5.--
Lumpkin, Henry	620	9/4	289.6.8	4.6.10
Lumpkin, John Est.	200	6/3	59.--.--	17.9
Lyne, William	1480	8/4	610.14.2	9.3.3
Lyne, William jr.	108	"	45.--.--	13.6
Lumpkin, William	305	14/6	221.2.6	3.6.5
Lefon, Francis	119	8/4	49.11.8	14.10
Lankford, Thomas	100	4/2	20.16.8	6.3
Lumpkin, Robert (D)	374	8/4	155.16.8	2.6.9
Longest, Caleb	97	7/10	37.19.10	11.6
Longest, Richard	140	"	54.16.8	16.6
Longest, John	100	"	39.3.4	11.9
Lumpkin, Anthony	216	6/3	67.10.--	1.0.4
Lumpkin, Jacob	916	"	286.5.0	4.5.11
do. Southerlands	271	5/3	71.2.9	1.1.4
do. from Milley Coleman	196	10/5	102.1.8	1.10.8
Lewis, Iveson	356	14/6	258.2.0	3.17.4¼
Lumpkin, Richard Est.	76¼	6/	22.17.6	6.10¼
Leigh, Lucy	101	24/10	125.8.2	1.17.7
Lumpkin, Robert jr.	233	5/3	61.3.3	18.4
Leigh, John Est.	199	24/10	247.1.10	3.14.2
Lyne, John	507	6/3	158.8.9	2.7.7
Lambeth, Thomas	100	3/2	15.16.8	4.[9]
Laughlin, James	126¾	"	26.8.2	8.--
Lambeth, Charles Est.	50	"	7.18.4	2.5
Motley, Edwin	815	10/5	428.2.6	6.8.6
McKentosh, William	126	4/2	26.5.--	7.10½
Martin, Thomas C.	680	14/6	493.--.--	7.7.11
do.	134½	7/3	48.15.1½	14.7½
Morgan, William	26	8/4	10.16.8	3.3
Mitchel, Ralph Est.	193	10/5	100.10.5	1.10.1½
Minor, William	149	8/4	62.1.8	18.8
Minor, John	137	"	57.1.8	17.2
Miller, Thomas	527	7/10	206.8.2	3.2.0
Mann, Augustine Est.	400	8/4	166.13.4	2.10.0
Mitchell, Robert	17	20/9	17.12.9	5.4
Mitchell, John	50	6/3	15.12.6	4.9
Mitchell, James Est.	650	13/	422.10.--	6.6.9
Mann, Robert	699	6/3	218.8.9	3.5.6½
McKendrie, Eliz[a.]	90	5/3	23.12.6	7.1
Moore, Lambeth	70	4/2	14.11.8	4.3¼
Morris, William	10	"	2.1.8	.7½
Moore, Benjamin	200	"	41.13.4	12.6
Merideth, Samuel	215	7/10	84.4.2	1.5.3
Moore, John	100	3/2	15.16.8	4.9
Major, Josiah	200	4/2	41.13.4	12.6
Mitchell, John Est.	270	5/3	70.17.6	1.1.4
do. part Rootes	200	9/11	99.3.4	1.9.8¾

[page 10, 1795] Persons owning lands	Quantity of land	Price per acre	Tot. Amt. Value Land	Tax on land 1½ percent
Macon, John Est.	892	16/7	739.12.4	11.1.10
Mansfield, William	75	"	62.3.9	18.7
Merideth, Ralph G.	567	14/6	411.1.6	6.3.5½
Muire, Richard	93	12/6	58.2.6	17.6
Moore, Richard	145	6/3	45.6.3	13.8
McCarty, Joseph Est.	73	3/2	11.11.2	3.6
Metcalf, John S.	265	14/6	196.5.10	2.18.1½
Metcalf, Tho[s.]	2[5]6	"	181.8.8	2.15.2¼
Mann, Mary	100	5/3	26.5.--	7.11
Martin, John	475	9/	312.15.--	3.3.1½
Mann, Joseph (son of Augt[ne.])	72	4/2	15.--.--	4.6
Nunn, Jane	180	7/3	65.5.0	19.7
Newbill, George Est.	500	8/4	208.6.8	3.2.6
Nunn, Thomas	130	7/3	47.2.6	14.1½
Nash, John Est.	100	6/3	31.5.0	9.5
Newcombe, Eliz[a.]	109	3/2	17.5.2	5.2
Newcombe, William	60	"	9.10.--	2.11
Newill, John	100	7/10	39.3.4	11.9
Orvill, John	100	6/3	31.5.--	9.5
Olliver, John	320	5/3	84.--.--	1.5.3
Overstreet, Gabriel	296	4/2	61.13.4	18.6
do. Haynes's	130	5/3	34.2.6	10.2
Oakes, Henry	198½	3/2	34.2.--	10.2¼
Oakes, William	80	4/2	16.13.4	5.--
Owin, Augustine	100	6/3	31.5.--	9.[5]
Pendleton, James	888½	8/7½	383.3.3¾	5.14.11½
do. Henry Wilmore	70	7/6	26.5.--	7.10½
Pitts, David Est.	420	9/4	196.--.--	2.18.10
Pitts, Obadiah	20	10/5	10.8.4	3.2
Phillips, Richard	230	7/3	83.7.6	1.5.1
Pollard, John Est.	235	9/4	109.13.4	1.12.11
do. of L. Smithey	384	7/3	139.4.--	2.1.10
Prewitt, Francis	99	9/4	46.4.--	13.11
Parker, John	264¼	7/	92.9.9	1.7.9
Pendleton, Phil	483	9/2	221.7.6	3.6.5
Perryman, A. Anthony Est.	130	7/3	47.2.6	14.2
Perryman, Phil	230	7/2	82.8.4	1.4.9
Pitts, Benjamin G.	100	5/4	26.13.4	8.--
Pynes, Clement	199¼	3/2	31.10.11½	9.5½
Pace, Benjamin	263	7/3	95.6.9	1.8.8
Pollard, Richard	389	8/4	162.1.8	2.8.7½
Prince, Francis	113	7/10	44.5.2	13.4
Pendleton, Benj[a.]	450	"	176.5.0	2.12.11
Pynes, Benjamin Est.	164	6/3	51.5.--	15.4½
Pynes, Benjamin jr.	100	"	31.5.--	9.5
Pynes, Robert	136	"	42.10.0	12.9
Pemberton, John	286	"	89.7.6	1.6.11½
Pollard, Robert	6	24/10	7.9.0	2.2¾
Price, Robert	630	6/3	196.17.6	2.19.1
Pigg, Rachel	108	14/[6]	[78.6.0]	1.3.6

[page 11, 1795] Persons owning lands	Quantity of land	Price per acre	Tot. Amt. Value Land	Tax on land 1½ percent
	[72]			
Pigg, John Est.	216	14/6	156.12.0	2.7.0
do.	180	7/3	65.5.--	19.7
Pollard, William	95	"	34.8.9	10.5
Peirce, Philip	100	3/2	15.16.8	4.9
Pierce, Thomas Est.	87	4/2	18.2.6	5.5¼
Price, Andrew	314	6/	94.4.--	1.8.3
Robertson, Rachel Est.	155	12/6	96.17.6	1.9.6
do.	260	7/3	94.5.0	1.8.5
Roane, Thomas	2033	18/8	1897.9.4	28.8.3
do. H. Carlton's	200	6/3	63.10.--	18.9
Roane, William	1585½	18/1½	1436.17.2	21.11.1
Row, Hansford & Wilson	390	6/3	121.17.6	1.16.5
Row, Thos. G. (orphan)	555	7/3	201.3.9	3.0.4
Row, Eliza.	665	20/9	689.18.9	10.7.--
Row, Francis (orphan)	612½	4/8	142.16.0	2.2.10
Read, Robert	14	5/3	3.3.6	0.1.1
Row, Richard Est.	550	8/4	229.3.4	3.8.9
Roane, ~~Roane~~ Spencer	1600	24/10	1926.13.4	28.18.--
Richeson, Elias	86	4/2	17.18.4	5.5
Row, Wm. & Moses	100	6/3	31.5.--	9.5
Richards, John	521½	4/8	124.8.--	1.17.6
Richerson, James	180	4/2	37.10.--	11.3
Richerson, William	181	"	37.14.2	11.4
Richerson, John Est.	101½	"	21.2.11	6.5
Roane, Major	687½	3/8	128.18.1½	1.18.8
Raines, Giles	60	3/2	9.10.--	2.11
Robinson, Benja. Est.	1300	8/4	541.13.4	8.[2.6]
Roane, Charles	200	14/6	145.--.--	2.3.6
do. Dragon Swamp	70	17/	59.10.--	17.[11]
Robbins, ~~Charles~~ William	40	6/3	12.10.--	3.[9]
Roy, Beverly	700	8/4	291.13.4	4.7.6
Ross, John (B. Minor to pay)	100	5/3	26.5.--	7.11
Richards, George	21	17/	17.17.--	5.4¼
Richeson, Willm. & R. Shephd.	80	10/5	41.13.4	12.6
Segar, Richard	406	7/3	147.3.6	2.4.2
[Satte]rwhite, George	164	6/3	51.5.--	15.1
Satterwhite, William	200	5/7½	56.5.--	16.10½
Spencer, Edward	245½	8/4	96.5.10	1.8.11
do. (S.M.)	582	7/3	210.19.6	3.3.3½
Schools, John	83½	7/10	32.14.1	9.9½
Seayres, Frankey	338	9/4	157.14.8	2.7.2
Schools, Gabriel	169	6/3	52.16.3	15.11
Skelton, William	362	8/2½	148.11.5	2.4.7
Smith, John (D)	190	7/6	71.5.--	1.1.4
Starling, Jane	360	7/10	141.--.--	2.2.4
Starling, Rodderick	213	8/2	86.19.6	1.6.[2]
Skelton, Thomas	294	8/4	122.10.--	1.16.[9]
Scott, Benja.	200	9/4	93.6.8	1.8.[0]
Saunders, George	200	7/3	72.10.--	1.1.[9]
Shepherd, William	140	9/4	65.6.8	19.[8]
Semple, John W.	574	15/	430.10.--	6.9.1
Smith, M[olley]	30	4/2	6.5.0	1.11

[page 12, 1795] Persons owning lands	Quantity of land	Price per acre	Tot. Amt. Value Land	Tax on land 1½ percent
Smith, John (L.H.)	100	5/3	26.5.0	7.11
Smith, Lewis	96	7/6	36.0.0	10.9¾
Swinton, George	750	13/6	506.5.--	7.11.11
Stone, Sarah	300	7/3	108.15.--	1.12.8
Stone, Daniel	52	3/2	8.4.8	2.6
Smith, Larkin	1254¼	31/1	1949.6.3½	29.4.10
Smith, Henry	400	6/3	130.--.--	1.18.--
Smith, William	[193]	7/10	20.15.2	1.2.[2]½
Smith, James	80	3/2	12.13.4	3.10
Smith, James jr.	101	7/10	39.11.2	11.10½
Stevens, George Est.	430	"	168.8.4	2.10.6½
Stevens, Tho[s.] (orphan)	75	"	29.8.4	8.10
Stevens, John do.	"	"	"	8.10
Stevens, George	"	"	"	8.10
Smith, William (Mill)	200	3/2	31.13.4	9.6
Shackelford, Jn[o.] Est.	214	7/3	77.11.6	1.3.3½
Starke, Richard Est.	350	5/8	99.3.4	1.9.9
Stone, Robert Est.	200	4/2	41.13.4	12.6
Stone, Job	100	"	20.16.8	6.3
Stone, John Est.	357	6/3	93.14.3	1.18.2
Smith, Robert	421	10/5	219.5.5	3.5.10
Smith, Samuel	110	"	57.5.10	17.2¼
Simpkins, Nimrod	60	3/2	9.10.--	2.11
[S]ears, Philip	83	4/2	17.5.10	5.3
[S]pencer, Thomas	300	10/5	156.5.0	2.6.11
do.	225	4/2	53.2.6	15.11
[Sha]ckelford, William Est.	700	14/6	527.10.--	7.18.6
[Se]ward, Benjamin	115	3/2	18.4.2	5.6
[St]edman, Christ[r.] Sen[r.]	191	5/3	50.2.9	15.1
[Sm]ith, Thomas (orphan)	485	14/6	351.12.6	5.5.5
Saddler, John	150	6/3	46.17.6	14.6
Shackelford, Alex[r.]	60	4/2	12.10.--	3.9
Steadman, Christ[r.] jr.	260	5/3	65.5.--	1.0.6
Shackelford, Jn[o.] (R)	482	8/4	200.16.8	3.0.3
Shackelford, Lyne	351	6/3	109.13.9	1.12.10¾
[Sh]ackelford, Lyne jr.	50	"	15.12.6	4.8
[Sh]ackelford, John (Mac)	283	6/2	87.5.2	1.6.[2¼]
Scott, Anderson	330	16/7	273.12.6	4.2.2
do. of Charles Williams	214	11/2	44.14.8	13.4½
Shepherd, John	190	3/2	30.1.8	9.3
Seward, Lucy & Eliz[a.] Est.	110	4/2	22.18.4	6.10
Semple, Robert B.	154	7/10	60.6.4	18.1
Stone, William	74¼	3/2	11.15.3½	3.6½
Seward, Edward	81½	5/3	21.6.6¾	6.4¾
Sthreshley, William	155½	6/3	48.11.10½	14.7
Sears, Thomas	123	6/7	40.9.9	12.2
Stratton Major Parish	300	10/	150.--.--	2.5.--
[Tr]ice, William	140	7/3	50.15.0	15.3
[T]aylor, James	50	6/3	15.12.6	4.9
Taylor, Edmond	294	8/14	122.10.--	1.16.9
Temple, Joseph	918	10/5	478.2.6	7.3.6
Tunstall, Molley	250	"	130.4.2	1.19.--¾

[page 13, 1795] Persons owning lands	Quantity of land	Price per acre	Tot. Amt. Value Land	Tax on land 1½ percent
	[73]			
Tunstall, Richard jr. Est.	1097	7/3	397.13.3	5.19.3
Tunstall, John	200	18/8	186.13.4	2.16.--
Tignor, William	130	7/10	50.18.4	15.4½
Tureman, Benj[a.]	70	3/2	11.1.8	3.4
Tureman, George	50	"	7.18.4	2.4½
Taliaferro, William	1000	14/6	725.--.--	10.17.6
Townley, Robert (Ed. Willi[s.] to pay)	200	6/3	62.10.--	18.9
do. Anderson's	117	14/6	84.16.6	1.5.5
Taliaferro, Phil	990	8/4	412.10.--	6.3.9
do. (D. Cook)	374½	12/6	234.7.6	3.10.4
Trice, Edward	206	5/3	54.2.6	16.3
Thruston, Armstead	145	4/3	30.16.3	9.3
Taliaferro, Richard Est.	300	5/3	78.15.--	1.3.8
Thruston, Batcheldor	200	3/2	31.13.4	9.6
Turner, Benj[a.]	36	4/2	7.10.--	2.3
Temple, Humph[y.]	178	31/3	278.2.6	4.3.5¼
do. of W[m.] Tunstall	100	15/	75.--.--	1.2.6
Tunstall, William Est.	438	21/	459.18.--	6.18.0
Tunstall, Richard (Purdy)	269½	8/4	112.15.10	1.13.9
Townley, Ann	79	4/2	16.9.2	5.--
Turner, Henry	100	"	20.16.8	6.3
Vass, Thomas	250	5/3	65.12.6	19.9
Wyatt, Henry	200	7/3	72.10.--	1.1.9
White, Henry	100	8/4	41.13.4	12.6
Willmore, Thomas	150	10/5	78.2.6	1.3.6
do. D. Farthing's	19	7/10	7.8.10	2.2½
Wright, James	[124½]	5/3	32.13.8	[9.10]
Wyatt, Joseph	68	8/4	25.--.--	7.6
Walden, John Est.	105	12/6	65.12.6	19.9
Wilson, Isaac	200	6/3	62.10.--	18.9
Wilson, Benj[a.] Est.	200	7/3	72.10.--	1.1.9
Wiltshire, Joseph	74	"	26.16.6	8.--
Wright, Isaac	183	6/3	57.3.9	17.[2]
Wyatt, John	100	7/10	39.3.4	11.3
Watkins, William	37	4/2	7.14.2	2.4
Watkins, Joseph	156	6/7	51.7.--	15.5
Walker, Henry Est.	150	5/3	39.7.6	11.10
Ware, John Est.	562	7/3	203.14.6	3.1.2
Walker, Humph[y.]	820	33/2	1355.14.2	20.7.10
Wright, William	175	5/3	45.18.9	13.10
Watts, Edward	250	7/3	90.12.6	1.7.3
do. W. Watts Est.	113	5/	28.5.--	8.5½
Watts, John	293	7/10	114.15.2	1.14.6
do. Pemberton's	45	6/3	14.1.3	4.2½
Watts, Kauffman	300	5/3	78.15.--	1.3.8
do. Burch's Est.	157	5/9	45.2.9	13.6¼
Watts, James	350	4/2	72.18.4	1.1.11
do. W. Watts Est.	60	15/	45.--.--	13.6
Williams, Howard	283	4/2	58.19.2	17.9
do. new ent[ry]	43	17/	36.11.--	10.11½
[Wyatt, Thomas] [page torn]	206	7/10	81.2.--	1.4.4½

[page 14, 1795] Persons owning lands	Quantity of land	Price per acre	Tot. Amt. Value Land	Tax on land 1½ percent
	[74]			
Wyatt, John Est.	103	6/3	32.3.9	9.8
Wyatt, William	29¾	7/3	10.15.8	3.8
Williams, Howard Est.	300	6/3	93.15.--	1.8.1
Williams, Charles	336	4/2	70.--.--	1.1.--
Walton, James	80	"	16.3.4	5.--
Walton, Mary	60	"	12.10.--	3.9
Willis, Joel	94	7/10	35.5.--	10.7
Walton, Eliza.	60	3/2	9.10.--	2.11
Walton, John	176	5/3	46.4--	13.11
Walton, William Est.	66	4/2	13.15.--	4.2
Walton, Thomas Est.	66	"	"	4.2
Ware, John	75	5/3	19.13.9	5.11
Ware, Arther Est.	83	4/2	17.5.10	5.3
Waring, Robert (P)	542	10/9	291.6.6	4.7.3¾
Walden, Richard	180	10/5	93.15.--	1.8.1½
Walden, Lewis	150	3/2	23.15--	7.3
do. of T. Dudley	84½	6/3	28.2.3½	8.5
Wright, Edward	60½	6/8	20.3.4	6.3¼
Wright, James	124	"	41.6.8	12.4¾
Ware, Robert S.	89½	11/9	52.13.--	15.10
Williams, George	40	4/2	8.6.8	2.6
Watkins, Phil	197	5/3	51.14.3	15.7
Wyatt, Richard	175	12/6	109.7.6	1.12.9¾
Ware, Robert jr. Est.	100	4/2	20.6.8	6.3
Williams, Eliza.	16½	3/2	2.12.9	9½
White, James Est.	200	6/3	62.10.--	18.9
Watkins, Eliza.	100	3/2	15.16.8	4.9
Warren, Catharine	175	"	27.14.2	8.[4]
Ware, Robert (preacher)	112	"	17.14.8	5.4
Wedderburn, Lydia	350	6/3	109.7.6	1.12.10
Whitting, Beverly Est.	2447¾	7/10	866.18.9½	13.--.--
Webbly, John	173	5/3	45.8.3	13.8
do. B. & F. Collier	268½	4/2	55.18.9	16.9¼
do. Wm. Dillard jr.	89½	"	18.12.11	5.7
Ware, Robert jr.	100	8/4	41.13.4	12.6
Ware, William	"	"	"	12.6
Walden, Edward Est.	373	5/3	97.18.3	1.9.5
Waller, Edward Est.	133½	3/2	21.2.9	6.5
Whayne, William	154½	7/10	60.10.3	18.1¾
Waller, Robert	113	3/7	20.5.11	6.1
Wyatt, John (taylor)	30	5/3	7.17.6	2.5
Williamson, Abner	100	3/2	15.16.8	4.9
Ware, Nicho.	100	3/2	15.16.8	4.9
Walden, Samuel	80	7/10	36.6.8	9.4½
Walden, John Senr.	100	5/3	26.5.--	7.10½
Ware, John (son of Kitt)	296	7/3	107.3.0	1.12.1
Young, Henry	640	18/8	597.6.8	8.19.3
				1365.[ ]
	William Fleet			227.11.6

[remainder of page dark and torn away]

King & Queen. Wm. Fleet, Wm. Courtney, Land 1795. Entd. Stated.

[page 15, 1795] Persons owning lands	Quantity of land	Price per acre	Tot. Amt. Value Land	Tax on land 1½ percent
				£136[5].12.0
				~~£227.10.10~~
[arithmetic omitted]				~~£37.10.6?~~

Errors Excepted by
William Fleet and Wm. Courtney, Commrs. tax
£227.12 @ 5/

List of the land within the County of King & Queen
with the tax thereon at one and a half percent
for the year 1796

[page 1, 1796] Persons owning lands	Quantity of land	Price per acre	Tot. Amt. Value Land	Tax on land 1½ percent
	[75]			
Atkins, Joseph	66	4/2	13.15.0	4.1½
Alexander, Benjamin	202	9/4	94.5.4	1.8.4
do. James Halbert	124	6/2	38.15.0	11.7½
Acre, Seaton [Acra]	52	9/4	24.5.4	7.3½
Alexander, Elisha	105	10/5	54.13.9	16.8
Anderson, Churchill Est.	636	7/3	230.11.3	3.9.2
Anderson, Paulin	498	14/6	361.1.0	5.9.4
Atkins, John	135	4/6	30.7.6	9.1½
Abbott, Jacob	112	7/10	43.17.4	13.2
Anderson, Richard Est.	460	5/3	120.15.0	1.16.3
Atkins, Lewis	60	8/4	25.0.0	7.6
Anderson, Francis	458	10/9	246.3.6	3.13.10½
Armistead, Thomas	29	8/4	12.1.8	3.7½
Bray, James	234	7/10	91.13.0	1.7.6
Brown, Henry Jun$^{r.}$	100	12/	60.0.0	18.--
Beverley, Robert	2474	10/5	1288.8.10	19.6.7
				41.2.2
Brown, Henry	760½	7/4½	280.8.8½	4.4.1½
Baylor, Gregory est.	720	14/6	522.0.0	7.16.7
Bland, John & Lucy	166	8/4	69.3.4	1.0.9
Bates, James	358	11/	149.3.4	2.4.9
do.	42	4/2	8.15.0	2.7½
Barton, John Est.	125	"	[7]6.0.10	1.2.9¾
Brooking, Frances	930	10/5	484.7.6	7.5.4
Baylor, John Est.	380	14/3	270.15.0	4.1.2½
Boughton, Thomas (Essex)	130	9/4	60.13.4	18.3
Boughton, John	200	8/4	83.6.8	1.5.0
Boughton, Henry (Essex)	88	6/3	27.10.0	8.3
Broach, John	72	4/2	15.0.0	4.6
Burton, Thomas Est.	170	5/3	44.12.6	13.5
Bohannon, Ann	197	4/6	44.6.6	13.3½
Brown, William	75	7/10	29.7.6	8.10
Bagby, John Est.	330	7/3	119.12.6	1.15.10½
Bagby, Richard	260	"	94.5.0	1.8.3½
Bagby, Thomas	"	"	"	1.8.3½
Brooke, Richard	1539¾	29/-	2232.12.9	33.9.10
Brumley, Robert	225	5/3	59.1.3	17.9
Brumley, John	60	7/10	23.10.3	7.0½
Bird, George B.	60	6/3	18.5.0	5.7½
Broach, William	20	7/10	7.16.8	2.4
Bird, William	532	7/3	197.17.0	2.18.0¼
do. Dragon Swamp	88½	17/	70.4.6	1.1.0
Brown, John	50	7/4½	18.8.9	5.6½
				117.11.7

[page 2, 1796] Persons owning lands	Quantity of land	Price per acre	Tot. Amt. Value Land	Tax on land 1½ percent
Bird, Philemon	1157½	6/3	361.14.4½	5.8.6
Bird, Mary	619	"	193.8.9	2.18.1
Brett, John Est.	446	18/	401.8.0	6.0.5
Burch, James	70	7/3	25.7.6	7.8
Bird, Anthony A.	275	3/2	43.10.10	13.1
Burch, Vincent	100	4/2	20.16.8	6.3
Byne, John Est.	336	4/2	70.0.0	1.1.0
do. Dragon Swamp	2¼	17/	1.18.3	6¾
Barbara Bird	266 2/3	24/10	331.2.2½	4.16.0
Bird, Robert	533 1/4	24/10	662.4.5½	9.12.0
do. Guy Smith	189½	3/2	30.0.1	1.9.6
Bourn, Richard Est.	150	"	23.15.0	7.2
Boyd, John	115	18/8	107.6.8	1.12.3
do. Sones's	382	24/10	474.6.4	7.2.4
Bray, Richard Est.	93	7/10	36.8.6	10.11
Bird, John Est.	100	3/2	15.16.8	4.9
Bowden, William	69	6/6	22.2.9	6.8
Bew, William	117	3/2	18.10.6	5.7
Boyd, Spencer Est.	1428	10/5	770.15.0	11.11.[2]
Berkeley, Edmund	762	5/3	200.0.6	3.0.0
Bland, John	60	12/6	37.10.0	11.3
Bohannan, William	130	5/3	34.2.6	10.3
Bland, William	100	9/11	49.11.8	14.10½
Bohannan, Wm. (St. Stephens)	33	5/3	8.13.3	2.8
				58.12.8
Bourn, Mill	159½	"	41.14.3	12.6
Bullman, Ann	100	5/3	26.5.0	7.11
Briggs, John (W. Finney)	170	4/2	35.8.4	10.8
Belote, Laban	384½	"	80.2.1	1.4.0
Bland, William Senr.	225	3/8¼	41.9.8¼	12.6
Bland, Ralph	146	5/3	38.6.6	11.6
Bowden, William jr.	100	4/2	20.16.8	6.3
do. of Sykes & Dudley's	34	3/2	5.7.8	1.8
Bowden, John	100	4/2	20.16.8	6.3
Bland, William Est.	250	"	52.1.8	15.8
Bland, Thomas	412	3/2	75.4.8	1.2.6¾
Bowden, George	236	5/3	61.19.0	18.7
do. of Wm. Dillard	[3]0	4/2	6.5.0	1.10½
Burch, William	45	3/2	7.8.6	2.1½
Brown, Thomas Est.	454	12/6	283.15.0	4.5.1
Banks, James	58	7/3	21.0.6	6.3½
Bristow, Bartholomew	33½	3/2	5.6.1	1.7
Beard, David	450	9/4	210.0.0	3.3.0
Bristow, George	100	3/2	15.16.8	4.8
Broach, James & Wm. Mansfield	200	16/7	165.16.8	2.9.9
Bates, William	81	7/9½	31.10.1	9.5¼
Banks, Andrew	125	12/6	78.2.6	1.3.5
Brightwell, John Est.	70	4/2	14.11.8	4.4½
Banks, William Est.	365	"	76.0.10	1.2.9¾
				79.17.1

[page 3, 1796] Persons owning lands	Quantity of land	Price per acre	Tot. Amt. Value Land	Tax on land 1½ percent
	[76]			
Crafton, Thomas	145	9/4	67.13.4	1.0.3½
Crafton, James	59	"	27.6.0	8.9½
Crafton, John	171	"	81.16.8	1.4.6½
Cooke, Mary	200	8/4	83.6.8	1.5.0
Chick, Richard Est.	491	7/3	177.19.9	2.13.5
Chapman, George Est.	200	7/10	78.6.8	1.3.6
do. Wm. Hoskins	39	10/5	20.6.3	6.1
Campbell, William	907	7/3	328.15.9	4.18.7½
Crane, John	136	6/3	42.--.--	12.7
Cluverius, Benjamin	419	20/9	434.14.3	6.10.5
Carlton, Henry	280	7/10	109.13.4	1.12.10
do John Baylor est.	257	14/6	186.6.6	2.15.10½
Clayton, Thomas Est.	275	7/3	99.13.9	1.9.1
Carlton, Benoni	72¾	"	26.7.4	0.8.0
do. of Wilson Row	49	6/3	15.3.1½	4.6¼
Campbell, Whitacar	318	7/10	124.11.--	1.17.6
Cleveley, Thomas	200	"	76.6.8	1.3.6
Crow, Nathaniel Est.	200	6/3	62.10.0	18.9
Craine, George est.	30	7/3	10.7.6	3.4
Carlton, Joel	53½	6/3	16.14.5	5.1
Cooke, John	100	7/3	36.5.0	10.10½
Cooper, Ann	60	3/2	9.10.0	2.11
Carlton, Thomas (Swamp)	200	7/10	78.6.8	1.3.6
Carlton, Noah	100	"	39.3.4	11.9
Carlton, John (Schoolmr.)	100	6/3	31.5.0	9.5
Campbell, Sarah	296	12/6	185.0.0	2.15.6
				36.15.8
Carlton, Christopher Senr.	37½	6/3	11.14.5	3.7
Carlton, Richard Est.	139	7/	48.13.--	14.7
Cothern, James	36½	3/2	5.15.7	1.8¾
Carlton, William (Sho[e])	309¾	11/6	178.1.2½	2.13.5
Carlton, Robert Est.	148	5/	37.--.--	11.1
Carlton, Richard	250	7/3	90.12.6	1.7.3
Carlton, Christopher jr.	100		36.5.0	10.11
Cooper, Henry	50	4/2	10.8.4	3.2
Carlton, Thomas (Taylor)	100	6/3	31.5.0	9.5
Cardwell, John Est.	150	4/2	31.5.0	9.5
Cardwell, John	"	"	"	9.5
Cardwell, William	77	"	15.11.6	4.7¼
Cardwell, Thomas	110	"	22.18.4	6.11
Cooke, John Est.	300	4/2	62.10.0	18.9
Collins, Thomas	329½	7/	115.6.6	1.14.7
do. Palmers	350	7/3	126.17.6	1.18.1
do. of Ro: S. Ware	86	11/9	50.10.6	15.2
Carlton, John jr.	235	4/2	48.19.2	14.9
Campbell, William	238	3/2	37.13.8	11.4
Collier, Charles	200	3/2	31.13.4	9.6
Curtis, Ann Est.	414	5/3	108.13.6	1.12.7
				53.15.11

[page 4, 1796] Persons owning lands	Quantity of land	Price per acre	Tot. Amt. Value Land	Tax on land 1½ percent
Collier, John	100	4/2	20.16.8	6.3
Corbin, John T. Est.	2390	11/1¾	1332.11.4	19.19.9½
do. New Dragon bridge	125	12/8	78.2.6	1.3.5
Crouch, James	130	3/2	20.11.8	6.3
Chapman, Phil	200	7/10	78.6.8	1.3.6
Crittenden, Thomas	126	13/6	85.1.0	1.5.6
do. Dragon Swamp	36	17/	30.12.0	9.2
Collins, Joyeux Est.	140	10/5	72.18.4	1.1.10
Crittenden, Zachariah	34 1/3	14/6	24.17.6	7.6
Cary, Wilson Est.	1820	16/7	1509.1.8	22.12.9
Collier, John (Cobler)	150	5/3	39.7.6	11.10
Campbell, James	130	5/9¼	37.10.0	11.3
Crittenden, Rich[d.] Est.	178	5/3	46.14.6	14.1
Corr, Avarilla	79	"	20.14.9	6.2½
Collier, Catharine Est.	750	5/3	196.17.6	2.19.1
Clegg, Isaiah	241	4/2	50.4.2	15.0½
Cooke, Dawson	282	3/2	44.13.0	13.6
Curry, Ann	100	4/2	20.16.8	6.3
Curry, John	55	3/2	8.14.2	2.7½
Courtney, William	200	7/10	78.6.8	1.3.6
Cooke, Thomas	240	3/2	38.0.0	11.5
Cook, Thomas jr.	96	"	15.0.4	4.6½
Carlton, Humphrey	175	7/	61.5.0	18.4
Carlton, Thomas Est.	235	6/3	73.8.9	1.2.1
Carlton, Beverley Est.	160	4/2	33.6.8	10.1
				60.[5].9
Corr, John jr.	64	7/3	23.4.0	6.4½
Campbell, John	400	12/6	250.0.0	3.15.0
Curry, James	70	4/2	18.16.0	4.7
Corr, John Sen[r.]	213	3/2	33.15.6	10.1½
do. John Corr jr.	90	7/3	32.12.6	9.9
Cooke, Henry	49¼	10/5	25.10.5	7.8
Crittenden, Francis (riv[r.])	105 2/3	14/6	76.12.2	1.3.0
Clark, John	144	5/	36.--.--	10.9½
Cannady, William	100	6/3	31.5.0	9.5
Corr, Thomas R.	157½	5/3	41.6.10½	12.4¼
Cook, William	65	5/5	17.12.1	5.3½
Cooke, James	65	8/9	28.8.9	8.6½
Carter, Jesse	395	10/	196.1.0	2.18.9½
Dew, William Est.	935	14/6	677.17.6	10.3.5
Dew, Thomas	331	12/6	68.19.2	1.0.8
Dowling, William Est.	264	8/4	110.--.--	1.13.0
Dix, Gabriel	338	6/3	105.12.6	1.11.8
Deshazo, William	60	4/2	12.10.0	3.9
Durham, Joseph	155	4/3	32.5.5	9.8
Deshazo, Peter Est.	192	7/4	70.8.0	1.1.1½
Deshazo, Larkin	87	7/3	31.4.10	8.11½
Dickie, James Est.	512	8/4	213.6.8	3.4.0
Dunbar, David	366	"	152.10.0	2.5.9
				9[4].10.--

[Page out of sequence on microfilm, after L-M]

[page 5, 1796] Persons owning lands	Quantity of land	Price per acre	Tot. Amt. Value Land	Tax on land 1½ percent
	[79]			
Dunn, Richard	150	4/2	31.5.0	9.4½
Dalley, John Est.	200	3/2	31.13.4	9.6
Dobbins, Charles Est.	147	5/3	38.11.9	11.7
Dean, Benjamin	50	"	13.2.6	4.0
Dillard, William jr. Est.	100	3/2	15.16.8	4.9
Dunn, Agrippa	140	5/3	36.15.0	11.1
Dudley, Peter Est.	530	7/3¼	186.18.4	2.16.1
Didlake, Mary	278	8/4	115.16.8	1.14.9
Durham, Robert Est.	50	"	10.8.4	3.2
Didlake, Margret Est.	65	4/2	13.10.10	4.1
Dunn, Thomas	50½	6/3	15.15.7½	4.9
Dillard, William S[r.]	276	12/6	172.10.0	2.11.9
Durham, George	50	4/2	10.8.4	3.2
Durham, Thomas Est.	85	3/2	13.9.2	4.2
Doumagin, Richard Est.	66	5/5	17.17.6	5.4
Digges, Frances	175	5/3	45.13.9	13.10
Doumagin, Richard	55	5/5	14.17.11	4.5½
Didlake, George Est.	114	10/5	59.7.6	17.10
Dungee, John	110	3/2	17.8.1	5.3
Dudley, William jr.	290	14/6	210.5.0	3.3.1
do. L. Wedderburn	315½	6/3	98.11.10½	1.9.6¾
Damm, John Est.	55	"	17.3.9	5.2
Dudley, William	180	7/10	70.10.0	1.1.2
Damm, William	25	4/2	5.4.2	1.6½
Douglas, John	239	7/	83.13.0	1.5.1
				20.2.6
Didlake, John	1200	7/3	435.0.0	6.10.6
Dudley, Ann	141	"	51.2.3	15.4
Dudley, Guilford	70	"	25.7.6	7.7
Didlake, James	278	8/4	115.16.8	1.14.9
Didlake, Edward	56	10/5	25.0.0	7.6
Dudley, Banks	230	3/2	36.8.4	10.11
Didlake, William	26¼	4/2	7.9.4½	2.2¾
Downey, Michael	50	10/5	26.0.10	7.9¾
Didlake, Royston	206	3/6½	36.7.4	11.1
Dillard, Thomas	49	15/	36.15.0	11.0
Dudley, Thomas	267½	6/3	81.17.8½	1.4.7
Dillard, William	392	15/	294.0.0	4.8.2
Dillard, Nicholas	75	4/2	15.12.6	4.9
Dillard, Benjamin Est.	148	5/3	48.17.0	14.7¾
Drummond, John	150	6/3	46.17.6	14.6
Dixon, Michael	414¾	15/5	320.0.0	4.16.0
Dabney, Benjamin	400	14/6	290.0.0	4.7.0
of. Phil Taliaferro	72	8/4	30.0.0	10.[0]¾
Davis, Stage	311	6/9	105.2.7½	1.11.4[½]
do. of Tho[s.] Foster	50	4/2	10.8.4	3.[ ]
Dally, George	174¼	3/2	27.11.9½	8.3[¼]
				51.3.8

[Page out of sequence on microfilm, after L-M]

[page 6, 1796] Persons owning lands	Quantity of land	Price per acre	Tot. Amt. Value Land	Tax on land 1½ percent
Dudley, Henry F.	50	5/3	13.2.6	3.11
Dunn, John (Essex, Dragon)	73	17/	62.1.0	18.7
Eubank, John	469	10/4	242.6.4	3.12.9
do. James Grafton	111	6/3	34.13.9	10.5
do. Thomas Dew	178½	12/6	111.5.0	1.13.4½
Eubank, Henry	171	5/3	44.17.9	13.6
Edwards, Thomas Est.	66	4/2	13.15.0	4.2
Eubank, William Est.	28¾	5/3	7.11.0	2.4
Eubank, Richard Sen[r.]	196	7/	68.12.0	1.0.7
Eubank, Thomas (S.S.)	100	5/9	28.15.0	8.7½
Eubank, Richard Est.	227	4/2	47.5.10	14.3
Eubank, Richard Jun[r.]	112¼	7/	39.5.7½	11.9¼
do. of Thomas Jeffries	12¾	7/3	4.12.5	1.4½
Evans, Ambrose	234½	7/10	91.13.0	1.7.6
Fogg, Frederick	298	8/4	124.3.4	1.17.3
Fleet, Baylor	862	12/6	538.15.8	8.1.7½
Fauntleroy, Sam[l.] G.	2069	20/	2069.0.0	31.0.8½
Fleet, John	260	6/3	81.5.0	1.6.4½
Faulconer, Thomas	220	"	68.15.0	1.0.6¼
Fogg, Thomas Est.	200	"	62.10.0	18.9
Fogg, James	120	"	37.10.0	11.3
Fox, Joseph S.	13	7/3	4.14.--	1.5
Frazer, William Est.	45½	20/9	46.[13].9	14.1
Fleet, William	352	"	365.4.0	5.9.6[½]
				63.4.8
Fisher, James Est.	110	3/2	17.18.4	5.3
Foster, Thomas	87¾	4/2	18.2.6	5.5¼
Faulkner, Mary	333	6/3	104.1.4	1.11.3
Fauntleroy, Thomas	486	10/	243.--.--	3.12.10¾
do. of H. Todd's	500	18/	460.--.--	6.18.0
do. W[m.] Bowden's	183	7/	64.1.--	19.2½
Farrinholtz, David	151¼	6/6	49.1.6	14.8½
Faulkner, Benjamin	100	4/2	20.16.8	6.3
Grafton, Sally & Ann	132	9/4	61.12.0	18.6
Gale, John	615	7/5½	229.13.9	3.8.8½
Goleman, Thomas (Essex)	948½	9/-	426.16.6	6.8.0
Garnett, Rice	297	7/3	107.13.4	1.12.4
Gatewood, Chaney	829	10/5	437.17.11	6.10.6
do. Gardner's	100	7/3	36.5.0	10.11
do. Noel's	362½	14/6	262.16.3	3.18.10
do. W. Harwood	225	4/2	46.17.6	14.1
do. Tho[s.] Eubank	300	14/6	217.10.0	3.5.3
Garnett, Joshua Est.	325	8/4	134.3.4	2.0.3
Graves, Edward Est.	200	6/3	62.10.0	18.9
Gatewood, Joseph	445	10/5	231.15.5	3.9.7
Gale, Matthew	323	11/5	184.7.7	2.15.4
Gatewood, John	160	8/4	66.13.4	[4].--.--
Garnett, Reuben	1026¾	8/10	453.8.0	6.15.7
Gwathmey, Temple	600	35/3	1057.10.--	15.17.3
				138.1.7

[page 7, 1796] Persons owning lands	Quantity of land	Price per acre	Tot. Amt. Value Land	Tax on land 1½ percent
	[77]			
Garlick, Samuel	454	24/10	563.14.4	8.9.2
Garlick, John	893	29/	1294.17.--	19.18.5
Griffith, Joseph	50	6/3	15.12.6	4.9
Gresham, Samuel	400	7/3	145.--.--	2.3.6
Guthrie, William	46¾	"	16.18.11¾	5.1
Garrett, Robert	100	4/2	20.16.8	6.3
Gaines, Francis	356	14/6	258.2.0	3.17.5
Gaines, Henry Est.	1517	20/4	1542.5.8	23.2.8
Gresham, Thomas	339¼	6/3	106.0.4	1.11.10
Gresham, Philemon	200	"	62.10.0	18.9
Gresham, John D	200	7/10	78.6.8	1.3.6
Gresham, Wm. (brickl r.)	100	4/2	20.16.8	6.3
do. W.C. Row	40	6/3	13.3.4	4.0
Gardner, Elizabeth	100	6/3	31.5.0	9.5
Gibson, Richard	156½	3/2	24.16.7	7.4
Gibson, Banks	56½	"	8.18.11	2.7
Gibson, John Est.	219¾	"	34.15.11	10.6
Griffith, Milly	50	6/3	15.12.6	4.9
Gresham, Machem	100	5/3	26.5.0	7.10½
do. of Ambros[e] Gresham	4	17/	3.8.0	1.[9]
Gresham, Ambrose	80	"	21.0.0	6.3½
do. New Entry	[26]	17/	25.13.0	6.6
Gresham, John jr.	80	5/3	21.0.0	6.3½
Graves, Thomas	50½	7/3	18.6.1½	5.5½
Griffin, William Est.	859	14/6	622.15.6	9.6.10
Garlick, Camm Est.	1100	6/3	343.15.0	5.3.2
				80.9.7
Garrett, Richard	50	3/2	7.8.4	2.4
Garrett, James	230	4/2	47.18.4	14.4½
Garrett, William jr.	100	"	20.16.8	6.3
Gardner, Anthony	638	11/	350.11.8	5.5.3
do. Dragon Swamp	67½	17/	57.7.6	17.2½
Gresham, Lumpkin	315	7/3	114.3.9	1.13.3
Garrett, Robert	200	7/	70.0.0	1.1.0
do. W. Hunt's Est.	170	6/3	53.2.6	15.11
Gatewood, William (*Tuck o.*)	220	3/2	34.14.6	10.6
Gresham, William jr.	329½	8/4	137.5.10	2.1.2¼
Gaines, Robert (Estate)	537¾	20/9	558.8.7¾	8.7.6
do. Ann Curtis	50	5/3	13.2.6	3.11
Gatewood, Wm. (son of Jno.)	132	10/	66.0.0	19.9½
Gleason, Patrick	134	8/4	55.16.8	16.9
Gatewood, Gabriel	78	10/5	40.12.6	12.2½
Guthrie, James	60	12/6	37.10.0	11.3
Guthrie, Richard Est.	60	"	"	11.3
Glaspe, James	210	5/3	55.2.6	16.7
Groom, Mary	173	3/2	27.17.10	8.5
Garrett, George	88½	5/3	23.4.7½	6.11½
Guthrie, Rachel	50	8/4	20.16.8	6.3
Goldman, Martin	140	4/2	29.3.4	8.9
Groom, Zachariah Est.	187	3/2	29.12.2	8.10½
				[illegible]

[page 8, 1796] Persons owning lands	Quantity of land	Price per acre	Tot. Amt. Value Land	Tax on land 1½ percent
Gulley, Philip Est.	50	3/2	7.18.4	2.4
Garrett, William (Shoe)	225	3/4¾	37.19.4	11.4½
Gramshill, Henry	25	3/2	3.19.2	1.2¼
Garrett, Ann Watts	112	5/	28.--.--	8.4¾
Garrett, Richard	100	4/2	20.16.8	6.3
Guthrie, Richard	162	3/2	25.13.0	7.8
Hill, William	1191	14/6	928.9.6	13.18.7
Hitchcock, Thomas	140	4/2	29.3.4	8.9
Hoskins, Samuel	345	6/3	107.16.3	1.12.3
Hutcherson, Charles	531	7/1	188.1.3	2.16.5
Hoskins, William	252	7/10	98.14.0	1.9.7
do. of Geo. Kauffman	583	14/6	422.13.6	6.6.10
Heskew, John	61	5/3	16.0.3	4.10
Heskew, John jr.	50	6/3	15.12.6	4.8
do. Clement Pynes	10	3/2	1.11.8	5½
Hill, Robert	1281	8/2	523.1.6	7.16.11
Hill, Edward	1200	18/8	1120.--.--	16.16.0
Hoomes, Benjamin	447	12/6	278.8.4	4.3.9¾
do. of Martha Cary	462	4/4	96.5.--	1.8.11
Hutson, William Est.	112	3/2	17.14.8	5.4
Hemmingway, John jr.	267	4/2	55.12.6	16.8½
Hemmingway, Samuel	"	"	"	16.8½
Hemmingway, John Sr.	266	"	55.8.4	16.7½
Hare, William	217	5/3	56.19.3	16.1
Harwood, Christ[r.] Est.	294	24/10	365.1.0	5.9.6
				68.6.3
Harwood, John Sen[r.]	25	5/3	4.7.6	1.3½
Harwood, William est.	240	30/	360.--.--	5.8.0
Hill, Thomas	300	26/11	403.15.--	6.1.2
Hart, James	150	3/2	23.15.--	7.2
Holderby, John	100	4/2	20.16.8	6.3
do. W[m.] Hoskins	108¾	7/10	42.6.0	12.8
Hart, Anthony	190	5/3	49.17.6	15.0
do. of Sundry Persons	259½	3/2	41.1.9	12.4
Hart, Gregory	200	11/	31.3.4	9.6
Hart, William	250	3/3½	41.2.11	12.4
Harwood, John Jun[r.]	109	10/5	56.15.5	17.0
Hunt, William Est.	560	6/3	175.--.--	2.12.6
Henry, Samuel H. Est.	1900	14/6	1377.10.0	20.13.3
Halyard, William	190	5/3	49.17.6	15.0
Hoskins, John	767	10/7	399.9.7	5.19.10
do. Boughton	100	8/4	41.13.4	12.6
Hall, Corbin	80	6/3	25.--.--	[9].6
Hurt, West	14	5/3	3.3.6	1.1
Hoskins, Robert	287	6/	86.2.--	1.5.10
Hart, Alden	127	"	26.9.2	7.11¼
Howerton, Heritage	122¼	20/9	126.16.7¼	1.18.0½
Holt, Richard	123	14/3	87.12.9	1.6.3½
Hutson, William (S.[S.])	50	4/2	10.8.4	3.1½
Hutcherson, John	73¼	8/9	32.0.11¼	9.7¼
				119.11.5

[page 9, 1796] Persons owning lands	Quantity of land	Price per acre	Tot. Amt. Value Land	Tax on land 1½ percent
	[78]			
Jones, Thomas	255	4/2	53.2.6	15.11
Jeffries, Thomas	63	7/3	22.16.9	6.10
do. John Harwood Jr.	38¼	10/5	19.15.10¾	5.11
Jones, John Est.	300	8/11	133.15.0	2.--.1½
Jeffries, Edward	70	3/2	11.1.8	3.4
Jones, James	160	14/6	116.--.--	1.14.10
Jones, James Est.	196	10/5	102.1.8	1.10.8
Jones, William Est.	241	15/10	190.15.10	2.17.3
do. L. Smith	35¾	31/1	55.11.2	16.8
Jeffries, Ambrose	337	7/10	124.18.10	1.17.6
Jeffries, Robert	60	"	23.10.--	7.1
Jeffries, Bernard Est.	30	4/2	6.5.0	1.11
Jordan, Thomas Est.	100	4/2	20.16.8	6.3
Johnson, Thomas	112	3/2	17.14.8	5.4
Jameson, David Est.	50	"	7.18.4	2.5
Jones, Rawleigh	63	31/1	93.18.3	1.9.4
Kemp, John	296	7/3	107.3.0	1.12.1
Kemp, John (S. Stephens)	178	7/3	64.2.2	19.2
Kauffman, John jr.	38	10/5	19.15.10	5.11½
do. John Kauffman	471	18/8	439.12.0	6.11.11
Keeling, James	113¼	7/3	41.0.0¾	12.4
do. Ro. Hill	23	8/2	9.7.10	2.10
				35.5.8
Kennedy, Archibald	38¼	4/2	7.19.4	2.4½
do. Benjamin Hoomes	227¾	7/10	89.4.2	1.6.9¾
Kennedy, Ann	70¼	4/2	14.11.8	4.6¾
Kennedy, Ann jr.	150	12/6	97.10.0	1.9.3
do. Holderby	33¾	4/2	7.0.6	2.1¼
Kennedy, Lucy	37½	"	7.16.2	2.4
Kay, Christopher	116	6/3	30.0.9	9.1½
Kidd, Bartholomew	136	5/3	35.14.0	10.8
Kidd, Benjamin	111	13/6	74.18.2	1.2.5½
do. Crittendens	60	"	40.10.0	12.1¾
do. Dragon Swamp	36	17/	30.12.0	9.2
Kidd, John	370	7/3	134.2.6	2.0.3
do. Lumpkin & Peirce	60	4/2	12.10.0	3.9
do. Tho[s.] Dillard	45	14/6	32.12.6	9.10
Lumpkin, Joyce	213	7/10	83.8.2	1.5.0
Lumpkin, Henry	620	9/4	289.6.8	4.6.10
Lumpkin, John Est.	200	6/3	59.0.0	17.9
Lyne, William jr.	108	"	45.--.--	13.6
do. Lotts in Dunkirk annual rent			150.--.--	1.0.10
Lyne, William	1480	8/4	610.14.2	9.3.3
Lumpkin, William	305	14/6	221.2.6	3.6.5
do. Thomas Dew	26½	12/6	16.5.0	4.10½
Lefon, Francis	119	8/4	49.11.8	14.10
Lankford, Tho[s.] Est.	100	4/2	20.16.8	6.3
				56.10.0

[page 10, 1796] Persons owning lands	Quantity of land	Price per acre	Tot. Amt. Value Land	Tax on land 1½ percent
Lumpkin, Robert Senr.	374	8/4	155.16.8	2.6.9
Longest, Caleb	97	7/10	37.19.10	11.6
Longest, Richard	140	"	54.16.8	16.6
Longest, John	100	"	39.3.4	11.9
Lumpkin, Anthony	216	6/3	67.10.0	1.0.4
Lumpkin, Jacob Est.	916	"	286.5.0	4.5.11
do. Southerland	271	5/3	71.2.9	1.1.4
do. Colemans	196	10/5	102.1.8	1.10.8
Lewis, Iveson	356	14/6	258.2.0	3.17.4¼
Lumpkin, Richard Est.	76¼	6/	22.17.6	6.10½
Leigh, Lucy	101	24/10	125.8.2	1.17.7
Lumpkin, Robert jr.	233	5/3	61.3.3	18.4
Leigh, John	199	24/10	247.1.10	3.14.2
Lyne, John	507	6/3	158.8.9	2.7.7
Lambeth, Thomas	100	3/2	15.16.8	4.9
Laughlin, James	126¾	"	26.8.2	8.0
Lambeth, Charles Est.	50	"	7.18.4	2.5
Motley, Edwin	815	10/5	428.2.6	6.8.6
McKentosh, William	126	4/2	26.5.0	7.10½
Martin, Thomas C.	680	14/6	493.--.--	7.7.11
do.	134½	7/3	48.15.1½	14.7½
Morgan, William	3	6/3	18.9	3¼
Mitchel, Ralph est.	193	10/5	100.10.5	1.10.1½
Minor, William	149	8/4	62.1.8	18.8
Minor, John	137	"	57.1.8	17.2
Minor, Thomas	288	7/10	225.6.0	1.13.10
Moody, Lewis	239	"	93.12.1	1.8.1
				47.9.--
Mann, Augustine est.	400	8/4	166.13.4	2.10.0
Mitchell, Robert	17	20/9	17.12.9	5.4
Mitchell, John	50	6/3	15.12.6	4.9
Mitchell, James est.	650	13/	422.10.0	6.6.9
Mann, Robert	699	6/3	218.8.9	3.5.6¼
McKendree, Elizabeth	90	5/3	23.12.6	7.1
Moore, Lambeth	70	4/2	14.11.8	4.3¼
Morris, William	10	"	2.1.8	7½
Moore, Benjamin	200	"	41.13.4	12.6
Merideth, Samuel	215	7/10	84.4.2	1.5.3
Moore, John	100	3/2	15.16.8	4.9
Major, Josiah	200	4/2	41.13.4	12.6
Mitchell, John est.	270	5/3	70.17.6	1.1.4
do. Rootes	200	9/11	99.13.4	1.9.8¼
Macon, John Est.	892	16/7	739.12.4	11.1.10
do. Lotts in Dunkirk annual rent			95.0.0	15.8¼
Montague, William	214	4/2	44.11.8	13.4½
Mansfield, William	75	"	62.3.9	18.7
Merideth, Ralph G.	567	14/6	411.1.6	6.3.5½
Muire, Richard	93	12/6	58.2.6	17.6
				86.9.9

[page 11, 1796] Persons owning lands	Quantity of land	Price per acre	Tot. Amt. Value Land	Tax on land 1½ percent
	[80]			
Moore, Richard	145	6/3	45.6.3	13.8
McCarty, Joseph Est.	73	3/2	11.11.2	3.6
Metcalf, John S.	265	14/6	196.5.10	2.18.1½
Metcalf, Thomas	256	"	181.8.8	2.15.2¼
Mann, Mary	100	5/3	26.5.0	7.11
Martin, John	475	9/	312.15.0	3.3.1½
Nunn, Jane	180	7/3	65.5.0	19.7
Newbill, George est.	500	8/4	208.6.8	3.2.6
Nunn, Thomas	130	7/3	47.2.6	14.1½
Nash, John est.	100	6/3	31.5.0	9.5
Newcombe, Elizabeth	109	3/2	17.5.2	5.2
Newcombe, William	60	"	9.10.0	2.11
Newill, John	100	7/10	39.3.4	11.9
Orvill, John	100	6/3	31.5.--	9.5
Oliver, John	320	5/3	84.--.--	1.5.3
Overstreet, Gabriel	296	4/2	61.13.4	18.9
do. Haynes	130	5/3	34.2.6	10.2
Oaks, Henry	198½	3/2	34.2.0	10.2¾
Oaks, William	80	4/2	16.13.4	5.0
Owen, Augustine	100	6/3	31.5.--	9.5
				20.15.2
Pendleton, James	888½	8/7½	383.3.3¾	5.14.11½
do. H. Wilmore	70	7/6	26.5.0	7.10½
Pitts, David est.	420	9/4	196.--.--	2.18.10
Pitts, Obediah	20	10/5	10.8.4	3.2
Philips, Richard	230	7/3	83.7.6	1.5.1
Pollard, John Est.	235	9/4	109.13.4	1.12.11
do. L. Smithey	384	7/3	139.4.0	2.1.10
Prewitt, Francis	99	9/4	46.4.0	13.11
Parker, John	264¼	7/	92.9.9	1.7.9
Prewitt, Richard	102	7/3	36.12.3	11.0
Pendleton, Philip	483	9/2	221.7.6	3.6.5
Perryman, Anthony est.	130	7/3	47.2.6	14.2
Perryman, Philip	218	7/2	78.2.4	1.1.9
Pitts, Benjamin G.	100	5/4	26.13.4	8.0
Pynes, Clement	189	3/2	30.6.10	9.1
Pace, Benjamin	263	7/3	95.6.9	1.8.8
Pollard, Richard	389	8/4	162.1.8	2.8.7½
Prince, Francis	113	7/6	44.5.2	13.4
Pendleton, Benjamin	450	"	176.5.0	2.12.11
Pynes, Benjamin est.	164	6/3	51.5.0	9.5
Pynes, Robert	136	"	42.10.0	12.9
Pynes, Benjamin jr.	100	"	31.5.0	9.5
Pemberton, John	286	"	89.7.6	1.6.11½
Pollard, Robert	6	24/10	7.9.0	2.2¾
				53.1[5].9

[page 12, 1796] Persons owning lands	Quantity of land	Price per acre	Tot. Amt. Value Land	Tax on land 1½ percent
Price, Robert	630	6/3	196.17.6	2.19.1
Pigg, Rachel	108	14/6	78.6.0	1.3.6
Pigg, John est.	216	14/6	156.12.0	2.7.0
do.	180	7/3	65.5.0	19.7
Pollard, William	95	"	34.8.9	10.5
Pierce, Philip	83	3/2	13.2.10	2.7½
Pierce, Beverley	25¾	4/2	5.7.3½	1.7
do. [of] Phil Pierce	17	3/2	2.13.10	9½
Pierce, Thomas est.	87	4/2	18.2.6	5.5¼
Price, Andrew	314	6/	94.4.--	1.8.3
Robertson, Rachel est.	155	12/6	96.17.6	1.9.6
do.	260	7/3	94.5.0	1.8.5
Roane, Thomas	2033	18/8	1897.9.4	28.8.3
do. H. Carlton's	200	6/3	63.10.0	18.9
Roane, William	1585	18/1½	1436.17.2	21.11.1
Row, Hansford & Wilson	341	6/3	105.14.7	1.10.8½
Row, Tho$^{s.}$ G. (orphan)	555	7/3	201.3.9	3.0.4
Row, Elizabeth	665	20/9	689.18.9	10.7.0
Row, Frances (orphan)	612½	4/8	142.16.0	2.2.10
Row, Richard est.	550	8/4	229.3.4	3.8.9
Roane, Spencer	1600	24/10	1926.13.4	28.18.0
Ryland, Josiah	160	7/10	62.13.4	18.9½
Riddle, Vaughan	55	5/5	13.16.3	4.0½
Richeson, Elias Est.	86	4/2	17.18.4	5.5
				114.10.2
Row, William & Moses	[6]0	6/3	18.15.0	5.7½
Richards, John	57[1]½	4/8	124.8.0	1.17.6
Richerson, James	180	4/2	37.10.0	11.3
Richerson, William	369½	"	76.17.6	1.3.0
Richerson, John Est.	101½	"	21.2.1	6.5
Roane, Major	687½	3/8	128.18.1½	1.18.8
Raines, Giles	60	3/2	9.10.0	2.11
Robinson, Benjamin Est.	1300	8/4	541.13.4	8.2.6
Roane, Charles	200	14/6	145.0.0	2.3.6
do. Dragon Swamp	70	17/	59.10.0	17.11
Robbins, William	40	6/3	12.10.0	3.9
Roy, Beverley	700	8/4	291.13.4	4.7.6
Ross, John (B. Minor to pay)	100	5/3	26.5.0	7.11
Richards, George	21	17/	17.17.--	5.4¼
Richerson, [Will$^{m.}$] & R. Shepherd	24	10/5	8.6.6	2.6
Segar, Richard	406	7/3	147.3.6	2.4.2
Satterwhite, George	164	6/3	51.5.0	15.1
Satterwhite, William	200	5/7½	56.5.0	16.10½
Spencer, Edward est.	245½	8/4	96.5.10	1.8.11
do. (S.M.)	582	7/3	210.19.6	3.3.3½
Schools, John	156	8/4	65.0.0	19.6
				146.14.4

[page 13, 1796] Persons owning lands	Quantity of land	Price per acre	Tot. Amt. Value Land	Tax on land 1½ percent
	[81]			
Schools, Jn$^{o.}$ & James	16	7/1	5.13.4	1.8¼
Seayres, Frankey	338	9/4	157.14.8	2.7.2
Schools, Gabriel est.	169	6/3	52.16.3	15.11
Skelton, William	362	8/2½	148.11.5	2.4.7
do. of Phil Perryman	12	7/2	4.6.0	1.3½
Smith, John (D)	190	7/6	71.5.0	1.1.4
Sterling, Jane	360	7/10	141.0.0	2.2.4
Sterling, Rhoderick	313	8/2	127.16.2	1.18.4
Skelton, Thomas	294	8/4	122.10.0	1.16.9
Scott, Benjamin est.	200	9/4	93.6.8	1.8.0
Saunders, George	200	7/3	72.10.0	1.1.9
Shepherd, William	140	9/4	65.6.8	19.8
Semple, John Walker	574	15/	430.10.--	6.9.1
Smith, M[olley]	30	4/2	6.5.0	1.11
Smith, John (L.H.)	100	5/3	26.5.0	7.11
Smith, Lewis	96	7/6	36.0.0	10.9¾
Swinton, George	750	13/6	506.5.0	7.11.11
Stone, Sarah	300	7/3	108.15.0	1.12.8
Stone, Daniel	52	3/2	8.4.8	2.6
Smith, Larkin	1254¼	31/1	1949.6.3½	29.4.10
Smith, Henry	400	6/3	130.--.--	1.18.0
Smith, William	53	7/10	20.15.2	6.2¼
Smith, James	80	3/2	12.13.4	3.10
Smith, James jr.	101	7/10	39.11.2	11.10½
Stevens, George Est.	430	"	168.8.4	2.10.6½
Stevens, Thomas (orphan)	75	"	29.8.4	8.10
Stevens, John do.	"	"	"	8.10
				68.8.7
Stevens, George do.	"	"	"	8.10
Smith, William (Mill)	200	3/2	31.13.4	9.6
Shackelford, John est.	114	7/3	40.18.2	12.3
Starke, Richard est.	350	5/8	99.3.4	1.9.9
Stone, Robert est.	200	4/2	41.13.4	12.6
Stone, Job	100	"	20.16.8	6.3
Stone, John Est.	357	6/3	93.14.3	1.18.2
Smith, Robert	421	10/5	219.5.5	3.5.10
Smith, Samuel	110	"	57.5.10	17.2¼
Simpkins, Nimrod	60	3/2	9.10.0	2.11
Sears, Philip	83	4/2	17.5.10	5.3
Shackelford, William est.	700	14/6	527.10.0	7.18.6
Spencer, Thomas	300	10/5	156.5.0	2.6.11
do.	225	4/2	53.2.6	15.11
Seward, Benjamin	115	3/2	18.4.2	5.6
Stedman, Christ$^{r.}$ S$^{r.}$	191	5/3	50.2.9	15.1
Smith, Thomas (orphan)	485	14/6	351.12.6	5.5.5
Sadler, John	150	6/3	46.17.6	14.6
Shackelford, Alex$^{r.}$	60	4/2	12.10.0	3.9
Stedman, Christ$^{r.}$ jr.	260	5/3	65.5.0	1.0.6
Shackelford, John (R)	482	8/4	200.16.8	3.0.3
Shackelford, William	351	6/3	109.13.9	1.12.10¾
Shackelford, Lyne	50	"	15.12.6	4.8
				103.1.--

[page 14, 1796] Persons owning lands	Quantity of land	Price per acre	Tot. Amt. Value Land	Tax on land 1½ percent
Shackelford, John (Mc)	283	6/2	87.5.2	1.6.2¼
Scott, Anderson	330	16/7	273.12.6	4.2.2
Shepherd, John	190	3/2	30.1.8	9.3
Seward, Lucy & Elizabeth	100	4/2	22.18.4	6.10
Semple, Robert B.	253	10/5	131.15.1	1.19.6½
Stone, William	74¼	3/2	11.15.3½	3.6½
Seward, Edward	81½	5/3	21.6.6¾	6.4¾
Sthreshley, William	155½	6/3	48.11.10½	14.7
Sears, Thomas	123	6/7	40.9.9	12.2
Stratton Major Parish	300	10/	150.0.0	2.5.0
Trice, William	140	7/3	50.15.0	15.3
Taylor, James	50	6/3	15.12.6	4.9
Taylor, Edmond	294	8/14	122.10.0	1.16.9
Temple, Joseph	918	10/5	478.2.6	7.3.6
Tunstall, Molly Est.	250	"	130.4.2	1.19.0¾
Tunstall, Richard jr. Est.	1097	7/3	397.13.3	5.19.3
Tunstall, John est.	200	18/8	186.13.4	2.16.0
Tignor, William	130	7/10	50.18.4	15.4½
Tureman, Benjamin	70	3/2	11.1.8	3.4
Tureman, George	50	"	7.18.4	2.4½
Taliaferro, William	1000	14/6	725.0.0	10.17.6
Townley, Robert	200	6/3	62.10.0	18.9
do. Anderson's	117	14/6	84.16.6	1.5.5
Taliaferro, Philip	940	8/4	391.13.4	5.17.6
do. D. Cooke	374½	12/6	234.7.6	3.10.4
Trice, Edward est.	206	5/3	54.2.6	16.3
				57.7.0
Thurston, Armstead	145	4/3	30.16.3	9.3
Taliaferro, Richard est.	300	5/3	78.15.0	1.3.8
Thurston, Batcheldor	200	3/2	31.13.4	9.6
Turner, Benjamin	36	4/2	7.10.0	2.3
Temple, Humphrey	178	31/3	278.2.6	4.3.5¼
do. W^m. Tunstall	100	15/	75.0.0	1.2.6
Tunstall, William est.	438	21/	459.18.0	6.18.0
Tunstall, Richard (Purdy)	269½	8/4	112.15.10	1.13.9
Townley, Ann	79	4/2	16.9.2	5.[0]
Turner, Henry Est.	100	"	20.16.8	6.3
Vass, Thomas	250	5/3	65.12.6	19.9
Wyatt, Henry	200	7/3	72.10.0	1.1.9
White, Henry	100	8/4	41.13.4	12.6
Willmore, Thomas	150	10/5	78.2.6	1.3.6
do. D. Farthing	19	7/10	7.8.10	2.2½
Wright, James	124½	5/3	32.13.8	9.10
Wyatt, Joseph	68	8/4	25.0.0	7.6
Walden, John est.	105	12/6	65.12.6	19.9
Wilson, Isaac	200	6/3	62.10.0	18.9
Wilson, Benjamin est.	200	7/3	72.10.0	1.1.9
Wiltshire, Joseph	74	"	26.16.6	8.0
				82.5.4

[page 15, 1796] Persons owning lands	Quantity of land	Price per acre	Tot. Amt. Value Land	Tax on land 1½ percent
	[82]			
Wright, Isaac	183	6/3	57.3.9	17.2
Wyatt, John	100	7/10	39.3.4	11.3
Watkins, William	37	4/2	7.14.2	2.4
Watkins, Joseph	156	6/7	51.7.--	15.5
Walker, Henry est.	150	5/3	39.7.6	11.10
Walker, Philip	110	9/4	51.6.8	15.4¾
Wood, William	2	7/10	15.8	0.2¾
Ware, John Est.	562	7/3	203.14.6	3.1.2
Walker, Humphrey	820	33/2	1355.14.2	20.7.10
Wright, William	175	5/3	45.18.9	13.10
Watts, Edward	250	7/3	90.12.6	1.7.3
do. W. Watts Est.	113	5/	28.5.0	8.5½
Watts, John	293	7/10	114.15.2	1.14.6
do. Pemberton	45	6/3	14.1.3	4.2½
Watts, Kauffman	300	5/3	78.15.0	1.3.8
do. Burch's Est.	157	5/9	45.2.9	13.6¼
Watts, James	350	4/2	72.18.4	1.1.11
do. W. Watts Est.	60	15/	45.--.--	13.6
Williams, Howard	283	4/2	58.19.2	17.9
do. New Entry	43	17/	36.11.0	10.11½
Wyatt, Thomas	206	7/10	81.2.0	1.4.4½
Wyatt, John Est.	103	6/3	32.3.9	9.8
Wyatt, William	29¾	7/3	10.15.8	3.8
Williams, Howard Est.	300	6/3	93.15.0	1.8.1
				39.18.0
Williams, Charles	336	4/2	70.--.--	1.1.0
Walton, James	80	"	16.3.4	5.0
Walton, Mary	60	"	12.10.0	3.9
Willis, Joel	94	7/10	35.5.0	10.7
Walton, Elizabeth	60	3/2	9.10.0	2.11
Walton, John	176	5/3	46.4.0	13.11
Walton, William est.	66	4/2	13.15.0	4.2
Walton, Thomas est.	"	"	"	4.2
Ware, John Est.	75	5/3	19.13.9	5.11
Ware, Arther Est.	83	4/2	17.5.10	5.3
Waring, Robert P.	542	10/9	291.6.6	4.7.3¾
Walden, Richard	180	10/5	93.15.--	1.8.1½
Walden, Lewis	150	3/2	23.15.0	7.3
do. T. Dudley	84½	6/3	28.2.3½	8.5
Wright, Edward	60½	6/8	20.3.4	6.3¼
Wright, James	124	"	41.6.8	12.4¾
Williams, George	40	4/2	8.6.8	2.6
Watkins, Philip	197	5/3	51.14.3	15.7
Wyatt, Richard	175	12/6	109.7.6	1.12.9¾
Ware, Robert jr. est.	100	4/2	20.6.8	6.3
Williams, Elizabeth	16½	3/2	2.12.9	9½
White, James Est.	200	6/3	62.10.0	18.9
Watkins, Elizabeth	100	3/2	15.16.8	4.9
Warren, Catharine Est.	175	"	27.14.2	8.4
				55.14.2

[page 16, 1796] Persons owning lands	Quantity of land	Price per acre	Tot. Amt. Value Land	Tax on land 1½ percent
Ware, Robert (B)	112	3/2	[17].14.8	5.4
Wedderburn, Lydia	350	6/3	[109].7.6	1[0].12.10
Whiteing, Beverley Est.	2447¾	7/10	[86]6.18.9½	13.0.0
Webbly, John	173	5/3	45.8.3	13.8
do. B. & F. Collier	268½	4/2	55.18.9	16.9¼
do. W. Dillard jr.	89½	"	18.12.11	5.7
Ware, Robert jr.	100	8/4	41.13.4	12.6
Walden, Edward Est.	373	5/3	97.18.3	1.9.5
Ware, William	100	8/4	41.13.4	12.6
Waller, Edward Est.	133½	3/2	21.2.9	6.5
Waller, George	87	"	13.15.6	4.1½
Whayne, William	154½	7/10	60.10.3	18.1¾
Waller, Robert	113	3/7	20.5.11	6.1
Wyatt, John (Taylor)	30	5/3	7.17.6	2.5
Williamson, Abner	100	3/2	15.16.8	4.9
Ware, Nicholas	"	"	"	4.9
Walden, Samuel	80	7/10	36.6.8	9.4½
Walden, John Sen[r.]	100	5/3	26.5.--	7.10½
Young, Henry	640	18/8	597.6.8	8.19.3
				3[0].[5].9

William Courtney, Comm[r.]
Beverley Roy, Comm[r.]

List of Land within the County of King & Queen with the tax thereon at one and a half p'cent for the year 1797

[page 1, 1797] Persons owning lands	Quantity of land	Price per acre	Tot. Amt. Value Land	Tax on land 1½ percent
	[83]			
Atkins, Joseph	66	4/2	13.15.0	4.1½
Alexander, Benjamin	202	9/4	94.5.4	1.8.4
do. James Halbert	124	6/2	38.15.--	11.7½
Acre, Seaton	52	9/4	24.5.4	7.3½
Alexander, Elisha	338	"	157.14.8	2.7.2
Anderson, Churchill Esta.	636	7/3	230.11.--	3.9.2
Anderson, Pauling Est.	498	14/6	361.1.0	5.9.4
Atkins, John	135	4/6	30.7.6	9.1½
Abbott, Jacob	112	7/10	43.17.4	13.2
Anderson, Richard Esta.	460	5/3	120.15.--	1.16.3
Atkins, Lewis	60	8/4	25--.--	7.6
Anderson, Francis	458	10/9	246.3.6	3.13.10½
Armistead, Thomas	29	8/4	12.1.8	3.7½
Bray, James	234	7/10	91.13.0	1.7.6
Broach, Benoni	48	10/5	25.4.--	7.7
Brown, Henry jr.	100	12/	60.--.--	18.--
Beverley, Robert	2444	10/5	1262.16.4	18.15.11
Brown, Henry	760½	7/4½	280.8.8½	4.4.1½
Baylor, Gregory Esta.	720	14/6	522.--.--	7.16.7
Bland, John & Lucy	166	8/4	69.3.4	1.--.9
Bates, James	358	11/	149.3.4	2.4.9
do.	42	4/2	8.15.--	0.2.7½
Barton, John Esta.	125	"	26.--.10	7.10
				58.6.3
Banks, William Esta.	365	"	76.0.10	1.2.9¾
Brooking, Frances	930	10/5	484.7.6	7.5.4
Baylor, John Est.	229	14/3	163.3.6	2.9.--
Boughton, Thomas, Essex	130	9/4	60.13.4	18.3
Boughton, John	200	8/4	83.6.8	1.5.--
Boughton, Henry, Essex	88	6/3	27.10.--	8.3
Broach, John	72	4/2	15.--.--	4.6
Burton, Thomas Esta.	170	5/3	44.12.6	13.5
Bohannon, Ann	197	4/6	44.6.6	13.3½
Brown, William	75	7/10	29.7.6	8.10
Bagby, John Esta.	330	7/3	119.12.6	1.15.10½
Bagby, Richard	260	"	94.5.--	1.8.3½
Bagby, Thomas	"	"	"	1.8.3½
Brooke, Richard	1539¾	29/-	2232.12.9	33.9.10
Brumley, Robert	225	5/3	59.1.3	17.9
Brumley, John	60	7/10	23.10.--	7.0½
Bird, George B.	60	6/3	18.5.--	5.7½
Broach, William	20	7/10	7.16.8	2.4
Bird, William	532	7/3	197.17.--	2.18.0¼
do. Dragon Swamp	88½	17/	70.4.6	1.1.--
Brown, John	50	7/4½	18.8.9	5.6½
Bird, Philemon	1157½	6/3	361.14.4½	5.8.6
do. Mary Bird	619	"	193.8.9	2.18.1
Brett, John Est.	308	18/	277.4.0	4.3.2
				130.4.3

[page 2, 1797] Persons owning lands	Quantity of land	Price per acre	Tot. Amt. Value Land	Tax on land 1½ percent
Burch, James	70	7/3	25.7.6	7.8
Burch, Vincent	100	4/2	20.16.8	6.3
Bird, Anthony A.	275	3/2	43.10.10	13.1
Byne, John Esta.	336	4/2	70.--.--	1.1.0
do. Dragon Swamp	2¼	17/	1.18.3	6¾
Bird, Barbara Esta.	266 2/3	24/10	331.2.2½	4.16.0
Bird, Robert Esta.	533 1/4	24/10	662.4.5½	9.12.0
do. Guy Smith	189½	3/2	30.0.1	9.--
Bourn, Richard Esta.	150	"	23.15.--	7.2
Boyd, John	115	18/8	107.6.8	1.12.3
do. Soanes's	382	24/10	474.6.4	7.2.4
Bray, Richard Esta.	93	7/10	36.8.6	10.11
Bird, John Esta.	100	3/2	15.16.8	4.9
Bowden, William	69	6/6	22.2.9	6.8
Bew, William	117	3/2	18.10.6	5.7
Boyd, Spencer Esta.	1428	10/5	770.15.--	11.11.2
Birkley, Edmond	762	5/3	200.0.6	3.0.0
Bland, John	60	12/6	37.10.0	11.3
Bohannan, William	130	5/3	34.2.6	10.3
Bland, William	100	9/11	49.11.8	14.10½
Bohannan, William (S. Stephens)	33	5/3	8.13.3	2.8
Bourn, Mills	159½	"	41.14.3	12.6
Bullman, Ann	100	5/3	26.5.--	7.11
do. of Agatha Moore	20	"	5.5.--	1.7½
Briggs, John (W. Finney's)	170	4/2	35.8.4	10.8
Belote, Laban	384½	"	80.2.6	1.4.--
Bland, William Sen[r.]	225	3/8¼	41.9.8¼	12.6
Bland, Ralph	146	5/3	38.6.6	11.6
Bowden, William jr.	100	4/2	20.16.8	6.3
do. Sykes & Dudley	34	3/2	5.7.8	1.8
do. of Lyne Shackelford	½	6/3	3.1½	5.[ ]
Bowden, John	100	4/2	20.16.8	6.3
Bland, William Esta.	250	"	52.1.8	15.8
Bland, Thomas	412	3/2	75.4.8	1.2.6¾
Bowden, George	236	5/3	61.19.--	18.7
do. of W[m.] Dillard	30	4/2	6.5.0	1.10½
Burch, William	45	3/2	7.8.6	2.1½
Brown, Thomas Esta.	445	12/6	283.15.--	4.5.1
Banks, James	22	7/3	7.19.6	2.5
Bristow, Bartholo[w.]	33½	3/2	5.6.1	1.7
Beard, David	450	9/4	210.--.--	3.3.--
Bristow, George	100	3/2	15.16.8	4.8
Bates, William	81	7/9½	31.10.1	9.5½
Banks, Andrew	125	12/6	78.2.6	1.3.5
Brightwell, John Esta.	70	4/2	14.11.8	4.4½
Burton, James	89	"	18.10.10	5.7
Crafton, Thomas	145	9/4	67.13.4	1.0.3½
Crafton, James	59	"	27.6.--	8.9½
Crafton, John	171	"	81.16.8	1.4.6½
Chick, Richard Esta.	491	7/3	177.19.9	2.13.5
Chapman, George Esta.	200	7/10	78.6.8	1.3.6
do. W[m.] Hoskins	39	10/5	20.6.3	6.1
				68.17.5

[page 3, 1797] Persons owning lands	Quantity of land	Price per acre	Tot. Amt. Value Land	Tax on land 1½ percent
	[84]			
Campbell, William	907	7/3	328.15.9	4.18.7½
Crane, John	136	6/3	42.--.--	12.7
Cleverius, Benjamin	419	20/9	434.14.3	6.10.5
Carlton, Henry Esta.	280	7/10	109.13.4	1.12.10
do Jno. Baylor Esta.	257	14/6	186.6.6	2.15.10½
Clayton, Thomas Esta.	275	7/3	99.13.9	1.9.1
Carlton, Benoni	72¾	"	26.7.4	8.--
do. of Wilson Row	49	6/3	15.3.1½	4.6¼
Campbell, Whitacar	318	7/10	124.11.--	1.17.6
Cleveley, Thomas	200	"	76.6.8	1.3.6
Crow, Nathaniel Esta.	200	6/3	62.10.--	18.9
Craine, George Esta.	30	7/3	10.7.6	3.4
Carlton, Joel	53½	6/3	16.14.5	5.1
Cooke, John	100	7/3	36.5.0	10.10½
Cooper, Ann	60	3/2	9.10.0	2.11
Carlton, Thomas (Swamp)	200	7/10	78.6.8	1.3.6
Carlton, Noah	100	"	39.3.4	11.9
Carlton, John (School)	100	6/3	31.5.--	9.5
Campbell, Sarah	296	12/6	185.--.--	2.15.6
Carlton, Christopher Senr.	37½	6/3	11.14.5	3.7
do. James Laughlin	126	3/2	26.8.2	8.--
Carlton, Richard Esta.	139	7/	48.13.--	14.7
Cothern, James	36½	3/2	5.15.7	1.8¾
Carlton, William (shoe)	309¾	11/6	178.1.2½	2.13.5
Carlton, Robert Esta.	148	5/	37.--.--	11.1
Carlton, Christopher jr.	100		36.5.--	10.11
do. Jno. Stone Esta.	159½	5/3	41.14.9	12.6
Carlton, Richard	250	7/3	90.12.6	1.7.3
Cooper, Henry	50	4/2	10.8.4	3.2
Carlton, Thomas (Taylor)	100	6/3	31.5.--	9.5
Cardwell, John Esta.	150	4/2	31.5.--	9.5
				36.19.2
Cardwell, John	"	"	"	9.5
Cardwell, William	77	"	15.11.6	4.7¼
Cardwell, Thomas	110	"	22.18.4	6.11
Cook, John	300	4/2	62.10.--	18.9
Collins, Thomas	329½	7/	115.6.6	1.14.7
do. Palmers	350	7/3	126.17.6	1.18.1
do. of Ro: S. Ware	86	11/9	50.10.6	15.2
Carlton, John jr.	235	4/2	48.19.2	14.9
Campbell, William	238	3/2	37.13.8	11.4
Curtis, Ann Esta.	414	5/3	108.13.6	1.12.7
Cook, Moses	100	8/4	41.13.4	12.6
Cook, Ann Cross	"	"	"	12.6
Corbin, Richard	2390	11/1¾	1332.11.4	19.19.9½
do. new Dragon bridge	125	12/8	78.2.6	1.3.5
Corr, James	100	6/2	30.16.8	9.3
Crouch, James	130	3/2	20.11.8	6.3
Chapman, Philip	200	7/10	78.6.8	1.3.6
Crittenden, Thomas	126	13/6	85.1.0	1.5.6
do. Dragon Swamp	36	17/	30.12.0	9.2
Collins, Joyeux Esta.	140	10/5	72.18.4	1.1.10
Crittenden, Zachy.	34 1/3	14/6	24.17.6	7.6
Cary, Wilson M. Esta.	1820	16/7	1509.1.8	22.12.9
Collier, John (Cobler)	150	5/3	39.7.6	11.10
Collier, John	100	4/2	20.16.8	6.3
				97.7.5

[page 4, 1797] Persons owning lands	Quantity of land	Price per acre	Tot. Amt. Value Land	Tax on land 1½ percent
Campbell, James	130	5/9¼	37.10.0	11.3
do. of Richard Garrett	70	3/2	11.1.8	3.4
Crittenden, Richard Esta.	178	5/3	46.14.6	14.1
Corr, Avarilla	79	"	20.14.9	6.2½
Collier, Catharine Esta.	750	"	196.17.6	2.19.1
Clegg, Isaiah	241	4/2	50.4.2	15.0½
Cook, Dawson	282	3/2	44.13.--	13.6
Curry, Ann	100	4/2	20.16.8	6.3
Curry, John	55	3/2	8.14.2	2.7½
Courtney, William	200	7/10	78.6.8	1.3.6
Cook, Thomas	240	3/2	38.--.--	11.5
Cook, Thomas jr.	96	"	15.--.4	4.6½
Carlton, Humphrey	175	7/	61.5.--	18.4
Carlton, Thomas Esta.	235	6/3	73.8.9	1.2.1
Carlton, Beverley Esta.	160	4/2	33.6.8	10.1
Coor, John jr. [Corr]	64	7/3	23.4.--	6.4½
Campbell, John	400	12/6	250.--.--	3.15.--
Curry, James	70	4/2	18.16.--	4.7
Coor, John Senr. [Corr]	213	3/2	33.15.6	10.1½
do. J. Corr jr.	90	7/3	32.12.6	9.9
Cook, Henry	49¼	10/5	25.10.5	7.8
Crittenden, Francis (River)	105 2/3	14/6	76.12.2	1.3.0
Clark, John	144	5/	36.0.0	10.9½
Cannady, William	100	6/3	31.5.0	9.5
Corr, Thomas R.	157½	5/3	41.6.10½	12.4¼
Cook, William	65	5/5	17.12.1	5.3½
Cooke, James	65	8/9	28.8.9	8.6½
Carter, Jesse	393	10/	196.1.--	2.18.9½
				23.3.8
Dew, William Esta.	935	14/6	677.17.6	10.3.5
Dew, Thomas	331	12/6	68.19.2	1.0.8
Dowling, William Esta.	264	8/4	110.--.--	1.13.--
Dix, Gabriel	338	6/3	105.12.6	1.11.8
Deshazo, William jr.	60	4/2	12.10.--	3.9
Durham, Joseph	155	4/3	32.5.5	9.8
Deshazo, Peter Esta.	192	7/4	70.8.--	1.1.1½
Deshazo, Larkin	87	7/3	31.4.10	8.11½
Dickie, James Esta.	512	8/4	213.6.8	3.4.0
Dunbar, David	366	"	152.10.--	2.5.9
Dunn, Richard	150	4/2	31.5.0	9.4½
Dalley, John Esta.	200	3/2	31.13.4	9.6
Dobbins, Charles Esta.	147	5/3	38.11.9	11.7
Dean, Benjamin	50	"	13.2.6	4.--
Dillard, William jr. Esta.	100	3/2	15.16.8	4.9
Dudley, Peter Esta.	530	7/3¼	186.18.4	2.16.1
Didlake, Mary	278	8/4	115.16.8	1.14.9
Durham, Robert Esta.	50	"	10.8.4	3.2
Didlake, Margret Esta.	65	4/2	13.10.10	4.1
Dunn, Thomas	50½	6/3	15.15.7½	4.9
Dillard, William Senr.	276	12/6	172.10.--	2.11.9
Durham, George	50	4/2	10.8.4	3.2
Durham, Thomas Esta.	85	3/2	13.9.2	4.2
Doumagin, Richard Esta.	66	5/5	17.17.6	5.4
Digges, Frances	175	5/3	45.13.9	13.10
				15.9.7

[page 5, 1797] Persons owning lands	Quantity of land	Price per acre	Tot. Amt. Value Land	Tax on land 1½ percent
	[85]			
Dumagin, Richard	55	5/5	14.17.11	4.5½
Didlake, George Esta.	114	10/5	59.7.6	17.10
Dungee, John	110	3/2	17.8.4	5.3
Dudley, William jr.	290	14/6	210.5.0	3.3.1
do. of L. Wedderburn	315½	6/3	98.11.10½	1.9.6¾
Damm, John Esta.	55	"	17.3.9	5.2
Dudley, William	180	7/10	70.10.--	1.1.2
Damm, William	25	4/2	5.4.2	1.6½
Douglas, John	239	7/	83.13.--	1.5.1
Didlake, John	1200	7/3	435.--.--	6.10.6
Dudley, Ann	141	"	51.2.3	15.4
Dudley, Guilford	106	"	38.8.6	11.6
Didlake, Edward	56	10/5	25.--.--	7.6
Dudley, Banks	230	3/2	36.8.4	10.11
Downey, Michael	50	10/5	26.--.10	7.9¾
Didlake, Royston	206	3/6½	36.7.4	11.1
Dillard, Thomas	49	15/	36.15.--	11.--
Dillard, William	392	15/	294.--.--	4.8.2
Dudley, Thomas	267½	6/3	81.17.8½	1.4.7
Dillard, Nicholas	75	4/2	15.12.6	4.9
Dillard, Benjamin Esta.	148	5/3	48.17.--	14.7¾
Drummond, John	150	6/3	46.17.6	14.6
Dixon, Michel	414¾	15/5	320.--.--	4.16.0
Dabney, Benjamin	400	14/6	290.--.--	4.7.0
of. Phil Taliaferro	72	8/4	30.--.--	10.0¾
Davis, Stage	311	6/9	105.2.7½	1.11.4½
do. Thos. Foster	50	4/2	10.8.4	3.1½
do. of Wm. Didlake	24	"	5.--.--	1.6
Dally, George	174¼	3/2	27.11.9½	8.3¼
Dudley, Henry F.	50	5/3	13.2.6	3.11
Dunn, John, Essex, Dragon	73	17/	62.1.--	18.7
				£39.5.2
Eubank, Richard Esta.	117	4/2	24.3.9	7.3
Eubank, John	469	10/4	242.6.4	3.12.9
do. James Grafton	111	6/3	34.13.9	10.5
do. Thomas Dew	178½	12/6	111.5.--	1.13.4½
Eubank, Henry	171	5/3	44.17.9	13.6
Edwards, Thomas Esta.	66	4/2	13.15.--	4.2
Eubank, William Esta.	28¾	5/3	7.11.--	2.4
Eubank, Richard Senr.	196	7/	68.12.--	1.0.7
Eubank, Thomas	110	4/2	22.18.4	6.10½
Eubank, Richard jr.	112¼	7/	39.5.7½	11.9¼
do. Thos. Jeffries	12¾	7/3	4.12.5	1.4½
do. of Agrippa Dunn	147	5/3	38.11.9	17.4
Evans, Ambrose	234½	7/10	91.13.--	1.7.6
Fogg, Fredrick	298	8/4	124.3.4	1.17.3
Fleet, Baylor	862	12/6	538.15.8	8.1.7½
Fauntleroy, Samuel G.	2069	20/	2069.--.--	31.--.8½
Fleet, John Esta.	260	6/3	81.5.--	1.6.4½
Faulconer, Thomas	220	"	68.15.--	1.0.6¼
Fogg, Thomas Esta.	200	"	62.10.--	18.9
Fogg, James	120	"	37.10.--	11.3
Fox, Joseph S.	13	7/3	4.14.3	1.5
				95.12.2

[page 6, 1797] Persons owning lands	Quantity of land	Price per acre	Tot. Amt. Value Land	Tax on land 1½ percent
Frazier, William Esta.	45	20/9	46.13.6	14.6
Fleet, William	352	"	365.4.--	5.9.6½
Fisher, James Esta.	110	3/2	17.18.4	5.3
Foster, Thomas	87¾	4/2	18.2.6	5.5¼
Faulkner, Mary	333	6/3	104.1.4	1.11.3
Fauntleroy, Thomas	486	10/	243.--.--	3.12.10¾
do. H. Todd	500	18/	460.--.--	6.18.--
do. W. Bowden	183	7/	64.1.--	19.2½
Farenholtz, David	151¼	6/6	49.1.6	14.8½
Faulkner, Benjamin	200	4/2	41.13.4	12.6
Grafton, Sally & Ann	132	9/4	61.12.0	18.6
Gale, John	615	7/5½	229.13.9	3.8.8½
Goleman, Thomas, Essex	948½	9/-	426.16.6	6.8.0
Garnett, Rice	297	7/3	107.13.4	1.12.4
Gatewood, Chaney	829	10/5	437.17.11	6.10.6
do. Gardner's	100	7/3	36.5.--	10.11
do. Noel's	362½	14/6	262.16.3	3.18.10
do. Harwood	225	4/2	46.17.6	14.1
do. Thomas Eubank	300	14/6	217.10.--	3.5.3
Garnett, ~~Rice~~ Joshua Esta.	325	8/4	134.3.4	2.--.3
Graves, Edward	200	6/3	62.10.--	18.9
Gatewood, Joseph	445	10/5	231.15.5	3.9.7
Gale, Mathew	323	11/5	184.7.7	2.15.4
Gatewood, John	160	8/4	66.13.4	[1].--.--
Garnett, Reuben	876½	8/10	387.2.5	5.16.2
Gwathmey, Temple	600	35/3	1057.10.--	15.17.3
Garlick, Samuel	454	24/10	563.14.4	8.9.2
Garlick, John	893	29/	1294.17.0	19.18.5
				108.15.4
Griffith, Joseph	50	6/3	15.12.6	4.9
Gresham, Samuel	400	7/3	145.--.--	2.3.6
Guthrie, William	46¾	"	16.18.11¾	5.1
Garrett, Robert	100	4/2	20.16.8	6.3
Gaines, Francis	356	14/6	258.2.0	3.17.5
Gaines, Henry Esta.	1517	20/4	1542.5.8	23.2.8
Gresham, Thomas	339¼	6/3	106.0.4	1.11.10
do. Thos. Stevens (orphan)	78	7/10	30.11.10	9.2
Gresham, Philemon	200	"	62.10.--	18.9
Gresham, John D	200	7/10	78.6.8	1.3.6
Gresham, William (Brickr.)	100	4/2	20.16.8	6.3
do. W.C. Row	40	6/3	13.3.4	4.--
Gardner, Elizabeth	100	"	31.5.--	9.5
Gibson, Richard	156½	3/2	24.16.7	7.4
Gibson, Banks	56½	"	8.18.11	2.7
Gibson, John	219¾	"	34.15.11	10.6
Griffith, Milley	50	6/3	15.12.6	4.9
Gresham, Machem	100	5/3	26.5.--	7.10½
do. of Ambrose Gresham	4	17/	3.8.--	1.[9]
Gresham, Ambrose	80	"	21.--.--	6.3½
do. Dragon	22	17/	18.5.--	5.6
Gresham, John jr.	80	5/3	21.--.--	6.3½
do. Ambrose Gresham	4	17/	3.8.--	1.--
Graves, Thomas	50	7/3	18.6.1½	5.5½
do. of Edward Wright	15¾	6/8	5.5.--	1.7
Griffin, William Esta.	859	14/6	622.15.6	9.6.10
Garlick, Camm Esta.	1100	6/3	343.15.--	5.3.2
Garrett, James	230	4/2	47.18.4	14.4½
				162.2.5

[page 7, 1797] Persons owning lands		Quantity of land	Price per acre	Tot. Amt. Value Land	Tax on land 1½ percent
		[86]			
Gardner, Anthony		638	11/	350.11.8	5.5.3
do. Dragon		67½	17/	57.7.6	17.2½
Gresham, Lumpkin		265	7/3	96.1.3	1.8.10
Garrett, Robert		200	7/	70.--.--	1.1.--
do. W. Hunt's Esta.		170	6/3	53.2.6	15.11
Gresham, William jr.		329	8/4	137.5.10	2.1.2¼
do. W. Gatewood		46	3/2	7.5.8	2.2
Gresham, George		141	"	22.6.6	6.8
Gaines, Robert Esta.		537¾	20/9	558.8.7¾	8.7.6
do. Ann Curtis		50	5/3	13.2.6	3.11
Gatewood, William (*Tuck*o.)		33	3/2	5.4.6	1.7
Gatewood, William, son of Jno.		132	10/	66.0.0	19.9½
Gleason, Patrick		134	8/4	55.16.8	16.9
Gatewood, Gabriel		78	10/5	40.12.6	12.2½
Guthrie, James		60	12/6	37.10.--	11.3
Guthrie, Richard Esta.		"	"	"	11.3
Glaspe, James		210	5/3	55.2.6	16.7
Groom, Mary		173	3/2	27.17.10	8.5
Garrett, George		88½	5/3	23.4.7½	6.11½
Guthrie, Rachel		50	8/4	20.16.8	6.3
Goldman, Martin		140	4/2	29.3.4	8.9
Groom, Zachy. Esta.		187	3/2	29.12.2	8.10½
Gulley, Phil Esta.		50	3/2	7.18.4	2.4
Garrett, William (shoe)		225	3/4¾	37.19.4	11.4½
Gramshill, Henry		25	3/2	3.19.2	1.2¼
Garrett, Ann Watts		112	5/	28.--.--	8.4¾
Garrett, Richard		100	4/2	20.16.8	6.3
Guthrie, Richard		162	3/2	25.13.--	7.8½
Hill, William		1342½	14/6	972.19.--	14.11.10½
Hitchcock, Thomas		140	4/2	29.3.4	8.9
Hoskins, Samuel		345	6/3	107.16.3	1.12.3
do. Elisha Alexander		57	10/5	29.13.9	8.10
Hutcherson, Charles	[subtotal £45.17.3]	531	7/1	188.1.3	2.16.5
Hoskins, William		252	7/10	98.14.--	1.9.7
do. George Kauffman		583	14/6	422.13.6	6.6.10
Heskew, John Esta.		61	5/3	16.--.3	4.10
Heskew, John jr.		50	6/3	15.12.6	4.8
do. Clemt. Pynes		10	3/2	1.11.8	5½
Hill, Robert Esta.		1281	8/2	523.1.6	7.16.11
Hill, Edward		1200	18/8	1120.--.--	16.16.--
Hoomes, Benjamin		372	12/6	232.10.--	3.9.9
do. Glebe		462	4/4	96.5.--	1.8.11
do. Ann Ken[n]edy		150	12/6	97.10.--	1.9.3
Hutson, William Esta.		112	3/2	17.14.8	5.4
Hemingway, John jr.		267	4/2	55.12.6	16.8½
Hemingway, Samuel		"	"	"	16.8½
Hemingway, John Senr.		266	"	55.8.4	16.7½
Hare, William		217	5/3	56.19.3	16.1
Harwood, Christopher Esta.		294	24/10	365.1.--	5.9.6
Harwood, John Senr.		25	5/3	4.7.6	1.3½
Harwood, William Esta.		240	30/	360.--.--	5.8.--
Hill, Thomas		300	26/11	403.15.--	6.1.2
Hart, James		150	3/2	23.15.--	7.2
Holderby, John		100	4/2	20.16.8	6.3
do. W. Hoskins		108¾	7/10	42.6.--	12.8
Hart, Anthony		190	5/3	49.17.6	15.--
do. of Sundry Persons		259½	3/2	41.1.9	12.4
					111.5.8

[page 8, 1797] Persons owning lands	Quantity of land	Price per acre	Tot. Amt. Value Land	Tax on land 1½ percent
Hart, Gregory	200	11/	31.3.4	9.6
Hart, William	250	3/3½	41.2.11	12.4
Harwood, John jr.	109	10/5	56.15.5	17.--
Hunt, William Esta.	560	6/3	175.--.--	2.12.6
Henry, Samuel Esta.	1900	14/6	1377.10.--	20.13.3
Henry, James	75	12/6	46.17.6	14.--½
Hurt, James	33	10/5	17.3.9	5.2
Halyard, William	190	5/3	49.17.6	15.--
Hoskins, John	767	10/7	399.9.7	5.19.10
do. Boughtons	100	8/4	41.13.4	12.6
Hunt, West	14	5/3	3.3.6	1.1
Hoskins, Robert	287	6/	86.2.--	1.5.10
Hart, Alden	127	"	26.9.2	7.11¼
Howerton, Heritage	122¼	20/9	126.16.7¼	1.18.0½
Holt, Richard	123	14/3	87.12.9	1.6.3½
Hutson, William (S.M.)	50	4/2	10.8.4	3.1½
Hutcherson, John	73¼	8/9	32.0.11¼	9.7¼
Hart, Vincent	75	6/6	24.7.6	7.4
Jones, Thomas	255	4/2	53.2.6	15.11
Jeffries, Thomas	63	7/3	22.16.9	6.10
do. Jn°. Harwood jr.	38¼	10/5	19.15.10	5.11
Jones, John Esta.	300	8/11	133.15.--	2.--.1½
Jeffries, Edward	70	3/2	11.1.8	3.4
Jones, James	160	14/6	116.--.--	1.14.10
do. James Jones Esta.	196	10/5	102.1.8	1.10.8
Jones, William Esta.	241	15/10	190.15.10	2.17.3
do. L. Smith	35¾	31/1	55.11.2	16.8
Jeffries, Ambrose	337	7/10	124.18.10	1.17.6
Jeffries, Robert	110	7/6	41.5.0	12.4
Jeffries, Bernard Esta.	30	4/2	6.5.--	1.11
Jordan, Thomas Esta.	100	"	20.16.8	6.3
Johnson, Thomas	112	3/2	17.14.8	5.4
Jameson, David Esta.	50	"	7.18.4	2.[5]
Jones, Rawleigh	63	31/1	93.18.3	1.9.4
				£53.7.1
Kemp, John (S.M.)	296	7/3	107.3.--	1.12.1
Kemp, John (St. Stephens)	178	7/3	64.2.2	19.2
Kauffman, Jn°. jr. Esta.	38	10/5	19.15.10	5.11½
do. Jn°. Kauffman's Esta.	471	18/8	439.12.--	6.11.11
Keeling, James Esta.	113¼	7/3	41.--.--¾	12.4
do. Robert Hill	23	8/2	9.7.10	2.10
Kennedy, Arch[d].	38¼	4/2	7.19.4	2.4½
do. B. Hoomes	227¾	7/10	89.4.2	1.6.9¾
Kennedy, Ann	70¼	"	14.11.8	4.6¾
Kennedy, Ann jr.	33¼	"	7.0.6	2.1¼
Kennedy, Lucy	37½	"	7.16.2	2.4
Kay, Christopher	116	6/3	30.--.9	9.1½
Kidd, Bartholo[w].	136	5/3	35.14.--	10.8

[see next page]

[page 8 (*continued*), 1797] Persons owning lands	Quantity of land	Price per acre	Tot. Amt. Value Land	Tax on land 1½ percent
Kidd, Benjamin	111	13/6	74.18.2	1.2.5½
do. Crittendens	60	"	40.10.--	12.1¾
do. Dragon	36	17/	30.12.--	9.2
Kidd, John	370	7/3	134.2.6	2.--.3
do. Lumpkin & Peirce	60	4/2	12.10.0	3.9
do. Thomas Dillard	45	14/6	32.12.6	9.10
King, Dice	18	8/4	7.10.--	2.3
Lumpkin, James	213	7/10	83.8.2	1.5.0
Lumpkin, Henry	620	9/4	289.6.8	4.6.10
Lumpkin, John Esta.	200	6/3	59.--.--	17.9
Lyne, William	1480	8/4	610.14.2	9.3.3
Lyne, William jr., Lotts in Dunkirk annual rent			150.--.--	1.--.10
Lumpkin, William	305	14/6	221.2.6	3.6.5
do. of Thos. Dew	26½	12/6	16.5.--	4.10½
Lefon, Francis	119	8/4	49.11.8	14.10
				92.8.11

[page 9, 1797] Persons owning lands	Quantity of land	Price per acre	Tot. Amt. Value Land	Tax on land 1½ percent
	[87]			
Lankford, Thomas Esta.	100	4/2	20.16.8	6.3
Lumpkin, Robert Sen[r.]	374	8/4	155.16.8	2.6.9
Longest, Caleb	97	7/10	37.19.10	11.6
Longest, Richard	140	"	54.16.8	16.6
Longest, John	100	"	39.3.4	11.9
Lumpkin, Anthony	216	6/3	67.10.--	1.0.4
Lumpkin, Jacob Esta.	916	"	286.5.--	4.5.11
do. Southerland's	271	5/3	71.2.9	1.1.4
do. Coleman's	196	10/5	102.1.8	1.10.8
Lewis, Iveson	356	14/6	258.2.--	3.17.4¼
Lumpkin, Richard Esta.	76¼	6/	22.17.6	6.10½
Leigh, Lucy	101	24/10	125.8.2	1.17.7
Lumpkin, Robert jr.	233	5/3	61.3.3	18.4
Leigh, John Esta.	199	24/10	247.1.10	3.14.2
Lyne, John	507	6/3	158.8.9	2.7.7
Lambouth, Thomas [Lambeth]	100	3/2	15.16.8	4.9
Lambouth, Charles Esta.	50	"	7.18.4	2.5
Motley, Edwin	815	10/5	428.2.6	6.8.6
McKentosh, William	126	4/2	26.5.--	7.10½
Martin, Thomas C.	680	14/6	493.--.--	7.7.11
do.	134½	7/3	48.15.1½	14.7½
Morgan, William	3	6/3	18.9	3¼
Mitchel, Ralph Esta.	193	10/5	100.10.5	1.10.1½
Minor, William	149	8/4	62.1.8	18.8
Minor, John	137	"	57.1.8	17.2
Minor, Thomas	288	7/10	225.6.--	1.13.10
Moody, Lewis	239	"	93.12.1	1.8.1
Mann, Joseph jr.	400	8/4	166.13.4	2.10.--
Mitchell, John	50	6/3	15.12.6	4.9
Mitchell, James Esta.	650	13/	422.10.0	6.6.9
Mann, Robert	699	6/3	218.8.9	3.5.6¼
				£59.14.2
McKendree, Elizabeth	90	5/3	23.12.6	7.1
Moore, Lambouth	70	4/2	14.11.8	4.3¼
Morris, William	10	"	2.1.8	7½
Moore, Benjamin	200	"	41.13.4	12.6
Merideth, Samuel	215	7/10	84.4.2	1.5.3
Moore, John	100	3/2	15.16.8	4.9
Major, Josiah	200	4/2	41.13.4	12.6
Mitchell, John Esta.	270	5/3	70.17.6	1.1.4
do. Root[e]s	200	9/11	99.13.4	1.9.8¼
Moore, Agatha	60	4/2	12.10.--	3.9
Moore, Rachel	120	"	25.--.--	7.6
Macon, John Esta.	1092	16/7	905.9.--	13.11.7
do. Lotts in Dunkirk			95.--.--	15.8¼
Montague, William	214	4/2	44.11.8	13.4½
Merideth, Ralph G.	567	14/6	411.1.6	6.3.5½
Muire, Richard	93	12/6	58.2.6	17.6

[see next page]

[page 9 (*continued*), 1797] Persons owning lands	Quantity of land	Price per acre	Tot. Amt. Value Land	Tax on land 1½ percent
Moore, Richard	145	6/3	45.6.3	13.8
McCarty, Joseph Esta.	73	3/2	11.11.2	3.6
Metcalf, John S.	265	14/6	196.5.10	2.18.1½
Metcalf, Thomas	256	"	181.8.8	2.15.2¼
Mann, Mary	100	5/3	26.5.--	7.11
Martin, John	475	9/	312.15.--	3.3.1½
Nunn, Jane	180	7/3	65.5.--	19.7
Newbill, George Esta.	500	8/4	208.6.8	3.2.6
Nunn, Thomas	130	7/3	47.2.6	14.1½
Nash, John Esta.	100	6/3	31.5.--	9.5
Newcombe, Eliz[a].	109	3/2	17.5.2	5.2
Newcombe, William	60	"	9.10.--	2.11
Newill, John	100	7/10	39.3.4	11.9
				104.12.--

[page 10, 1797] Persons owning lands	Quantity of land	Price per acre	Tot. Amt. Value Land	Tax on land 1½ percent
Orvill, John	100	6/3	31.5.--	9.5
Olliver, John	320	5/3	84.--.--	1.5.3
Overstreet, Gabriel	296	4/2	61.13.4	18.9
do. Hayses	130	5/3	34.2.6	10.2
Oaks, Henry	198½	3/2	34.2.0	10.2¾
Oaks, William	80	4/2	16.13.4	5.--
Owen, Augustine Esta.	100	6/3	31.5.--	9.5
Pendleton, James	888½	8/7½	383.3.3¾	5.14.11½
do. H. Wilmore	70	7/6	26.5.--	7.10½
Pitts, David Esta.	420	9/4	196.--.--	2.18.10
Pitts, Obadiah	20	10/5	10.8.4	3.2
Philips, Richard	230	7/3	83.7.6	1.5.1
Pollard, John Esta.	235	9/4	109.13.4	1.12.11
do. L. Smithey	384	7/3	139.4.--	2.1.10
Prewitt, Frances	99	9/4	46.4.--	13.11
Parker, John	264¼	7/	92.9.9	1.7.9
Prewitt, Richard	102	7/3	36.12.3	11.--
Pendleton, Phil	483	9/2	221.7.6	3.6.5
Perryman, Anthony Est.	130	7/3	47.2.6	14.2
Perryman, Phil	218	7/2	78.2.4	1.1.9
Pitts, Benjamin G.	100	5/4	26.13.4	8.--
Pynes, Clement	189	3/2	30.6.10	9.1
Pace, Benjamin	263	7/3	95.6.9	1.8.8
Pollard, Richard	389	8/4	162.1.8	2.8.7½
Prince, Francis	113	7/6	44.5.2	13.4
Pendleton, Benjamin	450	"	176.5.--	2.12.11
Pynes, Benjamin Esta.	164	6/3	51.5.--	15.3
Pynes, Robert	136	"	42.10.--	12.9
Pynes, Benjamin	100	"	31.5.--	9.5
Pemberton, John	165	"	51.11.3	15.5½
Pemberton, Philip	121	"	37.16.3	11.4
Pollard, Robert	6	24/10	7.9.--	2.2¾
Palmer, Charles	104	18/	93.12.--	1.8.[0]
				39.2.5
Price, Robert	630	6/3	196.17.6	2.19.1
Pigg, Rachel	108	14/6	78.6.--	1.3.6
Pigg, John Esta.	216	14/6	156.12.--	2.7.0
do.	180	7/3	65.5.--	19.7
Pollard, William	95	"	34.8.9	10.5
Pierce, Philip	83	3/2	13.2.10	2.7½
Pierce, Beverley	25¾	4/2	5.7.3½	1.7
do. of Phil Pierce	17	3/2	2.13.10	9½
Pierce, Thomas Esta.	87	4/2	18.2.6	5.5¼
Price, Andrew	314	6/	94.4.--	1.8.3

[page 10 (*continued*), 1797] Persons owning lands	Quantity of land	Price per acre	Tot. Amt. Value Land	Tax on land 1½ percent
Robertson, Rachel Esta.	155	12/6	96.17.6	1.9.6
do.	260	7/3	94.5.--	1.8.5
Roane, Thomas	2033	18/8	1897.9.4	28.8.3
do. H. Carlton's	200	6/3	63.10.--	18.9
do. Jn°. Brett's	34¾	18/	31.5.6	9.[ ]½
Roane, William Esta.	1585½	18/1½	1436.17.2	21.11.1
Row, Hansford & Wilson	341	6/3	105.14.7	1.10.8½
Row, Thomas (orphan)	555	7/3	201.3.9	3.0.4
Row, Elizabeth	665	20/9	689.18.9	10.7.--
Row, Francis (orphan)	612½	4/8	142.16.--	2.2.10
Row, Richard Esta.	550	8/4	229.3.4	3.8.9
Roane, Spencer	1600	24/10	1926.13.4	28.18.--
Ryland, Josiah	160	7/10	62.13.4	18.9½
Riddle, Vaughan	51	5/5	13.16.3	4.0½
Richerson, Elias Esta.	86	4/2	17.18.4	5.5
Row, William & Moses	60	6/3	18.15.--	5.7½
Richards, John	571½	4/8	124.8.--	1.17.6
Richerson, James	180	4/2	37.10.--	11.3
				156.16.3

[page 11, 1797] Persons owning lands	Quantity of land	Price per acre	Tot. Amt. Value Land	Tax on land 1½ percent
	[88]			
Richerson, William	369½	"	76.17.6	1.3.--
Richerson, William jr.	150	5/3	39.7.6	11.9¼
Richerson, John Esta.	101½	"	21.2.1	6.5
Roane, Major	687½	3/8	128.18.1½	1.18.8
Rains, Giles	60	3/2	9.10.--	2.11
Robinson, Benjamin Esta.	1300	8/4	541.13.4	8.2.6
Roane, Charles	200	14/6	145.--.--	2.3.6
do. Dragon	70	17/	59.10.--	17.11
Robbins, William	40	6/3	12.10.--	3.9
Roy, Beverley	700	8/4	291.13.4	4.7.6
Ross, John (B. Minor to pay)	100	5/3	26.5.--	7.11
Richards, George	21	17/	17.17.--	5.4¼
Richerson & Shepherd	24	10/5	8.6.6	2.6
Segar, Richard	406	7/3	147.3.6	2.4.2
Satterwhite, George	164	6/3	51.5.--	15.1
Satterwhite, William	200	5/7½	56.5.--	16.10½
Spencer, Edward Esta.	245½	8/4	96.5.10	1.8.11
do. S.M.	582	7/3	210.19.6	3.3.3½
Schools, John	156	8/4	65.--.--	19.6
Schools, John & James	16	7/1	5.13.4	1.8¼
Schools, Gabriel Esta.	169	6/3	52.16.3	15.11
Skelton, William	362	8/2½	148.11.5	2.4.7
do. of Phil Perryman	12	7/2	4.6.--	1.3½
Smith, John (D)	190	7/6	71.5.--	1.1.4
Sterling, Rodrick	360	7/10	141.--.--	2.2.4
do.	313	8/2	127.16.2	1.18.4
do. Wm. Lyne	56½	8/4	23.6.8	7.--
Skelton, Thomas	294	8/4	122.10.--	1.16.9
Scott, Benjamin Esta.	200	9/4	93.6.8	1.8.--
Saunders, George	200	7/3	72.10.--	1.1.9
Shepherd, William	140	9/4	65.6.8	19.8
Smith, Molley	30	4/2	6.5.--	1.11
Smith, John jr.	100	5/3	26.5.--	7.11
Smith, Lewis	96	7/6	36.--.--	10.9¾
Swinton, George	750	13/6	506.5.--	7.11.11
Stone, Sarah	300	7/3	108.15.--	1.12.8
Stone, Daniel	52	3/2	8.4.8	2.6
Smith, Larkin	1254¼	31/1	1949.6.3½	29.4.10
Smith, Henry	400	6/3	130.--.--	1.18.--
Smith, William	53	7/10	20.15.2	6.2½
Smith, James Esta.	80	3/2	12.13.4	3.10
Smith, James	101	7/10	39.11.2	11.10
Smith, Ambrose	92¾	8/4	38.6.8	11.6
Stevens, George Esta.	430	"	168.8.4	2.10.6½
Stevens, John (orphan)	75	"	29.8.4	8.10
Stevens, George (orphan)	"	"	"	8.10
Smith, William (Mill)	200	3/2	31.13.4	9.6

[page 11 (*continued*), 1797] Persons owning lands	Quantity of land	Price per acre	Tot. Amt. Value Land	Tax on land 1½ percent
Shackelford, John Esta.	114	7/3	40.18.2	12.3
Starke, Richard Esta.	350	5/8	99.3.4	1.9.9
Stone, Robert Esta.	200	4/2	41.13.4	12.6
Stone, Job	100	"	20.16.8	6.3
Stone, John Esta.	48½	5/3	12.12.--	3.9
Smith, Robert	325	10/5	169.5.5	2.10.9
Samuel Smith	110	"	57.5.10	17.2¼
do. Dragon	4	17/	3.8.--	1.--
Smith, John (son of Robt.)	80	10/5	41.13.4	12.6
do. Dragon	12	17/	10.8.--	2.1
Simkins, Nimrod	60	3/2	9.10.--	2.11
				98.12.10

[page 12, 1797] Persons owning lands	Quantity of land	Price per acre	Tot. Amt. Value Land	Tax on land 1½ percent
Sears, Philip	83	4/2	17.5.10	5.3
Shackelford, William Esta.	700	14/6	527.10.--	7.18.6
Spencer, Thomas	300	10/5	156.5.--	2.6.11
do.	225	4/2	53.2.6	15.11
Seward, Benjamin	115	3/2	18.4.2	5.6
Stedman, Christopher Sen[r.]	191	5/3	50.2.9	15.1
Smith, Thomas (orphan)	485	14/6	351.12.6	5.5.5
Saddler, John	150	6/3	46.17.6	14.6
Shackelford, Alexander	60	4/2	12.10.--	3.9
Stedman, Christopher jr.	260	5/3	65.5.--	1.0.6
Shackelford, John (R)	482	8/4	200.16.8	3.--.3
Shackelford, William	351	6/3	109.13.9	1.12.10¾
Shackelford, Lyne	50	"	15.12.6	4.8
Shackelford, John (Mc)	283	6/2	87.5.2	1.6.2¼
Scott, Anderson	330	16/7	273.12.6	4.2.2
Shepherd, John	192	3/2	30.1.8	9.3
Seward, Lucy & Eliz[a.] Esta.	100	4/2	22.18.4	6.10
Semple, Robert B.	253	10/5	131.15.1	1.19.6½
Stone, William	74¼	3/2	11.15.3½	3.6½
Seward, Edward	81½	5/3	21.6.6¾	6.4¾
Sthreshley, William	155½	6/3	48.11.10½	14.7
Sears, Thomas	123	6/7	40.9.9	12.2
Stratton Major Parish	300	10/	150.--.--	2.5.0
Trice, William	147	7/3	50.15.--	15.3
Taylor, James	50	6/3	15.12.6	4.9
Taylor, Edmond	294	8/14	122.10.--	1.16.9
Temple, Joseph	918	10/5	478.2.6	7.3.6
Tunstall, Molley Esta.	250	"	130.4.2	1.19.0¾
Tunstall, Richard jr. Esta.	1097	7/3	397.13.3	5.19.3
Tunstall, John Esta.	200	18/8	186.13.4	2.16.0
Tignor, William	130	7/10	50.18.4	15.4½
				58.4.9
Tureman, Benjamin	70	3/2	11.1.8	3.4
Tureman, George	50	"	7.18.4	2.4½
Taliaferro, William	1000	14/6	725.--.--	10.17.6
Townley, Robert (E. Williams to pay)	200	6/3	62.10.--	18.9
do. Anderson's	117	14/6	84.16.6	1.5.5
Taliaferro, Philip	940	8/4	391.13.4	5.17.6
do. D. Cook	374½	12/6	234.7.6	3.10.4
Trice, Edward Esta.	206	5/3	54.2.6	16.3
Thruston, Armstead	145	4/3	30.16.3	9.3
Taliaferro, Jn[o.] Baytop	296	5/3	77.14.--	1.2.3½
Temple, William	430	15/	322.10.--	4.16.9
Thruston, Batcheldor	200	3/2	31.13.4	9.6
Turner, Benjamin	36	4/2	7.10.--	2.3
Temple, Humphry	178	31/3	278.2.6	4.3.5¼
do. W. Tunstall	100	15/	75.--.--	1.2.6
Tunstall, William Esta.	438	21/	459.18.--	6.18.0
Tunstall, Richard (Purdy)	132½	8/4	55.--.--	16.[ ]

[page 12 (*continued*), 1797] Persons owning lands	Quantity of land	Price per acre	Tot. Amt. Value Land	Tax on land 1½ percent
Tunstall, Thomas C.	137	"	57.1.8	19.1½
Townley, Ann	79	4/2	16.9.2	5.--
Turner, Henry Esta.	100	"	20.16.8	6.3
Upshaw, James (Essex)	125	8/10	55.4.2	16.6¾
do. of Robert Beverley	30	10/5	15.12.6	4.8
Vass, Thomas	250	5/3	65.12.6	19.9
Wyatt, Henry	200	7/3	72.10.--	1.1.9
White, Henry	100	8/4	41.13.4	12.6
Wilmore, Thomas	150	10/5	78.2.6	1.3.6
do. D. Farthing	19	7/10	7.8.10	2.2½
Wright, James	124	5/3	32.13.8	9.10
Wyatt, Joseph	68	8/4	25.0.0	7.6
				109.5.3

[page 13, 1797] Persons owning lands	Quantity of land	Price per acre	Tot. Amt. Value Land	Tax on land 1½ percent
	[89]			
Walden, John Esta.	105	12/6	65.12.6	19.9
Wilson, Isaac	200	6/3	62.10.--	18.9
Wilson, Benjamin Esta.	200	7/3	72.10.--	1.1.9
Wiltshire, Joseph Esta.	74	"	26.16.6	8.--
Wright, Isaac	183	6/3	57.3.9	17.2
Wyatt, John	100	7/10	39.3.4	11.3
Watkins, William	37	4/2	7.14.2	2.4
Watkins, Joseph	156	6/7	51.7.--	15.5
Walker, Henry Esta.	150	5/3	39.7.6	11.10
Walker, Philip	110	9/4	51.6.8	15.4¾
Wood, William	2	7/10	15.8	2¾
Ware, John Esta.	562	7/3	203.14.6	3.1.2
Walker, Hump[y.]	820	33/2	1355.14.2	20.7.10
Wright, William	175	5/3	45.18.9	13.10
Watts, Edward	250	7/3	90.12.6	1.7.3
do. W. Watts Esta.	113	5/	28.5.--	8.5½
Watts, John	293	7/10	114.15.2	1.14.6
do. Pemberton	45	6/3	14.1.3	4.2
Watts, Kauffman	300	5/3	78.15.--	1.3.8
do. of Thomas Eubank	100	5/9	28.15.--	8.7½
do. Burch's Esta.	157	5/9	45.2.9	13.6¼
Watts, James	350	4/2	72.18.4	1.1.11
do. W. Watts Esta.	60	15/	45.--.--	13.6
Williams, Howard	283	4/2	58.19.2	17.9
do. Dragon	43	17/	36.11.--	10.10½
Wyatt, Thomas	206	7/10	81.2.--	1.4.4½
Wyatt, John Esta.	103	6/3	32.3.9	9.8
Wyatt, William	29¾	7/3	10.15.8	3.8
Williams, Howard Esta.	300	6/3	93.15.--	1.8.1
Williams, Charles	336	4/2	70.--.--	1.1.--
Walton, James	80	"	16.3.4	5.--
				£45.0.2
Walton, Mary	60	"	12.10.--	3.9
Willis, Joel	94	7/10	35.5.--	10.7
Walton, Elizabeth	60	3/2	9.10.--	2.11
Walton, John	176	5/3	46.4.--	13.11
Walton, William Esta.	66	4/2	13.15.--	4.2
Walton, Thomas Esta.	"	"	"	4.2
Ware, John	75	5/3	19.13.9	5.11
Ware, Arther Esta.	83	4/2	17.5.10	5.3
Waring, Robert P.	542	10/9	291.6.6	4.7.3¾
Walden, Richard	180	10/5	93.15.--	1.8.1½
Walden, Lewis	150	3/2	23.15.--	7.3
do. T. Dudley	84½	6/3	28.2.3½	8.5
Wright, Edward	60½	6/8	20.3.4	6.3¼
Wright, James	124	"	41.6.8	12.4¾
Williams, George	40	4/2	8.6.8	2.6
Watkins, Philip	197	5/3	51.14.3	15.7
Wyatt, Richard	175	12/6	109.7.6	1.12.9¾
Ware, Robert jr. Esta.	100	4/2	20.6.8	6.3
Williams, Elizabeth	16½	3/2	2.12.9	9½

[page 13 (*continued*), 1797] Persons owning lands	Quantity of land	Price per acre	Tot. Amt. Value Land	Tax on land 1½ percent
White, James Esta.	200	6/3	62.10.00	18.9
Watkins, Elizabeth	100	3/2	15.16.8	4.9
Warren, Catharine Esta.	175	"	27.14.2	8.4
Ware, Robert (B)	112	3/2	17.14.8	5.4
Wedderburn, Lydia	350	6/3	109.7.6	1.12.10
Whiting, Beverley Esta.	2447¾	7/10	866.18.9½	13.--.--
Webley, John	173	5/3	45.8.3	13.8
do. B. & F. Collier	268½	4/2	55.18.9	16.9¼
do. W. Dillard jr.	89½	"	18.12.11	5.7
Ware, Robert jr.	100	8/4	41.13.4	12.6
Ware, William	"	"	"	12.6
				77.9.3

[page 14, 1797] Persons owning lands	Quantity of land	Price per acre	Tot. Amt. Value Land	Tax on land 1½ percent
Walding, Edward Esta.	338	5/3	88.14.6	[4].6.9
Walding, Benjamin	35	"	9.3.9	2.9
Waller, Edward Esta.	133½	3/2	21.2.9	6.5
Waller, George	87	"	13.15.6	4.1½
Whayne, William	154½	7/10	60.10.3	18.1¾
Waller, Robert	113	3/7	20.5.11	6.1
Wyatt, John (Taylor)	30	5/3	7.17.6	2.5
Williamson, Abner	100	3/2	15.16.8	4.9
Ware, Nicholas	"	"	"	4.9
Walding, Samuel	80	7/10	36.6.8	9.4½
Walding, John Sen[r.]	100	5/3	26.5.--	7.10½
Young, Henry	640	18/8	597.6.8	8.19.3
				1374.5.11

¼ is £343.11.5
[arithmetic omitted]

William Courtney & Beverley Roy, Comm[rs.]

List of Land within the County of King & Queen with the Tax thereon for the year 1798

[page 1, 1798] Persons owning lands	Quantity of land	Price per acre	Tot. Amt. Value Land	Tax on land @ 7/6
	[90]			
Atkins, Joseph	66	4/2	13.15.0	1.0½
Alexander, Benjamin	202	9/4	94.5.4}	
do. James Halbert	124	6/2	38.15.--}	10.--
Acre, Seaton	52	9/4	24.5.4	1.5
Alexander, Elisha	338	"	157.14.8	11.0½
Anderson, Churchill Esta.	636	7/3	230.11.--	17.3½
Anderson, Pauling Esta.	498	14/6	361.1.0	1.7.4
Atkins, John	135	4/6	30.7.6	0.2.4
Abbott, Jacob	112	7/10	43.17.4	0.3.3¾
Anderson, Richard Esta.	460	5/3	120.15.--	9.--
Atkins, Lewis	60	8/4	25.--.--	1.10½
Anderson, Frances	458	10/9	246.3.6	18.5½
Bray, James	156	7/10	60.13.8	4.7½
Broach, Benoni	48	10/5	25.4.0	2.--
Brown, Henry Jun[r.]	100	12/	60.--.--	4.7
Beverley, Robert	2444	10/5	1262.16.4	4.14.--
Brown, Henry	760½	7/4½	280.8.8½	1.1.0½
Baylor, Gregory Esta.	720	14/6	522.0.0}	
do. of Bland, John & Lucy	166	8/4	69.3.4}	2.3.4
Bates, James	358	11/	149.3.4}	
do.	42	4/2	8.15.0}	11.11
Barton, John Esta.	125	"	26.--.10	2.0
Braxton, Carter (including marsh)	484½	10/5	252.6.10	0.19.0¾
Banks, William Esta.	365	"	76.0.10	5.9
Brooking, Frances	930	10/5	484.7.6	1.16.5
Boughton, Thomas (Essex)	130	9/4	60.13.4	4.7
Boughton, John	200	8/4	83.6.8	6.9
Boughton, Henry (Essex)	88	6/3	27.10.0	3.7
Broach, John	72	4/2	15.0.0	1.2
Burton, Thomas Esta.	170	5/3	44.12.6	3.4
Bohannon, Ann	197	4/6	44.6.6	3.3
Brown, William	75	7/10	29.7.6	3.9
Bagby, John Esta.	330	7/3	119.12.6	9.--
Bagby, Richard	260	"	94.5.0	7.1
Bagby, Thomas	"	"	"	7.1
do. of (Jacob Lumpkin) Esta.	235	6/3	73.8.9	5.6
Brizendine, Armstead	50	4/3	10.12.6	.10
Brooke, Richard	1539¾	29/-	2232.12.9	8.7.6
Brumley, Robert	225	5/3	59.1.3	4.5
Brumley, John	60	7/10	23.10.0	1.1
Bird, George B.	60	6/3	18.5.0	1.5
Broach, William	20	7/10	7.16.8	.7
				28.18.9

[page 2, 1798] Persons owning lands	Quantity of land	Price per acre	Tot. Amt. Value Land	Tax on land @ 7/6
Bird, William	532	7/3	197.17.0}	
do. Dragon Swamp	88½	17/	70.4.6}	19.9½
Brown, John	50	7/4½	18.8.9	1.4
Bird, Philemon	1776½	6/3	555.13.1½	2.1.8
Brett, John Estate	308	18/	277.4.--	1.0.9½
Burch, James [Burck]	70	7/3	25.7.6	1.10½
Burch, Vincent	100	4/2	20.16.8	1.7
Bird, Anthony Armstead	275	3/2	43.10.10}	
do. of Wm. Montague	44	4/2	9.3.4}	3.10½
Blake, Thomas	40	6/3	12.10.--	.11
Byne, John Esta.	336	4/2	70.--.--}	
do. Dragon (Swamp)	2¼	17/	1.18.3}	5.4½
Bird, Barbara Esta.	266 2/3	24/10	331.2.2½	1.4.--
Bird, Robert Esta.	533 1/4	"	662.4.5½}	
do. Guy Smith	189½	3/2	30.1.0}	2.10.3
Bourn, Richard Esta.	150	"	23.15.--	1.9½
Boyd, John	115	18/8	107.6.8}	
do. Soan's	382	24/10	474.6.4}	3.13.9
Bray, Richard Esta.	93	7/10	36.8.6	2.8
Bird, John Esta.	100	3/2	15.16.8	1.8
Bew, William	117	3/2	18.10.6	1.6
Bowden, William	69	6/6	22.2.9	1.8¼
Boyd, Spencer Esta.	1428	10/5	770.15.0	2.7.--
Berkley, Edmond	762	5/3	200.0.6	15.--
Bland, John	60	12/6	37.10.--	2.10
Bohannan, William	130	5/3	34.2.6	2.7
Bland, William	100	9/11	49.11.8	3.8½
Bohannan, William (S. Stephs.)	33	5/3	8.13.3	.8
Bourn, Mills	159½	"	41.14.3	3.2
				16.8.11
Bullman, Ann	100	"	26.5.--}	
do. of Agatha Moore	20	"	5.5.--}	2.3
Briggs, John (Wm. Finney's)	170	4/2	35.8.4	2.8
Belote, Laban	384½	"	80.2.6	6.--
Bland, William Senr.	225	3/8¼	41.9.8¼	3.1½
Bland, Ralph	146	5/3	38.6.6	2.10½
Bowden, William Junr.	100	4/2	20.16.8}	
do. Sykes & Dudley	34	3/2	5.7.8}	
do. Lyne Shackelford	½	6/3	3.1½}	2.2
Bowden, John	100	4/2	20.16.8	1.7
Bland, William Esta.	250	"	52.1.8	3.11
Bland, Thomas	412	3/2	75.4.8	5.8
Bowden, George	236	5/3	61.19.0}	
do. of Wm. Dillard	30	4/2	6.5.--}	5.1
Burch, William	45	3/2	7.8.6	.6½
Banks, James	22	7/3	7.19.6	.7½
Bristow, Bartholomew	33½	3/2	5.6.1	.6
Bristow, George	100	"	15.16.8	1.2
Bates, William	81	7/9½	31.10.1	2.4
Banks, Andrew	125	12/6	78.2.6	5.10
Brightwell, John Esta.	70	4/2	14.11.8	1.1
Burton, James	89	"	18.10.10	1.6
Crafton, Thomas	119	9/4	55.10.8	4.1½
Crafton, James	59	"	27.6.--	2.2
Crafton, John	171½	"	54.12.--	4.1
				19.8.4

[page 3, 1798] Persons owning lands	Quantity of land	Price per acre	Tot. Amt. Value Land	Tax on land @ 7/6
	[91]			
Chapman, George Esta.	200	7/10	78.6.8}	
do. of Wm. Hoskins	39	10/5	20.6.3}	7.6
Campbell, William	907	7/3	328.15.9	1.4.8
Crane, John	136	6/3	42.--.--	3.3
Cleverius, Benjamin	419	20/9	434.14.3	1.12.8
Carlton, Henry Esta.	280	7/10	109.13.4}	
do John Baylor Esta.	257	14/6	186.6.6}	1.2.2
Cole, G. Thomas	30	9/4	14.--.--	1.0½
do. for John Lumpkin's Esta.	75	6/3	23.8.9	1.9½
Carlton, Lewis	100	8/4	41.3.4	3.2
Clayton, Thomas Esta.	275	7/3	99.13.9	7.3½
Carlton, Benoni	72¾	"	26.7.4}	
do. of Wilson Row	49	6/3	15.3.1½}	3.1½
Campbell, Whitacar	318	7/10	124.11.--	9.4½
Cleveley, Thomas	200	"	76.6.8	5.11
Crow, Nathaniel Esta.	200	6/3	62.10.0	4.8
Crane, George Esta.	30	7/3	10.7.6	.10
Courtney, Thomas	183¼	10/5	95.6.3	7.3½
Carlton, Joel	53½	6/3	16.14.5	1.4½
Cooke, John	100	7/3	36.5.--	2.8½
Carlton, Thomas (Swamp)	200	7/10	78.6.8	5.11
Carlton, Noah	100	"	39.3.4	2.11½
Cook, Henry	260	5/3	68.5.--	5.1½
Carlton, John (Schoolm.)	100	6/3	31.5.--	2.4
Campbell, Sarah Esta.	296	12/6	185.--.--	9.4½
Carlton, Christopher Senr.	37½	6/3	11.14.5}	
do. of James Laughlin	126½	3/2	26.8.2}	3.—
				8.7.6
Carlto[n], Richard Esta.	139	7/	48.13.--	3.9
Cothern, James	36½	3/2	5.15.7	.5
Carlton, William (Shoe)	309¾	11/6	178.1.2½	13.4
Carlton, Robert Esta.	148	5/	37.--.--	2.4½
Carlton, Richard	250	7/3	90.12.6	6.10½
Carlton, Christopher Junr.	100		36.5.--}	
do. John Stone's Esta.	159½	5/3	41.14.9}	5.10
Cooper, Henry	50	4/2	10.8.4	0.9½
Carlton, Thomas (Taylor)	100	6/3	31.5.--	2.4
Cardwell, John Esta.	150	4/2	31.5.--	2.4
Cardwell, John	"	"	"	2.4
Cardwell, William	77	"	15.11.6	1.2
Cardwell, Thomas	110	"	22.18.4	61.8½
Cook, John Esta.	300	4/2	62.10.--	4.8
Collins, Thomas	329½	7/	115.6.6}	
do. Palmers	350	7/3	126.17.6}	
do. of Robt. S. Ware	86	11/9	50.10.6}	1.1.11
Carlton, John Jr.	235	4/2	48.19.2	3.8
Campbell, William	238	3/2	37.13.8	2.10½
Curtis, Ann Esta.	414	5/3	108.13.6	7.9
Cooke, Moses	100	8/4	41.13.4	3.1½
Cooke, Ambrose	"	"	"	3.1½
Corbin, Richard	2390	11/1¾	1332.11.4}	
do. New Dragon Bridge	125	12/6	78.2.6}	5.5.9½
Corr, James	100	6/3	30.16.8	2.4
Crouch, James	130	3/2	20.11.8	1.7
Chapman, Philip	200	7/10	78.6.8	5.10½
Crittenden, Thomas	126	13/6	85.1.--}	
do. Dragon Swamp	36	17/	30.12.--}	8.7¾
				£19.1.11

[page 4, 1798] Persons owning lands	Quantity of land	Price per acre	Tot. Amt. Value Land	Tax on land @ 7/6
Collins, Joyeux Esta.	140	10/5	72.18.4	5.5
Crittenden, Zacha$^{y.}$	34¼	14/6	24.17.10	1.10½
Cary, Wilson M. Esta.	1820	16/7	1509.1.8	5.13.2
Collier, John (Cobler)	150	5/3	39.7.6	3.0
Collier, John	100	4/2	20.16.8	1.7
Campbell, James	130	5/9¼	37.10.--}	
do. of Rich$^{d.}$ Garrett	70	3/2	11.1.8}	3.7
Crittenden, Rich$^{d.}$ Esta.	178	5/3	46.14.6	3.6
Corr, Avarilla	79	"	20.14.9	1.7
Collier, Catharine Esta.	750	"	196.17.6	14.10
Clegg, Isaiah	241	4/2	50.4.2	3.9
Cooke, Dawson	282	3/2	44.13.--	3.4½
Curry, Ann	100	4/2	20.16.8	1.7
Curry, John	55	3/3	8.14.2	.8
Courtney, William	200	7/10	78.16.8	5.10½
Cooke, Thomas	240	3/2	38.--.--	2.10
Cooke, Thomas Jun$^{r.}$	96	"	15.0.4	1.1½
Carlton, Humphrey	175	7/	61.5.--	4.7
Carlton, Thomas Esta.	235	6/3	73.8.9	5.6½
Carlton, Beverley Esta.	160	4/2	33.6.8	2.6½
Corr, John jr.	64	7/3	23.4.0}	
do. of Thomas Dudley	197½	6/3	61.14.4½}	6.5
Campbell, John	400	12/6	250.--.--	18.9
Curry, James	70	4/2	18.16.--	1.2
				10.6.9
Corr, John Sen$^{r.}$	213	3/2	33.15.6}	
do. J. Corr jr.	90	7/3	32.12.6	4.11½
Cooke, Henry	49¼	10/5	25.10.5	7.8
Crittenden, Francis (River)	105$_{2/3}$	14/6	76.12.2	5.9
Clark, John	144	5/	36.--.--	2.8
Cannady, William	100	6/3	31.5.--	2.4
Corr, Thomas (R)	157½	5/3	41.6.10½	3.1
Cook, William	65	5/5	17.12.1	1.4
Cooke, James	65	8/9	28.8.9	2.1½
Dew, William Esta.	935	14/6	677.17.6	2.10.10
Dew, Thomas	331	12/6	68.19.2	5.2
Dowling, William Esta.	264	8/4	110.--.--	8.3
Dix, Gabriel	338	6/3	105.12.6	7.11
Deshazo, William jr.	60	4/2	12.10.--	.11
Durham, Joseph	105	4/3	21.12.6	1.7
Deshazo, Peter Esta.	192	7/4	70.8.0	5.11
Deshazo, Larkin	87	7/3	31.4.10	2.4
Dickie, James	512	8/4	213.6.8	16.--
Dunbar, David	366	"	152.10.0	12.3
Dunn, Richard	150	4/2	31.5.--	2.4
Dalley, John Esta.	200	3/2	31.13.4	2.4½
Dobbins, Charles Esta.	147	5/3	38.11.9	2.11
Dean, Benjamin	50	"	13.2.6	1.--
Dillard, William Esta.	100	3/2	15.16.8	1.2
Dudley, Peter Esta.	530	7/3¼	186.18.4	14.1½
Didlake, Mary	278	8/4	115.16.8	8.8½
Durham, Robert	50	4/2	10.8.4	.9¾
				£18.15.6

[page 5, 1798] Persons owning lands	Quantity of land	Price per acre	Tot. Amt. Value Land	Tax on land @ 7/6
	[92]			
Didlake, Margret Esta.	65	4/2	13.10.10	1.1½
Dunn, Thomas	50½	6/3	15.15.7½	1.2
Dillard, [William] Senr.	226	12/6	141.5.--	8.7
Dillard, George	50	"	31.5.--	2.4
Durham, George	50	4/2	10.8.4	.9½
Durham, Thomas Esta.	85	3/2	13.9.2	1.0½
Dumagin, Richard Esta.	66	5/5	17.17.6	1.4
Diggs, Frances	175	5/3	45.13.9}	
do. of Thos. Brushwood	180	4/2	37.10.--}	6.3½
Dumagin, Richard	55	5/5	14.17.11	1.2
Didlake, George Esta.	114	10/5	59.7.6	4.4½
Dungee, John	110	3/2	17.8.4	1.4
Dudley, William jr.	290	14/6	210.5.0}	
do. of L. Wedderburn	315½	6/3	98.11.10½}	1.3.2
Damm, John Esta.	55	"	17.3.9	1.3½
Dudley, William	180	7/10	70.10.--	5.3½
Damm, William	25	4/2	5.4.2	.4½
Douglas, John	239	7/	83.13.--	6.3
Didlake, John	1200	7/3	435.--.--	1.12.7½
Dudley, Ann	141	"	51.2.3	3.0
Dudley, Guilford	106	"	38.8.6	2.10½
Didlake, Edward	56	10/5	25.--.--	1.10½
Dudley, Banks	230	3/2	36.8.4	2.9
Downey, Michael Esta.	50	10/5	26.--.10	1.11½
				5.11.10
Didlake, Royston	206	3/6½	36.7.4	2.9
Dillard, Thomas	49	15/	36.15.--	2.9½
Dillard, William	259½	"	194.4.--	14.7
Dudley, Thomas	70	6/3	21.17.6	1.8
Dillard, Nicholas	75	4/2	15.12.6	1.2½
Dillard, Benjamin Esta.	148	5/3	48.17.0	3.8
Drummond, John Esta.	150	6/3	46.17.6	3.7
Dixon, Michael	414¾	15/5	320.--.--	1.4.--
Dabney, Benjamin	400	14/6	290.--.--}	
do. Phil. Taliaferro	72	8/4	30.--.--}	1.4.3
Davis, Stage	311	6/9	105.2.7½}	
do. Thos. Foster	50	4/2	10.8.4}	
do. of W^m. Didlake	24	"	5.--.--}	9.--
Dally, George	174¼	3/2	27.11.9½	2.--
Dudley, Henry F.	50	5/3	13.2.6	1.--
Dunn, John (Essex), (Draggon)	73	17/	62.1.--	4.8
Eubank, Richard Esta.	117	4/2	24.3.9	1.10
Eubank, John Esta.	469	10/4	242.6.4}	
do. James Grafton	111	6/3	34.13.9}	
do. Thos. Dew	178½	12/6	111.5.--}	1.9.2
Eubank, Henry	171	5/3	44.17.9	4.1½
Edwards, Thomas Esta.	66	4/2	13.15.0	1.5½
Eubank, William Esta.	28¾	5/3	7.11.0	.7
Eubank, Richard Senr.	196	7/	68.12.0	5.1½
Eubank, Thomas	110	4/2	22.18.4	1.8½
				£12.10.7

[page 6, 1798] Persons owning lands	Quantity of land	Price per acre	Tot. Amt. Value Land	Tax on land @ 7/6
Eubank, Richard Jun[r.]	112¼	7/	39.5.7½}	
do. of Tho[s.] Jeffries	12¾	7/3	4.12.5}	
do. of Agrippa Dunn	147	5/3	38.11.9}	7.7
Evans, Ambrose	234½	7/10	91.13.0	6.10½
Fogg, Frederick	298	8/4	124.3.4	9.4½
Fogg, Thomas	107	6/3	33.8.8	2.6
Fleet, Baylor	862	12/6	538.15.8	2.0.4¾
Fauntleroy, Samuel G.	2069	20/	2069.--.--	7.15.2
Fleet, John Esta.	260	6/3	81.5.0	6.7
Faulkner, Thomas	220	"	68.15.0	5.1½
Fogg, Thomas Esta.	93	"	29.1.3	2.2
Fogg, James	120	"	37.10.0	2.10
Fox, Joseph S.	13	7/3	4.14.3	.4½
Frazier, William Esta.	45	20/9	46.13.6	3.6
Fleet, William	352	"	365.4.0	1.8.4¼
Fisher, James	110	3/2	17.18.4	1.4
Foster, Thomas	87¾	4/2	18.2.6	1.4½
Faulkner, Mary	333	6/3	104.1.4	7.10
Fauntleroy, Thomas	486	10/	243.0.0}	
do. H. Todd	500	18/	460.0.0}	
do. W. Bowden	183	7/	64.1.0}	
Farenholtz, David	151¼	6/6	49.1.6	3.7½
Faulkner, Benjamin	533	4/2	111.0.10	8.4
				14.3.4
Grafton, Sally & Ann	132	9/4	61.12.0	4.7
Gale, John	264	7/5	97.18.0	7.4
Gale, William	351	7/5	130.3.3	9.10
Goleman, Thomas (Essex)	948½	9/	426.16.6	1.12.--
Garnett, Rice	297	7/3	107.13.4	8.1
Gatewood, Chaney	829	10/5	437.17.11}	
do. Gardner's	100	7/3	36.5.0}	
do. Nole's [Noel's]	362½	14/6	262.16.3}	
do. Harwood	225	4/2	46.17.6}	
do. T. Eubank	300	14/6	217.10.0}	
do. [J]ohn Walden Esta.	120	12/6	75.0.0}	4.0.6½
Garnett, Joshua Esta.	325	8/4	134.3.4	10.1
Graves, Edward Esta.	200	6/3	62.10.0	4.8
Gatewood, Joseph	445	10/5	231.15.5	17.4½
Gale, Mathew	323	11/5	184.7.7	13.9½
Gatewood, John	160	8/4	66.13.4	5.0
Garnett, Reuben	876½	8/10	387.2.5	1.9.0½
Gwathmey, Temple	600	35/3	1057.10.0	3.19.3½
Garlick, Samuel	454	24/10	563.14.4	1.6.3½
Garlick, John	893	29/	1294.17.0	4.19.7½
Griffith, Joseph	50	6/3	15.12.6	1.2
Gresham, Samuel	432½	7/3	156.15.7½	11.9
Guthrie, William	46¾	"	16.18.11¾	1.3½
do. L. Smith, ½ acre Meetg. H.	½	"	"	"
Garrett, Robert	100	4/2	20.16.8	1.6
Gaines, Francis	356	14/6	258.2.0	19.4
Gaines, Henry Esta.	1517	20/4	1542.5.8	5.15.8
				43.11.6

[page 7, 1798] Persons owning lands	Quantity of land	Price per acre	Tot. Amt. Value Land	Tax on land @ 7/6
	[93]			
Gresham, Thomas	339¼	6/3	106.0.4}	
do. Thos. Stephens (orphan)	78	7/10	30.11.10}	10.3
Gresham, Philemon	200	"	62.10.0	4.8
Gresham, John D	200	7/10	78.6.8	5.10½
Gresham, William (Brickr.)	100	4/2	20.16.8}	
do. W.C. Row	40	6/3	13.3.4}	2.7
Gardner, Elizabeth	100	"	31.5.0	2.4
Gibson, Richard	156½	3/2	24.16.7	1.9½
Gibson, Banks	56½	"	8.18.11	.7½
Gibson, John	219¾	"	34.15.11	0.2.7½
Griffith, Milley	50	6/3	15.12.6	1.2
Gresham, Machem	100	5/3	26.5.0}	
do. of Ambrose Gresham	4	17/	3.8.0}	2.2½
Gresham, Ambrose	80	"	21.--.--}	
do. Dragon	22	17/	18.5.0}	2.11
Gresham, John jr.	80	5/3	21.0.0}	
do. A. Gresham	4	17/	3.8.0}	1.10
Graves, Thomas	50½	7/3	18.6.1½}	
do. of Edward Wright	15¾	6/8	5.5.0}	1.9
Griffin, William Esta.	859	14/6	622.15.6	2.0.8
Garlick, Camm Esta.	1100	6/3	343.15.0	1.5.9½
Garrett, James	230	4/2	47.18.4	3.7
Gardner, Anthony	638	11/	350.11.8}	
do. Dragon Swamp	67½	17/	57.7.6}	1.10.7
Gresham, Lumpkin	265	7/3	96.1.3	7.2½
Garrett, Robert	200	7/	70.0.0}	
do. Wm. Hunt's Esta.	170	6/3	53.2.6}	9.2½
				7.17.8
Gresham, William jr.	329	8/4	137.5.10}	
do. William Gatewood	46	3/2	7.5.8}	12.7½
do. from Chick	69	7/3	25.0.3}	
Gresham, George	141	3/2	22.6.6	1.8
Gaines, Robert Esta.	537¾	20/9	558.8.7¾}	
do. Ann Curtis	50	5/3	13.2.6}	2.7.10
Gatewood, William (*Tucko.*)	33	3/2	5.4.6	.4½
Gatewood, William (son of Jno.)	132	10/	66.0.0	6.[ ]
Gleason, Patrick	134	8/4	55.16.8	4.2½
Gatewood, Gabriel	78	10/5	40.12.6	1.0½
Garrett, William jr.	120	4/2	25.0.0	1.10½
Guthrie, James	60	12/6	37.10.0	2.10
Guthrie, Richard Esta.	60	"	"	2.10
Glaspe, James Esta.	210	5/3	55.2.6	4.1½
Groom, Mary	173	3/2	27.17.10	2.1
Garrett, George	88½	5/3	23.4.7½	1.8½
Guthrie, Rachel	50	8/4	20.16.8	1.6
Goldman, Martin	140	4/2	29.3.4	2.2½
Groom, Zachary Esta.	187	3/2	29.12.2	2.3
Gully, Philip	50	"	7.18.4	[11].7
Garrett, William (Shoe)	225	3/4¾	37.19.4	2.10
Gramshill, Henry	25	3/2	3.19.2	.4
Garrett, Ann Watts	112	5/	28.0.0	2.1
Garrett, Richard	100	4/2	20.16.8	1.6
Guthrie, Richard	162	3/2	25.13.0	1.11
Hill, William	1342½	14/6	972.19.0	3.12.11
Hitchcock, Thomas	140	4/2	29.3.4	2.2
				16.17.2

[page 8, 1798] Persons owning lands	Quantity of land	Price per acre	Tot. Amt. Value Land	Tax on land @ 7/6
Hoskins, Samuel Esta.	345	6/3	107.16.3}	
do. Elisha Alexander	57	10/5	29.13.9}	10.3
Hutcherson, Charles	531	7/1	188.1.3	14.1
Hoskins, William	252	7/10	98.14.0}	
do. of George Kauffman	583	14/6	422.13.6}	1.19.1
Heskew, John Esta.	61	5/3	16.--.3	1.2
Heskew, John Jr.	50	6/3	15.12.6}	
do. Clemt. Pynes	10	3/2	1.11.8}	1.4
Hill, Robert Esta.	1281	8/2	523.1.6	1.19.2½
Hill, Edward	1200	18/8	1120.0.0	4.4.0
Hoomes, Benjamin	372	12/6	232.10.0}	
do. Glebe	462	4/4	96.5.0}	
do. Ann Ken[n]edy	75	12/6	46.17.6}	[11].8.--
Hutson, William Esta.	112	3/2	17.14.8	1.4
Hemingway, John jr.	267	4/2	55.12.6	4.2
Hemingway, Samuel	"	"	"	4.2
Hemingway, John Senr.	266	"	55.8.4	4.1½
Hare, William Esta.	217	5/3	56.19.3	4.2
Harwood, Christopher Esta.	294	24/10	365.1.0	1.17.4½
Hill, Thomas	300	26/11	403.15.0	1.10.3½
Hart, James	150	3/2	23.15.0	1.9½
Holderby, John	100	4/2	20.16.8}	
do. of Wm. Hoskins	108¾	7/10	42.6.0}	4.8½
Hart, Anthony	190	5/3	49.17.6}	
do. of Sundry Persons	259½	3/2	41.1.9}	6.10
do. of Elizabeth Watkins	100	"	15.16.8}	1.2
				15.7.3
Hart, Gregory	200	11/	31.3.4	1.2.4½
Hart, William	250	3/3½	41.2.11	3.1
Harwood, John Jr.	109	10/5	56.15.5	4.3
Hunt, William Esta.	560	6/3	175.0.0	13.1½
Henry, Samuel Esta.	1900	14/6	1377.10.0	5.3.4
Henry, James	75	12/6	46.17.6	3.6
Hurt, James	33	10/5	17.3.9	1.3½
Halyard, William	190	5/3	49.17.6	3.9
Hoskins, John	767	10/7	399.9.7}	
do. Boughtons	100	8/4	41.13.4}	1.10.7
Hunt, West	14	5/3	3.3.6	.3
Hoskins, Robert	287	6/	86.2.0	6.4½
do. of Robt. Smith (Mortgage)	127	4/2	26.9.2	1.11½
Hart, Alden				
Howerton, Heritage	122¼	20/9	126.16.7¼	4.6¼
Howerton, John	269½	5/3	70.14.10½	5.3½
Holt, William	123	14/3	87.12.9	6.7
Hutson, William (S.M.)	50	4/2	10.8.4	.10
Hutcherson, John	73¼	8/9	32.0.11¼	2.4¼
Hart, Vincent	75	6/6	24.7.6	1.10
Halyard, John	1	5/9¼	5.9¼	½
Howerton, George	76¼	6/	22.17.6	1.8½
Jones, Thomas	255	4/2	53.2.6	3.11½
Jeffries, Thomas	63	7/3	22.16.9}	
do. Jno. Harwood jr.	38¼	10/5	19.15.10}	2.11½
Jones, John Esta.	300	8/11	133.15.0	10.0½
Jeffries, Edward	70	3/2	11.1.8	.9½
Jones, James	160	14/6	116.0.0}	
do. James Jones Esta.	196	10/5	102.1.8}	16.4½
				26.18.5

[page 9, 1798] Persons owning lands	Quantity of land	Price per acre	Tot. Amt. Value Land	Tax on land @ 7/6
	[94]			
Jones, William Esta.	241	15/10	190.15.10}	
do. L. Smith	35¾	31/1	55.11.2}	18.5½
Jeffries, Ambrose	337	7/10	124.18.10	9.4½
Jeffries, Robert	110	7/6	41.5.0	3.1
Jeffries, Gawin	30	4/2	6.5.0	.5½
Jordan, Thomas Esta.	100	"	20.16.8	1.8
Johnson, Thomas	112	3/2	17.14.8	1.4
Jameson, David Esta.	50	"	7.18.4	0.7½
Jones, Rawleigh	63	31/1	93.18.3	7.4
Kemp, John	296	7/3	107.3.0	8.--
Kemp, John (St. Stephens)	178	7/3	64.2.2	4.9
Kauffman, John jr. Esta.	38	10/5	19.15.10}	
do. John Kauffman's Esta.	471	18/8	439.12.0}	1.13.5½
Keeling, James Esta.	113¼	7/3	41.0.0¾}	
do. Rob[t.] Hill	23	8/2	9.7.10}	3.9½
Kennedy, Arch[d.] Esta.	38¼	4/2	7.19.4	1.1½
Kennedy, Ann	70¼	7/10	14.11.8	1.1½
Kennedy, Ann jr.	33¼	"	7.--.6	.6¼
Kennedy, Lucy	37½	"	7.16.2	.6¾
Kay, Christopher	116	6/3	30.0.9	2.3½
Kidd, Bartholomew	136	5/3	35.14.0}	
do. of W. Dillard	132½	4/2	27.12.1}	1.2.1½
Kidd, Benjamin	111	13/6	74.18.2}	
do. Crittendens	60	"	40.10.0}	11.0
do. Dragon Swamp	36	17/	30.12.0}	_____
Kidd, John	370	7/3	134.2.6}	6.11.1
do. Lumpkin & Pearce	60	4/2	12.10.0}	
do. Tho[s.] Dillard	45	14/6	32.12.6}	13.5½
King, Dicey	18	8/4	7.10.0	.6½
Lumpkin, James	213	7/10	83.8.2	6.3
Lumpkin, Henry	400	9/4	186.13.4	14.--
Lumpkin, John Esta.	125	6/3	35.11.3	2.8
Lyne, William	1480	8/4	610.14.2	2.5.10
Lyne, William Jun[r.], Lotts in Dunkirk annual rent			150.0.0	1.11.3
Lumpkin, William	305	14/6	221.2.6}	
do. of Tho[s.] Dew	26½	12/6	16.5.0}	15.4
Lefon, Francis	119	8/4	49.11.8	3.8
Lumpkin, Henry [Senr.]	190	9/4	88.13.4	6.7½
Lankford, Thomas Esta.	100	4/2	20.16.8	1.8
Lumpkin, Robert Sen[r.]	374	8/4	155.16.8	11.8½
Lumpkin, John Ware	140	7/10	54.16.8	4.1½
Longest, Caleb	97	"	37.19.10	2.10½
Longest, Rich[d.]	227¾	"	89.4.2	6.8½
Longest, John	100	"	39.3.4	3.--
Lumpkin, Anthony	216	6/3	67.10.0	5.1¼
Lumpkin, Jacob Esta. fm. L. Gresham	100	7/3	36.5.0	2.8½
Lumpkin, Jacob (orphan)	681	6/3	212.16.3	15.8
Lewis, Iveson	356	14/6	258.2.0	19.4
Leigh, Lucy	101	24/10	125.8.2	10.4½
Lumpkin, Robert Jun[r.]	233	5/3	61.3.3	4.7
Leigh, John Esta.	199	24/10	247.1.10	18.6½
				18.17.1

[page 10, 1798] Persons owning lands	Quantity of land	Price per acre	Tot. Amt. Value Land	Tax on land @ 7/6
Lyne, John	507	6/3	158.8.9	11.10½
Lambouth, Thomas	100	3/2	15.16.8	1.2½
Lambouth, Charles Esta.	50	"	7.18.4	.7½
Motley, Edwin	815	10/5	428.2.6	1.12.1½
McKentosh, William	126	4/2	26.5.0	1.11½
Martin, Thomas C.	680	14/6	493.0.0}	
do.	134½	7/3	48.15.1½}	2.--.7½
Mo[r]gin, William	3	6/3	18.9	.1
Mitchell, Ralph Esta.	193	10/5	100.10.5	7.7¼
Minor, William	149	8/4	62.1.8	4.7½
Minor, John	137	"	57.1.8	4.3
Minor, Thomas	288	7/10	225.6.0	8.4
Mo[o]dy, Lewis	239	"	93.12.2	7.[0]
Mann, Joseph Jun[r.]	400	8/4	166.13.4	12.6
Mitchell, John	50	6/3	15.12.6	1.2¼
Mitchell, Sally	391	13/	254.3.0	19.0½
Mitchell, James orphan	225	"	146.5.0	11.3½
Mann, Robert Esta.	699	6/3	218.8.9	16.4½
McKendree, Elizabeth	90	5/3	23.12.6	2.3
Moore, Lambouth	70	4/2	14.11.8	1.0¾
Morris, William	10	"	2.1.8	.2½
Moore, Benjamin	200	"	41.13.4	3.1½
Merideth, Samuel	215	7/10	84.4.2	6.4
Moore, John	100	3/2	15.16.8	1.2½
Major, Josiah	200	4/2	41.13.4	3.1½
				9.18.--
Mitchell, John Esta.	270	5/3	70.17.6}	
do. of Rootes	200	9/11	99.13.4}	12.9
Moore, Agatha	60	4/2	12.10.0	.11
Macon, John Esta.	1092	16/7	905.9.0}	
do. Lotts in Dunkirk			95.0.0}	4.3.7
Montague, William	170	4/2	35.8.4	2.8
Merideth, Ralph G. Esta.	567	14/6	411.1.6	1.10.10
Muire, Richard	93	12/6	58.2.6	2.10½
Moore, Richard	145	6/3	45.6.3	3.5
McCarty, Joseph Esta.	73	3/2	11.11.2	.10½
Metcalf, John S.	265	14/6	196.5.10	14.6
Metcalf, Thomas	256	14/6	181.8.8	13.9½
Mann, Mary	100	5/3	26.5.0	2.11¼
Martin, John	475	9/	312.15.0	15.9¼
Nunn, Jane	180	7/3	65.5.0	4.10½
Newbill, George Esta.	500	8/4	208.6.8	15.7½
Nunn, Thomas	130	7/3	47.2.6	3.6¼
Nash, John Esta.	100	6/3	31.5.0	2.4
Newbill, William	450	9/4	210.--.--	15.9
Newcomb, Eliz[a.]	109	3/2	17.5.2	4.3¼
Newcomb, William	60	"	9.10.0	.8½
Newill, John	100	7/10	39.3.4	2.11½
Omealy, John	368¾	30/	554.2.6	2.1.6½
Orvill, John	100	6/3	31.5.0	2.4
Oliver, John	320	5/3	84.0.0	6.3
Overstreet, Gabriel	296	4/2	61.13.4	4.8
do. Hayses	130	5/3	34.2.6	2.6½
				£24.7.3

[page 11, 1798] Persons owning lands	Quantity of land	Price per acre	Tot. Amt. Value Land	Tax on land @ 7/6
	[95]			
Oakes, Henry	198½	3/2	34.2.0	2.6
Oakes, William	80	4/2	16.13.4	1.3
Owin, Augustine Esta.	100	6/3	31.5.0	2.4
Pendleton, James	888½	8/7½	383.3.3¾	1.8.8½
do. Wilmore's	70	7/6	26.5.0	1.11½
Pitts, David Esta.	420	9/6	196.0.0	14.6¼
Pitts, Obadiah	20	10/5	10.8.4	.10
Phillips, Richard	230	7/3	83.7.6	6.9½
Pollard, John Esta.	235	9/4	109.13.4}	
do. of Leo[d.] Smithy	384	7/3	139.4.0}	18.11
Prewitt, Frances	99	9/4	46.4.0	3.6
Parker, John	264¼	7/	92.9.9	6.11
Prewitt, Richard	102	7/3	36.12.3	2.9
Pendleton, Phillip	483	9/2	221.7.6	16.7
Perryman, Anthony Est.	130	7/3	47.2.6	3.6½
Perryman, Philip	218	7/2	78.2.4	5.5
Pitts, Benjamin G.	100	5/4	26.13.4	2.0
Pynes, Clement	189	3/2	30.6.10	2.3
Pace, Benjamin	263	7/3	95.6.9	7.2
Pollard, Richard	389	8/4	162.1.8	12.0
Prince, Francis	113	7/6	44.5.2	3.4
Pendleton, Benjamin	450	"	176.5.0	13.2½
Pynes, Benjamin Esta.	164	6/3	51.5.0	3.9½
				8.--.3
Pynes, Robert	111½	"	34.13.9	2.7
Pynes, Benjamin	100	"	31.5.0	2.4
Pemberton, John	165	"	51.11.3	3.10
Pemberton, Philip	121	"	37.16.3	2.9½
Pollard, Robert	6	24/10	7.9.0	.6¾
Palmer, Charles	104	18/	93.12.0	7.0
Price, Robert	630	6/3	196.17.6	14.9
Pigg, Rachel	108	14/6	78.6.0	5.10½
Pigg, John Esta.	216	14/6	156.12.0}	
do.	180	7/3	65.5.0}	16.7½
Pollard, William	95	"	34.8.9	2.7
Pierce, Philip	83	3/2	13.2.10	.7½
Pierce, Beverley	25¾	4/2	5.7.3½}	
do. of Phill Peirce	17	3/2	2.17.10}	.7
Pierce, Thomas	87	4/2	18.2.6	1.4
Price, Andrew	314	6/	94.4.0	7.1
Robinson, Rachel Esta.	155	12/6	96.17.6}	
do.	260	7/3	94.5.0}	14.5½
Roane, Thomas	2033	18/8	1897.9.4}	
do. H. Carlton's	200	6/3	63.10.0}	
do. Brett's	34¾	18/	31.5.6}	
do. of Robt. Pynes	24½	6/3	7.9.1½}	7.9.8
Roane, William Esta.	1585½	18/1½	1436.17.2	5.7.9
Row, Hansford & Wilson	341	6/3	105.14.7	7.8
Row, Thomas G. (orphan)	555	7/3	201.3.9	15.0
				26.3.4

[page 12, 1798] Persons owning lands	Quantity of land	Price per acre	Tot. Amt. Value Land	Tax on land @ 7/6
Row, Elizabeth	665	20/9	689.18.9	2.11.9
Row, Francis (orphan)	612½	4/8	142.16.0	10.8
Row, Richard Esta.	450	8/4	188.0.0	14.1
Roane, Spencer	1600	24/10	1926.13.4	7.4.6
Ryland, Joseph	487½	7/3	176.10.9	13.2½
Ryland, Josiah	160	7/10	62.13.4	4.8
Riddle, Vaughn	51	5/5	13.16.3	1.--
Richerson, Elias Esta.	86	4/2	17.18.4	1.4
Row, William & Moses	60	6/3	18.15.0	1.5
Richards, John	571½	4/8	124.8.0}	
do. of R. Smith	236¾	10/5	122.18.4}	18.7
Richerson, James	180	4/2	37.10.0	2.9½
Richerson, William	369½	"	76.17.6	5.9
Richerson, William Jun[r.]	150	5/3	39.7.6	2.11
Richerson, John Esta.	101½	"	21.2.1	1.7
Roane, Major	687½	3/8	128.18.1½	9.8
Rains, Giles	60	3/2	9.10.0	.7½
Robinson, Benjamin Esta.	1300	8/4	541.13.4	2.--.7
Roane, Charles	200	14/6	145.0.0}	
do. Dragon Swamp	70	17/	59.10.0}	15.4
Roy, Beverley	700	8/4	291.13.4}	
do. Tho[s.] Brown	454	12/6	283.15.0}	2.3.1½
Ross, John (B. Minor) to pay	100	5/3	26.5.0	1.11½
Richerson & R. Shepherd	24	10/5	8.6.6	.7½
				19.6.2
Segar, Richard	406	7/3	147.3.6	11.0½
Saterwhite, George	164	6/3	51.5.0	3.9
Saterwhite, William	200	5/7½	56.5.0	4.2½
Spencer, Edward Esta.	245½	8/4	96.5.10}	
do. S.M.	582	7/3	210.19.6}	1.3.0½
Schools, John	156	8/4	65.0.0	4.10½
Schools, John & James	16	7/1	5.13.4	.4½
Schools, Gabriel Esta.	169	6/3	52.16.3	3.11½
Skelton, William	362	8/2½	148.11.5}	
do. Phil Per[r]yman	12	7/2	4.6.--}	11.5½
Smith, John (D)	190	7/6	71.5.0	5.3¾
Starling, Roderick	360	7/10	141.--.--}	
do.	313	8/2	127.16.2}	
do. of W[m.] Lyne	56½	8/4	23.6.8}	1.1.11
Skelton, Thomas	294	"	122.10.0	9.2
Scott, Benjamin Esta.	200	9/4	93.6.8	7.--
Saunders, George	200	7/3	72.10.0	5.5¼
Shepherd, William	140	9/4	65.6.8	4.11
Smith, Molley	30	4/2	6.5.0	.5¼
Smith, John Jun[r.]	100	5/3	26.5.0	1.11½
Smith, Lewis	96	7/6	36.0.0	2.8½
Swinton, George Esta.	750	13/6	506.5.0	1.13.11½
Stone, Sarah	300	7/3	108.15.0	8.2
Stone, Daniel	52	3/2	8.4.8	.7½
Smith, Larkin	1254¼	31/1	1949.6.3½	7.6.2½
Smith, Henry	400	6/3	130.0.0	9.6
Smith, William	53	7/10	20.15.2	1.6½
				35.7.7

[page 13, 1798] Persons owning lands	Quantity of land	Price per acre	Tot. Amt. Value Land	Tax on land @ 7/6
	[96]			
Smith, James Esta.	80	3/2	12.13.4	.11½
Smith, James jr.	101	7/10	39.11.2	2.11¼
Smith, Ambrose	92¾	8/4	38.6.8	2.10½
Stevens, George Esta.	430	7/10	168.8.4	12.7½
Stephens, John (orphan)	75	"	29.8.4	2.2½
Stephens, George (do.)	"	"	"	2.2½
Smith, William (Mill) Esta.	200	3/2	31.13.4	2.4½
Shackelford, John Esta.	114	7/3	40.18.2	3.1
Starke, Richard Esta.	350	5/8	99.3.4	7.5½
Stone, Robert Esta.	200	4/2	41.13.4	3.1½
Stone, Job	100	"	20.16.8	1.6½
Stone, John Esta.	48½	5/3	12.12.0	.11½
Smith, Robert	89	10/5	46.7.1	3.6
Samuel Smith	110	"	57.5.10}	
do. of R. Smith (Dragon)	4	17/	3.8.0}	4.6½
Smith, John (son of Rob[t.])	80	10/5	41.13.4}	
do. Dragon	12	17/	10.8.0}	3.8
Simpkins, Nimrod Esta.	60	3/2	9.10.0	.8½
Sears, Philip	83	4/2	17.5.10	1.3¾
Shackelford, William Esta.	700	14/6	527.10.0	1.19.7½
Spencer, Thomas	192	10/5	85.16.8	6.5¼
Seward, Benjamin	115	3/2	18.4.2	1.4½
Steadman, Christopher Sen[r.]	191	5/3	50.2.9	3.9¾
Smith, Thomas (orphan)	485	14/6	351.12.6	1.6.4
Shackelford, Richd. T	26	8/4	12.1.8	.11½
Sadler, John	150	6/3	46.17.6	3.7½
				6.18.3
Shackelford, Alexander	60	4/2	12.10.0	1.11¼
Stedman, Christopher jr.	260	5/3	65.5.0	5.1½
Shackelford, John (R)	482	8/4	200.16.8	15.0½
Shackelford, William	351	6/3	109.13.9	8.2½
Shackelford, Lyne	50	"	15.12.6	1.2
Shackelford, John (M)	283	6/2	87.5.2	6.6½
Scott, Anderson	330	16/7	273.12.6	17.9¾
Shepherd, John	192	3/2	30.1.8	2.4
Seward, Lucy & Eliz[a.] Esta.	100	4/2	22.18.4	1.8½
Semple, Robert B.	253	10/5	131.15.1	9.10½
Stone, William	74¼	3/2	11.15.3½	.10½
Seward, Edward	81½	5/3	26.6.6¾	1.7
Sthreshley, William	155½	6/3	48.11.10½	3.7½
Seares, Thomas	123	6/7	40.9.9	3.0½
Seagar, John (Lotts in Dunkirk)			150.0.0	1.0.10
Throgmorton, James	300	6/3	78.15.0	5.10½
Trice, William	140	7/3	50.15.0	3.9 ¾
Taylor, James	50	6/3	15.12.6	1.2
Taylor, Edmond	294	8/14	122.10.0	9.10½
Temple, Joseph	918	10/5	478.2.6	1.15.10½
Tunstall, Rich[d.] Jun[r.] Esta.	1097	7/3	397.13.3	1.19.10½
Tignor, William	130	7/10	50.18.4	3.10
Tureman, Benjamin	70	3/2	11.1.8	.10
				16.19.1

[page 14, 1798] Persons owning lands	Quantity of land	Price per acre	Tot. Amt. Value Land	Tax on land @ 7/6
Tureman, George	50	2/3	7.18.4	.7
Taliaferro, William	1000	14/6	725.--.--	2.14.4½
Townley, Robert	200	6/3	62.10.0}	
do. Anderson's	117	14/6	84.16.6}	11.0½
Tali[a[]ferro, Philip	940	8/4	391.13.4}	
do. D. Cooke	374½	12/6	234.7.6}	2.7.10
Trice, Edward Esta.	206	5/3	54.2.6	4.1
Thurston, Armstead	145	4/3	30.16.3	2.4
Taliaferro, John (B)	296	5/3	77.14.0	5.6
Temple, William	430	15/	322.10.0	1.4.2
Thurston, Batcheldor	200	3/2	31.13.4	2.4½
Turner, Benjamin	36	4/2	7.10.0	.7
Temple, Humphrey	178	31/3	278.2.6}	
do. W. Tunstall	100	15/	75.0.0}	
do. Jn°. Do. Esta.	200	18/8	18.13.4}	2.--.5½
Tunstall, William Esta.	438	21/	459.18.0	1.14.6
Tunstall, Richard Purdy	132½	8/4	55.0.0	4.1½
Tunstall, Thomas C.	137	"	57.1.8	5.4
Townley, Ann	79	4/2	16.9.2	1[c].3
Turner, Henry Esta.	100	"	20.16.8	1.6½
Upshaw, James	125	8/10	55.4.2}	
do. of R. Beverley	30	10/5	15.12.6}	5.3½
Vass, Thomas	250	5/3	65.12.6	4.11
				12.10.3
Wyatt, Henry	200	7/3	72.10.0	5.5
White, Henry	100	8/4	41.13.4	3.4½
Wyatt, Joseph	68	"	25.0.0	1.10½
Wilson, Isaac	200	6/3	62.10.0	4.8
Wilson, Benjamin Esta.	200	7/3	72.10.0	5.5
Wiltshire, Joseph Esta.	74	"	26.16.6	2.0
Wyatt, John	100	7/10	39.3.4	2.10
Watkins, William	37	4/2	7.14.2	.7
Watkins, Joseph	156	6/7	51.7.0	3.10
Walker, Henry Esta.	150	5/3	39.7.6	2.11½
Walker, Philip	110	9/4	51.6.8	3.10
Ware, John Esta.	562	7/3	203.14.6	15.3¼
Walker, Humphrey	820	33/2	1355.14.2	5.2.--
Wright, William	175	5/3	45.18.9	3.5¼
Watts, Edward	250	7/3	90.12.6}	
do. W. Watts Esta.	113	5/	28.5.0}	8.10½
Watts, John	293	7/10	114.15.2}	
do. Pemberton	45	6/3	14.1.3}	9.8
Watts, Kauffman	300	5/3	[7]8.15.0}	
do. of Thos. Eubank	100	5/9	28.15.0}	
do. Burches Esta.	157	"	45.2.9}	11.5
Watts, James	350	4/2	72.18.4}	
do. W. Watts Esta.	60	15/	45.0.0}	8.10
Williams, Howard	283	4/2	58.19.2}	
do. Dragon Swamp	43	17/	36.11.0}	7.1½
Wyatt, Thomas	206	7/10	81.2.0}	
do. of Joshua Boughton	60	3/2	9.10.0}	6.10
				23.--.6

[page 15, 1798] Persons owning lands	Quantity of land	Price per acre	Tot. Amt. Value Land	Tax on land @ 7/6
	[97]			
Wyatt, John Esta.	103	6/3	32.3.9	2.4½
Wyatt, William	29¾	7/3	10.15.8	.11
Williams, Montague	300	6/3	93.15.0	7.--
Williams, Charles	336	4/2	70.0.0	5.3
Walton, James	80	"	16.3.4	1.3
Walton, Mary	60	"	12.10.0	.11
~~Walton, Elizabeth~~				
Willis, Joel	94	7/10	35.5.0	2.7½
Walton, Elizabeth	60	3/2	9.10.0	.9
Walton, John	176	5/3	46.4.0	3.6
Walton, William Esta.	66	4/2	13.15.0	1.0½
Walton, Thomas Esta.	"	"	"	1.0½
Ware, John	75	5/3	19.13.9	1.5½
Ware, Arther Esta.	83	4/3	17.5.10	1.4
Waring, Robert P.	542	10/9	291.6.6	1.1.10
Walden, Richard	180	10/5	93.15.0	7.0½
Walden, Lewis	150	3/2	23.15.0}	
do. T. Dudley	84½	6/3	28.2.3}	3.11
Wright, Edward	367½	"	114.17.2	6.10
Williams, George	40	4/2	8.6.8	.7½
Watkins, Philip	197	5/3	51.14.3	3.10½
Wyatt, Richard	175	12/6	109.7.6	8.2¼
Ware, Robert Jun[r.] Esta.	100	4/2	20.6.8	1.6¾
Williams, Elizabeth	16½	3/2	2.12.9	.3
White, James Esta.	200	6/3	62.10.0	4.8½
Warren, Catharine	175	3/2	27.14.2	2.1
Ware, Robert (B)	112	"	17.14.8	1.4
Wedderburn, Lidia	350	6/3	109.7.6	8.2½
Whiting, Beverley Esta.	2447¾	7/10	866.18.9½	3.5.0
Webley, John	173	5/3	45.8.3}	
do. B. & Francis Collier	268½	4/2	55.18.9}	
do. W[m.] Dillard Jun[r.]	89½	"	18.12.11}	9.--
Ware, Robert Jun[r.]	100	8/4	41.13.4	3.1¼
Ware, William	"	"	"	3.1¼
Walden, Edward Esta.	338	5/3	88.14.6	6.7¾
Walden, Benjamin	35	"	9.3.9	.8¼
Waller, Edward Esta.	133½	3/2	21.2.9	1.7¼
Waller, George	87	"	13.15.6	1.0½
Whayne, William	154½	7/10	60.10.3	4.6¼
Waller, Robert	113	3/7	20.5.11	1.6¼
Wyatt, John (Taylor)	30	5/3	7.17.6	.7¼
Williamson, Abner	100	3/2	15.16.8	1.2¼
Ware, Nicholas	"	"	"	1.2¼
Walden, Samuel	80	7/10	36.6.8	2.4
Walden, John Sen[r.]	100	5/3	26.5.0	1.11½
Young, Henry	640	18/8	597.6.8	2.2.3¾
[arithmetic omitted]				12.5.8
				£343.12.8

Land valuation $304713.67 @ 48 [c]ts. $1462.62
Amount of [tax] on Land within the District of B. Roy, Commr., K[in]g & Queen, Decr. '98 at 7/6.
[cover] King & Queen, Beverley Roy, Land, 1798, entd., added.

List of Land within the County of King & Queen with the Tax thereon for the year 1798

DUPLICATE

[page 1, 1798 Duplicate] Persons owning lands	Quantity of land	Price per acre	Tot. Amt. Value Land	Amt. of tax @ 7/6
	[98]			
Atkins, Joseph	66	4/2	13.15.0	1.0½
Alexander, Benjamin	202	9/4	94.5.4}	
do. James Halbert	124	6/2	38.15.--}	10.--
Acre, Seaton	52	9/4	24.5.4	1.5
Alexander, Elisha	338	"	157.14.8	11.0½
Anderson, Churchill Esta.	636	7/3	230.11.--	17.3½
Anderson, Pauling Esta.	498	14/6	361.1.0	1.7.4
Atkins, John	135	4/6	30.7.6	2.4
Abbott, Jacob	112	7/10	43.17.4	3.3¾
Anderson, Richard Esta.	460	5/3	120.15.--	9.--
Atkins, Lewis	60	8/4	25--.--	1.10½
Anderson, Frances	458	10/9	246.3.6	18.5½
Bray, James	156	7/10	60.13.8	4.7½
Broach, Benoni	48	10/5	25.4.0	2.--
Brown, Henry jr.	100	12/	60.--.--	4.7
Beverley, Robert	2444	10/5	1262.16.4	4.14.--
Brown, Henry	760½	7/4½	280.8.8½	1.1.0½
Baylor, Gregory's Esta.	720	14/6	522.0.0}	
Bland, John & Lucy	166	8/4	69.3.4}	2.4.3
Bates, James	358	11/	149.3.4}	
do. [subtotal 13.19.6]	42	4/2	8.15.0}	11.11
Barton, John Esta.	125	"	26.--.10	0.2.0
Braxton, Carter (including marsh)	484½	10/5	252.6.10	0.19.0¾
Banks, William Esta.	365	"	76.0.10	5.9
Brooking, Frances	930	10/5	484.7.6	1.16.5
Boughton, Thomas (Essex)	130	9/4	60.13.4	4.7
Boughton, John	200	8/4	83.6.8	6.9
Boughton, Henry (Essex)	88	6/3	27.10.0	3.7
Broach, John	72	4/2	15.0.0	1.2
Burton, Thomas Esta.	170	5/3	44.12.6	3.4
Bohannon, Ann	197	4/6	44.6.6	3.3
Brown, William	75	7/10	29.7.6	3.9
Bagby, John Esta.	330	7/3	119.12.6	9.--
Bagby, Richard	260	"	94.5.0	7.1
Bagby, Thomas	"	"	"}	
do. Jacob Lumpkin's Esta.	235	6/3	73.8.9}	12.7
Brizendine, Armstead	50	4/3	10.12.6	.10
Brooke, Richard	1539¾	29/-	2232.12.9	8.7.6
Brumley, Robert	225	5/3	59.1.3	4.5
Brumley, John	60	7/10	23.10.0	1.10
Bird, George B.	60	6/3	18.5.0	1.5
Broach, William	20	7/10	7.16.8	.7
Bird, William	532	7/3	197.17.0}	
do. Dragon Swamp	88½	17/	70.4.6}	19.9½
Brown, John	50	7/4½	18.8.9	1.4
Bird, Philemon	1776½	6/3	555.13.1½	2.1.8
Brett, John Estate	308	18/	277.4.--	1.0.9½
				£32.18.0

[page 2, 1798 Duplicate] Persons owning lands	Quantity of land	Price per acre	Tot. Amt. Value Land	Amt. of tax @ 7/6
Bird, Anthony A.	275	3/2	43.10.10}	
do. of Wm. Montague	44	4/2	9.3.4}	3.10½
Blake, Thomas	40	6/3	12.10.--	.11
Byne, John Esta.	336	4/2	70.--.--}	
do. Dragon Swamp	2¼	17/	1.18.3}	5.4½
Bird, Barbara Esta.	266 2/3	24/10	331.2.2½	1.4.--
Bird, Robert Esta.	533 1/4	"	662.4.5½}	
do. Guy Smith	189½	3/2	30.--.1}	2.10.3
Bourn, Richard Esta.	150	"	25.15.--	1.9½
Boyd, John	115	18/8	107.6.8}	
do. Soanse's	382	24/10	474.6.4}	3.13.9
Bray, Richard Esta.	93	7/10	36.8.6	2.8
Bird, John Esta.	100	3/2	15.16.8	1.8
Bew, William	117	3/2	18.10.6	1.6
Bowden, William	69	6/6	22.2.9	1.8¼
Boyd, Spencer Esta.	1428	10/5	770.15.0	2.7.0
Berkley, Edmond	762	5/3	200.0.6	15.--
Bland, John	60	12/6	37.10.--	2.10
Bohannan, William	130	5/3	34.2.6	2.7
Bland, William	100	9/11	49.11.8	3.8½
Bohannan, William (St. Stephs.)	33	5/3	8.13.3	.8
Bourn, Mills	159½	"	41.14.3	3.2
Bu[ll]man, Ann	100	"	26.5.--}	
do. of Agatha Moore	20	"	5.5.--}	2.5
Briggs, John (W. Finney's)	170	4/2	35.8.4	2.8
Belote, Laban	384½	"	80.2.6	6.--
Bland, William Senr.	225	3/8¼	41.9.8¼	3.1½
Bland, Ralph	146	5/3	38.6.6	2.10½
Bowden, William jr.	100	4/2	20.16.8}	13.2.6
do. Sykes & Dudley	34	3/2	5.7.8}	
do. Lyne Shackelford	½	6/3	3.1½}	2.2
Bowden, John	100	4/2	20.16.8	1.7
Bland, William Esta.	250	"	52.1.8	3.11
Bland, Thomas	412	3/2	75.4.8	5.8
Bowden, George	236	5/3	61.19.0}	
do. of William Dillard	30	4/2	6.5.--}	5.1
Burch, William	45	3/2	7.8.6	.6½
Banks, James	22	7/3	7.19.6	.7½
Bristow, Bartholow.	33½	3/2	5.6.1	.6
Bristow, George	100	3/2	15.16.8	1.2
Bates, William	81	7/9½	31.10.1	2.4
Banks, Andrew	125	12/6	78.2.6	5.10
Brightwell, John Esta.	70	4/2	14.11.8	1.1
Burton, James	89	"	18.10.10	1.6
Crafton, Thomas	119	9/4	55.10.8	4.1½
Crafton, James	59	"	27.6.0	2.2
Crafton, John	117½	"	54.12.--	4.1
Chapman, George Esta.	200	7/10	78.6.8}	
do. of Wm. Hoskins	39	10/5	20.6.3}	7.6
				£15.12.4

[page 3, 1798 Duplicate] Persons owning lands	[99]	Quantity of land	Price per acre	Tot. Amt. Value Land	Amt. of tax @ 7/6
Campbell, William		907	7/3	328.15.9	1.4.8
Crane, John		136	6/3	42.--.--	3.3
Cleverius, Benjamin		419	20/9	434.14.3	1.12.8
Carlton, Henry Esta.		280	7/10	109.13.4}	
do Jno. Baylor's Esta.		257	14/6	186.6.6}	1.2.2
Cole, G. Thomas		30	9/4	14.--.--}	
do. of Jno. Lumpkin's Esta.		75	6/3	23.8.9}	2.10
Carlton, Lewis		100	8/4	41.3.4	3.2
Clayton, Thomas Esta.		275	7/3	99.13.9	7.3½
Carlton, Benoni		72¾	"	26.7.4}	
do. of W. Row		49	6/3	15.3.1½}	3.1½
Campbell, Whitacar		318	7/10	124.11.0	9.4½
Cleveley, Thomas		200	"	76.6.8	5.11
Crow, Nathaniel Esta.		200	6/3	62.10.0	4.8
Crane, George Esta.		30	7/3	10.7.6	.10
Courtney, Thomas		183¼	10/5	95.6.3	7.3½
Carlton, Joel		53½	6/3	16.14.5	1.4½
Cook, John		100	7/3	36.5.--	2.8½
Carlton, Thomas (Swamp)		200	7/10	78.6.8	5.11
Carlton, Noah		100	"	39.3.4	2.11½
Cook, Henry		260	5/3	68.5.--	5.1½
Carlton, John (School)		100	6/3	31.5.--	2.4
Campbell, Sarah Esta.		296	12/6	185.--.--	9.4½
Carlton, Christopher		37½	6/3	11.14.5}	
do. of James Laughlin		126½	3/2	26.8.2}	3.--
Carlton, Richard Esta.		139	7/	48.13.--	3.9
Cotharn, James		36½	3/2	5.15.7	.5
Carlton, William (Shoe)		309¾	11/6	178.1.2½	13.4
Carlton, Robert Esta.		148	5/	37.--.--	2.4½
Carlton, Richard		250	7/3	90.12.6	6.10½
Carlton, Christopher jr.		100		36.5.--}	9.6.9
do. Jno. Stone's Esta.		159½	5/3	41.14.9}	5.10
Cooper, Henry		50	4/2	10.8.4	.9½
Carlton, Thomas (Taylor)		100	6/3	31.5.--	2.4
Cardwell, John Esta.		150	4/2	31.5.--	2.4
Cardwell, John		"	"	"	2.4
Cardwell, William		77	"	15.11.6	1.2
Cardwell, Thomas		110	"	22.18.4	1.8½
Cook, John Esta.		300	4/2	62.10.--	4.8
Collins, Thomas		329	7/	115.6.6}	
do. Palmers		350	7/3	126.17.6}	
do. of Robt. S. Ware		86	11/9	50.10.6}	1.1.11
Carlton, John Jr.		235½	4/2	48.19.2	3.8
Campbell, William		238	3/2	37.13.8	2.10½
Curtis, Ann Esta.		[1]14	5/3	29.19.6	2.2½
Cooke, Moses		100	8/4	41.13.4	3.1½
Cooke, Ambrose		"	"	"	3.1½
Corbin, Richard		2390	11/1¾	1332.11.4}	
do. New Dragon Bridge		125	12/8	78.2.6}	5.5.9½
Corr, James		100	6/2	30.16.8	2.4
Crouch, James		130	3/2	20.11.8	1.7
Chapman, Phil		200	7/10	78.6.8	5.10½
Crittenden, Thomas		126	13/6	85.1.0}	
do. Dragon Swamp		36	17/	30.12.0}	8.7¾
Collins, Joyeux Esta.		140	10/5	72.18.4	5.5
Crittenden, Zachay.		34 2/3	14/6	24.17.10	1.10½
Cary, Wilson M. Esta.		1820	16/7	1509.1.8	5.13.2
Collier, John (Cobler)		150	5/3	39.7.6	3.--
Collier, John [subtotal £24.14.1]		100	4/2	20.16.8	1.7

[page 4, 1798 Duplicate] Persons owning lands	Quantity of land	Price per acre	Tot. Amt. Value Land	Amt. of tax @ 7/6
Campbell, James	130	5/9¼	37.10.0}	
do. of Richard Garrett	70	3/2	11.1.8}	3.7
Crittenden, Richard Esta.	178	5/3	46.14.6	3.6
Corr, Avarilla	79	"	20.14.9	1.7
Collier, Catharine Esta.	750	"	196.17.6	14.10
Clegg, Isaiah	241	4/2	50.4.2	3.9
Curry, Ann	100	"	20.16.8	1.7
Cook, Dawson	282	3/2	44.13.--	3.4½
Curry, John	55	3/2	8.14.2	.8
Courtney, William	200	7/10	78.6.8	5.10½
Cook, Thomas	240	3/2	38.--.--	2.10
Cook, Thomas jr.	96	"	15.0.4	1.1½
Carlton, Humph[y.]	175	7/	61.5.--	4.7
Carlton, Thomas Esta.	235	6/3	73.8.9	5.6½
Carlton, Beverley Esta.	160	4/2	33.6.8	2.6½
Corr, John jr.	64	7/3	23.4.--}	
do. of Tho[s.] Dudley	197½	6/3	61.14.4½}	6.5
Campbell, John	400	12/6	250.--.--	18.9
Curry, James	70	4/2	18.16.0	1.2
Corr, John Sen[r.]	213	3/2	33.15.6}	
do. Jn[o.] Corr jr.	90	7/3	32.12.6}	4.11½
Cooke, Henry	49¼	10/5	25.10.5	1.11½
Crittenden, Francis (river)	105 2/3	14/6	76.12.2	5.9
Clark, John	144	5/	36.--.--	2.8
Cannady, William	100	6/3	31.5.--	2.4
Corr, Thomas (R)	157½	5/3	41.6.10½	3.1
Cook, William	65	5/5	17.12.1	1.4
Cooke, James	65	8/9	28.8.9	2.1½
				5.5.10
Dew, William Esta.	935	14/6	677.17.6	2.10.10
Dew, Thomas	331	12/6	68.19.2	5.2
Dowling, William Esta.	264	8/4	110.--.--	8.3
Dix, Gabriel	338	6/3	105.12.6	7.11
Deshazo, William jr.	60	4/2	12.10.--	.11
Durham, Joseph	105	4/3	21.12.6	1.7
Deshazo, Peter Esta.	192	7/4	70.8.--	5.11
Deshazo, Larkin	87	7/3	31.4.10	2.4
Dickie, James	512	8/4	213.6.8	16.--
Dunbar, David	366	"	152.10.--	12.3
Dunn, Richard	150	4/2	31.5.--	2.4
Dalley, John Esta.	200	3/2	31.13.4	2.4½
Dobbins, Charles Esta.	147	5/3	38.11.9	2.11
Dean, Benjamin	50	"	13.12.6	1.--
Dillard, William Esta.	100	3/2	15.16.8	1.2
Dudley, Peter Esta.	530	7/3¼	186.18.4	14.1½
Didlake, Mary	278	8/4	115.16.8	8.8½
Durham, Robert Esta.	50	4/2	10.8.4	.9¾
Didlake, Margret Esta.	65	"	13.10.10	1.0½
Dunn, Thomas	50½	6/3	15.15.7½	1.2
Dillard, William Sen[r.]	226	12/6	141.5.--	8.7
Dillard, George	50	"	31.5.--	2.4
Durham, George	50	4/2	10.8.4	.9¾
Durham, Thomas Esta.	85	3/2	13.9.2	1.0½
Dumagin, Richard Esta.	66	5/5	17.17.6	1.4
Diggs, Frances	175	5/3	45.13.9}	
do. of Tho[s.] Brushwood	180	4/2	37.10.--}	6.3½
				£13.13.--

[page 5, 1798 Duplicate] Persons owning lands	Quantity of land	Price per acre	Tot. Amt. Value Land	Amt. of tax @ 7/6
	[100]			
Dumagin, Richard	55	5/5	14.17.11	1.2
Didlake, George Esta.	114	10/5	59.7.6	4.4½
Dungee, John	110	3/2	17.8.4	1.4
Dudley, William jr.	290	14/6	210.5.0}	
do. of L. Wedderburn	315½	6/3	98.11.10½}	1.3.2
Damm, John Esta.	55	"	17.3.9	1.3½
Dudley, William	180	7/10	70.10.--	5.3½
Damm, William	25	4/2	5.4.0	.4½
Douglass, John	239	7/	83.13.--	6.3
Didlake, John	1200	7/3	435.--.--	1.12.7½
Dudley, Ann	141	"	51.2.3	3.10
Dudley, Guilford	106	"	38.8.6	2.10½
Didlake, Edward	56	10/5	25.--.--	1.10½
Dudley, Banks	230	3/2	36.8.4	2.9
Downey, Michael Esta.	50	10/5	26.0.10	1.11½
Didlake, Royston	206	3/6½	36.7.4	2.9
Dillard, Thomas	49	15/	36.15.--	2.9½
Dillard, William	259½	"	194.5.--	14.7
Dudley, Thomas	70	6/3	21.17.6	1.8
Dillard, Nicholass	75	4/2	15.12.6	1.2½
Dillard, Benjamin Esta.	148	5/3	48.17.--	3.8
Drummond, John	150	6/3	46.17.6	3.7
Dixon, Michael	414¾	15/5	320.--.--	1.4.--
Dabney, Benjamin	400	14/6	290.--.--}	
do. of Phil Taliaferro	72	8/4	30.--.--}	1.4.3
Davis, Stage	311	6/9	105.2.7½}	
do. Thos. Foster	50	4/2	10.8.4}	
do. Wm. Didlake	24	"	5.--.--}	9.—
				8.16.8
Dally, George	174¼	3/2	27.11.9½	2.--
Dudley, Henry F.	50	5/3	13.2.6	1.--
Dunn, John (Essex), Dragon	73	17/	62.1.--	4.8
Eubank, Richard Esta.	117	4/2	24.3.9	1.10
Eubank, John Esta.	469	10/4	242.6.4}	
do. James Grafton	111	6/3	34.13.9}	
do. Thomas Dew	178½	12/6	111.5.0}	1.9.2
Eubank, Henry	171	5/3	44.17.9	4.1½
Edwards, Thomas Esta.	66	4/2	13.15.--	1.0½
Eubank, William Esta.	28¾	5/3	7.11.--	.7
Eubank, Richard Senr.	196	7/	68.12.--	5.1½
Eubank, Thomas	110	4/2	22.18.4	1.8½
Eubank, Richard jr.	112¼	7/	39.5.7½}	
do. Thomas Jeffries	12¾	7/3	4.12.5}	
do. Agrippa Dunn	147	5/3	38.11.9}	7.7
Evans, Ambrose	234½	7/10	91.13.0	6.10½
Fogg, Frederick	298	8/4	124.3.4	9.4½
Fogg, Thomas	107	6/3	33.8.8	2.6
Fleet, Baylor	862	12/6	538.15.8	2.0.4¾
Fauntleroy, Samuel G.	2069	20/	2069.--.--	7.15.2
Fleet, John Esta.	260	6/3	81.5.0	6.7
Faulkner, Thomas	220	"	68.15.--	5.1½
Fogg, Thomas	93	"	29.1.3	2.2
Fogg, James	120	"	37.10.0	2.10
Fox, Joseph S.	13	7/3	4.14.3	.4½
				£23.0.2

[page 6, 1798 Duplicate] Persons owning lands	Quantity of land	Price per acre	Tot. Amt. Value Land	Amt. of tax @ 7/6
Frazier, William Esta.	45	20/9	46.13.6	3.6½
Fleet, William	352	"	365.4.0	1.8.4¼
Fisher, James Esta.	110	3/2	17.18.4	1.4
Foster, Thomas	87¾	4/2	18.2.6	1.4½
Faulkner, Mary	333	6/3	104.1.4	7.10
Fauntleroy, Thomas	486	10/	243.--.--}	
do. H. Todd	500	18/	460.--.--}	
do. W. Bowden	183	7/	64.1.0}	2.17.3
Farenholtz, David	151¼	6/6	49.1.6	3.7½
Faulkner, Benjamin	533	4/2	111.0.10	8.4
Grafton, Sally & Ann	132	9/4	61.12.0	4.7½
Gale, John	264	7/5	97.18.--	7.4
Gale, William	351	7/5	130.3.3	9.10
Goleman, Thomas, Essex	948½	9/-	426.16.6	1.12.0
Garnett, Rice	297	7/3	107.13.4	8.1
Gatewood, Chaney	829	10/5	437.17.11}	
do. Gardner's	100	7/3	36.5.--}	
do. Noel's	362½	14/6	262.16.3}	
do. Harwood	225	4/2	46.17.6}	
do. T. Eubank's	300	14/6	217.10.--}	
do. Jn°. Walden's Esta.	120	12/6	75.--.--}	4.0.6½
Garnett, Joshua Esta.	325	8/4	134.3.4	10.1
Graves, Edward Esta.	200	6/3	62.10.--	4.8
Gatewood, Joseph	445	10/5	231.15.5	17.4½
Gale, Mathew	323	11/5	184.7.7	13.9½
Gatewood, John	160	8/4	66.13.4	5.--
Garnett, Reuben	876½	8/10	387.2.5	1.9.0½
Gwathmey, Temple	600	35/3	1057.10.--	3.19.3½
Garlick, Samuel	454	24/10	563.14.4	1.6.3½
Garlick, John	893	29/	1294.17.0	4.19.7½
Griffith, Joseph	50	6/3	15.12.6	1.2
Gresham, Samuel [subtotal 27.12.1]	432½	7/3	156.15.7½	11.9
Guthrie, William	46¾	"	16.18.11¾}	
do. Lewis Smith, Meet[g]. House	½	"	3.7[¼]}	1.3
Garrett, Robert	100	4/2	20.16.8	1.6
Gaines, Francis	356	14/6	258.2.--	19.4
Gaines, Henry Esta.	1517	20/4	1542.5.8	5.15.8
Gresham, Thomas	339¼	6/3	106.0.4}	
do. T. Stevens orphan	78	7/10	30.11.10}	10.3
Gresham, Philemon	200	"	62.10.0	4.8
Gresham, Jn°. D	200	7/10	78.6.8	5.10½
Gresham, William brick[r].	100	4/2	20.16.8}	
do. W.C. Row	40	6/3	13.3.4}	2.7
Gardner, Elizabeth	100	"	31.5.--	2.4
Gibson, Richard	156½	3/2	24.16.7	1.9½
Gibson, Banks	56½	"	8.18.11	.7½
Gibson, John	219¾	"	34.15.11	2.7½
Griffith, Milley	50	6/3	15.12.6	1.2
Gresham, Machem	100	5/3	26.5.0}	
do. Ambrose Gresham	4	17/	3.8.0}	2.2½
Gresham, Ambrose	80	"	21.--.--}	
do. Dragon	22	17/	18.5.0}	2.11
Gresham, John jr.	80	5/3	21.--.--}	
do. of Ambrose Gresham, Dragon	4	17/	3.8.0}	1.10
Graves, Thomas	50½	7/3	18.6.1½}	
do. of Edw[d]. Wright	15¾	6/8	5.5.0}	1.9
Griffin, William Esta.	859	14/6	622.15.6	2.0.8
Garlick, Camm Esta.	1100	6/3	343.15.0	1.5.9½
Garrett, James [subtotal 40.--.6]	230	4/2	47.18.4	3.7

[page 7, 1798 Duplicate] Persons owning lands	Quantity of land	Price per acre	Tot. Amt. Value Land	Amt. of tax @ 7/6
	[101]			
Gardner, Anthony	638	11/	350.11.8}	
do. Dragon	67½	17/	57.7.6}	1.10.7
Gresham, Lumpkin	265	7/3	96.1.3	7.2½
Garrett, Robert	200	7/	70.0.0}	
do. William Hunt Esta.	170	6/3	53.2.6}	9.2½
Gresham, William jr.	329	8/4	137.5.10}	
do. William Gatewood	46	3/2	7.5.8}	
do. Chick	69	7/3	25.0.3}	12.7½
Gresham, George	141	"	22.6.6	1.8
Gaines, Robert Esta.	537¾	20/9	558.8.7¾}	
do. Ann Curtis	50	5/3	13.2.6}	2.7.10
Gatewood, William (*Tuck*o.)	33	3/2	5.4.6	.4½
Gatewood, William son of Jno.	132	10/	66.--.--	.6
Gleason, Patrick	134	8/4	55.16.8	4.2½
Gatewood, Gabriel	78	10/5	40.12.6	1.0½
Garrett, William jr.	120	4/2	25.--.--	1.10½
Guthrie, James	60	12/6	37.10.0	2.10
Guthrie, Richard Esta.	60	"	"	2.10
Glaspe, James Esta.	210	5/3	55.2.6	4.1½
Groom, Mary	173	3/2	27.17.10	2.1
Garrett, George	88½	5/3	23.4.7½	1.8½
Guthrie, Rachel	50	8/4	20.16.8	1.6
Goldman, Martin	140	4/2	29.3.4	2.2½
Groom, Zachary. Esta.	187	3/2	29.12.2	2.3
Gully, Philip	50	3/2	7.18.4	.7
Garrett, William shoe	225	3/4¾	37.19.4	2.10
Gramshill, Henry	25	3/2	3.19.2	.4
Garrett, Ann Watts	112	5/	28.--.--	2.1
Garrett, Richard	100	4/2	20.16.8	1.6
Guthrie, Richard	162	3/2	25.13.--	1.11
Hill, William	1342½	14/6	972.19.0	3.12.11½
Hitchcock, Thomas	140	4/2	29.3.4	2.2
Hoskins, Samuel Esta.	345	6/3	107.16.3}	11.6.7
of Elisha Alexander	57	10/5	29.13.9}	10.3
Hutcherson, Charles	531	7/1	188.1.3	14.1
Hoskins, William	252	7/10	98.14.0}	
do. of George Kauffman	583	14/6	422.13.6}	1.19.1
Heskew, John Esta.	61	5/3	16.0.3	1.2
Heskew, John jr.	50	6/3	15.12.6}	
do. Clemt. Pynes	10	3/2	1.11.8}	1.4
Hill, Robert Esta.	1281	8/2	523.1.6	1.19.2½
Hill, Edward	1200	18/8	1120.--.--	4.4.--
Hoomes, Benjamin	372	12/6	232.10.0}	
do. Glebe	462	4/4	96.5.--}	
do. Ann Ken[n]edy	75	12/6	46.17.6}	1.8.--
Hutson, William Esta.	112	3/2	17.14.8	1.4
Hemingway, John jr.	267	4/2	55.12.6	4.2
Hemingway, Samuel	"	"	"	4.2
Hemingway, John Senr.	266	"	55.8.4	4.1½
Hare, William Esta.	217	5/3	56.19.3	4.2
Harwood, Christopher Esta.	294	24/10	365.1.--	1.7.4½
Hill, Thomas	300	26/11	403.15.0	1.10.3½
Hart, James	150	3/2	23.15.0	1.9½
Holderby, John	100	4/2	20.16.8}	
do. of Wm. Hoskins	108¾	7/10	42.6.0}	4.8½
Hart, Anthony	190	5/3	49.17.6}	
do. of Sundry Persons	259½	3/2	41.1.9}	
do. of Eliza. Watkins [subtotal 26.13.10]	100	"	15.16.8}	8.--

[page 8, 1798 Duplicate] Persons owning lands	Quantity of land	Price per acre	Tot. Amt. Value Land	Amt. of tax @ 7/6
Hart, Gregory	200	11/	31.3.4	2.4½
Hart, William	250	3/3½	41.2.11	3.1
Harwood, John Jr.	109	10/5	56.15.5	4.3
Hunt, William Esta.	560	6/3	175.--.--	13.1
Henry, Samuel Esta.	1900	14/6	1377.10.0	5.3.4
Henry, James	75	12/6	46.17.6	3.6
Hurt, James	33	10/5	17.3.9	1.3½
Halyard, William	190	5/3	49.17.6	3.9
Hoskins, John	767	10/7	399.9.7}	
do. Boughtons	100	8/4	41.13.4}	1.10.7
Hunt, West	14	5/3	3.3.6	.3
Hoskins, Robert	287	6/	86.2.--	6.4½
do. of Robt. Smith (Mortgage)				
Hart, Aulden	127	4/2	26.9.2	1.11½
Howerton, Heritage	122¼	20/9	126.16.7¼	4.6¼
Howerton, John	269½	5/3	70.14.1[0]½	5.3½
Holt, William	123	14/3	87.12.9	6.7
Hutson, William (S.M.)	50	4/2	10.8.4	.10
Hutcherson, John	73¼	8/9	32.0.11¼	2.4¼
Hart, Vincent	75	6/6	24.7.6	1.10
Halyard, John	1	5/9¼	5.9¼	½
Howerton, George	76¼	6/	22.17.6	1.8½
Jones, Thomas	255	4/2	53.2.6	3.11½
Jeffries, Thomas	63	7/3	22.16.9}	
do. Jno. Harwood jr.	38¼	10/5	19.15.10}	2.11½
Jones, John Esta.	300	8/11	133.15.--	10.0½
Jeffries, Edward	70	3/2	11.1.8	.9½
Jones, James	160	14/6	116.0.0}	
do. James Jones Esta.	196	10/5	102.1.8}	16.4½
Jones, William Esta.	241	15/10	190.15.10}	11.11.2
do. L. Smith	35¾	31/1	55.11.2}	18.5½
Jeffries, Ambrose	337	7/10	124.18.10	9.4½
Jeffries, Robert	110	7/6	41.5.--	3.1
Jeffries, Gawin	30	4/2	6.5.--	.5½
Jordan, Thomas Esta.	100	"	20.16.8	1.8
Johnson, Thomas	112	3/2	17.14.8	1.4
Jameson, David Esta.	50	"	7.18.4	0.7½
Jones, Rawleigh	63	31/1	93.18.3	7.4
Kemp, John	296	7/3	107.3.--	8.--
Kemp, John, St. Stephens	178	"	64.2.2	4.9
Kauffman, John jr. Esta.	38	10/5	19.15.10}	
do. Jno. Kauffman Esta.	471	18/8	439.12.0}	1.13.5½
Keeling, James Esta.	113¼	7/3	41.0.0¾}	
do. Robt. Hill	23	8/2	9.7.10}	3.9½
Kennedy, Arch^d. Esta.	38¼	4/2	7.19.4	1.1½
Kennedy, Ann	70¼	7/10	14.11.8	1.1½
Kennedy, Ann jr.	33¼	"	7.0.6	.6¼
Kennedy, Lucy	37½	"	7.16.2	.6¾
Kay, Christopher	116	6/3	30.0.9	2.3½
Kidd, Bartholo^w.	136	5/3	35.14.0}	
do. of William Dillard jr.	132½	4/2	27.12.1}	1.2.1½
Kidd, Benj^a.	111	13/6	74.18.2}	
do. Crittendens	60	"	40.10.--}	
do. Dragon Swamp	36	17/	30.12.--}	11.--
Kidd, John	370	7/3	134.2.6}	
do. Lumpkin & Peirce	60	4/2	12.10.--}	
do. Thos. Dillard	45	14/6	32.12.6}	13.5½
King, Dicey	18	8/4	7.10.0	.6½
				18.15.9

[page 9, 1798 Duplicate] Persons owning lands	Quantity of land	Price per acre	Tot. Amt. Value Land	Amt. of tax @ 7/6
	[102]			
Lumpkin, James	213	7/10	83.8.2	6.3
Lumpkin, Henry	400	9/4	186.13.4	14.--
Lumpkin, John Esta.	125	6/3	35.11.3	2.8
Lyne, William	1480	8/4	610.14.2	2.5.10
Lyne, William jr., Lotts in Dunkirk annual rent			150.--.--	1.11.3
Lumpkin, William	305	14/6	221.2.6}	
do. of Thos. Dew	26½	12/6	16.5.0}	15.4
Lefon, Francis	119	8/4	49.11.8	3.8
Lumpkin, Henry jr.	190	9/4	88.13.4	6.7½
Lankford, Thomas Esta.	100	4/2	20.16.8	1.8
Lumpkin, Robert Senr.	374	8/4	155.16.8	11.8½
Lumpkin, John Ware	140	7/10	54.16.8	4.1½
Longest, Caleb	97	"	37.19.10	2.10½
Longest, Richard	227¼	"	89.4.2	6.8½
Longest, John	100	"	39.3.4	3.--
Lumpkin, Anthony	216	6/3	67.10.--	5.1¼
Lumpkin, Jacob Esta. from L. Gresham	100	7/3	36.5.0	2.8½
Lumpkin, Jacob (orphan)	681	6/3	212.16.3	15.8
Lewis, Iveson	356	14/6	258.2.--	19.4
Leigh, Lucy	101	24/10	125.8.2	10.4½
Lumpkin, Robert jr.	233	5/3	61.3.3	4.7
Leigh, John Esta.	199	24/10	247.1.10	18.6½
Lyne, John	507	6/3	158.8.9	11.10½
Lambouth, Thomas	100	3/2	15.16.8	1.2½
Lambouth, Charles Esta.	50	"	7.18.4	.7½
Motley, Edwin	815	10/5	428.2.6	1.12.1½
McKentosh, William	126	4/2	26.5.--	1.11½
Martin, Thomas C.	680	14/6	493.--.--}	
do.	134½	7/3	48.15.1½}	2.0.7½
Morgan, William	3	6/3	18.9	.1
Mitchel, Ralph Esta. [subtotal 16.--.6]	193	10/5	100.10.5	7.7¼
Minor, William	149	8/4	62.1.8	4.7½
Minor, John	137	"	57.1.8	4.3
Minor, Thomas	288	7/10	225.6.--	8.4
Moody, Lewis	239	"	93.12.2	7.--
Mann, Joseph jr.	400	8/4	166.13.4	12.6
Mitchell, John	50	6/3	15.12.6	1.2¼
Mitchell, Salley	391	13/	254.3.--	19.0½
Mitchell, James (Orphan)	225	"	146.5.--	11.3½
Mann, Robert Esta.	699	6/3	218.8.9	16.4½
McKendree, Eliza.	90	5/3	23.12.6	2.3
Moore, Lambouth	70	4/2	14.11.8	1.0¾
Morris, William	10	"	2.1.8	.2½
Moore, Benjamin	200	"	41.13.4	3.1½
Merideth, Samuel	215	7/10	84.4.2	6.4
Moore, John	100	3/2	15.16.8	1.2½
Major, Josiah	200	4/2	41.13.4	3.1½
Mitchel, John Esta.	270	5/3	70.17.6}	
do. Rootes	200	9/11	99.13.4}	18.9
Moore, Agatha	60	4/2	12.10.--	.11
Macon, John Esta.	1092	16/7	905.9.0}	
do. Lotts in Dunkirk			95.0.0}	4.3.7
Montague, William	170	4/2	35.8.4	2.8
Merideth, Ralph G. Esta.	567	14/6	411.1.6	1.10.10
Muire, Richard	93	12/6	58.2.6	2.10½
Moore, Richard	145	6/3	45.6.3	3.5
McCarty, Joseph Esta.	73	3/2	11.11.2	.10½
Metcalf, John S. [page total £29.2.5]	265	14/6	196.5.10	14.6

[page 10, 1798 Duplicate] Persons owning lands	Quantity of land	Price per acre	Tot. Amt. Value Land	Amt. of tax @ 7/6
Metcalf, Thomas	256	14/6	181.8.8	13.9¼
Mann, Mary	100	5/3	26.5.--	2.11¼
Martin, John	475	9/	312.15.--	15.9¼
Nunn, Jane	180	7/3	65.5.0	4.10½
Newbill, George Esta.	500	8/4	208.6.8	15.7½
Nunn, Thomas	130	7/3	47.2.6	3.6¼
Nash, John Esta.	100	6/3	31.5.--	2.4
Newbill, William	450	9/4	210.--.--	15.9
Newcomb, Eliz[a.]	109	3/2	17.5.2	1.3¼
Newcomb, William	60	"	9.10.--	.8½
Newill, John	100	7/10	39.3.4	2.11½
Omealy, John	368¾	30/	554.2.6	2.1.6½
Orvill, John	100	6/3	31.5.--	2.4
Oliver, John	320	5/3	84.--.--	6.3
Overstreet, Gabriel	296	4/2	61.13.4	4.8
do. Hayses	130	5/3	34.2.6	2.6½
Oakes, Henry	198½	3/2	34.2.0	2.6
Oaks, William	80	4/2	16.13.4	1.3
Owin, Augustine Esta.	100	6/3	31.5.--	2.4
Pendleton, James	888½	8/7½	383.3.3¼}	
do. Wilmore's	70	7/6	26.5.0}	1.10.8
Pitts, David Esta.	420	9/4	196.--.--	14.6¼
Pitts, Obadiah	20	10/5	10.8.4	.10
Phillips, Richard	230	7/3	83.7.6	6.9½
Pollard, John Esta.	235	9/4	109.13.4}	
do. of Leo[d.] Smithy	384	7/3	139.4.0}	18.11
Prewitt, Frances [subtotal 10.14.8]	99	9/4	46.4.--	3.6
Parker, John [page torn]	264¼	7/	92.9.9	6.11
Prewitt, Richard	102	7/3	36.12.3	2.9
Pendleton, Phillip	483	9/2	221.7.6	16.7
Perryman, Anthony Est.	130	7/3	47.2.6	3.6½
Perryman, Philip	218	7/2	78.2.4	5.5
Pitts, Benjamin G.	100	5/4	26.13.4	2.--
Pynes, Clement	189	3/2	30.6.10	2.3
Pace, Benjamin	263	7/3	95.6.9	7.2
Pollard, Richard	389	8/4	162.1.8	12.--
Prince, Francis	113	7/6	44.5.2	3.4
Pendleton, Benjamin	450	"	176.5.0	13.2½
Pynes, Benjamin Esta.	164	6/3	51.5.--	3.9½
Pynes, Robert	111½	"	34.13.9	2.7
Pynes, Benjamin	100	"	31.5.--	2.4
Pemberton, John	165	"	51.11.3	3.10
Pemberton, Phil	121	"	37.16.3	2.9½
Pollard, Robert	6	24/10	7.9.--	.0¾
Palmer, Charles	104	18/	93.12.--	7.--
Price, Robert	630	6/3	196.17.6	14.9
Pigg, Rachel	108	14/6	78.6.--	5.10½
Pigg, John Esta.	216	14/6	156.12.0}	
do.	180	7/3	65.5.0}	16.7½
Pollard, William	95	"	34.8.9	2.7
				17.16.--

[page 11, 1798 Duplicate] Persons owning lands	Quantity of land	Price per acre	Tot. Amt. Value Land	Amt. of tax @ 7/6
	[103]			
Pierce, Philip	83	3/2	13.2.10	.7½
Peirce, Beverley	25¾	4/2	5.7.3½}	
do. of Phil Peirce	17	3/2	2.13.10}	.7
Peirce, Thomas	87	4/2	18.2.6	1.4
Price, Andrew	314	6/	94.4.--	7.1
Robinson, Rachel Esta.	155	12/6	96.17.6}	
do.	260	7/3	94.5.--}	14.5½
Roane, Thomas	2033	18/8	1897.9.4}	
do. Carlton's	200	6/3	63.10.0}	
do. Brett's	34¾	18/	31.5.6}	
do. R. Pynes	24½	6/3	7.9.1½}	7.9.8
Roane, William Esta.	1585½	18/1½	1436.17.2	5.7.9
Row, Hansford & Wilson	341	6/3	105.14.7	7.8
Row, Thomas G. (orphan)	555	7/3	201.3.9	15.--
Row, Elizabeth	665	20/9	689.18.9	2.11.9
Row, Francis (Orphan)	612½	4/8	142.16.0	10.8
Row, Richard Esta.	450	8/4	188.0.0	14.1
Roane, Spencer	1600	24/10	1926.13.4	7.4.6
Ryland, Joseph	487½	7/3	176.10.9	13.2½
Ryland, Josiah	160	7/10	62.13.4	4.8
Riddle, Vaughn	51	5/5	13.16.3	1.--
Richerson, Elias Esta.	86	4/2	17.18.4	1.4
Row, William & Moses	60	6/3	18.15.--	1.5
Richards, John	571½	4/8	124.8.0}	
do. of Robt. Smith	236¾	10/5	122.18.4}	18.7
Richerson, James	180	4/2	37.10.0	2.9½
Richerson, William	369½	"	76.17.6	5.9
Richerson, William jr.	153	5/3	39.7.6	2.11
Richerson, John Esta. [subtotal 28.16.6]	101½	"	21.2.1	1.7
Roane, Major	687½	3/8	128.18.1½	9.8
Rains, Giles	60	3/2	9.10.--	.7½
Roberson, Benjamin Esta.	1300	8/4	541.13.4	2.0.7
Roane, Charles	200	14/6	145.0.0}	
do. Dragon Swamp	70	17/	59.10.--}	15.4
Roy, Beverley	700	8/4	291.13.4}	
do. Thos. Brown	454	12/6	283.15.0}	2.3.1½
Ross, John (B. Minor to pay)	100	5/3	26.5.0	1.11½
Richerson & R. Shepherd	24	10/5	8.6.6	.7½
Segar, Richard	406	7/3	147.3.6	11.0½
Satterwhite, George	164	6/3	51.5.0	3.9
Satterwhite, William	200	5/7½	56.5.0	4.2½
Spencer, Edward Esta.	245½	8/4	96.5.10}	
do. S.M.	582	7/3	210.19.6}	1.3.0½
Schools, John	156	8/4	65.--.--	4.10½
Schools, John & James	16	7/1	5.13.4	.4½
Schools, Gabriel Esta.	169	6/3	52.16.3	3.11½
Skelton, William	362	8/2½	148.11.5}	
do. Phil Perryman	12	7/2	4.6.--}	11.5½
Smith, John (D)	190	7/6	71.5.0	5.3¾
				£37.18.--

[page 12, 1798 Duplicate] Persons owning lands	Quantity of land	Price per acre	Tot. Amt. Value Land	Amt. of tax @ 7/6
Starling, Roderick	360	7/10	14.--.--}	
do.	313	8/2	127.16.2}	
do. of Wm. Lyne	56½	8/4	23.6.8}	1.1.11
Skelton, Thomas	294	8/4	122.10.0	9.2
Scott, Benjamin Esta.	200	9/4	93.6.8	7.--
Saunders, George	200	7/3	72.10.--	5.5¼
Shepherd, William	140	9/4	65.6.8	4.11
Smith, Molley	30	4/2	6.5.--	.5¼
Smith, John jr.	100	5/3	26.5.--	1.11½
Smith, Lewis	96	7/6	36.--.--	2.8½
Swinton, George Esta.	750	13/6	506.5.0	1.13.11¼
Stone, Sarah	300	7/3	108.15.0	8.2
Stone, Daniel	52	3/2	8.4.8	.7½
Smith, Larkin	1254¼	31/1	1949.6.3½	7.6.2½
Smith, Henry	400	6/3	130.--.--	9.6
Smith, William	53	7/10	20.15.2	1.6½
Smith, James Esta.	80	3/2	12.13.4	.11½
Smith, James jr.	101	7/10	39.11.2	2.11¼
Smith, Ambrose	92¾	8/4	38.6.8	2.10½
Stevens, George Esta.	430	"	168.8.4	12.7½
Stephens, John (orphan)	75	"	29.8.4	2.2½
Stephens, George Do.	"	"	"	2.2½
Smith, William (Mill) Esta.	200	3/2	31.13.4	2.4½
Shackelford, John Esta.	114	7/3	40.18.2	3.1
Starke, Richard Esta.	350	5/8	99.3.4	7.5½
Stone, Robert Esta.	200	4/2	41.13.4	3.1½
Stone, Job	100	"	20.16.8	1.6½
Stone, John Esta.	48½	5/3	12.12.0	.11¼
Smith, Robert	89	10/5	46.7.1	3.6
Samuel Smith	110	"	57.5.10}	
do. of R. Smith (Dragon)	4	17/	3.8.--}	4.6½
Smith, John (son of Robt.)	80	10/5	41.13.4}	15.3.10
do. Dragon	12	17/	10.8.0}	3.8
Simkins, Nimrod Esta.	60	3/2	9.10.--	.8½
Sears, Philip	83	4/2	17.5.10	1.3¾
Shackelford, William Esta.	700	14/6	527.10.--	1.19.7½
Spencer, Thomas	192	10/5	85.16.8	6.5¼
Seward, Benjamin	115	3/2	18.4.2	1.4½
Steadman, Christopher Senr.	191	5/3	50.2.9	3.9¾
Smith, Thomas (Orphan)	485	14/6	351.12.6	1.6.4
Shackelford, Richard T	26	8/4	12.1.8	.11½
Saddler, John	150	6/3	46.17.6	3.7½
Shackelford, Alexander	60	4/2	12.10.--	1.11¼
Stedman, Christopher jr.	260	5/3	65.5.--	5.1½
Shackelford, John (Roman)	482	8/4	200.16.8	15.0½
Shackelford, William	351	6/3	109.13.9	8.2½
Shackelford, Ly[n]e	50	"	15.12.6	1.2
Shackelford, John (M)	283	6/2	87.5.2	6.6½
Scott, Anderson ~~Anderson~~	330	16/7	273.12.6	17.9¾
Shepherd, John	192	3/2	30.1.8	2.4
Seward, Lucy & Eliza. Esta.	100	4/2	22.18.4	1.8½
Semple, Robt. B.	253	10/5	131.15.1	9.10½
Stone, William	74¼	3/2	11.15.3½	.10½
Seward, Edward	81½	5/3	21.6.6¾	1.7
Sthreshley, William	155½	6/3	48.11.10½	3.7½
				23.7.6

[page 13, 1798 Duplicate] Persons owning lands	Quantity of land	Price per acre	Tot. Amt. Value Land	Amt. of tax @ 7/6
	[104]			
Seares, Thomas	123	6/7	40.9.9	3.0½
Seagar, John, Lotts in Dunkirk			150.--.--	1.0.10
Throgmorton, James	300	6/3	78.15.0	5.10½
Trice, William	140	7/3	50.15.0	3.9 ¾
Taylor, James	50	6/3	15.12.6	1.2
Taylor, Edmond	294	8/14	122.10.--	9.10½
Temple, Joseph	918	10/5	478.2.6	1.15.10½
Tunstall, Richard jr. Esta.	1097	7/3	397.13.3	1.9.10½
Tignor, William	130	7/10	50.18.4	3.10
Tureman, Benjamin	70	3/2	11.1.8	.10
Tureman, George	50	"	7.18.4	.7
Taliaferro, William	1000	14/6	725.--.--	2.14.4½
Townley, Robert	200	6/3	62.10.0}	
do. Anderson's	117	14/6	84.16.6}	11.0½
Taliaferro, Philip	940	8/4	391.13.4}	
do. D. Cook	374½	12/6	234.7.6}	2.7.10
Trice, Edward Esta.	206	5/3	54.2.6	4.1
Thruston, Armstead	145	4/3	30.16.3	2.4
Taliaferro, John B	296	5/3	77.14.0	5.6
Temple, William	430	15/	322.10.0	1.4.2
Thruston, Batcheldor	200	3/2	31.13.4	2.4½
Turner, Benjamin	36	4/2	7.10.0	.7
Temple, Humphry	178	31/3	278.2.6}	
do. William Tunstall	100	15/	75.--.--}	
do. Jn°. Tunstall Esta.	200	18/8	18.13.4}	2.0.5½
Tunstall, William Esta.	438	21/	459.18.0	1.14.6
Tunstall, Richard (Purdy)	132½	8/4	55.--.--	4.1½
Tunstall, Thomas C.	137	"	57.1.8	5.4
Townley, Ann	79	4/2	16.9.2	1.3
Turner, Henry Esta.	100	"	20.16.8	1.6½
Upshaw, James, Essex	125	8/10	55.4.2}	
do. of R. Beverley [subtotal 17.19.8]	30	10/5	15.12.6}	5.3½
Vass, Thomas	250	5/3	65.12.6	4.11
Wyatt, Henry	200	7/3	72.10.--	5.5
White, Henry	100	8/4	41.13.4	3.4½
Wyatt, Joseph	68	8/4	25.--.--	1.10½
Wilson, Isaac	200	6/3	62.10.--	4.8
Wilson, Benjamin Esta.	200	7/3	72.10.0	5.0
Wiltshire, Joseph Esta.	74	"	26.16.6	0.2.0
Wyatt, John	100	7/10	39.3.4	2.10
Watkins, William	37	4/2	7.14.2	.7
Watkins, Joseph	156	6/7	51.7.0	3.10
Walker, Henry Esta.	150	5/3	39.7.6	2.11½
Walker, Philip	110	9/4	51.6.8	3.10
Ware, John Esta.	562	7/3	203.14.6	15.3¼
Walker, Humphry	820	33/2	1355.14.2	5.2.0
Wright, William	175	5/3	45.18.9	3.5¼
Watts, Edward	250	7/3	90.12.6}	
do. W. Watts Esta.	113	5/	28.5.--}	8.10½
Watts, John	293	7/10	114.15.2}	
do. Pemberton [page total 27.0.7]	45	6/3	14.1.3}	9.8

[page 14, 1798 Duplicate] Persons owning lands	Quantity of land	Price per acre	Tot. Amt. Value Land	Amt. of tax @ 7/6
Watts, Kauffman	300	5/3	78.15.0}	
do. of Thomas Eubank	100	5/9	28.15.0}	
do. Burches Esta.	157	5/9	45.2.9}	11.5
Watts, James	350	4/2	72.18.4}	
do. W. Watts Esta.	60	15/	45.0.0}	8.10
Williams, Howard	283	4/2	58.19.2}	
do. Dragon Swamp	43	17/	36.11.0}	7.1½
Wyatt, Thomas	206	7/10	81.2.0}	
do. of Joshua Boughton	60	3/2	9.10.0}	6.10
Wyatt, John Esta.	103	6/3	32.3.9	2.4½
Wyatt, William	29¾	7/3	10.15.8	.11
Williams, Montague	300	6/3	93.15.0	7.--
Williams, Charles	336	4/2	70.--.--	5.3
Walton, James	80	"	16.3.4	1.3
Walton, Mary	60	"	12.10.0	.11
Willis, Joel	94	7/10	35.5.0	2.7½
Walton, Elizabeth	60	3/2	9.10.0	.9
Walton, John	176	5/3	46.4.0	3.6
Walton, William Esta.	66	4/2	13.15.0	1.0½
Walton, Thomas Esta.	"	"	"	1.0½
Ware, John	75	5/3	19.13.9	1.5½
Ware, Arther Esta.	83	4/2	17.5.10	1.4
Wareing, Robert P.	542	10/9	291.6.6	1.1.10
Walding, Richard	180	10/5	93.15.0	7.0½
Walding, Lewis	150	3/2	23.15.0}	
do. T. Dudley	84½	6/3	28.2.3½}	3.11
				4.16.5
Wright, Edward	367½	"	114.17.2	6.10
Williams, George	40	4/2	8.6.8	.7½
Watkins, Philip	197	5/3	51.14.3	3.10½
Wyatt, Richard	175	12/6	109.7.6	8.2¼
Ware, Robert jr. Esta.	100	4/2	20.6.8	1.6¾
Williams, Eliz[a.]	16½	3/2	2.12.9	.3
White, James Esta.	200	6/3	62.10.0	4.8½
Warren, Catherine	175	"	27.14.2	2.1
Ware, Robert (B)	112	3/2	17.14.8	1.4
Wedderburn, Lydia	350	6/3	109.7.6	8.2½
Whiting, Beverley's Esta.	2447¾	7/10	866.18.9½	3.5.--
Webley, John	173	5/3	45.8.3}	
do. B. & Francis Collier	268½	4/2	55.18.9}	
do. W[m.] Dillard jr.	89½	"	18.12.11}	9.0
Ware, Robert jr.	100	8/4	41.13.4	3.1¼
Ware, William	"	"	"	3.1¼
Walding, Edward Esta.	338	5/3	88.14.6	6.7¾
Walding, Benjamin	35	"	9.3.9	.8¼
Waller, Edward Esta.	133½	3/2	21.2.9	1.7¼
Waller, George	87	"	13.15.6	1.0½
Whayne, William	154½	7/10	60.10.3	4.6¼
Waller, Robert	113	3/7	20.5.11	1.6¼
Wyatt, John (Taylor)	30	5/3	7.17.6	.7¼
				11.10.10

[page 15, 1798 Duplicate] Persons owning lands	Quantity of land	Price per acre	Tot. Amt. Value Land	Amt. of tax @ 7/6
	[105]			
Williamson, Abner	100	3/2	15.16.8	1.2¼
Ware, Nicholas	"	"	"	1.2¼
Walden, Samuel	80	7/10	36.6.8	2.4
Walden, John Sen[r.]	100	5/3	26.5.--	1.11½
Young, Henry	640	18/8	597.6.8	2.2.3¾
				2.9.--

William Courtney & Beverley Roy, Commissioners

[arithmetic omitted]

Land valuation $3.06.300 @ 48 cents $1470.24
[cover] King & Queen, Wm. Courtney, Land & prop., 1798, entd. 31 July '98. Added [ ].

List of Land Within the County of King & Queen with the Tax thereon for the year 1799

[page 1, 1799] Persons Names Owning Land	Quantity of land	Price per acre	Tot. Amt. Value Land	Amt. Tax Thereon
	[106]			Dols. Cents
Atkins, Joseph	66	4/2	13.15.0	
Alexander, Benjamin	202	9/4	94.5.4}	
do. Jas. Halbert	124	6/2	38.15.0}	
Acre, Seaton	52	9/4	24.5.4	
Alexander, Elisha	338	"	157.14.8	
Anderson, Churchill Esta.	636	7/3	230.11.0	
Anderson, Pauling Esta.	498	14/6	361.1.0	
Atkins, John	135	4/6	30.7.6	
Abbott, Jacob	112	7/10	43.17.4	
Anderson, Richard Esta.	460	5/3	120.15.0	
Atkins, Lewis	60	8/4	25.0.0	
Anderson, Francis	458	10/9	246.3.6	
do. of Rich[d.] T. Shackelford	26	8/9	12.1.8	
			1399.12.3	
Bray, James	128¾	7/10	55.8.6	
Brown, Samuel	33¼	4/3	7.1.2	
Broach, Benoni	48	10/5	25.4.0	
Brown, Henry Jun[r.]	100	12/	60.0.0	
Beverley, Robert	2444	10/5	1262.16.4	
Brown, Henry	760½	7/4½	280.8.8½	
Baylor, Gregory Esta.	256	14/6	185.12.0	
Bland, John & Lucy	166	8/4	69.3.4	
Bates, James	358	11/	149.3.4}	
Do.	42	4/2	8.15.0}	
Do. of Rice Garnett	89	7/3	32.5.3}	
Barton, John Esta.	125	"	26.0.10	
Braxton, Carter (including marsh)	484½	10/5	252.6.10	
Banks, William Esta.	365	"	76.0.10	
Brooking, Francis	930	10/5	484.7.6	
Boughton, Thomas, Essex	130	9/4	60.13.4	
Boughton, John	200	8/4	83.6.8	
Boughton, Henry, Essex	88	6/3	27.10.0	
Broach, John	72	4/2	15.0.0	
Burton, Thomas Esta.	170	5/3	44.12.6	
Bohannon, Ann	197	4/6	44.6.6	
Brown, William	75	7/10	29.7.6	
Bagbey, John Esta.	330	7/3	119.12.9	
Bagbey, Richard	260	"	94.5.0	
Bagbey, Thomas	"	"	94.5.0}	
Do. of Jacob Lumpkin	235	6/3	73.8.9}	
Brizendine, Armstead	50	4/3	10.12.6	
Brooke, Richard	1539¾	29/-	2232.12.9	
Brumley, Robert	225	5/3	59.1.3	
Brumley, John	60	7/10	23.10.0	
			7386.10.4	

[page 2, 1799] Persons Names Owning Land	Quantity of land	Price per acre	Tot. Amt. Value Land	Amt. Tax Thereon Dol. Cents
Bird, George B.	60	6/3	18.5.0	
Broach, William	20	7/10	7.16.8	
Bird, William	532	7/3	197.17.0}	
Do. Dragon Swamp	88½	17/	70.4.6}	
Brown, John	50	7/4½	18.8.9	
Bird, Philemon	1776½	6/3	555.13.1½	
Brett, John	236	18/	212.8.0	
Burch, James	70	7/3	25.7.6	
Burch, Vincent	100	4/2	20.16.8	
Bird, Anthony Armistead	275	3/2	43.10.10}	
Do. of Wm. Montague	44	4/2	9.3.4}	
Blake, Thomas	40	6/3	12.10.0	
Byne, John Esta.	336	4/2	70.0.0}	
Do. Dragon Swamp	2¼	17/	1.18.3}	
Bird, Barbara Esta.	266 2/3	24/10	331.2.2½	
Bird, Robert Esta.	533 1/4	"	662.4.5¼}	
Do. Guy Smith	189½	3/2	30.0.1}	
Bourn, Richard Esta.	150	"	23.15.0	
Boyd, John	115	18/8	107.6.8}	
do. Soane's	382	24/10	474.6.4}	
Bray, Richard Esta.	93	7/10	36.8.6	
Bird, John Esta.	100	3/2	15.16.8	
Bew, William	117	"	18.10.6	
Bowden, William	69	6/6	22.2.9	
Boyd, Spencer Esta.	1419	10/5	739.6.5	
Berkley, Edmond	762	5/3	200.0.6	
Bland, John	60	12/6	37.10.0	
Bohannan, William	130	5/3	34.2.6	
Bland, William	100	9/11	49.11.8	
			4046.13.9	
Bohannan, William, St. Stephens	33	5/3	8.13.3	
Bourn, Mills	159½	"	41.14.3	
Bullman, Ann	100	5/3	26.5.0}	
Do. of Agatha Moore	20	"	5.5.0}	
Belote, Laban	384½	"	80.2.6	
Bland, William Senr.	225	3/8¼	41.9.8¼	
Bland, Ralph	146	5/3	38.6.8	
Do. of Finney & Buckner	170	4/2	35.8.[ ]	
Bowden, William Junr.	100	4/2	20.16.8}	
Do. Sykes & Dudley	34	3/2	5.7.8}	
Do. Lyne Shackelford	½	6/3	3.1½}	
Bowden, John	100	4/2	20.16.8	
Bland, William Esta.	250	"	52.1.8	
Bland, Thomas	412	3/2	75.4.8	
Bowden, George	236	5/3	61.19.0}	
Do. of Wm. Dillard	30	4/2	6.5.0}	
Burch, William	45	3/2	7.8.6	
Banks, James	22	7/3	7.19.6	
Bristow, Bartholomew	33½	3/2	5.6.1	
Bristow, George	100	3/2	15.16.8	
Bates, William	81	7/9½	31.10.1}	
Do. of Rice Garnett	117	7/3	42.8.4}	
Banks, Andrew	125	12/6	78.2.6	
Brightwell, John Esta.	70	4/2	14.11.8	
Burton, James	89	"	18.10.10	
			4788.7.0	

[page 3, 1799] Persons Names Owning Land	Quantity of land	Price per acre	Tot. Amt. Value Land	Amt. Tax Thereon
	[107]			Dols. Cents
Crafton, Thomas	119	9/4	55.10.8	
Crafton, James	59	"	27.10.8	
Crafton, John	117½	"	54.12.0	
Chapman, John Esta. Sold				
Campbell, William	907	7/3	328.15.9	
Crane, John	136	6/3	40.2.6	
Cleverius, Benjamin	419	20/9	434.14.3	
Carlton, Henry Esta.	280	7/10	109.13.4}	
Do. John Baylor Esta.	257	14/6	186.6.6}	
Cole, Thomas G.	30	9/4	14.0.0}	
Do. J. Lumpkin's Esta.	75	6/3	23.8.9}	
Carlton, Lewis	100	8/4	41.3.4}	
Do. Wm. Tignor	130	7/10	50.18.4}	
Clayton, Thomas Esta.	275	7/3	99.13.9	
Carlton, Benoni	72¾	"	26.7.4}	
Do. of W. Row	49	6/3	15.3.1½}	
Campbell, Whitacar	318	7/10	124.11.0	
Cleveley, Thomas	171	"	66.19.6	
Crow, Nathaniel Esta.	200	6/3	62.10.0	
Crane, George Esta.	30	7/3	10.7.6	
Courtney, Thomas	183¼	10/5	95.6.3	
Carlton, Joel	53½	6/3	16.14.5	
Cooke, John	100	7/3	36.5.0	
Carlton, Thomas (Swamp)	200	7/10	78.6.8	
Carlton, Noah	100	"	39.3.4	
Cooke, Henry	260	5/3	68.5.0	
Carlton, John, School	100	6/3	31.5.0	
Campbell, Sarah Esta.	296	12/6	185.0.0	
			2322.14.0	
Carlton, Christopher	37½	6/5	11.14.5}	
Do. of Jas. Laughlin	186½	3/2	26.8.2}	
Carlton, Richard Esta.	139	7/	48.13.--	
Cothern, James	36½	3/2	5.15.7	
Carlton, William (Shoe)	309¾	11/6	178.1.2½	
Carlton, Robert Esta.	148	5/	37.0.0	
Carlton, Richard	250	7/3	90.12.6	
Carlton, Christopher Junr.	100		36.5.0}	
Do. John Stone Esta.	159½	5/3	41.14.9}	
Cooper, Henry	50	4/2	10.8.4	
Carlton, Thomas (Taylor)	100	6/3	31.5.0	
Cardwell, John Esta.	150	4/2	31.5.0	
Cardwell, John	"	"	31.5.0	
Cardwell, William	77	"	15.11.6	
Cardwell, Thomas	100	"	22.18.4	
Cook, John Esta.	300	4/2	62.10.0	
Collins, Thomas	329½	7/	115.6.6}	
Do. Palmers	350	7/3	126.17.6}	
Do. R.S. Ware	86	11/9	50.10.6}	
Carlton, John Junr.	235	4/2	48.19.2	
Campbell, William	238	3/2	37.13.8	
Curtis, Ann Esta.	414	5/3	108.13.6	
Cooke, Moses	100	8/4	41.13.4	
Cooke, Ambrose	"	"	41.13.4	
Corbin, Richard	2390	11/1¾	1332.11.4}	
do. New Dragon Bridge	125	12/8	78.2.6}	
			4986.3.1	

[page 4, 1799] Persons Names Owning Land	Quantity of land	Price per acre	Tot. Amt. Value Land	Amt. Tax Thereon Dols. Cents
Corr, James	100	6/2	30.16.8	
Crouch, James	130	3/2	20.11.8	
Chapman, Philip	200	7/10	78.6.8	
Crittenden, Thomas	126	13/6	85.1.0}	
Do. Dragon Swamp	36	17/	30.12.0}	
Collins, Joyeux	140	10/5	72.18.4	
Crittenden, Zachariah	34 1/3	14/6	24.17.10	
Cary, Wilson M.	1820	16/7	1509.1.8	
Collier, John	100	4/2	20.16.8	
Campbell, James	130	5/9¼	37.10.--}	
Do. Rich[d.] Garrett	70	3/2	11.1.8}	
Crittenden, Richard Esta.	178	5/3	46.14.6	
Corr, Avarilla	79	"	20.14.9	
Collier, Catharine Esta.	750	"	196.17.6	
Clegg, Isaiah	241	4/2	50.4.2	
Cooke, Dawson	282	3/2	44.13.0	
Curry, Ann	100	4/2	20.16.8	
Curry, John	55	3/2	8.14.2	
Courtney, William	200	7/10	78.16.8	
Cooke, Thomas	240	3/2	38.0.0	
Cooke, Thomas Jun[r.]	96	"	15.0.4	
Carlton, Humphrey	127½	7/	44.10.9	
Carlton, Thomas Esta.	235	6/3	73.8.9	
Carlton, Beverley Esta.	160	4/2	33.6.8	
Corr, John Jun[r.] [subtotal 2774.17.1]	500	7/3	181.5.0}	
Do. T. Dudley	197½	6/3	61.14.4½}	
Campbell, John	400	12/6	250.0.0	
Curry, James	70	4/2	18.16.0	
Corr, John Sen[r.]	213	3/2	33.15.6}	
Do. John Corr Jun[r.]	90	7/3	32.12.6}	
Cooke, Henry	49¼	10/5	25.10.5	
Crittenden, Francis (River)	105 2/3	14/6	76.12.2	
Clark, John	144	5/	36.0.0}	
Do. of Sam[l.] Hemingway	254½	4/2	53.0.3}	
Cannady, William	100	6/3	31.5.0	
Corr, Thomas R	157½	5/3	41.6.10½	
Cooke, William	65	5/5	17.12.1	
Cooke, James	65	8/9	28.8.9	
Courtney, Fanny & Children	78	7/10	30.10.--	
Crowe, John	121	5/3	31.19.3¾	
Dew, William Esta.	935	14/6	677.17.6	
Dew, Thomas	331	12/6	68.19.2	
Dowling, William Esta.	264	8/4	110.0.0	
Dix, Gabriel	338	6/3	105.12.6	
Deshazo, William Jun[r.]	60	4/2	12.10.0	
Durham, Joseph	105	4/3	21.12.6	
Deshazo, Peter Esta.	192	7/4	70.8.0	
Deshazo, Larkin	87	7/3	31.4.10}	
Do. of J. Crane	6	6/3	1.17.6}	
Dunbar, David	366	"	152.10.--	
Dunn, Richard	150	4/2	31.5.0	
			4827.17.2	

[page 5, 1799] Persons Names Owning Land	Quantity of land	Price per acre	Tot. Amt. Value Land	Amt. Tax Thereon
	[108]			Dols. Cents
Dalley, John Esta.	200	3/2	31.13.4	
Dobbins, Charles	147	5/3	38.11.9	
Dean, Benjamin	50	"	13.2.6	
Dillard, William Esta.	100	3/2	15.16.8	
Dudley, Peter Esta.	530	7/3¼	186.18.4	
Dumagin, Richard	66	5/5	17.17.6	
Didlake, Mary	278	8/4	115.16.8	
Durham, Robert Esta.	50	"	10.8.4	
Didlake, Margret Esta.	65	4/2	13.10.10	
Dunn, Thomas	50½	6/3	15.15.7½	
Dillard, William Sen[r.]	226	12/6	141.5.0	
Dillard, George	50	"	31.5.0	
Durham, George	50	4/2	10.8.4	
Durham, Thomas Esta.	85	3/2	13.9.2	
Dumagin, Richard	55	5/5	14.17.11	
Didlake, George Esta.	114	10/5	59.7.6	
Dungie, John	110	3/2	17.8.4	
Dudley, William Jun[r.]	290	14/6	210.5.0}	
Do. of L. Wedderburn	315½	6/3	98.11.10}	
Damm, John Esta.	55	"	17.3.9	
Dudley, James	180	7/10	70.10.0	
Dame, William	25	4/2	5.4.2	
Douglas, John	239	7/	83.13.0	
Didlake, John	1200	7/3	435.0.0	
Dudley, Ann	141	"	51.2.3	
Dudley, Guilford	106	"	38.8.6	
Didlake, Edward	56	10/5	25.0.0	
Dudley, Banks	230	3/2	36.8.4	
Downey, Michael Esta.	50	10/5	26.0.10	
Didlake, Royston	206½	3/6½	36.7.4	
Dillard, Thomas	49	15/	36.15.0	
			1918.12.9	
Dillard, William	259½	"	194.5.0	
Dudley, Thomas	70	6/3	21.17.6	
Dillard, Nicholas	75	4/2	15.12.6	
Dillard, Benjamin Esta.	148	5/3	48.17.0	
Drummond, John Esta.	150	6/3	46.17.6	
Dixon, Michael	414¾	15/5	320.0.0	
Dabney, Benjamin	400	14/6	290.0.0}	
Do. [P.] Taliaferro	72	8/4	30.0.0}	
Davis, Stage	311	6/9	105.2.7½}	
Do. T. Foster	50	4/2	10.8.4}	
Do. W. Didlake	24	"	5.0.0}	
Dally, George	174¼	3/2	27.11.9½	
Dudley, Henry	50	5/3	13.2.6	
Dunn, John (Essex), Dragon	73	17/	62.1.0	
Diggs, Frances	175	5/3	45.13.9}	
Do. T. Brushwood	180	4/2	37.10.0}	
Eubank, Richard Esta.	117	4/2	24.3.9	
Eubank, John Esta.	469	10/4	242.6.4}	
Do. Jas. Grafton	111	6/3	34.13.9}	
Do. T. Dew	178½	12/6	111.5.6}	
Eubank, Henry	171	5/3	44.17.9	
Edwards, Thomas Esta.	66	4/2	13.15.0	
			3663.14.3	

[page 6, 1799] Persons Names Owning Land	Quantity of land	Price per acre	Tot. Amt. Value Land	Amt. Tax Thereon Dols. Cents
Eubank, William Esta.	28¾	5/3	7.11.0	
Eubank, Richard Senr.	196	7/	68.12.0	
Eubank, Thomas	110	4/2	22.18.4	
Eubank, Richard Junr.	112¼	7/	39.5.7¼}	
Do. T. Jeffries	12¾	7/3	4.12.5}	
Do. A. Dunn	147	5/3	38.11.9}	
Evans, Ambrose	195	7/10	56.10.0	
Eubank, Warner	115	3/2	18.4.2	
Fogg, Frederick	298	8/4	124.3.4	
Fogg, Thomas	107	6/3	33.8.8	
Fleet, Baylor	862	12/6	538.15.8	
Fauntleroy, Samuel G.	2069	20/	2069.0.0	
Fleet, John Esta.	260	6/3	81.5.0	
Faulkner, Thomas	220	"	68.15.0	
Fogg, Thomas Esta.	93	"	29.1.3	
Fogg, James	120	"	37.10.0	
Fox, Joseph S.	13	7/3	4.14.3}	
Do. of T. Garnett	28	7/10	10.19.4}	
Frazer, William Esta.	45	20/9	46.13.6	
Fleet, William	352	"	365.4.0	
Fisher, James Esta.	110	3/2	17.18.4	
Foster, Thomas	87¾	4/2	18.2.6	
Faulkner, Mary	333	6/3	104.1.4	
Fauntleroy, Thomas	486	10/	243.0.0}	
Do. Henry Todd	500	18/	460.0.0}	
Do. W^m. Bowden	183	7/	64.1.0}	
Farinholtz, David	151¼	6/6	49.1.6	
Faulkner, Benjamin	533	4/2	111.0.10}	
Do. W^m. Boyd	9½	10/5	4.10.9}	
Do. A. Gardner	3	17/	2.11.0}	
			4739.12.1	
Grafton, Sally & Ann	132	9/4	61.12.0	
Gale, John	264	7/5	97.18.0	
Goleman, Thomas (Essex)	948½	9/-	426.16.6	
Gatewood, Chaney	829	10/5	437.17.11}	
Do. Gardner's	100	7/3	36.5.0}	
Do. Nole's [Noel's]	362½	14/6	262.16.3}	
Do. Harwood's	225	4/2	46.17.6}	
Do. T. Eubank	300	14/6	217.10.0}	
Do. [J.] Walden Esta.	120	12/6	75.0.0}	
Garnett, Joshua Esta.	325	8/4	134.3.4	
Graves, Edward Esta.	200	6/3	62.10.0	
Gatewood, Joseph	445	10/5	231.15.5	
Gale, Mathew	323	11/5	184.7.7	
Gatewood, John	160	8/4	66.13.4	
Garnett, Reuben	876½	8/10	387.2.5}	
Do. of W. Halbert & G. Gatewood	28	10/5	14.12.10}	
Gwathmey, Temple	600	35/3	1057.10.0	
Garlick, Samuel	454	24/10	563.14.4}	
Do. Leon[ard] Tunstall	550	6/3	171.17.6}	
Garlick, John	893	29/	1294.17.0	
Griffith, Joseph	50	6/3	15.12.6	
Gresham, Samuel	432½	7/3	156.15.7½	
Do. Rice Garnett	157	"	56.18.1}	
			10700.15.2	

[page 7, 1799] Persons Names Owning Land	Quantity of land	Price per acre	Tot. Amt. Value Land	Amt. Tax Thereon
	[109]			Dols. Cents
Guthrie, William	46¾	"	16.18.11¾}	
do. L. Smith, ½ acre Meeting House	½	"	3.7½}	
Garrett, Robert	100	4/2	20.16.8	
Gaines, Francis	356	14/6	258.2.0	
Gaines, Henry Esta.	1517	20/4	1542.5.8	
Gresham, Thomas	339¼	6/3	106.0.4}	
do. T. Stephens	78	7/10	30.11.10}	
do. of Jas. Bray	38¼	"	14.19.8}	
Gresham, Philemon	200	"	62.10.0	
Gresham, John D	200	7/10	78.6.8	
Gresham, William (Bricklayer)	100	4/2	20.16.8}	
Do. W.C. Row	40	6/3	13.3.4}	
Gardner, Elizabeth	100	"	31.5.0	
Gibson, Richard	156½	3/2	24.16.7	
Gibson, Banks	56½	"	8.18.11	
Gibson, John	104¾	"	14.14.4½	
Griffith, Milley	50	6/3	15.12.6	
Gresham, Machem	100	5/3	26.5.0}	
Do. of Ambrose Gresham	4	17/	3.8.0}	
Gresham, Ambrose	80	"	21.0.0}	
Do. Dragon	22	17/	18.5.0}	
Gresham, John Jun[r.]	80	5/3	21.0.0}	
Do. A. Gresham	4	17/	3.8.0}	
Graves, Thomas	50½	7/3	18.6.1½}	
Do. of Edw[d.] Wright	15¾	6/8	5.5.0}	
Griffin, William Esta.	859	14/6	622.15.6	
Garlick, Camm Esta.	550	6/3	[171].17.6	
Garrett, James	230	4/2	47.18.4	
Gardner, Anthony	638	11/	350.11.8}	
Do. Dragon Swamp	67½	17/	57.7.6}	
Gresham, Lumpkin	265	7/3	96.1.3	
			3724.11.6	
Garrett, Robert	200	7/	70.0.0}	
Do. W[m.] Hunt's Esta.	170	6/3	53.2.6}	
Gresham, William Jun[r.]	329	8/4	137.5.10}	
Do. W[m.] Gatewood	46	3/2	7.5.8}	
Do. of Chick	69	7/3	25.0.3}	
Gresham, George	141	"	22.6.6	
Gaines, Robert Esta.	537¾	20/9	558.8.7¾}	
Do. Ann Curtis	50	5/3	13.2.6}	
Gatewood, William, *Tuckaho*	33	3/2	5.4.6	
Gatewood, William, son of Jn[o.]	132	10/	66.0.0	
Gleason, Patrick	134	8/4	55.16.8	
Gatewood, Gabriel	78	10/5	40.12.6}	
Do. W[m.] Halbert	50	"	26.10.0}	
Guthrie, James	60	12/6	37.10.0	
Guthrie, Richard	60	"	37.10.0	
Garrett, Edward	210	15/3	55.2.6}	
Do. Edw[d.] Trice Esta.	489½	"	188.9.10}	
Groom, Mary	173	3/2	27.17.10	
Garrett, George	88½	5/3	23.4.7½	
Guthrie, Rachel	50	8/4	20.16.8	
Goldman, Martin	140	4/2	29.3.4	
Groom, Zachary, [ ] Waller	187	3/2	29.12.2	
Gully, Philip	50	3/2	7.18.4	
Garrett, William (Shoe)	225	3/4¾	37.19.4	
			5251.11.7	

[page 8, 1799] Persons Names Owning Land	Quantity of land	Price per acre	Tot. Amt. Value Land	Amt. Tax Thereon Dols. Cents
Gramshill, Henry	25	3/2	3.19.2	
Garrett, Ann Watt[s]	112	5/	28.0.0	
Garrett, Richard	100	4/2	20.16.8	
Guthrie, Richard	162	3/2	25.13.0	
Gale, William	351	7/5	130.3.3	
Garrett, William Jun[r.]	120	4/2	25.0.0	
Gilman, Richard	100	5/3	26.5.0	
Hill, William	1342½	14/6	972.19.0	
Hitchcock, Thomas	140	4/2	29.3.4	
Hoskins, Samuel Esta.	345	6/3	107.16.3}	
Do. Elisha Alexander	57	10/5	29.13.9}	
Hutcherson, Charles	531	7/1	188.1.3	
Hoskins, William	583	14/6	422.13.6}	
Heskew, John Esta.	61	5/3	16.0.3	
Heskew, John Jun[r.]	50	6/3	15.12.6}	
do. Clem[t.] Pynes	10	3/2	1.11.8}	
Hill, Robert Esta.	1281	8/2	523.1.6	
Hill, Edward	1200	18/8	1120.0.0	
Hoomes, Benjamin	372	12/6	232.10.0}	
do. Glebe	462	4/4	96.5.0}	
do. Ann Ken[n]edy	75	12/6	46.17.6}	
Hutson, William Esta.	112	3/2	17.14.8	
Hemingway, John Jun[r.]	267	4/2	55.12.6	
Hemingway, Samuel	12¾	"	2.13.1½	
Hemingway, John Sen[r.]	154	"	32.1.4	
Hare, William Esta.	217	5/3	56.19.3	
Harwood, Christopher Esta.	194	24/10	240.17.8	
Harwood, Priscilla [subtotal 4612.1.1]	165	18/	148.10.0	
Hill, Thomas Esta.	300	26/11	403.15.0	
Hart, James	150	3/2	23.15.0	
Holderby, John	100	4/2	20.16.8}	
Do. of W[m.] Hoskins	108¾	7/10	42.6.0}	
Hart, Anthony	190	5/3	49.17.6}	
Do. of Sundry Persons	259½	3/2	41.1.9}	
Do. of Eliz[a.] Watkins	100	"	15.16.8}	
Hart, Gregory	200	11/	31.3.4	
Hart, William	250	3/3½	41.2.11	
Harwood, John Jun[r.]	109	10/5	56.15.5	
Hunt, William Esta.	560	6/3	175.0.0	
Henry, Samuel Esta.	1900	14/6	1377.10.0	
Henry, James	75	12/6	46.17.6	
Hurt, James	33	10/5	17.3.9	
Halyard, William	190	5/3	49.17.6	
Hoskins, John	767	10/7	399.9.7}	
Do. Boughtons	100	8/4	41.13.4}	
Hurt, West	14	5/3	3.3.6	
Hoskins, Robert	287	6/	86.2.0	
Do. of Robt. Smith, Mortgage				
Hart, Alden	127	4/2	26.9.2	
Howerton, Heritage	122¼	20/9	126.16.7¼	
Howerton, John	269½	5/3	70.14.10½	
Holt, William	123	14/3	87.12.9	
Hutson, William	50	4/2	10.8.4	
Hutcherson, John	73¼	8/9	32.0.11¼	
Hart, Vincent	75	6/6	24.7.6	
Halyard, John	1	5/9¼	5.9¼	
Howerton, George	76¼	6/	22.17.6	
			7937.11.10	

[page 9, 1799] Persons Names Owning Land	Quantity of land	Price per acre	Tot. Amt. Value Land	Amt. Tax Thereon
	[110]			Dols. Cents
Jones, Thomas	255	4/2	53.2.6	
Jeffries, Thomas	63	7/3	22.16.9}	
Do. J. Harwood	38¼	10/5	19.15.10}	
Jones, John Esta.	300	8/11	133.15.0	
Jeffries, Edward	70	3/2	11.1.8	
Jones, James	160	14/6	116.0.0}	
Do. Jas. Jones Esta.	196	10/5	102.1.8}	
Jones, William Esta.	241	15/10	190.15.10}	
Do. L. Smith	35¾	31/1	55.11.2}	
Jeffries, Ambrose	337	7/10	124.18.10	
Jeffries, Robert	110	7/6	41.5.0	
Jeffries, Gawin	30	4/2	6.5.0	
Jordan, Thomas Esta.	100	"	20.16.8	
Johnson, Thomas	112	3/2	17.14.8	
Jameson, David Esta.	50	"	7.18.4	
Jones, Rawley D.	63	31/1	93.18.3	
Kemp, John	296	7/3	107.3.0	
Kemp, John, St. Stephens	178	7/3	64.2.2	
Kauffman, John [Junr.]	38	10/5	19.15.10}	
Do. Kauffman John Esta.	471	18/8	439.1.0}	
Keeling, James Esta.	113¼	7/3	41.0.0¾}	
Do. Rob[t.] Hill	23	8/2	9.7.10}	
Kennady, Archibald Esta.	38¼	4/2	7.19.4	
Kennady, Ann	70¼	"	14.11.8	
Kennady, Ann Jun[r.]	33¼	"	7.0.6	
Kennady, Lucy [subtotal 1794.15.6]	37½	"	7.16.2	
Kay, Christopher	116	6/3	30.0.9	
Kidd, Bartholomew	136	5/3	35.14.0}	
Do. of W[m.] Dillard Jun[r.]	132½	4/2	27.12.1}	
Kidd, Benjamin	111	13/6	74.18.2}	
Do. Crittendens	60	"	40.10.0}	
Do. Dragon Swamp	36	17/	30.12.0}	
Kidd, John	370	7/3	134.2.6}	
Do. Lumpkin & Pearce	60	4/2	12.10.0}	
Do. T. Dillard	45	14/6	32.12.6}	
King, Dicey	18	8/4	7.10.0	
Lumpkin, James	213	7/10	83.8.2	
Lumpkin, Henry	400	9/4	186.13.4	
Lumpkin, John Esta.	125	6/3	35.11.3	
Lyne, William	1480	8/4	610.14.2	
Lyne, William Jun[r.], £70, } Lotts in Dunkirk annual rent}				
Lumpkin, William	305	14/6	221.2.6}	
Do. T. Dew	26½	12/6	16.5.0}	
Lefon, Francis	119	8/4	49.11.8	
Lankford, Thomas Esta.	100	4/2	20.16.8	
Lumpkin, Robert Sen[r.]	374	8/4	155.16.8	
Lumpkin, Henry Jun[r.]	190	9/4	88.13.4	
Lumpkin, John Ware	140	9/10	54.16.8	
Longest, Caleb	97	"	37.19.10	
Longest, Richard	227¾	"	89.4.2	
			3872.10.11	

[page 10, 1799] Persons Names Owning Land	Quantity of land	Price per acre	Tot. Amt. Value Land	Amt. Tax Thereon Dols. Cents
Longest, John	100	"	39.3.4	
Lumpkin, Anthony	216	6/3	67.10.0	
Lumpkin, Jacob Esta. from. L. Gresham	100	7/3	36.5.0	
Lumpkin, Jacob, orphan	681	6/3	212.16.3	
Lewis, Iveson	356	14/6	258.2.0	
Leigh, Lucy	101	24/10	125.8.2	
Lumpkin, Robert Jun[r.]	233	5/3	61.3.3	
Leigh, John Esta.	199	24/10	247.1.10	
Lyne, John	507	6/3	158.8.9	
Lambouth, Thomas	100	3/2	15.16.8	
Lambouth, Charles Esta.	50	"	7.18.4	
Motley, Edwin	815	10/5	428.2.6	
Martin, Thomas C.	680	14/6	493.0.0}	
do.	134½	7/3	48.15.1½}	
Morgln, William	3	6/3	18.9	
Mitchell, Ralph Esta.	193	10/5	100.10.5	
Minor, William	149	8/4	62.1.8	
Minor, John	137	"	57.1.8	
Minor, Thomas	288	7/10	225.6.0}	
Do. of John Chapman	239	8/5	100.0.3}	
Moody, Lewis	239	"	93.12.2	
Mann, Joseph Jun[r.]	400	8/4	166.13.4	
Mitchell, John	50	6/3	15.12.6	
Mitchell, Sally	391	13/	254.3.0	
Mitchell, James, orphan	225	"	146.5.0	
Mann, Robert Esta.	699	6/3	218.8.9	
McKendree, Elizabeth	90	5/3	23.12.6	
Moore, Lambouth	70	4/2	14.11.8	
Morris, William [subtotal 3685.10.6]	10	"	2.1.8	
Moore, Benjamin	200	"	41.13.4	
Merideth, Samuel	215	7/10	84.4.2	
Moore, Lodowick, John & Richard	100	3/2	15.16.8	
Major, Josiah	200	4/2	41.13.4	
Mitchell, John Esta.	270	5/3	70.17.6}	
Do. Rootes	200	9/11	99.13.4}	
Moore, Agatha	60	4/2	12.10.0	
Macon, John Esta.	1092	16/7	905.9.0}	
Do. Lotts in Dunkirk, £66				
Montague, William	170	4/2	35.8.4	
Merideth, Ralph G. Esta.	567	14/6	411.1.6	
Muire, Richard	93	12/6	58.2.6	
Moore, Richard Esta.	145	6/3	45.6.3	
McCarty, Joseph Esta.	73	3/2	11.11.2	
Metcalf, John S.	265	14/6	196.5.10	
Metcalf, Thomas	256	"	181.8.8	
Mann, Mary	100	5/3	26.5.0	
Martin, John	475	9/	312.15.0	
Mead, Joseph, Lotts in Dunkirk, annual rent			6.0.0	
Nunn, Jane	180	7/3	65.5.0	
Newbill, George	500	8/4	208.6.8	
Nunn, Thomas	130	7/3	47.2.6	
Nash, John Esta.	100	6/3	31.5.0	
Newbill, William	450	9/4	210.0.0}	
Do. of David Beard	560	8/4	233.6.8}	
Newcomb, Eliz[a.]	109	3/2	17.5.2	
Newcomb, William	60	"	9.10.0	
Newill, John	100	7/10	39.3.4	
			£7003.16.5	

[page 11, 1799] Persons Names Owning Land		Quantity of land	Price per acre	Tot. Amt. Value Land	Amt. Tax Thereon
		[111]			Dols. Cents
Omealy, John		368¾	30/	554.2.6	
Orvill, John		100	6/3	31.5.0	
Oliver, John		320	5/3	84.0.0	
Overstreet, Gabriel		296	4/2	61.13.4}	
Do. Hayses		130	5/3	34.2.6}	
Oaks, Henry		198½	3/2	34.2.0	
Oaks, William		80	4/2	16.13.4	
Owin, Augustine Esta.		100	6/3	31.5.0	
Oliver, William		59	4/2	12.3.10	
Pendleton, James		888½	8/7½	383.3.3¾}	
Do. Wilmore's		70	7/6	26.5.0}	
Do. Phil. Pendleton		120	9/2	53.0.0}	
Do. Wm. McKentosh		125	4/2	26.1.10}	
Pitts, David		420	9/4	196.0.0	
Pitts, Obadiah		20	10/5	10.8.4	
Phillips, Richard		230	7/3	83.7.6	
Pollard, John Esta.		235	9/4	109.13.4}	
Do. Leod. Smithy		384	7/3	139.4.0}	
Prewitt, Frances		99	9/4	46.4.0	
Parker, John		264¼	7/	92.9.9	
Prewitt, Richard		102	7/3	36.12.3	
Pendleton, Phillip		360	9/2	165.0.0	
Perryman, Anthony Est.		130	7/3	47.2.6	
Perryman, Philip		218	7/2	78.2.4	
Pitts, Benjamin G.		100	5/4	26.13.4	
Pynes, Clement		18[9]	3/2	30.6.10	
Pace, Benjamin		263	7/3	95.6.9	
Pollard, Richard		389	8/4	162.1.8	
				2666.10.2	
Prince, Francis		113	7/6	44.5.2	
Pendleton, Benjamin		450	"	176.5.0	
Pynes, Benjamin Esta.		164	6/3	51.5.0	
Pynes, Robert		111½	"	34.13.9	
Pynes, Benjamin		100	"	31.5.0	
Pemberton, John		165	"	51.11.3	
Pemberton, Philip		121	"	37.16.3	
Pollard, Robert		6	24/10	7.9.0	
Palmer, Charles		104	18/	93.12.0	
Price, Robert		630	6/3	196.17.6	
Pigg, Rachel		108	14/6	78.6.0	
Pigg, John Esta.		216	14/6	156.12.0}	
Do.		180	7/3	65.5.0}	
Pollard, William		95	"	34.8.9	
Pearce, Philip		83	3/2	13.2.10	
Pearce, Beverley		25¾	4/2	5.7.3½}	
Do. of Phil Pearce		17	3/2	2.13.10}	
Pearce, Thomas Esta.		87	4/2	18.2.6	
Price, Andrew		314	6/	94.4.0	
Quarles, Francis W., Lotts in Dunkirk	£15				
Robinson, Rachel Esta.		155	12/6	96.17.6}	
Do.		260	7/3	94.5.0}	
Roane, Thomas		2033	18/8	1897.9.4}	
Do. H. Carlton		200	6/3	63.10.0}	
Do. Brett's		34¾	18/	31.5.6}	
Do. Robt. Pynes	___	24½	6/3	7.9.1½}	
	£15			6050.8.8	

[page 12, 1799] Persons Names Owning Land	Quantity of land	Price per acre	Tot. Amt. Value Land	Amt. Tax Thereon Dols. Cents	
~~Roane, William Esta.~~	~~1585½~~	~~18/1½~~	~~1436.17.2~~		Chargd. to T. Bland
Row, Hansford & Wilson	341	6/3	105.14.7		
Row, Thomas orphan G.	555	7/3	201.3.9		
Row, Elizabeth	665	20/9	689.18.9		
Row, Francis (Orphan)	612½	4/8	142.16.--		
Row, Richard Esta.	450	8/4	188.0.0		
Roane, Spencer	1600	24/10	1926.13.4		
Ryland, Joseph	487½	7/3	176.10.9		
Ryland, Josiah	160	7/10	62.13.4}		
Do. of Wm. Temple	27½	15/	20.12.6}		
Riddle, Vaughn	51	5/5	13.16.3		
Richerson, Elias Esta.	86	4/2	17.18.4		
Row, Wm. & Moses	60	6/3	18.15.0		
Richards, John	571	4/8	124.8.0}		
Do. of R. Smith	236¾	10/5	122.18.4}		
Richerson, James	180	4/2	37.10.0		
Richerson, William	369½	"	76.17.6		
Richerson, William Junr.	150	5/3	39.7.6		
Richerson, John Esta.	101½	"	21.2.1		
Roane, Major	687½	3/8	128.18.1½		
Rains, Giles	60	3/2	9.10.0		
Robinson, Benjamin Esta.	1300	8/4	541.13.4		
Roane, Charles	200	14/6	145.0.0}		
Do. Dragon Swamp	70	17/	59.10.0}		
Roy, Beverley	700	8/4	291.13.4}		
do. T. Brown	454	12/6	283.15.0}		
Ross, John (B. Minor to pay)	100	5/3	26.5.0		
Richerson & R. Shepherd	24	10/5	8.6.6		
Roane, Thomas Junr.	564	14/6	408.18.0		
Do. of Wm. Roane's Esta.	1585½	18/1½	1436.17.2		
Half the Tax of the above 2 Tracts} of land to be paid by [Lewis] Roane}			7325.2.5		
Segar, Richard	406	7/3	147.3.6		
Saterwhite, George	164	6/3	51.5.0		
Saterwhite, William	200	5/7½	56.5.0		
Spencer, Edward Esta.	45½	8/4	78.19.2}		
Do. S.M.	582	7/3	210.19.6}		
Schools, John	156	8/4	65.0.0		
Schools, John & Jas.	16	7/1	5.13.4		
Schools, Gabriel Esta.	169	6/3	52.16.3		
Skelton, William	362	8/2½	148.11.5}		
Do. Phil Perryman	12	7/2	4.6.0}		
Smith, John (D)	190	7/6	71.5.0		
Starling, Roderick	360	7/10	14.0.0}		
Do.	313	8/2	127.16.2}		
Do. Wm. Lyne	56½	8/4	23.6.8}		
Do. H. Walker	46	5/3	12.1.6}		
Skelton, Thomas	294	8/4	122.10.0		
Scott, Benjamin Esta.	200	9/4	93.6.8		
Sanders, George	200	7/3	72.10.0		
Shepherd, William	140	9/4	65.6.8		
Smith, Molly	30	4/2	6.5.0		
Smith, John Junr.	100	5/3	26.5.0		
Smith, Lewis	96	7/6	36.0.0		
Swinton, George Esta.	750	13/6	506.5.0		
			9389.19.3		

[page 13, 1799] Persons Names Owning Land	Quantity of land [112]	Price per acre	Tot. Amt. Value Land	Amt. Tax Thereon Dols. Cents
Stone, Sarah	300	7/3	108.15.0	
Stone, Daniel	52	3/2	8.4.8	
Smith, Larkin	1254¼	31/1	1949.6.3½	
Smith, Henry	400	6/3	130.0.0	
Smith, William	53	7/10	20.15.2	
Smith, James Esta.	80	3/2	12.13.4	
Smith, James Jun[r.]	101	7/10	39.11.2	
Smith, Ambrose	92¾	8/4	38.6.8	
Stevens, George Esta.	430	"	168.8.4	
Stephens, George orphan	75	"	29.8.4	
Smith, William (Mill) Esta.	200	3/2	31.13.4	
Shackelford, John Esta.	114	7/3	40.18.2	
Starke, Richard Esta.	350	5/8	99.3.4	
Stone, Robert Esta.	200	4/2	41.13.4	
Stone, Job	100	"	20.16.8	
Stone, John Esta.	48½	5/3	12.12.0	
Smith, Robert	89	10/5	46.7.1	
Smith, Samuel	110	"	57.5.10}	
do. of R. Smith, Dragon	4	17/	3.8.0}	
Smith, John (son of Rob[t.])	80	10/5	41.13.4}	
do. Dragon	12	17/	10.8.0}	
Simpkins, Nimrod Esta.	60	3/2	9.10.0	
Sears, Philip	83	4/2	17.5.10	
Shackelford, William Esta.	700	14/6	527.10.0	
Spencer, Thomas	300	10/5	156.5.0	
do.	255	4/2	53.3.6}	
Seward, Benjamin	115	3/2	18.4.2	
Steadman, Christopher Sen[r.]	191	5/3	50.2.9	
Smith, Thomas	485	14/6	351.12.6	
Sadler, John	150	6/3	46.17.6	
Shackelford, Alexander	60	4/2	12.10.0	
Stedman, Christopher	260	5/3	65.5.0	
Shackelford, John (R)	482	8/4	200.16.8	
			4420.9.11	
Shackelford, William	351	6/3	109.13.9	
Shackelford, Lyne	300	"	93.15.0	
Shackelford, John (M)	283	6/2	87.5.2}	
Do. of John Collier's [Legatees]	150	5/3	39.7.6}	
Scott, Anderson	330	16/7	273.12.6	
Shepherd, John	192	3/2	30.1.8	
Seward, Lucy & Eliz[a.] Esta.	100	4/2	22.18.4	
Semple, Robert B.	253	10/5	131.15.1	
Stone, William	74¼	3/2	11.15.3½	
Seward, Edward	81½	5/3	21.6.6¾	
Sthreshley, William	155½	6/3	48.11.10½	
Sears, Thomas	123	6/7	40.9.9	
Segar, John (Lotts in Dunkirk)				
Schools, George	200	8/4	83.6.8	
Throgmorton, James	200	5/3	52.10.0	
Trice, William	140	7/3	50.15.0	
Taylor, James	50	6/3	15.12.6	
Taylor, Edmond	294	8/14	122.10.0	
Temple, Joseph	918	10/5	478.2.6	
Tunstall, Richard Jun[r.] Esta.	1097	7/3	397.13.3	
Tureman, Benjamin	70	3/2	11.1.8	
Tureman, George	50	2/3	7.18.4	
			6555.12.2	

[page 14, 1799] Persons Names Owning Land	Quantity of land	Price per acre	Tot. Amt. Value Land	Amt. Tax Thereon Dols. Cents
Taliaferro, William	1000	14/6	725.0.0	
Townley, Robert	200	6/3	62.10.0}	
Do. Anderson's	117	14/6	84.16.6}	
Taliaferro, Philip	940	8/4	391.13.4}	
Do. D. Cooke	374½	12/6	234.7.6}	
Thurston, Armstead	111¾	4/3	23.15.1½	
Taliaferro, John B	296	5/3	77.14.0	
Temple, William	402½	15/	301.17.6	
Thurston, Batcheldor	200	3/2	31.13.4	
Turner, Benjamin	36	4/2	7.10.0	
Temple, Humphrey	178	31/3	278.2.6}	
Do. Wm. Tunstall	100	15/	75.0.0}	
Do. J. Tunstall Esta.	200	18/8	185.16.8}	
Do. R. Tunstall & others	574	20/	602.14.0}	
Tunstall, Richard (Purdy)	132½	8/4	55.0.0	
Tunstall, Thomas C.	137	"	57.1.8	
Townley, Ann	79	4/2	16.9.2	
Turner, Henry Esta.	100	"	20.16.8	
Tunstall, Richard G.	206½	7/10	73.3.7	
Upshaw, James (Essex)	125	8/10	55.4.2}	
Do. of R. Beverley	30	10/5	15.12.6}	
Vass, Thomas	250	5/3	65.12.6	
			3441.10.8	
Wyatt, Henry	200	7/3	72.10.0	
White, Henry	100	8/4	41.13.4	
Wyatt, Joseph	68	8/4	25.0.0	
Wilson, Isaac	200	6/3	62.10.0	
Wilson, Benjamin Esta.	200	7/3	72.10.0	
Wiltshire, Joseph	74	"	26.16.6	
Wyatt, John	100	7/10	39.3.4	
Watkins, William	37	4/2	7.14.2	
Watkins, Joseph	156	6/7	51.7.0	
Walker, Philip	110	9/4	51.6.8	
Ware, John Esta.	562	7/3	203.14.6	
Walker, Humphrey	820	33/2	1355.14.2	
Wright, William	130	5/3	33.12.6	
Watts, Edward	250	7/3	90.12.6}	
Do. W. Watts Esta.	113	5/	28.5.0}	
Watts, John	293	7/10	114.15.2}	
Do. Pemberton	45	6/3	14.1.3}	
Watts, Kauffman	300	5/3	78.15.0}	
Do. T. Eubank	100	5/9	28.15.0}	
Do. Burches Esta.	157	5/9	45.2.9}	
Do. of Hemingway	112	4/2	23.6.4}	
Watts, James	350	4/2	72.18.4}	
Do. W. Watts Esta.	60	15/	45.0.0}	
Williams, Howard	224	4/2	46.13.4}	
Do. Dragon Swamp	43	17/	36.11.0}	
Wyatt, Thomas	206	7/10	81.2.0}	
Do. of J. Boughton	60	3/2	9.10.0}	
Wyatt, John Esta.	103	6/3	32.3.9	
Wyatt, William	48¾	7/3	17.1.3	
			6249.15.6	

[page 15, 1799] Persons Names Owning Land	Quantity of land [113]	Price per acre	Tot. Amt. Value Land	Amt. Tax Thereon Dols. Cents
Williams, Montague	300	6/3	93.15.0	
Williams, Charles	336	4/2	70.0.0	
Walton, James	80	"	16.13.4	
Walton, Mary	60	"	12.10.0	
Willis, Joel	94	7/10	35.5.0	
Walton, Elizabeth	60	3/2	9.10.0	
Walton, John	176	5/3	46.4.0	
Walton, William Esta.	66	4/2	13.15.0	
Walton, Thomas Esta.	66	"	13.15.0	
Ware, John	75	5/3	19.13.9	
Ware, Arther	83	4/2	17.15.10	
Waring, Robert P.	542	10/9	291.6.6	
Walden, Richard Esta.	180	10/5	93.15.0	
Walden, Lewis	150	3/2	23.15.0}	
Do. T. Dudley	84½	6/3	28.2.3½}	
Wright, Edward	569	"	177.3.9	
Williams, George	40	4/2	8.6.8	
Watkins, Philip	197	5/3	51.14.3	
Wyatt, Richard	175	12/6	109.7.6	
Ware, Robert Jun[r.] Esta.	100	4/2	20.6.8	
Williams, Elizabeth	16½	3/2	2.12.9	
White, James Esta.	200	6/3	62.10.0	
Warren, Catharine	175	"	27.14.2	
Ware, Robert (B)	112	3/2	17.14.8	
Wedderburn, Lydia	350	6/3	109.7.6	
			1372.14.7	
Whiting, Beverley Esta.	2447¾	7/10	866.18.9	
Webley, John Esta.	173	5/3	45.8.3}	
Do. B. & F. Collier	268½	4/2	55.18.9}	
Do. W[m.] Dillard Jun[r.]	89½	"	18.12.11}	
Ware, Robert Jun[r.]	100	8/4	41.13.4	
Ware, William	"	"	41.13.4	
Walden, Edward Esta.	338	5/3	88.14.6	
Walden, Benjamin	35	"	9.3.9	
Waller, Edward Esta.	133½	3/2	21.2.9	
Waller, George Esta.	87	"	13.15.6	
Whayne, William	154½	7/10	60.10.3	
Waller, Robert	113	3/7	20.5.11	
Wyatt, John (Taylor)	30	5/3	7.17.6	
Williamson, Abner	100	3/2	15.16.8	
Ware, Nicholas	"	"	15.16.8	
Walden, Samuel	80	7/10	36.6.8	
Walden, John Sen[r.]	100	5/3	26.5.0	
Young, Henry	640	18/8	597.6.8	
[arithmetic omitted]			3356.1.9	
			£92020.15.1	

Yearly rent Lotts £151.0.0, [tax] $7:80 Lotts
$306,735.84 valuation, $1472.33 Land

List of Land Within the County of King & Queen with the Tax thereon for the year 1800

[page 1, 1800] Persons Names Owning Land	Quantity of land	Price per acre	Tot. Amt. Value Land	Amt. Tax Thereon Dols. Cents
	[114]			
Atkins, Joseph	66	4/2	13.15.0	
Allexander, Benjamin	202	9/4	94.5.4}	
Do. Jas. Halbert	124	6/2	38.15.0}	
Acre, Seaton	52	9/4	24.5.[4]	
Alexander, Elisha	338	"	157.14.8	
Anderson, Churchill Esta.	636	7/3	230.11.0	
Anderson, Pauling Esta.	498	14/6	361.1.0	
Atkins, John	135	4/6	30.7.6	
Abbott, Jacob	112	7/10	43.17.4	
Anderson, Richard Esta.	460	5/3	120.15.0	
Atkins, Lewis	60	8/4	25.0.0	
Anderson, Francis	458	10/9	246.3.6}	
Do. of Rich[d.] T. Shackelford	26	8/4	12.1.8}	
Bray, James	128¾	7/10	55.8.6	
Brown, Samuel	33¼	4/3	7.1.2	
Broach, Benoni	48	10/5	25.4.0	
Brown, Henry Jun[r.]	100	12/	60.0.0	
Beverley, Robert	2444	10/5	1262.16.4	
Brown, Henry	728	7/4½	269.19.0	
Baylor, Gregory	256	14/6	185.12.0	
Bland, John & Lucy	166	8/4	69.3.4	
Bates, James	358	11/	149.3.4}	
			3482.19.8	
Do. Do.	42	4/2	8.15.0}	
Do. of Rice Garnett	89	7/3	32.5.3}	
Barton, John Esta.	125	"	26.0.10	
Braxton, Carter	484½	10/5	252.6.10	
Banks, William Esta.	365	"	76.0.10	
Brooking, Francis	930	10/5	484.7.6	
Boughton, Thomas, Essex	130	9/4	60.13.4	
Boughton, John	200	8/4	83.6.8	
Boughton, Henry, Essex	88	6/3	27.10.0	
Broach, John	72	4/2	15.0.0	
Burton, Thomas Esta.	170	5/3	44.12.6	
Bohannon, Ann	197	4/6	44.6.6	
Brown, William	75	7/10	29.7.6	
Bagbey, John Esta.	330	7/3	119.12.9	
Bagbey, Richard	260	"	94.5.0	
Bagbey, Thomas	260	"	94.5.0	
Do. of Jacob Lumpkin	235	6/3	73.8.9	
Brizendine, Armstead	50	4/3	10.12.6	
Brooke, Richard	1539¾	29/-	2232.12.9	
Brumley, Robert	225	5/3	59.1.3	
Brumley, John	60	7/10	23.10.0	
Bird, George B.	60	6/3	18.5.0	
Broach, William	20	7/10	7.16.8	
Bird, William	532	7/3	197.17.0}	
Do. Dragon Swamp	88½	17/	70.4.6}	
Brown, John	50	7/4½	18.8.9	
Bird, Philemon	1776½	6/3	555.13.1½	
	15883		8323.15.5	

[page 2, 1800] Persons Names Owning Land	Quantity of land	Price per acre	Tot. Amt. Value Land	Amt. Tax Thereon Dol. Cents
Brett, John	178¼	18/2	160.8.6	
Burch, James	70	7/3	25.7.6	
Burch, Vincent	100	4/2	20.16.8}	
Do. of Wm. Hoskins in St. Stephens	50	14/6	36.5.0}	
Bird, Anthony Armistead	275	3/2	43.10.10}	
Do. of Wm. Montague	44	4/2	9.3.4}	
Blake, Thomas	40	6/3	12.10.0	
Byne, John Esta.	336	4/2	70.0.0}	
Do. Dragon Swamp	2¼	17/	1.18.3}	
Bird, Barbara Esta.	266 2/3	24/10	331.2.2½	
Bird, Robert Esta.	533 1/4	"	662.4.5¼}	
Do. Guy Smith	189	3/2	30.0.1}	
Bourn, Richard Esta.	150	"	23.15.0	
Boyd, John	115	18/8	107.6.8}	
do. Soane's	382	24/10	474.6.4}	
Bray, Richard Esta.	93	7/10	36.8.6	
Bird, John Esta.	100	3/2	15.16.8	
Bew, William	117	"	18.10.6	
Bowden, William	69	6/6	22.2.9	
Boyd, Spencer Esta.	1419	10/5	739.6.5	
Berkley, Edmond	762	5/3	200.0.6	
Bland, John	60	12/6	37.10.0	
Bohannan, William	130	5/3	34.2.6	
Bland, William	100	9/11	49.11.8	
Bohannan, William, St. Stephens	33	5/3	8.13.3	
Bourn, Mills	159½	"	41.14.3	
Bullman, Ann	100	"	26.5.0}	
Do. of Agatha Moore	20	"	5.5.0}	
Belote, Laban	384½	"	80.2.6	
Bland, William Senr.	225	3/8¼	41.9.8¼	
Bland, Ralph	146	5/3	38.6.8	
Do. of Finney & Buckner	170	4/2	35.8.4	
			3438.8.11	
Bowden, William Junr.	100	4/2	20.16.8}	
Do. Sykes & Dudley	34	3/2	5.7.8}	
Do. Lyne Shackelford	½	6/3	3.1½}	
Bowden, John	100	4/2	20.16.8	
Bland, William Esta.	250	"	52.1.8	
Bland, Thomas	412	3/2	75.4.8	
Bowden, George	236	5/3	61.19.0}	
Do. of Wm. Dillard	30	4/2	6.5.0}	
Burch, William	45	3/2	7.8.6	
Banks, James	22	7/3	7.19.6	
Bristow, Bartholomew	33½	3/2	5.6.1	
Bristow, George	100	3/2	15.16.8	
Bates, William	81	7/9½	31.10.1}	
Do. of Rice Garnett	117	7/3	42.8.4}	
Banks, Andrew	125	12/6	78.2.6	
Brightwell, John Esta.	70	4/2	14.11.8	
Burton, James	89	"	18.10.10	
Broach, George	32	14/6	23.11.3	
Bland, William	300	7/3	108.15.0	
Bird, Janett & Frances	230	10/5	119.15.10	
of John Richards				
Do. of Robert Smith, Dragon}				
Swamp, partly in Essex}	60			
Bird, Philemon & John Smith	[1]	7/10	0.7.10	
	9287		4155.7.5	

[page 3, 1800] Persons Names Owning Land	Quantity of land	Price per acre	Tot. Amt. Value Land	Amt. Tax Thereon
	[115]			Dols. Cents
Crafton, Thomas	119	9/4	55.10.8	
Crafton, James	59	"	27.10.8	
Crafton, John	117½	"	54.12.0	
Campbell, William	890	7/3	322.12.6	
Crane, John	130	6/3	40.2.6	
Cleverius, Benjamin	419	20/9	434.14.3	
Carlton, Henry Esta.	280	7/10	109.13.4}	
Do. John Baylor Esta.	257	14/6	186.6.6}	
Cole, Thomas G.	30	9/4	14.0.0}	
Do. of J. Lumpkin's Esta.	75	6/3	23.8.9}	
Do. of Francis Lumpkin	70			
Carlton, Lewis	100	8/4	41.3.4}	
Do. of Wm. Tignor	130	7/10	50.18.4}	
Clayton, Thomas Esta.	275	7/3	99.13.9	
Campbell, Whitacar	318	7/10	124.11.0	
Cleveley, Thomas	171	"	66.19.6	
Crow, Nathaniel Esta.	200	6/3	62.10.0	
Crane, George Esta.	30	7/3	10.17.6	
Courtney, Thomas	183¼	10/5	95.6.3	
Carlton, Joel	53½	6/3	16.14.5	
Cooke, John	100	7/3	36.5.0	
Carlton, Thomas (Swamp)	200	7/10	78.6.8	
Carlton, Noah	100	"	39.3.4	
Cooke, Henry	260	5/3	68.5.0	
Carlton, John, School	100	6/3	31.5.0	
Campbell, Sarah Esta.	296	12/6	185.0.0	
Carlton, Christopher Senr.	37½	6/5	11.14.5}	
Do. of Jas. Laughlin	186½	3/2	26.8.2}	
Carlton, Richard Esta.	139	7/	48.13.0	
Cothern, James	36½	3/2	5.15.7	
			2367.11.5	
Carlton, William (Shoe)	309¾	11/6	178.1.2½	
Carlton, Robert Esta.	148	5/	37.0.0	
Carlton, Richard	250	7/3	90.12.6	
Carlton, Christopher Junr.	100		36.5.0}	
Do. John Stone Esta.	159½	5/3	41.14.9}	
Cooper, Henry	50	4/2	10.8.4	
Carlton, Thomas (Taylor)	100	6/3	31.5.0	
Cardwell, John Esta.	150	4/2	31.5.0	
Cardwell, John	150	"	31.5.0	
Cardwell, William	77	"	15.11.6	
Cardwell, Thomas	100	"	22.18.4	
Cooke, John Esta.	300	4/2	62.10.0	
Collins, Thomas	329½	7/	115.6.6}	
Do. Palmers	350	7/3	126.17.6}	
Do. R.S. Ware	86	11/9	50.10.6}	
Carlton, John Junr.	235	4/2	48.19.2	
Campbell, William	238	3/2	37.13.8	
Curtis, Ann Esta.	414	5/3	108.13.6	
Cooke, Moses	100	8/4	41.13.4	
Cooke, Ambrose	100	"	41.13.4	
Corbin, Richard	2390	11/1¾	1332.11.4}	
Do. New Dragon Bridge	125	12/8	78.2.6}	
Do. Shackelford's	300	14/6	217.10.0}	
Corr, James	100	6/2	30.16.8	
	14764		5186.17.0	

[page 4, 1800] Persons Names Owning Land	Quantity of land	Price per acre	Tot. Amt. Value Land	Amt. Tax Thereon Dols. Cents
Crouch, James	130	3/2	20.11.8	
Chapman, Philip	200	7/10	78.6.8	
Crittenden, Thomas	126	13/6	85.1.0}	
Do. Dragon Swamp	36	17/	30.12.0}	
Collins, Joyeux	140	10/5	72.18.4	
Crittenden, Zachariah	34½	14/6	24.17.10	
Cary, Wilson M.	1820	16/7	1509.1.8	
Collier, John	100	4/2	20.16.8	
Campbell, James	130	5/9¼	37.10.0}	
Do. Richard Garrett	70	3/2	11.1.8}	
Crittenden, Richard Esta.	178	5/3	46.14.6	
Corr, Avarilla	79	"	20.14.9	
Collier, Catharine	750	"	196.17.6	
Clegg, Isaiah	241	4/2	50.4.2	
Cooke, Dawson	282	3/2	44.13.0	
Curry, John	155	4/8	31.0.0	
Courtney, Robert	200	7/10	78.16.8	
Cooke, Thomas	240	3/2	38.0.0	
Cooke, Thomas Jun[r.]	96	"	15.0.4	
Carlton, Humphrey	127½	7/	44.10.9	
Carlton, Thomas Esta.	235	6/3	73.8.9	
Carlton, Beverley Esta.	160	4/2	33.6.8	
Corr, John Jun[r.]	500	7/3	181.5.0}	
Do. T. Dudley	197½	6/3	61.14.4½}	
Campbell, John	400	12/6	250.0.0	
Curry, James	70	4/2	18.16.0	
			3075.19.11	
Corr, John Sen[r.]	213	3/2	33.15.6}	
Do. J. Corr Jun[r.]	90	7/3	32.12.6}	
Cooke, Henry	49¼	10/5	25.10.5	
Crittenden, Francis, River	105 2/3	14/6	76.12.2	
Clarke, John	144	5/	36.0.0}	
Do. of Samuel Hemingway	254½	4/2	53.0.3}	
Cannady, William	100	6/3	31.5.0	
Corr, Thomas R	157½	5/3	41.6.10	
Cooke, William	65	5/5	17.12.1	
Cooke, James	65	8/9	28.8.9	
Courtney, Fanny & Children	78	7/10	30.10.0	
Crowe, John	121	5/3	31.19.3¾	
Cross, Joseph	103	6/3	32.6.10½	
Dew, William Esta.	935	14/6	677.17.6	
Dew, Thomas	331	12/6	68.19.2	
Dowling, William Esta.	264	8/4	110.0.0	
Dix, Gabriel	338	6/3	105.12.6	
Deshazo, William Jun[r.]	60	4/2	12.10.0	
Durham, Joseph	105	4/3	21.12.6}	
Do. of Rich[d.] Dunn	10	4/2	2.1.8}	
Deshazo, Peter Esta.	192	7/4	70.8.0	
Deshazo, Larkin	87	7/3	31.4.10}	
Do. of J. Crane	6	6/3	1.17.6}	
Do. of Benj[a.] Hoomes	450	4/4	97.10.0}	
Dunbar, David	366	"	152.10.0	
Dalley, John Esta.	200	3/2	31.13.4	
	11587		4930.15.6	

[page 5, 1800] Persons Names Owning Land	Quantity of land [116]	Price per acre	Tot. Amt. Value Land	Amt. Tax Thereon Dols. Cents
Dobbins, Charles Esta.	147	5/3	38.11.9	
Dean, Benjamin	50	"	13.2.6	
Dillard, William Esta.	100	3/2	15.16.8	
Dudley, Peter Esta.	530	7/3¼	186.18.4	
Dumagin, Richard	66	5/5	17.17.6	
Didlake, Mary	278	8/4	115.16.8	
Durham, Robert Esta.	50	"	10.8.4	
Didlake, Margret	65	4/2	13.10.10	
Dunn, Thomas	50½	6/3	15.15.7½	
Dillard, William Senr.	226	12/6	141.5.0	
Dillard, George	50	"	31.5.0	
Durham, George	50	4/2	10.8.4	
Durham, Thomas Esta.	85	3/2	13.9.2	
Dumagin, Richard	55	5/5	14.17.11	
Didlake, George Esta.	114	10/5	59.7.6	
Dungie, John	110	3/2	17.8.4	
Dudley, William Junr.	290	14/6	210.5.0}	
Do. of L. Wedderburn	315½	6/3	98.11.10}	
Damm, John Esta.	55	"	17.3.9	
Dudley, James	180	7/10	70.10.0	
Dame, William	25	4/2	5.4.2	
Douglas, John	239	7/	83.13.0	
Didlake, John	1200	7/3	435.0.0	
Dudley, Ann	141	"	51.2.3	
Dudley, Guilford	106	"	38.8.6	
Didlake, Edward	56	10/5	25.0.0	
Dudley, Banks	230	3/2	36.8.4	
Downey, Michael Esta.	50	10/5	26.0.10	
			1813.12.1	
Didlake, Royston	206	3/6½	36.7.4	
Dillard, Thomas	49	15/	36.15.0	
Dillard, William	259½	"	194.5.0	
Dudley, Thomas	70	6/3	21.17.6	
Dillard, Nicholas	75	4/2	15.12.6	
Dillard, Benjamin Esta.	148	5/3	48.17.0	
Drummond, John Esta.	150	6/3	46.17.6	
Dixon, Michael	414¾	15/5	320.0.0	
Dabney, Benjamin	400	14/6	290.0.0}	
Do. of Phil Taliaferro	72	8/4	30.0.0}	
Davis, Stage	311	6/9	105.2.7½}	
Do. of T. Foster	50	4/2	10.8.4}	
Do. of W^m. Didlake	24	"	5.0.0}	
Dally, George	174¼	3/2	27.11.9½	
Dudley, Henry	50	5/3	13.2.6	
Dunn, John (Essex), Dragon	73	17/	62.1.0	
Diggs, Frances	175	5/3	45.13.9}	
Do. T. Brushwood	180	4/2	37.10.0}	
Durham, John	25	3/2	3.9.4	
Eubank, Richard Esta.	117	4/2	24.3.9	
Eubank, John Esta.	469	10/4	242.6.4}	
Do. Jas. Grafton	111	6/3	34.13.9}	
Do. T. Dew	178½	12/6	111.5.6}	
	8685		3576.12.6	

[page 6, 1800] Persons Names Owning Land	Quantity of land	Price per acre	Tot. Amt. Value Land	Amt. Tax Thereon Dols. Cents
Eubank, Henry	171	5/3	44.17.9	
Edwards, Thomas Esta.	66	4/2	13.15.0	
Eubank, William Esta.	28¾	5/3	7.11.0	
Eubank, Richard Sen[r.]	196	7/	68.12.0	
Eubank, Thomas	110	4/2	22.18.4	
Eubank, Richard Jun[r.]	112¼	7/	39.5.7¼}	
Do. of T. Jeffries	12¾	7/3	4.12.5}	
Do. of A. Dunn	147	5/3	38.11.9}	
Evans, Ambrose	195	7/10	56.10.0	
Eubank, Warner	115	3/2	18.4.2	
Fogg, Frederick	298	8/4	124.3.4	
Fogg, Thomas	107	6/3	33.8.8	
Fleet, Baylor	862	12/6	538.15.8	
Fauntleroy, Samuel G.	2069	20/	2069.0.0	
Fleet, John Esta.	260	6/3	81.5.0	
Faulkner, Thomas	220	"	68.15.0	
Fogg, Thomas Esta.	93	"	29.1.3	
Fogg, James	120	"	37.10.0	
Fox, Joseph S.	13	7/3	4.14.3}	
Do. of T. Garnett	28	7/10	10.19.4}	
Frazier, William	45	20/9	46.13.6	
Fleet, William	352	"	365.4.0	
Fisher, James Esta.	110	3/2	17.18.4	
Foster, Thomas	87¾	4/2	18.2.6	
			3760.8.10	
Faulkner, Mary	333	6/3	104.1.4	
Fauntleroy, Thomas	486	10/	243.0.0}	
Do. of H. Todd	500	18/	460.0.0}	
Do. of W[m.] Bowden	183	7/	64.1.0}	
Farinholtz, David	151¼	6/6	49.1.6	
Faulkner, Benjamin	533	4/2	111.0.10}	
Do. of W[m.] Boyd	9½	10/5	4.10.9}	
Do. of A. Gardner	3	17/	2.11.0}	
Grafton, Sally & Ann	132	9/4	61.12.0	
Gale, John [Jr.?]	264	7/5	97.18.0	
Do. of W[m.] Gale	7	"	2.13.11}	
Gatewood, Chaney	829	10/5	437.17.11}	
Do. Gardner's	100	7/3	36.5.0}	
Do. Nole's	362½	14/6	262.16.3}	
Do. Harwood's	125	4/2	46.17.6}	
Do. T. Eubank	300	14/3	217.10.0}	
Do. [J.] Walden Esta.	120	12/6	75.0.0}	
Do. W[m.] Lyne, Lotts in Dunkirk				
Garnett, Joshua	325	8/4	134.3.4	
Graves, Edward Esta.	200	6/3	62.10.0	
Gatewood, Joseph	445	10/5	231.15.5	
Gale, Matthew	323	11/5	184.7.7	
	11550		6650.2.2	

[page 7, 1800] Persons Names Owning Land	Quantity of land	Price per acre	Tot. Amt. Value Land	Amt. Tax Thereon
	[117]			Dols. Cents
Gatewood, John	160	8/4	66.13.4	
Garnett, Reuben	876½	8/10	387.2.5}	
Do. of W. Halbert & Gatewood	28	10/5	14.12.10}	
Gwathmey, Temple	600	35/3	1057.10.0	
Garlick, Samuel	454	24/10	463.14.4}	
Do. of Leonard Tunstall	550	6/3	171.17.6}	
Garlick, John	893	29/	1294.17.0	
Griffith, Joseph	50	6/3	15.12.6	
Gresham, Samuel	432½	7/3	156.15.7½	
Do. of Rice Garnett	157	"	56.18.1}	
Guthrie, William	46¾	"	16.18.11¾}	
Do. of L. Smith	½	"	3.7½}	
Do. of Wm. Campbell	17	"	6.3.3}	
Do. of Saml. Walden	27	7/10	10.11.3}	
Garrett, Robert	100	4/2	20.16.8	
Gaines, Francis	356	14/6	258.2.0	
Gaines, Harry Esta.	1517	20/4	1542.5.8	
Gresham, Thomas	339	6/3	106.0.4}	
Do. T. Stephens	78	7/10	30.11.10}	
Do. Jas. Bray	38¼	"	14.19.8}	
Gresham, Philemon	200	"	62.10.0	
Gresham, John D	200	7/10	78.6.8	
Gresham, William, Bricklayer	100	4/2	20.16.8}	
Do. of W.C. Row	40	6/3	13.3.4}	
Gardner, Elizabeth	100	"	31.5.0	
Gibson, Richard	156½	3/2	24.16.7	
Gibson, Banks	56½	"	8.8.11	
Gibson, John	104¾	"	14.14.4½	
Griffith, Milley	50	6/3	15.12.6	
			5963.1.2	
Gresham, Machem	100	5/3	26.5.0}	
Do. of A. Gresham	4	17/	3.8.0}	
Gresham, Ambrose	80	"	21.0.0}	
Do. Dragon Swamp	22	17/	18.5.0}	
Gresham, John Junr.	79	5/3	20.14.9}	
Do. A. Gresham, Dragon	4	17/	3.8.0}	
Graves, Thomas	50½	7/3	18.6.1½}	
Do. of Edwd. Wright	15¾	6/8	5.5.0}	
Griffin, William Esta.	859	14/6	622.15.6	
Garlick, Camm Esta.	550	6/3	171.17.6	
Garrett, James	230	4/2	48.18.4	
Gardner, Anthony	638	11/	350.11.8}	
Do. Dragon Swamp	67½	17/	57.7.6}	
Gresham, Lumpkin	255	7/3	92.8.9	
Garrett, Robert	200	7/	70.0.0}	
Do. Wm. Hunt's Esta.	170	6/3	53.2.6}	
Gresham, William Junr.	329	8/4	137.5.10}	
Do. of Wm. Gatewood	46	3/2	7.5.8}	
Do. of Chick	69	7/3	25.0.3}	
Gresham, George	141	"	22.6.6	
Gaines, Robert Esta.	537¾	20/9	558.8.7¾}	
Do. Ann Curtis	50	5/3	13.2.6}	
Gatewood, William, Tucko.	33	3/2	5.4.6	
Gatewood, William, son of Jno.	132	10/	66.0.0	
Gleson, Patrick	134	8/4	55.16.8	
	12524		8437.15.4	

[page 8, 1800] Persons Names Owning Land	Quantity of land	Price per acre	Tot. Amt. Value Land	Amt. Tax Thereon
				Dols. Cents
Gatewood, Gabriel	78	10/5	40.12.6}	
Do. Halbert	50	"	26.10.0}	
Guthrie, James	60	12/6	37.10.0	
Guthrie, Richard	60	"	37.10.0	
Do. Do.	162	3/2	25.13.0}	
Garrett, Edward	210	15/3	55.2.6}	
Do. of Edw[d.] Trice Esta.	489½	"	128.9.10}	
Groom, John	173	3/2	27.17.10	
Garrett, George	88½	5/3	23.4.7½	
Guthrie, Rachel	50	8/4	20.16.8	
Goldman, Martin	140	4/2	29.3.4	
Gully, Philip	50	3/2	7.18.4	
Garrett, William (Shoe)	225	3/4¾	37.19.4	
Gramshill, Henry	25	3/2	3.9.2	
Garrett, Ann Watt[s]	112	5/	28.0.0	
Garrett, Richard	100	4/2	20.16.8	
Gale, William	344	7/5	127.11.4	
Garrett, William Jun[r.]	120	4/2	25.0.0	
Groom, Richard	50	"	10.8.4	
Hill, William	1310¼	14/6	949.11.4½	
Hawes, Walker	97	"	70.6.6	
Hitchcock, Thomas	140	4/2	29.3.4	
Hoskins, Samuel Esta.	345	6/3	107.16.3}	
Do. of Elisha Alexander	57	10/5	25.13.9}	
Hutcherson, Charles	531	7/1	188.1.3	
			2084.6.0	
Hoskins, William	533	14/6	366.8.6	
Heskew, John Esta.	61	5/3	16.0.3	
Heskew, John Jun[r.]	50	6/3	15.12.6}	
do. Clement Pynes	10	3/2	1.11.8}	
Hill, Robert Esta.	1281	8/2	523.1.6	
Hill, Edward	1200	18/8	1120.0.0	
Hoomes, Benjamin	372	12/6	232.10.0}	
do. Ann Ken[n]edy	75	"	46.17.6}	
Hutson, William Esta.	112	3/2	17.14.6	
Hemingway, John Jun[r.]	67	4/2	13.19.2	
Hemingway, Samuel	12¾	"	2.13.1½	
Hemingway, John Sen[r.]	154	"	32.1.4	
Hare, William Esta.	217	5/3	56.19.3	
Harwood, Christopher Esta.	194	24/10	240.17.8	
Harwood, Priscilla	165	18/	148.10.0	
Hill, Thomas Esta.	300	26/11	403.15.0	
Hart, James	150	3/2	23.15.0	
Holderby, John	100	4/2	20.16.8}	
Do. of W[m.] Hoskins	108¾	7/10	42.6.0}	
Hart, Anthony	190	5/3	49.17.6}	
Do. of Sundrie Persons	359½	3/2	56.18.5}	
Hart, Gregory	200	11/	31.3.4	
Hart, William	250	3/3½	41.2.11	
Harwood, John Jun[r.]	109	10/5	56.15.5½	
Hunt, William Esta.	560	6/3	175.0.0	
	11895		5790.13.3	

[page 9, 1800] Persons Names Owning Land	Quantity of land [118]	Price per acre	Tot. Amt. Value Land	Amt. Tax Thereon Dols. Cents
Henry, Samuel Esta.	1900	14/6	1377.10.0	
Henry, James	75	12/6	46.17.6	
Hurt, James	33	10/5	17.3.9	
Halyard, William	190	5/3	49.17.6	
Hoskins, John	767	10/5	399.9.7}	
Do. Boughtons	100	8/4	41.13.4}	
Hurt, West	14	5/3	3.3.6	
Hoskins, Robert	287	6/	86.2.0	
Do. Robt. Smith, Mor[t]gage				
Hart, Alden	127	4/2	26.9.2	
Howerton, Heritage	122¼	20/9	126.16.7¼	
Howerton, John	269½	5/3	70.14.10½	
Holt, William	123	14/3	87.12.9	
Hutson, William	50	4/2	10.8.4	
Hutcherson, John	73¼	8/9	32.0.11¼	
Hart, Vincent	75	6/6	24.7.6	
Halyard, John	1	5/9¼	5.9¼	
Howerton, George	76¼	6/	22.17.6	
Jones, Thomas	255	4/2	53.2.6	
Jeffries, Thomas	63	7/3	22.16.9}	
Do. of J. Harwood Jun[r.]	38¼	10/5	19.15.10}	
Jones, John Esta.	300	8/11	133.15.0	
Jeffries, Edward	70	3/2	11.1.8	
Jones, James	160	14/6	116.0.0}	
Do. of Jas. Jones Esta.	196	10/5	102.1.8}	
Jones, Jas. Jr., Fleet & Gilmore	125	5/3	33.16.3}	
Jones, William	241	15/10	190.15.10}	
Do. of L. Smith	35¾	31/1	55.11.2}	
Jeffries, Ambrose	337	7/10	124.18.10	
			3346.16.1	
Jeffries, Robert	110	7/6	41.5.0	
Do. of Lumpkin Gresham	10	7/3	3.12.6}	
Jeffries, Gowin	60	4/2	12.10.0	
Jordan, Thomas Esta.	100	"	20.16.8	
Johnson, Thomas	72	3/2	11.8.0	
Jameson, David Esta.	50	"	7.18.4	
Jones, Rawleigh	63	31/1	93.18.3	
Jeffries, Thomas	57¾	18/	51.19.6	
Kemp, John	296	7/3	107.3.0	
Kemp, John, St. Stephens	178	7/3	64.2.2	
Kauffman, John Junr.	38	10/5	19.15.10}	
Do. John Kauffman Esta.	471	18/8	439.1.0}	
Keeling, Mary	78½	8/	31.8.0	
Kennadey, Archibald Esta.	38¼	4/2	7.19.4	
Kennadey, Ann	70¼	7/10	14.11.8	
Kennadey, Ann Jun[r.]	33¼	"	7.0.6	
Kennadey, Lucy	37½	"	7.16.2	
Kay, Christopher	116	6/3	36.6.0}	
Do. of T. Goleman Esta.	416½	9/	187.8.6}	
Kidd, Bartholomew	136	5/3	35.14.0}	
Do. of William Dillard J[r.]	132½	4/2	27.12.1}	
Kidd, Benjamin	111	13/6	74.18.2}	
Do. of Crittenden	60	"	40.10.0}	
Do. Dragon Swamp	36	17/	30.12.0}	
	8876		4722.0.10	

[page 10, 1800] Persons Names Owning Land	Quantity of land	Price per acre	Tot. Amt. Value Land	Amt. Tax Thereon Dols. Cents
Kidd, John Esta.	370	7/3	134.2.6}	
Do. Lumpkin & Pearce	60	4/2	12.10.0}	
Do. of T. Dillard	45	14/6	32.12.6}	
King, Dicey	18	8/4	7.10.0	
Kidd, Henry	81½	5/3	26.6.6.¾	
Lumpkin, James	213	7/10	83.8.2	
Lumpkin, Henry	400	9/4	186.13.4	
Lumpkin, John Esta.	125	6/3	35.11.3	
Lyne, William Jun[r.]}				
Lotts in Dunkirk annual rent}				
Lumpkin, William	305	14/6	221.2.6}	
Do. of T. Dew	26½	12/6	16.5.0}	
Lefon, Francis	119	8/4	49.11.8	
Lankford, Thomas Esta.	100	4/2	20.16.8	
Lumpkin, Robert Sen[r.]	374	8/4	155.16.8	
Lumpkin, Henry Jun[r.]	190	9/4	88.13.4	
Lumpkin, John Ware	140	7/10	54.16.8	
Longest, Caleb	97	"	37.19.10	
Longest, Richard	227¾	"	89.4.2	
Longest, John	100	"	39.3.4	
Lumpkin, Anthony	216	6/3	67.10.0	
Lumpkin, Jacob Esta.	100	7/3	36.5.0	
Lumpkin, Jacob, orphan	681	6/3	212.16.3	
Lewis, Iveson	356	14/6	258.2.0	
Leigh, Lucy	101	24/10	125.8.2	
			1992.5.6	
Lumpkin, Robert	323	5/3	84.15.9	
Leigh, John Esta.	199	24/10	247.1.10	
Lyne, John Esta.	507	6/3	158.8.9	
Lambouth, Thomas	100	3/2	15.16.8	
Lambouth, Charles Esta.	50	"	7.18.4	
Motley, Edwin	815	10/5	428.2.8	
Martin, Thomas C.	583	14/6	422.13.6}	
Do.	134½	7/3	48.15.1½}	
Morgin, William	3	6/3	18.9	
Mitchell, Ralph Esta.	193	10/5	100.10.5	
Minor, William	149	8/4	62.1.8	
Minor, John	137	"	57.1.8	
Minor, Thomas	288	7/10	112.16.0}	
Do. of J. Chapman	239	8/5	100.0.3}	
Moody, Lewis	239	"	93.12.2	
Mann, Joseph Jun[r.]	400	8/4	166.13.4	
Mitchell, John	50	6/3	15.12.6	
Mitchell, Sally	391	13/	254.3.0	
Mitchell, James, orphan	225	"	146.5.0	
Mann, Robert Esta.	699	6/3	218.8.9	
Moore, Lambeth	70	4/2	14.11.8	
Morris, William	10	"	2.1.8	
Moore, Benjamin	200	"	41.13.4	
Merideth, Samuel	215	7/10	84.4.2	
Moore, Lodowick, John & Richard	100	3/2	15.16.8	
Major, Josiah	200	4/2	41.13.4	
Mitchell, John Esta.	270	5/3	70.17.6}	
Do. Rootes	200	9/11	99.13.4}	
	11435		5104.13.3	

[page 11, 1800] Persons Names Owning Land	Quantity of land [119]	Price per acre	Tot. Amt. Value Land	Amt. Tax Thereon Dols. Cents
Moore, Aggatha	60	4/2	12.10.0	
Macon, John Esta.	1092	16/7	905.9.0}	
Do. Lotts in Dunkirk anuel rent			66.0.0}	
Montague, William	170	4/2	35.8.4	
Merideth, Ralph G. Esta.	567	14/6	411.1.6	
Muire, Richard	93	12/6	58.2.6	
Moore, Richard Esta.	145	6/3	45.6.3	
McCarty, Joseph Esta.	73	3/2	11.11.2	
Metcalf, John S.	265	14/6	196.5.10	
Metcalf, Thomas	256	"	181.8.8	
Mann, Mary	100	5/3	26.5.0	
Martin, John	475	9/	213.15.0	
Mead, Joseph, Lotts in Dunkirk, annual rent			0.0.0	£6.0.0
Mahon, Thomas	101	6/3	31.11.3	
Mahon, William	103½	"	32.3.9	
Nunn, Jane	180	7/3	65.5.0	
Newbill, George	500	8/4	208.6.8	
Nunn, Thomas	130	7/3	47.2.6	
Nash, John Esta.	100	6/3	31.5.0	
Newbill, William	450	9/4	210.0.0}	
Do. of David Beard	560	8/4	233.6.8}	
Newcomb, William	169	3/2	26.15.2	
Newill, John	100	7/10	39.3.4	
Omealy, John	368¼	30/	553.7.6	
Or[v]ill, John	100	6/3	31.5.0	
Oliver, John	320	5/3	84.0.0	
Overstreet, Gabriel	296	4/2	61.13.4}	
Do. Hayes	130	5/3	34.2.6}	
			3952.10.11	
Oaks, Henry	198½	3/2	34.2.0	
Oaks, William	80	4/2	16.13.4	
Owin, Augustine Esta.	100	6/3	31.5.0	
Oliver, William	59	4/2	12.3.10	
Pendleton, James	888½	8/7½	383.3.3¾}	
Do. Wilmore's	70	7/6	26.5.0}	
Do. Phill Pendleton	120	9/2	53.0.0}	
Do. of Wm. McKentosh	125	4/2	26.1.10}	
Pitts, David	420	9/4	196.0.0	
Pitts, Obadiah	20	10/5	10.8.4	
Philips, Richard	230	7/3	83.7.6	
Pollard, John Esta.	235	9/4	109.13.4}	
Do. Leonard Smithy	384	7/3	139.4.0}	
Prewitt, Francis	99	9/4	46.4.0	
Parker, John	264¼	7/	92.9.9}	
Do. Goleman's Esta.	532	9/	239.10.0}	
Prewitt, Richard	102	7/3	36.12.3	
Pendleton, Philip	360	9/2	165.0.0	
Perryman, Philip	218	7/2	78.2.4	
Pitts, Benjamin G.	100	5/4	26.13.4	
Pynes, Clement				
Pace, Benjamin	263	7/3	95.6.9	
Pollard, Richard	389	8/4	162.1.8	
	12127		5915.16.5	

[page 12, 1800] Persons Names Owning Land	Quantity of land	Price per acre	Tot. Amt. Value Land	Amt. Tax Thereon Dols. Cents
Pendleton, Benjamin	450	7/10	176.5.0	
Pynes, Benjamin Esta.	164	6/3	51.5.0	
Pynes, Robert	111½	"	34.13.9	
Pynes, Benjamin	100	"	31.5.0	
Pemberton, John	165	"	51.11.3	
Pemberton, Philip	121	"	37.16.3	
Pollard, Robert				
Palmer, Charles	104	18/	93.12.0	
Price, Robert	630	6/3	196.17.6	
Pigg, Rachel Esta.	108	14/6	78.6.0	
Pigg, John Esta.	216	14/6	156.12.0}	
Do.	180	7/3	65.5.0}	
Pollard, William	95	"	34.8.9	
Pearce, Philip	83	3/2	13.2.10	
Pearce, Beverley	25¾	4/2	5.7.3½}	
Do. of Phil Pearce	17	3/2	2.13.10}	
Pearce, Thomas Esta.	87	4/2	18.2.6	
Price, Andrew	314	6/	94.4.0	
Perryman, Richard	110	7/3	39.7.6	
Prewitt, Tunstall	58½	8/	23.8.0	
Quarles, Francis W., Lotts in Dunkirk, annual rent				15.0.0
Robinson, Rachel Esta.	155	12/6	96.17.6}	
Do. Do.	260	7/3	94.5.0}	
Roane, Thomas Esta.	2033	18/8	1897.9.4}	
Do. of H. Carlton	200	6/3	63.10.0}	
Do. of Brett's	34¾	18/	31.5.6}	
Do. of Robt. Pynes	24½	6/3	7.9.1½}	
Row, Hansford & Wilson	341	6/3	105.14.7	
			3480.14.5	
Rowe, Thomas, orphan G.	555	7/3	201.3.9	
Rowe, Elizabeth	665	20/9	689.18.9	
Rowe, Francis, orphan	612½	4/8	142.16.0	
Row, Richard Esta.	450	8/4	188.0.0	
Roane, Spencer	1600	24/10	1926.13.4	
Ryland, Joseph	487½	7/3	176.10.9	
Ryland, Josiah	160	7/10	62.13.4}	
Do. of Wm. Temple	27½	15/	20.12.6}	
Do. of Francis Prince Esta.	113	7/10	44.5.2}	
Do. of Henry Brown	34½	7/4¾	12.14.1½}	
Riddle, Vaughn	51	5/5	13.16.3	
Richerson, Elias Esta.	86	4/2	17.18.4	
Row, William & Moses	60	6/3	18.15.0	
Richards, John	571	4/8	124.8.0	
Richerson, James	180	4/2	37.10.0	
Richerson, William	369½	"	76.17.6	
Richerson, William Junr.	150	5/3	39.7.6	
Richerson, John Esta.	101½	"	21.2.1	
Roane, Major	687½	3/8	128.18.1½	
Raines, Giles	60	3/2	9.10.0	
Robinson, Benjamin Esta.	1300	8/4	541.13.4	
Roane, Charles	200	14/6	145.0.0}	
Do. Dragon Swamp	70	17/	59.10.0}	
Roy, Beverley	700	8/4	291.13.4}	
do. T. Brown	454	12/6	283.15.0}	
	15932		875[1].16.6	

[page 13, 1800] Persons Names Owning Land	Quantity of land [120]	Price per acre	Tot. Amt. Value Land	Amt. Tax Thereon Dols. Cents
Ross, John (B. Minor to pay)	100	5/3	26.5.0	
Richerson & R. Shepherd	24	10/5	8.6.6	
Roane, Thomas	564	14/6	408.18.0	
Do. of Wm. Roane's Esta.	792¾	78/1½	718.8.7	
Roane, Samuel	792¾	"	718.8.7	
Segar, Richard	406	7/3	147.3.6	
Saterwhite, George	164	6/3	51.5.0	
Saterwhite, William	200	5/7½	56.5.0	
Spencer, Edward Esta.	45½	8/4	78.19.2}	
Do. in Stratton Major Parish	582	7/3	210.19.6}	
Schools, John	156	8/4	65.0.0	
Schools, John & James	16	7/1	5.13.4	
Schools, Gabriel Esta.	169	6/3	52.16.3	
Skelton, William	362	8/2½	148.11.5}	
Do. of Phill Perryman	12	7/2	4.6.6}	
Smith, John (D)	190	7/6	71.5.0	
Starling, Roderick	360	7/10	141.0.0}	
Do.	313	8/2	127.16.2}	
Do. of Wm. Lyne	56½	8/4	23.6.8}	
Do. of H. Walker	46	5/3	12.1.6}	
Skelton, Thomas	294	8/4	122.10.0	
Scott, Benjamin Esta.	200	9/4	92.6.8	
Sanders, George	200	7/3	70.10.8	
Shepherd, William	140	9/4	65.6.8	
Smith, Molly	30	4/2	6.5.0	
Smith, John Junr.	100	5/3	26.5.0	
			3398.19.8	
Smith, Lewis	96	7/6	36.0.0	
Swinton, George Esta.	750	13/6	506.5.0	
Stone, Sarah	300	7/3	108.15.0	
Stone, Daniel	52	3/2	8.4.8	
Smith, Larkin	1254¼	31/1	1949.6.3½	
Smith, Henry	400	6/3	130.0.0	
Smith, William	53	7/10	20.15.2	
Smith, James Esta.	80	3/2	12.13.4	
Smith, James Junr.	101	7/10	39.11.2	
Smith, Ambrose	92¾	8/4	38.6.8	
Stevens, George Esta.	430	"	168.8.4	
Stephens, George	75	"	29.8.4	
Smith, William (Mill) Esta.	200	3/2	31.13.4	
Shackelford, John Esta.	114	7/3	40.18.2	
Starke, Richard Esta.	350	5/8	99.3.4	
Stone, Robert Esta.	200	4/2	41.13.4	
Stone, Job	100	"	20.16.8	
Stone, John Esta.	48½	5/3	12.12.0	
Smith, Robert	89	10/5	46.7.1	
Smith, Samuel	110	"	57.5.10}	
do. R. Smith, Dragon	4	17/	3.8.0}	
Smith, John, son of Robt.	80	10/5	41.13.4}	
do. Dragon	12	17/	10.8.0}	
Simpkins, Nimrod Esta.	60	3/2	9.10.0	
	11367		6862.2.8	

[page 14, 1800] Persons Names Owning Land	Quantity of land	Price per acre	Tot. Amt. Value Land	Amt. Tax Thereon Dols. Cents
Sears, Philip	83	4/2	17.5.10	
Shackelford, William Esta.	400	14/6	310.0.0	
Spencer, Thomas	300	10/5	156.5.0}	
Do. Do.	255	4/2	53.3.6}	
Seward, Benjamin	115	3/2	18.4.2	
Steadman, Christopher	191	5/3	50.2.9}	
Do Do.	260	"	65.5.0}	
Smith, Thomas	485	14/6	351.12.6	
Sadler, John	150	6/3	46.17.6	
Shackelford, Alexander	60	4/2	12.10.0	
Shackelford, John (R)	482	8/4	216.8.0	
Shackelford, William	351	6/3	109.13.9	
Shackelford, John (M)	283	6/2	87.5.2}	
Do. of John Collier's Legatees	150	5/3	39.7.6}	
Scott, Anderson	330	16/7	273.12.6	
Shepherd, John	192	3/2	30.1.8	
Semple, Robert	253	10/5	131.15.1	
Stone, William	74¼	3/2	11.15.3½	
Sthreshley, William	155½	6/3	48.11.10½	
Sears, Thomas	123	6/7	40.9.9	
Segar, John, Lotts in Dunkirk, anuel rent			40.0.0	
Schools, George	200	8/4	83.6.8	
Throgmorton, James	200	5/3	52.10.0	
Trice, William	140	7/3	50.15.0	
Taylor, James	50	6/3	15.12.6	
Taylor, Edward	294	8/14	122.10.0	
Temple, Joseph	918	10/5	478.2.6	
			2873.1.8	
Tunstall, Richard Jun[r.] Esta.	1097	7/3	397.13.3	
Tureman, Benjamin	70	3/2	11.1.8	
Tureman, George	50	2/3	7.18.4	
Taliaferro, William	1000	14/6	725.0.0	
Townley, Robert	200	6/3	62.10.0}	
Do. Anderson's	117	14/6	84.16.6}	
Taliaferro, Philip Esta.	940	8/4	391.13.4}	
Do. of D. Cooke	374½	12/6	234.7.6}	
Thurston, Armstead	111¾	4/3	23.15.1½	
Taliaferro, John B	296	5/3	77.14.0	
Temple, William	402½	15/	301.17.6	
Thurston, Batcheldor	200	3/2	31.13.4	
Turner, Benjamin	36	4/2	7.10.0	
Temple, John of Temple, Humphrey	178	31/3	278.2.6}	
Temple, Humphrey Estate				
of W[m.] Tunstall	100	15/	75.0.0}	
Do. J. Tunstall Esta.	200	18/8	185.16.8}	
Do. R. Tunstall & others	574	20/	602.14.0}	
Tunstall, Richard (Purdy)	132½	8/4	55.0.0	
Tunstall, Thomas C.	137	"	57.1.8	
Townley, Ann	79	4/2	16.9.2	
Turner, Henry Esta.	100	"	20.16.8	
Tunstall, Richard G.	206½	7/10	73.3.7	
Upshaw, James (Essex)	125	8/10	55.4.2}	
Do. of R. Beverley	30	10/5	15.12.6}	
Vass, Thomas	250	5/3	65.12.6	
	13507		6731.5.7	

[page 15, 1800] Persons Names Owning Land	Quantity of land	Price per acre	3441.10.8 Tot. Amt. Value Land	Amt. Tax Thereon
	[121]			Dols. Cents
Wyatt, Henry	200	7/3	72.10.0	
White, Henry	100	8/4	41.13.4	
Wyatt, Joseph	68	8/4	25.0.0	
Wilson, Isaac	200	6/3	62.10.0	
Wilson, Benjamin Esta.	200	7/3	72.10.--	
Wiltshire, Joseph	74	"	26.16.6	
Wyatt, John	100	7/10	39.3.4	
Watki[n]s, William	37	4/2	7.14.2	
Watkins, Joseph	156	6/7	51.7.0	
Walker, Philip	110	9/4	51.6.8	
Ware, John Esta.	262	7/3	95.19.6	
Walker, Humphrey	820	33/2	1355.14.2	
Wright, William	130	5/3	33.12.6	
Watts, Edward	250	7/3	90.12.6}	
Do. William Watts Esta.	113	5/	28.5.0}	
Watts, John	293	7/10	114.15.2}	
Do. Pemberton	45	6/3	14.1.3}	
Watts, Kauffman	300	5/3	78.15.0}	
Do. of T. Eubank	100	5/9	28.15.0}	
Do. of Burches Esta.	157	5/9	45.2.9}	
Do. of Hemingway	112	4/2	23.6.4}	
Do. of John & Daniel Hemingway	200	"	40.15.8}	
Watts, James	350	4/2	72.18.4}	
Do. William Watts Esta.	60	15/	45.0.0}	
Williams, Howard	224	4/2	46.13.4}	
Do. Dragon Swamp	43	17/	36.11.0}	
Wyatt, Thomas Thomas [sic]	206	7/10	81.2.0}	
Do. of J. Boughton	60	3/2	9.10.0}	
Wyatt, John Esta. [subtotal 2723.15.3]	103	6/3	32.3.9	
Wyatt, William	48¾	7/3	17.1.3	
Williams, Montague	300	6/3	93.15.0	
Williams, Charles	336	4/2	70.0.0	
Walton, James	80	"	16.13.4	
Walton, Mary	60	"	12.10.0	
Willis, Joel	94	7/10	35.5.0	
Walton, Elizabeth	60	3/2	9.10.0	
Walton, John	176	5/3	46.4.0	
Walton, William Esta.	66	4/2	13.15.0	
Walton, Thomas Esta.	"	"	13.15.0	
Ware, John	75	5/3	19.13.9	
Ware, Arther	83	4/2	17.15.10	
Waring, Robert P.	542	10/9	291.6.6	
Walden, Richard Esta.	180	10/5	93.15.0	
Walden, Lewis	150	3/2	23.15.0}	
Do. of T. Dudley	84½	6/3	28.2.3½}	
Wright, Edward	567	"	177.3.9	
Williams, George	40	4/2	8.6.8	
Watkins, Philip	197	5/3	51.14.3	
Wyatt, Richard	175	12/6	109.7.6	
Ware, Robert Junr. Esta.	100	4/2	20.16.8	
Williams, Elizabeth	16½	3/2	2.12.9	
White, James Esta.	200	6/3	62.10.0	
Warren, Catharine Esta.	175	"	27.14.2	
Ware, Robert (B)	112	3/2	17.14.8	
Wedderburn, Lydia	350	6/3	109.7.6	
Whiting, Beverley Esta.	2447¾	7/10	866.18.9	
	11788		4980.19.10	

[page 16, 1800] Persons Names Owning Land	Quantity of land	Price per acre	Tot. Amt. Value Land	Amt. Tax Thereon Dols. Cents
Webley, John Esta.	173	5/3	45.8.3}	
Do. of B. & F. Colliers	268½	4/2	55.18.9}	
Do. of Wm. Dillard Junr.	89½	"	18.12.11}	
Ware, Robert Junr.	100	8/4	41.13.4	
Ware, William	"	"	41.13.4	
Walden, Edward Esta.	338	5/3	88.14.6	
Walden, Benjamin	3[5]	"	9.3.9	
Waller, Edward Esta.	133½	3/2	21.2.9	
Waller, George	87	"	13.15.6	
Whayne, William	154½	7/10	60.10.3	
Waller, Robert	113	3/7	20.5.11}	
Do. of Groom's Esta.	187	3/2	29.12.2}	
Wyatt, John, Taylor	30	5/3	7.17.6	
Williamson, Abner	100	3/2	15.16.8	
Ware, Nicholas	100	"	15.16.8	
Walden, Samuel	53	7/10	20.15.2	
Walden, John Senr.	100	5/3	26.5.0	
Webb, James	140¾	4/2	29.6.6	
Do. Do.	7	4/2	1.9.2	
Wyatt, George	112	7/6	40.0.0	
	2242			
Young, Henry	640	18/8	597.6.8	
			1181.4.9	

183,349 acres land, King & Queen, 1800
added, stated

List of land within the district of William Fleet, Commissioner in the County of King and Queen for the year 1801

LIST A

[page 1, List A, 1801] Persons Names Owning Lands	Quantity of land [122]	Price per acre	Total Amount Land	Amt. Tax Thereon in Dols. Cents
Anderson, Richard estate	460	5/3	120.15.0	
Atkins, Lewis	60	8/4	25.0.0	
Anderson, Francis	458	10/9	246.3.6}	
do. of Rich[d.] T. Shackelford	26	8/4	12.1.8}	
Brown, Samuel	33¼	4/3	7.1.2	
Banks, William estate	365	4/2	76.0.10	
Brooke, Richard	1539¾	29/-	2232.12.9	
Brumley, Robert	225	5/3	59.1.3	
Bird, William	532	7/3	179.17.0}	
do. dragon swamp	88½	17/	70.4.6}	
Bird, Philemon	1693	6/3	529.11.3	
Brett, Nancy	50	18/	45.0.0	
Burch, James	70	7/3	25.7.6	
Burch, Vincent	100	4/2	20.16.8}	
do. W[m.] Hoskins	50	3/2	7.18.4}	
Bird, Anthony A.	275	3/2	43.10.10}	
do. of W[m.] Montague	44	4/2	9.3.4}	
Byne, John estate	336	4/2	70.0.0}	
do. dragon swamp	2¼	17/	1.18.3	
			3892.13.10	
Bird, Robert estate	780	24/10	993.6.8}	
do. Guy Smith	189½	3/2	30.0.1}	
Bourn, Richard estate	150	"	23.15.0	
Boyd, John	115	18/8	107.6.8}	
do. Soane's	382	24/10	474.6.4}	
Bray, Richard estate	93	7/10	36.8.6	
Bird, John estate	100	3/2	15.16.8	
Bew, William estate	117	"	18.0.6	
Boyd, Robert	1119	9/3	517.10.3	
Boyd, William	300	15/	225.0.0	
Berkley, Edmund	762	5/3	200.0.6	
Bland, John	60	12/6	37.10.0	
Bland, William	100	9/11	49.11.8	
Bourn, Mills	159½	"	41.14.3}	
do. Tho[s.] Jordan's estate	33 1/3	4/2	6.18.10½}	
Bullman, Ann	120	5/3	31.10.0	
Belote, Laban	384½	"	80.2.6	
Bland, William Sen[r.]	225	3/8¼	41.9.8¼	
Bland, Ralph	146	53	38.6.8}	
do. Finney & Buckner	170	4/2	35.8.4}	
Bowden, William Junr.	100	"	20.16.8}	
do. Sykes & Dudley	34	3/2	5.7.8}	
Bowden, John	100	4/2	20.16.8	
			£6833.17.11	

[page 2, List A, 1801] Persons Names Owning Lands	Quantity of land	Price per acre	Total Amount Land	Amt. Tax Thereon in Dols. Cents
Bland, William estate	250	4/2	52.1.8	
Bland, Thomas	412	3/2	75.4.8	
Bowden, George	236	5/3	61.19.0}	
Do. Wm. Dillard	30	4/2	6.5.0}	
Banks, James	22	7/3	7.19.6	
Bristow, Bartholomew	33½	3/2	5.6.1	
Bristow, George	100	3/2	15.16.8	
Banks, Andrew	125	12/6	78.2.6	
Brightwell, John estate	70	4/2	14.11.8	
Burton, James estate	89	"	18.10.10	
Bland, William (younger)	300	7/3	108.15.0	
Bird, Janett & Frances	230	10/5	119.15.10}	
do. Ro. Smith (dragon)	60	17/	51.0.0}	
Bird, Philemon & John Smith	1	7/10	7.10	
Breedlove, John	37¾	15/	28.6.3	
Brushwood, George	188	4/2	39.3.4	
Bird, Parmenas	132¼	11/8	77.4.7	
Bray, Peter	51¼	6/3	16.0.3¾	
Bland, John	212	5/3	55.13.0	
Carlton, Thomas (Swamp)	200	7/10	78.6.8}	
do. Philemon Bird	83½	6/3	26.1.10½}	
Carlton, Noah	100	"	39.3.4	
Cooke, Henry	260	5/3	68.5.0}	
do.	49¼	10/5	25.10.5}	
Carlton, John (Schoolr.)	100	6/3	31.5.0	
Campbell, James T. (orphan)	296	12/6	185.0.0	
			1285.15.11	
Carlton, Christopher Senr.	37½	6/5	11.14.5}	
do. Jas. Laughlin	126½	3/2	26.8.2}	
Carlton, Richard estate	139	7/	48.13.0	
Cauthorn, James	36½	3/2	5.15.7	
Carlton, William (Shoe)	309¾	11/6	178.1.2½	
Carlton, Christopher (youngr.)	148	5/	37.0.0	
Carlton, Christopher Junr.	100		36.5.0}	
do. John Stone's estate	159½	5/3	41.14.9}	
Carlton, Richard	250	7/3	90.12.6	
Cooper, Henry	50	4/2	10.8.4	
Carlton, Thomas (Taylor)	100	6/3	31.5.0	
Cardwell, James	150	4/2	31.5.0	
Cardwell, John	150	"	31.5.0	
Cardwell, William esta.	77	"	15.11.6	
Cardwell, Thomas	110	"	22.18.4	
Cooke, John estate	300	4/2	62.10.0	
Collins, Thomas	329½	7/	115.6.6}	
do. Ro. S. Ware	84½	11/9	49.12.10½}	
Carlton, John Junr.	235	4/2	48.19.2	
Campbell, William	238	3/2	37.13.8	
Corbin, Richard	2390	11/1¾	1332.11.4}	
do. new dragon bridge	125	12/8	78.2.6}	
do. Shackelford	300	14/6	217.10.0}	
Corr, James	100	6/2	30.16.8	
Crouch, James	130	3/2	20.11.8	
Collins, Joyeux	140	10/5	72.18.4	
			3971.6.4	

[page 3, List A, 1801] Persons Names Owning Lands	Quantity of land [123]	Price per acre	Total Amount Land	Amt. Tax Thereon in Dols. Cents
Crittenden, Zachariah	34½	14/6	24.17.10	
Collier, John	100	4/2	20.16.8	
Cary, Wilson M.	1820	16/7	1509.1.8	
Campbell, James	130	5/9½	37.10.--}	
do. Richard Garrett	70	3/2	11.1.8}	
Crittenden, Richard estate	178	5/3	46.14.6	
Corr, Thomas R.	236½	"	62.1.7	
Collier, Joseph	468	"	112.17.0	
Collier, Benjamin	75	"	19.13.9	
Clegg, Isaiah	241	4/2	50.4.2	
Cooke, Dawson	282	3/2	44.13.0	
Curry, John	155	4/8	31.0.0	
Cooke, Thomas	240	3/2	38.--.--	
Cooke, Thomas Jun[r.]	96	"	15.0.4	
Carlton, Humphry	175	7/	61.5.0}	
do. John Wyatt's estate	48½	6/3	15.3.1½}	
Carlton, Thomas Esta.	235	6/3	73.8.9	
Carlton, Beverley Esta.	160	4/2	33.6.8	
Corr, John Jun[r.]	503½	7/3	182.10.4½}	
do. Tho[s.] Dudley	197½	6/3	61.14.4½}	
Campbell, John	400	12/6	250.--.--	
Curry, James	70	4/2	18.16.--	
Corr, John Sen[r.]	213	3/2	33.15.6}	
do. John Corr Jun[r.]	90	7/3	32.12.6}	
Crittenden, Franc[i]s (River)	$105_{2/3}$	14/6	76.12.2	
Clarke, John	144	5/	36.--.--}	
do. Sam[l.] Hemingway	254½	4/2	53.0.3}	
Cooke, John estate	100	7/3	36.5.0	
			2988.8.2	
Dillard, William estate [sic]	100	3/2	15.16.8	
Didlake, Mary	278	8/4	115.16.8}	
do. John Gardner's esta.	302	6/9	101.13.3}	
Durham, Newman	50	4/2	10.8.4	
Dunn, Thomas	50½	6/3	15.15.7½	
Dillard, William Sen[r.]	226	12/6	141.5.0	
Dillard, George	50	"	31.5.0	
Durham, George	50	4/2	10.8.4	
Durham, Thomas estate	85	3/2	13.9.2	
Dungie, John	110	3/2	17.8.4	
Dudley, William	290	14/6	210.5.0}	
do. L. Wedderburn	315½	6/3	98.11.10}	
Dame, John estate	55	"	17.3.9	
Dudley, James	180	7/10	70.10.--	
Dame, William	25	4/2	5.4.2	
Douglas, John	239	7/	83.13.0	
Didlake, John	1200	7/3	435.--.--	
Dudley, Ann	141	"	51.2.3	
Dudley, Guilford	106	"	38.8.6	
Didlake, Edward	56	10/5	25.--.--	
Dudley, Banks	230	3/2	36.8.4	
Downey, Michael estate	50	10/5	26.0.10	
			4559.7.2	

[page 4, List A, 1801] Persons Names Owning Lands	Quantity of land	Price per acre	Total Amount Land	Amt. Tax Thereon in Dols. Cents
Didlake, Royston	206	3/6½	36.7.4	
Dillard, Thomas	49	15/	36.15.--	
Dillard, William Jun[r.]	221¾	"	165.18.9	
Dudley, Thomas	70	6/3	21.17.6	
Dillard, Nicholas	75	4/2	15.12.6	
Dillard, Benjamin estate	148	5/3	48.17.0	
Drummond, John estate	150	6/3	46.17.6	
Dixon, Michael	414¾	15/5	320.--.--	
Dabney, Benjamin	400	14/6	290.--.--}	
do. of P. Taliaferro	72	8/4	30.--.--}	
Davis, Stage	311	6/9	105.2.7½}	
do. Tho[s.] Foster & Didlake	74	4/2	15.8.4}	
Dunn, John (Essex, dragon)	73	17/	62.1.0	
Diggs, Frances	175	5/3	45.13.9}	
Dean, Benjamin	50	5/3	13.12.6	
Eubank, Richard estate	117	4/2	24.3.9	
Eubank, William estate	28¾	5/3	7.11.--	
Eubank, Richard Sen[r.]	196	7/	68.12.--	
Eubank, Thomas	110	4/2	22.18.4	
Eubank, Richard Jun[r.]	112¼	7/	39.5.7½}	
do. Tho[s.] Jeffries	12¾	7/3	4.12.5}	
do. A. Dunn	147	5/3	39.11.9}	
Eubank, Warner	115	3/2	18.4.2	
do. John Hemmingway Jun[r.]	4	4/2	16.8	
			1479.6.11	
Fleet, Baylor	862	12/6	538.15.8	
Fleet, John estate	260	6/3	81.5.--	
Frazier, William estate	45	20/9	46.13.6	
Fleet, William	352	"	365.4.0	
do. Ben. Gaines	183	6/3	57.3.9}	
Fisher, James estate	110	3/2	17.18.4	
Foster, Thomas	87¾	4/2	18.2.6	
Faulkner, Mary	333	6/3	104.1.4	
Fauntleroy, Thomas	486	10/	243.--.--}	
do. H. Todd	500	18/	460.--.--}	
do. W[m.] Bowden	183	7/	64.1.--}	
Farrinholtz, David	151¼	6/6	49.1.6	
Faulkner, Benjamin	533	4/2	111.0.10}	
do. W[m.] Boyd	9½	10/5	4.10.9}	
do. A. Gardner	3	17/	2.11.--}	
Fargerson, Thomas	62	10/5	32.5.10	
Faucett, Vincent	46½	"	24.4.4½	
Garlick, Camm estate	917	6/3	286.11.3	
Garrett, Robert	100	4/2	20.16.8	
Gaines, Francis	356	14/6	258.2.0	
Gresham, Philemon	200	6/3	62.10.--	
Gresham, John (D) esta.	200	7/10	78.6.8	
			4405.2.10	

[page 5, List A, 1801] Persons Names Owning Lands	Quantity of land [124]	Price per acre	Total Amount Land	Amt. Tax Thereon in Dols. Cents
Gresham, William (B.L.)	100	4/2	20.16.8}	
do. W. Row	40	6/3	13.3.4}	
Gardner, Elizabeth	100	"	31.5.--	
Gibson, Richard	156½	3/2	24.16.7	
Gibson, Eubank	56½	"	8.18.11	
Gibson, Philip	129¼	"	20.9.3½	
Gresham, Mecham	100	5/3	26.5.--}	
do. A. Gresham	4	17/	3.8.--}	
Gresham, Ambrose	80	5/3	21.--.—}	
do. dragon swamp	22	17/	18.5.--}	
Gresham, John (B.L.)	79	5/3	20.14.9}	
do. A. Gresham	4	17/	3.8.--}	
Griffin, William estate	859	14/6	622.15.6	
Garrett, James	230	4/2	48.18.4	
Gardner, Anthony	638	11/	350.11.8}	
do. dragon swamp	67½	17/	57.7.6}	
Garrett, Robert	200	7/	70.--.--}	
do. Wm. Hunt	170	6/3	53.2.6}	
Gaines, Robert estate	537¾	20/9	558.8.7¾}	
do. Ann Curtis	50	5/3	13.2.6}	
Guthrie, James	60	12/6	37.10.--	
Guthrie, Richard	60	"	37.10.--	
do.	162	3/2	[2]5.13.0}	
Garrett, Edward	210	15/3	55.2.6}	
do. Ed. Trice esta.	489½	"	128.9.10}	
			2271.2.5	
Groom, John	173	3/2	27.17.10	
Garrett, George	88½	5/3	23.4.7½	
Guthrie, Rachel	50	8/4	20.16.8	
Goleman, Martin	140	4/2	29.3.4	
Gully, Philip estate	50	3/2	7.18.4	
Garrett, William (Shoe)	2[2]5	3/4¾	37.19.4}	
do. Geo. B. Bird	60	6/3	18.15.--}	
do. Henry [F.] Dudley	50	5/3	13.2.6}	
Gramshill, Henry	25	3/2	3.9.2	
Garrett, Ann Watts	112	5/	28.--.--	
Garrett, Richard	100	4/2	20.16.8	
Garrett, William Junr.	120	"	25.--.--	
Groom, Richard	414	5/3	108.13.6	
Garrett, Edward Junr.	150	6/3	46.17.6	
Gaines, Benjamin	360	20/4	366.--.--	
Gaines, Harry	360	"	366.--.--	
Hoskins, William estate	296	20/	296.--.--}	
do. balance Bray's	2	7/10	15.8}	
Hoomes, Benjamin	447	12/6	279.7.6	
Hemingway, John Junr.	263	4/2	54.15.10	
Hare, William esta.	217	5/3	56.19.3	
Harwood, Christopher estate	194	24/10	240.17.8	
Harwood, Priscilla	165	18/	148.10.--	
Hart, James	150	3/2	23.15.--	
Holderby, John	100	4/2	20.16.8	
Holderby, John Junr.	108¾	7/10	42.6.--	
			4579.10.5	

[page 6, List A, 1801] Persons Names Owning Lands	Quantity of land	Price per acre	Total Amount Land	Amt. Tax Thereon in Dols. Cents
Hart, Anthony	190	5/3	49.17.6}	
do. of Sundry Persons	359½	3/2	56.18.5}	
Hart, Gregory	200	11/	31.3.4	
Hart, William estate	250	3/3½	41.2.11	
Harwood, John estate	109	10/5	56.15.5½	
Henry, Samuel H. Esta.	1900	14/6	1377.10.0	
Henry, James	75	12/6	46.17.6	
Hurt, James	33	10/5	17.3.9	
Halyard, William	190	5/3	49.17.6	
Hoskins, Robert	287	6/	86.2.0	
Hart, Alden	127	4/2	26.9.2	
Howerton, Heritage estate	122½	20/9	126.16.7¼	
Howerton, John	269½	5/3	70.14.10½	
Hutson, William	50	4/2	10.8.4	
Hart, Vincent	75	6/6	24.7.6	
Halyard, John	187½	5/3	49.4.4½	
Hog[g], William & legatees of} Holt, Richeson}	50	18/-	45.--.--	
Jones, Thomas	255	4/2	53.2.6	
Jeffries, Thomas (B.L.)	63	7/3	22.16.9}	
do. John Harwood	38¼	10/5	19.15.10}	
do. John Brett's esta.	57¾	18/-	51.19.6}	
Jones, James Junr.	125	5/3	33.16.3	
Jeffries, Gawin	60	4/2	12.10.--	
Jordan, Robert	66 2/3	4/2	13.18.10	
Jones, Mary	300	26/11	403.15.0	
			2778.13.9	
Kemp, John	296	7/3	107.3.0	
Kauffman, Richard (orphan)	176	26/-	228.16.--	
do. in Stanhope's neck	38	10/5	19.15.10}	
Kauffman, Sambo, Humphry} & Lucy (free negroes)	167	7/6	62.5.0	
Kidd, Henry	81½	5/3	26.6.6¾}	
do. Lambeth Moore	50	4/2	10.8.8}	
Kennedy, Arch^d. estate	38¼	4/2	7.19.4	
Kennedy, Ann	70¼	7/10	14.11.8	
Kennedy, Ann Junr.	33¾	"	7.0.6	
Kennedy, Lucy	37½	"	7.16.2	
Kidd, Bartholomew	136	5/3	35.14.0}	
do. W^m. Dillard J^r.	132½	4/2	27.12.1}	
Kidd, Benjamin	111	13/6	74.18.2}	
do. Crittenden	60	"	40.10.--}	
do. dragon swamp do.	36	17/	30.12.--}	
Kidd, John estate	370	7/3	134.2.6}	
do. Lumpkin & Peirce	60	4/2	12.10.--}	
do. Thos. Dillard	45	14/6	32.12.6}	
King, Dicey estate	18	8/4	7.10.--	
Lumpkin, Jacob (orphan)	681	6/3	212.16.3	
Lewis, Iveson	356	14/6	258.2.0	
			4137.13.2	

[page 7, List A, 1801] Persons Names Owning Lands	Quantity of land	Price per acre	Total Amount Land	Amt. Tax Thereon in Dols. Cents
	[125]			
Leigh, Lucy	101	24/10	125.8.2	
Leigh, John estate	133	"	165.2.10	
Lambeth, Thomas	100	3/2	15.16.8	
Leigh, Richard estate	560	6/3	175.--.--	
Morgan, William	3	6/3	18.9	
Mitchell, Ralph estate	193	10/5	100.10.5	
Mitchell, Sally	391	13/	254.3.0	
Mitchell, James (orphan)	225	"	146.5.0	
Moore, Lambeth	20	4/2	4.3.4	
Morris, William	10	"	2.1.8	
Moore, Benjamin	200	"	41.13.4	
Moore, Lodowick, John & Richard	100	3/2	15.16.8	
Major, Josiah	2[9]0	4/2	41.13.4	
Mitchell, John estate	270	5/3	70.17.--}	
Do. Rootes	200	9/11	99.13.4}	
Moore, Agatha	40	4/2	8.6.8	
Montague, William	170	"	35.8.4	
Merideth, Ralph G. estate	567	14/6	411.1.6	
Muire, Richard	93	12/6	58.2.6}	
do. John Leigh's estate	66	24/10	81.19.--}	
Moore, Richard Esta.	145	6/3	45.6.3	
McCarty, Joseph estate	73	3/2	11.11.2	
Metcalfe, John S. estate	265	14/6	196.5.10	
Metcalfe, Thomas	256	"	181.8.8	
Madereas, John	34½	6/3	10.15.7½	
Milby, Richard	175	3/2	27.14.2	
			2326.4.5	
Newcomb, William	169	3/2	26.15.2	
Orvill, John	100	6/3	31.5.0	
Oliver, John	320	5/3	84.--.--	
Overstreet, Gabriel estate	296	4/2	61.13.4}	
do. Haynes's	130	5/3	34.2.6}	
Oakes, Henry	198½	3/2	34.2.--	
Oakes, William	80	4/2	16.13.4	
Oliver, William	59	"	12.[3].10	
Oakes, Ann	60	"	12.10.--	
Pitts, Benjamin G.	100	5/4	26.13.4	
Pace, Benjamin	263	7/3	95.6.9	
Pynes, Benjamin estate	164	6/3	51.5.--	
Pynes, Robert	111½	"	34.13.9	
Pynes, Benjamin	100	"	31.5.--	
Pemberton, John	165	"	51.11.3	
Pemberton, Philip	121	"	37.17.6	
Pollard, Robert	6	24/10	7.9.--}	
do. John J. O'Mealy	367	30/	550.10.--}	
Palmer, Charles	107¾	18/	96.19.6	
Price, Robert	630	6/3	196.17.6	
Pigg, John estate	324	14/6	234.18.--}	
do.	180	7/3	65.5.--}	
			4120.1.2	

[page 8, List A, 1801] Persons Names Owning Lands	Quantity of land	Price per acre	Total Amount Land	Amt. Tax Thereon in Dols. Cents
Peirce, Philip	83	3/2	13.2.10	
Peirce, Beverley	25¾	4/2	5.7.3½}	
do. of Phil Peirce	17	3/2	2.13.10}	
Peirce, Thomas estate	87	4/2	18.2.6	
Price, Andrew estate	314	6/	94.4.--	
Palmer, Roger	152	7/3	55.2.--	
Roane, Thomas estate	2033	18/8	1897.9.4}	
do. H. Carlton	200	6/3	63.10.--}	
do. Brett's	34¾	18/	31.5.6}	
do. Ro. Pynes	24½	6/3	7.9.1½}	
Row, Elizabeth	665	20/9	689.18.9	
Row, Francis (orphan)	612½	4/8	142.16.0	
Richerson, Elias estate	86	4/2	17.18.4	
Row, William & Moses	60	6/3	18.15.--	
Richards, John	571	4/8	124.8.--	
Richeson, James	180	4/2	37.10.--	
Richeson, William	369½	"	76.17.6	
Richeson, William Jun$^{r.}$	150	5/3	39.7.6	
Richeson, John estate	101½	"	21.2.1	
Roane, Major	687½	3/8	128.18.1½	
do. John Lyne's esta.	455¾	6/3	142.8.5¼	
do. Palmer	9	7/3	3.5.3	
			3630.11.4	
Raines, Giles	60	3/2	9.10.--	
Robinson, Benjamin estate	1300	8/4	541.13.4	
Roane, Charles	133	19/	126.7.0}	
do. dragon swamp	70	17/	59.10.--}	
Roy, Beverley	700	8/4	291.13.4}	
do. T. Brown	454	12/6	283.15.--}	
Ross, John (Ben Minor to pay)	100	5/3	26.5.--	
Richeson, James Jun$^{r.}$	250	5/3	65.12.6	
Spencer, Susanna & John	416	7/3	150.16.0	
Spencer, Ann	166	"	60.3.6	
Starke, Richard estate	350	5/8	99.3.4	
Stone, Robert estate	200	4/2	41.13.4	
Stone, Job	100	"	20.16.8	
Smith, Robert	89	10/5	46.7.1	
Smith, John (son of Robert)	88	"	45.16.8}	
do. dragon swamp	12	17/	10.8.--}	
Simpkins, Young	60	3/2	9.10.—	
Sears, Philip	83	4/2	17.5.10	
Shackelford, William estate	400	14/6	310.--.—	
Spencer, Thomas	300	10/5	156.5.--}	
do.	255	4/2	53.2.6}	
Sword, Benjamin	115	3/2	18.4.2	
Stedman, Christopher	260	5/3	65.5.--	
Smith, Thomas G.	485	14/6	351.12.6	
Sadler, John	150	6/3	46.17.6	
Shackelford, Alexander	60	4/2	12.10.--	
Shackelford, John (R)	482	8/4	216.8.--	
Shackelford, William	351	6/3	109.13.9}	
do. Wyatt's (lease)	30	5/3	7.17.6}	
			6883.13.10	

[page 9, List A, 1801] Persons Names Owning Lands	Quantity of land [126]	Price per acre	Total Amount Land	Amt. Tax Thereon in Dols. Cents
Shackelford, John (Mc)	283	6/2	87.5.2}	
do. John Collier (Cobler)	150	5/3	39.7.6}	
Sears, Thomas	123	6/7	40.9.9	
Shackelford, Benjamin	189	7/3	67.0.3}	
do. John Halyard (lease)	1	5/9½	5.9½	
Shepherd, John	67	6/	20.2.0	
Smith, John (Doctor)	½	30/	15.—	
Southurn, John	150	4/2	31.5.--	
Tureman, Benjamin	70	3/2	11.1.8	
Tureman, George	50	"	7.18.4	
Taliaferro, William	1000	14/6	725.--.--	
Townley, Robert	200	6/3	62.10.--}	
do. Anderson's	117	14/6	84.16.6}	
Taliaferro, Philip estate	940	8/4	391.13.4	
Taliaferro, James B.	374½	12/6	234.7.6}	
do. John B. Taliaferro	296	5/3	77.14.--	
Thruston, Armstead	111¾	4/3	23.15.1	
Thruston, Batcheldor	200	3/2	31.13.4	
Turner, Benjamin	36	4/2	7.10.--	
Townley, Ann	79	4/2	16.9.2	
Turner, Henry estate	100	"	20.16.8	
Tunstall, Richard G.	206½	7/10	73.3.7	
Taylor, William [subtotal 2067.9.7]	40	6/3	12.10.--	
Watts, Edward estate	250	7/3	90.12.6}	
do. W. Watts esta.	113	5/	28.5.--}	
Watts, John	293	7/10	114.15.2}	
do. Pemberton	45	6/3	14.1.3}	
Watts, Kauffman	300	5/3	78.15.--}	
do. Eubank & Burch	257	5/9	73.17.9}	
do. John & Danl. Hemingway	312	4/2	64.3.0}	
Watts, James	350	"	72.18.4}	
do. W. Watts esta.	60	15/	45.--.--}	
Williams, Howard	224	4/2	46.13.4}	
do. dragon swamp	43	17/	36.11.--}	
Wyatt, Thomas	206	7/10	81.2.--}	
do. Boughton	60	3/2	9.10.--}	
Wyatt, William	48¾	7/3	17.1.3	
Williams, Montague	300	6/3	93.15.0	
Williams, Charles estate	336	4/2	70.--.--	
Walton, James	80	"	16.13.4}	
do. Thos. Walton's esta.	66	"	13.15.--}	
Walton, Elizabeth	60	3/2	9.10.--	
Walton, John	176	5/3	46.4.--	
Walton, William estate	66	4/2	13.15.--	
Ware, John estate	75	5/3	19.13.9	
Ware, Arther estate	83	4/2	17.15.10	
Waring, Robert P. estate	542	10/9	291.6.6	
Walden, Richard estate	180	10/5	93.15.--	
Walden, Lewis estate	150	3/2	23.15.--}	
do. T. Dudley	84½	6/3	28.2.3½}	
Williams, George	40	4/2	8.6.8	
			3586.13.6	

[page 10, List A, 1801] Persons Names Owning Lands	Quantity of land	Price per acre	Total Amount Land	Amt. Tax Thereon in Dols. Cents
Watkins, Philip	197	5/3	51.14.3	
Wyatt, Richard	175	12/6	109.7.6	
Ware, Robert Jun[r.] estate	100	4/2	20.16.8	
Williams, Elizabeth	16½	3/2	2.12.9	
White, James estate	200	6/3	62.10.0	
Ware, Robert (P)	112	3/2	17.14.8	
Wedderburn, Lydia	350	6/3	109.7.6	
Whiting, Beverley estate	2447¾	7/10	866.18.9	
Webbley, John estate	173	5/3	45.8.3}	
do. Collier & Dillard	358	4/2	74.11.8}	
Ware, Robert Jun[r.]	100	8/4	41.13.4	
Ware, William	100	"	41.13.4	
Walden, Benjamin	373	5/3	97.18.3	
Waller, Edward estate	133½	3/2	21.2.9	
Waller, George estate	87	"	13.15.6	
Waller, John	65	3/7	11.12.11	
Waller, Robert	48	3/7	8.12.--}	
do. Groom's estate	187	3/2	29.12.2}	
Ware, Nicholas	100	"	15.16.8	
Walton, Beverly	47½	7/10	18.12.1	
Watts, George [K]	36	26/	46.16.--	
Wyatt, Smith	29¾	7/3	10.15.8	
			1719.2.8	

The foregoing list is as correct as I can make it from the imperfect state in which the one for the last year stands.
[signed] Wm. Fleet, Commissioner

ForThe Auditor of Public Acco[ts.], of Richmond.

[page]

Amount Land within the Dist. of Wm. Fleet, Commissioner in the County of King & Queen, 1801

[arithmetic omitted]

$149321.50
$716.73 land @ 48 cts.

A List of Land within the District of Robert
B. Hill, Commissioner, in the County of King and Queen
for the year 1801
LIST B

[page 1, List B, 1801] Persons names owning Land	Quantity of land	Price per acre	Tot. Amt. Valuation
	[127]		
Atkins, Joseph Esta.	66	4/2	£13.15.0
Allexander, Benjamin	202	9/4	94.5.4}
Do. of James Halbert	124	6/2	38.15.0}
Lott in Dunkirk, annual rent			18.--.-}
Do. of Joseph Meede, Do.			4.10.0}
Acre, Seaton	52	9/4	24.5.4
Alexander, Elisha	338	"	157.14.8
Anderson, Churchill	636	7/3	230.11.0}
Do. of Paulin Anderson's Estate	96	20/9	99.12.0}
Atkins, John	135	4/6	30.7.6
Abbott, Jacob	112	7/10	43.17.4
Anderson, Sarah of P. Anderson's Esta.	86	20/9	89.3.9
Barton, John Estate	125	4/2	26.0.10
Bray, James	128¾	7/10	55.8.6
Broach, Benoni	48	10/5	25.4.0
Brown, Henry Jun[r.]	100	12/	60.--.--
4.6.8.7			1011.10.3
Beverley, Robert Estate	2444	10/5	1262.16.4
Brown, Henry	570	7/4½	210.3.9
Bland, John and Lucy	166	8/4	69.3.4
Bates, James	358	11/	149.3.4
Do.	42	4/2	8.15.0
Do. of Rice Garnett	89	7/3	32.5.3
Braxton, Carter	484½	10/5	252.6.10
Brooking, Frances	930	"	484.7.6
Boughton, Thomas (Essex)	130	9/4	60.13.4
Boughton, John	200	8/4	83.6.8
Boughton, Henry (Essex)	88	6/3	27.10.0
Burton, John	170	5/3	44.12.6
Bohannon, Ann Esta.	197	4/6	44.6.6
Brown, William	75	7/10	29.7.6}
Do. of Clem Pynes	18¼	3/2	2.17.9}
Bagby, John Esta.	330	7/3	119.12.9
Bagby, Richard	260	"	94.5.0
Bagby, Thomas	260	"	94.5.0}
Do. of Jacob Lumpkin	235	6/3	73.8.9}
Brizendine, Armistead	86 2/3	8/4	35.17.6
Bromley, John	60	7/10	23.10.0
Broach, William	20	"	7.16.8
9.11.11.10			[£] 4222.1.6

[page 2, List B, 1801] Persons names owning Land		Quantity of land	Price per acre	Tot. Amt. Valuation
Brown, John		50	7/4½	18.8.9
Bohannan, William		130	5/3	34.2.6
Bohannan, William, St. Stephens		33	5/3	8.13.3
Bates, William		81	7/9½	31.10.1}
Do. of Rice Garnett		117	7/3	42.8.4}
Broach, George		32½	14/6	23.11.3
Beadles, Justin		20	6/3	6.5.0
Blackburn, Mary (Heirs) of P. Anderson		86	20/9	89.4.6
Crafton, Thomas		119	9/4	55.10.8
Crafton, James		59	"	27.10.8
Crafton, John		117½	"	54.12.0
Crane, John		130	6/3	40.2.6
Do. of Clem Pynes		14	3/2	2.4.4
Do. of John Ware's Esta.		49¼	7/3	17.17.0¾
Cleverius, Benjamin		419	20/9	434.14.3
Carlton, Henry Esta.		280	7/10	109.13.4
Do. of John Baylor's Esta.		257	14/6	186.6.6
Cole, G. Thomas		30	9/4	14.0.0
Do. of John Lumpkin's Esta.		75	6/3	23.8.9
of Frances Lumpkin		70	6/3	21.17.6
Carlton, Lewis		100	8/4	41.3.4
Clayton, Thomas Esta.		275	7/3	99.13.9
Crane, George Esta.		30	7/3	10.17.6
Courtney, Thomas		156	7/10	61.2.0
Carlton, Joel		53½	6/3	16.14.5
Cooke, Moses		100	8/4	41.13.4
	9.11.12.9			1512.15.7
Cooke, Ambrose		100	"	41.13.4
Chapman, Philip Esta.		200	7/10	78.6.8
Courtney, Robert		330½	"	132.19.5
Cannaday, William		100	6/3	31.8.0
Cooke, William		65	5/5	17.12.1
Cooke, James		65	8/9	28.8.9
Courtney, Fanny and Children		78	7/10	30.10.0
Cross, Joseph		103½	6/3	32.6.10½
Campbell, William		868¼	7/3	314.14.9¾
Campbell, Whitaker		406	7/10	159.0.4
Crow, John		121	5/3	31.19.2¼
Crow, Nathaniel Esta.		200	6/3	62.10.0
Dew, William Esta.		935	14/6	677.17.6
Dew, Thomas		331	12/6	206.17.6
Duling, William Esta.		264	8/4	110.0.0
Dix, Gabriel		338	6/3	105.12.6
Deshazo, William Jun[r.]		60	4/2	12.10.0
Durham, Joseph		105	4/3	21.12.6
Do. of Rich[d.] Dunn		10	4/2	2.1.8
Deshazo, John		192	7/4	70.8.0
Deshazo, Larkin		87	7/3	31.4.10
Do. of John Crane		6	6/3	1.17.6
of Benjamin Hoomes		430¾	4/4	93.4.5
	9.12.8.8			3807.8.5

[page 3, List B, 1801] Persons names owning Land	Quantity of land	Price per acre	Tot. Amt. Valuation
	[128]		
Dunbar, David	366	8/4	152.10.0
Dudley, Peter Esta.	530	7/3¼	186.18.4
Dalley, George	174¼	3/2	27.11.9½
Durham, John	25	3/2	3.19.4
Dickie, James	512	8/4	213.6.8
Deshazo, Unity	71	7/10	27.16.3
Deshazo, Polly orphan	41	"	16.1.2
Dally, John Esta.	200	3/2	31.13.4
Dobbins, Charles Esta.	147	5/3	38.11.9
Donagin, Rich[d.] Esta. [Dumagin]	55	"	14.17.11
Eubank, John Esta.	469	10/4	242.6.4
Do. of James Grafton	111	6/3	34.13.9
Do. of Tho[s.] Dew	178½	12/6	111.5.6
Eubank, Henry	171	5/3	44.17.9
Edwards, Thomas	66	4/2	13.15.0
Evans, Ambrose	195	7/10	56.10.0
Fleet, William	512	12/	307.4.0
Fogg, Frederick	298	8/4	124.3.4
Fogg, Thomas	107	6/3	33.8.8
8.11.9.5			1699.8.4
Fauntleroy, G. Samuel	2069	20/	2069.0.0
Falkner, Thomas	220	6/3	68.15.0
Fogg, Thomas Esta.	93	6/3	29.1.3
Fogg, James	120	6/3	37.10.0
Fox, S. Joseph of H. Brown	158	7/4	57.18.8
Do. of Thomas Garnett	28	7/10	10.19.4
" of Cleaveley	39	"	15.5.6
" of Pollard	94	7/3	34.1.6
Grafton, Sally and Ann	132	9/4	61.12.0
Gayle, John	264	7/5	97.18.0
Do. of W[m.] Gayle	7¼	"	2.13.11
Gatewood, Chaney	829	10/5	437.17.11
Do. Gardner's	100	7/3	36.5.0
Do. Noel's	362½	14/6	262.16.3
Do. Harwood's	125	4/2	46.17.6
Do. Eubank's	300	14/3	217.10.0
Do. Walden's Esta.	120	12/6	75.0.0
Do. W[m.] Lyne, Lotts in Dunkirk			
of W[m.] Lyne, Dunkirk Lott, annual rent			20.0.0
5.9.11.8			5280.10.2

[page 4, List B, 1801] Persons names owning Land	Quantity of land	Price per acre	Tot. Amt. Valuation
Garnett, Joshua Esta.	325	8/4	134.3.4
Gatewood, Joseph	445	10/5	231.15.5
Gayle, Matthew Esta.	323	11/5	184.7.7
Gatewood, John	160	8/4	66.13.4
Garnett, Reuben	876½	8/10	387.2.5
Do. of Halbert & Gatewood	28	10/5	14.12.10
Gwathmey, Temple	600	35/3	1057.10.0
Garlick, Samuel	454	24/10	463.14.4
Garlick, John	839	29/	1216.11.0
Griffith, Joseph	50	6/3	15.12.6
Gresham, Samuel	432½	7/3	156.15.7½
Do. of Rice Garnett	157	7/3	56.18.1
Guthrie, William	91¼	7/5	33.14.7
Gaines, Harry Esta.	481½	20/4	489.10.6
Gaines, B. Robert	481½	"	489.10.6
Gresham, Thomas Esta.	455¼	6/8	151.13.4
Griffith, Milly	50	6/3	15.12.6
Graves, Thomas	66¼	7/3	23.18.6
Gresham, Lumpkin	255	"	92.8.9
Gresham, William Jun[r.]	242 1/3	8/4	101.5.0
Do. of W[m.] Gatewood	46	3/2	7.5.8
" of Chick	69	7/3	25.0.3
Gresham, George	141	3/2	22.6.6
Gatewood, William (*Tuck[o.]*)	33	"	5.4.6
10.12.12.10			5443.7.—
Gatewood, William (Son of Jn[o.])	132	10/	66.0.0
Gleason, Patrick	134	8/4	55.16.8
Gatewood, Gabriel	78	10/5	40.12.6
Do. of Halbert	50	"	26.10.0
Gayle, William	344	7/5	127.11.4
Hill, William	1310¼	14/6	949.11.4½
Hawes, Walker	97	"	70.6.6
Hitchcock, Thomas	140	4/2	29.3.4
Hoskins, Samuel Esta.	345	6/3	107.16.3
Do. of Elisha Alexander	57	10/5	25.13.9
Hutcherson, Charles Esta.	531	7/1	188.1.3
Heskew, John Esta.	61	5/3	16.0.3
Heskew, John	50	6/3	15.12.6
Do. Clem Pynes	10	3/2	1.11.8
" of L. Deshazo	19¼	4/4	4.2.4
Hill, Edward	1200	18/8	1120.0.0
Hoskins, John	767	10/5	399.9.7
Do. Boughtons	100	8/4	41.13.4
" of Semple & Fleet	2	10/5	1.0.10
7.8.10.7			8730.0.5

[page 5, List B, 1801] Persons names owning Land	Quantity of land	Price per acre	Tot. Amt. Valuation
	[129]		
Hurt, West	14	5/3	3.3.6
Holt, William	123	14/3	87.12.9
Hutchason, John	73¼	8/9	32.0.11¼
Howerton, George	76¼	6/	22.17.6
Hall, Corbin	72	4/2	15.0.0
Hill, B. Robert	322	8/2	131.9.8
Hill, Richard	332	"	135.11.4
Hill, G. Mary	360	"	147.0.0
Hill, Robert Esta.	420	"	171.10.0
Hoomes, John, Lott in Dk., anl. rent			40.0.0
Jones, John Esta.	300	8/11	133.15.0
Jeffries, Edward	70	3/2	11.1.8
Jeffries, Ambrose	337	7/10	131.19.10
Jeffries, Robert	110	7/6	41.5.0
Do. of Lumpkin Gresham	10	7/3	3.12.6
" of Jacob Lumpkin	5	"	1.16.3
Jones, James	160	14/6	116.0.0
Do. of James Jones Esta.	196	10/5	102.1.8
Jones, William Esta.	241	15/10	190.15.10
Do. of L. Smith	35	31/1	55.11.2
Johnson, Thomas	72	3/2	11.8.0
Jones, Rawleigh	63	31/1	93.18.3
7.9.6.7			1679.10.10
Kemp, John	178	7/3	64.2.2
Keeling, Mary	78½	8/	31.8.0
Kay, Christopher	116	6/3	36.6.0
Do. of T. Goleman	416½	9/	187.8.6
Lumpkin, James	213	7/10	83.8.2
Lumpkin, Henry	400	9/4	186.13.4
Lumpkin, John Esta.	125	6/3	35.11.3
Lyne, William Esta.	305	14/6	221.2.6
Do. of T. Dew	26½	12/6	16.5.0
Lafon, Francis	119	8/4	49.11.8
Lankford, Thomas Esta.	100	4/2	20.16.8
Lumpkin, Robert Sen[r.]	374	8/4	155.16.8
Lumpkin, Henry Jun[r.]	190	9/4	88.13.4
Lumpkin, W. John Esta.	140	7/10	54.16.8
Do. of John Ware's Esta.	118½	7/3	42.15.6
Longest, Caleb	97	7/10	37.19.10
Longest, Richard	227¾	"	89.4.2
Longest, John	100	"	39.3.4
Lumpkin, Anthony Esta.	216	6/3	67.10.0
7.10.11.10			3188.3.7

[page 6, List B, 1801] Persons names owning Land	Quantity of land	Price per acre	Tot. Amt. Valuation
Lumpkin, Robert Jun$^{r.}$	323	5/3	84.15.9
Lumpkin, Wilson	122½	9/4	57.3.4
Lumpkin, William Jun$^{r.}$	183¼	10/5	95.6.3
Lumpkin, John	112	3/2	17.14.8
Lyne, William	1480	8/4	610.14.2
Motley, Edwin	815	10/5	428.2.6
Do. of J.W. Semple	155	12/6	96.17.6
Martin, C. Thomas	583	14/6	422.13.6
Do.	134½	7/3	48.15.1½
Minor, William	149	8/4	62.1.8
Minor, John	137	"	57.1.8
Minor, Thomas Esta.	288	7/10	112.16.0
Moody, Lewis	239	"	93.12.2
Mann, Joseph Jun$^{r.}$	400	8/4	166.13.4
Mitchell, John	50	6/3	15.12.6
Mann, Robert Esta.	699	6/3	218.8.9
Merideth, Samuel	215	7/10	84.4.2
Macon, John Esta.	1092	16/7	905.9.0
Do. Lotts in Dunkirk, anl. rent			55.0.0
Mann, Mary	100	5/3	26.5.0
Martin, John	475	9/	213.15.0
Mahon, Thomas	101	6/3	31.11.3
Mahon, William	103½	"	32.3.9
8.10.11.10			3936.13."
Nunn, Moses	318	7/4½	117.5.3
Nunn, Thomas	130	7/3	47.2.6
Do. of Brizendine	49	4/3	10.8.3
Newbill, William	1060	8/4	441.13.4
Newell, John Esta.	100	7/10	39.3.4
Nash, John Esta.	100	6/3	31.5.0
Owen, Augustine Esta.	100	6/3	31.5.0
Pendleton, James	888½	8/7½	383.3.3¾
Do. Wilmore's	70	7/6	26.5.0
Do. Phill Pendleton's	120	9/2	53.0.0
Do. W$^{m.}$ Intosh	125	4/2	26.1.10
Pitts, David	420	9/4	196.0.0
Pitts, Obadiah	20	10/5	10.8.4
Philips, James	230	7/3	83.7.6
Pollard, John Esta.	235	9/4	109.13.4
Do. Smithy's	384	7/3	139.4.0
Prewitt, Frances	99	9/4	46.4.0
11.10.9.7			5733.3."

[page 7, List B, 1801] Persons names owning Land	Quantity of land	Price per acre	Tot. Amt. Valuation
	[130]		
Parker, John	264¼	7/	92.9.9
Do. Gouldman's	532	9/	239.8.0
Prewitt, Richard	102	7/3	36.12.3
Pendleton, Philip	360	9/2	165.0.0
Do. Lott in Dunkirk, annual rent			3.0.0
Perryman, Philip	218	7/2	78.2.4
Pynes, Clement	99	3/2	15.13.6
Pollard, Richard	389	8/4	162.1.8
Pendleton, Benjamin Esta.	450	7/10	176.5.0
Perryman, Richard	110	7/3	39.7.6
Prewitt, Tunstall	58½	8/	23.8.0
Pollard, Joseph	200	6/3	62.10.0
*			
Quarles, W. Fran^s., Lotts in Dunkirk, annual rents			51.0.0
Rowe, G. Thomas orphan	555	7/3	201.3.9
Row, Richard Esta.	450	8/4	188.0.0
Roane, Spencer	954	24/10	1184.11.0
Ryland, Joseph	487½	7/3	176.10.9
Ryland, Josiah	160	7/10	62.13.4
Do. of Will. Temple	27½	15/	20.12.6
" of Fra^s. Prince Esta.	113	7/10	44.5.2
" of H. Brown	34½	7/4½	12.14.1½
Riddle, Vaughan	51	5/5	13.16.3
	5.8.9.10		3049.4.10
Roane, Thomas	1074¾	17/2	922.9.10½
Roane, Samuel	1074¾	"	922.9.10½
Row, Handsford	160½	6/3	50.3.1½
Row, Wilson	160½	"	50.3.1½
Smith, William	53	7/10	20.15.2
Do. of James Smith Esta.	25	3/2	3.19.2
Segar, Richard	406	7/3	147.3.6
Satterwhite, George	164	6/3	51.5.0
Satterwhite, William	200	5/7½	56.5.0
Schools, John	156	8/4	65.0.0
Schools, Gabriel Esta.	174	6/3	54.7.6
Skelton, William	362	8/2½	148.11.5
Do. of Phil. Perryman	12	7/2	4.6.0
Smith, John (D^e)	190	7/6	71.5.0
Starling, Roderick	360	7/10	141.0.0
Do.	313	8/2	127.16.2
Do. of W^m. Lyne	56½	8/4	23.6.8
" of H. Walker	46	5/3	12.1.6
Saunders, George	200	7/3	70.10.8
Shepherd, William	140	9/4	65.6.8
Smith, Molly	30	4/2	6.5.0
	7.7.8.8		6063.15.5

[page 8, List B, 1801] Persons names owning Land		Quantity of land	Price per acre	Tot. Amt. Valuation
Smith, John Jun[r.]		100	5/3	26.8.0
Smith, Lewis		96	7/6	36.0.0
Swinton, Ann		750	13/6	506.5.0
Stone, Sarah		300	7/3	108.15.0
Stone, Daniel		52	3/2	8.4.8
Smith, Larkin		1254¼	31/1	1949.6.3½
Smith, Henry		400	6/3	130.0.0
Smith, Ambrose		92¾	8/4	38.6.8
Stevens, George Esta.		430	7/10	168.8.4
Stevens, George orphan		75	"	29.8.4
Smith, William Esta. Mill		200	3/2	31.13.4
Shackelford, John Esta.		114	7/3	40.8.2
Shepherd, John		192	3/2	30.1.8
Stone, William		74¼	3/2	11.15.3½
Sthreshley, William		155½	6/3	48.11.10
Schools, George		200	8/4	83.6.8
Smith, John, of J. Garlick		54	29/	78.6.0
Smith, Jane, of J. Smith's Esta.		25	3/2	3.19.2
Smith, Philip, orphan of Do.		12½	"	1.19.7
Smith, James		101	7/10	39.11.2
Do. of James Smith's Esta.		12½	3/2	1.19.7
	6.9.11.6			3372.11.9
Scott, Anderson		330	16/7	273.12.6
Do. of P. Anderson's Legatees		248	20/9	257.6.0
Semple, B. Robert		253	10/5	131.15.1
Do. of Spencer Roane		155	24/10	192.9.2
Trice, William		140	7/3	50.15.0
Taylor, James		50	6/3	15.12.6
Taylor, Edmund		294	8/14	122.10.0
Temple, Joseph		918	10/5	478.2.6
Tunstall, Richard Jun[r.] Esta.		1097	7/3	397.13.3
Temple, William		402¼	15/	301.17.6
Temple, John		178	31/3	278.2.6
Temple, Humphrey Esta. of W.T.		100	15/	75.0.0
Do. J. Tunstall		200	18/8	185.16.8
" of R. Tunstall & others		574	21/	602.14.0
Tunstall, Richard (Purdy Esta.)		132½	8/4	55.0.0
Tunstall, C. Thomas		137	"	57.1.8
Upshaw, James (Essex)		125	8/10	55.4.2
Do. of R. Beverley		30	10/5	15.12.6
Wyatt, Henry		200	7/3	72.10.0
~~White, Henry~~		~~100~~	~~8/4~~	~~41.13.4~~
Wilson, Isaac Estate		200	6/3	62.10.0
	5.9.9.11.			7053.16.9

[page 9, List B, 1801] Persons names owning Land	Quantity of land	Price per acre	Tot. Amt. Valuation
	[131]		
Wilson, Benjamin Esta.	200	7/3	72.10.0
Wyatt, John Esta.	100	7/10	39.3.4
Watkins, Joseph	63	6/7	20.14.9
Do. Wiltshire's Esta.	71	7/3	26.19.9
Walker, Philip	110	9/4	51.6.8
Walker, Humphrey	820	33/2	1355.14.2
Wright, William	130	5/3	33.12.6
Willis, Joel	94	7/10	35.5.0
Wright, Edward	567	6/3	177.3.9
Whayne, William	154½	7/10	60.10.3
Wyatt, George	122	7/6	45.15.0
Webb, James	140¾	4/2	29.6.6
Do.	7	4/2	1.9.2
Wheeley, Carriol, of Wm. Campbell	21¾	7/3	7.17.8¼
Do. Ware's Estate	15½	7/3	5.12.4½
Watkins, Joseph Junr.	93¼	8/4	38.17.1
Wilson, M. George	52½	9/4	24.10.0
Wyatt, Robert	50	7/3	18.2.6
Watkins, John	152	8/4	63.6.8
Watkins, Philip	107	4/2	22.5.10
Young, Henry	640	18/8	597.6.8
8.10.10.8			2727.9.7

[signed] Ro. B. Hill, Commissioner

*Pollard, Richard & Brown, Henry omitted (of Wm. Wood)	50	8/	20.0.0

[page]
Valuation of Land in the Coty. of King & Queen & District of Robt. B. Hill, Commr. for the year 1801.

[arithmetic omitted]
£46806.8.10
Land $748.89 @ 48 cts.

[cover]
Ro. B. Hill's Land List for 1801, For The Auditor
added, stated, Added

List of land within the district of Richard T. Shackelford, Commissioner in the County of King & Queen for the year 1802

LIST A

[page 1, List A, 1802] Persons Names Owning Lands	Quantity of land [133]	Price per acre	Total Amount Land	Amt. Tax Thereon in Dols. Cents
Anderson, Richard est.	460	5/3	120.15.0	
Atkins, Lewis	60	8/4	25.0.0	
Anderson, Francis	458	10/9	246.3.6}	
do. Richd. T. Shackelford	26	8/4	12.1.8}	
Anderson, Beverley	¾	5/3	3.11¼	
Brown, Samuel	33¼	4/3	7.1.2	
Banks, William est.	365	4/2	76.0.10	
Brooke, Richard	1539¾	29/-	2232.12.9	
Brumley, Robert	225	5/3	59.1.3	
Bird, William est.	532	7/3	197.17.0}	
do. Dragon Swamp	88½	17/	70.4.6}	
Bird, Philemon	1693	6/3	529.11.3	
Brett, Nancy	50	18/	45.0.0	
Burch, James	70	7/3	25.7.6	
Burch, Vincent	100	4/2	20.16.8}	
do. Wm. Hoskins	50	3/2	7.18.4}	
Bird, Anthony A.	275	3/2	43.10.10}	
do. of Wm. Montague	44	4/2	9.3.6}	
Byne, John est.	336	4/2	70.0.0}	
do. Dragon Swamp	2¼	17/	1.18.3	
Bird, Robert est.	780	24/10	993.6.8}	
do. Guy Smith	189½	3/2	30.0.1}	
Bourn, Richard est.	150	3/2	23.15.0	
			4847.9.8	
Boyd, John	115	18/8	107.6.8}	
do. Soane's	382	24/10	474.6.4}	
Bray, Richard estate	93	7/10	36.8.6	
Bird, John est.	71	3/2	11.4.10	
Bew, William estate	117	"	18.0.6	
Boyd, Robert	1119	9/3	517.10.3	
Boyd, William	300	15/	225.0.0	
Berkley, Edmund est.	762	5/3	200.0.6	
Bland, John	60	12/6	37.10.0	
Bland, William	100	9/11	49.11.8	
Bourn, Mills	159½	5/3	41.14.3}	
do. Thos. Jordan's estate	33 1/3	4/2	6.18.10½}	
Bullman, Ann	120	5/3	31.10.0	
Belote, Laban	384½	4/2	80.2.6	
Bland, William Senr.	225	3/8¼	41.9.8¼	
Bland, Ralph	146	53	38.6.8}	
do. Finney & Buckner	170	4/2	35.8.4}	
Bowden, William	100	"	20.16.8}	
do. Sykes	34	3/2	5.7.8}	
Bowden, John	100	4/2	20.16.8	
Bland, William est.	250	"	52.1.8	
Bland, Thomas	412	3/2	75.4.8	
Bowden, George	236	5/3	61.19.0}	
do. William Dillard	30	4/2	6.5.0}	
Banks, James	22	7/3	7.19.6	
Bristow, Bartholomew	33½	3/2	5.6.1	
Bristow, George	100	3/2	15.16.8	
			7071.12.9	

[page 2, List A, 1802] Persons Names Owning Lands	Quantity of land	Price per acre	Total Amount Land	Amt. Tax Thereon in Dols. Cents
Banks, Andrew	125	12/6	78.2.6	
Brightwell, John est.	70	4/2	14.11.8	
Burton, James estate	89	"	18.10.10	
Bland, William (Younger)	300	7/3	108.15.0	
Bird, Janet & Frances	230	10/5	119.15.10}	
do. Ro. Smith (Dragon)	60	17/	51.0.0}	
Bird, Philemon & Jn°. Smith	1	7/10	7.10	
Breedlove, John	37¾	15/	28.6.3	
Brushwood, George	188	4/2	39.3.4}	
do. Ro. Ware	112	3/2	17.14.8}	
Bird, Parmenas	132¼	11/8	77.4.7	
Bray, Peter	51¼	6/3	16.0.3¾	
Bland, John	212	5/3	55.13.0	
Carlton, Thomas (Swamp)	200	7/10	78.6.8}	
do. Philemon Bird	83½	6/3	26.1.10½}	
Carlton, Noah	100	"	39.3.4	
Cooke, Henry	260	5/3	68.5.0}	
Ditto	49¼	10/5	25.10.5}	
Carlton, John (School[r.])	100	6/3	31.5.0}	
do. Baylor Fleet	2	12/6	1.5.0}	
Campbell, James T. (orphan)	296	12/6	185.0.0	
Carlton, Christopher Sen[r.]	37½	6/5	11.14.5}	
do. James Laughlin	126½	3/2	26.8.2}	
Carlton, Richard estate	139	7/	48.13.0	
Cauthern, James	36½	3/2	5.15.7	
Carlton, William (Shoemk[r.])	309¾	11/6	178.1.2½	
Carlton, Christopher (younger)	148	5/	37.0.0	
Carlton, Richard	250	7/3	90.12.6	
Carlton, Christopher Jun[r.]	100	"	36.5.0}	
do. John Stone estate	159½	5/3	41.14.9}	
Cooper, Henry	50	4/2	10.8.4	
			1566.15.11	
Carlton, Thomas (Taylor)	100	6/3	31.5.0	
Cardwell, James	150	4/2	31.5.0	
Cardwell, John	150	"	31.5.0	
Cardwell, William estate	77	"	15.11.6	
Cardwell, Thomas	110	"	22.18.4	
Cooke, John estate	300	4/2	62.10.0	
Collins, Thomas	281½	7/	98.10.6}	
do. Ro. S. Ware	84½	11/9	49.12.10½}	
do. Metcalfe & Levert	289½	14/6	209.17.9}	
Carlton, John Jun[r.]	235	4/2	48.19.2	
Campbell, William	238	3/2	37.13.8	
Corbin, Richard	2390	11/1¾	1332.11.4}	
do. New Dragon bridge	125	12/8	78.2.6}	
do. Shackelfords	300	14/6	217.10.0}	
do. Dixon's	416¾	15/5	321.10.10}	
Corr, James	100	6/2	30.16.8	
Crouch, James	105¼	3/2	16.13.3½	
Collins, Joyeux	140	10/5	72.18.4	
Clayton, James	260	5/3	65.5.0	
Crittenden, Zachariah	34½	14/6	24.17.10	
Collier, John	100	4/2	20.16.8	
Cary, Wilson M.	1820	16/7	1509.1.8	
			5896.8.9	

[page 3, List A, 1802] Persons Names Owning Lands	Quantity of land [134]	Price per acre	Total Amount Land	Amt. Tax Thereon in Dols. Cents
Campbell, James	130	5/9½	37.10.0}	
do. Rich[d.] Garrett	70	3/2	11.1.8}	
do. Benjamin Moore	100	4/2	20.16.8}	
Crittenden, Richard estate	178	5/3	46.14.6	
Corr, Thomas R.	236½	"	62.1.7	
Collier, Joseph	468	"	112.17.0	
Collier, Benjamin	75	"	19.13.9	
Clegg, Isaiah	241	4/2	50.4.2	
Cooke, Dawson	282	3/2	44.13.0	
Curry, John	155	4/8	31.0.0	
Cooke, Thomas	240	3/2	38.0.0	
Cooke, Thomas Jun[r.]	96	"	15.0.4	
Carlton, Humphry	175	7/	61.5.0}	
do. John Wyatt's est.	48½	6/3	15.3.1½}	
Carlton, Thomas estate	235	6/3	73.8.9	
Corr, John Jun[r.]	503½	7/3	182.10.4½}	
do. Thomas Dudley	197½	6/3	61.14.4½}	
Campbell, John	400	12/6	250.0.0	
Curry, James	70	4/2	18.16.0	
Corr, John Sen[r.]	213	3/2	33.15.6}	
do. John Corr Jun[r.]	90	7/3	32.12.6}	
Crittenden, Frances (River)	105 2/3	14/6	76.12.2	
Clarke, John	144	5/	36.0.0}	
do. Sam[l.] Hemmingway	254½	4/2	53.0.3}	
Cooke, John Jun[r.] estate	100	3/2	15.16.8	
Clayton, Reubin	160	4/2	33.6.8	
			1433.14.0	
Didlake, William est.	100	3/2	15.16.8	
Didlake, Mary	278	8/4	115.16.8}	
do. John Gardner esta.	302	6/9	101.13.3}	
Durham, Newman	50	4/2	10.8.4	
Dunn, Thomas	50½	6/3	15.15.7½	
Dillard, William Sen[r.]	226	12/6	141.5.0	
Dillard, George	50	"	31.5.0	
Durham, Thomas estate	85	3/2	13.9.2	
Dungie, John est.	110	3/2	17.8.4	
Dudley, William est.	290	14/6	210.5.0	
do. L. Wedderburn	315½	6/3	98.11.10	
Dame, John estate	55	"	17.3.9	
Dudley, James	180	7/10	70.10.0	
Dame, William	25	4/2	5.4.2	
Douglas, John	239	7/	83.13.0	
Didlake, John	1200	7/3	435.0.0	
Dudley, Ann	141	"	51.2.3	
Dudley, Guilford	106	"	38.8.6	
Didlake, Edward	56	10/5	20.3.4	
Dudley, Banks	230	3/2	36.8.4	
Downey, Michael estate	50	10/5	26.0.10	
Didlake, Royston	206	3/6½	36.7.4	
Dillard, Thomas	49	15/	36.15.0	
Dillard, William Jun[r.]	221¾	"	165.18.9	
			3237.9.2	

[page 4, List A, 1802] Persons Names Owning Lands	Quantity of land	Price per acre	Total Amount Land	Amt. Tax Thereon in Dols. Cents
Dudley, Thomas	70	6/3	21.17.6	
Dillard, Nicholas	75	4/2	15.12.6	
Dillard, Benjamin est.	148	5/3	48.17.0	
Drummond, John estate	150	6/3	46.17.6	
Dabney, Benjamin	400	14/6	290.0.0	
do. P. Taliaferro	150	8/4	62.10.0	
Davis, Stage	311	6/9	105.2.7½}	
do. Foster & Didlake	74	4/2	15.8.4}	
do. Eliz[a.] M. Davis	10	6/9	3.7.6}	
Dunn, John (Essex), Dragon	73	17/	62.1.0	
Digges, Frances	175	5/3	45.13.9}	
Dean, Benjamin	50	5/3	13.12.6	
Dillard, Thomas A.	29	3/2	4.11.10	
Eubank, Warner	115	"	18.4.2	
do. John Hemmingway Jun[r.]	4	4/2	16.8	
Eubank, Richard estate	117	"	24.3.9	
Eubank, William estate	28¾	5/3	7.11.0	
Eubank, Richard Sen[r.]	196	7/	68.12.0	
Eubank, Thomas	110	4/2	22.18.4	
Eubank, Richard Jun[r.]	112¼	7/	39.5.7½}	
do. Thomas Jeffries	12¾	7/3	4.12.5}	
do. A. Dunn	147	5/3	38.11.9}	
Fleet, Baylor	860	12/6	537.10.8	
Fleet, John estate	260	6/3	81.5.0	
			1579.3.0	
Frazer, William estate	45	20/9	46.13.6	
Fleet, William	352	"	365.4.0	
do. Ben Gaines	183	6/3	57.3.9}	
Fisher, James estate	110	3/2	17.18.4	
Foster, Thomas	87¾	4/2	18.2.6	
Fauntleroy, Thomas	486	10/	243.0.2}	
do. H. Todds	500	18/	460.0.0}	
do. W[m.] Bowdens	183	7/	64.1.6}	
Farinholtz, David	151¼	6/6	49.1.6	
Faulkner, Benjamin	133	4/2	27.14.2}	
do. Mary Falkner	333	6/3	104.1.4}	
do. W. Boyd	9½	10/5	4.10.9}	
do. A. Gardner	3	17/	2.11.0}	
do. Southern	134½	4/2	28.0.5}	
Fargerson, Thomas	62	10/5	32.5.10}	
do. T. Collins	48	7/	16.16.6}	
Faucett, Vincent	46½	"	24.4.4½	
Fisher, William	30	5/3	7.17.6	
Graves, Elenor	163½	"	42.18.4½	
Garlick, Camm estate	917	6/3	286.11.3	
Garrett, Robert	100	4/2	20.16.8	
Gaines, Francis	356	14/6	258.2.0	
Gresham, Philemon	200	6/3	62.10.0	
Gresham, John (D) estate	200	7/10	78.6.8	
Gresham, William (B)	100	4/2	20.16.8}	
do. W. Row	40	6/3	13.3.4}	
Gardner, Anthony	638	11/	350.11.8	
do. dragon swamp	67½	17/	57.7.6	
			4339.13.2	

[page 5, List A, 1802] Persons Names Owning Lands	Quantity of land [135]	Price per acre	Total Amount Land	Amt. Tax Thereon in Dols. Cents
Gardner, Elizabeth	100	6/3	31.5.0	
Gibson, Richard	156½	3/2	24.16.7	
Gibson, Eubank	56½	"	8.18.11	
Gibson, Philip	129¼	"	20.9.3½	
Gresham, Meacham	100	5/3	26.5.0}	
do. A. Gresham	4	17/	3.8.0}	
Gresham, Ambrose	80	5/3	21.0.0}	
do. Dragon swamp	22	17/	18.5.0}	
Gresham, John (B)	79	5/3	20.14.9}	
do. A. Gresham	4	17/	3.8.0}	
Griffin, William est.	859	14/6	622.15.6	
Garrett, James	230	4/2	48.18.4	
Garrett, Robert	200	7/	70.0.0}	
do. Wm. Hunt	170	6/3	53.2.6}	
Gaines, Robert est.	537¾	20/9	558.8.7¾}	
do. A. Curtis	50	5/3	13.2.6}	
Guthrie, James	60	12/6	37.10.0	
Guthrie, Richard	60	"	37.10.0	
do. do.	162	3/2	25.13.0}	
Garrett, Edward	210	15/3	55.2.6}	
do. Edwd. Trice est.	489½	"	128.9.10}	
Groom, John	173	3/2	27.17.10	
Garrett, George	6½	5/3	1.14.1½	
Guthrie, Rachel	50	8/4	20.16.8	
Goldman, Martin	140	4/2	29.3.4	
Gully, Philip estate	50	3/2	7.18.4	
			1976.13.6	
Garrett, William (Shoemr.)	225	3/4¾	37.19.4}	
do. Geo. B. Bird	60	6/3	18.15.0}	
do. H.F. Dudley	50	5/3	13.2.6}	
Gramshill, Henry	25	3/2	3.9.2	
Garrett, Ann Watts	112	5/	28.0.0	
Garrett, Richard	100	4/2	20.16.8	
Garrett, William Junr.	120	"	25.0.0	
Groom, Richard	414	5/3	108.13.6	
Garrett, Edward Junr.	150	6/3	46.17.6	
Gaines, Benjamin	360	20/4	366.0.0	
Gaines, Harry	360	"	366.0.0	
Henderson, James	25	5/3	6.11.3	
Hoskins, William estate	296	20/	296.0.0}	
do. balance Bray's	2	7/10	15.8}	
Hoomes, Benjamin	372	12/6	232.10.0}	
do. Ann Kennedy	75	"	46.17.6}	
Hemmingway, John Junr.	263	4/2	54.15.10	
Hare, William estate	217	5/3	56.19.3	
Harwood, Christopher est.	194	24/10	240.17.8	
Harwood, Priscilla	165	18/	148.10.0	
Hart, James	150	3/2	23.15.0	
Holderby, John	73¼	4/2	15.5.2½	
Holderby, John Junr.	108¾	7/10	42.6.0	
Hart, Anthony	190	5/3	49.17.6}	
do. of Sundry Persons	359½	3/2	56.18.5}	
			4223.16.6	

[page 6, List A, 1802] Persons Names Owning Lands	Quantity of land	Price per acre	Total Amount Land	Amt. Tax Thereon in Dols. Cents
Hart, Gregory	200	3/2	31.3.4	
Hart, William estate	250	3/3½	41.2.11	
Harwood, John estate	109	10/5	56.15.5½	
Henry, Samuel H. estate	1900	14/6	1377.10.0	
Henry, James	75	12/6	46.17.6	
Hurt, James	33	10/5	17.3.9	
Halyard, William estate	126 2/3	5/3	33.5.0	
Hoskins, Robert	287	6/	86.2.0	
Hart, Alden	127	4/2	26.9.2	
Howerton, Heritage est.	122¼	20/9	126.16.7¼	
Howerton, John	269½	5/3	70.14.10½	
Hutson, William	50	4/2	10.8.4	
Hart, Vincent	75	6/6	24.7.6	
Halyard, John	187½	5/3	49.4.4½}	
do. William Halyard	63 1/3	"	16.12.6}	
Hogg, William & Legatees of}				
Holt, Richeson}	50	18/-	45.0.0	
Jones, Thomas	255	4/2	53.2.6	
Jeffries, Thomas (B)	63	7/3	22.16.9}	
do. John Harwood	38¼	10/5	19.15.10}	
do. John Brett's estate	57¾	18/-	51.19.6}	
Jones, James Junr.	100	5/3	26.5.0}	
do. Mary Jones	150	26/11	201.17.6}	
Jeffries, Gawin	60	4/2	12.10.0	
Jordan, Robert	66 2/3	4/2	13.18.10	
Jones, Mary	150	26/11	201.17.6	
Ison, George	140¼	5/3	36.16.3¾	
Kemp, John	296	7/3	107.3.0	
			2808.3.1	
Kauffman, Richard (orphan)	176	26/-	228.16.0}	
do. in Stanhope's Neck	38	10/5	19.15.10}	
Kauffman, Sambo, Humphry}				
& Lucy, free negroes	167	7/6	62.5.0	
Kidd, Henry	81½	5/3	26.6.6¾	
Kennedy, Archibald est.	38¼	4/2	7.19.4	
Kennedy, Ann	33¼	"	6.18.6½	
Kennedy, Ann Junr.	33¾	"	7.0.6	
Kennedy, Lucy	37½	"	7.16.2	
Kidd, Bartholomew	136	5/3	35.14.0}	
do. William Dillard Junr.	132½	4/2	27.12.1}	
Kidd, Benjamin	111	13/6	74.18.2}	
do. Crittenden	60	"	40.10.0}	
do. Dragon swamp	36	17/	30.12.0}	
Kidd, John estate	370	7/3	134.2.6}	
do. Lumpkin & Pierce	60	4/2	12.10.0}	
do. Thos. Dillard	45	14/6	32.12.6}	
King, Dicey estate	18	8/4	7.10.0	
Lumpkin, Jacob (orphan)	681	6/3	212.16.3	
Lewis, Iveson	356	14/6	258.2.0	
Leigh, Lucy	101	24/10	125.8.2	
Leigh, John estate	133	"	165.2.10	
Lambeth, Thomas	100	3/2	15.16.8	
Leigh, Richard estate	560	6/3	175.0.0	
			4523.8.2	

[page 7, List A, 1802] Persons Names Owning Lands	Quantity of land [136]	Price per acre	Total Amount Land	Amt. Tax Thereon in Dols. Cents
Mitchell, Ralph estate	193	10/5	100.10.5	
Mitchell, Sally	391	13/	254.3.0	
Mitchell, James (orphan)	225	"	146.5.0	
Moore, Lambeth	20	4/2	4.3.4}	
do. John Holderby	26¾	"	5.11 5½}	
do. William Morris	10	"	2.1.8}	
do. Henry Kidd	50	"	10.8.4}	
Moore, Benjamin	100	"	20.16.8	
Moore, Lodowick, John & Richard	100	3/2	15.16.8	
Major, Josiah	200	4/2	41.13.4	
Mitchell, John estate	270	5/3	70.17.0}	
do. Rootes	200	9/11	99.13.4}	
Mann, Joseph Sen[r.]	231	6/3	72.3.9	
Moore, Agathy	40	4/2	8.6.8	
Montague, William	170	"	35.8.4	
Merideth, Ralph G. est.	567	14/6	411.1.6	
Muire, Richard	93	12/6	58.2.6}	
do. John Leigh's est.	66	24/10	81.19.0}	
Moore, Richard est.	145	6/3	45.6.8	
McCarty, Joseph est.	73	3/2	11.11.2	
Metcalfe, Thomas	256	"	181.8.8	
Maderias, John	34½	6/3	10.15.7½	
Milby, Richard	175	3/2	27.14.2	
Morgan, William	3	6/3	0.18.9	
Moore, John	37	4/2	7.14.2	
			1724.11.2	
Newcomb, William	169	3/2	26.15.2	
Orvill, John	100	6/3	31.5.0	
Oliver, John	320	5/3	84.0.0	
Overstreet, Gabriel est.	296	4/2	61.13.4}	
do. Haynes	130	5/3	34.2.6}	
Oaks, Henry	198½	3/2	34.2.0	
Oaks, William	80	4/2	16.13.4	
Oliver, William	59	"	12.5.10	
Oaks, Ann	60	"	12.10.0	
Pitts, Benjamin G.	100	5/4	26.13.4	
Pace, Benjamin	263	7/3	95.6.9	
Pynes, Benjamin est.	164	6/3	51.5.0	
Pynes, Robert	111½	"	34.13.9	
Pynes, Benjamin	100	"	31.5.0	
Pemberton, John	165	"	51.11.3	
Pemberton, Philip	121	"	37.17.6	
Pollard, Robert	6	24/10	7.9.0}	
do. John O'Mealy	367	30/	550.10.0}	
Palmer, Charles	107¾	18/	96.19.6	
Price, Robert	399	6/3	124.13.9	
Pigg, John est.	324	14/6	234.18.0}	
Ditto	180	7/3	65.5.0}	
Peirce, Philip	83	3/2	13.2.10	
Peirce, Beverley	25¾	4/2	5.7.3½}	
do. of Phil Peirce	17	3/2	2.13.10}	
			3467.10.2	

[page 8, List A, 1802] Persons Names Owning Lands	Quantity of land	Price per acre	Total Amount Land	Amt. Tax Thereon in Dols. Cents
Pierce, Thomas estate	87	4/2	18.2.6	
Palmer, Roger	314	6/	94.4.0	
Roane, Thomas estate	2033	18/8	1897.9.4}	
do. H. Carlton	200	6/3	63.10.0}	
do. Brett's	34¾	18/	31.5.6}	
do. Ro. Pynes	24½	6/3	7.9.1½}	
Rowe, Elizabeth	665	20/9	689.18.9	
Rowe, Francis (orphan)	612½	4/8	142.16.0	
Richason, Elias est.	86	4/2	17.8.4	
Rowe, William & Moses	60	6/3	18.15.0	
Richards, John	571	4/8	124.8.0	
Richeson, James	180	4/2	37.10.0	
Richeson, William	369½	"	76.17.6	
Richeson, William Jun[r.]	150	5/3	39.7.6	
Richeson, John est.	101½	"	21.2.1	
Roane, Major	687½	3/8	128.18.1½	
do. John Lyne's est.	455¾	6/3	142.8.5¼	
do. Palmer	9	7/3	3.5.3	
Raines, Giles	60	3/2	9.10.0	
Robinson, Benjamin est.	1300	8/4	541.13.4	
Roane, Charles	133	19/	126.7.0}	
do. Dragon swamp	70	17/	59.10.0}	
Roy, Beverley	700	8/4	291.13.4}	
do. T. Brown	454	12/6	283.15.0}	
Ross, John	100	5/3	26.5.0	
Richason, James Jun[r.]	250	5/3	65.12.6	
Spencer, Susanna & John	416	7/3	150.16.0	
Spencer, John	34	"	12.6.6	
			5120.14.0	
Spencer, Ann	166	"	60.3.6	
Starke, Richard estate	350	5/8	99.3.4	
Stone, Robert est.	200	4/2	41.13.4	
Stone, Job	100	"	20.16.8	
Smith, Robert	89	10/5	46.7.1	
Smith, John (son of Robert)	88	"	45.16.8}	
do. Dragon Swamp	12	17/	10.8.0}	
Simpkins, Young	60	3/2	9.10.0	
Sears, Philip	83	4/2	17.5.10	
Shackelford, William est.	400	14/6	310.0.0	
Spencer, Thomas	300	10/5	156.5.0}	
do.	225	4/2	53.2.6}	
Seward, Benjamin	115	3/2	18.4.2	
Smith, Thomas G.	485	14/6	351.12.6	
Sadler, John	150	6/3	46.17.6	
Shackelford, John (R)	482	8/4	216.8.0	
Shackelford, William	351	6/3	109.13.9}	
do. Wyatt's lease	30	5/3	7.17.6}	
Shackelford, John (Mc)	283	6/2	87.5.2}	
do. John Collier (Cobler)	150	5/3	39.7.6}	
Shackelford, Benjamin	189	7/3	67.0.3}	
do. Halyard's lease	1	5/9½	5.9½}	
do. Palmers	197¾	7/3	71.13.8¼}	
Shepherd, John	67	6/	20.2.0	
Smith, John Doct[r.]	½	30/	15.0	
			7028.8.8	

[page 9, List A, 1802] Persons Names Owning Lands	Quantity of land	Price per acre	Total Amount Land	Amt. Tax Thereon in Dols. Cents
	[137]			
Southern, John	15½	4/2	3.4.7	
Sears, Thomas	123	6/7	40.9.9	
Tureman, Elizabeth	24¾	3/2	3.18.4½	
Tureman, Benjamin	70	3/2	11.1.8	
Tureman, George	50	"	7.18.4	
Taliaferro, William	1000	14/6	725.0.0	
Townley, Robert	200	6/3	62.10.0}	
do. Anderson's	117	14/6	84.16.6}	
Taliaferro, Philip est.	662	8/4	275.16.8	
Taliaferro, James B.	374½	12/6	234.7.6}	
Thurston, Armistead	111¾	4/3	23.15.1	
Thurston, Batcheldor	200	3/2	31.13.4	
Turner, Benjamin	36	4/2	7.10.0	
Townley, Ann	79	4/2	16.9.2	
Turner, Henry est.	100	"	20.16.8	
Tunstall, Richard G.	206½	7/10	73.3.7	
Taylor, William	40	6/3	12.10.0}	
do. P. Taliaferro est.	200	8/4	83.6.8}	
Trice, Kitty White	82	5/3	21.10.6	
Watts, Edward est.	250	7/3	90.12.6}	
do. W. Watts est.	113	5/	28.5.0}	
Watts, John	293	7/10	114.15.2}	
do. Pemberton	45	6/3	14.1.3}	
Watts, Kauffman	270	5/3	70.17.6}	
do. Eubank & Burch	257	5/9	73.17.9}	
do. John & Danl. Hemmingway	312	4/2	64.3.0}	
Watts, James	350	"	72.18.4}	
do. W. Watts est.	60	15/	45.0.0}	
			2313.18.10	
Williams, Howard	224	4/2	46.13.4}	
do. Dragon Swamp	43	17/	36.11.0}	
Wyatt, Thomas	206	7/10	81.2.0}	
do. Boughtons	60	3/2	9.10.0}	
Wyatt, William	48¾	7/3	17.1.3	
Williams, Montague	300	6/3	93.15.0	
Williams, Charles estate	336	4/2	70.0.0	
Walton, James	80	"	16.13.4}	
do. Thos. Walton's est.	66	"	13.15.0}	
Walton, Elizabeth	60	3/2	9.10.0	
Walton, John	176	5/3	46.4.0	
Walton, William est.	66	4/2	13.15.0	
Ware, John est.	75	5/3	19.13.9	
Ware, Arther estate	83	4/2	17.15.10	
Waring, Robert P. est.	542	10/9	291.10.6	
Walden, Richard est.	180	10/5	93.15.0	
Walden, Lewis estate	150	3/2	23.15.0}	
do. T. Dudley	84½	6/3	28.2.3½}	
Williams, George	40	4/2	8.6.8	
Watkins, Philip	197	5/3	51.14.3	
Wyatt, Richard	175	12/6	109.7.6	
Ware, Robert Junr. est.	100	4/2	20.16.8	
Williams, Elizabeth	16½	3/2	2.12.9	
			3435.10.0	

[page 10, List A, 1802] Persons Names Owning Lands	Quantity of land	Price per acre	Total Amount Land	Amt. Tax Thereon in Dols. Cents
White, James est.	200	6/3	62.10.0	
Wedderburn, Lydia	350	"	109.7.6	
Whiting, Beverley est.	2447¾	7/10	866.18.9	
Webley, John est.	173	5/3	45.8.3}	
do. Collier & Dillard	358	4/2	74.11.8}	
Ware, Robert Jun[r.]	100	8/4	41.13.4	
Ware, William	100	"	41.13.4	
Walden, Benjamin	373	5/3	97.18.3	
Waller, Edward est.	133½	3/2	21.2.9	
Waller, George est.	87	"	13.15.6	
Waller, John	65	3/7	11.12.11	
Waller, Robert est.	48	3/7	8.12.0}	
do. Groom's est.	187	3/2	29.12.2}	
Ware, Nicholas	100	"	15.16.8	
Walton, Beverly	47½	7/10	18.12.1	
Watts, George [K]	36	26/	46.16.0	
Wyatt, Smith	29¾	7/3	10.15.8	
			1516.16.10	
			[44740.14.2]	

Rich[d.] T. Shackelford, Comr. Revenue

[page]

[arithmetic omitted]

715.84 Land

[cover]
King & Queen
Richd. T. Shackleford
1802
Land
stated
Added, S.L.

A List of Land within the District of Robert B. Hill, Commissioner in the upper District in the County of King and Queen for the year 1802 to wit

LIST B

[page 1, List B, 1802] Persons names owning Land	Quantity of Land	Price per acre	Tot. Amt. Value Land
	[139]		
Atkins, Joseph Esta.	66	4/2	£13.15.0
Alexander, Benjamin	202	9/4	94.5.4}
Do. of James Halbert	124	6/2	38.15.0}
Do. Lott in Dunk[k.], an[l.] rent			20.0.0}
Do. Do. of Joseph Meede			4.10.0}
Acre, Sceton	52	9/4	24.5.4
Alexander, Elisha	338	"	157.14.8
Anderson, Churchill	636	7/3	230.11.0}
Do. of P. Anderson's Este.	96	20/9	99.12.0}
Atkins, John	135	4/6	30.7.6
Abbott, Jacob	112	7/10	43.17.4
Anderson, Sarah	86	20/9	89.3.9
Barton, John Este.	125	4/2	26.0.10
Bray, James	128¾	7/10	55.8.6
Broach, Benoni	48	10/5	25.4.0
Beverley, Robert Estate [page torn]	2444	10/5	1262.16.4
Brown, Henry	570	7/4½	210.3.9
			2486.10.14
Bland, John	83	8/4	34.11.8
Bates, James	358	11/	149.3.4
Do.	42	4/2	8.15.0
Do. of Rice Garnett	89	7/3	32.5.3
Braxton, Carter	484½	10/5	252.6.10
Brooking, Frances	930	"	484.7.6
Boughton, Thomas, Essex	130	9/4	60.13.4
Boughton, John	200	8/4	83.6.8
Boughton, Henry, Essex	88	6/3	27.10.0
Burton, John	170	5/3	44.12.6
Bohannon, Ann Este.	197	4/6	44.6.6
Brown, William	75	7/10	29.7.6}
Do. of Clem Pynes	18¼	3/2	2.17.9}
Do. of Ware's Exors. &c.	196½	7/3	71.4.7½}
Bagby, John Este.	330	7/3	119.12.9
Bagby, Richard	260	"	94.5.0
Bagby, Thomas	260	"	94.5.0}
Do. of Jacob Lumpkin	235	6/3	73.8.9}
Brizendine, Armistead	86 2/3	8/4	35.17.6
Bromley, John	60	7/10	23.10.0
Broach, William	20	"	7.16.8
Brown, John	50	7/4½	18.8.9
Bohannan, William	163	5/3	42.15.9
Bates, William	81	7/9½	31.10.1}
Do. of Rice Garnett	117	7/3	42.8.4}
			[4395.17].4

[page 2, List B, 1802] Persons names owning Land	Quantity of Land	Price per acre	Tot. Amt. Value Land
Broach, George	32½	14/6	£23.11.3}
Do. of Hill and wife	43¼	"	31.7.1½}
Beadles, Justin	20	6/3	6.5.0
Blackburn, Mary, heirs of P.A. Este.	86	20/9	89.4.6
Boulware, Samuel	175¾	31/3	274.12.2¼
Crafton, Thomas	119	9/4	55.10.8
Crafton, James	59	"	27.10.8
Crafton, John	117½	"	54.12.0
Craine, John	130	6/3	40.2.6}
Do. of Clem Pynes	14	3/2	2.4.4}
Do. of John Ware's Este.	49¼	7/3	17.17.0¾}
Cleverius, Benjamin	419	20/9	434.14.3
Carlton, Henry Este.	280	7/10	109.13.4}
Do. of John Baylor's Este.	257	14/6	186.6.6}
Cole, G. Thomas	105	6/3	32.16.3
Carlton, Lewis	100	8/4	41.3.4
Clayton, Thomas Este.	275	7/3	99.13.9
Crane, George Este.	30	7/3	10.17.6
Courtney, Thomas	156	7/10	61.2.0
Carlton, Joel	53½	6/3	16.4.5
Cooke, Moses	100	8/4	41.13.4
Cooke, Ambrose	100	"	41.13.4
Chapman, M. George	250	7/10	87.18.4
Courtney, Robert	183½	7/10	71.17.5
Cannaday, William [subtotal 1889.16.0]	100	6/3	31.5.0
Cooke, William	65	5/5	17.12.1
Cooke, James	65	8/9	28.8.9
Courtney, Fanny & Children	78	7/10	30.10.0
Cross, Joseph	103½	6/3	32.6.10½
Campbell, William	868¼	7/3	314.14.9¾
Campbell, Whitaker	406	7/10	159.0.4
Crow, John	121	5/3	31.19.2¼
Crow, Nathaniel Este.	60	6/3	18.15.0
Dew, Thomas	331	12/6	206.17.6
Dew, William Este.	935	14/6	677.17.6
Duling, William Este.	264	8/4	110.0.0
Dix, Gabriel	338	6/3	105.12.6
Deshazo, William Jun[r.]	60	4/2	12.10.0
Durham, Joseph	105	4/3	21.12.6}
Do. of Richard Dunn	10	4/2	2.1.8}
Deshazo, John	192	7/4	70.8.0
Deshazo, Larkin	87	7/3	31.4.10}
Do. of John Craine	6	6/3	1.17.6}
Do. of Benjamin Hoomes	430¾	4/4	93.4.5}
Dunbar, David	366	8/4	152.10.0
Dudley, Peter Esta.	530	7/3¼	186.18.4
Dalley, George	174¼	3/2	27.11.9½
Durham, John	25	3/2	3.19.4
Dickie, James	512	8/4	213.6.8
			[4440].15.6

[page 3, List B, 1802] Persons names owning Land	Quantity of Land	Price per acre	Tot. Amt. Value Land
	[140]		
Deshazo, Unity	71	7/10	27.16.3
Deshazo, Polly orphan	41	"	16.1.2
Dally, John Este.	200	3/2	31.13.4
Dobbins, Charles Este.	147	5/3	38.11.9
Eubank, John Este.	469	10/4	242.6.4}
Do. of James Grafton	111	6/3	34.13.9}
Do. of T. Dew	178½	12/6	111.5.6}
Eubank, Henry	171	5/3	44.17.9
Edwards, Thomas	66	4/2	13.15.0
Evans, Ambrose	195	7/10	56.10.0
Fleet, William	512	12/	307.4.0
Fogg, Frederick	298	8/4	124.3.4
Fauntleroy, G. Samuel	2069	20/	2069.0.0
Falkner, Thomas	220	6/3	68.15.0
Fogg, James	120	6/3	37.10.0
Fox, S. Joseph of H. Brown	158	7/4	57.18.8}
Do. of Thomas Garnett	28	7/10	10.19.4}
Do. of Thomas Cleaveley	39	"	15.5.6}
Do. of William Pollard	94	7/3	34.1.6}
Grafton, Sally & Ann	132	9/4	61.12.0
Gayle, John	264	7/5	97.18.0
Do. of Wm. Gayle	7¼	"	2.13.11
Gatewood, Chaney	829	10/5	437.17.11
Do. Noell's	362½	14/6	262.16.3
" Harwood's	125	4/2	46.17.6
" Eubank's	300	14/3	217.10.0
" Walden's Este.	120	12/6	75.0.0
" Wm. Lyne, Lott in Dunkk., anl. rent			30.0.0
			4574.13.9
Garnett, Joshua Este.	325	8/4	134.3.4
Gatewood, Joseph	445	10/5	231.15.5
Gayle, Matthew Este.	323	11/5	184.7.7
Gatewood, John	160	8/4	66.13.4
Garnett, Reuben	876½	8/10	387.2.5}
Do. of Halbert & Gatewood	28	10/5	14.12.10}
Gwathmey, Temple	600	35/3	1057.10.0
Garlick, Samuel	454	24/10	463.14.4
Garlick, John	839	29/	1216.11.0
Griffith, Thomas	22¾	6/3	7.0.7½
Griffith, Joseph Este.	22¾	"	7.0.7½
Gresham, Samuel	432½	7/3	156.15.7½}
Do. of Rice Garnett	157	"	56.18.1}
Guthrie, William	91¼	7/5	33.14.7
Gaines, Harry Este.	481½	20/4	489.10.6
Gaines, B. Robert	481½	"	489.10.6
Gresham, Thomas Este.	455¼	6/8	151.13.4
Griffith, Milly	50	6/3	15.12.6
Graves, Thomas	66¼	7/3	23.18.6
Gresham, Lumpkin	255	"	92.8.9
Gresham, William Junr.	242 1/3	8/4	101.5.0
Do. of William Gatewood	46	3/2	7.5.8
" of Chick	69	7/3	25.0.3
			9988.18.6

[page 4, List B, 1802] Persons names owning Land	Quantity of Land	Price per acre	Tot. Amt. Value Land
Gresham, George	141	3/2	£22.6.6
Gatewood, William (*Tuck*o.)	33	"	5.4.6
Gatewood, William (Son of Jno.)	132	10/	66.0.0
Gleason, Patrick	134	8/4	55.16.8
Gatewood, Gabriel	78	10/5	40.12.6}
Do. of Halbert	50	"	26.10.0}
Gayle, William	344	7/5	127.11.4
Garnett, Henry	140	7/3	50.15.0}
Do. Lott in Dunkirk annual rent			70.0.0}
Hill, William Este.	1267	14/6	918.4.3
Hawes, Walker	97	"	70.6.6
Hitchcock, Thomas	140	4/2	29.3.4
Hoskins, Samuel Este.	345	6/3	107.16.3}
Do. Elisha Alexander	57	10/5	25.13.9}
Hutchason, Charles Este.	531	7/1	188.1.3
Heskew, John Este.	61	5/3	16.0.3
Heskew, John Junr. Este.	50	6/3	15.12.6}
Do. of Clem Pynes	10	3/2	1.11.8}
Do. of Larkin Deshazo	19¼	4/4	4.2.4}
Hill, Edward	1200	18/8	1120.0.0
Hoskins, John	767	10/5	399.9.7}
Do. of Boughtons	100	8/4	41.13.4}
Do. of Fleet & Semple	2	10/5	1.0.10}
Hurt, West	14	5/3	3.3.6
Holt, William	123	14/3	87.12.9
Hutchason, John	73¼	8/9	32.0.11¼
Howerton, George	76¼	6/	22.17.6
Hall, Corbin	72	4/2	15.0.0
			3564.7.0
Hill, B. Robert	322	8/2	131.9.8
Hill, Richard	332	"	135.11.4
Hill, G. Mary	360	"	147.0.0
Hill, Robert Este.	420	"	171.10.0
Hoomes, John, Lott in Dk., anl. rent			40.0.0
Jones, John Este.	300	8/11	133.15.0
Jeffries, Edward	70	3/2	11.1.8
Jeffries, Ambrose	237	7/10	92.16.6
Jeffries, Robert	110	7/6	41.5.0}
Do. of Lumpkin Gresham	10	7/3	3.12.6}
" of Jacob Lumpkin	5	"	1.16.3}
Jones, James Este.	160	14/6	116.0.0}
Do. of James Jones Este.	196	10/5	102.1.8}
Jones, William Este.	241	15/10	190.15.10}
Do. of L. Smith	35	31/1	55.11.2}
Johnson, Thomas	72	3/2	11.8.0
Jones, Rawleigh	63	31/1	93.18.3
Jeffries, John	100	7/10	39.3.4
Kemp, John	178	7/3	64.2.2
Keeling, Mary	78½	8/	31.8.0
Kay, Christopher	116	6/3	36.6.0
Do. of T. Gouldman	416½	9/	187.8.6
			5402.[7.10]

[page 5, List B, 1802] Persons names owning Land	Quantity of Land	Price per acre	Tot. Amt. Value Land
	[141]		
Lumpkin, James	213	7/10	83.8.2
Lumpkin, Henry	400	9/4	186.13.4
Lumpkin, John Este.	125	6/3	35.11.3
Lumpkin, William Este.	61½	13/6	61.17.6
Lafon, Francis	119	8/4	49.11.8
Lankford, Thomas Este.	100	4/2	20.16.8
Lumpkin, Robert Senr.	374	8/4	155.16.8
Lumpkin, Henry Junr.	190	9/4	88.13.4
Lumpkin, W. John Este.	140	7/10	54.16.8}
Do. of John Ware's Este.	118½	7/3	42.15.6}
Longest, Caleb	97	7/10	37.19.10
Longest, Richard	227¾	"	89.4.2
Longest, John	100	"	39.3.4
Lumpkin, Anthony Este.	216	6/3	67.10.0
Lumpkin, Robert Junr.	279¾	5/3	73.8.8¼
Lumpkin, Wilson	122½	9/4	57.3.4
Lumpkin, William Junr.	183¼	10/5	95.6.3
Lumpkin, John	112	3/2	17.14.8
Lyne, William	1480	8/4	610.14.2
Lumpkin, Richard	57½	5/3	15.1.10½
Longest, William	83	8/4	34.11.8
Lumpkin, Ann	47	13/6	31.14.6
Lumpkin, Elizabeth	51	13/6	34.8.6
Lumpkin, John, Kg. Wm.	105	"	70.17.6
			2054.19.2
Motley, Edwin	815	10/5	428.2.6}
Do. of John W. Semple & Uxor.	149	12/6	93.2.6}
Martin, C. Thomas	583	14/6	422.13.6
Do.	134½	7/3	48.15.1½
Minor, William	149	8/4	62.1.8
Minor, John	137	"	57.1.8
Minor, Thomas Este.	288	7/10	112.16.0
Moody, Lewis	239	"	93.12.2
Mann, Joseph Junr.	400	8/4	166.13.4}
Do. of Crows	140	6/3	43.15.0}
Mitchell, John	50	6/3	15.12.6
Mann, Robert Este.	699	6/3	218.8.9
Merideth, Samuel	215	7/10	84.4.2
Macon, John Este.	1092	16/7	905.9.0}
Do. Lotts in Dunkirk, annual rents			42.0.0}
Mann, Mary	100	5/3	26.5.0
Martin, John	475	9/	213.15.0}
Do. of Thomas Fogg	197	6/3	61.11.3}
Mahon, Thomas	101	6/3	31.11.3
Mahon, William	103½	6/3	32.3.9
Mahon, Benjamin	43¼	5/3	11.7.0¾
Nunn, Moses	318	7/4½	117.5.3
Nunn, Thomas	130	7/3	47.2.6
Do. of Brizendine	49	4/3	10.8.3
Newbill, William	1060	8/4	441.13.4
Newell, John Este.	100	7/10	39.3.4
Nash, John Este.	100	6/3	31.5.0
			5912.18.0

[page 6, List B, 1802] Persons names owning Land	Quantity of Land	Price per acre	Tot. Amt. Value Land
Owen, Augustine Este.	100	6/3	£31.5.0
Pendleton, James	888½	8/7½	383.3.3¾}
Do. Wilmore's	70	7/6	26.5.0}
Do. Phil Pendleton	120	9/2	53.0.0}
" Wm. McIntosh	125	4/2	26.1.10}
Pitts, David	420	9/4	196.0.0
Pitts, Obadiah	20	10/5	10.8.4
Phillips, James	230	7/3	83.7.6
Pollard, John Este.	235	9/4	109.13.4}
Do. of Leonard Smithy	384	7/3	139.4.0}
Prewitt, Frances	99	9/4	46.4.0
Parker, John	761¼	8/4	317.3.9
Prewitt, Richard	102	7/3	36.12.3
Pendleton, Philip	360	9/2	165.0.0}
Do. Lott in Dunkirk, annual rent			3.0.0}
Perryman, Philip	218	7/2	78.2.4
Pynes, Clement	99	3/2	15.13.6
Pollard, Richard	389	8/4	162.1.8
Pendleton, Benjamin Este.	450	7/10	176.5.0
Perryman, Richard	110	7/3	39.7.6
Prewitt, Tunstall	58½	8/	23.8.0
Pollard, Joseph	200	6/3	62.10.0
Pollard, Richard & Brown, Henry	50	8/	20.0.0
Quarles, W. Francis	154	17/2	132.1.8}
Do. Lott in Dunkirk, annual rent			9.0.0
			2344.18.0
Rowe, G. Thomas (orphan)	555	7/3	201.3.9
Row, Richard Este.	450	8/4	188.0.0
Roane, Spencer	954	24/10	1184.11.0
Ryland, Joseph	487½	7/3	176.10.9
Ryland, Josiah	160	7/10	62.13.4}
Do. of William Temple	27½	15/	20.12.6}
" of Francis Prince's Este.	113	7/10	44.5.2}
" of H. Brown	34½	7/4½	12.14.1¼}
Riddle, Vaughan	188	5/5	49.7.0
Roane, Thomas	920¾	17/2	790.8.2½
Roane, Samuel	1074¾	"	922.9.10½
Row, Handsford	160½	6/3	50.3.1½
Row, Wilson	160½	"	50.3.1½
Smith, William	53	7/10	20.15.2}
Do. of James Smith Este.	25	3/2	3.19.2}
Segar, Richard	406	7/3	147.3.6
Satterwhite, George	164	6/3	51.5.0
Satterwhite, William	200	5/7½	56.5.0
Schools, John	156	8/4	65.0.0}
Do. of Parker & Uxor.	35	"	14.11.8}
Schools, Gabriel Este.	174	6/3	54.7.6
			6511.7.0

[page 7, List B, 1802] Persons names owning Land	Quantity of Land	Price per acre	Tot. Amt. Value Land
	[142]		
Skelton, William	362	8/2½	£148.11.5
Do. of Phil Perryman	12	7/2	4.6.0
Smith, John D.	190	7/6	71.5.0
Starling, Roderick	360	7/10	141.0.0}
Do.	313	8/2	127.16.2}
" of Wm. Lyne	56½	8/4	23.6.8}
" of H. Walker	46	5/3	12.1.6}
Saunders, George	200	7/3	70.10.8
Shepherd, William	140	9/4	65.6.8
Smith, Molly	30	4/2	6.5.0
Smith, John Junr.	42½	5/3	11.3.1½
Smith, Lewis	96	7/6	36.0.0
Swinton, Ann	750	13/6	506.5.0
Stone, Sarah	300	7/3	108.15.0
Stone, Daniel	52	3/2	8.4.8
Smith, Larkin	1254¼	31/1	1949.6.3½
Smith, Henry	400	6/3	130.0.0
Smith, Ambrose	92¾	8/4	38.6.8
Stevens, George Este.	430	7/10	168.8.4
Stevens, George (orphan)	75	"	29.8.4
Smith, William Este. (Mill)	200	3/2	31.13.4
Shackelford, John Este.	114	7/3	40.8.2
Shepherd, John	192	3/2	30.1.8
Stone, William	74¼	3/2	11.15.3½
Sthreshley, William	155½	6/3	48.11.10
Schools, George [subtotal 3902.3.4]	200	8/4	83.6.8
Smith, John, of J. Garlick	54	29/	78.6.0
Smith, Jane, of Jas. Smith's Este.	25	3/2	3.19.2
Smith, Philip (orphan) of Do.	12½	"	1.19.7
Smith, James	101	7/10	39.11.2}
Do. of Jas. Smith's Este.	12½	3/2	1.19.7}
Scott, Anderson	330	16/7	273.12.6
Do. of P. Anderson's Este.	248	20/9	257.6.0
Semple, B. Robert	253	10/5	131.15.1}
Do. of Spencer Roane	155	24/10	192.9.2}
Trice, William Este.	140	7/3	50.15.0
Taylor, James	50	6/3	15.12.6
Taylor, Edmund	294	8/14	122.10.0
Temple, Joseph	918	10/5	478.2.6
Tunstall, Richard Junr. Este.	1097	7/3	397.13.3
Temple, William	402¼	15/	301.17.6
Temple, John	42	31/3	65.12.6
Temple, Humphrey Este.	100	15/	75.0.0
Do. of J. Tunstall	200	18/8	185.16.8
["] of R. Tunstall & others	574	21/	602.14.0
[Tuns]tall, Richard (Purdy Este.)	132½	8/4	55.0.0
[Tun]stall, C. Thomas	137	"	57.1.[8]
Upshaw, James (Essex)	125	8/10	55.[4.2]
[Do. of] R. Beverley	30	10/5	15.[12.6]
	[page torn]		73[61.13.10]

[page 8, List B, 1802] Persons names owning Land	Quantity of Land	Price per acre	Tot. Amt. Value Land
Wyatt, Henry	200	7/3	£72.10.0
Wilson, Isaac Este.	200	6/3	62.10.0
Wilson, Benjamin Esta.	200	7/3	72.10.0
Wyatt, John Este.	100	7/10	39.3.4
Watkins, Joseph	63	6/7	20.14.9
Do. of Wiltshire's Este.	71	7/3	26.19.9
Walker, Philip	110	9/4	51.6.8
Walker, Humphrey	820	33/2	1355.14.2
Wright, William	130	5/3	33.12.6
Willis, Joel	94	7/10	35.5.0
Wright, Edward	567	6/3	177.3.9
Whayne, William	154½	7/10	60.10.3
Wyatt, George	122	7/6	45.15.0
Webb, James	140¾	4/2	29.6.6
Do.	7	4/2	1.9.2
Wheeley, Carriol	21¾	7/3	7.17.8¼
Do. of Ware's Este.	15½	7/3	5.12.4½
Watkins, Joseph Jun[r.]	93¼	8/4	38.17.1
Wilson, M: George	52½	9/4	24.10.0
Wyatt, Robert	50	7/3	18.2.6
Watkins, John	152	8/4	63.6.8
Watkins, Philip	107	4/2	22.5.10
White, Henry	57	13/6	38.9.6
Young, Henry	640	18/8	597.6.8
			2900.14.[3]
			[46914.12.3]

Ro. B. Hill, Commissioner

King & Queen, 1802
added
Stated
Added, S.L.
for the
Auditor of Public Accounts, Richmond

[arithmetic omitted]

$750.64 Land

List of Land within the district of Richard T. Shackelford, Commissioner in the county of King & Queen for the year 1803

LIST A

[page 1, List A, 1803] Persons Names Owning Lands	Quantity of land [143]	Price per acre	Total Amount Land	Amt. Tax Thereon in Dols. Cents
Anderson, Richard est.	460	5/3	120.15.0	
Atkins, Lewis	60	8/4	25.0.0	
Anderson, Francis	458	10/9	246.3.6}	
do. Rich^d. T. Shackelford	26	8/4	12.1.8}	
Anderson, Beverley	¾	5/3	3.1½	
Brown, Samuel	33¼	4/3	7.1.2	
Banks, William est.	365	4/2	76.0.0	
Brooke, Richard	1539¾	29/-	2232.12.9	
Brumley, Robert	225	5/3	59.1.3	
Bird, William est.	532	7/3	197.17.0}	
do. Dragon Swamp	88½	17/	70.4.6}	
Bird, Philemon	1638¼	6/3	511.19.0¾	
Brett, Nancy	50	18/	45.0.0	
Burch, James	183	6/3	57.3.9	
Burch, Vincent	100	4/2	20.16.8}	
do. William Hoskins	50	3/3	7.18.4}	
Bird, Anthony A.	275	"	43.10.10}	
do. of William Montague	44	4/2	9.3.4}	
Byne, John est.	336	4/2	70.0.0}	
do. Dragon Swamp	2¼	17/	1.18.3	
Bird, Robert est.	780	24/10	993.6.8}	
do. Guy Smith	189½	3/2	30.0.1}	
Bourn, Richard est.	150	3/2	23.15.0	
			4861.12.8	
Boyd, John	115	18/8	107.6.8}	
do. Soane's	382	24/10	474.6.4}	
Bray, Richard est.	93	7/10	36.8.6	
Bird, John est.	71	3/2	11.4.10	
Bew, William est.	117	"	18.0.6	
Boyd, Robert	1119	9/3	517.10.3	
Boyd, William	300	15/	225.0.0	
Berkeley, Edmund est.	762	5/3	200.0.6	
Bland, John	60	12/6	37.10.0	
Bland, William	100	9/11	49.11.8	
Bourn, Mills	159½	5/3	41.14.3}	
do. Thos. Jordan's est.	33 1/3	4/2	6.18.10½}	
Bullman, Ann	120	5/3	31.10.0	
Belote, Laban	384½	4/2	80.2.6	
Bland, William Senr.	225	3/8¼	41.9.8¼	
Bland, Ralph	146	53	38.6.8}	
do. Finney & Buckner	170	4/2	35.8.4}	
Bowden, William	100	"	20.16.8}	
do. Sykes	34	3/2	5.7.8}	
Bland, W^m. est.	250	"	52.1.8	
Bland, Thomas	412	3/2	75.4.8	
Brooks, Merryman	100	7/10	39.3.4	
Bowden, George	236	5/3	61.19.0}	
do. William Dillard's	30	4/2	6.5.0}	
			7075.0.3	

[page 2, List A, 1803] Persons Names Owning Lands	Quantity of land	Price per acre	Total Amount Land	Amt. Tax Thereon in Dols. Cents
Banks, James	22	7/3	7.19.6	
Bristow, Bartholomew	33½	3/2	5.6.1	
Bristow, George	100	3/2	15.16.8	
Banks, Andrew	125	12/6	78.2.6	
Brightwell, John est.	70	4/2	14.11.8	
Burton, James est.	89	"	18.10.10	
Bland, William (younger)	300	7/3	108.15.0	
Bird, Janet & Frances	230	10/5	119.15.10}	
Do. Rob[t.] Smith (Dragon)	60	17/	51.0.0}	
Bird, Philemon & Jn[o.] Smith	1	7/10	7.10	
Breedlove, John	37¾	15/	28.6.3½	
Brushwood, George	188	4/2	39.3.4}	
do. Robert Ware	112	3/2	17.14.8}	
Bird, Parmenas	132¼	11/8	77.4.7	
Bray, Peter	51¼	6/3	16.0.3¾	
Bland, John	212	5/3	55.13.0	
Carlton, Thomas Sen[r.]	200	7/10	78.6.8}	
do. Philemon Bird	83½	6/3	26.1.10½}	
Carlton, Noah	100	7/10	39.3.4	
Cooke, Henry	260	5/3	68.5.0}	
Ditto	49¼	10/5	25.10.5}	
Carlton, John (S)	100	6/3	31.5.0}	
Campbell, James T. (orphan)	296	12/6	185.0.0	
Carlton, Christopher Sen[r.]	37½	6/3	11.14.5}	
Do. James Laughlin	126½	3/2	26.8.2}	
Carlton, Richard est.	139	7/	[48.13.0]	
Cauthern, James	36½	3/2	5.15.7	
			1179.17.1	
Carlton, William Sen[r.]	309¾	11/6	178.1.2½	
Carlton, Christopher (younger)	148	5/	37.0.0	
Carlton, Richard	250	7/3	90.12.6	
Carlton, Christopher Jun[r.]	100	"	36.5.0}	
do. John Stone est.	159½	5/3	41.14.9}	
Cooper, Henry	50	4/2	10.8.4	
Carlton, Thomas (Taylor)	100	6/3	31.5.0	
Cardwell, James	150	4/2	31.5.0	
Cardwell, John	150	"	31.5.0	
Cardwell, William est.	77	"	15.11.6	
Cardwell, Thomas est.	110	"	22.18.4	
Cooke, John est.	300	"	62.10.0	
Collins, Thomas	281½	7/	98.10.6}	
Do. Ro. S. Ware	84½	11/9	49.12.10½}	
Do. Metcalfe & Levert	289½	14/6	209.17.9}	
Carlton, John Jun[r.]	235	4/2	48.19.2	
Do. Baylor Fleet	2	12/6	1.5.0}	
Campbell, William	238	3/2	37.13.8	
Corbin, Richard	2390	11/1¾	1332.11.4}	
Do. Shackelfords	300	12/6	78.2.6}	
Do. Dixon's	416¾	15/5	321.10.10}	
Corr, James	100	6/2	30.16.8	
			3977.14.0	

[page 3, List A, 1803] Persons Names Owning Lands	Quantity of land	Price per acre	Total Amount Land	Amt. Tax Thereon in
	[144]			Dols. Cents
Crouch, James	105¼	3/2	16.13.3½	
Collins, Joyeux	140	10/5	72.18.4	
Clayton, James	260	5/3	65.5.0	
Crittenden, Zachariah	34½	14/6	24.17.10	
Collier, John	100	4/2	20.16.8	
Cary, Wilson est.	1820	16/7	1509.1.8	
Campbell, James	130	5/9½	37.10.0}	
Do. Rich[d.] Garrett	70	3/2	11.1.8}	
Do. Benjamin Moore	100	4/2	20.16.8}	
Crittenden, Richard est.	178	5/3	46.14.6	
Corr, Thomas R.	236½	"	62.1.7	
Collier, Joseph	468	"	112.17.0	
Collier, Benjamin	75	"	19.13.9	
Clegg, Isaiah est.	241	4/2	50.4.2	
Cooke, Dawson	282	3/2	44.13.0	
Curry, John	155	4/8	31.0.0	
Cooke, Thomas	240	3/2	38.0.0	
Cooke, Thomas Jun[r.]	96	"	15.0.4	
Carlton, Humphry	175	7/	61.5.0}	
Do. John Wyatt's est.	48½	6/3	15.3.1½}	
Carlton, Thomas est.	235	6/3	73.8.9	
Corr, John Jun[r.]	503½	7/3	182.10.4½}	
Do. Tho[s.] Dudley's	197½	6/3	61.14.4½}	
Campbell, John	400	12/6	250.0.0	
Curry, James	70	4/2	18.16.0	
Corr, John Sen[r.]	213	3/2	33.15.6}	
Do. John Corr Jun[r.]	90	7/3	32.12.6}	
			2928.11.1	
Crittenden, Frances (River)	$105_{1/3}$	14/6	76.12.2	
Clarke, John	144	5/	36.0.0}	
Do. Sam[l.] Hemmingway	254½	4/2	53.0.3}	
Cooke, John est.	100	3/2	15.16.8	
Clayton, Maria H., Sally K. Clayton} and Polly R. Clayton}	72	9/11	35.14.0	
Didlake, William est.	100	3/2	15.16.8	
Didlake, Mary est.	278	8/4	115.16.8}	
Do. John Gardner est.	173	6/9	53.7.9	
Durham, Newman	50	4/2	10.8.4	
Dunn, Thomas	50½	6/3	15.15.7½	
Dillard, William Sen[r.]	226	12/6	141.5.0	
Dillard, George	50	"	31.5.0	
Durham, Thomas est.	85	3/2	13.9.2	
Dungie, John est.	110	"	17.8.4	
Dudley, William est.	290	14/6	210.5.0}	
Do. L. Wedderburn	315½	6/3	98.11.10}	
Damm, John est.	55	"	17.3.9	
Dudley, James	180	7/10	70.10.0	
Daniel, John	134¾	4/2	28.1.5½	
Damm, William	25	4/2	5.4.2	
Douglas, John	239	7/	83.13.0	
			4873.15.11	

[page 4, List A, 1803] Persons Names Owning Lands	Quantity of land	Price per acre	Total Amount Land	Amt. Tax Thereon in Dols. Cents
Didlake, John	1200	7/3	435.0.0	
Dudley, Ann	141	"	51.2.3	
Dudley, Guilford	106	"	38.8.6	
Didlake, Edward	56	10/5	29.3.4	
Dudley, Banks est.	230	3/2	36.8.4	
Downey, Michael est.	50	10/5	26.0.10	
Didlake, Royston	206	3/6½	36.7.4	
Dillard, Thomas	49	15/	36.15.0	
Dillard, William Jun[r.]	207½	"	155.12.6	
Dudley, Thomas	70	6/3	21.17.6	
Dillard, Nicholas	75	4/2	15.12.6	
Drummond, John est.	150	6/3	46.17.6	
Dabney, Benjamin	400	14/6	290.0.0}	
Do. Phil Taliaferro's	150	8/4	62.10.0}	
Davis, Stage	74	4/2	15.8.4}	
do. Eliz[a.] M. Davis	10	6/9	3.7.6}	
Dunn, John (Essex), Dragon	73	17/	62.1.0	
Digges, Francis	175	5/3	45.13.9	
Dean, Benjamin	50	5/3	13.12.6	
Dillard, Thomas A.	29	3/2	4.11.10	
Durham, George est.	50	4/2	10.8.4	
			1436.18.10	
Eubank, Warner	115	"	18.4.2}	
Do. John Hemmingway Jun[r.]	4	4/2	16.8}	
Eubank, Richard est.	117	"	24.3.9	
Eubank, William est.	28¾	5/3	7.11.0	
Eubank, Richard Sen[r.]	196	7/	68.12.0	
Eubank, Thomas	110	4/2	22.18.4	
Eubank, Richard Jun[r.]	108¾	7/	38.1.1½}	
Do. Thomas Jeffries	12¾	7/3	4.12.5}	
Do. A. Dunn	147	5/3	38.11.9}	
Fleet, Baylor	860	12/6	537.10.8	
Frazer, William est.	45	20/9	46.13.6	
Fleet, William	352	"	365.4.0	
Fisher, James est.	110	3/2	17.18.4	
Foster, Thomas	87¾	4/2	18.2.6	
Fauntleroy, Thomas	486	10/	243.0.0}	
Do. H. Todds	500	18/	460.0.0}	
Do. W[m.] Bowdens	183	7/	64.1.0}	
Farinholtz, David	151¼	6/6	49.1.6	
Faulkner, Benjamin	133	4/2	27.14.2}	
Do. Mary Falkner	333	6/3	104.1.4}	
Do. W. Boyd	9½	10/5	4.10.9}	
Do. A. Gardner	3	17/	2.11.0}	
Do. Southern	134½	4/2	28.0.5}	
Fargerson, Thomas	62	10/5	32.5.10}	
Do. T. Collins	48	7/	16.16.0}	
Faucett, Vincent	46½	"	24.4.4½	
Fisher, William	30	5/3	7.17.6	
			3699.12.11	

[page 5, List A, 1803] Persons Names Owning Lands	Quantity of land [145]	Price per acre	Total Amount Land	Amt. Tax Thereon in Dols. Cents
Graves, Eleanor	163½	5/3	42.18.4½	
Garlick, Camm est.	917	6/3	286.11.3	
Garrett, Robert	100	4/2	20.16.8	
Gaines, Francis	356	14/6	258.2.0	
Gresham, Philemon	200	6/3	62.10.0	
Gresham, Mary	100	7/10	39.3.4	
Gresham, William (B)	100	4/2	20.16.8}	
Do. W. Row	40	6/3	13.3.4}	
Gardner, Anthony	638	11/	350.11.8	
Do. Dragon swamp	67½	17/	57.7.6	
Gardner, Elizabeth	100	6/3	31.5.0	
Gibson, Richard	156½	3/2	24.16.7	
Gibson, Eubank	56½	"	8.18.11}	
Do. R. Eubank Jun[r.]	3½	7/	1.4.6}	
Gibson, Philip	129½	3/2	20.9.3½	
Gresham, Meacham	100	5/3	26.5.0}	
Do. of Gresham A.	4	17/	3.8.0}	
Gresham, Ambrose	80	5/3	21.0.0}	
Do. Dragon Swamp	22	17/	18.5.0}	
Gresham, John (B)	79	5/3	20.14.9}	
Do. A. Gresham	4	17/	3.8.0}	
Griffin, William est.	859	14/6	622.15.6	
Garrett, James	230	4/2	48.18.4	
Garrett, Robert	200	7/	70.0.0}	
Do. P. Bird	54¾	6/3	172.2.¼}	
Do. W[m.] Hunt	170	"	53.2.6}	
Gaines, Robert est.	537¾	20/9	558.8.7¾}	
Do. A. Curtis	50	5/3	13.2.6}	
Guthrie, James [subtotal 2752.15.5]	60	12/6	37.10.0	
Guthrie, Richard	60	"	37.10.0	
Ditto Ditto	162	3/2	25.13.0}	
Garrett, Edward	210	15/3	55.2.6}	
Do. Edw[d.] Trice's	489½	"	128.9.10}	
Garrett, William (son of W[m.])	197¾	7/3	71.13.8¼	
Groom, John	173	3/2	27.17.10}	
Do. John Bowden	95	4/2	19.15.10}	
Garrett, George	6½	5/3	1.14.1½	
Guthrie, Rachel	50	8/4	20.16.8	
Goldman, Martin	140	4/2	29.3.4	
Gully, Philip est.	50	3/2	7.18.4	
Garrett, William Sen[r.]	225	3/4¾	37.19.4½}	
Do. Geo. B. Bird	60	6/3	18.15.0}	
Do. H.F. Dudley	50	5/3	13.2.6}	
Gramshill, Henry	25	3/2	3.19.2	
Garrett, Ann Watts	112	5/	28.0.0	
Garrett, Richard	100	4/2	20.16.8	
Garrett, William Jun[r.]	120	"	25.0.0	
Groom, Richard	414	5/3	108.13.6	
Garrett, Edward Jun[r.]	150	6/3	46.17.6	
Gaines, Benjamin	360	20/4	366.0.0	
Gaines, Harry	360	"	366.0.0	
			4213.14.3	

[page 6, List A, 1803] Persons Names Owning Lands	Quantity of land	Price per acre	Total Amount Land	Amt. Tax Thereon in Dols. Cents
Henderson, James	25	5/3	6.11.3	
Hoskins, William est.	296	20/	296.0.0}	
Do. balance Bray's	2	7/10	15.8}	
Hoomes, Benjamin	372	12/6	232.10.0}	
Do. Ann Kennedy's	75	"	46.17.6}	
Hemmingway, John Junr.	263	4/2	54.15.10	
Hare, William est.	217	5/3	56.19.3	
Harwood, Christopher est.	194	24/10	240.17.8	
Harwood, Priscilla	165	18/	148.10.0	
Hart, James	150	3/2	23.15.0	
Holderby, John	73¼	4/2	15.5.2½	
Holderby, John Junr.	108¾	7/10	42.6.0	
Hart, Anthony	190	5/3	49.17.6}	
do. of Sundry Persons	359½	3/2	56.18.5}	
Hart, Gregory	200	"	31.3.4	
Hart, William est.	250	3/3½	41.2.11	
Henry, Samuel H. est.	1900	14/6	1377.10.0	
Henry, James	75	12/6	46.17.6	
Hurt, James	33	10/5	17.3.9	
Halyard, William est.	63 1/3	5/3	16.12.6	
Hoskins, Robert	287	6/	86.2.0}	
Do. Ro. Smith	157¾	10/5	82.10.6¾}	
Hart, Alden	127	4/2	26.9.2	
Hutson, William	75¼	"	15.13.6½	
Howerton, Heritage est.	122¼	20/9	126.16.7¼	
Halyard, William	260	6/3	81.5.0	
Howerton, John	269½	5/3	70.14.10½	
Hart, Vincent	75	6/6	24.7.6	
Halyard, John	187½	5/3	49.4.4½}	
Do. William Halyard	63 1/3	"	16.12.6}	
Do. Wm. Halyard's est.	63 1/3	"	16.12.6}	
Hogg, William & Legatees of} of Holt, Richeson}	50	18/-	45.0.0	
			3444.7.11	
Jones, Thomas	255	4/2	53.2.6	
Jeffries, Thomas (B)	63	7/3	22.16.9}	
Do. John Harwood	38¼	10/5	19.15.10}	
Do. John Brett's estate	57¾	18/-	51.19.6}	
Jones, James Junr.	100	5/3	26.5.0}	
Do. Mary Jones	150	26/11	201.17.6}	
Jeffries, Going	60	4/2	12.10.0	
Jordan, Robert	66 2/3	4/2	13.18.10	
Jones, Mary	150	26/11	201.17.6	
Ison, George	140¼	5/3	36.16.3¾	
Inge, Vincent est.	33	8/4	13.15.0	
Kemp, John	296	7/3	107.3.0	
Kauffman, Richard (orphan)	176	26/-	228.16.0}	
Do. in Stanhope's Neck	38	10/5	19.15.10}	
Kauffman, Sambo, Humphry} and Lucy, free negroes	167	7/6	62.5.0	
Kidd, Henry est.	81½	5/3	26.6.6¾	
Kennedy, Archibald est.	38¼	4/2	7.19.4	
			4551.5.7	

[page 7, List A, 1803] Persons Names Owning Lands	Quantity of land [146]	Price per acre	Total Amount Land	Amt. Tax Thereon in Dols. Cents
Kennedy, Ann	33¼	4/2	6.18.6½	
Kennedy, Ann Jun[r.]	33¾	"	7.0.6	
Kennedy, Lucy	37½	"	7.16.2	
Kidd, Bartholomew	136	5/3	35.14.0}	
Do. of W[m.] Dillard Jun[r.]	132½	4/2	27.12.1}	
Do. of Robt. Lumpkin	95½	"	19.17.11}	
Kidd, Benjamin	111	13/6	74.18.2}	
Do. Crittenden's	60	"	40.10.0}	
Do. Dragon swamp	36	17/	30.12.0}	
Kidd, John est.	370	7/3	134.2.6}	
Do. Lumpkin & Pierce	60	4/2	12.10.0}	
Do. Tho[s.] Dillard	45	14/6	32.12.6}	
King, Dicey est.	18	8/4	7.10.0	
Lumpkin, Jacob (orphan)	681	6/3	212.16.3	
Lewis, Iveson	356	14/6	258.2.0	
Leigh, Lucy	101	24/10	125.8.2	
Leigh, John est.	133	"	165.2.10	
Leigh, Richard est.	560	6/3	175.0.0	
Mitchell, Ralph est.	193	10/5	100.10.5	
Mitchell, Sally	391	13/	254.3.0	
Mitchell, James (orphan)	225	"	146.5.0	
Moore, Lambeth	20	4/2	4.3.4}	
Do. of John Holderby	26¾	"	5.11 5½}	
Do. of Kidd & Morris	60	"	12.10.0}	
Moore, Benjamin	100	"	20.16.8	
			1918.3.6	
Moore, Lodowick, John & Richard	100	3/2	15.16.8	
Major, Josiah	200	4/2	41.13.4	
Mitchell, John est.	270	5/3	70.17.0}	
do. Rootes	128	9/11	63.9.3}	
Mann, Joseph Sen[r.]	231	6/3	72.3.9	
Moore, Aggathy	40	4/2	8.6.8	
Montague, William	170	"	35.8.4	
Meredith, Ralph G. est.	462	14/6	334.19.0	
Muire, Richard	93	12/6	58.2.6}	
do. John Leigh's est.	66	24/10	81.19.0}	
Moore, Richard est.	145	6/3	45.6.8	
McCarty, Joseph est.	73	3/2	11.11.2	
Metcalfe, Thomas	256	"	181.8.8	
Maderias, John	34½	6/3	10.15.7½	
Milby, Richard	175	3/2	27.14.2	
Morgan, William	3	6/3	0.18.9	
Moore, John	37	4/2	7.14.2	
Newcomb, William	169	3/2	26.15.2}	
do. Benj[a.] Dillard est.	148	5/3	48.17.0}	
Orvill, John	100	6/3	31.5.0	
Oliver, John	320	5/3	84.0.0	
			3177.5.4	

[page 8, List A, 1803] Persons Names Owning Lands	Quantity of land	Price per acre	Total Amount Land	Amt. Tax Thereon in Dols. Cents
Overstreet, Gabriel est.	296	4/2	61.13.4}	
do. Haynes	130	5/3	34.2.6}	
Oaks, Henry	198½	3/2	34.2.0	
Oaks, William	80	4/2	16.13.4	
Oliver, William	59	"	12.5.10	
Oaks, Ann	60	"	12.10.0	
Pitts, Benjamin G.	100	5/4	26.13.4	
Pace, Benjamin est.	263	7/3	95.6.9	
Pynes, Benjamin est.	164	6/3	51.5.0	
Pynes, Robert	111½	"	34.13.9	
Pynes, Benjamin	100	"	31.5.0	
Pemberton, John	165	"	51.11.3	
Pemberton, Philip est.	121	"	37.17.6	
Pollard, Robert	6	24/10	7.9.0}	
do. John O'Mealy's	367	30/	550.10.0}	
Palmer, Charles	107¾	18/	96.19.6	
Price, Robert	399	6/3	124.13.9	
Pigg, John est.	324	14/6	234.18.0}	
Ditto	180	7/3	65.5.0}	
Pierce, Philip	83	3/2	13.2.10	
Pierce, Beverley	25¾	4/2	5.7.3½}	
do. Philip Pierce	17	3/2	2.13.10}	
Pierce, Thomas est.	87	4/2	18.2.6	
Palmer, Roger	314	6/	94.4.0	
			1713.5.3	
Roane, Thomas est.	2033	18/8	1897.9.4}	
do. H. Carlton	200	6/3	63.10.0}	
do. Brett's	34¾	18/	31.5.6}	
do. Ro. Pynes	24½	6/3	7.9.1½}	
Rowe, Elizabeth	665	20/9	689.18.9	
Rowe, Francis (orphan)	612½	4/8	142.16.[0]	
Richason, Elias est.	86	4/2	17.8.4	
Rowe, William & Moses	60	6/3	18.15.0	
Richards, John	571	4/8	124.8.0	
Richeson, James	180	4/2	37.10.0	
Richeson, William	369½	"	76.17.6	
Roane, Thomas (Middlesex)	14¼	15/	10.13.9	
Richason, William Jun[r.]	118½	5/3	31.2.1½}	
do. of Ro. Stone	101	4/2	21.0.10}	
Richason, John est.	101½	5/3	26.12.10½	
Roane, Major est.	687½	3/8	128.18.1½	
do. John Lyne est.	455¾	6/3	142.8.5¼}	
do. Palmer	9	7/3	3.5.3}	
Raines, Giles	60	3/2	9.10.0	
Robinson, Benjamin est.	1300	8/4	541.13.4	
			5735.7.6	

[page 9, List A, 1803] Persons Names Owning Lands	Quantity of land [147]	Price per acre	Total Amount Land	Amt. Tax Thereon in Dols. Cents
Roane, Charles	133	19/	126.7.0}	
do. Dragon swamp	70	17/	59.10.0}	
Roy, Beverley	700	8/4	291.13.4}	
do. T. Browns	454	12/6	283.15.0}	
do. Corbins	125	"	78.2.6}	
Richason, James Jun[r.]	250	5/3	65.12.6	
Rowsey, William	88	7/3	31.18.0	
Spencer, Susanna & John	416	"	150.16.0	
Spencer, John	34	"	12.6.6	
Spencer, Ann	116	"	60.3.6	
Starke, Richard est.	350	5/8	99.3.4	
Stone, Robert est.	99	4/2	20.12.6	
Stone, Robert	31½	5/3	8.5.4½	
Stone, Job	100	"	20.16.8	
Smith, John (son of Rob[t.])	88	"	45.16.8}	
do. Dragon Swamp	12	17/	10.8.0}	
Smith, Francis	150	3/2	23.5.0	
Simpkins, Young	60	"	9.10.0	
Sears, Philip	83	4/2	17.5.10	
Shackelford, William est.	400	14/6	310.0.0	
Spencer, Thomas	300	10/5	158.5.0}	
Ditto	225	4/2	53.2.6}	
Ditto	117	6/9	39.9.9}	
Seward, Benjamin	115	3/2	18.4.2	
Smith, Thomas G.	485	14/6	351.12.6	
			2346.1.7	
Sadler, John	150	6/3	46.17.6	
Shackelford, Zachariah	200	"	62.10.0	
Shackelford, John (R)	401¼	8/4	167.3.10	
Shackelford, William	151	6/3	47.3.9}	
do. Wyatt's lease	30	5/3	7.16.6}	
Shackelford, John (Mc)	283	6/2	87.5.2}	
do. John Collier (Cobler)	150	5/3	39.7.6}	
Shackelford, Benjamin	189	7/3	67.0.0}	
do. Halyard's lease	1	5/9½	0.5.9½}	
Shepherd, John	67	6/	20.2.0	
Smith, John Doct[r.]	½	30/	15.0	
Spencer, Meacham	323	6/9	109.0.3	
Southern, John	15½	4/2	3.4.7	
Sears, Thomas	123	6/7	40.9.9}	
do. H. Williams	42¼	4/2	8.17.1}	
Smith, Robert Jun[r.]	30	10/5	15.12.6}	
do. Dragon Swamp	8	17/	6.14.0}	
Tureman, Elizabeth	24¾	3/2	3.18.4½	
Tureman, Benjamin est.	70	3/2	11.1.8	
Tureman, George	50	"	7.18.4	
Taliaferro, William	1000	14/6	725.0.0	
			3824.7.2	

[page 10, List A, 1803] Persons Names Owning Lands	Quantity of land	Price per acre	Total Amount Land	Amt. Tax Thereon in Dols. Cents
Townley, Robert	200	6/3	62.10.0}	
do. Anderson's	117	14/6	84.16.6}	
Taliaferro, Philip est.	662	8/4	275.16.8	
Taliaferro, James B.	374½	12/6	234.7.6}	
Thurston, Armistead	111 1/3	4/3	23.15.1	
Thurston, Batchelder	200	3/2	31.13.4	
Turner, Benjamin	36	4/2	7.10.0	
Townley, Ann	79	"	16.9.2	
Turner, Henry est.	100	"	20.16.8	
Tunstall, Richard G.	206½	7/10	73.3.7	
Taylor, William	40	6/3	12.10.0}	
do. P. Taliaferro est.	200	8/4	83.6.8}	
Trice, Kitty White	82	5/3	21.10.6	
Watts, Edward est.	250	7/3	90.12.6}	
do. W. Watts est.	113	5/	28.5.0}	
Watts, John	293	7/10	114.15.2}	
do. Pembertons	45	6/3	14.1.3}	
Watts, Kauffman	270	5/3	70.17.6}	
do. Eubank & Burch	257	5/9	73.17.9}	
do. Jn°. & Danl. Hemmingway	312	4/2	64.3.0}	
Watts, James	350	"	72.8.4}	
do. W. Watts est.	60	15/	45.0.0}	
Williams, Howard	181½	4/2	37.16.3	
do. Dragon Swamp	43	17/	36.11.0}	
Wyatt, Thomas	206	7/10	81.2.0}	
do. Boughtons	60	3/2	9.10.0}	
			1687.5.5	
Wyatt, William	48¾	7/3	17.1.3	
Williams, Montague	300	6/3	93.15.0	
Williams, Charles est.	336	4/2	70.0.0	
Walton, James	80	"	16.13.4}	
do. Thoˢ. Walton's est.	66	"	13.15.0}	
Walton, Elizabeth	60	3/2	9.10.0	
Walton, John est.	176	5/3	46.4.0	
Walton, William est.	66	4/2	13.15.0	
Ware, John est.	75	5/3	19.13.9	
Ware, Arther estate	83	4/2	17.5.10	
Waring, Robert P. est.	542	10/9	291.10.6	
Walden, Richard est.	180	10/5	93.15.0	
Walden, Lewis est.	150	3/2	23.15.0}	
do. T. Dudleys	84½	6/3	28.[3].3½}	
Williams, George	40	4/2	8.6.8	
Watkins, Philip	197	5/3	51.14.3	
Wyatt, Richard	175	12/6	109.7.6	
Ware, Robert Junʳ. est.	100	4/2	20.16.8	
Williams, Elizabeth	16½	3/2	2.12.9	
White, James est.	200	6/3	62.10.0	
			2697.0.2	

[page 11, List A, 1803] Persons Names Owning Lands	Quantity of land	Price per acre	Total Amount Land	Amt. Tax Thereon in Dols. Cents
	[148]			
Wedderburn, Lydia	350	"	109.7.6	
Whiting, Beverley est.	2447¾	7/10	866.18.9	
Webley, John est.	173	5/3	45.8.3}	
do. Collier & Dillard	358	4/2	74.11.8}	
Ware, Robert Jun$^{r.}$	100	8/4	41.13.4	
Ware, William	100	"	41.13.4	
Walden, Benjamin	373	5/3	97.18.3	
Waller, Edward est.	133½	3/2	21.2.9	
Waller, George est.	87	"	13.15.6}	
do. Jn$^{o.}$ Shackelfords	47¾	8/4	19.17.11}	
Waller, John	65	3/7	11.12.11	
Waller, Robert est.	48	3/7	8.12.0}	
do. Groom's est.	187	3/2	29.12.2}	
Ware, Nicholas	100	"	15.16.8	
Walton, Beverley	47½	7/10	18.12.1	
Watts, George K.	36	26/	46.16.0	
Wyatt, Smith	29¾	7/3	10.15.8	
Willis, Robert	105	14/6	75.2.6	
Williams, Christopher	100	5/3	25.5.0	
			1574.12.3	
			[44599.15.4]	

Richd. T. Shackelford, C[ommr. Reve]nue

$713.58 [Land]

[arithmetic omitted]

[cover]

King & Queen
R. Shackleford
Land
1803
26 Ap. 1804
added & stated
entd.

A List of Land within the District of Robert B. Hill, Commissioner in the upper District in the County of King and Queen for the year 1803 to wit

LIST B

[page 1, List B, 1803] Persons names owning Land	Quantity of Land	Price per acre	Tot. Amt. Value Land	Rents
	[149]			
Atkins, Joseph Esta.	66	4/2	£13.15.0	
Alexander, Benjamin	202	9/4	94.5.4	
Do. of James Halbert	124	6/2	38.15.0	
Lott in Dunk[k.], an[l.] rent				£20
Do. of Jos. Meede Do.			4.10.0	
Acre, Seeton	52	9/4	24.5.4	
Alexander, Elisha	338	9/4	157.14.8	
Anderson, Churchill	636	7/3	230.11.0	
Atkins, John	135	4/6	30.7.6	
Abbott, Jacob	112	7/10	43.17.4	
Anderson, Sarah	86	20/9	89.3.9	
Barton, John Este.	125	4/2	26.0.10	
Bray, James	118½	7/10	46.4.4	
Broach, Benoni	48	10/5	25.4.0	
Brown, Henry Jun[r.]	100	12/-	60.0.0	
Beverley, Robert Este.	2444	10/5	1262.16.4	
Brown, Henry	570	7/4½	210.3.9	
Bland, John	83	8/4	34.11.8	
Bates, James	358	11/	149.3.4	
Do.	42	4/2	8.15.0	
Do. of Rice Garnett	89	7/3	32.5.3	
Braxton, Carter	484½	10/5	252.6.10	
Brooking, Frances	930	10/5	484.7.6	
Boughton, Thomas (Essex)	130	9/4	60.13.4	
Boughton, John	200	8/4	83.6.8	
Boughton, Henry (Essex)	88	6/3	27.10.0	
Burton, John	170	5/3	44.12.6	
Bohannon, Ann Este.	197	4/6	44.6.6	
Brown, William	18¼	3/2	2.17.9½	
Do. of Ware's Exors. &c.	196½	7/3	71.4.7½	
Bagby, John Este.	330	7/3	119.12.9	
Bagby, Richard	260	"	94.5.0	
Bagby, Thomas	260	"	94.5.0	
Do. of Jacob Lumpkin	235	6/3	73.8.9	
Brizendine, Armistead	86 2/3	8/4	35.17.6	
Bromley, John	60	7/10	23.10.0	
Broach, William	20	7/10	7.16.8	
			$4102.10.10	£20.

[page 2, List B, 1803] Persons names owning Land	Quantity of Land	Price per acre	Tot. Amt. Value Land	Rents
Brown, John	50	7/4½	£18.8.9	
Bohannan, William	163	5/3	42.15.9	
Bates, William	81	7/9½	31.10.1	
Do. of Rice Garnett	117	7/3	42.8.4	
Broach, George	32½	14/6	23.11.3	
Do. of Hill and Uxor.	43¼	14/6	31.7.1½	
Beadles, Justin	20	6/3	6.5.0	
Boulware, Samuel	175¾	31/3	274.12.2¼	
Crafton, Thomas	119	9/4	55.10.8	
Crafton, James	59	"	27.10.8	
Crafton, John	117½	"	54.12.0	
Crane, John	130	6/3	40.2.6	
Do. of Clem Pynes	14	3/2	2.4.4	
" of Ware's Este.	49¼	7/3	17.17.0¾	
" of Ware's Exors. &c.	71	"	29.14.9	
Cleverius, Benjamin	419	20/9	434.14.3	
Carlton, John	257	14/6	186.6.6	
Cole, G. Thomas	105	6/3	32.16.3	
Carlton, Lewis	100	8/4	41.3.4	
Do. of H. Carlton's Este.	150	7/10	58.15.0	
Clayton, Thomas Este.	275	7/3	99.13.9	
Crane, George Este.	30	7/3	10.17.6	
Courtney, Thomas	156	7/10	61.2.0	
Carlton, Joel	53½	6/3	16.4.5	
Cooke, Moses	100	8/4	41.13.4	
Cooke, Ambrose	100	8/4	41.13.4	
Chapman, M. George	250	7/10	87.18.4	
Courtney, Robert	183½	7/10	71.17.5	
Cannaday, William	100	6/3	31.5.0	
Cooke, William	65	5/5	17.12.1	
Cooke, James	65	8/9	28.8.9	
Courtney, Fanny & Children	78	7/10	30.10.0	
Cooke, William	65	5/5	17.12.1	
Cross, Joseph	103½	6/3	32.6.10½	
Campbell, William	868¼	7/3	314.14.9¾	
Campbell, Whitaker	406	7/10	159.0.4	
Crow, John	121	5/3	31.19.2¼	
Crow, Nathaniel Este.	60	6/3	18.15.0	
Crouch, Edmund	74¼	7/10	29.1.9	
Campbell, John, of E. Hill	74¼	18/8	69.6.0	
Cauthorn, Vincent, of W.B. Tunstall	10	8/4	4.3.4	
Do. of T.C. Tunstall	33	"	13.15.0	
Crane, Nathaniel	66	3/2	10.9.0	
Carlton, Thomas	297	7/10	116.6.6	
Dew, Thomas	331	12/6	206.17.6	
Dew, William Este.	935	14/6	677.17.6	
			£3665.18.6	15.23.2

[page 3, List B, 1803] Persons names owning Land	Quantity of Land	Price per acre	Tot. Amt. Value Land	
	[150]			
Duling, William Este.	264	8/4	£110.0.0	
Dix, Gabriel	338	6/3	105.12.6	
Deshazo, William Jun$^{r.}$	60	4/2	12.10.0	
Durham, Joseph	105	4/3	21.12.6	
Do. of Dunn	10	4/2	2.1.8	
Deshazo, John	188	7/4	68.18.8	
Deshazo, Larkin	87	7/3	31.4.10	
Do. of John Crane	6	6/3	1.17.6	
Do. of Benjamin Hoomes	430¾	4/4	93.4.5	
Dunbar, David	366	8/4	152.10.0	
Dudley, Peter Este.	530	7/3¼	186.18.4	
Dalley, George	174¼	3/2	27.11.9½	
Durham, John	25	3/2	3.19.4	
Dickie, James	512	8/4	213.6.8	
Deshazo, Unity	71	7/10	27.16.3	
Deshazo, Polly (orphan)	41	"	16.1.2	
Dally, John Este.	200	3/2	31.13.4	
Dobbins, Charles Este.	147	5/3	38.11.9	
Dobson, Pitman	136	10/2¾	69.5.4	
Eubank, Henry	171	5/3	44.17.9	
Edwards, Thomas	66	4/2	13.15.0	
Evans, Ambrose	195	7/10	56.10.0	
Eubank, James	111	10/2¾	56.10.9¾	
Eubank, Peter	127	"	67.13.9¾	
Eubank, William	130	"	69.4.6	
Eubank, John	136	"	69.5.4	
Fogg, James	120	6/3	37.10.0	
Fleet, William	512	12/	307.4.0	
Fogg, Frederick	298	8/4	124.3.4	
Fauntleroy, G. Samuel	2069	20/	2069.0.0	
Do. of P.A. Blackburn &c.	57 1/3	20/9	59.9.8	
" of Fran$^{s.}$ Anderson	28 2/3	20/9	29.14.10	
Fox, S. Joseph of H. Brown	158	7/4	57.18.8	
Do. of T. Garnett	28	7/10	10.19.4	
" of T. Cleaveley	39	"	15.5.6	
" of Pollard	94	7/3	31.1.6	
Fogg, Thomas	223	10/2¾	114.9.1¼	
Falkner, Thomas	220	6/3	68.15.0	
Grafton, Sally & Ann	132	9/4	61.12.0	
Gayle, John	264	7/5	97.18.0	
Do. of William Gayle	7¼	"	2.13.11	
Gatewood, Chaney	829	10/5	437.17.11	
Do. Noell's	362½	14/6	262.16.3	
" Harwood's	125	4/2	46.17.6	
" Eubank's	300	14/3	217.10.0	
" Walden's Este.	120	12/6	75.0.0	
" W$^{m.}$ Lyne, Lott in Dunk$^{k.}$, anl. rent			~~33.0.0~~	£30.
" Samuel Roane	1070	17/2	913.8.4	
Garnett, Joshua Este.	325	8/4	134.3.4	
Gatewood, Joseph	445	10/5	231.15.5	___
18.25.25.18			$6999.16.10	£33.

[page 4, List B, 1803] Persons names owning Land	Quantity of Land	Price per acre	Tot. Amt. Value Land	
Gayle, Matthew Este.	323	11/5	£184.7.7	
Gatewood, John	160	8/4	66.13.4	
Garnett, Reuben	656½	8/10	289.19.1	
Do. of Halbert &c.	28	10/5	14.12.10	
" of Gatewood & wife	50	10/5	26.0.10	
Garnett, M. Reuben	220	8/10	97.3.4	
Gwathmey, Temple	600	35/3	1057.10.0	
Garlick, Samuel	454	24/10	463.14.4	
Garlick, John Este.	839	29/	1216.11.0	
Griffith, Thomas	22¾	6/3	7.0.7½	
Griffith, Joseph Este.	22¾	"	7.0.7½	
Gresham, Samuel	432½	7/3	156.15.7½	
Do. of Rice Garnett	157	"	56.18.1	
Guthrie, William	91¼	7/5	33.14.7	
Gaines, Harry Este.	481½	20/4	489.10.6	
Gaines, B. Robert	481½	"	489.10.6	
Gresham, Thomas Este.	455¼	6/8	151.13.4	
Griffith, Milly	50	6/3	15.12.6	
Graves, Thomas	66¼	7/3	23.18.6	
Gresham, Lumpkin	233	"	85.3.9	
Gresham, William Junr.	242 1/3	8/4	101.5.0	
Do. of Wm. Gatewood	46	3/2	7.5.8	
" of Chick	69	7/3	25.0.3	
Gresham, George	141	3/2	22.6.6	
Gatewood, William (*Tucko.*)	33	3/2	5.4.6	
Gleason, Patrick	134	8/4	55.16.8	
Gatewood, Gabriel	78	10/5	40.12.6	
Gayle, William	344	7/5	127.11.4	
Garnett, Henry	140	7/3	50.15.0	
Do. Lott in D'Kirk anl. rent			~~70.0.0~~	40.
Hill, William Este.	1267	14/6	918.4.3	
Hawes, Walker	97	"	70.6.6	
Hitchcock, Thomas	140	4/2	29.3.4	
Hoskins, Samuel Este.	345	6/3	107.16.3	
Do. of Elisha Alexander	57	10/5	25.13.9	
Hutchason, Charles Este.	531	7/1	188.1.3	
Heskew, John Este.	61	5/3	16.0.3	
Heskew, John Junr. Este.	50	6/3	15.12.6	
Do. of Clem Pynes	10	3/2	1.11.8	
Do. of Larkin Deshazo	19¼	4/4	4.2.4	
Hill, Edward	1125¾	18/8	1050.14.0	
Hoskins, John	767	10/5	399.9.7	
Do. Boughtons	100	8/4	41.13.4	
" of Fleet & Semple	2	10/5	1.0.10	
" of Semple	18 1/8	10/5	9.8.9½	
Hurt, West	14	5/3	3.3.6	
Holt, William	123	14/3	87.12.9	
Hutchason, John	73¼	8/9	32.0.11¼	
Howerton, George	76¼	6/	22.17.6	
	21.22.25.18		$8[394].1.8	£40.

[page 5, List B, 1803] Persons names owning Land	Quantity of Land	Price per acre	Tot. Amt. Value Land	Rents
	[151]			
Hall, Corbin	72	4/2	£15.0.0	
Hill, B. Robert	322	8/2	131.9.8	
Hill, Richard	277	8/2	113.2.2	
Hill, G. Mary	360	"	147.0.0	
Hill, Robert Este.	420	"	171.10.0	
Hoomes, John, Lott in D'Kirk, rent			~~30.0.0~~	£30.
Hoskins, Thomas	55	8/2	22.9.2	
Jones, John Este.	300	8/11	133.15.0	
Jeffries, Edward	70	3/2	11.1.8	
Jeffries, Ambrose	237	7/10	92.16.6	
Jeffries, Robert	110	7/6	41.5.0	
Do. of L. Gresham	10	7/3	3.12.6	
" of Jacob Lumpkin	5	7/3	1.16.3	
" of Lumpkin Gresham	20	7/3	7.5.0	
Jones, James Este.	160	14/6	116.0.0	
Do.	196	10/5	102.1.8	
Jones, Rawleigh Este.	63	31/1	93.18.3	
Do. of Wm. Jones Este.	135¾	17/10	121.0.10½	
Jeffries, John Este.	100	7/10	39.3.4	
Johnson, Thomas	72	3/2	11.8.0	
Kemp, John	178	7/3	64.2.2	
Keeling, Mary	78½	8/	31.8.0	
Kay, Christopher	116	6/3	36.6.0	
Do. of T. Gouldman	416½	9/	107.8.6	
Lumpkin, James	213	7/10	83.8.2	
Lumpkin, Henry	400	9/4	186.13.4	
Lumpkin, John Este.	125	6/3	35.11.3	
Lumpkin, William Este.	61½	13/6	41.10.3	
Lafon, Francis	119	8/4	49.11.8	
Lankford, Thomas Este.	100	4/2	20.16.8	
Lumpkin, Robert Senr.	374	8/4	155.16.8	
Lumpkin, Henry Junr.	190	9/4	88.13.4	
Lumpkin, W. John Este.	140	7/10	54.16.8	
Do. of John Ware's Este.	118½	7/3	42.15.6	
Longest, Caleb	97	7/10	37.19.10	
Longest, Richard	227¾	"	89.4.2	
Longest, John	100	"	39.3.4	
Lumpkin, Anthony Este.	216	6/3	67.10.0	
Lumpkin, Robert Junr.	279¾	5/3	73.8.8¼	
Lumpkin, Wilson	122½	9/4	57.3.4	
Lumpkin, William Junr.	183¼	10/5	95.6.3	
Lumpkin, John	112	3/2	17.14.8	
Lyne, William	1480	8/4	610.14.2	
Lumpkin, Richard	57½	5/3	15.1.10½	
Longest, William	83	8/4	34.11.8	
Lumpkin, Ann	47	13/6	31.14.6	
Lumpkin, Elizabeth	51	13/6	34.8.6	
Lumpkin, John, Kg. Wm.	105	13/6	70.17.6	
	16.22.21.19		£3650.0.8	£30.

[page 6, List B, 1803] Persons names owning Land	Quantity of Land	Price per acre	Tot. Amt. Value Land	
Motley, Edwin	815	10/5	£428.2.6	
Do. of Semple & wife	149	12/6	93.2.6	
Martin, C. Thomas	583	14/6	422.13.6	
Do.	134½	7/3	48.15.1½	
Minor, William	149	8/4	62.1.8	
Minor, John	137	"	57.1.8	
Minor, Thomas Este.	288	7/10	112.16.0	
Moody, Lewis	239	7/10	93.12.2	
Mann, Joseph Junr.	400	8/4	166.13.4	
Do. of Crows	140	6/3	43.15.0	
Mitchell, John	50	6/3	15.12.6	
Mann, Robert Este.	699	6/3	218.8.9	
Merideth, Samuel	215	7/10	84.4.2	
Macon, John Este.	1092	16/7	905.9.0	
Do. Lotts in D'Kirk rent			~~40.0.0~~	£40.
Mann, Mary	100	5/3	26.5.0	
Martin, John	475	9/	213.15.0	
Do. of Fogg	197	6/3	61.11.3	
Mahon, Thomas	101	6/3	31.11.3	
Mahon, William	103½	6/3	32.3.9	
Mahon, Benjamin	43¼	5/3	11.7.0¾	
Nunn, Moses	318	7/4½	117.5.3	
Nunn, Thomas	130	7/3	47.2.6	
Do. of Brizendine	49	4/3	10.8.3	
Newbill, William	1060	8/4	441.13.4	
Newell, John Este.	100	7/10	39.3.4	
Nash, John Este.	100	6/3	31.5.0	
Noell, Phil & Skelton, Reuben & Thos.	275	8/4	114.11.8	
Owen, Augustine Este.	100	6/3	£31.5.0	
Pendleton, James	888½	8/7½	383.3.3¾	
Do. Wilmore's	70	7/6	26.5.0	
" Wm. McIntosh	125	4/2	26.1.10	
Pitts, David	420	9/4	196.0.0	
Pitts, Obadiah	20	10/5	10.8.4	
Phillips, James	230	7/3	83.7.6	
Pollard, John Este.	235	9/4	109.13.4	
Do. of Leonard Smithy	384	7/3	139.4.0	
Prewitt, Frances	99	9/4	46.4.0	
Parker, John	761¼	8/4	317.3.9	
Prewitt, Richard	102	7/3	36.12.3	
Pendleton, Philip	360	9/2	165.0.0	
Do. Lott in D'Kirk, anl. rent			~~3.0.0~~	£3.
Perryman, Philip	218	7/2	78.2.4	
Do. of George Dillard & wife	215	7/2	77.0.10	
Pynes, Clement	99	3/2	15.13.6	
Pollard, Richard	389	8/4	162.1.8	
Pendleton, Benjamin Este.	450	7/10	176.5.0	
	14.16.22.19		£6010.2.2	£43.

[page 7, List B, 1803] Persons names owning Land	Quantity of Land	Price per acre	Tot. Amt. Value Land	
	[152]			
Perryman, Richard	110	7/3	£39.7.6	
Prewitt, Tunstall	58½	8/	23.8.0	
Pollard, Joseph	200	6/3	62.10.0	
Pollard, Rich^d.^ & Brown, Henry	50	8/	20.0.0	
Quarles, W. Francis	154	17/2	£132.1.8	
Do. Lott in D'Kirk, anl. rent			~~9.0.0~~	£9.
Rowe, G. Thomas (orphan) decd.	555	7/3	201.3.9	
Row, Richard Este.	450	8/4	188.0.0	
Roane, Spencer	954	24/10	1184.11.0	
Ryland, Joseph	487½	7/3	176.10.9	
Ryland, Josiah	160	7/10	62.13.4	
Do. of Wm. Temple	27½	15/	20.12.6	
Do. of Prince's Este.	113	7/10	44.5.2	
" of H. Brown	34½	7/4½	12.14.1¼	
Riddle, Vaughan	188	5/5	49.7.0	
Roane, Thomas	920¾	17/2	790.8.2½	
Row, Handsford	160½	6/3	50.3.1½	
Row, Wilson	160½	"	50.3.1½	
Redd, James	200	7/3	72.10.0	
Row, Ovil	55½	9/4	25.18.0	
Smith, William	53	7/10	20.15.2	
Do. of James Smith's Este.	25	3/2	3.19.2	
Segar, Richard	406	7/3	147.3.6	
Satterwhite, George	164	6/3	51.5.0	
Satterwhite, William	118	5/7½	33.3.9	
Schools, John	156	8/4	65.0.0	
Do. of Parker & wife	35	"	14.11.8	
Schools, Gabriel Este.	174	6/3	54.7.6	
Skelton, William	362	8/2½	148.11.5	
Do. of Phil Perryman	12	7/2	4.6.0	
Smith, John (D^e.^)	190	7/6	71.5.0	
Starling, Roderick	360	7/10	141.0.0	
Do.	313	8/2	127.16.2	
" of Wm. Lyne	56½	8/4	23.6.8	
" of H. Walker	46	5/3	12.1.6	
Saunders, George	200	7/3	70.10.8	
Do. of Wyatts &c.	115	7/10	45.0.10	
Shepherd, William	140	9/4	65.6.8	
Smith, Molly	30	4/2	6.5.0	
Smith, John Junr.	42½	5/3	11.3.1½	
Smith, Lewis	96	7/6	36.0.0	
Swinton, Ann	750	13/6	506.5.0	
Stone, Sarah	300	7/3	108.15.0	
Stone, Daniel	52	3/2	8.4.8	
Smith, Larkin	1254¼	31/1	1949.6.3½	
Smith, Henry	400	6/3	130.0.0	
12.15.18.17			£7061.17.0	£9.

[page 8, List B, 1803] Persons names owning Land	Quantity of Land	Price per acre	Tot. Amt. Value Land
Smith, Ambrose	92¾	8/4	£38.6.8
Stevens, George Este.	430	7/10	168.8.4
Stevens, George orphan	75	"	29.8.4
Smith, William Este. (Mill)	200	3/2	31.13.4
Shackelford, John Este.	114	7/3	40.8.2
Shepherd, John	192	3/2	31.1.8
Stone, William	74¼	3/2	11.15.3½
Sthreshley, William	155½	6/3	48.11.10
Schools, George	200	8/4	83.6.8
Smith, John, of J. Garlick	54	29/	78.6.0
Smith, Jane, of J. Smith's Este.	25	3/2	3.19.2
Smith, Philip (orphan) of Do.	12½	"	1.19.7
Smith, James	101	7/10	39.11.2
Do. of James Smith's Este.	12½	3/2	1.19.7
Scott, Anderson	330	16/7	273.12.6
Do. of P. Anderson's Este.	248	20/9	257.6.0
" of C. Anderson & wife	96	"	99.12.0
Semple, B. Robert	235	10/5	122.6.3½
Do. of Spencer Roane	155	24/10	192.9.2
Stewart, James	120	9/2	55.0.0
Trice, William Este.	140	7/3	50.15.0
Taylor, James	50	6/3	15.12.6
Taylor, Edmund	294	8/14	122.10.0
Temple, Joseph	918	10/5	478.2.6
Tunstall, Richard Jun[r.] Este.	1097	7/3	397.13.3
Temple, William	402¼	15/	301.17.6
Temple, John	42	31/3	65.12.6
Temple, Humphrey Este.	100	15/	75.0.0
Do. of J. Tunstall	200	18/8	185.16.8
" of R. Tunstall &c.	574	21/	602.14.0
Tunstall, Rich[d.] (Purdy) Este.	222½	8/4	50.16.8
Tunstall, C. Thomas	104	8/4	43.6.8
Upshaw, James (Essex)	125	8/10	55.4.2
Do. of R. Beverley	30	10/5	15.12.6
Wilson, Isaac Este.	200	6/3	62.10.0
Wilson, Benjamin Esta.	200	7/3	72.10.0
Watkins, Joseph	63	6/7	20.14.9
Do. of Wiltshire's Este.	71	7/3	26.19.9
Walker, Philip	110	9/4	51.6.8
Walker, Humphrey	820	33/2	1355.14.2
Wright, William	130	5/3	33.12.6
Willis, Joel	94	7/10	35.5.0
Do. of W[m.] Jones' Este.	140¼	17/10	125.1.1½
14.22.19.19			5853.4.7

[page 9, List B, 1803] Persons names owning Land	Quantity of Land	Price per acre	Tot. Amt. Value Land	
	[153]			
Wright, Edward	567	6/3	£177.3.9	
Whayne, William	154½	7/10	60.10.3	
Wyatt, George	122	7/6	45.15.0	
Webb, James	147¾	4/2	30.15.8	
Wheeley, Carriol Este.	37¼	7/3	13.10.0¾	
Watkins, Joseph Jun[r.]	93¼	8/4	38.17.1	
Wyatt, Robert	50	7/3	18.2.6	
Watkins, John	152	8/4	63.6.8	
Watkins, Philip	107	4/2	22.5.10	
White, Henry	57	13/6	38.9.6	
Young, Henry	640	18/8	597.6.8	
			£1106.3.--	[£175.]
			[46843.15.3]	

Ro. B. Hill, Commr.

[arithmetic omitted]

[cover]
Ro. B. Hills Land Tax
Book for 1803 from
King & Queen for
The Auditor

[cover]
King & Queen
Rob: Hill
Land & propy.
1803
[9] Merchts. $135.95 entd.
29 Sep: 1803
entd.
Stated
added

A list of land within the district of Benjamin Shackelford,
Commissioner in the county of King & Queen for the year 1804

LIST A

[page 1, List A, 1804] Persons names owning land	Quantity of land [155]	Price per acre	Total Amount Land	Amt. Tax Thereon in Dols. Cents
Atkins, Lewis	60	8/4	25.0.0	
Anderson, Francis	348	10/9	187.3.8}	
do. Richard T. Shackelford	26	8/4	12.1.8}	
Anderson, Beverley	203½	3/2	32.4.5	
Adams, William	53¾	6/3	16.15.11¼	
Brown, Samuel	33¼	4/3	7.1.2	
Banks, William est.	365	4/2	76.0.0	
Brooke, Richard	1539¾	29/	2232.12.9	
Brumley, Robert	225	5/3	59.1.3	
Bird, William est.	532	7/3	197.17.0}	
do. Dragon Swamp	88½	17/	70.4.6}	
Bird, Philemon	1638¼	6/3	511.19.0¾	
Brett, Nancy	50	18/	45.0.0	
Burch, James	183	6/3	57.3.9	
Burch, Vincent	100	4/2	20.16.8}	
do. William Hoskins	50	3/3	7.18.4}	
Bird, Anth[y.] A.	275	"	43.10.10}	
do. William Montigue	44	4/2	9.3.4}	
Byne, John est.	336	"	70.0.0}	
do. Dragon Swamp	2¼	17/	1.18.3}	
Bird, Robert est.	780	24/10	993.6.8}	
do. Guy Smith	189½	3/2	30.0.10}	
Bourn, Richard est.	150	"	23.15.0	
Boyd, John	115	18/8	107.6.8}	
do. Sowne's	382	24/10	474.6.4}	
Bray, Richard est.	93	7/10	36.8.6	
Bird, John est.	71	3/2	11.4.10	
Bew, William est.	117	"	18.0.6	
Boyd, Robert	1119	9/3	517.10.3	
Boyd, William	300	15/	225.0.0}	
do. Frances Gains	367	14/6	266.1.6}	
Berkeley, Edmund est.	762	5/3	200.0.6	
Bland, John	60	12/6	37.10.0	
Bland, William	100	9/11	49.11.8	
Bourn, Mills	159½	5/3	41.14.3}	
do. Tho[s.] Jorden est.	33 1/4	4/2	6.18.10}	
			£6722.8.10	14.13.17.13

[page 2, List A, 1804] Persons names owning land	Quantity of land	Price per acre	Total Amount Land	Amt. Tax Thereon in Dols. Cents
Bullman, Ann	120	5/3	31.10.0	
Balote, Laban [Belote]	384½	4/2	80.2.6	
Bland, William Sen[r.]	225	3/8¼	41.9.8½	
Bland, Ralph	146	53	38.6.8}	
do. Finny & Buckner	170	4/2	35.8.4}	
Bowden, William	100	"	20.16.8}	
do. Sykes	34	3/2	5.7.8}	
Bland, William est.	250	4/2	52.1.8	
Bland, Thomas	412	3/2	75.4.8	
Brooks, Meriman	100	7/10	39.3.4	
Bowden, George	236	5/3	61.19.0}	
do. William Dillard's	30	4/2	6.5.0}	
Banks, James	22	7/3	7.19.6	
Bristow, Bartholomew	33½	3/2	5.6.1	
Bristow, George	100	"	15.16.8	
Banks, Andrew	125	12/6	78.2.6	
Brightwell, John est.	70	4/2	14.11.8	
Burton, James est.	89	"	18.10.10	
Bland, William (Younger)	300	7/3	108.15.0	
Bird, Janet & Frances	230	10/5	119.10.5}	
Do. Robert Smith (Dragon)	22½	17/	19.2.6}	
Breedlove, John	37¾	4/2	7.17.3½	
Brushwood, George	188	"	39.3.4}	
do. Wares	112	3/2	17.4.8}	
Bird, Parmenas	82	11/8	47.16.8	
Bray, Peter	51¼	6/3	16.0.3¾	
Bland, John	212	5/3	55.13.0	
Brooks, William	33	10/5	17.3.9	
Carlton, Thomas Sen[r.]	200	7/10	78.6.8}	
do. Philemon Bird	83½	6/3	26.1.10½}	
Carlton, Noah	100	7/10	39.3.4	
Cooke, Henry	260	5/3	68.5.0}	
do.	49¼	10/5	25.10.5}	
Carlton, John (S)	100	6/3	31.5.0	
Campbell, James T. (orphan)	296	12/6	185.0.0	
Carlton, Christopher Sen[r.]	37½	6/3	11.14.5}	
do. James Laughlin's	126½	3/2	26.8.2}	
Carlton, Richard est.	139	7/	48.13.0	
Cauthern, James	36½	3/2	5.15.7	
Collins, John est.	75	"	11.17.6	
			1634.10.4	165.23.[ ]

[page 3, List A, 1804] Persons names owning land	Quantity of land [156]	Price per acre	Total Amount Land	Amt. Tax Thereon in Dols. Cents
Carlton, William Sen$^{r.}$	309¾	11/6	178.1.2½	
Carlton, Christopher (Younger)	148	5/	37.0.0	
Carlton, Richard	250	7/3	90.12.6	
Carlton, Christopher Jun$^{r.}$	100	"	36.5.0}	
do. John Stone est.	159½	5/3	41.14.9}	
Cooper, Henry	50	4/2	10.8.4	
Carlton, Thomas (Taylor)	100	6/3	31.5.0	
Cardwell, James	150	4/2	31.5.0	
Cardwell, John	150	"	31.5.0	
Cardwell, William est.	77	"	15.11.6	
[Ca]rdwell, Thomas est.	110	"	22.18.4	
Cooke, John est.	300	"	62.10.0	
Collins, Thomas	281½	7/	98.10.6}	
do. Robert S. Ware	84½	11/9	49.12.10½}	
do. Metcalfe & Levert	289½	14/6	209.17.9}	
Carlton, John Jun$^{r.}$	235	4/2	48.19.2	
do. Baylor Fleet	2	12/6	1.5.0}	
Campbell, William	238	3/2	37.13.8	
Corbin, Richard	2390	11/1¾	1332.11.4}	
do. Shackelfords	300	12/6	78.2.6}	
do. Dixon's	416¾	15/5	321.10.10}	
Corr, James	100	6/2	30.16.8	
Crouch, James	105½	3/2	16.13.3½	
Collins, Joyeux	140	10/5	72.18.4	
Clayton, James	260	5/3	65.5.0	
Crittenden, Zachariah	34½	14/6	24.17.10	
Collier, John	100	4/2	20.16.8	
Cary, Wilson est.	1820	16/7	1509.1.8	
Campbell, James	130	5/9½	37.10.0}	
do. Richard Garrett	70	3/2	11.1.8}	
do. Benjamin Faulkner	55¼	7/3	20.0.6¾	
Crittenden, Richard est.	178	5/3	46.14.6	
Corr, Thomas R.	236½	"	62.1.7	
Collier, Joseph	468	"	112.17.0	
Collier, Benjamin	75	"	19.13.9	
Clegg, Isaiah est.	241	4/2	50.4.2	
Cooke, Dawson	78½	3/2	12.8.7	
do. Beverly Anderson	1	5/3	0.5.3	
			£4880.6.8	14.18.16.13

[page 4, List A, 1804] Persons names owning land	Quantity of land	Price per acre	Total Amount Land	Amt. Tax Thereon in Dols. Cents
Curry, John	155	4/	31.0.0	
Cooke, Thomas Sen$^{r.}$	240	3/2	38.0.0	
Cooke, Thomas Jun$^{r.}$	96	"	15.0.4	
Carlton, Humphrey	175	7/	61.5.0}	
do. John Watt's est.	48½	6/3	15.3.1½}	
Carlton, Thomas est.	235	"	73.8.9	
Corr, John Jun$^{r.}$ est.	503½	7/3	182.10.4½}	
do. Thomas Dudley's	197½	6/3	61.14.4½}	
Campbell, John	400	12/6	250.0.0	
do. Ralph G. Meredith est.	111½	14/6	80.16.9}	
Curry, James	70	4/2	14.11.8	
do. John Broach	71	"	14.15.10}	
do. Frances Webley	79	4/2	16.9.2}	
Corr, John Sen$^{r.}$	213	3/2	33.15.6}	
do. John Corr Jun$^{r.}$	90	7/3	32.12.6}	
Crittenden, Frances, River	105¾	14/6	76.12.2	
Clarke, John	144	5/	36.0.0}	
do. Samuel Hemingway	254½	4/2	53.0.3}	
Carlton, Lody	18½	3/2	2.15.7}	
Ditto	44	--	6.19.4}	
Cooke, John est.	100	"	15.16.8	
Clayton, Maria H., Sally K.} Clayton & Polly R. Clayton}	72	9/11	35.14.0	
Collins, Mason	110	3/2	17.8.4	
Didlake, William est.	100	"	15.16.8	
Didlake, Mary est.	278	8/4	115.16.8}	
do. John Gardner est.	173	6/9	53.7.9}	
Durham, Newman	50	4/2	10.8.4	
Dunn, Thomas	50½	6/3	15.15.7½	
Dillard, William Sen$^{r.}$	226	12/6	141.5.0	
Dillard, George	50	"	31.5.0	
Durham, Thomas est.	85	3/2	13.9.2	
Dickie, Barbara	1½	17/	1.5.6}	
do. Permenas Bird	50¼	11/8	29.6.3}	
do. W$^{m.}$ Bird Junr. Exr. Ro. Bird} & Beverley Roy & wife}	37½	17/	31.17.6}	
Dudley, William est.	290	14/6	210.5.0}	
do. Lydia Wedderburn	315½	6/3	98.11.10}	
			£1933.10.0	13.16.14.[ ]

[page 5, List A, 1804] Persons names owning land	Quantity of land [157]	Price per acre	Total Amount Land	Amt. Tax Thereon in Dols. Cents
Damm, John est.	55	"	17.3.9	
Dudley, James	180	7/10	70.10.0	
Daniel, John	109¾	4/2	22.17.3½	
Damm, William	25	"	5.4.2	
Douglas, John	239	7/	83.13.0	
Didlake, John	1200	7/3	435.0.0	
Dudley, Ann	141	"	51.2.3	
Dudley, Guilford	106	"	38.8.6	
Didlake, Edward	56	10/5	29.3.4	
Dudley, Banks est.	230	3/2	36.8.4	
Downey, Michael est.	50	10/5	26.0.10	
Didlake, Royston	206	3/6½	36.7.4	
Dillard, Thomas	49	15/	36.15.0	
Dillard, William Jun[r.]	207½	"	155.12.6	
Dudley, Thomas	70	6/3	21.17.6	
Dillard, Nicholas	75	4/2	15.12.6	
Drummond, John est.	150	6/3	46.17.6	
Davis, Stage	74	4/2	15.8.4}	
do. Eliz[a.] M. Davis	10	6/9	3.7.6}	
Dunn, John (Essex), draggon	73	17/	62.1.0	
Digges, Francis	175	5/3	45.13.9	
Dean, Benjamin	50	"	13.12.6	
Dillard, Thomas A.	29	3/2	4.11.10	
Durham, George est.	50	4/2	10.8.4	
Didlake, Philip	83	"	17.5.10	
Dabney, Benjamin	50	8/4	20.16.8	
Eubank, Richard est.	117	"	24.3.[9]	
Eubank, William est.	28¾	5/3	7.11.0	
Eubank, Richard Sen[r.]	196	7/	68.12.0	
Eubank, Thomas	110	4/2	22.18.4	
Eubank, Richard Jun[r.]	108¾	7/	38.1.1½}	
do. Thomas Jeffries	12¾	7/3	4.12.5}	
do. A. Dunn	147	5/3	38.11.9}	
Eubank, Warner	115	3/2	18.4.2}	
do. John Hemingway Jun[r.]	4	4/2	0.16.8}	
Fleet, Baylor	860	12/6	537.10.8	
Frazer, William est.	45	20/9	46.13.6	
Fleet, William	352	"	365.4.0	
			£2494.18.10	14.17.19.11

[page 6, List A, 1804] Persons names owning land	Quantity of land	Price per acre	Total Amount Land	Amt. Tax Thereon in Dols. Cents
Fisher, James est.	110	3/2	17.18.4	
Foster, Thomas	87¾	4/2	18.2.6	
Fauntleroy, Thomas	486	10/	243.0.0}	
do. Henry Todds	500	18/	450.0.0}	
do. William Bowdens	183	7/	64.1.0}	
Farinholtz, David	151¼	6/6	49.1.6	
Faulkner, Benjamin	100	4/2	20.16.8}	
do. Mary Faulkner	333	6/3	104.1.4}	
do. William Boyd	9½	10/5	4.10.9}	
do. Anthony Gardner	3	17/	2.11.0}	
do. John Southern	134½	4/2	28.0.5}	
do. James Campbell	29¾	7/3	10.15.8¼}	
do. Ditto Do.	112¼	4/2	23.7.8½}	
Fargerson, Thomas	62	10/5	32.5.10}	
do. Thomas Collins	48	7/	16.16.0}	
Faucett, Vincent	46½	10/5	24.4.4½	
Fisher, William	30	5/3	7.17.6	
Graves, Elinor	163½	5/3	42.18.4½	
Garlick, Camm est.	917	6/3	286.11.3	
Gresham, Philemon	200	"	62.10.0	
Gresham, Mary	100	7/10	39.3.4	
Gresham, William (B)	100	4/2	20.16.8}	
do. William Row	95	6/3	29.13.9}	
Gardner, Anthony	638	11/	350.11.8	
do. Dragon swamp	67½	17/	57.7.6	
do. Vincent Hart	73¾	6/6	23.19.4½	
Gardner, Elizabeth	100	6/3	31.5.0	
Gibson, Richard	156½	3/2	24.16.7	
Gibson, Eubank	56½	"	8.18.11}	
do. Rich[d.] Eubank Jun[r.]	3½	7/	1.4.6}	
Gibson, Philip	129½	3/2	20.9.3½	
Gresham, Meacham	100	5/3	26.5.0}	
do. of A. Gresham	4	17/	3.8.0}	
Gresham, Ambrose	80	5/3	21.0.0}	
do. Dragon Swamp	22	17/	18.5.0}	
Gresham, John (B)	79	5/3	20.14.9}	
do. A. Gresham	4	17/	3.8.0}	
			£2210.17.7	14.14.[ ].10

[page 7, List A, 1804] Persons names owning land	Quantity of land	Price per acre	Total Amount Land	Amt. Tax Thereon in
	[158]			Dols. Cents
Griffin, William est.	859	14/6	622.15.6	
Garrett, James	230	4/2	48.18.4}	
do. William Garrett	100	"	20.16.8}	
Garrett, Robert	200	7/	70.0.0}	
do. Philemon Bird	54¾	6/3	17.2.2¼}	
do. William Hunt	170	"	53.2.6}	
Gaines, Robert est.	537¾	20/9	558.8.7¾}	
do. A. Curtis	50	5/3	13.2.6}	
Guthrie, James	60	12/6	37.10.0	
Guthrie, Richard	60	"	37.10.0}	
Ditto	162	3/2	25.13.0}	
Garrett, Edward	210	5/3	55.2.6}	
do. Trice's	489½	"	128.9.10}	
Garrett, William (son of Wm.)	197¾	7/3	71.13.8¾	
Groom, John	173	3/2	27.17.10}	
do. John Bowdens	95	4/2	19.15.10}	
do. Robert Lumpkin	106¾	"	22.4.9¾}	
Garrett, George	6½	5/3	1.14.1½	
Guthrie, Rachel	50	8/4	20.16.8	
Goldman, Martin	140	4/2	29.3.4	
Garnett, James	100	"	20.16.8	
Gully, Philip est.	50	3/2	7.18.4	
Garrett, William Senr.	225	3/4¾	37.19.4½}	
do. George B. Bird	60	6/3	18.15.0}	
do. Henry F. Dudley	50	5/3	13.2.6}	
Gramshill, Henry	25	3/2	3.19.2	
Garrett, Ann Watts	112	5/	28.0.0	
Gilmore, Richard	414	5/3	108.13.6	
Garrett, Richard, York	100	4/2	20.16.8	
Garrett, William Junr.	120	"	25.0.0	
Garrett, Edward Junr.	150	6/3	46.17.6	
Gaines, Benjamin	360	20/4	366.0.0	
Gaines, Henry	360	"	366.0.0	
Gatewood, Philip	1	7/10	0.7.10	
Henderson, James	25	5/3	6.11.3	
Hoskins, William est.	296	20/	296.0.0}	
do. Balance Bray's	2	7/10	0.15.8}	
			$3249.11.4	14.18.18.11

[page 8, List A, 1804] Persons names owning land	Quantity of land	Price per acre	Total Amount Land	Amt. Tax Thereon in Dols. Cents
Hoomes, Benjamin	372	12/6	232.10.0}	
do. ad to make the above} agree with the record}	75	"	76.17.6}	
do. Ann Kennedy's	75	"	46.17.6}	
Hemmingway, John Jun[r.]	263	4/2	54.15.10	
Hare, William est.	217	5/3	56.19.3	
Harwood, Christopher	194	24/10	240.17.8	
Harwood, Priscilla	165	18/	148.10.0	
Hart, James	150	3/2	23.15.0	
Holderby, John	73¼	4/2	15.5.2½	
Holderby, John Jun[r.]	108¾	7/10	42.6.0	
Hart, Anthony	190	5/3	49.17.6}	
do. Sundry Persons	359½	3/2	56.18.5}	
Hart, Gregory	200	"	31.13.4	
Hart, William est.	250	3/3½	41.2.11	
Harwood, John est.	109	10/5	56.15.5	
Henry, Samuel H. est.	1900	14/6	1377.10.0	
Henry, James	75	12/6	46.17.6	
Halyard, William est.	63 1/3	5/3	16.12.6	
Hoskins, Robert	287	6/	86.2.0}	
Do. Robert Smith	157¾	10/5	82.10.6¾}	
Hart, Alden	127	4/2	26.9.2	
Hutson, William	75¼	"	15.13.6½	
do. John Daniel	25	"	5.4.2}	
Howerton, Heritage	122¼	20/9	126.16.7¼	
Halyard, William	260	6/3	81.5.0	
Howerton, John	269½	5/3	70.14.10½	
Hart, Vincent	1¼	6/6	0.8.1½}	
Ditto William Rouzey	88	7/3	31.18.0}	
Halyard, John	187½	5/3	49.4.4½}	
do. William Halyard	63 1/3	"	16.12.6}	
do. W[m.] Halyard est.	63 1/3	"	16.12.6}	
Hog[g], William & legatees} of Holt Richeson}	50	18/-	45.0.0	
Jones, Thomas	255	4/2	53.2.6	
Jeffries, Thomas (B)	63	7/3	22.16.9}	
do. John Harwood	25½	10/5	13.5.7½}	
do. Brett's est.	57¾	18/-	51.19.6}	
			£3382.7.3	13.[ ].[ ].14

[page 9, List A, 1804] Persons names owning land	Quantity of land	Price per acre	Total Amount Land	Amt. Tax Thereon in Dols. Cents
	[159]			
[Jo]nes, James Jun[r.]	100	5/3	26.5.0}	
do. Mary Jones	150	26/11	201.17.6}	
[Je]ffries, Going	60	4/2	12.10.0	
[Jo]rdin, Robert	66 2/3	"	13.18.10	
[Jo]nes, Mary	150	26/11	201.17.6	
[I]son, George	140¼	5/3	36.16.3¾	
[I]nge, Vincent est.	33	8/4	13.15.0	
Kemp, John	296	7/3	107.3.0	
Kauffman, Rich[d.] (orphan)	176	26/	228.16.0}	
do. in Stanhope's Neck	38	10/5	19.15.10}	
Kauffman, Sambo, Humphry} [&} Lucy, free negroes	167	7/6	62.5.0	
Kidd, John	81½	5/3	26.6.6¾	
Kennedy, Archibald est.	38¼	4/2	7.19.4	
Kennedy, Ann	33¼	4/2	6.18.6½	
Kennedy, Ann Jun[r.]	33¾	"	7.0.6	
Kennedy, Lucy	37½	"	7.16.2	
Kidd, Bartholomew	136	5/3	35.14.0}	
do. of William Dillard jr.	132½	4/2	27.12.1}	
do. of Robert Lumpkin	95½	"	19.17.11}	
Kidd, Benjamin	111	13/6	74.18.2}	
do. Crittenden's	60	"	40.10.0}	
do. Dragon Swamp	36	17/	30.12.0}	
Kidd, John est.	370	7/3	134.2.6}	
do. Lumpkin & Pierce	60	4/2	12.10.0}	
Do. Thomas Dillard	45	14/6	32.12.6}	
King, Dicey est.	18	8/4	7.10.0	
Lumpkin, Jacob (orphan)	681	6/3	212.16.3	
Lewis, Iveson	356	14/6	258.2.0	
Leigh, Lucy	101	24/10	125.8.2	
Leigh, John est.	133	"	165.2.10}	
do.	66	"	81.19.0}	
Leigh, Richard est.	560	6/3	175.0.0	
Mitchell, Ralph est.	193	10/5	100.10.5	
Mitchell, Sally	391	13/	254.3.0	
Mitchell, James (orphan)	225	13/	146.5.0	
			£2916.3.4	8.19.17.10

[page 10, List A, 1804] Persons names owning land	Quantity of land	Price per acre	Total Amount Land	Amt. Tax Thereon in Dols. Cents
Moore, Lambeth	20	4/2	4.3.4}	
do. of John Holderby	26¾	"	5.11 5½}	
do. of Kidd & Morris	60	"	12.10.0}	
Moore, Lodowick, John & Richard	100	3/2	15.16.8	
Major, Josiah	200	4/2	41.13.4	
Mitchel, John est.	270	5/3	70.17.0}	
do. Root[e]s	128	9/11	63.9.3}	
Mann, Joseph Sen[r.]	231	6/3	72.3.9	
Moore, Agatha	40	4/2	8.6.8	
Montague, William	170	"	35.8.4	
Meredith, Ralph G. est.	350½	14/6	254.2.3	
Muire, Richard	93	12/6	58.2.6}	
do. Richard Anderson est.	177	5/3	46.9.3}	
Mitchel, Richard	74¼	4/2	15.9.4½	
Moore, Richard est.	145	6/3	45.6.8	
McCarty, Joseph est.	73	3/2	11.11.2	
Metcalfe, Thomas	256	14/6	181.8.8	
Maderias, John	34½	6/3	10.15.7½	
Milby, Richard	175	3/2	27.14.2	
Morgan, William	3	6/3	0.18.9	
Moore, John	37	4/2	7.14.2	
Newcomb, William	169	3/2	26.15.2}	
do. Benjamin Dillards	148	5/3	48.17.0}	
do. Ditto	52	"	13.13.0}	
Orvil, John	100	6/3	31.5.0}	
Ditto	52	"	16.5.0}	
Oliver, John	320	5/3	84.0.0	
Overstreet, Gabriel	296	4/2	61.13.4}	
do. Haynes	130	5/3	34.2.6}	
Oakes, Henry	198½	3/2	34.2.0	
Oakes, William	80	4/2	16.13.4	
Oakes, Ann	60	"	12.10.0	
Oliver, William	59	"	12.5.10	
Pitts, Benjamin G.	100	5/4	26.13.4	
Pace, Benjamin est.	263	7/3	95.6.9	
			£1503.14.7	11.16.[ ].[ ]

[page 11, List A, 1804] Persons names owning land	Quantity of land	Price per acre	Total Amount Land	Amt. Tax Thereon in Dols. Cents
	[160]			
Pynes, Benjamin est.	164	6/3	51.5.0	
Pynes, Robert	111½	"	34.16.10½	
Pynes, Benjamin	46¼	"	14.9.0¾	
Pemberton, John	165	"	51.11.3	
Pollard, Robert	6	24/10	7.9.0}	
do. John Omealy's	367	30/	550.10.0}	
Palmer, Charles	107¾	18/	96.19.6}	
Ditto	104	"	93.12.0}	
Pigg, John est.	324	14/6	234.18.0}	
Ditto	180	7/3	65.5.0}	
Pemberton, John Junr.	121	6/3	37.17.6	
Pierce, Beverly	25¾	4/2	5.7.3½}	
do. Philip Pierce	17	3/2	2.13.10}	
Patterson, Joseph	62¾	"	9.18.8½	
Pierce, Philip	83	"	13.2.10	
Pierce, Thomas est.	87	4/2	18.2.6	
Pilsbury, George	109¾	10/9	58.19.9¾	
Palmer, Roger	314	6/	94.4.0	
Price, Robert	399	6/3	124.13.9	
Roane, Thomas est.	2033	18/8	1897.9.4}	
Do. H. Carltons	200	6/3	63.10.0}	
do. Brett's	34¾	18/	31.5.6}	
do. Robert Pynes	24½	6/3	7.9.1½}	
Rowe, Elizabeth	665	20/9	689.18.9	
Rowe, Francis (orphan)	612½	4/8	142.16.8	
Richason, James (son of Elias)	86	4/2	17.8.4	
Richards, John	571	4/8	124.8.0	
Richason, James	180	4/2	37.10.0	
Richason, William Senr.	181	"	37.14.2	
Roane, Thomas, Middlesex	14¼	15/	10.13.9	
Richason, William (son of Jas.)	188½	4/2	39.5.5	
Richason, William Junr.	118½	5/3	31.2.1½}	
ditto of Robert Stone	101	4/2	21.0.10}	
Richason, John est.	101½	5/3	26.12.10½	
Roane, Major	687½	3/8	128.18.1½	
do. John Lyne	455¾	6/3	142.8.5½}	
do. Palmer	9	7/3	3.5.3}	
			£5018.2.6	13.19.18.14

[page 12, List A, 1804] Persons names owning land	Quantity of land	Price per acre	Total Amount Land	Amt. Tax Thereon in Dols. Cents
Rains, Giles	60	3/2	9.10.0	
Robinson, Benjamin est.	1300	8/4	541.13.4	
Roane, Charles	133	19	126.7.0}	
do. Dragon Swamp	70	17/	59.10.0}	
Roy, Beverley	700	8/4	291.13.4}	
do. Thomas Browns	454	12/6	283.15.0}	
do. Corbins	125	"	78.2.6}	
Richason, James Jun[r.]	250	5/3	65.12.6	
Spencer, Susanna & John	416	7/3	150.16.0	
Spencer, John	34	"	12.6.6	
Spencer, Ann	116	"	60.3.6	
Stark, Richard est.	350	5/8	99.3.4	
Stone, Robert est.	24¾	4/2	5.3.1½	
Stone, Robert	31½	5/3	8.5.4½	
Stone, Job	100	4/2	20.16.8	
Smith, John son of Robert	88	10/5	45.16.8}	
do. Dragon Swamp	12	17/	10.8.0}	
Smith, Francis	150	3/2	23.5.0	
Simpkins, Young	60	"	9.10.0	
Sears, Philip	83	4/2	17.5.10	
Shackelford, William est.	400	14/6	310.0.0	
Spencer, Thomas	300	10/5	158.5.0}	
ditto	225	4/2	53.2.6}	
ditto	117	6/9	39.9.9}	
Seward, Benjamin	115	3/2	18.4.2	
Smith, Thomas G.	485	14/6	351.12.6	
do. Benjamin Dabney	400	"	290.0.0	
do. Ditto	100	8/4	41.13.4}	
Sadler, John	150	6/3	46.17.6	
Shackelford, Zachariah	200	"	62.10.0}	
Ditto Richard Anderson est.	177	5/3	46.9.3}	
Shackelford, John (R)	401¼	8/4	167.3.10	
Shackelford, William	151	6/3	47.3.9}	
do. Wyatt's lease	30	5/3	7.16.6}	
Shackelford, John (Mc)	283	6/2	87.5.2}	
do. John Collier (Cobler)	150	5/3	39.7.6}	
Shackelford, Benjamin	104	7/3	37.14.0}	
do. Halyard's lease	1	5/9½	0.5.9½}	
Shepherd, John	67	6/	20.2.0	
Smith, John Doct[r.]	½	30/	0.15.0	
			£3745.0.8	11.17.19.[ ]

[page 13, List A, 1804] Persons names owning land	Quantity of land [161]	Price per acre	Total Amount Land	Amt. Tax Thereon in Dols. Cents
Smith, Samuel	1	7/10	0.7.10}	
Ditto, Dragon	10	17/	8.10.0}	
Spencer, Meacham	323	6/9	109.0.3	
Southern, John	15½	4/2	3.4.7	
Sears, Thomas	123	6/7	40.9.9}	
do. H. Williams	42¼	4/2	8.17.1}	
Smith, Robert Jun[r.]	30	10/5	15.12.6	
Tureman, Elizabeth	24¾	3/2	3.18.4½	
Tureman, Benjamin est.	70	"	11.1.8	
Tureman, George	50	"	7.18.4	
[Ta]liaferro, William	1000	14/6	725.0.0	
[To]wnley, Robert	200	6/3	62.10.0}	
Do. Anderson's	117	14/6	84.16.6}	
Taliaferro, Philip est.	662	8/4	275.16.8	
Taliaferro, James B.	374½	12/6	234.7.6	
Thruston, Armstead	111 1/3	4/3	23.15.1	
Thruston, Batchelder	200	3/2	31.13.4	
Turner, Benjamin	36	4/2	7.10.0	
Townley, Ann	79	"	16.9.2	
Turner, Henry est.	100	"	20.16.8	
Tunstall, Richard G.	206½	7/10	73.3.7	
Taylor, William	40	6/3	12.10.0}	
do. Philip Taliaferro's est.	200	8/4	83.6.8}	
Trice, Kitty White	82	5/3	21.10.6	
Watts, Edward est.	250	7/3	90.12.6}	
do. W. Watts est.	113	5/	28.5.0}	
Watts, John	293	7/10	114.15.2}	
do. Pembertons	45	6/3	14.1.3}	
Watts, Kauffman	270	5/3	70.17.6}	
do. Eubank & Burch	257	5/9	73.17.9}	
do. John & Dl. Hemingway	312	4/2	64.3.4}	
Watts, James	350	"	72.8.4}	
do. William Watts est.	60	15/	45.0.0}	
Williams, Howard	181½	4/2	37.16.3}	
do. Dragon Swamp	43	17/	36.11.0}	
Wyatt, Thomas	206	7/10	81.2.0	
Wyatt, William	39¾	7/	13.18.3	
			£2525.14.4	12.18.15.13

[page 14, List A, 1804] Persons names owning land	Quantity of land	Price per acre	Total Amount Land	Amt. Tax Thereon in Dols. Cents
Williams, Montague	300	6/3	93.15.0	
Williams, Charles est.	336	4/2	70.0.0	
Walton, James	80	"	16.13.4}	
do. Thomas Walton's est.	66	"	13.15.0}	
Walton, Elizabeth	60	3/2	9.10.0	
Walton, John est.	176	5/3	46.4.0	
Walton, William est.	66	4/2	13.15.0	
Ware, John est.	75	5/3	19.13.9	
Waring, Robert P. est.	542	10/9	291.10.6	
Walden, Lewis	90	10/5	46.17.6	
Walden, Richard (son of Rich[d.])	90	10/5	46.17.6	
Walden, Lewis est.	150	3/2	23.15.0}	
do. Thomas Dudley's	84½	6/3	28.3.3½}	
Williams, George	40	4/2	8.6.8	
Wyatt, Richard	175	12/6	109.7.6	
Watkins, Philip	197	5/3	51.14.3	
Ware, Robert Jun[r.] est.	100	4/2	20.16.8	
Williams, Elizabeth	16½	3/2	2.12.9	
White, James est.	200	6/3	62.10.0	
Wedderburn, Lydia	350	6/3	109.7.6	
Whiting, Beverley est.	2447¾	7/10	866.18.9	
Webley, John est.	173	5/3	45.8.3}	
Ditto Collier & Dillard	279	4/2	58.2.6}	
Ware, Robert Jun[r.]	100	8/4	41.13.4	
Ware, William	100	"	41.13.4	
Walden, Benjamin	373	5/3	97.18.3}	
do. Richard Anderson's est.	120½	"	31.12.7½}	
Waller, Edward est.	133½	3/2	21.2.9	
Waller, George est.	87	"	13.15.6}	
do. John Shackelfords	47¾	8/4	19.17.11}	
Waller, John	65	3/7	11.12.11	
Waller, Robert est.	48	"	8.12.0}	
do. Groom's est.	187	3/2	29.12.2}	
Ware, Nicholas	100	"	15.16.8	
Walton, Beverly	47½	7/10	18.12.1	
			$2407.4.2	13.20.18.17

[page 15, List A, 1804] Persons names owning land	Quantity of land	Price per acre	Total Amount Land	Amt. Tax Thereon in Dols. Cents	
	[162]				
Watts, George K.	36	26/	46.16.0		
Wyatt, Smith	29¾	7/3	10.15.8}		
do. William Wyatts	9	7/	3.3.0}		
Willis, Robert	105	14/6	75.2.6		
Williams, Christopher	100	5/3	25.5.0		
			£161.2.2		1.2
			[44785.12.7]		

Benjamin Shackelford, Comr. revenue

[arithmetic omitted]

$716.58 Tax on Land

A List of Land within the District of Robert B. Hill, Commissioner in the upper District in the County of King & Queen for the year 1804 to wit

LIST B

[page 1, List B, 1804] Persons names owning Land	Quantity of Land	Price per acre	Tot. Amt. Value Land
	[163]		
Atkins, Joseph Este.	66	4/2	£13.15.0
Alexander, Benjamin	202	9/4	94.5.4
do. of James Halbert	124	6/2	38.15.0
do. Lott in D'kirk, an[l.] rent			20.0.0
do. of Joseph Meede			4.10.0
Acre, Seaton	52	9/4	24.5.4
Alexander, Elisha	338	9/4	157.14.8
Anderson, Churchill	636	7/3	230.11.0
Atkins, John	277	5/	69.5.0
Anderson, Sarah	86	20/9	89.3.9
Barton, John Este.	125	4/2	26.0.10
Bray, James	118½	7/10	46.4.4
Broach, Benoni	48	10/5	25.4.0
Brown, Henry Jun[r.]	100	12	60.0.0
Beverley, Robert Este.	2444	10/5	1262.16.4
Brown, Henry	526	7/4½	190.17.9
Bland, John	83	8/4	34.11.8
Bates, James	358	11/	149.3.4
do.	42	4/2	8.15.0
do. of Rice Garnett	89	7/3	32.5.3
Braxton, Carter	484½	10/5	252.6.10
do. of Robert B. Carter	132¼	10/5	68.17.7¼
Brooking, Frances	930	10/5	484.7.6
Boughton, Thomas, Essex	130	9/4	60.13.4
Boughton, John	106	8/4	44.3.2½
Boughton, Henry, Essex	88	6/3	27.10.0
Bohannan, Ann Este.	197	4/6	44.6.6
Brown, William	18¼	3/2	2.17.9½
do. of Ware's Exors. &c.	196½	7/3	71.4.7½
Bagby, John Este.	330	7/3	119.12.9
Bagby, Richard	260	"	94.5.0
Bagby, Thomas	260	"	94.5.0
do. of Jacob Lumpkin	235	6/3	73.8.9
Brizendine, Armistead	86 2/3	8/4	35.17.6
Bromley, John	60	7/10	23.10.0
Broach, William	20	7/10	7.16.8
Brown, John	50	7/4½	18.8.9
Bohannan, William	163	5/3	42.15.9
Bates, William	81	7/9½	31.10.1
do. of Rice Garnett	117	7/3	42.8.4
Broach, George	32½	14/6	23.11.3
do. of Hill & wife	43¼	"	31.7.1½
Boulware, Samuel	175¾	31/3	274.12.2¼
Beadles, Justin	20	6/3	6.5.0
Burnett, James, of Jn[o.] Boughton	65	8/4	27.1.8
Boulware, Lee, of Gresham &c.	153	7/3	55.9.3
Brown, William Jun[r.]	54	7/4	19.6.0
			£4656.2.0

16.20 [torn]

[page 2, List B, 1804] Persons names owning Land	Quantity of Land	Price per acre	Tot. Amt. Value Land	
Crafton, Thomas	119	9/4	£55.10.8	
Crafton, James	59	"	27.10.8	
Crafton, John	117½	"	54.12.0	
Crane, John	130	6/3	40.2.6	
do. of Clem Pynes	14	3/2	2.4.4	
do. of Ware's Este.	49¼	7/3	17.17.0¾	
do. of Ware's Exors.	71	"	29.14.9	
Cluverius, Benjamin	419	20/9	434.14.3	
Carlton, John	242	14/6	175.9.0	
Cole, G. Thomas	105	6/3	32.16.3	
Carlton, Lewis	100	8/4	41.3.4	
do. of H. Carlton's Este.	150	7/10	58.15.0	
Clayton, Thomas Este.	275	7/3	99.13.9	
Crane, George Este.	30	7/3	10.17.6	
Courtney, Thomas	156	7/10	61.2.0	
Carlton, Joel	53½	6/3	16.4.5	
Cooke, Moses	100	8/4	41.13.4	
Cooke, Ambrose	100	8/4	41.13.4	
Chapman, M. George	250	7/10	87.18.4	
Courtney, Robert	183½	7/10	71.17.5	
do. of Jacob Abbott	40½	"	15.13.4	
Cannada, William	100	6/3	31.5.0	
do. of George Satterwhite	15¼	"	4.15.3½	
Cooke, William	65	5/5	17.12.1	
Cooke, James	65	8/9	28.8.9	
Courtney, Fanny & Children	78	7/10	30.10.0	
Cross, Joseph	103½	6/3	32.6.10½	
Campbell, William	837¼	7/3	303.10.0¾	
Campbell, Whitaker	406	7/10	159.0.4	
Crow, John	121	5/3	31.19.2¼	
Crow, Nathaniel Este.	34½	6/3	10.15.7½	
Crouch, Edmund	74¼	7/10	29.1.9	
Campbell, William, of J. Campbell	74¼	18/8	69.6.0	
Cauthorn, Vincent, of Tunstalls	43	8/4	17.18.4	
Crane, Nathaniel	66	3/2	10.9.0	
Carlton, Thomas	297	7/10	116.6.6	
Dew, Thomas	331	12/6	206.17.6	
Dew, William Este.	935	14/6	677.17.6	
Duling, William Este.	264	8/4	110.0.0	
Dix, Gabriel	338	6/3	105.12.6	
Durham, Joseph	105	4/3	21.12.6	
do. of Dunn	10	4/2	2.1.8	
Deshazo, John	188	7/4	68.18.8	
Deshazo, Larkin	87	7/3	34.4.10	
do. of John Crane	6	6/3	1.17.6	
do. of Benjamin Hoomes	430¾	4/4	93.4.5	
Dunbar, David	366	8/4	152.10.0	
Dudley, Peter Este.	530	7/3¼	186.18.4	
Dally, George	174¼	3/2	27.11.9½	
Durham, John	25	3/2	3.19.4	
Dickie, James	512	8/4	213.6.8	
Deshazo, Unity	71	7/10	27.16.3	
Deshazo, Polly, orphan	41	"	16.1.2	
Dally, John Este.	200	3/2	31.13.4	
Dobbins, Charles Este.	147	5/3	38.11.9	
			$4331.3.9	20.30.4.[ ]

[page 3, List B, 1804] Persons names owning Land	Quantity of Land	Price per acre	Tot. Amt. Value Land	
	[164]			
Dobson, Pitman	136	10/2¾	£69.10.9¾	
Daniel, Leonard	81	7/10	26.14.6	
Eubank, Henry	171	5/3	44.17.9	
do. of Richard Eubank	26	"	6.16.6	
Edwards, Thomas	66	4/2	13.15.0	
Evans, Ambrose	195	7/10	56.10.0	
Eubank, James	111	10/2¾	56.15.5	
Eubank, Polly	127	"	64.19.1	
Eubank, William	130	"	66.9.9¼	
Eubank, John	136	"	69.10.9¾	
Fogg, James	120	6/3	37.10.0	
Fleet, William	512	12/	307.4.0	
Fogg, Frederick	298	8/4	124.3.4	
Fauntleroy, G. Samuel	2069	20/	2069.0.0	
Do. of P.A. Blackburn &c.	57¾	20/9	59.9.8	
do. of Francis Anderson	28 2/3	"	29.14.10	
Fox, S. Joseph	28	7/10	10.19.4	
do.	39	"	15.5.6	
do.	94	7/3	31.1.6	
Fogg, Thomas	223	10/2¾	114.2.1¾	
Falkner, Thomas	220	6/3	68.15.0	
Grafton, Sally & Ann	132	9/4	61.12.0	
Gayle, John	264	7/5	97.18.0	
do. of William Gayle	7¼	"	2.13.11	
Gatewood, Chaney	829	10/5	437.17.11	
do. Noell's	362½	14/6	262.16.3	
" Harwood's	125	4/2	46.17.6	
" Eubank's	300	14/3	217.10.0	
" Walden's Este.	120	12/6	75.0.0	
" Wm. Lyne, Lott in D'kirk, anl. rent			33.0.0	
" Saml. Roane	457	17/2	387.5.2	
Garnett, Joshua Este.	325	8/4	134.3.4	
Gatewood, Joseph	445	10/5	231.15.5	
do. of John Schools	70	8/4	29.3.4	
Gayle, Matthew Este.	323	11/5	184.7.7	
Gatewood, John	160	8/4	66.13.4	
Garnett, Reuben	656½	8/10	289.19.1	
do. of Halbert &c.	28	10/5	14.12.10	
" of Gabriel Gatewood &c.	50	10/5	26.0.10	
" of Do. Do.	20¾	"	10.16.1¼	
" of James Upshaw jr.	61	8/	24.8.0	
Garnett, M. Reuben	220	8/10	97.3.4	
Gwathmey, Temple	600	35/3	1057.10.0	
Garlick, Samuel Este.	454	24/10	463.14.4	
Garlick, John Este.	839	29	1216.11.0	
Griffith, Thomas	22¾	6/3	7.0.7½	
Griffith, Joseph Este.	22¾	"	7.0.7½	
Gresham, Samuel	432½	7/3	156.15.7½	
do. of Rice Garnett	157	"	56.18.1	
Guthrie, William	91¼	7/5	33.14.7	
do. of Rd. Hill	46	8/2	18.15.8	
do. of William Campbell	31	7/3	11.4.9	
Gaines, Harry Este.	481½	20/4	489.10.6	
Gaines, B. Robert	481½	"	489.10.6	
			$10083.5.11	20.28.3[ ].23

[page 4, List B, 1804] Persons names owning Land	Quantity of Land	Price per acre	Tot. Amt. Value Land	
Gresham, Thomas Este.	455¼	6/8	£151.13.4	
Griffith, Milly	50	6/3	15.12.6	
Graves, Thomas	66¼	7/3	23.18.6	
Gresham, Lumpkin	233	7/3	85.3.9	
Gresham, George	141	3/2	22.6.6	
Gatewood, William (*Tuck*o.)	33	3/2	5.4.6	
Gleason, Patrick	134	8/4	55.16.8	
Gatewood, Gabriel	57¼	10/5	29.16.4¾	
Gayle, William	344	7/5	127.11.4	
Garnett, Henry	25½	7/3	9.4.10½	
do. of Pendleton & wife	438	9/2	200.15.0	
Gatewood, William (son of Jno.)	132	10/	526.3.2	
Gatewood, Philip	613	17/2	526.3.2	
Gayle, Thomas, Lott D'kirk. anl. rent			9.0.0	
Garrett, Robert Junr.	33	8/4	13.15.0	
Gresham, Anthony	22	8/4	9.3.4	
Hill, William Este.	1267	14/6	918.4.3	
Hawes, Walker	97	"	70.6.6	
Hitchcock, Thomas	140	4/2	29.3.4	
Hoskins, Samuel Este.	345	6/3	107.16.3	
do. of Elisha Alexander	57	10/5	25.13.9	
Hutchason, William	200	7/1	70.16.8	
Hutchason, Charles	200	"	70.16.8	
Heskew, John Este.	61	5/3	16.0.3	
Heskew, John Junr. Este.	50	6/3	15.12.6	
do. of Clem Pynes	10	3/2	1.11.8	
do. of Larkin Deshazo	19¼	4/4	4.2.4	
Hill, Edward	1125¾	18/8	1050.14.0	
do. of Quarles	130¾	17/2	112.4.6½	
Hoskins, John	767	10/5	399.9.7	
do. of Boughtons	100	8/4	41.13.4	
" of Fleet & Semple	2	10/5	1.0.10	
" of Semple	18 1/8	"	9.8.9	
Hurt, West	14	5/3	3.3.6	
Holt, William	123	14/3	87.12.9	
Hutchason, John	73¼	8/9	32.0.11¼	
do. of C. Hutchason's Este.	131	7/1	46.7.11	
Hall, Corbin	72	4/2	15.0.0	
Hill, B. Robert	257	8/2	104.18.10	
Hill, Richard	194	"	79.4.4	
Hill, G. Mary	360	"	147.0.0	
Hill, Robert Este.	420	"	171.10.0	
Hoskins, Thomas	55	"	22.9.2	
Jones, John Este.	300	8/11	133.15.0	
Jeffries, Edward	70	3/2	11.1.8	
Jeffries, Ambrose	237	7/10	92.16.6	
Jeffries, Robert	110	7/6	41.5.0	
Do. of L. Gresham	10	7/3	3.12.6	
" of Jacob Lumpkin	5	7/3	1.16.3	
" of Lumpkin Gresham	20	7/3	7.5.0	
Jones, James Este.	160	14/6	116.0.0	
Do.	196	10/5	102.1.8	
Jones, Rawleigh Este.	63	31/1	93.18.3	
Do. of Wm. Jones Este.	135¾	17/10	121.0.10½	
			$5730.10.2	22.2[ ], 25.17

[page 5, List B, 1804] Persons names owning Land	Quantity of Land	Price per acre	Tot. Amt. Value Land
	[165]		
Jeffries, John Este.	100	7/10	£39.3.4
Johnson, Thomas	72	3/2	11.8.0
Jones, John, of Boughton & wife	29 1/8	8/4	12.1.9½
Kemp, John	178	7/3	64.2.2
Keeling, Mary	78½	8/	31.8.0
Kay, Christopher	116	6/3	36.6.0
do. of T. Gouldman	416½	9/	107.8.6
Lumpkin, James	213	7/10	83.8.2
Lumpkin, Henry	400	9/4	186.13.4
Lumpkin, John Este.	125	6/3	35.11.3
Lumpkin, William Este.	61½	13/6	41.10.3
Lafon, Francis	119	8/4	49.11.8
Lankford, Thomas Este.	100	4/2	20.16.8
Lumpkin, Robert Senr.	374	8/4	155.16.8
Lumpkin, Henry Junr.	190	9/4	88.13.4
Lumpkin, W. John Este.	140	7/10	54.16.8
do. of John Ware's Este.	118½	7/3	42.15.6
Longest, Caleb	97	7/10	37.19.10
Longest, Richard	227¾	"	89.4.2
Longest, John	100	"	39.3.4
Lumpkin, Anthony Este.	216	6/3	67.10.0
Lumpkin, Robert Junr.	279¾	5/3	73.8.8¼
Lumpkin, Wilson	122½	9/4	57.3.4
Lumpkin, William Junr.	183¼	10/5	95.6.3
Lumpkin, John	112	3/2	17.14.8
Lyne, William	1430	8/4	489.17.6
Lumpkin, Richard	178	5/3	46.14.6
Longest, William	83	8/4	34.11.8
Lumpkin, Ann	47	13/6	31.14.6
Lumpkin, Elizabeth	51	13/6	34.8.6
Lumpkin, John (King Wm.)	105	"	70.17.6
do. of Henry White & wife	57	"	38.9.6
Lyne, Edmund	50	8/4	20.16.8
Motley, Edwin	815	10/5	428.2.6
do. of Semple & wife	149	12/6	93.2.6
Martin, C. Thomas	583	14/6	422.13.6
do.	134½	7/3	48.15.1
Minor, William	149	8/4	62.1.8
Minor, John	137	"	57.1.8
Minor, Thomas Este.	288	7/10	112.16.0
Moody, Lewis	239	7/10	93.12.2
Mann, Joseph Junr.	400	8/4	166.13.4
do. of Crows	140	6/3	43.15.0
" of Allen & wife	25½	6/3	7.19.4½
Mitchell, John	50	6/3	15.12.6
Mann, Robert Este.	699	"	218.8.9
Meredith, Samuel	215	7/10	84.4.2
Macon, John Este.	1092	16/7	905.9.0
do. Lotts in D'Kirk anl. rent			40.0.0
do. do. do. do.			30.0.0
Mann, Mary	100	5/3	26.5.0
			$5263.4.1

19.[torn]

[page 6, List B, 1804] Persons names owning Land	Quantity of Land	Price per acre	Tot. Amt. Value Land	
Martin, John	475	9/	£213.15.0	
do. of Fogg	197	6/3	61.11.3	
do. of Satterwhite	88	6/3	27.10.0	
Mahon, Thomas	101	6/3	31.11.3	
Mahon, William	103½	6/3	32.3.9	
Mahon, Benjamin	43¼	5/3	11.7.0¾	
Mitchell, Richard, of Stone	74¼	3/2	11.15.1½	
Muse, Lawrence, Lott in D'kirk rent			60.0.0	
Nunn, Moses	318	7/4½	117.5.3	
Nunn, Thomas	130	7/3	47.2.6	
do. of Brizendine	49	4/3	10.8.3	
Newbill, William	1060	8/4	441.13.4	
Newell, John Este.	100	7/10	39.3.4	
Nash, John Este.	100	6/3	31.5.0	
Noll, Phil & Skelton, Reuben & Thos. [Noel]	275	8/4	114.11.8	
Newbill, Thomas, of Tunstalls	94¾	8/4	39.9.6	
Owen, Augustine Este.	100	6/3	31.5.0	
Pendleton, James	888½	8/7½	383.3.3¾	
do. of Wilmore	70	7/6	26.5.0	
" of McIntosh	125	4/2	26.1.10	
Pitts, David	420	9/6	196.0.0	
Phillips, James	230	7/3	83.7.6	
Pollard, John Este.	235	9/4	109.13.4	
do. of Leonard Smithy	384	7/3	139.4.0	
Prewitt, Frances	99	9/4	46.4.0	
Parker, John	761¼	8/4	317.3.9	
Prewitt, Richard	102	7/3	36.12.3	
Pendleton, Philip, of Brown &c.	156	7/4	57.4.0	
do. Lott in D'kirk, anl. rent			3.0.0	
Perryman, Philip	218	7/2	78.2.4	
do. of George Dillard & wife	215	7/2	77.0.10	
Pynes, Clement	99	3/2	15.13.6	
Pollard, Richard	389	8/4	162.1.8	
Pendleton, Benjamin Este.	450	7/10	176.5.0	
Perryman, Richard	110	7/3	39.7.6	
Prewett, Tunstall	58½	8	23.8.0	
Pollard, Joseph	200	6/3	62.10.0	
Pollard, Richard & Brown, Henry	50	8	20.0.0	
Parker, Gouldman, of Gresham	170	7/3	61.12.6	
Pitts, Obadiah	20	10/5	10.18.4	
Quarles, W. Francis	23¼	17/2	19.17.1½	
do. of Garnett	114½	7/3	41.10.1½	
Quarles, Isaac, King William	25¾	20	25.15.0	
Rowe, G. Thomas orphan decd.	555	7/3	201.3.9	
Row, Richard Este.	450	8/4	188.0.0	
Roane, Spencer	954	24/10	1184.11.0	
Ryland, Joseph	487½	7/3	176.10.9	
do. of Chick's Exors.	463	7/3	167.16.9	
			£5478.0.5	13.18.22.19

[page 7, List B, 1804] Persons names owning Land	Quantity of Land	Price per acre	Tot. Amt. Value Land
	[166]		
Ryland, Josiah	160	7/10	£62.13.4
do. of William Temple	27½	15/	20.12.6
" of Frans. Prince's Este.	107	7/10	41.18.2
" of H. Brown	34½	7/4½	12.14.1¼
" of James H. Row	226	8/4	92.3.4
Riddle, Vaughan	188	5/5	49.7.0
Roane, Thomas	920¾	17/2	790.8.2½
Row, Handsford	160½	6/3	50.3.1½
Row, Wilson	160½	6/3	50.3.1½
Redd, James	200	7/3	72.10.0
Row, Ovil	55½	9/4	25.18.0
Smith, William	53	7/10	20.15.2
do. of James Smith's Este.	25	3/2	3.19.2
Segar, Richard Este.	406	7/3	147.3.6
Satterwhite, George	60¾	6/3	18.19.8½
Satterwhite, William	118	5/7½	33.3.9
Schools, John	86	8/4	35.16.8
do. of Parker & wife	35	"	14.11.8
Schools, Gabriel Este.	174	6/3	54.7.6
Skelton, William	362	8/2½	148.11.5
do. of Phil Perryman	12	7/2	4.6.0
Smith, John De.	190	7/6	71.5.0
Starling, Roderick	360	7/10	141.0.0
do.	313	8/2	127.16.2
do. of Wm. Lyne	56½	8/4	23.6.8
" of H. Walker	46	5/3	12.1.6
" of Rob. B. Hill	65	8/2	26.10.10
Saunders, George	200	7/3	70.10.8
do. of Wyatts &c.	115	7/10	45.0.10
Shepherd, William	140	9/4	65.6.8
Smith, Molly	30	4/2	6.5.0
Smith, John Junr.	42½	5/3	11.3.1½
Smith, Lewis	96	7/6	36.0.0
do. of Richd. Hill	37	8/2	15.2.2
Swinton, Ann	750	13/6	506.5.0
Stone, Sarah	300	7/3	108.15.0
Stone, Daniel	52	3/2	8.4.8
Smith, Larkin	1254¼	31/1	1949.6.3½
Smith, Henry	400	6/3	130.0.0
Smith, Ambrose	92¾	8/4	38.6.8
Stevens, George Este.	430	7/10	168.8.4
Stevens, George orphan	75	"	29.8.4
Smith, William Este. (Mill)	200	3/2	31.13.4
Shackelford, John Este.	114	7/3	40.8.2
Shepherd, John	192	3/2	30.1.8
Sthreshley, William	155½	6/3	48.11.10
Schools, George	200	8/4	83.6.8
Smith, John, of Garlick	54	29/	78.6.0
Smith, Jane, of Smith's Este.	25	3/2	3.19.2
Smith, Philip orphan of Do.	12½	"	1.19.7
Smith, James	101	7/10	39.11.2
do. of James Smith's Este.	12½	3/2	1.19.7
			$5700.5.6

17.[ ].[ ].23

[page 8, List B, 1804] Persons names owning Land	Quantity of Land	Price per acre	Tot. Amt. Value Land	
Scott, Anderson	330	16/7	£273.12.6	
do. of P. Anderson's Este.	248	20/9	257.6.0	
do. of C. Anderson & wife	96	"	99.12.0	
Semple, B. Robert	235	10/5	122.6.3½	
do. of Spencer Roane	155	24/10	192.9.2	
Stuart, James	120	9/2	55.0.0	
Trice, William Este.	140	7/3	50.15.0	
Taylor, James	50	6/3	15.12.6	
Taylor, Edmund	294	8/14	122.10.0	
Temple, Joseph	918	10/5	478.2.6	
Tunstall, Richard jr. Este.	1097	7/3	397.13.3	
Temple, William	402¼	15/	301.17.6	
Temple, John	42	31/3	65.12.6	
Temple, Humphrey Este.	100	15/	75.0.0	
do. of J. Tunstall	200	18/8	185.16.8	
" of R. Tunstall &c.	574	21/	602.14.0	
Tunstall, Richard (Purdy) Este.	76¾	8/4	32.5.6	
Upshaw, James, Essex	125	8/10	55.4.2	
do. of R. Beverley	30	10/5	15.12.6	
" of Reuben Garnett	120	8/	48.0.0	
Wilson, Isaac Este.	200	6/3	62.10.0	
Wilson, Benjamin Este.	200	7/3	72.10.0	
Watkins, Joseph	63	6/7	20.14.9	
do. of Wiltshire's Este.	71	7/3	26.14.9	
Walker, Philip	110	9/4	51.6.8	
Walker, Humphrey	820	33/2	1355.14.2	
Wright, William	130	5/3	33.12.6	
Willis, Joel	94	7/10	35.5.0	
do. of Wm. Jones Este.	140¼	17/10	125.1.1½	
Wright, Edward	567	6/3	177.3.9	
Whayne, William	154½	7/10	60.10.3	
Wyatt, George	122	7/6	45.15.0	
Webb, James	209	4/2	43.10.10	
Wheely, Carriol Este.	37¼	7/3	13.10.0¾	
Watkins, Joseph Junr.	93¼	8/4	38.17.1	
Wyatt, Robert	50	7/3	18.2.6	
Watkins, John	152	8/4	63.6.8	
Watkins, Philip Este.	107	4/2	22.5.10	
Walton, Thomas, of Howerton	76¾	6/	23.0.6	
Young, Henry	640	18/8	597.6.8	
			£6334.--.2	13.18.[ ].19
			[47576.12.--]	

Ro. B. Hill, Commr.

Land List for 1804 for the Auditor
[arithmetic omitted]
$750.92 Land
$10.32 Lotts

A list of land within the district of Thomas Spencer, Commissioner in the county of King and Queen for the year Eighteen hundred and five
LIST A

[page 1, List A, 1805] Persons names owning land	Quantity of land [167]	Price per acre	Total Amount Land	Amt. Tax Thereon in Dols. Cents
Atkins, Lewis	60	8/4	25.0.0}	
Do. John B. Whiting	256½	7/10	100.0.0}	
Anderson, Francis est.	348	10/9	187.3.8}	
do. Rich[d.] T. Shackelford	26	8/4	12.1.8}	
Anderson, Beverly	203½	3/2	32.4.5	
Brown, Samuel	33¼	4/3	7.1.2	
Banks, William est.	365	4/2	76.0.0	
Brooke, Richard	1539¾	29/	2232.12.9	
Brumley, Robert	225	5/3	59.1.3	
Bird, William est.	532	7/3	197.17.0}	
Do. Dragon Swamp	88½	17/	70.4.6}	
Bird, Philemon	1638¼	6/3	511.19.0¾	
Brett, Nancy	50	18/	45.0.0	
Burch, James	183	6/3	57.3.9	
Burch, Vincent	100	4/2	20.16.8}	
Do. William Hoskins	50	3/3	7.18.4}	
Bird, Anthony A.	275	"	43.10.10}	
Do. W[m.] Montague	44	4/2	9.3.4}	
Byne, John est.	336	"	70.0.0}	
Do. Dragon Swamp	2¼	17/	1.18.3}	
Bird, Robert est.	780	24/10	993.6.8}	
Do. Guy Smith	189½	3/2	30.0.10}	
Bourn, Richard est.	150	"	23.15.0	
Boyd, John	115	18/8	107.6.8}	
Do. Sowne's	382	24/10	474.6.4}	
Bray, Richard est.	93	7/10	36.8.6	
Bird, John est.	71	3/2	11.4.10	
Bew, William est.	117	"	18.0.6	
Boyd, Robert	1119	9/3	517.10.3	
Boyd, William	300	15/	225.0.0}	
do. Francis Gaines	367	14/6	266.1.6}	
Burkeley, Edmund est.	762	5/3	200.0.6	
Bland, John	60	12/6	37.10.0	
Bland, William est.	100	9/11	49.11.8	
Bourn, Mills	159½	5/3	41.14.3}	
Do. Thomas Jordan's est.	33 1/3	4/2	6.18.10}	
Bullman, Ann	120	5/3	31.10.0	
Bew, Major	82	"	21.10.6	
			£6858.13.4¾	14.13.16.13

[page 2, List A, 1805] Persons names owning land	Quantity of land	Price per acre	Total Amount Land	Amt. Tax Thereon in Dols. Cents
Balote, Laban	384½	4/2	80.2.6	
Bland, William Sen.	225	3/8¼	41.9.8½}	
do. Wm. Dillard's	152¼	6/	45.13.6}	
Bland, Ralph	146	53	38.6.8}	
Do. Finny & Buckner	170	4/2	35.8.4}	
Do. N. Dillard, Dragon	4¼	17/	3.12.3}	
Bowden, William	100	4/2	20.16.8}	
Do. Sykes's	34	3/2	5.7.8}	
Bland, Robert	250	4/2	52.1.8	
Bland, Thomas	412	3/2	75.4.8	
Brooks, Meriman	100	7/10	39.3.4	
Bowden, George	205	5/3	53.16.3	
Banks, James	22	7/3	7.19.6	
Banks, Andrew	125	12/6	78.2.6	
Brightwell, John est.	70	4/2	14.11.8	
Burton, James est.	89	"	18.10.10	
Bland, William (Younger)	300	7/3	108.15.0}	
Do. Dawson Cooke	103	4/2	21.9.2}	
Bird, Janet & Frances	230	10/5	119.10.5}	
Do. Robt. Smith, Dragon	22½	17/	19.2.6}	
Breadlove, John	37¾	4/2	7.17.3	
Brushwood, George	188	"	39.3.4}	
Do. Wares	112	3/2	17.4.8}	
Bray, Peter	51¼	6/3	16.0.3¾	
Bland, John Jun.	212	5/3	55.13.0}	
Do. Overstreets	96	4/2	20.0.0}	
Broocke, William	33	10/5	17.3.9}	
Do. Parmenas Bird	83	11/8	48.8.4}	
Carlton, Thomas Sen.	200	7/10	78.6.8}	
Do. Philemon Bird	83½	6/3	26.1.10½}	
Carlton, Noah	100	7/10	39.3.4	
Cooke, Henry est.	260	5/3	68.5.0}	
Ditto	49¼	10/5	25.10.5}	
Collins, John est.	75	3/2	11.17.6	
Carlton, John (S)	100	6/3	31.5.0	
Campbell, James T. (Orph)	296	12/6	185.0.0	
Carlton, Christopher Sen.	37½	6/3	11.14.5}	
Do. James Laughlin's	126½	3/2	26.8.2}	
Carlton, Richard est.	139	7/	48.13.0	
Cauthern, James	36½	3/2	5.15.7	
Carlton, William Sen.	309¾	11/6	178.1.2½	
Carlton, Christopher (Young)	148	5/	37.0.0	
Carlton, Richard	250	7/3	90.12.6	
			£1964.10.1¼	2.11.17.24.15

[page 3, List A, 1805] Persons names owning land	Quantity of land [168]	Price per acre	Total Amount Land	Amt. Tax Thereon in Dols. Cents
Carlton, Christopher Jun.	100	7/3	36.5.0}	
Do. John Stone's est.	159½	5/3	41.14.9}	
Cooper, Henry	50	4/2	10.8.4	
Carlton, Thomas (T) est.	90 10/11	6/3	28.7.11½	
Cardwell, James	150	4/2	31.5.0	
Cardwell, John	150	"	31.5.0	
Cardwell, William est.	77	"	15.11.6	
Cardwell, Thomas est.	110	"	22.18.4	
Cooke, John est.	300	"	62.10.0	
Collins, Thomas	281½	7/	98.10.6}	
Do. Robert S. Ware	84½	11/9	49.12.6 }	
Do. Metcalfe & Levert	289½	14/6	209.17.9}	
Do. Jane Crittenden	60	13/6	40.10.0}	
Carlton, John Jun.	235	4/2	48.19.2}	
Do. Baylor Fleet	2	12/6	1.5.0}	
Campbell, William	238	3/2	37.13.8	
Corbin, Richard	2390	11/1¾	1332.11.4}	
Do. Shackelford's	300	12/6	78.2.6}	
Do. Dixon's	416¾	15/5	321.10.10}	
Corr, James	100	6/2	30.16.8	
Crouch, James	105½	3/2	16.13.3½	
Collins, Joyeux	140	10/5	72.8.4	
Clayton, James	260	5/3	65.5.0	
Crittenden, Zachariah	34½	14/6	24.17.10	
Collier, John	100	4/2	20.16.8	
Cary, Wilson J.	1820	16/7	1509.1.8	
Campbell, James	130	5/9½	37.10.0}	
Do. Richard Garrett's	70	3/2	11.1.8}	
Do. Benjamin Faulkner	55¼	7/3	20.0.6¾	
Crittenden, Richard est.	178	5/3	46.14.6	
Corr, Thomas R.	231¼	"	60.12.9}	
Do. John Shackelford Mc.	73=22 poles	"	19.4.3}	
Do. Benjamin Walden's	170	"	44.12.6}	
Collier, Joseph	468	"	112.17.0	
Collier, Benjamin	75	"	19.13.9	
Clegg, Isaiah est.	241	4/2	50.4.2	
Cooke, Dawson	1	5/3	5.3}	
Do. John B. Whiting's	24¾	7/10	9.13.10½}	
Curry, John	155	4/	31.0.0	
Cooke, Thomas Sen.	240	3/2	38.0.0	
Cooke, Thomas Jun.	96	"	15.0.4	
Carlton, Humphrey	175	7/	61.5.0}	
Do. John Watt's est.	48½	6/3	15.3.1½}	
Carlton, Thomas est.	235	"	73.8.9	
Corr, John est.	503½	7/3	182.10.4½}	
Do. Thomas Dudley's	197½	6/3	61.14.4½}	
			£5149.0.9¾	3.17.21.16

[page 4, List A, 1805] Persons names owning land	Quantity of land	Price per acre	Total Amount Land	Amt. Tax Thereon in Dols. Cents
Campbell, John Sen.	400	12/6	250.0.0	
Do. Ralph G. Meredith est.	111½	14/6	80.16.9}	
Curry, James	70	4/2	14.11.8	
Do. John Broach	71	"	14.15.10}	
Do. Frances Webley	79	"	16.9.2}	
Corr, John Sen.	213	3/2	33.15.6}	
Do. John Corr Jun.	90	7/3	32.12.6}	
Do. Dawson Cooke	5=6 poles	4/2	1.1.0}	
Do. Ditto	106	3/2	16.15.8}	
Crittenden, Frances (R)	105¾	14/6	76.12.2	
Clarke, John	144	5/	36.0.0}	
Do. Samuel Hemingway	254½	4/2	53.0.3}	
Carlton, Lody	44	3/2	6.19.4	
Cooke, John est.	100	"	15.16.8	
Clayton, Maria H., Sally} K. and Polly R. Clayton}	72	9/11	35.14.0	
Collins, Mason	110	3/2	17.8.4	
Carlton, Lewis	9 1/11	6/3	2.16.10	
Collins, James	120	4/2	25.0.0	
Campbell, John Jun.	50	"	10.8.4	
Didlake, William est.	100	3/2	15.16.8	
Didlake, James est.	278	8/4	115.16.8	
Dunn, Thomas	50½	6/3	15.15.7½	
Dillard, George	50	12/6	31.5.0}	
Do. William Dillard Sen.	226	"	141.5.0}	
Durham, Thomas est.	85	3/2	13.9.2	
Dickie, Barbara	1½	17/	1.5.6}	
Do. Parmenas Bird	50¼	11/8	29.6.3}	
Do. Wm. Bird Jun. Exor. Ro.} Bird & Beverley Roy & wife}	37½	17/	31.17.6}	
Dudley, William est.	290	14/6	210.5.0}	
Do. Lydia Wedderburn	315½	6/3	98.11.10}	
Damm, John est.	55	"	17.3.9	
Dudley, James	180	7/10	70.10.0	
Damm, William	25	4/2	5.4.2	
Douglas, John	239	7/	83.13.0	
Didlake, John	1200	7/3	435.0.0}	
Do. Halyard's	186	5/3	48.16.6}	
Dudley, Ann	141	7/3	51.2.3	
Dudley, Guilford	106	"	38.8.6	
Dudley, Banks est.	230	3/2	36.8.4	
Downey, Michael est.	50	10/5	26.0.10	
Didlake, Royston	206	3/6½	36.7.4}	
Do. George Bowden's	65	4/2	13.10.0}	
Dillard, William Jun. est.	207½	15/	155.12.6	
Dudley, Thomas	70	6/3	21.17.6	
Dillard, Nicholas	75	4/2	15.12.6	
			£2499.15.4½	16.20.19.13

[page 5, List A, 1805] Persons names owning land	Quantity of land [169]	Price per acre	Total Amount Land	Amt. Tax Thereon in Dols. Cents
Drummond, John est.	150	6/3	46.17.6	
Dunn, John, Essex, Dragon	73	17/	62.1.0	
Digges, Frances	105	5/3	27.11.3	
Dean, Benjamin	50	"	13.12.6	
Dillard, Thomas A.	29	3/2	4.11.10}	
Do. Young Simpkins	1	"	0.3.2}	
Durham, George est.	50	4/2	10.8.4}	
Do. Newham Durham's	50	"	10.8.4}	
Didlake, Philip	83	"	17.5.10}	
Do. Edward Didlake's	40	10/5	20.16.8}	
Eubank, Richard est.	117	8/4	24.3.9	
Eubank, William est.	28¾	5/3	7.11.0	
Eubank, Richard Sen.	196	7/	68.12.0	
Eubank, Thomas	110	4/2	22.18.4	
Eubank, Richard Jun.	108¾	7/	38.1.1½}	
Do. Thomas Jeffries	12¾	7/3	4.12.5}	
Do. A. Dunn	147	5/3	38.11.9}	
Do. Anty. Hart	87¼	3/2	13.10.3½}	
Eubank, Warner	115	"	18.4.2}	
Do. Jno. Hemingway Jun.	4	4/2	16.8}	
Eubank, Philip	135¾	"	28.5.7½	
Fleet, Baylor	860	12/6	537.10.8	
Frazer, William est.	45	20/9	46.13.6	
Fleet, William	352	"	365.4.0}	
Do. Richd. T. Kauffman	15	"	15.11.3}	
Fisher, James	111	3/2	17.11.6	
Foster, Thomas	87¾	4/2	18.2.6	
Fauntleroy, Thomas	486	10/	243.0.0}	
Do. Henry Todds	500	18/	450.0.0}	
Do. William Bowdens	183	7/	64.1.0}	
Farinholtz, David	151¼	6/6	49.1.6	
Do. Davis'es	219½	6/9	74.1.6	
Faulkner, Benjamin	100	4/2	20.16.8}	
Do. Mary Faulkner's	333	6/3	104.1.4}	
Do. William Boyd	9½	10/5	4.10.9}	
Do. Anty. Gardner	3	17/	2.11.0}	
Do. John Southern	134½	4/2	28.0.5}	
Do. James Campbell	29¾	7/3	10.15.8¼}	
Do. Do.	112¼	4/2	23.7.8½}	
Faugerson, Thomas	62	10/5	32.5.10}	
Do. Thomas Collins	48	7/	16.16.0}	
Faucett, Vincent	46½	10/5	24.4.4½	
Fisher, William	30	5/3	7.17.6	
			£2635.8.2¾	2.17.18.20.11

[page 6, List A, 1805] Persons names owning land	Quantity of land	Price per acre	Total Amount Land	Amt. Tax Thereon in Dols. Cents
Graves, Eleanor	163½	5/3	42.18.4½}	
Do. John B. Whiting	100=13 poles	7/10	39.4.0}	
Garlick, Camm est.	917	6/3	286.11.3	
Gresham, Philemon	200	"	62.10.0	
Gresham, Mary	100	7/10	39.3.4	
Gresham, William (B)	100	4/2	20.16.8}	
Do. William Rowe	95	6/3	29.13.9}	
Gardner, Anthony	638	11/	350.11.8}	
Do. Dragon Swamp	67½	17/	57.7.6}	
Do. Vincent Hart	73¾	6/6	23.19.4½	
Gardner, Elizabeth	100	6/3	31.5.0	
Gibson, Richard	156½	3/2	24.16.7	
Gibson, Eubank	56½	"	8.18.11}	
Do. Rich[d.] Eubank Jun.	3½	7/	1.4.6}	
Gibson, Philip	129½	3/2	20.9.3½	
Gresham, Meacham	100	5/3	26.5.0}	
Do. A. Gresham	4	17/	3.8.0}	
Gresham, Ambrose	80	5/3	21.0.0}	
Do. Dragon Swamp	22	17/	18.5.0}	
Gresham, John (B)	79	5/3	20.14.9}	
Do. A. Gresham's	4	17/	3.8.0}	
Griffin, William est.	859	14/6	622.15.6	
Garrett, James	230	4/2	48.18.4}	
Do. William Garrett	100	"	20.16.8}	
Garrett, Robert	200	7/	70.0.0}	
Do. Philemon Bird	54¾	6/3	17.2.2.¼}	
Do. William Hunt's	170	"	53.2.6}	
Do. Spencer Ware's	70	5/3	18.7.6}	
Do. Robert Reed's	26	4/2	5.8.4}	
Gaines, Robert est.	537¾	20/9	558.8.7¾}	
Do. A. Curtis	50	5/3	13.2.6}	
Guthrie, James	60	12/6	37.10.0	
Guthrie, Richard	60	"	37.10.0}	
Ditto	162	3/2	25.13.0}	
Garrett, Edward	210	5/3	55.2.6}	
Do. Trice's	489½	"	128.9.10}	
Garrett, William (son W[m.])	197¾	7/3	71.13.8¾	
Groom, John	173	3/2	27.17.10}	
Do. John Bowden's	95	4/2	19.15.10}	
Do. Robert Lumpkins's	106¾	"	22.4.9¾}	
Guthrie, Rachel	50	8/4	20.16.8	
Goldman, Martin	140	4/2	29.3.4	
Garnett, James	100	"	20.16.8	
Gully, Philip est.	50	3/2	7.18.4	
Garrett, William Sen.	225	3/4½	37.19.4½}	
Do. George B. Bird	60	6/3	18.15.0}	
Do. Henry F. Dudley	50	5/3	13.2.6}	
			£3135.3.6½	

[page 7, List A, 1805] Persons names owning land	Quantity of land [170]	Price per acre	Total Amount Land	Amt. Tax Thereon in Dols. Cents
Gramshill, Henry	25	3/2	3.19.2	
Garrett, Ann Watts	112	5/	28.0.0	
Gilmore, Richard	414	5/3	108.13.6	
Garrett, Richard	100	4/2	20.16.8	
Garrett, William Jun.	120	"	25.0.0	
Garrett, Edward Jun.	150	6/3	46.17.6	
Gaines, Benjamin	360	20/4	366.0.0}	
Do. Howard Williams	52½	4/2	10.8.9}	
Gaines, Henry	360	20/4	366.0.0	
Gatewood, Philip	1	7/10	7.10	
Guthrie, Major est.	100	5/	25.0.0	
Henderson, James	25	5/3	6.11.3	
Hoskins, William est.	296	20/	296.0.0}	
Do. Balance Bray's	2	7/10	15.8}	
Homes, Benjamin [Hoomes]	447	12/6	279.7.6}	
Do. Ann Kennedy's	75	"	46.17.6}	
Hemingway, John Jun.	263	4/2	54.15.10	
Hare, William est.	217	5/3	56.19.3	
Harwood, Christopher est.	194	24/10	240.17.8	
Harwood, Priscilla	165	18/	148.10.0	
Hart, James	150	3/2	23.15.0	
Holderby, John Sen.	73¼	4/2	15.5.2½	
Holderby, John Jun.	108¾	7/10	42.6.0	
Hart, Anthony	190	5/3	49.17.6}	
Do. balance of Sundry Persons	41	3/2	6.9.10}	
Hart, Gregory	200	"	31.13.4	
Hart, William est.	250	3/3½	41.2.11	
Harwood, John est.	109	10/5	56.15.5	
Henry, Samuel H. est.	1900	14/6	1377.10.0	
Henry, James	75	12/6	46.17.6	
Hoskins, Robert	287	6/	86.2.0}	
Do. Robert Smith's	157¾	10/5	82.10.6¾}	
Hart, Alden	77	4/2	16.0.10	
Do. .Anty. Hart's	231	3/2	36.11.6	
Hutson, William	75	"	15.13.6½}	
Do. John Daniel	25	"	5.4.2}	
Howerton, Heritage est.	122¼	20/9	126.16.7¼	
Halyard, William	260	6/3	81.5.0	
Howerton, John	269½	5/3	70.14.10½	
Hart, Vincent	1¼	6/6	8.1½}	
Do. William Rowzey's	88	7/3	31.18.0}	
Harris, Samuel	214¼	5/3	56.4.9¾	
Hogg, William & Legatees} of Holt Richason}	50	18/-	45.0.0	
Jones, Thomas	255	4/2	53.2.6	
Jeffries, Thomas (B)	63	7/3	22.16.9	
Do. John Harwood's	25½	10/5	13.5.7½	
Do. Brett's est.	57¾	18/	51.19.6}	
			£4619.5.2¼	4.18.23.21.18

[page 8, List A, 1805] Persons names owning land	Quantity of land	Price per acre	Total Amount Land	Amt. Tax Thereon in Dols. Cents
Jones, James Jun.	100	5/3	26.5.0}	
Do. Mary Jones	150	26/11	201.17.6}	
Jeffries, Going	60	4/2	12.10.0	
Jordan, Robert	66 2/3	"	13.18.10	
Jones, Mary	150	26/11	201.17.6	
Ison, George	140¼	5/3	36.16.3¾	
Inge, Vincent est.	33	8/4	13.15.0	
Kemp, John	296	7/3	107.0.3	
Kauffman, Richard T.	161	26/	209.6.0	
Kauffman, Sambo, Humphry} and Lucy, free Negroes	167	7/6	62.5.0	
Kidd, John	81¾	5/3	26.6.6¾	
Kennedy, Archibald est.	38¼	4/2	7.19.4	
Kennedy, Ann	33¼	"	6.18.6½	
Kennedy, Ann Jun.	33¾	"	7.0.6	
Kennedy, Lucy	37½	"	7.16.2	
Kidd, Bartholomew	136	5/3	35.14.0}	
Do. William Dillard Jun.	132½	4/2	27.12.1}	
Do. Robert Lumpkins's	95½	"	19.17.11}	
Kidd, Benjamin	111	13/6	74.18.2}	
Do. Dragon Swamp	36	17/	30.12.0}	
Kidd, John est.	370	7/3	134.2.6}	
Do. Lumpkin & Pierce	60	4/2	12.10.0}	
Do. Thomas Dillard	45	14/6	32.12.6}	
King, Dicey est.	18	8/4	7.10.0	
Lumpkin, Jacob	621	6/3	194.1.3	
Lewis, Iveson	356	14/6	258.2.0	
Leigh, Lucy	101	24/10	125.8.2	
Leigh, John est.	133	"	165.2.10}	
Ditto	66	"	81.19.0}	
Leigh, Richard est.	560	6/3	175.0.0	
Mitchell, Ralph est.	193	10/5	100.10.5	
Mitchell, Sally est.	391	13/	254.3.0	
Mitchell, James (Orphan)	225	"	146.5.0	
Moore, Lambuth	56¾	4/2	11.17.5½	
Moore, Lodawick, John and Richard	100	3/2	15.16.8	
Major, Josiah	200	4/2	41.13.4	
Mitchel, John est.	270	5/3	70.17.0}	
Do. Rootes's	128	9/11	63.9.3}	
Mann, Joseph Sen.	231	6/3	72.3.9	
Moore, Agathy	40	4/2	8.6.8	
Montague, William	170	"	35.8.4	
Meridith, Ralph G. est.	350½	14/6	254.2.3	
			£3390.18.--	12.20.20.13

[page 9, List A, 1805] Persons names owning land	Quantity of land [171]	Price per acre	Total Amount Land	Amt. Tax Thereon in Dols. Cents
Muire, Richard	93	12/6	58.2.6}	
Do. Richard Anderson est.	177	5/3	46.9.3}	
Mitchel, Richard	74¼	4/2	15.9.4½	
Moore, Richard est.	145	6/3	45.6.8	
McCarty, Joseph est.	73	3/2	11.11.2	
Metcalfe, Thomas	256	14/6	181.8.8	
Maderias, John	34½	6/3	10.15.7½	
Milby, Richard	175	3/2	27.14.2	
Morgan, William	3	6/3	0.18.9	
Moore, John	37	4/2	7.14.2	
Mann, John	179¼	7/10	74.7.5½	
Muire, William	125	5/3	32.16.3	
Newcomb, William	169	3/2	26.15.2}	
Do. Benj[a.] Dillard's	148	5/3	48.17.0}	
Do. Ditto	52	"	13.13.0}	
Noel, Silas M.	104	7/3	37.14.0	
Orvil, John	100	6/3	31.5.0}	
Ditto	52	"	15.12.6}	
Oliver, John	320	5/3	84.0.0	
Overstreet, Gabriel est.	80	4/2	16.13.4}	
Do. Haynes's	130	5/3	34.2.6}	
Oakes, Henry	198½	3/2	34.2.0	
Oakes, William	80	4/2	16.13.4	
Oliver, William	59	"	12.5.10	
Do. Howard Williams	62 7/8	"	13.1.11¾	
Oakes, Ann	60	"	12.10.0	
Oliver, Jn[o.] (said to belong to Philip Vass)	210	¾	35.0.0	
Oliver, Francis	89¼	4/2	18.11.10½	
Pitts, Benjamin G.	100	5/4	26.13.4	
Pace, Benjamin est.	263	7/3	95.6.9	
Pynes, Benjamin est.	164	6/3	51.5.0	
Pynes, Robert	111½	"	34.16.10½	
Do. William Adams	53¾	"	16.15.11¾	
Pynes, Benjamin	46¼	"	14.9.0¾	
Pemberton, John Sen.	90	"	28.2.3}	
Do. Jacob Lumpkin	60	"	18.5.0}	
Pollard, Robert	6	24/10	7.9.0}	
Do. John Omealy	367	30/	550.10.0}	
Palmer, Charles	107¾	18/	96.19.6}	
Ditto	104	"	93.12.0}	
Pigg, John est.	324	14/6	234.18.0}	
Do. Cockses	180	7/3	65.5.0}	
Pemberton, John Jun.	121	6/3	37.17.6	
Pierce, Beverly	25¾	4/2	5.7.3½}	
Do. Philip Pierce's	17	3/2	2.13.10}	
Patterson, Joseph	62¾	"	9.18.8½	
Pierce, Philip	83	"	13.2.10	
Pierce, Thomas est.	87	4/2	18.2.6	
			£2385.2.5¾	5.17.24.24.15

[page 10, List A, 1805] Persons names owning land	Quantity of land	Price per acre	Total Amount Land	Amt. Tax Thereon in Dols. Cents
Pilsbury, George	109¾	10/9	58.19.9¾	
Palmer, Roger	314	6/	94.4.0	
Price, Robert	399	6/3	124.13.9	
Pemberton, James	75	"	23.8.9	
Roane, Thomas est.	2033	18/8	1897.9.4}	
Do. H. Carlton's	200	6/3	63.10.0}	
Do. Brett's	34¾	18/	31.5.6}	
Do. Robert Pynes's	24½	6/3	7.9.1½}	
Rowe, Elizabeth	665	20/9	689.18.9	
Rowe, Francis (Orphan)	612½	4/8	142.16.8	
Richason, James (son of Elias)	86	4/2	17.8.4	
Richards, John	571	4/8	124.8.0	
Richason, James Sen.	180	4/2	37.10.0	
Richason, William Sen.	181	"	37.14.2	
Roane, Thomas (Middlesex)	14¼	15/	10.13.9	
Richason, William (son James)	188½	4/2	39.5.5	
Richason, William Jun.	118½	5/3	31.2.1½}	
Do. Robert Stone's	101	4/2	21.0.10}	
Richason, John est.	101½	5/3	26.12.10½	
Roane, Major est.	687½	3/8	128.18.1½	
Do. John Lynes's	455¾	6/3	142.8.5½}	
Do. Palmer's	9	7/3	3.5.3}	
Raines, Giles	60	3/2	9.10.0	
Robinson, Benjamin est.	1300	8/4	541.13.4	
Roane, Charles	133	19/	126.7.0}	
Do. Dragon Swamp	70	17/	59.10.0}	
Roy, Beverly	700	8/4	291.13.4}	
Do. Thomas Browns	454	12/6	283.15.0}	
Do. Corbins	125	"	78.2.6}	
Richason, James Jun.	250	5/3	65.12.6	
Richason, John Sen.	120	"	31.10.0	
Richason, John Jun.	50	4/2	10.8.4	
Spencer, John	416	7/3	150.16.0	
Spencer, Ann	116	"	60.3.6	
Stark, Richard est.	350	5/8	99.3.4	
Stone, Robert est.	24¾	4/2	5.3.1½	
Stone, Job	100	"	20.16.8	
Stone, Robert	31½	5/3	8.5.4½	
Smith, John (son of Rob$^{t.}$)	88	10/5	45.16.8}	
Do. Dragon Swamp	12	17/	10.8.0}	
Smith, Francis	150	3/2	23.5.0	
Simpkins, Young	59	"	9.6.10	
Sears, Philip	83	4/2	17.5.10	
Shackelford, William est.	400	14/6	310.0.0	
Spencer, Thomas	300	10/5	156.5.0}	
Ditto	225	4/2	53.2.6}	
Ditto	73	6/9	24.12.9}	
Ditto	71½	4/2	14.17.11}	
			£6261.3.6¼	4.17.22.23.18

[page 11, List A, 1805] Persons names owning land	Quantity of land [172]	Price per acre	Total Amount Land	Amt. Tax Thereon in Dols. Cents
Seward, Benjamin	115	3/2	18.4.2}	
Do. Loddy Carlton's	18½	"	2.17.1¾}	
Smith, Thomas G.	485	14/6	351.12.6}	
Do. Benjamin Dabney's	400	"	290.0.0}	
Do. Ditto	100	8/4	41.13.4}	
Sadler, John est.	150	6/3	46.17.6	
Shackelford, Zachariah	200	"	62.10.0}	
Do. Richard Anderson	177	5/3	46.9.3}	
Shackelford, John (R)	401¼	8/4	167.3.10	
Shackelford, William	151	6/3	47.3.9}	
Do. Wyatt's lease	30	5/3	7.16.6}	
Shackelford, John, Mc	283	6/2	87.5.2}	
Do. John Collier, Cobler	76¾	5/3	20.2.11¼}	
Do. Thomas R. Corr	5=30 poles	"	1.7.2¾	
Shackelford, Benjamin, Halyard's lease	1	5/9½	0.5.9½}	
Shepherd, John	67	6/	20.2.0	
Smith, John Doct[r.]	½	30/	0.15.0	
Smith, Samuel	1	7/10	0.7.10}	
Do., Dragon	10	17/	8.10.0}	
Spencer, Meacham	323	6/9	109.0.3	
Southern, John	15½	4/2	3.4.7	
Sears, Thomas	123	6/7	40.9.9	
Do. H. Williams	42¼	4/2	8.17.1	
Smith, Robert Jun.	30	10/5	15.12.6	
Smith, Lewis	44	10/6	23.2.0	
Seward, William	70	3/2	11.1.8	
Tureman, Elizabeth	24¾	"	3.18.4½	
Tureman, George	50	"	7.18.4	
Taliaferro, William	1000	14/6	725.0.0	
Townley, Robert	200	6/3	62.10.0}	
Do. Anderson's	117	14/6	84.16.6}	
Taliaferro, Philip est.	662	8/4	275.16.8	
Taliaferro, James B.	374½	12/6	234.7.6	
Thruston, Armstead	111 1/3	4/3	23.15.1	
Thruston, Bachelor	200	3/2	31.13.4	
Turner, Benjamin	36	4/2	7.10.0	
Townley, Ann	79	"	16.9.2	
Turner, Henry est.	100	"	20.16.8	
Tunstall, Richard G.	206½	7/10	73.3.7	
Taylor, William	40	6/3	12.10.0	
Do. Philip Taliaferro est.	200	8/4	83.6.8	
Watts, Edward est.	250	7/3	90.12.6}	
Do. W. Watts est.	113	5/	28.5.0}	
Watts, John	293	7/10	114.15.2}	
Do. Pembertons	45	6/3	14.1.3}	
			£3343.17.6¾	2.15.20.18.14

[page 12, List A, 1805] Persons names owning land	Quantity of land	Price per acre	Total Amount Land	Amt. Tax Thereon in Dols. Cents
Watts, Kauffman	270	5/3	70.17.6}	
Do. Eubank & Burch	257	5/9	73.17.9}	
Do. Jn[o.] & D. Hemingway	312	4/2	64.3.4}	
Watts, James	350	"	72.8.4}	
Do. W. Watts est.	60	15/	45.0.0}	
Williams, Howard	66 1/8	4/2	13.15.6¼}	
Do. Dragon Swamp	43	17/	36.11.0}	
Wyatt, Thomas	206	7/10	81.2.0	
Wyatt, William	39¾	7/	13.18.3	
Williams, Mountague	300	6/3	93.15.0	
Walton, James	80	4/2	16.8.4}	
Do. Tho[s.] Walton's est.	66	"	13.15.0}	
Williams, Charles est.	336	"	70.0.0	
Walton, Elizabeth	60	3/2	9.10.0	
Walton, John est.	176	5/3	46.4.0	
Walton, William est.	40	4/2	8.6.8	
Ware, John est.	75	5/3	19.3.9	
Waring, Robert P. est.	542	10/9	291.10.6	
Walden, Lewis	90	10/5	46.17.6	
Walden, Richard Jun.	90	10/5	46.17.6	
Walden, Lewis est.	150	3/2	23.15.0}	
Do. Thomas Dudley's	84½	6/3	28.3.3½}	
Williams, George	40	4/2	8.6.8	
Wyatt, Richard	175	12/6	109.7.6	
Watkins, Philip	197	5/3	51.14.3	
Ware, Robert Jun. est.	10¾	4/2	2.4.9½	
Williams, Elizabeth	16½	3/2	2.12.9	
White, James est.	200	6/3	62.10.0	
Wedderburn, Lydia	350	"	109.7.6	
Whiting, Beverly est.	1778	7/10	696.7.8	
Webley, John est.	173	5/3	45.8.3}	
Do. Collier & Dillard	279	4/2	58.2.6}	
Ware, Robert Jun.	100	8/4	41.13.4	
Ware, William	100	"	41.13.4	
Walden, Benjamin	203	5/3	53.5.9}	
Do. Richard Anderson's	120½	"	31.12.7½}	
Waller, Edward est.	133½	3/2	21.2.9	
Waller, George est.	87	"	13.15.6}	
Do. John Shackelford	47¾	8/4	19.17.11}	
Waller, John	65	3/7	11.12.11	
Waller, Robert est.	48	"	8.12.0	
Do. Groom's est.	187	3/2	29.12.2	
Ware, Nicholas	100	"	15.16.8	
			£2620.7.0¾	1.17.21.21.1[0]

[page 13, List A, 1805] Persons names owning land	Quantity of land [173]	Price per acre	Total Amount Land	Amt. Tax Thereon in Dols. Cents	
Walton, Beverly	47½	7/10	18.12.1		
Watts, George K.	36	26/	46.16.0		
Wyatt, Smith	29¾	7/3	10.15.8}		
Do. William Wyatt's	9	7/	3.3.0}		
Willis, Robert	105	14/6	75.2.6		
Williams, Christopher	100	5/3	26.5.0		
Walden, Charles	109¼	7/10	42.15.9		2.3.3
			£223.10.--		
			[44086.15.3¼]		

[arithmetic omitted]
$705.40 Tax on Land

[page]

A list of retail merchants within the District of Robert B. Hill one of the Commissioners of the revenue in the County of King and Queen to whom Licences have been issued since my last return to wit:

1805 April 27th	Edward Hill	$15.00
	John Temple	15.00
	Thomas Jeffries	15.00
	Geo. Minor for Jno. Johnson	15.00
" May 29	Joshua Ward	13.75
" August 10	Solomon Patten	10.84
		84.59

Ro. B. Hill, Comr.
August 10th 1805

At a Court held for King & Queen County at the Courthouse on Monday the 9th of September 1805. Robert B. Hill, one of the Commissioners of the revenue for this County, returned this list. Teste Robert Pollard, C.C.
A Copy Teste Robert Pollard, C.C.

A List of Land within the District of Robert B. Hill, Commissioner in the upper District in the County of King and Queen for the year 1805 to wit

LIST B

[page 1, List B, 1805] Persons names owning Land	Quantity of Land	Price per acre	Tot. Amt. Value Land	
	[174]			
Atkins, Joseph este.	66	4/2	[£]13.15.0	
Alexander, Benjamin	202	9/4	94.5.4	
do. of James Halbert	124	6/2	38.15.0	
do. Lot in Dunkirk, ann[l.] rent			20.0.0	
do. of Joseph Meede			4.10.0	
Acre, Seaton	52	9/4	24.5.4	
do. of Richard Eubank &c.	87¾	5/3	23.0.9	
Alexander, Elisha	338	9/4	157.14.8	
Anderson, Churchill	374	7/3	135.11.6	
Atkins, John	277	5/	69.5.0	
Anderson, Sarah	86	20/9	89.3.9	
Barton, John este.	125	4/2	26.0.10	
Broach, Benoni	48	10/5	25.4.0	
Brown, Henry jun[r.]	100	12/	60.0.0	
Beverley, Robert este.	2444	10/5	1262.16.4	
Brown, Henry	526	7/4½	190.17.9	
Bland, John	83	8/4	34.11.8	
Bates, James	358	11/	149.3.4	
do.	42	4/2	8.15.0	
do. of Rice Garnett	89	7/3	32.5.3	
Braxton, Carter	616¾	10/5	321.4.5¼	
Brooking, Frances	900	"	468.15.0	
Boughton, John	200 1/8	8/4	83.7.6½	
Brown, William	18¼	3/2	2.17.9½	
do. of Ware's Exors. &c.	196½	7/3	71.4.7½	
Bagby, Richard	260	"	94.5.0	
Bagby, Thomas	260	"	94.5.0	
do. of Jacob Lumpkin	235	6/3	73.8.9	
Brizendine, Armistead	86 2/3	8/4	35.17.6	
Bromley, John	60	7/10	23.10.0	
Broach, William	20	"	7.16.8	
Brown, John	50	7/4½	18.8.9	
Bohannan, William	163	5/3	42.15.9	
do. of Lumpkin Gresham	343	7/3	124.6.9	
Bates, William	81	7/9½	31.10.1	
do. of Rice Garnett	117	7/3	42.8.4	
Broach, George	75¾	14/6	54.18.4½	
Boulware, Samuel	175¾	31/3	274.12.2¼	
Boulware, Lee	153	7/3	55.9.3	
Brown, William jun[r.]	54	7/4	19.6.0	
Brown, Lewis	79	8/2	32.5.2	
Beadles, Justin	20	6/3	6.5.0	
do. of Henry Garnett	4	"	1.5.0	
Bagby, John	271	7/3	99.7.3	
Bagby, Robert	118	"	42.15.6	
Bohannan, Robert	50	4/6	11.5.0	
			£4593.11.[3]	20.21.19.[ ]

[page 2, List B, 1805] Persons names owning Land	Quantity of Land	Price per acre	Tot. Amt. Value Land	
Burnett, James	65	6/3	[£] 20.6.3	
Bray, James	195	7/10	76.7.6	
Crafton, Thomas	119	9/4	55.10.8	
Crafton, James	59	"	27.10.8	
Crafton, John	117½	"	54.12.0	
Crane, John	130	6/3	40.2.6	
do. of Clem Pynes	14	3/2	2.4.4	
do. of Ware's este.	49¼	7/3	17.17.0¾	
do. of Ware's Exors.	71	"	29.14.9	
Cleverius, Benjamin	419	20/9	434.14.3	
Carlton, John	242	14/6	175.9.0	
Cole, G. Thomas	105	6/3	32.16.3	
Carlton, Lewis	100	8/4	41.3.4	
Do. of H. Carlton's este.	150	7/10	58.15.0	
Clayton, Thomas este.	275	7/3	99.13.9	
Crane, George este.	30	7/3	10.17.6	
Courtney, Thomas	156	7/10	61.2.0	
Carlton, Joel	53½	6/3	16.4.5	
Cooke, Moses	100	8/4	41.13.4	
do. of Ambrose Cooke	100	"	41.13.4	
Chapman, M. George	250	7/10	87.18.4	
Courtney, Robert	183½	"	71.17.5	
do. of Jacob Abbott	40½	"	15.13.4	
Cannady, William	100	6/3	31.5.0	
do. of George Satterwhite	15¼	"	4.15.3½	
Cooke, William	65	5/5	17.12.1	
Cooke, James	65	8/9	28.8.9	
Courtney, Fanny & Children	78	7/10	30.10.0	
Cross, Joseph	103½	6/3	32.6.10½	
Campbell, William	837¼	7/3	303.10.0¾	
Campbell, Whitaker	406	7/10	159.0.4	
Crow, John	121	5/3	31.19.2¼	
Crow, Nathaniel este.	34½	6/3	10.15.7½	
Crouch, Edmund	74¼	7/10	29.1.9	
Campbell, William, of J. Campbell	74¼	18/8	69.6.0	
Cauthorn, Vincent, of Tunstalls	43	8/4	17.18.4	
Crane, Nathaniel	66	3/2	10.9.0	
Carlton, Thomas	297	7/10	116.6.6	
Dew, Thomas	331	12/6	206.17.6	
Dew, William este.	935	14/6	677.17.6	
Duling, William este.	264	8/4	110.0.0	
Dix, Gabriel	109	6/3	[5]4.1.5	
do. of R. Starling	416½	7/10	163.2.7	
Durham, Joseph	105	4/3	21.12.6	
do. of Dunn	10	4/2	2.1.8	
Deshazo, John	188	7/4	68.18.8	
Deshazo, Larkin	87	7/3	34.4.10	
do. of John Crane	6	6/3	1.17.6	
do. of Benjamin Hoomes	430¾	4/4	93.4.5	
Dunbar, David	366	8/4	152.10.0	
Dudley, Peter este.	530	7/3¼	186.18.4	
Dally, George	174¼	3/2	27.11.9½	
Durham, John	25	3/2	3.19.4	
Do. of Thomas Johnson	18¼	"	2.17.9½	
Dickie, James	512	8/4	213.6.8	
			$4408.4.1¼	4.21.29.[ ]

[page 3, List B, 1805] Persons names owning Land	Quantity of Land	Price per acre	Tot. Amt. Value Land
	[175]		
Deshazo, Unity	71	7/10	[£] 27.16.3
Deshazo, Polly, orphan	41	"	16.1.2
Dally, John este.	200	3/2	31.13.4
Dobbins, Charles este.	147	5/3	38.11.9
Dobson, Pitman	136	10/2¾	69.10.9¾
Daniel, Leonard	81	7/10	26.14.6
Deshazo, William	130	9/4	60.13.4
Eubank, Henry	171	5/3	44.17.9
do. of Richard Eubank	26	"	6.16.6
Edwards, Thomas	66	4/2	13.15.0
do. of Owen Gwathmey	185	8/2	75.10.10
Eubank, James	111	10/2¾	56.15.5
Eubank, Polly	127	"	64.19.1
Eubank, William	130	"	66.9.9¼
Eubank, John	136	"	69.10.9¾
Fogg, James	120	6/3	27.10.0
Fleet, William	512	12/	307.4.0
Fogg, Frederick	298	8/4	124.3.4
Fauntleroy, G. Samuel	2069	20/	2069.0.0
do. of P.A. Blackburn &c.	57 1/3	20/9	59.9.8
do. of Frances Anderson	28 2/3	"	29.14.10
do. of Vivion Brooking	30	10/5	15.12.6
Fox, S. Joseph	28	7/10	10.19.4
do.	39	"	15.5.6
do.	94	7/3	31.1.6
Fogg, Thomas	223	10/2¾	114.2.1¾
do. of Henry Lyne	352	8/4	146.13.4
Falkner, Thomas	220	6/3	68.15.0
Grafton, Sally & Ann	132	9/4	61.12.0
Gayle, John	170¾	7/5	63.6.4¾
do. of William Gayle	7¼	"	2.13.11
Gatewood, Chaney	829	10/5	437.17.11
do. of Noel's	362½	14/6	262.16.3
" Harwood's	125	4/2	46.17.6
" Eubank's	300	14/3	217.10.0
" Walden's Este.	120	12/6	75.0.0
" Wm. Lyne, lot in D'kirk, annl. rent			33.0.0
" Saml. Roane	457	17/2	387.5.2
Garnett, Joshua este.	325	8/4	134.3.4
Gatewood, Joseph	445	10/5	231.15.5
do. of John Schools	70	8/4	29.3.4
Gatewood, John	78	"	32.10.0

[page 3 *continued*, List B, 1805] Persons names owning Land	Quantity of Land	Price per acre	Tot. Amt. Value Land	
Garnett, Reuben	656½	8/10	289.19.1	
do. of Halbert &c.	28	10/5	14.12.10	
do. of Gabriel Gatewood &c.	50	"	26.0.10	
do. of do.	20¾	"	10.16.1¼	
do. of James Upshaw junr.	61	8/	24.8.0	
do. of Jno. Gatewood	52	8/4	21.13.4	
Garnett, M. Reuben	220	8/10	97.3.4	
Gwathmey, Temple	600	35/3	1057.10.0	
Garlick, Saml. este.	454	24/10	463.14.4	
Garlick, John este.	839	29	1216.11.0	
Griffith, Thomas	22¾	6/3	7.0.7½	
Griffith, Joseph Este.	22¾	"	7.0.7½	
Gresham, Samuel	432½	7/3	156.15.7½	
do. of Rice Garnett	157	"	56.18.1	
Guthrie, William	91¼	7/5	33.14.7	
do. of Richard Hill	46	8/2	18.15.8	
do. of William Campbell	31	7/3	11.4.9	
Gaines, Harry este.	481½	20/4	489.10.6	
Gaines, B. Robert	481½	"	489.10.6	
Gresham, Thomas este.	455¼	6/8	151.13.4	
			$10347.11.10	5.23.3.24.25.6

[page 4, List B, 1805] Persons names owning Land	Quantity of Land	Price per acre	Tot. Amt. Value Land
Griffith, Milly	50	6/3	15.12.6
Graves, Thomas	66¼	7/3	23.18.6
Gresham, George	141	3/2	22.6.6
Gatewood, William (*Tucko.*)	33	"	5.4.6
Gleason, Patrick	134	8/4	55.16.8
~~Gatewood, Gabriel~~	~~57¼~~	~~10/5~~	~~29.16.4¾~~
Gayle, William	344	7/5	127.11.4
Garnett, Henry	438	9/2	200.15.0
do. of Wilson Lumpkin	121	9/4	56.9.4
do. of Ovil Row	51½	"	23.12.8
Gatewood, William (Son of John)	132	10/	66.0.0
Gatewood, Philip	613	17/2	526.3.2
Gayle, Thomas, Lot Dunkirk, annl. rent			9.0.0
Garrett, Robert junr.	33	8/4	13.15.0
Gresham, Anthony	22	8/4	9.3.4
Gwathmey, Owen	82	8/2	33.9.8
Gresham, James	113	7/10	44.5.2
George, Cooper, of Tho. C. Tunstall	13	8/4	5.8.4
Gayle, Matthew este.	323	11/5	184.7.7
Gatewood, Robert, of Jno. Gatewood	30	8/4	12.10.0
Hill, William este.	1267	14/6	918.4.3
Hawes, Walker	97	"	70.6.6
Hitchcock, Thomas	140	4/2	29.3.4
Hoskins, Samuel este.	345	6/3	107.16.3
do. of Elisha Alexander	57	10/5	25.13.9
Hutchason, William	200	7/1	70.16.8
Heskew, John este.	61	5/3	16.0.3
Heskew, John junr. este.	50	6/3	15.12.6
do. of Clem Pynes	10	3/2	1.11.8
do. of Larkin Deshazo	19¼	4/4	4.2.4
Hill, Edward	1125¾	18/8	1050.14.0
do. of Quarles	130¾	17/2	112.4.6½
Hoskins, John	767	10/5	399.9.7
do. of Boughtons	100	8/4	41.13.4
" of Fleet & Semple	2	10/5	1.0.10
" of Semple	18 1/8	"	9.8.9½
" of Rowe &c.	446	7/3	161.13.6
Hurt, West	14	5/3	3.3.6
do. of Bohannan's este.	80	4/6	18.0.0
Holt, William	123	14/3	87.12.9
do. of Abram Wilson &c.	41	6/3	12.6.3
Hutchason, John	54¼	8/9	23.14.8¼
Hall, Corbin	72	4/2	15.0.0
Hill, B. Robert	257	8/2	104.18.10
do. of Richard Hill	103¾	"	42.7.3½
Hill, Henry	420	"	171.10.0
do. of Gwathmey	107	"	43.13.10
Hoskins, Thomas	55	"	22.9.2
Hutchason, Charles	200	7/1	70.16.8
Jones, John este.	300	8/11	133.15.0
Jeffries, Edward	70	3/2	11.1.8
Jeffries, Ambrose	237	7/10	92.16.6
Jeffries, Robert	110	7/6	41.5.0
do. of L. Gresham	10	7/3	3.12.6
do. of Jacob Lumpkin	5	7/3	1.16.3
do. of Lumpkin Gresham	20	"	7.5.0
			$8378.16.2¾

21.25.23.16

[page 5, List B, 1805] Persons names owning Land	[176]	Quantity of Land	Price per acre	Tot. Amt. Value Land
Jones, James este.		160	14/6	[£] 116.0.0
do.		196	10/5	102.1.8
Jones, Rawleigh este.		135¾	17/10	121.0.10½
Jeffries, John este.		100	7/10	39.3.4
Johnson, Thomas		53¾	7/2	19.5.2½
Jones, John, of Boughton & wife		29 1/8	6/3	9.2.0
Jones, John, of Roderick Starling		100	89/2	40.16.8
Kemp, John		178	7/3	64.2.2
do. of Hill's exors.		44¾	8/2	18.5.5
Keeling, Mary		78½	8/	31.8.0
Kay, Christopher		116	6/3	36.6.0
do. of T. Gouldman		416½	9/	107.8.6
Lumpkin, James		213	7/10	83.8.2
Lumpkin, Henry		400	9/4	186.13.4
Lumpkin, John este.		125	6/3	35.11.3
Lumpkin, William este.		61½	13/6	41.10.3
Lafon, Francis		119	8/4	49.11.8
Lankford, Thomas este.		100	4/2	20.16.8
Lumpkin, Robert Senr.		374	8/4	155.16.8
Lumpkin, Henry junr.		190	9/4	88.13.4
Lumpkin, W. John este.		140	7/10	54.16.8
do. of John Ware's este.		118½	7/3	42.15.6
Longest, Caleb		97	7/10	37.19.10
Longest, Richard		227¾	"	89.4.2
Longest, John		100	"	39.3.4
Lumpkin, Anthony este.		216	6/3	67.10.0
Lumpkin, Robert junr. este.		279¾	5/3	73.8.8¼
Lumpkin, William Junr.		183¼	10/5	95.6.3
Lumpkin, John		112	3/2	17.14.8
Lyne, William		1160	8/4	483.6.8
Lumpkin, Richard		178	5/3	46.14.6
Longest, William		83	8/4	34.11.8
Lumpkin, Ann		47	13/6	31.14.6
Lumpkin, Elizabeth		51	"	38.8.6
Lumpkin, John, Kg. Wm.		105	"	70.17.6
do. of Henry White & Wife		57	"	38.9.6
Lyne, Edmund		50	8/4	20.16.8
Longest, Daniel, of Pendleton's Admr.		156	7/4	57.4.0
Motley, Edwin		815	10/5	428.2.6
do. of Semple		149	12/6	93.2.6
Martin, C. Thomas		583	14/6	422.13.6
do.		134½	7/3	48.15.1
Minor, William		149	8/4	62.1.8
Minor, John		137	"	57.1.8
Miller, Anthony		171½	7/10	67.3.5
Moody, Lewis		239	"	93.12.2
Mann, Joseph junr.		400	8/4	166.13.4
do. of Crows		140	6/3	43.15.0
do. of Allen & wife		25½	"	7.19.4½
Mitchell, John		50	"	15.12.6
Mann, Robert este.		699	6/3	218.8.9
Meredith, Samuel		215	7/10	84.4.2
Macon, John este.		1092	16/7	905.9.0
do. lots in Dunkirk, annl. rent				40.0.0
do. do. do. do.				30.0.0
Mann, Mary		100	5/3	26.5.0
Martin, John		475	9	213.15.0
Ditto of Fogg		197	6/3	61.11.3
				$5793.9.7¾

21.26.30.25

[page 6, List B, 1805] Persons names owning Land	Quantity of Land	Price per acre	Tot. Amt. Value Land
Martin, John, of Satterwhite	88	6/3	[£] 27.10.0
do. of Major Taylor &c.	60	"	18.15.0
Mahon, Thomas	101	6/3	31.11.3
Mahon, William	103½	"	32.3.9
Mahon, Benjamin	43¼	5/3	11.7.0¾
Mitchell, Richard, of Stone	74¼	3/2	11.15.1½
Minor, Coleman, of Jn°. Gayle	9¾	7/5	34.11.7½
Nunn, Moses	318	7/4½	117.5.3
do. of William Byers &c.	15	"	5.10.7½
Nunn, Thomas	130	7/3	47.2.6
do. of Brizendine	49	4/3	10.8.3
Newbill, William	1060	8/4	441.13.4
Newell, John este.	100	7/10	39.3.4
Nash, John este.	100	6/3	31.5.0
Noel, Phill & Skelton, Reuben & Thomas	275	8/4	114.11.8
Newbill, Thomas, of Tunstalls	94¾	"	39.9.6
Pendleton, James	888½	8/7½	383.3.3¾
do. of Wilmore	70	7/6	26.5.0
do. of William McIntosh	125	4/2	26.1.10
Pitts, David	420	9/6	196.0.0
Pitts, Obadiah	20	10/5	10.8.4
Phillips, James	230	7/3	83.7.6
Pollard, John este.	235	9/4	109.13.4
do. of Leonard Smithy	384	7/3	139.4.0
Prewitt, Frances	99	9/4	46.4.0
Parker, John	761¼	8/4	317.3.9
Prewitt, Richard	102	7/3	36.12.3
Pendleton, Philip, lot in D'kirk, annl. rent			3.0.0
Perryman, Philip	218	7/2	78.2.4
do. of George Dillard & Wife	215	"	77.10.0
Pynes, Clement	99	3/2	15.13.6
Pollard, Richard	389	8/4	162.1.8
Pendleton, Benjamin este.	450	7/10	176.5.0
Perryman, Richard	110	7/3	39.7.6
Prewett, Tunstall	58½	8/	23.8.0
Pollard, Joseph	200	6/3	62.10.0
Pollard, Richard & Brown, Henry	50	8/	20.0.0
Parker, Gouldman, of Gresham	170	7/3	61.12.6
Quarles, W. Francis	23¼	17/2	19.17.1½
do. of Garnett	114½	7/3	41.10.1½
Quarles, Isaac, King Wm.	25¾	20/	25.15.0
Row, Richard este.	314	8/4	1[3]0.16.8
Roane, Spencer	954	24/10	1184.11.0
Ryland, Joseph	487½	7/3	176.10.9
Do. of Chick's exors.	463	"	167.16.9
Ryland, Josiah	160	7/10	62.13.4
do. of William Temple	27½	15/	20.12.6
do. of Francis Prince's este.	107	7/10	41.18.2
do. of H. Brown	34½	7/4½	12.14.1¼
do. of James H. Row	226	8/4	92.3.4
Riddle, Vaughan	188	5/5	49.7.0
Roane, Thomas	920¾	17/2	790.8.2½
Row, Hansford	160½	6/3	50.3.1½
Row, Wilson	160½	6/3	50.3.1½
Redd, James	200	7/3	72.10.0
Row, James H., of [C.] Anderson	262	"	94.19.6
do. of John Watkins &c.	152	8/4	63.6.8
			$6255.3.6¾

5.16.24.25.24

[page 7, List B, 1805] Persons names owning Land	Quantity of Land	Price per acre	Tot. Amt. Value Land	
	[177]			
Smith, William	53	7/10	[£] 20.15.2	
do. of James Smith's este.	25	3/2	3.19.2	
Segar, Richard este.	406	7/3	147.3.6	
Satterwhite, George	60¾	6/3	18.19.8½	
Satterwhite, William	118	5/7½	33.3.9	
Schools, John	86	8/4	35.16.8	
do. of Parker & Wife	35	"	14.11.8	
Schools, Gabriel este.	174	6/3	54.7.6	
Skelton, William Este.	289	8/2½	118.12.2½	
do. of Lyne	91	8/4	37.18.4	
do. of Phill Perryman	12	7/2	4.6.0	
Smith, John (De.)	190	7/6	71.5.0	
Starling, Roderick	324	8/2	132.6.0	
Saunders, George	200	7/3	70.10.8	
do. of Wyatts &c.	115	7/10	45.0.10	
Shepherd, William este.	140	9/4	65.6.8	
Smith, Molly	30	4/2	6.5.0	
Smith, John junr.	42½	5/3	11.3.1½	
Smith, Lewis	96	7/6	36.0.0	
do. of Richard Hill	37	8/2	15.2.2	
do. of do.	11¼	"	4.11.10½	
Swinton, Ann	750	13/6	506.5.0	
Stone, Sarah	300	7/3	108.15.0	
Stone, Daniel	52	3/2	8.4.8	
Smith, Larkin	1254¼	31/1	1949.6.3½	
Smith, Henry	400	6/3	130.0.0	
Smith, Ambrose	92¾	8/4	38.6.8	
Stevens, George este.	430	7/10	168.8.4	
Stevens, George, Orphan	75	"	29.8.4	
Smith, William este. (Mill)	200	3/2	31.13.4	
Shackelford, John este.	114	7/3	40.8.2	
Shepherd, John	192	3/2	30.1.8	
Sthreshley, William	155½	6/3	48.11.10	
Schools, George	200	8/4	83.6.8	
do. of John Hutchason	150	7/1	53.2.6	
Smith, John, of J. Garlick	54	29/	78.6.0	
Smith, Jane, of James Smith's este.	25	3/2	3.19.2	
Smith, Philip orphan of do.	12½	"	1.19.7	
Smith, James	101	7/10	39.11.2	
do. of James Smith's este.	12½	3/2	1.19.7	
Scott, Anderson	330	16/7	273.12.6	
do. of P. Anderson's Este.	248	20/9	257.6.0	
do. of Anderson & wife	96	"	99.12.0	
Semple, B. Robert	235	10/5	122.6.3½	
do. of Spencer Roane	155	24/10	192.9.2	
Stewart, James	120	9/2	55.0.0	
Skelton, William, of Wm. Skelton's este.	73	8/2½	29.19.2½	
Shepherd, William, of Wyatt & Wife	49½	7/6	18.11.3	
James Shackelford, of Joel Willis	63	31/1	97.18.3	
Shackelford, Leonard	113	6/3	35.6.3	
Trice, William este.	[140	7/3	50.15.0]	[covered]
Taylor, James	50	6/3	15.12.6	
Taylor, Edmund	294	8/4	122.10.0	
Temple, Joseph	918	10/5	478.2.6	
Tunstall, Richard junr. este.	1097	7/3	397.13.3	
Temple, William	402¼	15/	301.17.6	
Temple, John	42	31/1	65.12.6	
			$6913.3.1½	3.19.27.298.22

[page 8, List B, 1805] Persons names owning Land	Quantity of Land	Price per acre	Tot. Amt. Value Land	
Temple, Humphrey este.	100	15/	[£] 75.0.0	
do. of J. Tunstall	200	18/8	185.16.8	
do. of R. Tunstall este.	574	21/	602.14.0	
Tunstall, Richard (Purdy) este.	63¾	8/4	32.5.6	
Upshaw, James, Essex	125	8/10	55.4.2	
do. of R. Beverley	30	10/5	15.12.6	
do. of Reuben Garnett	120	8/	48.0.0	
Wilson, Abraham	159	6/3	49.13.9	
Wilson, Benjamin Este.	200	7/3	72.10.0	
Watkins, Joseph	63	6/7	20.14.9	
do. of Wiltshire's este.	71	7/3	26.14.9	
Walker, Philip	110	9/4	51.6.8	
Walker, Humphrey	820	33/2	1355.14.2	
Wright, William	130	5/3	33.12.6	
Willis, Joel	94	7/10	35.10.0	
do. of Wm. Jones' este.	140¼	17/10	125.1.1½	
Wright, Edward	567	6/3	177.3.9	
Whayne, William	154½	7/10	60.10.3	
Wyatt, George	122	7/6	27.3.9	
Webb, James	209	4/2	43.10.10	
Wheely, Carriol Este.	37¼	7/3	13.10.0¾	
Watkins, Joseph junr.	93¼	8/4	38.17.1	
Wyatt, Robert	50	7/3	18.2.6	
Watkins, John, of G. Dix	226	6/3	70.12.6	
Watkins, Philip este.	107	4/2	22.5.10	
Walton, Thomas, of Howerton	76¾	6/	23.0.6	
Williamson, Abner, of D. Walker & Wife	50¼	3/1	7.[ ].[ ]½	
Ward, Joshua, lot in D'kirk, annl. rent			60.0.0	
Young, Henry	640	18/8	597.6.8	
			$3945.13.4¾	1.11.12.[ ].12
			[47635.13.1¾]	

Ro. B. Hill, Comr.

$758.98 Tax on Land

[cover]

King & Queen
R. Hill
Land & prop.
1805
Misc. lott $84.59 entd.
28 Sep. 1805
Added, entd., stated
S.L.
Land Book for 1805
For Mr. Auditor

A list of land within the district of Thomas Spencer, Commissioner in the County of King & Queen for the year One thousand Eight hundred and six

LIST A

[page 1, List A, 1806] Persons names owning land	Quantity of land	Price per acre	Total Amount Land	Amt. Tax Thereon in Dols. Cents
	[178]			
Atkins, Lewis	60	8/4	25.0.0}	
Do. John B. Whiting	256½	7/10	100.0.0}	
Anderson, Francis est.	348	10/9	187.3.8}	
Do. Rich[d.] T. Shackelford	26	8/4	12.1.8}	
Anderson, Beverly	203½	3/2	32.4.5}	
Do. John B. Whiting	242¾	7/10	95.1.6½	
Brown, Samuel	33¼	4/3	7.1.2	
Banks, William est.	365	4/2	76.0.0	
Brooke, Richard	1539¾	29/	2232.12.9	
Brumley, Robert	225	5/3	59.1.3	
Bird, William est.	532	7/3	197.17.0}	
Do. Dragon Swamp	88½	17/	70.4.6}	
Bird, Philemon est.	1638¼	6/3	511.19.0¾	
Brett, Nancy	50	18/	45.0.0	
Burch, James est.	183	6/3	57.3.9	
Burch, Vincent	100	4/2	20.16.8}	
Do. W[m.] Hoskins	50	3/3	7.18.4}	
Bird, Anthony A.	275	"	43.10.10}	
Do. W[m.] Montague	44	4/2	9.3.4}	
Do. Rob[t.] Smith Sen.	8	10/5	4.4.4"	
Byne, John est.	336	4/2	70.0.0}	
Do. Dragon Swamp	2¼	17/	1.18.3}	
Do. Do., Grant to Jn[o.] Lyne	20 ¾	"	17.12.9}	
Do. Do. Do. Do.	14 ¾	"	12.10.9}	
Bird, Robert est.	780	24/10	993.6.8}	
Do. Guy Smith	189½	3/2	30.0.10}	
Bourn, Richard est.	150	"	23.15.0	
Boyd, John	115	18/8	107.6.8}	
Do. Sowne's	382	24/10	474.6.4}	
Bray, Richard est.	93	7/10	36.8.6	
Bird, John est.	71	3/2	11.4.10	
Bew, William est.	117	"	18.0.6	
Boyd, Robert	1119	9/3	517.10.3	
Boyd, William	300	15/	225.0.0}	
Do. Francis Gaines	367	14/6	266.1.6}	
Burkeley, Edmund est.	762	5/3	200.0.6	
Bland, John	60	12/6	37.10.0	
Bland, William est.	100	9/11	49.11.8	
Bourn, Mills	159½	5/3	41.14.3}	
Do. Tho[s.] Jordan's est.	33 1/3	4/2	6.18.10}	
Bullman, Ann	120	5/3	31.10.0	
Bew, Major W.	82	"	21.10.6	
Burton, Caty	58	3/2	9.3.8	
	14.19.15.17		£6997.6.6¼	

[page 2, List A, 1806] Persons names owning land	Quantity of land	Price per acre	Total Amount Land	Amt. Tax Thereon in Dols. Cents
Balote, Laban	384½	4/2	80.2.6	
Bland, William, Preacher	225	3/8¼	41.9.8½}	
do. William Dillard	152¼	6/	45.13.6}	
Bland, Ralph	146	53	38.6.8}	
Do. Finny & Buckner	170	4/2	35.8.4}	
Do. N. Dillard, Drag.	4¼	17/	3.12.3}	
Bowden, William	100	4/2	20.16.8}	
Do. Sykes's	34	3/2	5.7.8}	
Bland, Robert	250	4/2	52.1.8	
Bland, Thomas	412	3/2	75.4.8	
Brooks, Meriman	100	7/10	39.3.4	
Bowden, George	205	5/3	53.16.3	
Banks, James	22	7/3	7.19.6	
Banks, Andrew	125	12/6	78.2.6	
Brightwell, John est.	70	4/2	14.11.8	
Burton, James est.	89	"	18.10.10	
Bland, William, young	300	7/3	108.15.0}	
Do. Dawson Cooke	103	4/2	21.9.2}	
Bird, Janet & Frances	230	10/5	119.10.5}	
Do. Rob[t.] Smith, Drag.	22½	17/	19.2.6}	
Brushwood, George	138	4/2	39.3.4}	
Do. Wares	32¼	3/2	5.2.1½}	
Bray, Peter	51¼	6/3	16.0.3¾	
Bland, John Jun.	212	5/3	55.13.0}	
Do. Overstreets	96	4/2	20.0.0}	
Broocke, William	33	10/5	17.3.9	
Brooke, William, Essex	83	11/8	48.8.4	
Banks, John D.	150	6/3	46.17.6	
Carlton, Thomas Sen.	200	7/10	78.6.8}	
Do. Philemon Bird	83½	6/3	26.1.10½}	
Carlton, Noah	100	7/10	39.3.4	
Cooke, Henry est.	260	5/3	68.5.0}	
Do.	49¼	10/5	25.10.5}	
Collins, John est.	75	3/2	11.17.6	
Carlton, John S	100	6/3	31.5.0}	
Do. to agree with late survey	41	"	12.16.3}	
Campbell, James T., Orph.	296	12/6	185.0.0	
Carlton, Christopher Sen.	37½	6/3	11.14.5}	
Do. James Laughlin	126½	3/2	26.8.2}	
Carlton, Richard est.	139	7/	48.13.4	
Cauthern, James	36½	3/2	5.15.7	
Carlton, William Sen.	309¾	11/6	178.1.2½	
Carlton, Christopher, young	138¼	5/	34.11.3	
Carlton, Richard Sen.	250	7/3	90.12.6	
Carlton, Christopher Jun.	100	"	36.5.0	
16.26.19.17			£2048.0.7¾	

[page 3, List A, 1806] Persons names owning land	Quantity of land [179]	Price per acre	Total Amount Land	Amt. Tax Thereon in Dols. Cents
Cooper, Henry	50	4/2	10.8.4	
Carlton, Thomas (T) est.	72 8/11	6/3	22.14.4¾	
Cardwell, James	211	4/2	43.19.2}	
Do. John Richeson est.	106	5/3	27.16.6}	
Do. Cooke's est.	30	4/2	6.5.0}	
Do. Jo. Wyatt	8¼	"	1.14.4½	
Do. Richard Eubanks	117	8/4	48.15.0}	
Cardwell, John	150	4/2	31.5.0	
Cardwell, William est.	77	"	15.11.6	
Cardwell, Thomas est.	110	"	22.18.4	
Cooke, John est.	270	"	56.5.0	
Collins, Thomas	281½	7/	98.10.6}	
Do. Rob[t.] S. Ware	84½	11/9	49.12.6 }	
Do. Metcalf & Levert	289½	14/6	209.17.9}	
Do. Jane Crittenden	60	13/6	40.10.0}	
Carlton, John Jun.	235	4/2	48.19.2}	
Do. Baylor Fleet	2	12/6	1.5.0}	
Corbin, Richard	2390	11/1¾	1332.11.4}	
Do. Shackelford's	300	14/6	217.10.0}	
Do. Dixon's	416¾	15/5	321.10.10}	
Campbell, William	238	3/2	37.13.8	
Corr, James	100	6/2	30.16.8	
Crouch, James	105½	3/2	16.13.3½	
Clayton, James	260	5/3	65.5.0	
Crittenden, Zachariah	34½	14/6	24.17.10	
Cary, Wilson J.	1820	16/7	1509.1.8	
Collins, Joyeux	140	10/5	72.8.4}	
Do. H. & W. Robinson	37 1/3	8/4	15.11.1½	
Campbell, James	130	5/9½	37.10.0}	
Do. Rich[d.] Garrett	70	3/2	11.1.8}	
Do. Benj[a.] Faulkner	55¼	7/3	20.0.6¾}	
Corr, Thomas R.	231¼	5/3	60.12.9}	
Do. Jn[o.] Shackelford Mc.	73=28 poles	"	19.4.3}	
Do. Benj[a.] Walden	170	"	44.12.6}	
Crittenden, Richard est.	178	"	46.14.6	
Collier, Joseph	468	"	112.17.0	
Collier, Benjamin	75	"	19.13.9	
Clegg, Isaiah est.	241	4/2	50.4.2	
Curry, John	155	4/	31.0.0	
Cooke, Thomas est.	240	3/2	38.0.0	
Cooke, Thomas Jun.	96	"	15.0.4	
Cooke, Dawson	1	5/3	5.3}	
Do. Jn[o.] Whiting	24¾	7/10	9.13.10¾}	
Do. Do.	150	"	58.15.0}	
Do. Eleanor Graves	¼	"	1.11½}	
	13.21.22.15		£4944.14.10	

[page 4, List A, 1806] Persons names owning land	Quantity of land	Price per acre	Total Amount Land	Amt. Tax Thereon in Dols. Cents
Carlton, Humphrey	175	7/	61.5.0}	
Do. John Watt's est.	48½	6/3	15.3.1½}	
Corr, John est.	503½	7/3	182.10.4½}	
Do. Thomas Dudley	197½	6/3	61.14.4½}	
Do. Guildford Dudley	28½	7/3	10.6.7½	
Carlton, Thomas est.	235	6/3	73.8.9	
Campbell, John est.	400	12/6	250.0.0	
Do. Ralph G. Meredith	111½	14/6	80.16.8}	
Curry, James	70	4/2	14.11.8	
Do. John Broach	71	"	14.15.10}	
Do. Frances Webley	79	"	16.9.2}	
Corr, John Sen.	213	3/2	33.15.6}	
Do. John Corr Jun.	90	7/3	32.12.6}	
Do. Dawson Cooke	5=6 poles	4/2	1.1.0}	
Do. Ditto	106	3/2	16.15.8}	
Crittenden, Frances (Riv)	105¾	14/6	76.12.2	
Clarke, John	144	5/	36.0.0}	
Do. Saml. Hemingway	254¼	4/2	53.0.3}	
Carlton, Loddy	44	3/2	6.19.4	
Cooke, John est.	100	"	15.6.8	
Clayton, Maria H., Sally K.} and Polley R. Clayton}	72	9/11	35.14.0	
Collins, Mason	110	3/2	17.8.4	
Carlton, Lewis	$9_{1/11}$	6/3	2.16.10}	
Do. Baylor & Christo. Carlton	$18_{2/11}$	"	5.13.8}	
Collins, James	120	4/2	25.0.0}	
Do. Loddy Carlton to you and} James Overstreet}	125½	5/3	32.18.10½	
Campbell, John Jun.	50	4/2	10.8.4	
Corr, Jessee	37¾	"	7.17.3½	
Dillard, William est., apply to Frances Digges	100	3/2	15.16.8	
Didlake, James est.	278	8/4	115.16.8	
Dunn, Thomas	50½	6/3	15.15.7½	
Dillard, George	50	12/6	31.5.0}	
Do. William Dillard Sen.	226	"	141.5.0}	
Durham, Thomas est.	85	3/2	13.9.2	
Dickie, Barbara	1½	17/	1.5.6}	
Do. Parmenas Bird	50¼	11/8	29.6.3}	
Do. Robt. Bird Exors. &c.	37½	17/	31.17.6}	
Dudley, William est.	290	14/6	210.5.0}	
Do. Lydia Wedderburn	315½	6/3	98.11.10}	
Damm, John est.	55	"	17.3.9	
Dudley, James	180	7/10	70.10.0	
Damm, William est.	25	4/2	5.4.2	
Douglas, John	239	7/	83.13.0	
Didlake, John	1200	7/3	435.0.0}	
Do. Halyard's	186	5/3	48.16.6}	
Dudley, Guilford est.	69½	7/3	25.3.10½	
	14.19.22.17		$2581.7.[6]	

[page 5, List A, 1806] Persons names owning land	Quantity of land [180]	Price per acre	Total Amount Land	Amt. Tax Thereon in Dols. Cents
Dudley, Banks est.	230	3/2	36.8.4	
Downey, Michael est.	50	10/5	26.0.10	
Didlake, Royston	206	3/6½	36.7.4}	
Do. Geo. Bowden	65	4/2	13.10.0}	
Dillard, William Jun. est.	207½	15/	155.12.6	
Dudley, Thomas	70	6/3	21.17.6	
Dillard, Nicholas	75	4/2	15.12.6	
Dunn, John, Essex, Drag.	73	17/	62.1.0	
Digges, Frances	105	5/3	27.11.3	
Dean, Benjamin	28¼	"	7.8.3¾	
Dillard, Thomas A.	29	3/2	4.11.10}	
Do. Young Simpkins	1	"	3.2}	
Durham, George est.	50	4/2	10.8.4}	
Do. Newham Durham	50	"	10.8.4}	
Didlake, Philip	83	"	17.5.10}	
Do. Edward Didlake	40	10/5	20.16.8}	
Daniel, John	30	4/2	6.5.0	
Eubank, William est.	28¾	5/3	7.11.0	
Eubank, Richard Sen.	196	7/	68.12.0	
Eubank, Thomas	110	4/2	22.18.4	
Eubank, Philip	135¾	"	28.5.7½	
Eubank, Richard Jun.	108¾	7/	38.1.1½}	
Do. Thomas Jeffries	12¾	7/3	4.12.5}	
Do. A. Dunn	147	5/3	38.11.9}	
Do. Anty. Hart	87¼	3/2	13.10.3½}	
Eubank, Warner	115	"	18.4.2}	
Do. Jno. Hemingway Jun.	4	4/2	16.8}	
Fleet, Baylor	860	12/6	537.10.8	
Frazer, William est.	45	20/9	46.13.6	
Fleet, William	352	"	365.4.0}	
Do. Rich^d. T. Kauffman	15	"	15.11.3}	
Fisher, James	111	3/2	17.11.6	
Foster, Thomas	87¾	4/2	18.2.6	
Fauntleroy, Thomas	486	10/	243.0.0}	
Do. Henry Todd	500	18/	450.0.0}	
Do. W^m. Bowden	183	7/	64.1.0}	
Farinholtz, David	151¼	6/6	49.1.6}	
Do. Stage Davis	219½	6/9	74.1.6}	
Faulkner, Benjamin	100	4/2	20.16.8}	
Do. Mary Faulkner	333	6/3	104.1.4}	
Do. W^m. Boyd	9½	10/5	4.10.9}	
Do. Jno. Southern	134½	4/2	28.0.0}	
Do. Jas. Campbell	29¾	7/3	10.15.8¼}	
Do. Do.	112¼	4/2	23.7.8½}	
Do. Anty. Gardner	3	17/	2.11.0}	
Do. Do.	10=27 poles	17/	8.12.10½}	
Faugerson, Thomas	62	10/5	32.5.10}	
Do. Thos. Collins	48	7/	16.16.0}	
	12.23.20.18		£2846.7.6½	

[page 6, List A, 1806] Persons names owning land	Quantity of land	Price per acre	Total Amount Land	Amt. Tax Thereon in Dols. Cents
Faucet, Vincent	46½	10/5	24.4.4½	
Fisher, William	30	5/3	7.17.6	
Graves, Eleanor	163	"	42.15.9}	
Do. Jno. B. Whiting	100	7/10	39.3.4}	
Garlick, Camm est.	917	6/3	286.11.3	
Gresham, Philemon	200	"	62.10.0	
Gresham, Mary	100	7/10	39.3.4	
Gresham, William B	100	4/2	20.16.8}	
Do. W^m. Rowe	95	6/3	29.13.9}	
Gardner, Anthony	638	11/	350.11.8}	
Do. Dragon Swamp	57	17/	48.9.0}	
Do. Vincent Hart	73¾	6/6	23.19.4½}	
Gardner, Elizabeth	100	6/3	31.5.0	
Gibson, Richard	156½	3/2	24.16.7	
Gibson, Eubank	56½	"	8.18.11}	
Do. Rich^d. Eubank Jun.	3½	7/	1.4.6}	
Gibson, Philip	129½	3/2	20.10.3½	
Gresham, Meacham	100	5/3	26.5.0}	
Do. A. Gresham	4	17/	3.8.0}	
Gresham, Ambrose	79½	5/3	20.17.4½}	
Do. Dragon Swamp	22	17/	18.5.0}	
Gresham, John B	79	5/3	20.14.9}	
Do. A. Gresham	4	17/	3.8.0}	
Griffin, William est.	859	14/6	622.15.6	
Garrett, James	230	4/2	48.18.4}	
Do. W^m. Garrett	100	"	20.16.8}	
Garrett, Robert Sen.	200	7/	70.0.0}	
Do. Philemon Bird	54¾	6/3	17.2.2.¼}	
Do. William Hunt	170	"	53.2.6}	
Do. Spencer Ware	70	5/3	18.7.6}	
Do. Robert Reed	26	4/2	5.8.4}	
Gaines, Robert est.	537¾	20/9	558.8.7¾}	
Do. A. Curtis	50	5/3	13.2.6}	
Guthrie, James	60	12/6	37.10.0	
Guthrie, Richard	60	"	37.10.0}	
Do.	162	3/2	25.13.0}	
Garrett, Edward Sen.	210	5/3	55.2.6}	
Do. Trice's	489½	"	128.9.10}	
Garrett, William, son W^m.	197¾	7/3	71.13.8¾	
Groom, John	173	3/2	27.17.10}	
Do. John Bowden	95	4/2	19.15.10}	
Do. Robert Lumpkin	106¾	"	22.4.9¾}	
Do. Samuel Groom	50	"	10.8.4}	
Guthrie, Rachel	50	8/4	20.16.8	
Goldman, Martin	140	4/2	29.3.4	
Garnett, James	100	"	20.16.8	
Gully, Philip est.	50	3/2	7.18.4	
	13.22.24.18		£3098.11.9½	

[page 7, List A, 1806] Persons names owning land	Quantity of land	Price per acre	Total Amount Land	Amt. Tax Thereon in
	[181]			Dols. Cents
Garrett, William Sen.	225	3/4½	37.19.4½}	
Do. Geo. B. Bird	60	6/3	18.15.0}	
Do. Henry F. Dudley	50	5/3	13.2.6}	
Gramshill, Henry	25	3/2	3.19.2	
Gresham, James	112	5/	28.0.0	
Gilmore, Richard	414	5/3	108.13.6	
Garrett, Richard	100	4/2	20.16.8	
Garrett, William Jun.	120	"	25.0.0	
Garrett, Edward Jun.	150	6/3	46.17.6	
Gaines, Benjamin	360	20/4	366.0.0}	
Do. Howard Williams	52½	4/2	10.8.9}	
Gaines, Harry	360	20/4	366.0.0	
Gatewood, Philip	1	7/10	7.10	
Guthrie, Major est.	100	5/	25.0.0	
Gresham, William Jun.	31¾	6/3	9.18.4½	
Henderson, James	25	5/3	6.11.3	
Hoskins, William est.	296	20/	296.0.0}	
Do. Balance Bray's	2	7/10	15.8}	
Hoomes, Benjamin	447	12/6	279.7.6}	
Do. Ann Kennedy	75	"	46.17.6}	
Hemingway, John Jun.	250	4/2	52.1.8	
Hare, William est.	217	5/3	56.19.3	
Harwood, Christopher est.	194	24/10	240.17.8	
Harwood, Priscilla	165	18/	148.10.0	
Hart, James Sen.	150	3/2	23.15.0	
Holderby, John Sen.	73¼	4/2	15.5.2½	
Holderby, John Jun.	108¾	7/10	42.6.0	
Hart, Anthony	190	5/3	49.17.6}	
Do. balance sundry persons	41	3/2	6.9.10}	
Hart, Gregory	200	"	31.13.4	
Harwood, John est.	109	10/5	56.15.5	
Henry, Samuel H. est.	1900	14/6	1377.10.0	
Henry, James est.	75	12/6	46.17.6	
Hoskins, Robert	287	6/	86.2.0}	
Do. Robert Smith	157¾	10/5	82.10.6¾}	
Hart, Alden	77	4/2	16.0.10}	
Do. Anty. Hart	231	3/2	36.11.6}	
Hudson, William	75¼	4/2	15.13.6}	
Do. John Daniel	25	"	5.4.2}	
Howerton, Heritage est.	122¼	20/9	126.16.7¼	
Halyard, William	260	6/3	81.5.0	
Howerton, John	269½	5/3	70.14.10½	
Hart, Vincent	88	7/3	31.18.0	
Harris, Samuel	214¼	5/3	56.4.9¾	
Hogg, William & Legatees of Holt Richason	50	18/	45.0.0	
Hart, James Jun.	146	3/3 ½	24.0.7}	
Do. John Hart's	88	"	14.4.4}	
17.24.23.16			£4552.5.10¾	

[page 8, List A, 1806] Persons names owning land	Quantity of land	Price per acre	Total Amount Land	Amt. Tax Thereon in Dols. Cents
Hart, John	80	3/2	12.13.4	
Hart, Salley	119	3/3½	19.11.8½	
Hart, Robert	62	"	10.6.7	
Hemingway, John Sen.	125	4/2	26.0.10	
Jones, Thomas	255	"	53.2.6	
Jones, Thomas, Essex	735	7/10	287.17.6	
Jeffries, Thomas B	63	7/3	22.16.9}	
Do. John Harwood	25½	10/5	13.5.7½}	
Do. Brett's est.	57¾	18/	51.19.6}	
Jones, James	100	5/3	26.5.0}	
Do. Mary Jones	150	26/11	201.17.6}	
Jeffries, Going	60	4/2	12.10.0	
Jordan, Robert	66 2/3	"	13.18.10	
Jones, Mary	150	26/11	201.17.6	
Ison, George	140¼	5/3	36.16.3¾	
Inge, Vincent est.	33	8/4	13.15.0	
Kemp, John	296	7/3	107.0.3	
Kauffman, Richard T.	161	26/	209.6.0	
Kauffman, Sambo, Humphry} and Lucy, free negroes	167	7/6	62.5.0	
Kidd, John	81¾	5/3	26.6.6¾	
Kennedy, Archibald est.	38¼	4/2	7.19.4	
Kennedy, Ann	33¼	"	6.18.6½	
Kennedy, Ann Jun.	33¾	"	7.0.6	
Kennedy, Lucy	37½	"	7.16.2	
Kidd, Bartholomew	136	5/3	35.14.0}	
Do. Wm. Dillard Jun.	132½	4/2	27.12.1}	
Do. Robert Lumpkin	95½	"	19.17.11}	
Kidd, Benjamin	111	13/6	74.18.2}	
Do. Dragon Swamp	36	17/	30.12.0}	
Kidd, John est.	370	7/3	134.2.6}	
Do. Lumpkin & Pierce	60	4/2	12.10.0}	
Do. Thomas Dillard	45	14/6	32.12.6}	
King, Dicey est.	18	8/4	7.10.0	
Lumpkin, Jacob	589¼	6/3	184.10.9¾	
Lewis, Iveson	356	14/6	258.2.0}	
Do. Elizabeth Montague	3	17/	2.11.0}	
Leigh, Lucy	101	24/10	125.8.2	
Leigh, John est.	133	"	165.2.10}	
Do.	66	"	81.19.0}	
Leigh, Richard est.	560	6/3	175.0.0	
Mitchel, Salley est.	391	13/	254.3.0	
Mitchel, James, Orphan	225	"	146.5.0	
Moore, Lodawick, John and Richard	100	3/2	15.16.8	
Major, Josiah	200	4/2	41.13.4	
Mitchel, John est.	270	5/3	70.17.0}	
Do. Rootes	128	9/11	63.9.3}	
15.22.25.14			£3400.11.11¾	

[page 9, List A, 1806] Persons names owning land	Quantity of land [182]	Price per acre	Total Amount Land	Amt. Tax Thereon in Dols. Cents
Mann, Joseph Sen.	231	6/3	72.3.9	
Moore, Agathy	40	4/2	8.6.8	
Montague, William	170	"	35.8.4	
Meridith, Ralph G. est.	350½	14/6	254.2.3	
Muire, Richard	93	12/6	58.2.6}	
Do. Rich[d.] Anderson	177	5/3	46.9.3}	
Mitchel, Richard est.	74¼	4/2	15.9.4½	
Moore, Richard est.	145	6/3	45.6.8	
McCarty, Joseph est.	73	3/2	11.11.2	
Metcalf, Thomas	256	14/6	181.8.8	
Milby, Richard	175	3/2	27.14.2	
Morgan, William	3	6/3	0.18.9	
Moore, John est.	37	4/2	7.14.2	
Mann, John	179¼	7/10	74.7.5½	
Muire, William	125	5/3	32.16.3	
Newcomb, William	169	3/2	26.15.2}	
Do. Benj[a.] Dillard	148	5/3	48.17.0}	
Do. Do.	52	"	13.13.0}	
Noel, Silas M.	104	7/3	37.14.0	
Newbill, John	21¾	5/3	5.14.2¾	
Oliver, John, said to be sold to Philip Vass}				
N. Carolinia [sic]}	210	¾	35.0.0	
Orril, John	100	6/3	31.5.0}	
Do.	52	"	16.5.0}	
Oliver, John	320	5/3	84.0.0	
Oakes, Henry	198½	3/2	34.2.0	
Oakes, William	80	4/2	16.13.4	
Oliver, William	59	"	12.5.10}	
Do. Howard Williams	62 7/8	"	13.1.11¾}	
Oakes, Ann	60	"	12.10.0	
Oliver, Francis	40¾	"	8.9.9½}	
Do. James Medeiras	86	6/3	28.6.2}	
Pitts, Benjamin G.	100	5/4	26.13.4	
Pace, Benjamin est.	263	7/3	95.6.9	
Pynes, Benjamin est.	164	6/3	51.5.0	
Pynes, Robert	111½	"	34.16.10½}	
Do. William Adams	53¾	"	16.15.11¾}	
Pynes, Benjamin	46¼	"	14.9.0¾	
Pemberton, John Sen.	90	"	28.2.3}	
Do. Jacob Lumpkin	60	"	18.5.0}	
Pollard, Robert	6	24/10	7.9.0}	
Do. John Omealy	367	30/	550.10.0}	
Palmer, Charles	107¾	18/	96.19.6}	
Do.	104	"	93.12.0}	
Pigg, John est.	324	14/6	234.18.0}	
Do. Cockses	180	7/3	65.0.0}	
16.23.21.13			£2631.14.4	

[page 10, List A, 1806] Persons names owning land	Quantity of land	Price per acre	Total Amount Land	Amt. Tax Thereon in Dols. Cents
Pemberton, John Jun.	121	6/3	37.17.6	
Patterson, Joseph	62¾	3/2	9.18.8½	
Pierce, Philip	83	"	13.2.10	
Pierce, Thomas est.	87	4/2	18.2.6	
Pierce, Beverly	25¾	"	5.7.3½}	
Do. Philip Pierce	17	3/2	2.13.10}	
Pilsbury, George	109¾	10/9	58.19.9¾	
Palmer, Roger	314	6/	94.4.0	
Price, Robert	399	6/3	124.13.9	
Pemberton, James	75	"	23.8.9	
Roane, Thomas est.	2033	18/8	1897.9.4}	
Do. H. Carlton	200	6/3	63.10.0}	
Do. Brett's	34¾	18/	31.5.6}	
Do. Rob[t.] Pynes	24½	6/3	7.9.1½}	
Rowe, Elizabeth	665	20/9	689.18.9	
Rowe, Francis, Orph.	612½	4/8	142.16.8	
Richason, James, son Elias	86	4/2	17.8.4	
Richards, John	571	4/8	124.8.0	
Richason, James Sen.	180	4/2	37.10.0	
Richason, William Sen.	181	"	37.14.2	
Roane, Thomas, Middlesex	14¼	15/	10.13.9	
Richeson, William est.	188½	4/2	39.5.5	
Richeson, William Jun.	118½	5/3	31.2.1½}	
Do. Rob[t.] Stone	101	4/2	21.0.10}	
Roane, Major est.	687½	3/8	128.18.1½	
Do. John Lyne	455¾	6/3	142.8.5½}	
Do. Roger Palmer	9	7/3	3.5.3}	
" George Brushwood	79¾	3/2	12.12.6½}	
Raines, Giles	60	"	9.10.0	
Robinson, Benjamin est.	1263 2/3	8/4	526.10.6½	
Roane, Charles Sen.	133	19/	126.7.0}	
Do. Dragon Swamp [sic]	70/	17/	59.10.0}	
Roy, Beverly	700	8/4	291.13.4}	
Do. Thomas Brown	454	12/6	283.15.0}	
Do. Richard Corbin	125	"	78.2.6}	
Richeson, James son Jas.	250	5/3	65.12.6	
Richeson, John Sen.	120	"	31.10.0	
Richeson, John Jun.	50	4/2	10.8.4	
Spencer, John	416	7/3	150.16.0}	
Do. Eleanor Graves	½	7/10	3.11}	
Starke, Richard est.	350	5/8	99.3.4	
Stone, Robert est.	24¾	4/2	5.3.1½	
Stone, Robert	31½	5/3	8.5.4½	
Stone, Job	100	4/2	20.16.8	
Smith, John (Neck)	88	10/5	45.16.8}	
Do. Dragon Swamp	12	17/	10.8.0}	
Do. A. Gresham	½	5/3	2.7¼	
16.23.22.18			£5650.10.3	

[page 11, List A, 1806] Persons names owning land	Quantity of land [183]	Price per acre	Total Amount Land	Amt. Tax Thereon in Dols. Cents
Smith, Francis	150	3/2	23.5.0	
Simpkins, Young	59	"	9.6.10	
Sears, Philip	83	4/2	17.5.10}	
Do. Francis Oliver	48½	"	10.2.1}	
Shackelford, William est.	400	14/6	310.0.0	
Spencer, Thomas	300	10/5	156.5.0}	
Do.	255	4/2	53.2.6}	
Do. Stage Davis	71½	"	14.17.11}	
Do. Do.	73	6/9	24.12.9}	
Shackelford, Richard T. est.	300	10/	150.0.0	
Seward, Benjamin	115	3/2	18.4.2}	
Do. Loddy Carlton	18½	"	2.17.1¾}	
Smith, Thomas G.	485	14/6	351.12.6}	
Do. Benj[a.] Dabney	400	"	290.0.0}	
Do. Do.	100	8/4	41.13.4}	
Sadler, John est.	150	6/3	46.17.6	
Shackelford, Zachariah	200	"	62.10.0}	
Do. Rich[d.] Anderson	177	5/3	46.9.3}	
Shackelford, John R	401¼	8/4	167.3.10	
Shackelford, William	151	6/3	47.3.9}	
Do. Wyatt's lease	30	5/3	7.16.6}	
Do. Matt Wood	166	7/3	60.3.6}	
Shackelford, John, Mc	283	6/2	87.5.2}	
Do. John Collier C	76¾	5/3	20.2.11¼}	
Do. Tho[s.] R. Corr	5=30 poles	"	1.7.2¾	
Shackelford, Benjamin, Halyard's lease	1	5/9½	5.9½	
Shepherd, John	67	6/	20.2.0	
Smith, John Doct[r.]	½	30/	15.0	
Smith, Samuel	1	7/10	7.10}	
Do., Dragon	10	17/	8.10.0}	
Spencer, Meacham	323	6/9	109.0.3	
Sears, Thomas	123	6/7	40.9.9}	
Do. How[d.] Williams	42¼	4/2	8.17.1}	
Smith, Robert Jun.	30	10/5	15.12.6	
Stone, William	193½	"	100.10.5	
Smith, Lewis	44	10/6	23.2.0	
Seward, William	70	3/2	11.1.8	
Tureman, Elizabeth	24¾	"	3.18.4½	
Tureman, Benjamin est.	90¾	"	14.7.4½	
Tureman, George	50	"	7.18.4	
Taliaferro, William est.	1000	14/6	725.0.0	
Townley, Robert	200	6/3	62.10.0}	
Do. Anderson's	117	14/6	84.16.6}	
Taliaferro, Philip est.	462	8/4	192.10.0	
Taliaferro, James B.	374½	12/6	234.7.6	
13.17.18.16			£3684.7.1¼	

[page 12, List A, 1806] Persons names owning land	Quantity of land	Price per acre	Total Amount Land	Amt. Tax Thereon in Dols. Cents
Thruston, Armstead	111 1/3	4/3	23.15.1	
Thruston, Bachelor	200	3/2	31.13.4	
Turner, Benjamin	36	4/2	7.10.0	
Townley, Ann	79	"	16.9.2	
Turner, Henry est.	100	"	20.16.8	
Tunstall, Richard G.	206½	7/10	73.3.7	
Taylor, William	40	6/3	12.10.0}	
Do. Taliaferro est.	200	8/4	83.6.8}	
Do. Taliaferro Exors.	200	"	83.6.8}	
Watts, Edward est.	250	7/3	90.12.6}	
Do. W. Watts est.	113	5/	28.5.0}	
Watts, John	293	7/10	114.15.2}	
Do. Pembertons	45	6/3	14.1.3}	
Watts, Kauffman	270	5/3	70.17.6}	
Do. Eubank & Burch	257	5/9	73.17.9}	
Do. J. & D. Hemingway	187	4/2	38.19.2}	
Do. Christopher Carlton, younger]			}	
two tracts one 5½ the other 4¼ acres	9 ¾	5/	2.8.9}	
Watts, James	350	4/2	72.8.4}	
Do. W. Watts est.	60	15/	45.0.0}	
Williams, Howard	66 1/8	4/2	13.15.6¼}	
Do. Dragon Swamp	43	17/	36.11.0}	
Wyatt, Thomas	206	7/10	81.2.0	
Wyatt, William	39¾	7/	13.18.3	
Williams, Montague	300	6/3	93.15.0	
Walton, James	80	4/2	16.8.4}	
Do. Thos. Walton's est.	66	"	13.15.0}	
Williams, Charles est.	336	"	70.0.0	
Walton, John	176	5/3	46.4.0	
Walton, William est.	40	4/2	8.6.8	
Ware, John est.	75	5/3	19.13.9	
Waring, Robert P. est. [Wareing]	542	10/9	291.10.6	
Walden, Lewis	90	10/5	46.17.6	
Walden, Richard Jun.	90	10/5	46.17.6	
Walden, Lewis est.	150	3/2	23.15.0}	
Do. Thos. Dudley	84½	6/3	28.3.3½}	
Williams, George	40	4/2	8.6.8	
Wyatt, Richard	175	12/6	109.7.6	
Watkins, Philip	197	5/3	51.14.3	
Williams, Elizabeth	16½	3/2	2.12.9	
White, James est.	200	6/3	62.10.0	
Wedderburn, Lydia	350	"	109.7.6	
Whiting, Beverley est.	650¼	7/10	254.13.7½	
Webley, John est.	173	5/3	45.8.3}	
Do. Collier & Dillard	279	4/2	58.2.6}	
17.20.22.15			£2456.13.2¼	

[page 13, List A, 1806] Persons names owning land	Quantity of land	Price per acre	Total Amount Land	Amt. Tax Thereon in Dols. Cents
	[184]			
Ware, Robert Jun.	100	8/4	41.13.4	
Ware, William [T.]	100	"	41.13.4	
Walden, Benjamin	203	5/3	53.5.9}	
Do. Rich^d. Anderson	120½	"	31.12.7½}	
Waller, Edward est.	133½	3/2	21.2.9	
Waller, George est.	87	"	13.15.6}	
Do. John Shackelford	47¾	8/4	19.17.11}	
Waller, John	65	3/7	11.12.11	
Waller, Robert est.	48	"	8.12.0}	
Do. Groom's est.	187	3/2	29.12.2}	
Ware, Nicholas	100	"	15.16.8	
Walton, Beverly	47½	7/10	18.12.1	
Watts, George K.	36	26/	46.16.0	
Wyatt, Smith	29¾	7/3	10.15.8	
Do. Wm. Wyatt's	9	7/	3.3.0	
Willis, Robert	105	14/6	75.2.6	
Williams, Christopher	100	5/3	26.5.0	
Walden, Charles	109¼	7/10	42.15.9½	
			£512.5.0	
			[45414.16.7¼]	

[Land Tax] $725.65
[arithmetic omitted]

A List of Land within the District of Richard Pollard, Commissioner in the upper District in the County of King and Queen for the year 1806 to wit

LIST B

[page 1, List B, 1806] Persons names owning Land	Quantity of Land	Price per acre	Tot. Amt. Value Land
	[185]		
Atkins, Joseph este.	66	4/2	[£]13.15.0
Alexander, Benjamin	202	9/4	94.5.4
do. of James Halbert	124	6/2	38.15.0
do. lot in Dunkirk, an[l.] Rent			20.0.0
do. of Joseph Meede			4.10.0
Acre, Seaton	52	9/4	24.5.4
do. of Richard Eubank	87¾	5/3	23.0.9
Alexander, Elisha	338	9/4	157.14.8
Anderson, Churchill	374	7/3	135.11.6
Atkins, John	277	5/	69.5.0
Alexander, Robert	159½	9/2	73.2.1
Alexander, Richard, of Gabl. Dix	109	63	[5]4.1.3
Alexander, Henry	90	9/2	41.5.0
Barton, John este.	125	4/2	26.0.10
Broach, Benoni	48	10/5	25.4.0
Brown, Henry Jun[r.]	100	12/	60.0.0
Beverly, Robert este.	2444	10/5	1262.16.4
Brown, Henry	526	7/4½	190.17.9
Bland, John	83	8/4	34.11.8
Bates, James	358	11/	149.3.4
do.	42	4/2	8.15.0
do. of Rice Garnett	89	7/3	32.5.3
Braxton, Carter	616¾	10/5	321.4.5¼
Brooking, Robert	900	10/5	468.15.0
Boughton, John	200 1/8	8/4	83.7.6½
Brown, William	18¼	3/2	2.17.9½
do. of Ware's Exors.	196½	7/3	71.4.7½
Bagby, Richard	260	"	94.5.0
Bagby, Thomas	260	"	94.5.0
do. of Jacob Lumpkin	235	6/3	73.8.9
Brizendine, Armistead	86 2/3	8/4	35.17.6
	14.13.12.9		$3764.10.8¾

[page 2, List B, 1806] Persons names owning Land	Quantity of Land	Price per acre	Tot. Amt. Value Land
Brumley, John Este.	60	7/10	23.10.0
do. of John Dudley &c.	35	7/10	13.14.2
Broach, William	20	"	7.16.8
Brown, John	50	7/4½	18.8.9
Bohannan, William	163	5/3	42.15.9
do. of Lumpkin Gresham	343	7/3	124.6.9
Bates, William	81	7/9½	31.10.1
do. of Rice Garnett	117	7/3	42.8.4
Boulware, Samuel	175¾	31/3	274.12.2¼
Boulware, Lee	153	7/3	55.9.3
Brown, William Jun[r.]	54	7/4	19.6.0
Brown, Lewis	79	8/2	32.5.2
Beadles, Justin	20	6/3	6.5.0
do. of Henry Garnett	4	6/3	1.5.0
Bagby, John	271	7/3	99.7.3
Bagby, Robert	118	7/3	42.15.6
Bohannan, Robert	50	4/6	11.5.0
Burnett, James	65	6/3	20.6.3
Bray, James	195	7/10	76.7.6
Boulware, Thomas, of L. Boul.	139	3/2	22.0.2
Brown, Henry A., of Mitchael	50	6/3	15.12.6
Crafton, Thomas	119	9/4	55.10.8
Crafton, James	59	"	27.10.8
Crafton, John	117½	"	54.12.0
Craine, John	130	6/3	40.2.6
do. of Clem Pynes	14	3/2	2.4.4
do. of Ware's Estate	49¼	7/3	17.17.0¾
do. of Ware's Exors.	71	"	29.14.9
Cluverius, Benjamin	419	20/9	434.14.3
Carlton, John	242	14/6	175.9.0
Carlton, Milley, of Broach	75½	14/6	54.14.9
Cole, Thomas G.	105	6/3	32.6.3
do. of Wiatt & Phillips	101	"	31.11.3
Carlton, Lewis	100	8/4	41.3.4
do. of H. Carlton's este.	150	7/10	58.15.0
Clayton, Thomas este.	275	7/3	99.13.9
Craine, George este.	30	"	10.17.6
Courtney, Thomas	156	7/10	61.2.0
Carlton, Joel	53½	6/3	16.4.5
Cook, Moses	100	"	41.13.4
do. of Ambrose Cook	100	"	41.13.4
Chapman, George M.	250	7/10	87.18.4
	15.18.20.13		£2396.15.9

[page 3, List B, 1806] Persons names owning Land	Quantity of Land	Price per acre	Tot. Amt. Value Land
	[186]		
Cannady, William	100	6/3	31.5.0
do. of George Saterwhite	15¼	"	4.15.3½
do. of Mary Barby	52	"	16.5.0
Courtney, Robert	183½	7/10	71.17.5
do. of Jacob Abbot	40½	"	15.13.4
do. of Leonard Daniel	81	7/10	26.14.6
Cook, William	65	5/5	17.12.1
Cook, James	65	8/9	28.8.9
Courtney, Fanny & Children	78	7/10	30.10.0
Cross, Joseph	103½	6/3	32.6.10½
Campbell, William este.	837¼	7/3	303.10.0¾
Campbell, Whitaker	406	7/10	159.0.4
Crow, John	121	5/3	31.19.2¼
do. of Roderick Starling	65	5/3	17.1.3
Crouch, Edmund	74¼	7/10	29.1.9
Campbell, William, of J. Campbell	74¼	18/8	69.6.0
Cauthorn, Vincent F., of Tunstall	43	8/4	17.18.4
Craine, Nathaniel	66	3/2	10.9.0
Carlton, Thomas	297	7/10	116.6.6
Dew, Thomas	331	12/6	206.17.6
do. of William Dews este.	623½	14/6	451.13.6
Duling, William este.	264	8/4	110.0.0
Dix, Gabriel, of Rod[k.] Starling	416½	7/10	163.2.7
Durham, Joseph	105	4/3	21.12.6
do. of Dunn	10	4/2	2.1.8
Deshazo, John	188	7/4	68.18.8
Deshazo, Larkin	87	7/3	34.4.10
do. of John Craine	6	6/3	1.17.6
do. of Benjamin Hoomes	430¾	4/4	93.4.5
Dunbar, David	366	8/4	152.10.0
Dudley, Peter este.	435	7/3¼	158.2.9¾
Dally, George	174¼	3/2	27.11.9½
Durham, John	25	3/2	3.19.4
do. of Thomas Johnson	18¼	"	2.17.9½
Dickie, James	512	8/4	213.6.8
Deshazo, Unity	71	7/10	27.16.3
Dally, John este.	200	3/2	31.13.4
Dobbins, Charles este.	147	5/3	38.11.9
Dobson, Pitman	136	10/2¾	69.10.9¾
Do. of Nancy Grafton	1	9/4	0.9.4
Deshazo, William	130	9/4	60.13.4
Duling, Jesse, of Thomas Dew	311 2/3	14/6	225.19.6
Dillard, Thomas, of Swinton	588	13/6	396.18.0
	13.20.22.17		£3593.14.6½

[page 4, List B, 1806] Persons names owning Land	Quantity of Land	Price per acre	Tot. Amt. Value Land
Eubank, Henry	171	5/3	44.17.9
do. of Richard Eubank	26	"	6.16.6
Edwards, Thomas	66	4/2	13.15.0
do. of Owen Gwathmey	108	8/2	44.2.0
Edwards, John, of T. Edwards	77	"	31.8.10
Eubank, James	111	10/2¾	56.15.5
Eubank, Polly	127	"	64.19.1
Eubank, William	130	"	66.9.9¼
Eubank, John	136	"	69.10.9¾
Fogg, James	120	6/3	27.10.0
Fleet, William	512	12/	307.4.0
Fogg, Frederick	268	8/4	111.13.4
do. of Obediah Pitts	33	10/5	17.3.9
Fauntleroy, Samuel G.	2069	20/	2069.0.0
do. of P.A. Blackburn &c.	57 1/3	20/9	59.9.8
do. of Frances Anderson	28 2/3	"	29.14.10
do. of Vivion Brooking	30	10/5	15.12.6
Fox, Joseph S.	28	7/10	10.19.4
do.	39	"	15.5.6
do.	94	7/3	31.1.6
Fogg, Thomas	223	10/2¾	114.2.1¾
Falkner, Thomas	220	6/3	68.15.0
do. of Coleman Minor	30	7/5	11.2.6
Fogg, Thomas, of Henry Lyne	352	8/4	146.13.4
Fauntleroy, Samuel G., of Tho[s.] Miller	140	9/2	64.3.4
Grafton, Sally & Ann	131	9/4	61.2.8
Gayle, John	170¾	7/5	63.6.4¾
do. of William Gayle	7¼	"	2.13.11
Gatewood, Chaney	829	10/5	437.17.11
do. Noel's	362	14/6	262.16.3
" Harwood's	125	4/2	46.17.6
" Eubank's	300	14/3	217.10.0
" Walden's Estate	120	12/6	75.0.0
" William Lyne, lot in Dunkirk, anl. rent			33.0.0
Do. of Thomas Miller, 2 lots dunkirk do.			30.0.0
of Samuel Roane	457	17/2	387.5.2
Garnett, Joshua este.	325	8/4	135.8.4
Gatewood, Joseph	445	10/5	231.15.5
do. of John Schools	70	8/4	29.3.4
Gatewood, John	78	"	32.10.0
Garnett, Reuben	656½	8/10	289.19.1
do. of Halbert &c.	28	10/5	14.12.10
do. of Gabriel Gatewood &c.	50	"	26.0.10
do. of do.	20¾	"	10.16.1¼
do. of James Upshaw jr.	61	8/	24.8.0
do. of John Gatewood	52	8/4	21.13.4
17.23.22.16			£5932.2.11¾

[page 5, List B, 1806] Persons names owning Land	Quantity of Land	Price per acre	Tot. Amt. Value Land
	[187]		
Garnett, Reuben M.	220	8/10	97.3.4
Gwathmey, Temple	600	35/3	1057.10.0
Garlick, Samuel este.	454	24/10	463.14.4
Garlick, John Estate	839	29	1216.11.0
Griffith, Thomas	22¾	6/3	7.0.7½
Griffith, Joseph Estate	22¾	6/3	7.0.7½
Gresham, Samuel	432½	7/3	156.15.7½
do. of Rice Garnett	157	"	56.18.1
Guthrie, William	91¼	7/5	33.14.7
do. of Richard Hill	46	8/2	18.15.8
do. of William Campbell	31	7/3	11.4.9
Gaines, Harry estate	481½	20/4	489.10.6
Gaines, Robert B.	481½	20/4	489.10.6
Gresham, Thomas estate	455¼	6/8	151.13.4
Griffith, Milley	50	6/3	15.12.6
Graves, Thomas	66¼	7/3	23.18.6
Gatewood, William (*Tuck°.*)	33	"	5.4.6
Gleason, Patrick	134	8/4	55.16.8
Gayle, William	344	7/5	127.11.4
do. of Thomas Dew	162	7/2	53.1.2
Garnett, Henry	438	9/2	200.15.0
do. of Wilson Lumpkin	121	9/4	56.9.4
do. of Ovil Row	51½	"	23.12.8
do. lots in Dunkirk			38.0.0
Gatewood, William, Son of John	132	10/	66.0.0
Gatewood, Philip	613	17/2	526.3.2
Gayle, Thomas, lot dunkirk			9.0.0
Garrett, Robert Jun[r.]	33	8/4	13.15.0
Gresham, Anthony	22	8/4	9.3.4
Gwathmey, Owen	82	8/2	33.9.8
Gresham, James	113	7/10	44.5.2
George, Cooper, of Tho[s.] C. Tunstall	13	8/4	5.8.4
Gayle, Mathew este.	233	11/5	184.7.7
Gatewood, Robert, of John Gatewood	30	8/4	12.10.0
Garrit, Joseph, of George Gresham	141	7/3	51.2.3
Hill, William este.	1267	14/6	918.4.3
Hawes, Walker	97	"	70.6.6
do. of Thomas Miller	683	16/7	570.9.9
Hitchcock, Thomas	140	4/2	29.3.4
Hoskins, Samuel este.	345	6/3	107.16.3
do. of Elisha Alexander	57	10/5	25.13.9
Hutchason, William	200	7/1	70.16.8
Heskew, John este.	61	5/3	16.0.3
Heskew, John Jun[r.] este.	50	6/3	15.12.6
do. of Clem Pynes	10	3/2	1.11.8
do. of Larkin Deshazo	19¼	4/4	4.2.4
	5.16.24.20.17		£7642.16.4½

[page 6, List B, 1806] Persons names owning Land	Quantity of Land	Price per acre	Tot. Amt. Value Land
Hill, Edward	1125¾	18/8	1050.14.0
do. of Quarles	130¾	17/2	112.4.6½
Hoskins, John	767	10/5	399.9.7
do. of Boughtons	100	8/4	41.13.4
" of Fleet & Semple	2	10/5	1.0.10
" Semple	18 1/8	"	9.8.9½
" of Row &c.	447	7/3	160.0.9
Hoomes, Benjamin, P2 lots in dunkirk			12.0.0
Hurt, West	14	5/3	3.3.6
do. of Bohannan's este.	80	4/6	18.0.0
Holt, William	123	14/3	87.12.9
do. of Abraham Wilson &c.	41	6/3	12.6.3
Hutchason, John	54¼	8/9	23.14.8¼
Hall, Corbin este.	72	4/2	15.0.0
Hill, Robert B.	257	8/2	104.18.10
do. of Richard Hill	103¾	"	42.7.3½
Hill, Henry	420	"	171.10.0
do. of Gwathmey	107	"	43.13.10
Hoskins, Thomas	55	"	22.9.2
Hutchason, Charles	200	7/1	70.16.8
Hoskins, John Jun[r.], lot in dunkirk anl. Rent			33.0.0
Jones, John este.	300	8/11	133.15.0
Jeffries, Edward	70	3/2	11.1.8
Jeffries, Ambrose este.	237	7/10	92.16.6
Jeffries, Robert	110	7/6	41.5.0
do. of L. Gresham	10	7/3	3.12.6
do. of Jacob Lumpkin	5	"	1.16.3
do. of Lumpkin Gresham	20	"	7.5.0
do. of John Dudley &c.	39½	7/3¼	14.3.6¾
Jeffries, Thomas, of J. Smith	25	7/10	9.15.10
Jones, James este.	160	14/6	116.0.0
do.	196	10/5	102.1.8
Jones, Rawleigh este.	135¾	17/10	121.0.10½
Jeffries, John este.	100	7/10	39.3.4
Johnson, Thomas	53¾	7/2	19.5.2½
Jones, John, of Boughton &c.	29 1/8	6/3	9.2.0
Jones, John, of Roderick Starling	100	89/2	40.16.8
Kemp, John	178	7/3	64.2.6
do. of Hill's Exors.	44¾	8/2	18.5.5
Keeling, Mary	78½	8/	31.8.0
Kay, Christopher	116	6/3	36.6.0
do. of T. Gouldman	416½	9/	187.8.6
	13.17.16.16		£3536.6.1½

[page 7, List B, 1806] Persons names owning Land	Quantity of Land	Price per acre	Tot. Amt. Value Land
	[188]		
Lumpkin, James	213	7/10	83.8.10
Lumpkin, Henry	409	9/4	198.6.8
Lumpkin, John este.	125	6/3	35.11.3
Lumpkin, William este.	61½	13/6	41.10.3
Lafon, Francis	119	8/4	49.11.8
Lankford, Thomas este.	100	4/2	20.16.8
Lumpkin, Robert Sen[r.]	374	8/4	155.16.8
Lumpkin, Henry Jun[r.]	190	9/4	88.13.4
Lumpkin, John W. este.	140	7/10	54.16.8
do. of John Ware's este.	118½	7/3	42.15.6
do. of Pendleton	3	7/10	1.3.6
Longest, Richard	227¾	"	89.4.2
do. of John Dudley	20½	7/3	7.8.7½
Longest, Daniel, of Pendleton	156	7/4	57.4.0
Longest, John	100	7/10	39.3.4
Lumpkin, Anthony este.	216	6/3	67.10.0
Lumpkin, Robert Jun[r.] este.	297¾	5/3	73.8.8¼
Lumpkin, William Jun[r.]	183¼	10/5	95.6.3
Lyne, William	1160	8/4	483.6.8
Lumpkin, Richard	178	5/3	46.14.6
Longest, William	83	8/4	34.11.4
Lumpkin, Ann	47	13/6	31.14.6
Lumpkin, Elizabeth	51	"	38.8.6
Lumpkin, John (King W[m.])	105	"	70.17.6
do. of Henry White	57	"	38.9.6
Lyne, Edmund	50	8/4	20.16.8
Motley, Edwin	815	10/5	428.2.6
do. of Semple	149	12/6	93.2.6
Martin, Thomas C.	583	14/6	422.13.6
do.	134½	7/3	48.15.1
Minor, William	149	8/4	62.1.8
Minor, John	137	"	57.1.8
Miller, Anthony	171½	7/10	67.3.5
Moody, Lewis	239	7/10	93.12.2
Mann, Joseph Jun[r.]	400	8/4	166.13.4
do. of Crows	140	6/3	43.15.0
do. of Fielding S. Crow			
do. of Allen & wife	25½	6/3	7.19.4½
Mann, Robert este.	699	6/3	218.8.9
Meredith, Samuel	215	7/10	84.4.2
Mann, Mary	100	5/3	26.5.0
Martin, John	475	9/	213.15.0
do. of Fogg	197	6/3	61.11.3
21.22.20.17			£4961.19.7¼

[page 8, List B, 1806] Persons names owning Land	Quantity of Land	Price per acre	Tot. Amt. Value Land
[Martin, John], of Satterwhite	88	6/3	27.10.0
do. of Major Taylor &c.	60	6/3	18.15.0
Mahon, Thomas	101	6/3	31.11.3
Mahon, William	103½	"	32.3.9
Mahon, Benjamin	43¼	5/3	11.7.0¾
Mitchael, Richard, of Stone [Mitchell]	74¼	3/2	11.15.1½
Minor, Coleman, of John Gayle	63¼	7/5	23.9.1¼
Nunn, Moses	318	7/4½	117.5.3
do. of William Byers &c.	15	"	5.10.7½
Nunn, Thomas	130	7/3	47.2.6
do. of Brizendine	49	4/3	10.8.3
Newbill, William	1060	8/4	441.13.4
Newell, John este.	100	7/10	39.3.4
Nash, John este.	100	6/3	31.5.0
Noel, Phill & Skelton, Reuben	275	8/4	114.11.8
Newbil, Thomas, of Tunstall	94¾	"	39.9.6
Pendleton, James	888½	8/7½	383.3.3¾
do. of Wilmore	70	7/6	26.5.0
do. of Wm. McIntosh	125	4/2	26.1.10
Pitts, David	420	9/6	196.0.0
Pitts, Obadiah	20	10/5	10.8.4
Phillips, James	230	7/3	83.7.6
Pollard, John este.	235	9/4	109.13.4
do. of Leonard Smithey	384	7/3	139.4.0
Prewitt, Richard	102	7/3	36.12.3
do. of Prewit's este.	99	9/4	46.4.0
Parker, John	761¼	8/4	317.3.9
Pendleton, Phillip este., lot in Dunkirk			3.0.0
Perryman, Phillip	218	7/2	78.2.4
do. of Dillard	215	"	77.10.0
Pynes, Clement	99	3/2	15.13.6
Pollard, Richard	389	8/4	162.1.8
Pendleton, Benjamin este.	447	7/10	175.1.6
Perryman, Richard	110	7/3	39.7.6
Prewit, Tunstall	58½	8/	23.8.0
Pollard, Joseph	200	6/3	62.10.0
Pollard, Richard & Brown	50	8/	20.0.0
Parker, Gouldman, of Gresham	170	7/3	61.12.6
18.13.11			£3095.11.0¾

[page 8, List B, 1806] Persons names owning Land	Quantity of Land	Price per acre	Tot. Amt. Value Land
	[189]		
Quarles, Francis W.	23¼	17/2	19.17.1½
do. of Garnett	114½	7/3	41.10.1½
Quarles, Isaac (King Wm.)	25¾	20/	25.15.0
Row, Richard este.	88	8/4	36.13.4
Roane, Spencer	954	24/10	1184.11.0
Ryland, Joseph	487½	7/3	176.10.9
do. of Chick's Exors.	463	"	167.16.9
Ryland, Josiah	160	7/10	62.13.4
do. of Wm. Temple	27½	15/	20.12.6
do. of Francis Prince's este.	107	7/10	41.18.2
do. of H. Brown	34½	7/4½	12.14.1¼
do. of James H. Row	226	8/4	92.3.4
Riddle, Vaughan	188	5/5	49.7.0
Roane, Thomas	920¾	17/2	790.8.2½
Row, Hansford	162½	6/3	50.3.1½
Row, Wilson	162½	6/3	50.3.1½
Redd, James	200	7/3	72.10.0
Row, James H., of [C.] Anderson	262	"	94.19.6
do. of John Watkins &c.	152	8/4	63.6.8
do. lot in Dunkirk			6.0.0
Smith, William	53	7/10	20.15.2
do. of James Smith's este.	25	3/2	3.19.2
Segar, Richard este.	406	7/3	147.3.6
Satterwhite, George	60¾	6/3	18.19.8
Satterwhite, William	118	5/7½	33.3.9
Schools, John	86	8/4	35.16.8
do. of Frederick Fogg	30	"	12.10.0
do. of Parker & Wife	35	"	14.11.8
Schools, Gabriel este.	174	6/3	54.7.6
Skelton, William Este.	289	8/2½	118.12.2½
do. of Lyne	91	8/4	37.18.4
do. of Phil Perryman	12	7/2	4.6.0
Smith, John (drisdale)	142½	7/6	53.8.9
Saunders, George	200	7/3	70.10.8
do. of Wiatt &c.	115	7/10	45.0.10
Shepherd, William este.	140	9/4	65.6.8
Smith, Molly	30	4/2	6.5.0
Smith, John Junr.	42½	5/3	11.3.1½
Smith, Lewis	96	7/6	36.0.0
do. of Richard Hill	37	8/2	15.2.2
do. of do.	11¼	"	4.11.10½
16.17.19.13			£3868.15.10

[page 9, List B, 1806] Persons names owning Land	Quantity of Land	Price per acre	Tot. Amt. Value Land
Stone, Sarah	300	7/3	108.15.0
Stone, Daniel	52	3/2	8.4.8
Smith, Larkin	1154¼	31/1	1793.17.11¼
Smith, John, of Larkin Smith	100	31/1	155.[8].4
Smith, Henry	400	6/3	130.0.0
Smith, Ambrose	92¾	8/4	38.6.8
do. of John Smith (De.)	47½	7/6	17.16.3
Stevens, George este.	430	7/10	168.8.4
Stevens, George, Orphan	75	"	29.8.4
Smith, William este., Mill	200	3/2	31.13.4
Shackelford, John este.	114	7/3	40.8.2
Shepherd, John	192	3/2	30.1.8
Sthreshley, William	155½	6/3	48.11.10
Schools, George	200	8/4	83.6.8
do. of John Hutchason	150	7/1	53.2.6
Smith, John, of J. Garlick	54	29/	78.6.0
Smith, Jane, of Smith's este.	25	3/2	3.19.2
Smith, Philip, Orphan of do.	12½	"	1.19.7
Smith, James	76	7/10	29.15.4
do. of James Smith's este.	12½	3/2	1.19.7
Scott, Anderson	330	16/7	273.12.6
do. of P. Anderson's Este.	248	20/9	257.6.0
do. of Anderson and wife	96	"	99.12.0
Semple, Robert B.	235	10/5	122.6.3½
do. of Spencer Roane	155	24/10	192.9.2
Stewart, James	120	9/2	55.0.0
Skelton, William, of Wm. Skelton's este.	73	8/2½	29.19.2½
Shepherd, William, of George Wiatt	49½	7/6	18.11.3
Shackelford, James, of Joel Willis	63	31/1	97.18.8
Shackelford, Leonard	113	6/3	35.6.3
Trice, William este.	140	7/3	50.15.0
Taylor, James	50	6/8	15.12.6
Taylor, Edmund	249	8/4	122.10.0
Temple, Joseph	918	10/5	478.2.6
Tunstall, Richard Junr. este.	1097	7/3	397.13.3
Temple, William	402¼	15/	301.17.6
Temple, John	42	31/3	65.12.6
Temple, Humphrey este.	100	15/	75.0.0
do. of J. Tunstall	200	18/8	185.16.8
do. of R. Tunstall este.	574	21/	602.14.0
18.21.21.13			£6331.4.7¼

[page 10, List B, 1806] Persons names owning Land	Quantity of Land	Price per acre	Tot. Amt. Value Land
	[190]		
Tunstall, Richard (Purdy) este.	63¾	8/4	32.5.6
Temple, Joseph Junr., of Jno. Temple	2	30/	3.0.0
Upshaw, James (Essex)	125	8/10	55.4.2
do. of R. Beverly	30	10/5	15.12.6
do. of Reuben Garnett	120	8/	48.0.0
Wilson, Abraham	159	6/3	49.13.9
Wilson, Benjamin este.	200	7/3	72.10.0
Watkins, Joseph	63	6/7	20.14.9
do. of Wiltshire's este.	71	7/3	26.14.9
Walker, Phillip	110	9/4	51.6.8
Walker, Humphrey	820	33/2	1355.14.2
Wright, William	130	5/3	33.12.6
Willis, Joel	94	7/10	35.5.0
do. of William Jones este.	140¼	17/10	125.1.1½
Wright, Edward	567	6/3	177.3.9
Whayne, William este.	154½	7/10	60.10.3
Wiatt, George	122	7/6	45.15.0
Webb, James	209	4/2	43.10.10
Wheeley, Carriol este.	37¼	7/3	13.10.0¾
Watkins, Joseph Junr.	93¼	8/4	38.17.1
Wyatt, Robert	50	7/3	18.2.6
Watkins, John, of G. Dix	226	6/3	70.12.6
Watkins, Phillip este.	107	4/2	22.5.10
Walton, Thomas, of Howerton	76¾	6/	23.0.6
Williamson, Abner, of D. Walker &c.	50¼	3/2	7.19.1½
Ward, Joshoua, lot in dunkirk, anl. Rent			60.0.0
Watkins, Richard, of Rodk. Starling	187½	8/	75.0.0
Wilmore, Christopher	50	8/	20.0.0
Wilmore, John	130	"	52.0.0
Young, Henry	640	18/8	597.6.8
	12.13.11.9		£3250.8.11¾
			[47474.6.7]

Richard Pollard, Comr.

[arithmetic omitted]

[cover]

King & Queen
Rd. Pollard
1806
Land
29th Septr. 1806
Entd.
Added
Stated, Added
Richd. Pollard's List
of Land for 1805
$759.59 Tax on Land

A list of land within the district of Thomas Spencer, Commissioner in the County of King & Queen for the year one thousand eight hundred and seven

LIST A

[page 1, List A, 1807] Persons names owning land	Quantity of land	Price per acre	Total Amount Land	Amt. Tax Thereon in Dols. Cents
	[192]			
Atkins, Lewis	60	8/4	25.0.0}	
Do. John B. Whiting	256½	7/10	100.0.0}	
Anderson, Francis est.	384	10/9	187.3.8}	
Do. Rich[d.] T. Shackelford	26	8/4	12.1.8}	
Anderson, Beverley	203½	3/2	32.4.5}	
Do. Jn[o.] B. Whiting	242¾	7/10	95.1.6½	
Brown, Samuel	33¼	4/3	7.1.2	
Banks, William est.	365	4/2	76.0.0	
Brooke, Richard	1539¾	29/	2232.12.9	
Brumley, Robert	225	5/3	59.1.3	
Bird, William est.	532	7/3	197.17.0}	
Do. Dragon Swamp	88½	17/	70.4.6}	
Bird, Philemon est.	1638¼	6/3	511.19.0¾	
Brett, Nancy	50	18/	45.0.0	
Burch, James est.	183	6/3	57.3.9	
Burch, Vincent Est.	100	4/2	20.16.8}	
Do. William Hoskins	50	3/3	7.18.4}	
Bird, Anthony A.	275	"	43.10.10}	
Do. W[m.] Montague	44	4/2	9.3.4}	
Do. Robert Smith Sen.	8	10/5	4.4.4"	
Byne, John est.	336	4/2	70.0.0}	
Do. Dragon Swamp	2¼	17/	1.18.3}	
Do. Do., Grant to Jn[o.] Lyne	20 ¾	"	17.12.9}	
Do. Do. Do. Do.	14 ¾	"	12.10.9}	
Bird, Robert est.	780	24/10	993.6.8}	
Do. Guy Smith	189½	3/2	30.0.10}	
Bourn, Richard est.	150	"	23.15.0	
Boyd, John	115	18/8	107.6.8}	
Do. Sownes	382	24/10	474.6.4}	
Bray, Richard est.	93	7/10	36.8.6	
Bird, John est.	71	3/2	11.4.10	
Bew, William est.	117	"	18.0.6	
Boyd, Robert	1119	9/3	517.10.3	
Boyd, William	300	15/	225.0.0}	
Do. Francis Gaines	367	14/6	266.1.6}	
Burkeley, Edmund est.	762	5/3	200.0.6	
Bland, John, Porto.	60	12/6	37.10.0	
Bland, William est.	100	9/11	49.11.8	
Bourn, Mills	159½	5/3	41.14.3}	
Do. Thomas Jordan's est.	33 1/3	4/2	6.18.10}	
16.14.18.14			£6935.2.3	

[page 2, List A, 1807] Persons names owning land	Quantity of land	Price per acre	Total Amount Land	Amt. Tax Thereon in Dols. Cents
Bullman, Ann	120	5/3	31.10.0	
Bew, Major W.	82	"	21.10.6	
Burton, Caty	58	3/2	9.3.8	
Balote, Laban, H. Clegg's Est.	384½	4/2	80.2.6	
Bland, William, Preacher	225	3/8¼	41.9.8½}	
do. William Dillard	152¼	6/	45.13.6}	
Bland, Ralph	146	53	38.6.8}	
Do. Finny & Buckner	170	4/2	35.8.4}	
Do. N. Dillard, Dragon	4¼	17/	3.12.3}	
Bowden, William	100	4/2	20.16.8}	
Do. Sykes	34	3/2	5.7.8}	
Bland, Robert	250	4/2	52.1.8	
Bland, Thomas est.	412	3/2	75.4.8	
Brooks, Meriman	100	7/10	39.3.4	
Bowden, George	205	5/3	53.16.3	
Banks, James	22	7/3	7.19.6	
Banks, Andrew	125	12/6	78.2.6	
Brightwell, John est.	70	4/2	14.11.8	
Burton, James est.	89	"	18.10.10	
Bland, William, Younger	300	7/3	108.15.0}	
Do. Dawson Cooke	103	4/2	21.9.2}	
Bird, Janett & Frances	230	10/5	119.10.5}	
Do. Robt. Smith, Dragon	22½	17/	19.2.6}	
Brushwood, George	138	4/2	39.3.4}	
Do. Wares	32¼	3/2	5.2.1½}	
Bray, Peter	51¼	6/3	16.0.3¾	
Bland, John Jun.	212	5/3	55.13.0}	
Do. Overstreets	96	4/2	20.0.0}	
Broocke, William	33	10/5	17.3.9	
Brooke, William, Essex	83	11/8	48.8.4	
Banks, John D.	150	6/3	46.17.6	
Bird, Parmenas	100	5/3	28.6.8	
Carlton, Thomas Sen.	200	7/10	78.6.8}	
Carlton, Noah	100	"	39.3.4	
Cooke, Henry est.	260	5/3	68.5.0}	
Collins, John est.	75	3/2	11.17.6	
Carlton, John S	100	6/3	31.5.0}	
Do. to agree with late survey	41	"	12.16.3}	
Do. Loddy Carlton	44	3/2	6.19.4}	
Campbell, James T. (Orphan)	296	12/6	185.0.0	
Carlton, Christopher Sen.	37½	6/3	11.14.5}	
Do. James Laughlin	126½	3/2	26.8.2}	
Carlton, Richard est.	139	7/	48.13.4	
Cauthern, James	36½	3/2	5.15.7	
Carlton, William Sen.	309¾	11/6	178.1.2½	
Carlton, Christopher (Younger)	138¼	5/	34.11.3	
Carlton, Richard Sen.	250	7/3	90.12.6	
18.20.25.16			£2047.13.2	

[page 3, List A, 1807] Persons names owning land	Quantity of land [193]	Price per acre	Total Amount Land	Amt. Tax Thereon in Dols. Cents
Carlton, Christopher Jun.	100	"	36.5.0	
Cooper, Henry	50	4/2	10.8.4	
Carlton, Thomas (T) est.	72 8/11	6/3	22.14.4¾	
Cardwell, James	211	4/2	43.19.2}	
Do. Jn°. Richeson est.	106	5/3	27.16.6}	
Do. Jn°. Cooke's est.	30	4/2	6.5.0}	
Do. Joseph Wyatt	8¼	"	1.14.4½}	
Do. Rich[d]. Eubanks est.	117	8/4	48.15.0}	
Cardwell, John	150	4/2	31.5.0	
Cardwell, William est.	77	"	15.11.6	
Cardwell, Thomas est.	110	"	22.18.4	
Cooke, John est.	270	"	56.5.0	
Collins, Thomas	281½	7/	98.10.6}	
Do. R.S. Ware	84½	11/9	49.12.6 }	
Do. Metcalf & Levert	289½	14/6	209.17.9}	
Do. Jane Crittenden	60	13/6	40.10.0}	
Carlton, John Jun.	235	4/2	48.19.2}	
Do. Baylor Fleet	2	12/6	1.5.0}	
Corbin, Richard	2390	11/1¾	1332.11.4}	
Do. Shackelford's	300	14/6	217.10.0}	
Do. Dixons	416¾	15/5	321.10.10}	
Do. Dragon at new bridge	20	17/	17.0.0}	
Campbell, William	238	3/2	37.13.8	
Corr, James	100	6/2	30.16.8	
Crouch, James	105½	3/2	16.13.3½	
Clayton, James	260	5/3	65.5.0	
Crittenden, Zachariah	34½	14/6	24.7.10	
Cary, Wilson J.	1820	16/7	1509.1.8	
Collins, Joyeux	140	10/5	72.8.4}	
Do. H. & W. Robinson	37 1/3	8/4	15.11.1½	
Campbell, James	130	5/9½	37.10.0}	
Do. Rich[d]. Garrett	70	3/2	11.1.8}	
Do. Benj[a]. Faulkner	55¼	7/3	20.0.6¾}	
Corr, Thomas R.	231¼	5/3	60.12.9}	
Do. Jn°. Shackelford Mc.	73=28 poles	"	19.4.3}	
Do. Benj[a]. Walden	170	"	44.12.6}	
Crittenden, Richard est.	178	"	46.14.6	
Collier, Joseph	468	"	112.17.0	
Collier, Benjamin	75	"	19.13.9	
Clegg, Isaiah est.	241	4/2	50.4.2	
Curry, John	155	4/	31.0.0	
Cooke, Thomas Sen. est.	240	3/2	38.0.0	
Cooke, Thomas Jun.	96	"	15.0.4	
Cooke, Dawson	1	5/3	5.3}	
Do. Jn°. B. Whiting	24¾	7/10	9.13.10¾}	
Do. Do.	150	"	58.15.0}	
Do. Eleanor Graves	¼	"	1.11½}	
4.15.22.22.14			£5008.9.10	

[page 4, List A, 1807] Persons names owning land	Quantity of land	Price per acre	Total Amount Land	Amt. Tax Thereon in Dols. Cents
Carlton, Humphrey	175	7/	61.5.0}	
Do. Jn°. Watt's est.	28	6/3	8.7.0}	
Corr, John est.	503½	7/3	182.10.4½}	
Do. Thomas Dudley	197½	6/3	61.14.4½}	
Do. Guildford Dudley	28½	7/3	10.6.7½	
Carlton, Thomas est.	235	6/3	73.8.9	
Campbell, John est.	400	12/6	250.0.0	
Do. R.G. Meredith	111½	14/6	80.16.9}	
Curry, James	70	4/2	14.11.8	
Do. Jn°. Broach	71	"	14.15.10}	
Do. Frances Webley	79	"	16.9.2}	
Corr, John Sen.	213	3/2	33.15.6}	
Do. Jn°. Corr Jun.	90	7/3	32.12.6}	
Do. Dawson Cooke	5=6 poles	4/2	1.1.0}	
Do. Do.	106	3/2	16.15.8}	
Crittenden, Frances (Riv)	105¾	14/6	76.12.2	
Clarke, John	144	5/	36.0.0}	
Do. Saml. Hemingway	254¼	4/2	53.0.3}	
Cooke, John est.	100	3/2	15.6.8	
Clayton, Maria H., Sally K.} and Polley R. Clayton}	72	9/11	35.14.0	
Collins, Mason	110	3/2	17.8.4	
Carlton, Lewis	$9_{1/11}$	6/3	2.16.10}	
Do. Baylor & Christ°. Carlton	$18_{2/11}$	"	5.13.8}	
Collins, James	120	4/2	25.0.0}	
Do. Loddy Carlton to you and Overstreet	25½	5/3	32.18.10½	
Cauthern, Vincent F.	16¼	5/8	4.12.1	
Carlton, Nathan	83½	6/3	26.1.10½	
Dillard, William est., apply to Frances Digges	100	3/2	15.16.8	
Didlake, James est.	278	8/4	115.16.8	
Dunn, Thomas	50½	6/3	15.15.7½	
Dillard, George	50	12/6	31.5.0}	
Do. Wm. Dillard Sen.	226	"	141.5.0}	
Durham, Thomas est.	85	3/2	13.9.2	
Dickie, Barbara	1½	17/	1.5.6}	
Do. Parmenas Bird	50¼	11/8	29.6.3}	
Do. Robt. Bird Exors. &c.	37½	17/	31.17.6}	
Dudley, William est.	290	14/6	210.5.0}	
Do. Lydia Wedderburn	315½	6/3	98.11.10}	
Damm, John est.	55	"	17.3.9	
Dudley, James	180	7/10	70.10.0	
Damm, William est.	25	4/2	5.4.2	
Doughlas, John [sic]	239	7/	83.13.0	
Didlake, John	1200	7/3	435.0.0}	
Do. Halyard's	186	5/3	48.16.6}	
Dudley, Guildford est.	69½	7/3	25.3.10½	
3.17.21.19.14			£2580.0.5½	

[page 5, List A, 1807] Persons names owning land	Quantity of land [194]	Price per acre	Total Amount Land	Amt. Tax Thereon in Dols. Cents
Dudley, Banks est.	230	3/2	36.8.4	
Downey, Michael est.	50	10/5	26.0.10	
Didlake, Royston	206	3/6½	36.7.4}	
Do. George Bowden	65	4/2	13.10.0}	
Dillard, William Jun. est.	207½	15/	155.12.6	
Dudley, Thomas	70	6/3	21.17.6	
Dillard, Nicholas	75	4/2	15.12.6	
Dunn, John, Essex	73	17/	62.1.0	
Digges, Frances	105	5/3	27.11.3	
Dean, Benjamin	28¼	"	7.8.3¾	
Dillard, Thomas A.	29	3/2	4.11.10}	
Do. Young Simpkins	1	"	3.2}	
Durham, George est.	50	4/2	10.8.4}	
Do. Newham Durham	50	"	10.8.4}	
Didlake, Philip	83	"	17.5.10}	
Do. Edward Didlake	40	10/5	20.16.8}	
Daniel, John	30	4/2	6.5.0	
Eubank, William est.	28¾	5/3	7.11.0	
Eubank, Richard Sen.	196	7/	68.12.0	
Eubank, Thomas	110	4/2	22.18.4	
Eubank, Philip	135¾	"	28.5.7½	
Eubank, Richard Jun.	108¾	7/	38.1.1½}	
Do. Thomas Jeffries	12¾	7/3	4.12.5}	
Do. A. Dunn	147	5/3	38.11.9}	
Do. Anty. Hart	87¼	3/2	13.10.3½}	
Eubank, Warner	115	"	18.4.2}	
Do. Jn°. Hemingway Jun.	4	4/2	16.8}	
Fleet, Baylor	860	12/6	537.10.8	
Frazer, William est.	45	20/9	46.13.6	
Fleet, William	352	"	365.4.0}	
Do. Rich[d]. T. Kauffman	15	"	15.11.3}	
Fisher, John	111	3/2	17.11.6	
Foster, Thomas	87¾	4/2	18.2.6	
Fauntleroy, Thomas	486	10/	243.0.0}	
Do. Henry Todd	500	18/	450.0.0}	
Do. Willliam Bowden	183	7/	64.1.0}	
Farinholtz, David	151¼	6/6	49.1.6}	
Do. Staige Davis	219½	6/9	74.1.6}	
Faulkner, Benjamin	100	4/2	20.16.8}	
Do. Mary Faulkner	333	6/3	104.1.4}	
Do. William Boyd	9½	10/5	4.10.9}	
Do. Jn°. Southern	134½	4/2	28.0.5}	
Do. James Campbell	29¾	7/3	10.15.8¼}	
Do. Do.	112¼	4/2	23.7.8½}	
Do. Anty. Gardner	3	17/	2.11.0}	
Do. Do.	10=27 poles	17/	8.12.10½}	
Farguson, Thomas	62	10/5	32.5.10}	
Do. Thomas Collins	48	7/	16.16.0}	
	3.19.23.12		£2845.8.0½	

[page 6, List A, 1807] Persons names owning land	Quantity of land	Price per acre	Total Amount Land	Amt. Tax Thereon in Dols. Cents
Faucet, Vincent	46½	10/5	24.4.4½	
Fisher, William	30	5/3	7.17.6	
Graves, Eleanor	163	"	42.15.9}	
Do. Jn°. B. Whiting	100	7/10	39.3.4}	
Garlick, Camm est.	917	6/3	286.11.3	
Gresham, Philemon	200	"	62.10.0	
Gresham, Mary	100	7/10	39.3.4	
Gresham, William B	100	4/2	20.16.8}	
Do. William Rowe	95	6/3	29.13.9}	
Gardner, Anthony	638	11/	350.11.8}	
Do. Dragon Swamp	57	17/	48.9.0}	
Do. Vincent Hart	73¾	6/6	23.19.4½}	
Gardner, Elizabeth	100	6/3	31.5.0	
Gibson, Richard	156½	3/2	24.16.7	
Gibson, Eubank	56½	"	8.18.11}	
Do. Rich[d]. Eubank Jun.	3½	7/	1.4.6}	
Gresham, Meacham	100	5/3	26.5.0}	
Do. A. Gresham	4	17/	3.8.0}	
Gresham, Ambrose	79½	5/3	20.17.4}	
Do. Dragon Swamp	22	17/	18.5.0}	
Gresham, John B	79	5/3	20.14.9}	
Do. A. Gresham	4	17/	3.8.0}	
Garrett, James	280	4/2	48.18.4}	
Do. William Garrett	100	"	20.16.8}	
Garrett, Robert Sen.	200	7/	70.0.0}	
Do. Philemon Bird	54¾	6/3	17.2.2.¼}	
Do. William Hunt	170	"	53.2.6}	
Do. Spencer Ware	70	5/3	18.7.6}	
Do. Robert Read	26	4/2	5.8.4}	
Gaines, Robert est.	315½	20/9	327.16.11}	
Do. A. Curtis	50	5/3	13.2.6}	
Guthrie, James	60	12/6	37.10.0	
Guthrie, Richard	60	"	37.10.0}	
Do.	162	3/2	25.13.0}	
Garrett, Edward Sen.	210	5/3	55.2.6}	
Do. Trices	489½	"	128.9.10}	
Garrett, William, son W[m].	197¾	7/3	71.13.8¾	
Groom, John	173	3/2	27.17.10}	
Do. John Bowden	95	4/2	19.15.10}	
Do. Robert Lumpkin	106¾	"	22.4.9¾}	
Guthrie, Rachel	50	8/4	20.16.8	
Goldman, Martin	140	4/2	29.3.4	
Garnett, James	100	"	20.16.8	
Gully, Philip est.	50	3/2	7.18.4	
Garrett, William Sen.	225	3/4½	37.19.4½}	
Do. Geo. B. Bird	60	6/3	18.15.0}	
Do. Henry F. Dudley	50	5/3	13.2.6}	
Gramshill, Henry	25	3/2	3.19.2	
3.19.26.24.13			£2288.2.7¼	

[page 7, List A, 1807] Persons names owning land	Quantity of land [195]	Price per acre	Total Amount Land	Amt. Tax Thereon in Dols. Cents
Gresham, James	112	5/	28.0.0	
Do. Philip Gibson & Wife	129½	3/2	20.98.3¾	
Gilmore, Richard	414	5/3	108.13.6	
Garrett, Richard, apply to Wm. Garrett Sen.	100	4/2	20.16.8	
Garrett, William Jun.	120	"	25.0.0	
Garrett, Edward Jun.	150	6/3	46.17.6	
Gaines, Benjamin	360	20/4	366.0.0}	
Do. Howard Williams	52½	4/2	10.8.9}	
Do. Robert Gaines	222¼	20/9	230.11.8}	
Gaines, Harry	360	20/4	366.0.0	
Gatewood, Philip	1	7/10	7.10	
Guthrie, Major est., apply to Nick Ware} and Ewd. Garrett Sen.	100	5/	25.0.0	
Henderson, James	25	5/3	6.11.3	
Hoskins, William est.	296	20/	296.0.0}	
Do. Balance Bray's	2	7/10	15.8}	
Hoomes, Benjamin	447	12/6	279.7.6}	
Do. Ann Kennedy	75	"	46.17.6}	
Hemingway, John Jun.	250	4/2	52.1.8	
Hare, William est.	217	5/3	56.19.3	
Harwood, Christopher est.	194	24/10	240.17.8	
Harwood, Priscilla	165	18/	148.10.0	
Hart, James Sen.	150	3/2	23.15.0	
Holderby, John Sen.	73¼	4/2	15.5.2½	
Holderby, John Jun.	108¾	7/10	42.6.0	
Hart, Anthony	190	5/3	49.17.6}	
Do. balance sundry persons	41	3/2	6.9.10}	
Hart, Gregory	200	"	31.13.4	
Harwood, John est.	109	10/5	56.15.2	
Henry, Samuel H. est.	1900	14/6	1377.10.0	
Henry, James est.	75	12/6	46.17.6	
Hoskins, Robert	287	6/	86.2.0}	
Do. Robert Smith	157¾	10/5	82.10.6¾}	
Do. Do., Dragon	7¾=13 poles	17/	6.13.1¼}	
Do. Rob[t.] Smith Jun.	22	10/5	11.8.2}	
Hart, Alden	77	4/2	16.0.10}	
Do. Anty. Hart	231	3/2	36.11.6}	
Hudson, William	75¼	4/2	15.13.6}	
Do. Jn[o.] Daniel	25	"	5.4.2}	
Howerton, Heritage est.	122¼	20/9	126.16.7¼	
Halyard, William	260	6/3	81.5.0	
Howerton, John	269½	5/3	70.14.10½	
Hart, Vincent	88	7/3	31.18.0	
Harris, Samuel	214¼	5/3	56.4.9¾	
Hogg, William & Legatees of Holt Richeson	36	18/	32.8.0	
Hart, James Jun.	146	3/3½	24.0.7}	
Do. Jn[o.] Hart's	88	"	14.4.4}	
4.16.22.21.17			£4725.11.4½	

[page 8, List A, 1807] Persons names owning land	Quantity of land	Price per acre	Total Amount Land	Amt. Tax Thereon in Dols. Cents
Hart, John	80	3/2	12.13.4	
Hart, Salley	119	3/3½	19.11.8½	
Hart, Robert	62	"	10.6.7	
Hemingway, John Sen.	125	4/2	26.0.10	
Hill, Richard	69¾	5/8	19.15.3	
Jones, Thomas	255	4/2	53.2.6	
Jones, Thomas, Essex	735	7/10	287.17.6	
Jeffries, Thomas B	63	7/3	22.16.9}	
Do. John Harwood	25½	10/5	13.5.7½	
Do. Brett's est.	57¾	18/	51.19.6}	
Jones, James	100	5/3	26.5.0}	
Do. Mary Jones	150	26/11	201.17.6}	
Jeffries, Going	60	4/2	12.10.0	
Jordan, Robert	66 2/3	"	13.18.10	
Jones, Mary	150	26/11	201.17.6	
Ison, George	140¼	5/3	36.16.3¾	
Inge, Vincent est.	33	8/4	13.15.0	
Kemp, John	296	7/3	107.0.3	
Kauffman, Richard T.	161	26/	209.6.0	
Kauffman, Sambo, Humphrey} and Lucy, free negroes	167	7/6	62.5.0	
Kidd, John	81¾	5/3	26.6.6¾	
Kennedy, Archibald est.	38¼	4/2	7.19.4	
Kennedy, Ann	33¼	"	6.18.6½	
Kennedy, Ann Jun.	33¾	"	7.0.6	
Kennedy, Lucy	37½	"	7.16.2	
Kidd, Bartholomew	136	5/3	35.14.0}	
Do. Wm. Dillard Jun.	132½	4/2	27.12.1}	
Do. Robt. Lumpkin	95½	"	19.17.11}	
Kidd, Benjamin	111	13/6	74.18.2}	
Do. Dragon Swamp	36	17/	30.12.0}	
Kidd, John est.	370	7/3	134.2.6}	
Do. Lumpkin & Pierce	60	4/2	12.10.0}	
Do. Thomas Dillard	45	14/6	32.12.6}	
King, Dicey est.	18	8/4	7.10.0	
Lumpkin, Jacob	589¼	6/3	184.10.9¾	
Lewis, Iveson	356	14/6	258.2.0}	
Do. Eliza. Montague	3	17/	2.11.0}	
Leigh, Lucy	101	24/10	125.8.2	
Leigh, John est.	133	"	165.2.10}	
Do.	66	"	81.19.0}	
Leigh, Richard est.	560	6/3	175.0.0	
Lattany, Catharine R.	271	10/9	145.13.3	
Lewis, John, Gloster	818	14/6	593.1.0	
Mitchel, Salley est.	391	13/	254.3.4	
Mitchel, James, Orphan	225	"	146.5.0	
Moore, Lodawick, John and Richard	100	3/2	15.16.8	
3.15.24.23.14			£3982.4.3¾	

[page 9, List A, 1807] Persons names owning land	Quantity of land [196]	Price per acre	Total Amount Land	Amt. Tax Thereon in Dols. Cents
Major, Josiah	200	4/2	41.13.4	
Mitchel, John est.	270	5/3	70.17.0}	
Do. Rootes	128	9/11	63.9.3}	
Mann, Joseph Sen.	231	6/3	72.3.9	
Moore, Agathy	40	4/2	8.6.8	
Montague, William	170	"	35.8.4	
Muire, Richard	93	12/6	58.2.6}	
Do. Rich[d.] Anderson	177	5/3	46.9.3}	
Mitchell, Richard est.	74¼	4/2	15.9.4½	
Moore, Richard est.	145	6/3	45.6.8	
McCarty, Joseph est.	73	3/2	11.11.2	
Metcalf, Thomas	256	14/6	181.8.8	
Milby, Richard	175	3/2	27.14.2	
Morgan, William	3	6/3	.18.9	
Moore, John est.	37	4/2	7.14.2	
Mann, John	179¼	7/10	74.7.5½	
Muire, William	125	5/3	32.16.3	
Muse, Thomas, Middlesex	30	17/	25.10.0	
Meridith, George	74	14/6	53.3.3	
Meridith, Austin	114	"	82.13.0	
Meridith, Samuel	75	"	53.17.6	
Newcomb, William	169	3/2	26.15.2}	
Do. Benj[a.] Dillard	148	5/3	48.17.0}	
Do. of Do.	52	"	13.13.0}	
Noel, Silas M.	104	7/3	37.14.0	
Newbill, John	21¾	5/3	5.14.2¾	
Norman, John	60	4/2	12.10.0	
Oliver, John, said to be sold to Philip Vass} of N[o.] Carolinia [sic]}	210	¾	35.0.0	
Orrill, John est.	100	6/3	31.5.0}	
Do.	52	"	16.5.0}	
Oliver, John	320	5/3	84.0.0	
Oakes, Henry	198½	3/2	34.2.0	
Oakes, William	80	4/2	16.13.4	
Oliver, William	59	"	12.5.10}	
Do. Howard Williams	62 7/8	"	13.1.11¾}	
Oakes, Ann	60	"	12.10.0	
Oliver, Francis	40¾	"	8.9.9½}	
Do. James Medearas	86	6/3	28.6.2}	
Pitts, Benjamin G.	100	5/4	26.13.4	
Pace, Benjamin est.	263	7/3	95.6.9	
Pynes, Benjamin est.	164	6/3	51.5.0	
Pynes, Robert	111½	"	34.16.10½}	
Do. William Adams	53¾	"	16.15.11¾}	
Pynes, Benjamin	46¼	"	14.9.0¾	
Pemberton, John Sen.	90	"	28.2.3}	
Do. Jacob Lumpkin	60	"	18.5.0}	
5.14.22.22.16			£1732.7.3	

[page 10, List A, 1807] Persons names owning land	Quantity of land	Price per acre	Total Amount Land	Amt. Tax Thereon in Dols. Cents
Pollard, Robert	6	24/10	7.9.0}	
Do. John Omealy	367	30/	550.10.0}	
Do. William Garrett Sen.	49¼	10/5	25.12.0}	
Palmer, Charles	107¾	18/	96.19.6}	
Do.	104	"	93.12.0}	
Do. Mattox & Richeson	14	"	12.12.0}	
Pigg, John est.	324	14/6	234.18.0}	
Do. Cockses	180	7/3	65.0.0}	
Pemberton, John Jun.	121	6/3	37.17.6	
Patterson, Joseph	62¾	3/2	9.18.8½	
Pierce, Philip	83	"	13.2.10	
Pierce, Thomas est.	87	4/2	18.2.6	
Pierce, Beverly	25¾	"	5.7.3½}	
Do. Philip Pierce	17	3/2	2.13.10}	
Pilsbury, George	109¾	10/9	58.19.9¾	
Palmer, Roger	314	6/	94.4.0	
Price, Robert	399	6/3	124.13.9	
Pemberton, James	75	"	23.8.9	
Quarles, John, Middlesex	10	17/	8.10.0	
Roane, Thomas est.	1481	21/1¾	1565.16.11¾}	
Do. H. Carlton	200	6/3	63.10.0}	
Do. Bretts	34¾	18/	31.5.6}	
Do. Robert Pynes	24½	6/3	7.9.1½}	
Rowe, Elizabeth	665	20/9	689.18.9	
Rowe, Francis, Orphan	612½	4/8	142.16.8	
Richason, James (son Elias)	86	4/2	17.8.4	
Richards, John	571	4/8	124.8.0	
Richason, James Sen.	180	4/2	37.10.0	
Richason, William Sen.	181	"	37.14.2	
Roane, Thomas, Middlesex	14¼	15/	10.13.9	
Richeson, William est.	188½	4/2	39.5.5	
Richeson, William Jun.	118½	5/3	31.2.1½}	
Do. Robert Stone	101	4/2	21.0.10}	
Roane, Major est.	687½	3/8	128.18.1½	
Do. John Lyne	455¾	6/3	142.8.5½}	
Do. Roger Palmer	9	7/3	3.5.3}	
" George Brushwood	79¾	3/2	12.12.6½}	
Raines, Giles	60	"	9.10.0	
Robinson, Benjamin est.	1263 2/3	8/4	526.10.6½	
Roane, Charles Sen.	133	19/	126.7.0}	
Do. Dragon Swamp	70/	17/	59.10.0}	
Roy, Beverly	700	8/4	291.13.4}	
Do. Thomas Brown	454	12/6	283.15.0}	
Do. Richard Corbin	125	9/10	61.9.2}	
Richeson, James (son James)	250	5/3	65.12.6	
Richeson, John Sen.	120	"	31.10.0	
Richeson, John Jun.	50	4/2	10.8.4	
5.16.24.23.17			£6056.17.10½	

[page 11, List A, 1807] Persons names owning land	Quantity of land [197]	Price per acre	Total Amount Land	Amt. Tax Thereon in Dols. Cents
Robinson, Mary H.	542	14/6	393.9.0	
Robins, William, Gloster	50	7/10	19.11.8	
Spencer, John	416	7/3	150.16.0}	
Do. Eleanor Graves	½	7/10	3.11}	
Starke, Richard est.	164	5/8	46.9.4	
Stone, Robert est.	24¾	4/2	5.3.1½	
Stone, Robert	31½	5/3	8.5.4½	
Stone, Job est.	100	4/2	20.16.8	
Smith, John (Neck)	88	10/5	45.16.8}	
Do. Dragon Swamp	12	17/	10.8.0}	
Do. A. Gresham	½	5/3	2.7¼	
Smith, Francis	150	3/2	23.5.0	
Simpkins, Young	59	"	9.6.10	
Sears, Philip	83	4/2	17.5.10}	
Do. Francis Oliver	48½	"	10.2.1}	
Shackelford, William est.	400	14/6	310.0.0	
Spencer, Thomas	300	10/5	156.5.0}	
Do.	255	4/2	53.2.6}	
Do. Staige Davis	73	6/9	24.12.9}	
Do. of Do., Foster's tract	71½	4/2	14.17.11}	
Shackelford, Richard T. est.	300	10/	150.0.0	
Seward, Benjamin	115	3/2	18.4.2}	
Do. Loddy Carlton	18½	"	2.17.1¾}	
Smith, Thomas G.	485	14/6	351.12.6}	
Do. Benj[a.] Dabney	400	"	290.0.0}	
Do. of Do.	100	8/4	41.13.4}	
Sadler, John est.	150	6/3	46.17.6	
Shackelford, Zachariah est.	200	"	62.10.0}	
Do. Rich[d.] Anderson	177	5/3	46.9.3}	
Shackelford, John R	401¼	8/4	167.3.10	
Shackelford, William	151	6/3	47.3.9}	
Do. Wyatt's lease	30	5/3	7.16.6}	
Do. Matt Wood	166	7/3	60.3.6}	
Shackelford, John, Mc	283	6/2	87.5.2}	
Do. John Collier C	76¾	5/3	20.2.11¼}	
Do. T.R. Corr	5=30 poles	"	1.7.2¾	
Shackelford, Benjamin, Halyard's lease	1	5/9½	5.9½	
Shepherd, John	67	6/	20.2.0	
Smith, John Doct[r.]	½	30/	15.0	
Smith, Samuel	1	7/10	7.10}	
Do., Dragon	10	17/	8.10.0}	
Spencer, Meacham	323	6/9	109.0.3	
Sears, Thomas	123	6/7	40.9.9}	
Do. How[d.] Williams	42¼	4/2	8.17.1}	
Stone, William	193½	10/5	100.10.5	
Smith, Lewis	44	10/6	23.2.0	
Seward, William	70	3/2	11.1.8	
Shackelford, Benjamin	31¾	6/3	9.18.4½	
4.18.19.18.13			£3054.7.3½	

[page 12, List A, 1807] Persons names owning land	Quantity of land	Price per acre	Total Amount Land	Amt. Tax Thereon in Dols. Cents
Tureman, Elizabeth	24¾	3/2	3.18.4½	
Tureman, Benjamin est.	90¾	"	14.7.4½	
Tureman, George	50	"	7.18.4	
Taliaferro, William est.	1000	14/6	725.0.0	
Townley, Robert	200	6/3	62.10.0}	
Do. Anderson's	117	14/6	84.16.6}	
Taliaferro, Philip est.	662	8/4	275.16.3	
Taliaferro, James B.	374½	12/6	234.7.6	
Thruston, Armstead	111 1/3	4/3	23.15.1	
Thruston, Bachelor	200	3/2	31.13.4	
Turner, Benjamin	36	4/2	7.10.0	
Townley, Ann	79	"	16.9.2	
Turner, Henry est.	100	"	20.16.8	
Tunstall, Richard G.	206½	7/10	73.3.7	
Taylor, William	40	6/3	12.10.0}	
Do. Taliaferro Exors.	200	8/4	83.6.8}	
Todd, William	552	12/	331.4.0	
Trebill, John, Essex	75	14/6	53.17.6	
Watts, Edward est.	250	7/3	90.12.6}	
Do. Wm. Watts est.	113	5/	28.5.0}	
Watts, John	293	7/10	114.15.2}	
Do. Pembertons	45	6/3	14.1.3}	
Watts, Kauffman	270	5/3	70.17.6}	
Do. Eubank & Burch	257	5/9	73.17.9}	
Do. Jno. & D. Hemingway	187	4/2	38.19.2}	
Do. Christo. Carlton, younger]	5½	5/	1.7.6}	
Do. of Do.	4¼	"	1.1.3}	
Watts, James	350	4/2	72.8.4}	
Do. Wm. Watts est.	60	15/	45.0.0}	
Williams, Howard	66 1/8	4/2	13.15.6}	
Do. Dragon Swamp	43	17/	36.11.0}	
Wyatt, Thomas	206	7/10	81.2.0	
Wyatt, William	39¾	7/	13.18.3	
Williams, Montague	300	6/3	93.15.0	
Walton, James	80	4/2	16.8.4}	
Do. Thos. Walton's est.	66	"	13.15.0}	
Walton, John	176	5/3	46.4.0	
Walton, William est.	40	4/2	8.6.8	
Ware, John est.	75	5/3	19.13.9	
Walden, Lewis	90	10/5	46.17.6	
Walden, Richard Jun.	90	10/5	46.17.6	
Walden, Lewis est.	150	3/2	23.15.0}	
Do. Thos. Dudley	84½	6/3	28.3.3½}	
12.23.19.16			£3103.8.11½	

[page 13, List A, 1807] Persons names owning land	Quantity of land	Price per acre	Total Amount Land	Amt. Tax Thereon in Dols. Cents
	[198]			
Williams, George	40	4/2	8.6.8	
Wyatt, Richard	175	12/6	109.7.6	
Wattkins, Philip	197	5/3	51.14.3	
Williams, Elizabeth	16½	3/2	2.12.9	
White, James est.	200	6/3	62.10.0	
Wedderburn, Lydia	350	"	109.7.6	
Whiting, Beverley est.	600¼	7/10	235.1.11½	
Webley, John est.	173	5/3	45.8.3}	
Do. Collier & Dillard	279	4/2	58.2.6}	
Ware, Robert Jun.	100	8/4	41.13.4	
Ware, William [T.]	100	"	41.13.4	
Walden, Benjamin	203	5/3	53.5.9}	
Do. Rich[d.] Anderson	120½	"	31.12.7½}	
Waller, Edward est.	133½	3/2	21.2.9	
Waller, George est.	87	"	13.15.6}	
Do. Jn[o.] Shackelford	47¾	8/4	19.17.11}	
Waller, John	65	3/7	11.12.11	
Waller, Robert est.	48	"	8.12.0}	
Do. Groom's est.	187	3/2	29.12.2}	
Ware, Nicholas	100	"	15.16.8	
Walton, Beverley	47½	7/10	18.12.1	
Watts, George K.	36	26/	46.16.0	
Wyatt, Smith	29¾	7/3	10.15.8}	
Do. W[m.] Wyatt's	9	7/	3.3.0}	
Do. H. Carlton	20½	6/8	6.8.1½}	
Willis, Robert	105	14/6	75.2.6	
Williams, Christopher	100	5/3	26.5.0	
Walden, Charles	109¼	7/10	42.15.9½	
Ware, John	37¾	4/2	7.17.3½	
Wareing, Frank, orphan	271	10/9	145.13.3	
Williams, Thomas	144	4/2	30.0.0	
Williams, John	192	"	40.0.0	
Walton, William Jun.	110	"	22.18.2	
2.13.16.15.9			£1447.13.2½	
			[45807.6.7½]	

Thomas Spencer, Comr. Revenue

[Land Tax] $732.93
[arithmetic omitted]

A List of Land within the District of Richard Pollard, Commissioner in the up[p]er District in the County of King & Queen for the year 1807 to Wit

LIST B

[page 1, List B, 1807] Persons names owning Land	Quantity of Land	Price per acre	Tot. Amt. Value Land
	[199]		
Alexander, Benjamin	202	9/4	94.5.4
Do. of Richard Prewit	90	"	46.4.0
Do. of Halbert	124	6/2	38.15.0
Do. lott in Dunkirk			20.0.0
Do. of Meede			4.10.0
Atkins, Joseph Estate	66	4/2	13.15.0
Acre, Seaton	52	9/4	24.5.4
Do. of Eubank &c.	87¾	5/3	23.0.9
Alexander, Elisha	338	9/4	157.14.8
Anderson, Churchill	374	7/3	135.11.6
Do. of Campbell	155¼	"	56.5.6¾
Atkins, John	277	5/	69.5.0
Alexander, Robert	144¼	9/2	66.2.3½
Alexander, Richard, of Dix	109	63	[5]4.1.3
Alexander, Henry	90	9/2	41.5.0
Barton, John Estate	125	4/2	26.0.10
Broach, Benoni	48	10/5	25.4.0
Brown, Henry Jun[r.]	100	12/	60.0.0
Beverly, Robert Estate	1341	10/5	698.8.9
Beverly, Mackenzie	698½	"	363.16.0 ½
Brown, Henry	526	7/4½	190.17.9
Bland, John	83	8/4	34.11.8
Bates, James	358	11/	196.18.0
Do.	42	4/2	8.15.0
Do. of Rice Garnett	89	7/3	32.5.3
Braxton, Carter	616¾	10/5	321.4.5¼
Boughton, John	200 1/3	8/4	83.7.6½
Brown, William	18¼	3/2	2.17.9½
Do. of Ware's Exors.	196½	7/3	71.4.7½
Bagby, Richard	260	"	94.5.0
Do. of Benjamin Nash &c.	62¼	6/3	19.9.0¾
Bagby, Thomas	260	"	94.5.0
Do. of Jacob Lumpkin	235	6/3	73.8.9
4.9.12.15.16			£3221.19.10¼

[page 2, List B, 1807] Persons names owning Land	Quantity of Land	Price per acre	Tot. Amt. Value Land
Brizendine, Armstead	86 2/3	8/4	35.17.6
Brumley, John Estate	60	7/10	23.10.0
Do. of John Dudley	35	7/10	13.14.2
Broach, William	20	"	7.16.8
Brown, John	50	7/4½	18.3.9
Bohannan, William	163	5/3	42.15.9
Do. of Lumpkin Gresham	343	7/3	124.6.9
Bates, William	81	7/9½	31.10.1
Do. of Rice Garnett	117	7/3	42.8.4
Boulware, Samuel	175¾	31/3	274.12.2¼
Boulware, Lee	153	7/3	55.9.3
Brown, William Jun[r.]	54	7/4	19.6.0
Brown, Lewis	79	8/2	32.5.2
Beadles, Justin	20	6/3	6.5.0
Do. of Henry Garnett	4	"	1.5.0
Bagby, John	271	7/3	99.7.3
Bagby, Robert	118	7/3	42.15.6
Bohannan, Robert	50	4/6	11.5.0
Burnett, James	195	7/10	76.7.6
Boulware, Thomas	139	3/2	22.0.2
Brown, Henry A., of Mitchael	50	6/3	15.12.6
Buckner, Francis	839	29/	1216.10.0
Crafton, Thomas	119	9/4	55.10.8
Crafton, James	119½	"	55.15.4
Crafton, John	117	"	54.7.4
Craine, John	251	6/3	78.8.9
Do.	27	3/2	4.5.6
Do.	56	7/3	20.6.0
Cluverius, Benjamin	419	20/9	434.14.3
Carlton, John	242	14/6	175.9.0
Carlton, Milley	75½	14/6	54.14.9
Cole, Thomas G.	105	6/3	32.6.3
Do. of Wiatt & Phillips	101	"	31.11.3
Carlton, Lewis	100	8/4	41.3.4
Do. of Carlton's este.	150	7/10	58.15.0
Clayton, Reuben	275	7/3	99.13.9
Craine, George Estate	30	7/3	10.17.6
Carleton, Benoni	231	8/4	96.5.0
Courtney, Thomas	156	7/10	61.2.0
Carlton, Joel	53½	6/3	16.4.5
Cook, Moses	100	"	41.13.4
Do. of Ambrose Cook	100	"	41.13.4
Chapman, George M.	250	7/10	87.18.4
Cannady, William	100	6/3	31.5.0
Do. of Saterwhite	15¼	"	4.15.3½
Do. of M. Barby	52	"	16.5.0
	13.21.20.17		£3797.12.8¾

[page 3, List B, 1807] Persons names owning Land	Quantity of Land	Price per acre	Tot. Amt. Value Land
	[200]		
Courtney, Robert	183½	7/10	71.17.5
Do. of Abbot	40½	"	15.13.4
Do. of Daniel	81	"	26.14.6
Cook, William	65	5/5	17.12.1
Cook, James	65	8/9	28.8.9
Courtney, Fanny & Children	78	7/10	30.10.0
Cross, Joseph	103½	6/3	32.6.10½
Campbell, Mary	375	7/3	135.18.9
Campbell, Whitaker	406	7/10	159.0.4
Crow, John	121	5/3	31.19.2¼
Do. of Roderick Starling	65	5/3	17.1.3
Crouch, Edmund	74¼	7/10	29.1.9
Campbell, William, of Jn°. Campbell	74¼	18/8	69.6.0
Cauthorn, Vincent F.	43	8/4	17.18.4
Craine, Nathaniel	66	3/2	10.9.0
Carleton, Thomas	297	7/10	116.6.6
Dew, Thomas	331	12/6	206.17.6
Do. of William Dews Estate	623½	14/6	451.13.6
Do. of Thomas Dillard	426	13/6	287.11.0
Duling, William Estate	264	8/4	110.0.0
Dix, Gabriel	416½	7/10	163.2.7
Durham, Joseph	105	4/3	21.12.6
Do. of Dunn	10	4/2	2.1.8
Deshazo, Larkin	87	7/3	34.4.10
Do. of Craine	6	6/3	1.17.6
Do. of Hoomes	403¾	4/4	93.4.5
Do. of Campbell & Wife	99	7/3	35.17.9
Deshazo, John	188	7/4	68.18.8
Dunbar, David	366	8/4	152.10.0
Dudley, Peter Estate	435	7/3¼	158.2.9¾
Dalley, George	174¼	3/2	27.11.9½
Durham, John	25	"	3.19.2
Do. of Thomas Johnson	18¼	"	2.17.9½
Dickie, James	512	8/4	213.6.8
Deshazo, Unity	71	7/10	27.16.3
Dalley, John Estate	200	3/2	31.13.4
Dobbins, Charles Estate	147	5/3	38.11.9
Dobson, Pitman	136	10/2¾	69.10.9¾
Do. of Nancy Grafton	1	9/4	0.9.4
Deshazo, William	130	"	60.13.4
Duling, Jesse, of Thomas Dew	311 2/3	14/6	225.19.6
Davis, Peter B.	171	7/10	66.19.6
2.18.23.20.14			£3367.8.4½

[page 4, List B, 1807] Persons names owning Land	Quantity of Land	Price per acre	Tot. Amt. Value Land
Eubank, Henry	171	5/3	44.17.9
Do. of Richard Eubank	26	"	6.16.6
Edwards, Thomas	66	4/2	13.15.0
Do. of Owen Gwathmey	108	8/2	44.2.0
Edwards, John, of Thomas Edwards	77	"	31.8.10
Eubank, James	111	10/2¾	56.15.5
Eubank, Polly	127	"	64.19.1
Eubank, William	130	"	66.9.9¼
Eubank, John	136	"	69.10.9¾
Fogg, James	120	6/3	37.10.0
Fleet, William	512	12/	307.4.0
Fogg, Frederick	268	8/4	111.13.4
Do. of Obediah Pitts	33	10/5	17.3.9
Fauntleroy, Samuel G.	2069	20/	2069.0.0
Do. of Miller &c.	145	9/2	66.9.2
Do. of Blackburn &c.	57 1/3	20/9	59.9.8
Do. of Francis Anderson	28 2/3	"	29.14.10
Do. of Brooking	30	10/5	15.12.6
Fox, Joseph S. Estate	28	7/10	10.19.4
Do.	39	"	15.5.6
Do.	94	7/3	31.1.6
Fogg, Thomas	223	10/2¾	114.2.1¾
Do. of Henry Lyne	352	8/4	146.13.4
Faulkner, Thomas	220	6/3	68.15.0
Do. of Coleman Minor	30	7/5	11.2.6
Grafton, Sally & Ann	123¾	9/4	57.15.0
Gayle, John	170¾	7/5	63.6.4¾
Do. of William Gayle	7¼	"	2.13.11
Gatewood, Chaney	829	10/5	437.17.11
Do. Noels	362	14/6	262.16.3
Do. Harwoods	125	4/2	46.17.6
Do. Eubanks	300	14/3	217.10.0
Do. Walden's Estate	120	12/6	75.0.0
Do. of Lyne's lott in Dunkirk, anl. rent			33.0.0
Do. of Miller, 2 [lots] No. 17 & 18			30.0.0
Do. of Roane	457	17/2	387.5.2
Garnett, Joshua Estate	325	8/4	135.8.4
Gatewood, Joseph	445	10/5	231.15.5
Do. of John Schools	70	8/4	29.3.4
Do. of Gabriel Schools Estate	70	6/3	21.17.6
Gatewood, John	78	8/4	32.10.0
Garnett, Reuben	395	8/10	174.9.2
Do. of Upshaw	61	8/	24.8.0
Do. of Gabriel Gatewood	78	10/5	40.12.6
Do. of John Gatewood	107	8/4	44.11.8
	2.15.22.22.17		£5859.9.7½

[page 5, List B, 1807] Persons names owning Land	Quantity of Land	Price per acre	Tot. Amt. Value Land
	[201]		
Do. of Roane	43	10/5	22.7.11
Garnett, Reuben M.	220	8/10	97.3.4
Gwathmey, Temple	600	35/3	1057.10.0
Griffith, Thomas	22¾	6/3	7.0.7½
Griffith, Joseph Estate	22¾	"	7.0.7½
Garlick, Samuel Estate	432½	7/3	156.15.7½
Do. of Rice Garnett	157	"	56.18.1
Guthrie, William	91¼	7/5	33.14.7
Do. of Richard Hill	46	8/2	18.15.8
Do. of William Campbell	31	7/3	11.4.9
Gaines, Betty	481½	20/4	489.10.6
Gaines, Robert B.	481½	20/4	489.10.6
Gresham, Thomas	505	6/8	168.6.8
Griffith, Milley	50	6/3	15.12.6
Graves, Thomas	66¼	7/3	23.18.6
Gatewood, William (*Tuck*$^{o.}$)	33	"	5.4.6
Gleason, Patrick	134	8/4	55.16.8
Gayle, William	344	7/5	127.11.4
Do. of Thomas Dew	162	7/2	53.1.2
Garnett, Henry Jun$^{r.}$	438	9/2	200.15.0
Do. of Wilson Lumpkin	121	9/4	56.9.4
Do. of Ovil Row	51½	"	23.12.8
Do. of Benoni Carleton	83	8/4	34.11.8
Do. lots in Dunkirk			38.0.0
Do. Do. of James H. Row, A. Rent			6.0.0
Gatewood, William, Son of John	132	10/	66.0.0
Gatewood, Phillip	613	17/2	526.3.2
Gayle, Thomas, loit in Dunkirk, A. Rent			9.0.0
Garrett, Robert Jun$^{r.}$	33	8/4	13.15.0
Gresham, Anthony	22	8/4	9.3.4
Gwathmey, Owen	82	8/2	33.9.8
George, Cooper, of Tunstall	13	8/4	5.8.4
Gayle, Mathew Estate	233	11/5	184.7.7
Gatewood, Robert, of J. Gatewood	30	8/4	12.10.0
Garret, Joseph, of George Gresham	141	7/3	51.2.3
Hill, William Estate	1267	14/6	918.4.3
Hawes, Walker	97	"	70.6.6
Do. of Miller &c.	683	16/7	570.9.9
Hitchcock, Thomas	140	4/2	29.3.4
Hoskins, Samuel Estate	345	6/3	107.16.3
Do. of Elisha Alexander	57	10/5	25.13.9
Hutchason, William	200	7/1	70.16.8
Heskew, Gallaman Estate	71½	5/3	18.14.10½
Heskew, John Estate	50	6/3	15.12.6
Do. of Clement Pynes	10	3/2	1.11.8
Do. of Larkin Deshazo	19¼	4/4	4.2.4
Hill, Edward	1125¾	18/8	1050.14.0
2.19.21.24.16			£7057.12.0

[page 6, List B, 1807] Persons names owning Land	Quantity of Land	Price per acre	Tot. Amt. Value Land
Hill, Richard	133 1/3	17/2	112.4.6½
Hoskins, John	767	10/5	399.9.7
Do. of Boughton	100	8/4	41.13.4
Do. of Fleet & Semple	2	10/5	1.0.10
Do. of Semple	18 1/8	"	9.8.9½
Do. of Row &c.	447	7/3	160.0.9
Hoomes, Benjamin, P lotts in Dunkirk			12.0.0
Hurt, West	14	5/3	3.3.6
Do. of Bohannan's Estate	80	4/6	18.0.0
Holt, William	123	14/3	87.12.9
Do. of Wilson &c.	41	6/3	12.6.3
Hutchason, John	54¼	8/9	23.14.8¼
Hall, Corbin Estate	72	4/2	15.0.0
Hill, Robert B.	257	8/2	104.18.10
Do. of Richard Hill	103¾	"	42.7.3½
Hill, Henry	420	"	171.10.0
Do. of Gwathmey	107	"	43.13.10
Hoskins, Thomas	55	"	22.9.2
Hutchason, Charles	200	7/1	70.16.8
Hoskins, John Jun[r]., lott in Dunkirk			33.0.0
Do. of Miller & [Micon] 2 Lotts No. 6 & 7			3.0.0
Haynes, Anthony, of Campbell &c.	208	7/3	75.0.0
Jones, John Estate	300	8/11	133.15.0
Jeffries, Edward	70	3/2	11.1.8
Jeffries, Robert, of Ambrose Jeffries Estate	237	7/10	92.16.8
Do.	110	7/6	41.5.0
Do. of Gresham &c.	74	7/3	28.13.6¾
Jeffries, Thomas, of J. Smith	25	7/10	9.15.10
Jones, James Estate	160	14/6	116.0.0
Do.	196	10/5	102.1.8
Jones, Rawleigh Estate	135¾	17/10	121.0.10½
Jeffries, John Estate	100	7/10	39.3.4
Johnson, Thomas	53¾	7/2	19.5.2½
Jones, John, of Boughton	29 1/8	6/3	9.2.0
Jones, John, of R. Starling	100	89/2	40.16.8
Kemp, John	178	7/3	64.2.6
Do. of Hill's Exors.	44¾	8/2	18.5.5
Keeling, Mary	78½	8/	31.8.0
Kay, Christopher	116	6/3	36.6.0
Do. of T. Gouldman	416½	9/	187.8.6
Lumpkin, James	213	7/10	83.8.10
Lumpkin, Henry	409	9/4	198.6.8
Lumpkin, William Estate	61½	13/6	41.10.6
	3.17.16.18.15		£2889.4.8½

[page 7, List B, 1807] Persons names owning Land	Quantity of Land	Price per acre	Tot. Amt. Value Land
	[202]		
Lafon, Francis	119	8/4	49.11.8
Lankford, Thomas Estate	100	4/2	20.16.8
Lumpkin, Henry Jun[r.]	190	9/4	88.13.4
Lumpkin, John W. Estate	140	7/10	54.16.8
Do. of Ware's Estate	118½	7/3	42.15.6
Do. of Pendleton	3	7/10	1.3.6
Longest, Richard	221¾	"	89.4.2
Do. of Dudley	20½	7/3	7.8.7½
Do. of John Longest	112½	7/10	43.17.4
Longest, Daniel, of Pendleton	156	7/4	57.4.0
Lumpkin, Anthony Estate	216	6/3	67.10.0
Lumpkin, Robert Jun[r.] Estate	297¾	5/3	73.8.8¼
Lumpkin, William Jun[r.]	183¼	10/5	95.6.3
Lyne, William	1160	8/4	483.6.8
Lumpkin, Richard	178	5/3	46.14.6
Longest, William	83	8/4	34.11.4
Lumpkin, Ann	47	13/6	31.14.6
Lumpkin, Elizabeth	51	"	38.8.6
Lumpkin, John (King W[m.])	105	"	70.17.6
Do. of White	57	"	38.9.6
Lyne, Edmund	50	8/4	20.16.8
Lumpkin, John, of Rob[t.] Lumpkin's Estate	32	8/4	13.6.8
Lumpkin, Spencer	1[3]1¼	"	54.13.9
Lumpkin, Thomas	219	"	91.5.0
Loving, John, of Beverly	204½	10/5	106.10.2½
Langham, Edmund	41	7/10	16.1.2
Motley, Edwin	815	10/5	428.2.6
Do. of Semple	149	12/6	93.2.6
Martin, Thomas C.	583	14/6	422.13.6
Do.	134½	7/3	48.15.1
Minor, William	149	8/4	62.1.8
Minor, John	137	"	57.1.8
Moody, Lewis	239	7/10	93.12.2
Mann, Joseph Jun[r.]	400	8/4	166.13.4
Do. of Crows	140	6/3	43.15.0
Do. of Allen & wife	25½	6/3	7.19.4½
Mann, Robert Estate	699	6/3	218.8.9
Meridith, Samuel	215	7/10	84.4.2
Mann, Mary	100	5/3	26.5.0
Martin, John	475	9/	213.15.0
Do. of Fogg	197	6/3	61.11.3
Do. of Satterwhite	88	6/3	27.10.0
Do. of Major Taylor &c.	60	6/3	18.15.0
Mahon, Thomas	101	6/3	31.11.3
Mahon, William	103½	"	32.3.9
Mahon, Benjamin	43¼	5/3	11.7.0¾
Mitchael, Richard, of Stone [Mitchell]	74¼	3/2	11.15.1½
Minor, Coleman	63¼	7/5	23.9.1¼
	3.17.24.23.21		£3923.7.8¾

[page 8, List B, 1807] Persons names owning Land	Quantity of Land	Price per acre	Tot. Amt. Value Land
Nunn, Moses	318	7/4½	117.5.3
Do. of Wm. Byers &c.	15	"	5.10.7½
Do. of Campbell & Wife	17	7/10	6.13.2
Do. of Wheeley Estate	24½	7/3	8.17.7½
Nunn, Thomas	130	7/3	47.2.6
Do. of Brizendine	49	4/3	10.8.3
Newbil, William	1060	8/4	441.13.4
Newil, John Estate	100	7/10	39.3.4
Nash, John Estate	100	6/3	31.5.0
Noel, Phillip & Skelton, Reuben	275	8/4	114.11.8
Pendleton, James	888½	8/7½	383.3.3¾
Do. of Wilmore	70	7/6	26.5.0
Do. of McIntosh	125	4/2	26.1.10
Pitts, David	420	9/6	196.0.0
Pitts, Obediah	20	10/5	10.8.4
Do. of Levi Pitts	104	9/6	49.8.0
Phillips, James	230	7/3	83.7.6
Do. of Ann Grafton	7 ¼	9/4	3.7.8
Pollard, John Estate	235	9/4	109.13.4
Do. of Leonard Smithey	384	7/3	139.4.0
Prewitt, Richard	102	"	36.12.3
Parker, John	761¼	8/4	317.3.9
Pendleton, Phillip Est., of Pendleton's Est.	447	7/10	173.1.6
Do. lott in Dunkirk			3.0.0
Perryman, Phillip	218	7/2	78.2.4
Do. of Dillard	215	"	77.10.0
Pollard, Richard	389	8/4	162.1.8
Perryman, Richard	110	7/3	39.7.6
Prewit, Dunstan	58½	8/	23.8.0
Pollard, Joseph	200	6/3	62.10.0
Pollard, Richard & Brown	50	8/	20.0.0
Parker, Gouldman	170	7/3	61.12.6
Quarles, Isaac (K. Wm.)	25¾	20/	25.15.0
Roane, Spencer	954	24/10	1184.11.0
Ryland, Joseph	467¾	7/3	169.10.2¼
Ryland, Josiah	160	7/10	62.13.4
Do. of William Temple	27½	15/	20.12.6
Do. of Prince's Estate	107	7/10	41.18.2
Do. of H. Brown	34½	7/4½	12.14.1¼
Do. of Jas. H. Row	226	8/4	92.3.4
Riddle, Vaughan	188	5/5	49.7.0
Roane, Thomas	920¾	17/2	790.8.2½
	3.13.17.20.17		£5336.2.0

[page 8, List B, 1807] Persons names owning Land	Quantity of Land	Price per acre	Tot. Amt. Value Land
	[203]		
Row, Hansford	162½	6/3	50.3.1½
Row, Wilson	162½	6/3	50.3.1½
Redd, James	200	7/3	72.10.0
Row, James H., of C. Anderson	262	"	94.19.6
Do. of John Watkins &c.	152	8/4	63.6.8
Roy, Wiley, of Saml. Garlick's Estate	454	24/10	463.14.4
Schools, James, of Gab[l.] School's Estate	70	6/3	21.17.6
Smith, William	53	7/10	20.15.2
Do. of James Smith's Estate	25	3/2	3.19.2
Segar, John	406	7/3	147.3.6
Schools, John	86	8/4	35.16.8
Do. of Fogg	30	"	12.10.0
Do. of Parker & Wife	35	"	14.11.8
Smith, John (D) Estate	142½	7/6	53.8.9
Saunders, George	200	7/3	70.10.8
Do. of Wiatt &c.	115	7/10	45.0.10
Shepherd, William Estate	140	9/4	65.6.8
Smith, Molly	30	4/2	6.5.0
Smith, John Jun[r.]	42½	5/3	11.3.1½
Smith, Lewis	96	7/6	36.0.0
Do. of Richard Hill	48¼	8/2	19.14.0½
Stone, Sarah	300	7/3	108.15.0
Stone, Daniel	52	3/2	8.4.8
Smith, Larkin	1154¼	31/1	1793.17.11¼
Smith, John H., of L. Smith	100	"	155.8.4
Smith, Henry	400	6/3	130.0.0
Smith, Ambrose	92¾	8/4	38.6.8
Do. of John Smith	47½	7/6	17.16.3
Stevens, George Estate	430	7/10	168.8.4
Stevens, George, Orphan	75	"	29.8.4
Smith, William Estate (Mill)	200	3/2	31.13.4
Shepherd, John	192	3/2	30.1.8
Do. of James Gresham & Wife	113	7/10	34.5.2
Sthreshley, William	155½	6/3	48.11.10
Schools, George	200	8/4	83.6.8
Do. of John Hu[t]chason	150	7/1	53.2.6
Do. of Gabriel School's Estate	34	6/3	10.12.6
Smith, John, of J. Garlick	54	29/	78.6.0
Smith, Jane, of James Smith's Estate	25	3/2	3.19.2
Smith, Philip, Orphan of Do.	12½	"	1.19.7
Smith, James	76	7/10	29.15.4
Do. of James Smith's Estate	12½	3/2	1.19.7
Scott, Anderson	330	16/7	273.12.6
Do. of P. Anderson's Estate	248	20/9	257.6.0
Do. of Anderson & Wife	96	"	99.12.0
Semple, Robert B.	235	10/5	122.6.3½
Do. of Spencer Roane	155	24/10	192.9.2
Stewart, James	120	9/2	55.0.0
Skelton, William	73	8/2½	29.19.2½
Skelton, Meriwether	60	"	24.10.0
3.18.24.24.21			£5351.16.0¼

[page 9, List B, 1807] Persons names owning Land	Quantity of Land	Price per acre	Tot. Amt. Value Land
Shepherd, William, of G. Wiatt	49½	7/6	18.11.3
Shackelford, James, of Willis	63	31/1	97.18.8
Do. of Benjamin Shackelford &c.	114	7/3	40.8.2
Shackelford, Leonard	113	6/3	35.6.3
Samuel, Thomas, of Beverly	100	10/5	52.1.8
Samuel, Thomas Jun$^{r.}$, of Tho$^{s.}$ Samuel	100	10/5	52.1.8
Schools, Thomas, of W$^{m.}$ Satterwhite's Estate	118	5/7 ½	33.3.9
Satterwhite, George Estate	60¾	6/3	18.19.8
Skelton, Lucy, Rachael, Fanny &c.	142	8/4	59.3.4
Skelton, William Estate	238	8/2½	97.13.7
Trice, William Estate	140	7/3	50.15.0
Taylor, James	50	6/8	15.12.6
Taylor, Edmund	249	8/4	122.10.0
Temple, Joseph	918	10/5	478.2.6
Tunstall, Richard Estate	1097	7/3	397.13.3
Temple, William	402¼	15/	301.17.6
Temple, John	42	31/3	65.12.6
Do. of Robert Alexander	15¼	10/	7.12.6
Temple, Humphrey Estate	100	15/	75.0.0
Do. of J. Tunstall	200	18/8	185.16.8
Do. of R. Tunstall's Estate	574	21/	602.14.0
Tunstall, Richard (Purdie) Estate	63 ¾	8/4	26.11.3
Temple, Joseph Jun$^{r.}$	2	30/	3.0.0
Tunstall, Richard (Purdy) este.	63¾	8/4	32.5.6
Temple, Joseph Jun$^{r.}$, of Jn$^{o.}$ Temple	2	30/	3.0.0
Upshaw, James Estate (Essex)	125	8/10	55.4.2
Do. of Beverly	30	10/5	15.12.6
Do. of Garnett	120	8/	48.0.0
Wilson, Abraham	159	6/3	49.13.9
Wilson, Benjamin Estate	200	7/3	72.10.0
Watkins, Joseph Est., of Wilthire's Estate	71	7/3	26.14.9
Walker, Phillip	110	9/4	51.6.8
Walker, Humphrey	820	33/2	1355.14.2
Wright, William	130	5/3	33.12.6
Willis, Joel	94	7/10	35.5.0
Do. of William Jones Estate	140¼	17/10	125.1.1½
Wright, Edward	567	6/3	177.3.9
Whayne, William Estate	154½	7/10	60.10.3
Wiatt, George	122	7/6	45.15.0
Webb, James	209	4/2	43.10.10
Wheeley, Carrol Estate	12½	7/3	4.10.7½
Watkins, Joseph Jun$^{r.}$	93¼	8/4	38.17.1
Watkins, John, of Dix	226	6/3	70.12.6
	15.19.20.18		£5148.13.3

[page 10, List B, 1807] Persons names owning Land		Quantity of Land	Price per acre	Tot. Amt. Value Land
		[204]		
Watkins, Phillip Estate		107	4/2	22.5.10
Walton, Thomas, of Howerton		76¾	6/	23.0.6
Williamson, Abner Estate		50¼	3/2	7.19.1½
Ward, Joshoua, lott in Dunkirk				60.0.0
Watkins, Richard, of Starling		187½	8/	75.0.0
Wilmore, Christopher		50	8/	20.0.0
Wilmore, John		130	"	52.0.0
Watkins, Benjamin		27¾	5/	6.18.9
Watkins, Nancy		21¾	6	6.10.6
Watkins, William		28¾	5/	7.3.9
Watkins, Betsey		7¾	17/	6.11.9
Watkins, Mary		7½	17/	6.7.6
Watkins, Philip, Yr.		55¾	5/	13.18.9
Young, Henry		640	18/8	597.6.8
	6.5.6.4			£905.3.1½
				[46858.9.6]

[arithmetic omitted]

$749.74 Tax on hand

Richard Pollard, Comr.

[cover]
King & Queen
Richard Pollard
1807
Land & Taxble. propy.
9 Merchts. Lics., $112.—4
Entd.
30th Septr. 1807
Added
Stated

INDEX

Heritage Books by Wesley E. Pippenger:

Alexander Family: Migrations from Maryland

Alexandria (Arlington) County, Virginia Death Records, 1853–1896

Alexandria City and Arlington County, Virginia Records Index: Vol. 1

Alexandria City and Arlington County, Virginia Records Index: Vol. 2

Alexandria County, Virginia Marriage Records, 1853–1895

Alexandria, Virginia Marriage Index, January 10, 1893 to August 31, 1905

Alexandria, Virginia Marriages, 1870–1892

Alexandria, Virginia Town Lots, 1749–1801
Together with the Proceedings of the Board of Trustees, 1749–1780

Alexandria, Virginia Wills, Administrations and Guardianships, 1786–1800

Alexandria, Virginia 1808 Census (Wards 1, 2, 3, and 4)

Alexandria, Virginia Death Records, 1863–1896

Alexandria, Virginia Hustings Court Orders, Volume 1, 1780–1787

Allen-Lewis and Davison-Ridgeway Families: Migrations to Missouri

Connections and Separations: Divorce, Name Change and Other
Genealogical Tidbits from the Acts of the Virginia General Assembly

Daily National Intelligencer *Index to Deaths, 1855–1870*

Daily National Intelligencer, *Washington, District of Columbia*
Marriages and Deaths Notices (January 1, 1851 to December 30, 1854)

Dead People on the Move: Reconstruction of the Georgetown Presbyterian Burying Ground,
Holmead's (Western) Burying Ground, and Other Removals in the District of Columbia

Death Notices from Richmond, Virginia Newspapers, 1841–1853

District of Columbia Ancestors: A Guide to Records of the District of Columbia

District of Columbia Death Records: August 1, 1874–July 31, 1879

District of Columbia Foreign Deaths, 1888–1923

District of Columbia Guardianship Index, 1802–1928

District of Columbia Interments (Index to Deaths) January 1, 1855 to July 31, 1874

District of Columbia Marriage Licenses, Register 1: 1811–1858

District of Columbia Marriage Licenses, Register 2: 1858–1870

District of Columbia Marriage Records Index
June 28, 1877 to October 19, 1885: Marriage Record Books 11 to 20
Wesley E. Pippenger and Dorothy S. Provine

District of Columbia Marriage Records Index
October 20, 1885 to January 20, 1892: Marriage Record Books 21 to 30

District of Columbia Marriage Records Index
January 20, 1892 to August 30, 1896: Marriage Record Books 31 to 40

District of Columbia Marriage Records Index
August 31, 1896 to December 17, 1900: Marriage Record Books 41 to 65

District of Columbia Probate Records, 1801–1852

District of Columbia: Original Land Owners, 1791–1800

Early Church Records of Alexandria City and Fairfax County, Virginia

Essex County, Virginia Buildings in Photographs

Essex County, Virginia Consolidated Index to Wills and Fiduciary Accounts, Etc., 1692–1903

Essex County, Virginia Death Records, 1856–1896

Essex County, Virginia Deed Abstracts, 1786–1805, Deed Books 33 to 36

Essex County, Virginia Deed Abstracts, 1805–1819, Deed Books 37 to 39

Essex County, Virginia Guardianship and Orphans Records, 1707–1888: A Descriptive Index

Essex County, Virginia Index to Court Orders, 1702–1715

Essex County, Virginia Land Tax Lists, 1782–1814

Essex County, Virginia Marriage Bonds, 1804–1850, Annotated

Essex County, Virginia Marriage Records, Transcripts of Consents Affidavits, Minister Returns, and Marriage Licenses, Volume 1: 1850–1872
Suzanne P. Derieux and Wesley E. Pippenger

Essex County, Virginia Marriage Records, Transcripts of Consents Affidavits, Minister Returns, and Marriage Licenses, Volume 2: 1873–1883
Suzanne P. Derieux and Wesley E. Pippenger

Essex County, Virginia Newspaper Notices, 1738–1938

Essex County, Virginia Newspaper Notices, Vol. 2, 1735–1952

Essex County, Virginia Will Abstracts, 1751–1842 and Estate Records Index, 1751–1799

Georgetown, District of Columbia 1850 Federal Population Census (Schedule I) and 1853 Directory of Residents of Georgetown

Georgetown, District of Columbia Marriage and Death Notices, 1801–1838

Husbands and Wives Associated with Early Alexandria, Virginia (and the Surrounding Area), 3rd Edition, Revised

Index to District of Columbia Estates, 1801–1929

Index to District of Columbia Land Records, 1792–1817

Index to Virginia Estates, 1800–1865: Volumes 4, 5 and 6

John Alexander, a Northern Neck Proprietor, His Family, Friends and Kin

King and Queen County, Virginia Land Tax Lists, 1782–1807

Legislative Petitions of Alexandria, 1778–1861

Marriage and Death Notices from Alexandria, Virginia Newspapers, 1784–1852

Pippenger and Pittenger Families

Proceedings of the Orphan's Court, Washington County, District of Columbia, 1801–1808

Richmond County, Virginia Marriage Records, 1854–1890, Annotated

Stafford County, Virginia Land Tax Lists, 1782–1805

Tappahannock and Essex County, Virginia in Early Photographs

The Georgetown Courier *Marriage and Death Notices: Georgetown, District of Columbia, November 18, 1865 to May 6, 1876*

The Georgetown Directory for the Year 1830: to which is appended, a Short Description of the Churches, Public Institutions, and the Original Charter of Georgetown, and Extracts of the Laws Pertaining to the Chesapeake and Ohio Canal Company

The Virginia Gazette and Alexandria Advertiser: *Volume 1, September 3, 1789 to November 11, 1790*

The Virginia Journal and Alexandria Advertiser:
Volume I (February 5, 1784 to January 27, 1785)

Volume II (February 3, 1785 to January 26, 1786)

Volume III (March 2, 1786 to January 25, 1787)

Volume IV (February 8, 1787 to May 21, 1789)

The Washington and Georgetown Directory of 1853

Tombstone Inscriptions of Alexandria, Volumes 1–5

Virginia's Lost Wills: An Index

Westmoreland County, Virginia Marriage Records, 1850–1880, Annotated

www.ingramcontent.com/pod-product-compliance
Lightning Source LLC
Chambersburg PA
CBHW080410270326
41929CB00018B/2965
9780788406454